Lecture Notes in Artificial Intelligence   11529

Subseries of Lecture Notes in Computer Science

Series Editors

Randy Goebel
University of Alberta, Edmonton, Canada
Yuzuru Tanaka
Hokkaido University, Sapporo, Japan
Wolfgang Wahlster
DFKI and Saarland University, Saarbrücken, Germany

Founding Editor

Jörg Siekmann
DFKI and Saarland University, Saarbrücken, Germany

More information about this series at http://www.springer.com/series/1244

Alfredo Cuzzocrea · Sergio Greco ·
Henrik Legind Larsen · Domenico Saccà ·
Troels Andreasen · Henning Christiansen (Eds.)

Flexible Query Answering Systems

13th International Conference, FQAS 2019
Amantea, Italy, July 2–5, 2019
Proceedings

 Springer

Editors
Alfredo Cuzzocrea
University of Calabria
Rende, Italy

Sergio Greco
University of Calabria
Rende, Italy

Henrik Legind Larsen
Legind Technologies
Esbjerg, Denmark

Domenico Saccà
University of Calabria
Rende, Italy

Troels Andreasen
Roskilde University
Roskilde, Denmark

Henning Christiansen
Roskilde University
Roskilde, Denmark

ISSN 0302-9743   ISSN 1611-3349 (electronic)
Lecture Notes in Artificial Intelligence
ISBN 978-3-030-27628-7   ISBN 978-3-030-27629-4 (eBook)
https://doi.org/10.1007/978-3-030-27629-4

LNCS Sublibrary: SL7 – Artificial Intelligence

This Springer imprint is published by the registered company Springer Nature Switzerland AG
The registered company address is: Gewerbestrasse 11, 6330 Cham, Switzerland

Preface

This volume contains the papers presented at the 13th International Conference on Flexible Query Answering Systems (FQAS 2019), held during July 2–5, 2019, in Amantea, Calabria.

FQAS is the premier conference focusing on the key issue in the information society of providing easy, flexible, and intuitive access to information to everybody. In targeting this issue, the conference draws on several research areas, such as information retrieval, database management, data science, information filtering, knowledge representation, knowledge discovery, analytics, soft computing, management of multimedia information, and human-computer interaction. The guiding topic of the FQAS conferences are innovative query systems aimed at providing easy, flexible, and human-friendly access to information. Such systems are becoming increasingly important due to the huge and always growing number of users, as well as the growing amount of available information. Thus, works related to the concepts of data science, data streams querying etc., were welcomed. This year, FQAS had a special theme: "flexible querying and analytics for smart cities and smart societies in the age of big data." This provided a unique opportunity to focalize on emerging research trends that have been leading the research scene for several years.

This year FQAS received a significant number of submissions from over several countries. Most papers were reviewed by three Program Committee members. The committee finally decided to accept 33 papers. We are thankful to all the researchers that helped in the review process and made this possible. The conference program featured three invited talks, namely: "Logic, Machine Learning, and Security" by V. S. Subrahmanian, Dartmouth College, Nil, USA; "Personal Big Data, GDPR and Anonymization" by Josep Domingo-Ferrer, Universitat Rovira i Virgili, Spain; and "Querying Databases with Ontologies: 17 Years Later" by Enrico Franconi, Free University of Bozen-Bolzano, Italy. In addition to this, the conference program was also comprised of two tutorials, namely: "Supervised Learning for Prevalence Estimation" by Alejandro Moreo and Fabrizio Sebastiani, ISTI-CNR, Pisa, Italy; and "Approaches to Computational Models of Argumentation" by Matthias Thimm, Universitat Koblenz-Landau, Germany.

We are very grateful to our institutions that actively supported the organization of the conference. These were:

- Dipartimento di Science Politiche e Sociali, University of Calabria, Italy;
- Dipartimento di Ingegneria Informatica, Modellistica, Elettronica e Sistemistica, University of Calabria, Italy;
- Department of Electronic Systems, Aalborg University, Denmark;
- Istituto di Calcolo e Reti ad Alte Prestazioni, National Research Council, Italy;

- Centro di Competenza, ICT-SUD, Italy;
- Dipartimento di Ingegneria e Architettura, University of Trieste, Italy.

July 2019

Alfredo Cuzzocrea
Sergio Greco
Henrik Legind Larsen
Domenico Saccà
Troels Andreasen
Henning Christiansen

Organization

General Chairs

Henrik Legind Larsen   Aalborg University, Denmark
Domenico Saccà   University of Calabria, Italy

Program Chairs

Alfredo Cuzzocrea   University of Calabria, Italy
Sergio Greco   University of Calabria, Italy

Special Session Chairs

Nicolas Spyratos   University of Paris-South, France
Volker Hoffmann   SINTEF Digital, Norway

Panel Chair

Carlos Ordonez   University of Huston, USA

Tutorial Chairs

Ladjel Bellatreche   ENSMA, France
Carson Leung   University of Manitoba, Canada

Industrial Track Chair

Hassane Essafi   CEA, France

Publicity Chair

Wookey Lee   INHA University, South Korea

Local Organization Chairs

Marco Calautti   The University of Edinburgh, UK,
     and University of Calabria, Italy
Enzo Mumolo   University of Trieste, Italy

Steering Committee

Henrik Legind Larsen, Denmark
Henning Christiansen, Denmark
Troels Andreasen, Denmark

International Advisory Board

Adnan Yazici, Turkey
Fred Petry, USA
Gabriella Pasi, Italy
Henri Prade, France
Janusz Kacprzyk, Poland
Jesus Cardenosa, Spain
Jorgen Fischer Nilsson, Denmark
Maria Amparo Vila, Spain
Maria J. Martin-Bautista, Spain
Nicolas Spyratos, France
Olivier Pivert, France
Panagiotis Chountas, UK
Slawomir Zadrozny, Poland
Zbigniew W. Raś, USA

Program Committee

Gianvincenzo Alfano	University of Calabria, Italy
Giovanni Amendola	University of Calabria, Italy
Troels Andreasen	Roskilde University, Denmark
Ignacio J. Blanco	University of Granada, Spain
Patrice Buche	INRA, France
Henrik Bulskov	Roskilde University, Denmark
Marco Calautti	The University of Edinburgh, UK, and University of Calabria, Italy
Panagiotis Chountas	University of Westminster, UK
Henning Christiansen	Roskilde University, Denmark
Alfredo Cuzzocrea	University of Calabria, Italy
Florian Daniel	Politecnico di Milano, Italy
Agnieszka Dardzinska-Glebocka	Bialystok University of Technology, Poland
Guy De Tre	Ghent University, Belgium
Sergio Greco	University of Calabria, Italy
Allel Hadjali	LIAS/ENSMA, France
Hlne Jaudoin	IRISA-ENSSAT, France
Etienne Kerre	Ghent University, Belgium
Marzena Kryszkiewicz	Warsaw University of Technology, Poland

Contents

Argumentation-Based Query Answering

Data Mining and Knowledge Discovery

Advanced Flexible Query Answering Methodologies and Techniques

Flexible Query Answering Methods and Techniques

Flexible Intelligent Information-Oriented and Network-Oriented Approaches

Big Data Veracity and Soft Computing

Invited Talks

Logic, Machine Learning, and Security

V. S. Subrahmanian$^{(\boxtimes)}$

Department of Computer Science,
Institute for Security, Technology, and Society,
Dartmouth College, Hanover, NH 03755, USA
vs@dartmouth.edu

Abstract. Logic stands at the very heart of computer science. In this talk, I will argue that logic is also an essential part of machine learning and that it has a fundamental role to play in both international security and counter-terrorism. I will first briefly describe the use of logic for high-level reasoning in counter-terrorism applications and then describe the BEEF system to explain the forecasts generated by virtually any machine learning classifier. Finally, I will describe one use of logic in deceiving cyber-adversaries who may have successfully compromised an enterprise network.

Keywords: Logic · Deception · Counter-terrorism ·
Machine learning · AI · Cybersecurity

1 Introduction

In this talk, I will describe the role of logic in 3 broad areas: the use of logic in counter-terrorism applications, the use of logic to explain the results generated by very diverse and potentially very complex machine learning classification algorithms, and the role of logic in deceiving malicious hackers who may have successfully entered an enterprise network.

2 Logic for Counter-Terrorism

Since approximately 2004, my research group (then at the University of Maryland College Park) and I have worked on the problem of predicting the behaviors of terrorist groups and reshaping their behavior when the forecasts of their behavior were not to our liking. The key aspect of our work was to develop forecasts that were: (i) accurate, and (ii) easily explainable to policy makers. As policy makers are drawn from diverse backgrounds ranging from lawyers to social scientists to business people, the explanations had to be both easy to grasp and compelling. We turned immediately to probabilistic logic programs [6] and temporal probabilistic logic programs [3]. We wrote the first ever paper on computational predictive models in counter-terrorism. The paper, about Hezbollah,

© Springer Nature Switzerland AG 2019
A. Cuzzocrea et al. (Eds.): FQAS 2019, LNAI 11529, pp. 3–6, 2019.
https://doi.org/10.1007/978-3-030-27629-4_1

presented probabilistic rules about Hezbollah's behavior [7] that were simple enough for journalists and Hezbollah to understand—so much so that Hezbollah even issued a comment to the Beirut Daily Star about the paper on Oct 22 2008[1]. The fact that Hezbollah could understand our paper gave us the confidence to believe that we were on the right track—and later, we were able to develop the first ever thorough study of terrorist group behavior by analyzing Lashkar-e-Taiba, the terrorist group that carried out the infamous 2008 Mumbai attacks [11]. This was quickly followed by a similar study of the Indian Mujahideen [10] using temporal probabilistic rules. Our group put out several live forecasts of the behaviors of these two groups which were mostly correct. We subsequently developed methods to reshape the behaviors of these groups and formulate policies against them. For instance, in citesimari2013parallel, we showed that a form of abduction could be used to generate policies that would reduce—with maximal possible probability—the different types of attacks that the group would carry out. Later, we showed how to combine temporal probabilistic rules and game theoretic reasoning to show that strategically disclosing the behavioral rules we had learned about the groups could help reshape the action of the group to help deter/influence them [8,9].

3 Logic for Explaining Forecasts Generated by Machine Learning Classifiers

More recently, the field of "explainable" machine learning has become very important. Machine learning classifiers such as support vector machines [2] and ensemble classifiers such as random forest [1] often generate highly accurate forecasts, but explaining them in plain English can be a major challenge. In the second part of my talk, I will describe a system called BEEF (Balanced English Explanation of Forecasts) developed by us [4]. Given any machine learning algorithm (in a black box) and given a forecast F made by that algorithm, BEEF introduces the concept of a balanced explanation. A balanced explanation consists of arguments both *for* and *against* the forecast. The need for balanced explanations was motivated by my prior work on counter-terrorism where I was repeatedly asked to provide explanations for both why the forecasts we made were correct as well as to explain why they may be incorrect. We show that the problem of generating balanced explanations has both a geometric and a logical interpretation. We built out a prototype system and ran experiments showing that BEEF provides intuitive explanations that were deemed more compelling by human subjects than other methods.

4 Logic for Deceiving Cyber-Adversaries

Today, most enterprises are aware that they need to be ready to be the target of cyber-attacks. When malicious hackers successfully enter a network, they often

---

[1] http://www.dailystar.com.lb/News/Lebanon-News/2008/Oct-22/54721-us-academics-design-software-to-predict-hizbullah-behavior.ashx.

move laterally in the network by scanning nodes in the network, understanding what kinds of vulnerabilities exist in the scanned nodes, and then move through the network by exploiting those vulnerabilities. As they move from node to node, they may carry out a host of malicious activities ranging from reconnaissance and surveillance to exfiltration of data or intellectual property, to planting malware and backdoors, or carrying out denial of service attacks. I will discuss one way to disrupt the hacker's ability to damage an enterprise even after the enterprise has been compromised. We introduce the idea of generating fake scan results [5] that lead a hacker away from the crown jewels of an enterprise and minimize the expected damage caused by the hacker.

5   Conclusion

This talk describes results generated by my research group along with several students, postdocs, and colleagues. Our work shows that logic is a rich and fertile mechanism for helping humans understand the behavior of both humans and programs and has demonstrated the potential to help secure us—both in the physical world and in cyberspace.

Acknowledgement. Different parts of this work were supported by ONR grants N000141612739, N00014-16-1-2918, N00014-18-1-2670 and N00014-16-1-2896.

References

1. Breiman, L.: Random forests. Mach. Learn. **45**, 5–32 (2001)
2. Cortes, C., Vapnik, V.: Support vector machine. Mach. Learn. **20**, 273–297 (1995)
3. Dekhtyar, A., Dekhtyar, M.I., Subrahmanian, V.: Temporal probabilistic logic programs. In: ICLP, vol. 99, pp. 109–123 (1999)
4. Grover, S., Pulice, C., Simari, G.I., Subrahmanian, V.: BEEF: balanced English explanations of forecasts. IEEE Trans. Comput. Soc. Syst. **6**(2), 350–364 (2019)
5. Jajodia, S., et al.: A probabilistic logic of cyber deception. IEEE Inf. Forensics Secur. **12**(11), 2532–2544 (2017)
6. Khuller, S., Martinez, M.V., Nau, D., Sliva, A., Simari, G.I., Subrahmanian, V.S.: Computing most probable worlds of action probabilistic logic programs: scalable estimation for 10 30,000 worlds. Ann. Math. Artif. Intell. **51**(2–4), 295–331 (2007)
7. Mannes, A., Michael, M., Pate, A., Sliva, A., Subrahmanian, V.S., Wilkenfeld, J.: Stochastic opponent modeling agents: a case study with Hezbollah. In: Liu, H., Salerno, J.J., Young, M.J. (eds.) Social Computing, Behavioral Modeling, and Prediction, pp. 37–45. Springer, Boston (2008). https://doi.org/10.1007/978-0-387-77672-9_6
8. Serra, E., Subrahmanian, V.: A survey of quantitative models of terror group behavior and an analysis of strategic disclosure of behavioral models. IEEE Trans. Comput. Soc. Syst. **1**(1), 66–88 (2014)
9. Simari, G.I., Dickerson, J.P., Sliva, A., Subrahmanian, V.: Parallel abductive query answering in probabilistic logic programs. ACM Trans. Comput. Logic (TOCL) **14**(2), 12 (2013)

10. Subrahmanian, V.S., Mannes, A., Roul, A., Raghavan, R.: Indian Mujahideen: Computational Analysis and Public Policy. TESECO. Springer, Cham (2013). https://doi.org/10.1007/978-3-319-02818-7
11. Subrahmanian, V.S., Mannes, A., Sliva, A., Shakarian, J., Dickerson, J.P.: Computational Analysis of Terrorist Groups: Lashkar-e-Taiba. Springer, New York (2012). https://doi.org/10.1007/978-1-4614-4769-6

Personal Big Data, GDPR
and Anonymization

Josep Domingo-Ferrer[✉]

Department of Computer Science and Mathematics,
CYBERCAT-Center for Cybersecurity Research of Catalonia,
UNESCO Chair in Data Privacy,
Universitat Rovira i Virgili,
Av. Països Catalans 26, 43007 Tarragona, Catalonia, Spain
josep.domingo@urv.cat

Abstract. Big data are analyzed to reveal patterns, trends and associations, especially relating to human behavior and interactions. However, according to the European General Data Protection Regulation (GDPR), which is becoming a *de facto* global data protection standard, any intended uses of personally identifiable information (PII) must be clearly specified and explicitly accepted by the data subjects. Furthermore, PII cannot be accumulated for secondary use. Thus, can exploratory data uses on PII be GDPR-compliant? Hardly so.

Resorting to anonymized data sets instead of PII is a natural way around, for anonymized data fall outside the scope of GDPR. The problem is that anonymization techniques, based on statistical disclosure control and privacy models, use algorithms and assumptions from the time of small data that must be thoroughly revised, updated or even replaced to deal with big data.

Upgrading big data anonymization to address the previous challenge needs to empower users (by giving them useful anonymized data), subjects (by giving them control on anonymization) and controllers (by simplifying anonymization and making it more flexible).

Keywords: Big data · GDPR · Anonymization

Last century, Kafka, Orwell, Huxley and Böll wrote novels on dystopian societies. They were premonitory of what can be achieved and is achieved with big data in our century (*e.g.* social credit system in China, [8]). Without going that far, even in liberal democracies, big data can be very privacy-invasive [4,13]. To protect citizens, the European Union has promoted the General Data Protection Regulation (GDPR, [5]), that is quickly being adopted as a *de facto* global privacy standard by Internet companies [6,7]. GDPR limits the collection, processing and sharing of personally identifiable information (PII) and requires a privacy-by-design approach on the controllers' side [1,3].

Nonetheless, the surge of big data analytics has brought a lot of progress and opportunities and is here to stay: one can hardly expect the private (and even

© Springer Nature Switzerland AG 2019
A. Cuzzocrea et al. (Eds.): FQAS 2019, LNAI 11529, pp. 7–10, 2019.
https://doi.org/10.1007/978-3-030-27629-4_2

the public) sector to refrain from harnessing big data on people for a great deal of secondary purposes (other than the purpose at collection time). These include data exploration, machine learning and other forms of knowledge extraction. Satisfying the GDPR legal obligations towards subjects is very difficult in such a scenario where a host of controllers exchange and merge big data for secondary use to extract knowledge.

According to GPDR, anonymization is the tool that allows turning PII-based big data into big data *tout court*, and hence legitimately circumventing the legal restrictions applicable to PII. As repeatedly aired in the media [2,10,12], just suppressing direct identifiers (names, passport numbers, etc.), let alone replacing them by pseudonyms, is not enough to anonymize a data set. Anonymizing for privacy requires further data modification beyond identifier suppression, which may decrease utility. On the other hand, attaining good levels of utility and privacy for PII-based big data is essential to conciliate law with reality.

In this talk, I will first survey the main current limitations of the state of the art in big data anonymization:

1. *Unjustified* de facto *trust in controllers.* Twenty years ago, National Statistical Institutes (NSIs) and a few others were the only data controllers explicitly gathering data on citizens, and their legal status often made them trusted. In contrast, in the current big data scenario, a host of controllers collect PII and it is no longer reasonable to assume the subject trusts all of them to keep her data confidential and/or anonymize them properly in case of release [9].

2. Ad hoc *anonymization methods.* Many privacy models have been proposed (k-anonymity, l-diversity, t-closeness, ϵ-differential privacy, etc.) and each privacy model is satisfied using a specific statistical disclosure control (SDC) method, or a few specific ones. For example, k-anonymity is reached via generalization or microaggregation, and DP via noise addition. Life would be easier if a unified masking approach existed that, under proper parameterization, could be used to attain a broad range of privacy models. This would empower controllers in centralized anonymization and subjects in local anonymization.

3. *Difficulty of merging and exploring anonymized big data.* Even if subjects decide to accept centralized anonymization by the controllers, none of the main families of privacy models in use manages to satisfy all the desiderata of big data anonymization that we identified in [11]: (i) *protection* against disclosure no matter the amount of background information available to the attacker; (ii) *utility* of the anonymized microdata for exploratory analyses; (iii) *linkability* of records corresponding to the same or similar individuals across several anonymized data sets; (iv) *composability*, that is, preservation of privacy guarantees after repeated application of the model or linkage of anonymized data sets; and (v) *low computational cost.* Utility and linkability are needed to empower the *users/data analysts*, protection and composability are desired by *subjects*, and low cost is desired by *controllers*. On the other hand, it is hard for controllers holding data sets to engage in joint exploratory analysis without disclosing any of their data to other controllers. Note that cryptographic secure multi-party computation (MPC) is of limited use here,

because it is intended for specific calculations planned in advance, rather than exploratory analyses. Furthermore, while MPC ensures input confidentiality, it gives exact outputs that can lead to disclosure by inference (for example if the outputs are the mean and the variance of the inputs, and the variance is very small, it can be inferred that the inputs are very close to the mean).

Thus, the grand challenge is to obtain anonymized big data that can be validly used for exploratory analyses, knowledge extraction and machine learning while *empowering subjects, users and controllers*:

– Subjects must be given control and even agency on how their data are anonymized. Local anonymization gives maximum agency to the subject. However, it is ill-suited for privacy models relying on hiding the subject's record in a group of records, such as k-anonymity and its extensions, because these need to cluster the contributions of several subjects. If we obviate this shortcoming and go for local anonymization, randomized response and *local* DP are natural approaches. Unfortunately, the current literature on both approaches focuses on obtaining statistics on the data from subjects, rather than multi-dimensional full sets of anonymized microdata that are valid for exploratory analysis. The latter is precisely what is wanted. Centralized DP can indeed produce anonymized data sets preserving some dependences between the original attributes, but the challenge is to avoid centralizing anonymization at the *untrusted* controller.
– Users should receive anonymized data that are analytically useful.
– Controllers should be given more unified approaches to anonymization, allowing them to engage in multi-controller exploratory computation.

I will conclude the talk with some hints on how to tackle the above grand challenge.

Acknowledgment and Disclaimer. Partial support to this work has been received from the European Commission (project H2020-700540 "CANVAS"), the Government of Catalonia (ICREA Acadèmia Prize to J. Domingo-Ferrer and grant 2017 SGR 705), and from the Spanish Government (project RTI2018-095094-B-C21). The author is with the UNESCO Chair in Data Privacy, but the views in this paper are his own and are not necessarily shared by UNESCO.

References

1. D'Acquisto, G., Domingo-Ferrer, J., Kikiras, P., Torra, V., de Montjoye, Y.-A., Bourka, A.: Privacy by design in big data – an overview of privacy enhancing technologies in the era of big data analytics. European Union Agency for Network and Information Security (ENISA) (2015)
2. Barbaro, M., Zeller, T.: A face is exposed for AOL searcher no. 4417749. New York Times (2006)
3. Danezis, G., et al.: Privacy and data protection by design – from policy to engineering. European Union Agency for Network and Information Security (ENISA) (2015)

4. Duhigg, C.: How companies learn your secrets. New York Times Mag. (2012)
5. General Data Protection Regulation. Regulation (EU) 2016/679. https://gdpr-info.eu
6. General Data Protection Regulation (GDPR). Google cloud whitepaper, May 2018
7. Lomas, N.: Facebook urged to maked GDPR its "baseline standard" globally. Techcrunch, 9 April 2018
8. Ma, A.: China has started ranking citizens with a creepy 'social credit' system - here's what you can do wrong, and the embarrassing, demeaning ways they can punish you. Business Insider, 8 April 2018
9. Rogaway, P.: The moral character of cryptographic work. Invited talk at Asiacrypt 2015. http://web.cs.ucdavis.edu/~rogaway/papers/moral.pdf
10. Solon, O.: 'Data is a fingerprint': why you aren't as anonymous as you think online. The Guardian (2018)
11. Soria-Comas, J., Domingo-Ferrer, J.: Big data privacy: challenges to privacy principles and models. Data Sci. Eng. 1(1), 21–28 (2015)
12. Sweeney, L.: Simple demographics often identify people uniquely. Carnegie Mellon University, Data privacy work paper 3, Pittsburgh (2000)
13. Yu, S.: Big privacy: challenges and opportunitiesof privacy study in the age of big data. IEEE Access 4, 2751–2763 (2016)

Tutorials

Tutorial: Supervised Learning for Prevalence Estimation

Alejandro Moreo and Fabrizio Sebastiani$^{(\boxtimes)}$

Istituto di Scienza e Tecnologie dell'Informazione, Consiglio Nazionale delle Ricerche, 56124 Pisa, Italy
{alejandro.moreo,fabrizio.sebastiani}@isti.cnr.it

Abstract. *Quantification* is the task of estimating, given a set σ of unlabelled items and a set of classes $\mathcal{C}$, the relative frequency (or "prevalence") $p(c_i)$ of each class $c_i \in \mathcal{C}$. Quantification is important in many disciplines (such as e.g., market research, political science, the social sciences, and epidemiology) which usually deal with aggregate (as opposed to individual) data. In these contexts, classifying individual unlabelled instances is usually not a primary goal, while estimating the prevalence of the classes of interest in the data is. Quantification may in principle be solved via classification, i.e., by classifying each item in σ and counting, for all $c_i \in \mathcal{C}$, how many such items have been labelled with c_i. However, it has been shown in a multitude of works that this "classify and count" (CC) method yields suboptimal quantification accuracy, one of the reasons being that most classifiers are optimized for classification accuracy, and not for quantification accuracy. As a result, quantification has come to be no longer considered a mere byproduct of classification, and has evolved as a task of its own, devoted to designing methods and algorithms that deliver better prevalence estimates than CC. The goal of this tutorial is to introduce the main supervised learning techniques that have been proposed for solving quantification, the metrics used to evaluate them, and the most promising directions for further research.

1 Motivation

Quantification (also known as "supervised prevalence estimation" [2], or "class prior estimation" [5]) is the task of estimating, given a set σ of unlabelled items and a set of classes $\mathcal{C} = \{c_1, \ldots, c_{|\mathcal{C}|}\}$, the relative frequency (or "prevalence") $p(c_i)$ of each class $c_i \in \mathcal{C}$, i.e., the fraction of items in σ that belong to c_i. When each item belongs to exactly one class, since $0 \leq p(c_i) \leq 1$ and $\sum_{c_i \in \mathcal{C}} p(c_i) = 1$, p is a *distribution* of the items in σ across the classes in $\mathcal{C}$ (the *true distribution*), and quantification thus amounts to estimating p (i.e., to computing a *predicted distribution* $\hat{p}$).

Quantification is important in many disciplines (such as e.g., market research, political science, the social sciences, and epidemiology) which usually deal with aggregate (as opposed to individual) data. In these contexts, classifying individual unlabelled instances is usually not a primary goal, while estimating the

© Springer Nature Switzerland AG 2019
A. Cuzzocrea et al. (Eds.): FQAS 2019, LNAI 11529, pp. 13–17, 2019.
https://doi.org/10.1007/978-3-030-27629-4_3

prevalence of the classes of interest in the data is. For instance, when classifying the tweets about a certain entity (e.g., a political candidate) as displaying either a Positive or a Negative stance towards the entity, we are usually not much interested in the class of a specific tweet: instead, we usually want to know the fraction of these tweets that belong to the class [9].

Quantification may in principle be solved via classification, i.e., by classifying each item in σ and counting, for all $c_i \in C$, how many such items have been labelled with c_i. However, it has been shown in a multitude of works (see e.g., [1,3,7–9,12]) that this "classify and count" (CC) method yields suboptimal quantification accuracy. Simply put, the reason of this suboptimality is that most classifiers are optimized for classification accuracy, and not for quantification accuracy. These two notions do not coincide, since the former is, by and large, inversely proportional to the sum $(FP_i + FN_i)$ of the false positives and the false negatives for c_i in the contingency table, while the latter is, by and large, inversely proportional to the absolute difference $|FP_i - FN_i|$ of the two.

One reason why it seems sensible to pursue quantification directly, instead of tackling it via classification, is that classification is a more general task than quantification: after all, a perfect classifier is also a perfect quantifier, while the opposite is not true. To see this consider that a binary classifier h_1 for which $FP = 20$ and $FN = 20$ (FP and FN standing for the "false positives" and "false negatives", respectively, that it has generated on a given dataset) is worse than a classifier h_2 for which, on the same test set, $FP = 18$ and $FN = 20$. However, h_1 is intuitively a better binary quantifier than h_2; indeed, h_1 is a perfect quantifier, since FP and FN are equal and thus, when it comes to class frequency estimation, compensate each other, so that the distribution of the test items across the class and its complement is estimated perfectly. In other words, a good quantifier needs to have small *bias* (i.e., needs to distribute its errors as evenly as possible across FP and FN). A training set might thus contain information sufficient to generate a good quantifier but not a good classifier, which means that performing quantification via "classify and count" might be a suboptimal way of performing quantification. In other words, performing quantification via "classify and count" looks like a violation of "Vapnik's principle" [21], which asserts that

> If you possess a restricted amount of information for solving some problem, try to solve the problem directly and never solve a more general problem as an intermediate step. It is possible that the available information is sufficient for a direct solution but is insufficient for solving a more general intermediate problem.

As a result, quantification is no longer considered a mere byproduct of classification, and has evolved as a task of its own, devoted to designing methods (see [10] for a survey) for delivering better prevalence estimates than CC.

There are further reasons why quantification is now considered as a task of its own. One such reason is that, since the goal of quantification is different from that of classification, quantification requires evaluation measures different from those used for classification. A second reason is the growing awareness that quantification is going to be more and more important; with the advent of big data, more and more application contexts are going to spring up in which we will simply be happy with analyzing data at the aggregate level and we will not be able to afford analyzing them at the individual level.

2   Format and Detailed Schedule

The structure of the lectures is as follows (each section also indicates the main bibliographic material discussed within the section):

1. Introduction/Motivation [17]
   (a) Solving quantification via "Classify and Count"
   (b) Concept drift and distribution drift
   (c) Vapnik's principle
   (d) The "paradox of quantification"
2. Applications of quantification in machine learning, data mining, text mining, and NLP [9,12]
   (a) Sentiment quantification
   (b) Quantification in the social sciences
   (c) Quantification in political science
   (d) Quantification in epidemiology
   (e) Quantification in market research
   (f) Quantification in ecological modelling
3. Evaluation of quantification algorithms [19]
   (a) Desirable properties for quantification evaluation measures
   (b) Evaluation measures for quantification
   (c) Experimental protocols for evaluating quantification
4. Supervised learning methods for binary and multiclass quantification [1,3,7, 8,11,12,15,18]
   (a) Aggregative methods based on general-purpose learners
   (b) Aggregative methods based on special-purpose learners
   (c) Non-aggregative methods
5. Advanced topics [4,6,13,14,16,20]
   (a) Ordinal quantification
   (b) Quantification for networked data
   (c) Quantification for data streams
   (d) Cross-lingual quantification
6. Conclusions.

References

1. Barranquero, J., Díez, J., del Coz, J.J.: Quantification-oriented learning based on reliable classifiers. Pattern Recogn. **48**(2), 591–604 (2015). https://doi.org/10.1016/j.patcog.2014.07.032
2. Barranquero, J., González, P., Díez, J., del Coz, J.J.: On the study of nearest neighbor algorithms for prevalence estimation in binary problems. Pattern Recogn. **46**(2), 472–482 (2013)
3. Bella, A., Ferri, C., Hernández-Orallo, J., Ramírez-Quintana, M.J.: Quantification via probability estimators. In: Proceedings of the 11th IEEE International Conference on Data Mining (ICDM 2010), Sydney, AU, pp. 737–742 (2010)
4. Da San Martino, G., Gao, W., Sebastiani, F.: Ordinal text quantification. In: Proceedings of the 39th ACM Conference on Research and Development in Information Retrieval (SIGIR 2016), Pisa, IT, pp. 937–940 (2016)
5. du Plessis, M.C., Niu, G., Sugiyama, M.: Class-prior estimation for learning from positive and unlabeled data. Mach. Learn. **106**(4), 463–492 (2017)
6. Esuli, A., Moreo, A., Sebastiani, F.: Cross-lingual sentiment quantification (2019). arXiv:1904.07965
7. Esuli, A., Sebastiani, F.: Optimizing text quantifiers for multivariate loss functions. ACM Trans. Knowl. Discov. Data **9**(4), Article ID 27 (2015)
8. Forman, G.: Quantifying counts and costs via classification. Data Min. Knowl. Discov. **17**(2), 164–206 (2008)
9. Gao, W., Sebastiani, F.: From classification to quantification in tweet sentiment analysis. Soc. Netw. Anal. Min. **6**(19), 1–22 (2016)
10. González, P., Castaño, A., Chawla, N.V., del Coz, J.J.: A review on quantification learning. ACM Comput. Surv. **50**(5), 74:1–74:40 (2017)
11. González-Castro, V., Alaiz-Rodríguez, R., Alegre, E.: Class distribution estimation based on the Hellinger distance. Inf. Sci. **218**, 146–164 (2013)
12. Hopkins, D.J., King, G.: A method of automated nonparametric content analysis for social science. Am. J. Polit. Sci. **54**(1), 229–247 (2010)
13. Kar, P., Li, S., Narasimhan, H., Chawla, S., Sebastiani, F.: Online optimization methods for the quantification problem. In: Proceedings of the 22nd ACM SIGKDD International Conference on Knowledge Discovery and Data Mining (KDD 2016), San Francisco, US, pp. 1625–1634 (2016)
14. Maletzke, A.G., dos Reis, D.M., Batista, G.E.: Combining instance selection and self-training to improve data stream quantification. J. Braz. Comput. Soc. **24**(12), 43–48 (2018)
15. Milli, L., Monreale, A., Rossetti, G., Giannotti, F., Pedreschi, D., Sebastiani, F.: Quantification trees. In: Proceedings of the 13th IEEE International Conference on Data Mining (ICDM 2013), Dallas, US, pp. 528–536 (2013)
16. Milli, L., Monreale, A., Rossetti, G., Pedreschi, D., Giannotti, F., Sebastiani, F.: Quantification in social networks. In: Proceedings of the 2nd IEEE International Conference on Data Science and Advanced Analytics (DSAA 2015), Paris, FR (2015)
17. Moreno-Torres, J.G., Raeder, T., Alaiz-Rodríguez, R., Chawla, N.V., Herrera, F.: A unifying view on dataset shift in classification. Pattern Recogn. **45**(1), 521–530 (2012)
18. Saerens, M., Latinne, P., Decaestecker, C.: Adjusting the outputs of a classifier to new a priori probabilities: a simple procedure. Neural Comput. **14**(1), 21–41 (2002)

19. Sebastiani, F.: Evaluation measures for quantification: an axiomatic approach. Inf. Retrieval J. (2019, to appear)
20. Tang, L., Gao, H., Liu, H.: Network quantification despite biased labels. In: Proceedings of the 8th Workshop on Mining and Learning with Graphs (MLG 2010), Washington, US, pp. 147–154 (2010)
21. Vapnik, V.: Statistical Learning Theory. Wiley, New York (1998)

Algorithmic Approaches to Computational Models of Argumentation

Matthias Thimm[✉]

Institute for Web Science and Technologies (WeST),
University of Koblenz-Landau, Koblenz, Germany
thimm@uni-koblenz.de

1 Introduction

Computational models of argumentation [1] are approaches for non-monotonic reasoning that focus on the interplay between arguments and counterarguments in order to reach conclusions. These approaches can be divided into either *abstract* or *structured* approaches. The former encompass the classical abstract argumentation frameworks following Dung [8] that model argumentation scenarios by directed graphs, where vertices represent arguments and directed links represent attacks between arguments. In these graphs one is usually interested in identifying *extensions*, i.e., sets of arguments that are mutually acceptable and thus provide a coherent perspective on the outcome of the argumentation. On the other hand, structured argumentation approaches consider arguments to be collections of formulas and/or rules which entail some conclusion. The most prominent structured approaches are ASPIC+ [16], ABA [22], DeLP [13], and *deductive argumentation* [2]. These approaches consider a knowledge base of formulas and/or rules as a starting point.

2 Algorithms for Abstract Argumentation

According to [6], algorithms for solving reasoning problems in abstract argumentation can generally be categorised into two classes: *reduction-based* approaches and *direct* approaches.

Reduction-based approaches such as ASPARTIX-D [10,12] and ArgSemSAT [5] translate the given problem for abstract argumentation—such as determining a single stable extension—into another formalism and use dedicated (and mature) systems for that formalism to solve the original problem. For example, ASPARTIX encodes the problem of finding a stable extension in abstract argumentation into the question of finding an answer set of an answer set program [14]. Due to the direct relationship of answer sets and stable models the answer set program only needs to model the semantics of the abstract argumentation framework in a faithful manner and represent the actual framework.

© Springer Nature Switzerland AG 2019
A. Cuzzocrea et al. (Eds.): FQAS 2019, LNAI 11529, pp. 18–21, 2019.
https://doi.org/10.1007/978-3-030-27629-4_4

ASPARTIX-D then makes use of the Potassco ASP solvers[1] to solve the reduced problem and translate their output back to the original question. Similarly, ArgSemSAT decodes the problem as a SAT instance and uses the Glucose[2] SAT solver to solve the latter. Internally, solvers such as the Potassco ASP solvers and SAT solvers make use of sophisticated search strategies such as *conflict-driven nogood learning* or *conflict-driven clause learning*, see [3,14] for details.

Direct approaches to solve reasoning problems in abstract argumentation are inspired by similar search strategies but directly realise these algorithms for abstract argumentation. For example, solvers such as ArgTools [17] and heureka [15] are based on the DPLL (Davis-Putnam-Logemann-Loveland) backtracking algorithm from SAT solving [3, Chapter 3]. Basically, they exhaustively explore the search space of all possible sets of arguments to determine, e.g., a stable extension but include various optimisations and specific search strategies to prune the search space as much as possible to keep runtime low. Another direct solver, EqArgSolver [18], uses a different approach though, and is inspired by an iteration scheme originally designed to solve problems for probabilistic argumentation [11]. For a more detailed discussion of the different approaches to solving problems in abstract argumentation see [4].

Recently, approximate methods for reasoning problems in abstract argumentation have been introduced as well [20]. The algorithms of [20] follow the paradigm of *stochastic local search*, i.e., incomplete optimisation algorithms that aim at reaching an optimal value of a target function by small random changes of the parameters, see e.g. [3, Chapter 6] for a deeper discussion in the context of solving the satisfiability problem (SAT). The core idea of these algorithms is as follows. Considering the labelling approach to the semantics of abstract argumentation frameworks, they start from a labelling that randomly assigns the acceptability status in and out to all arguments of the input argumentation framework. As long as this labelling is not stable—i.e. as long as the arguments labelled in do not form a stable extension—one mislabelled argument is selected and its acceptability status is flipped. Albeit being a simple idea it can outperform traditional algorithms, in particular on *random* instances with little structure.

3 Algorithms for Structured Argumentation

Queries are answered in structured argumentation approaches, e.g. in the case of ASPIC+ [16], by determining all arguments constructible from the knowledge base, identifying attacks between these arguments using e.g. contradictions between conclusions of different arguments, and resolving the conflicts by representing the constructed arguments and attacks as an abstract argumentation framework and relying on reasoning methods for this abstract case. Computationally, reasoning with structured argumentation approaches can be quite

---

[1] http://potassco.sourceforge.net.
[2] http://www.labri.fr/perso/lsimon/glucose/.

demanding as both checking whether a set of formulas and/or rules is an argument can be challenging and the number of arguments in a knowledge base may be super-polynomial (and even infinite in some approaches). Some formal analyses on this, in particular regarding the approach of ABA, can be found in [7,9]. Existing solvers for ASPIC+ that implement complete reasoning procedures are, e.g., TOAST [19] and EPR[3]. See [4] for a survey on sound and complete algorithms and implementations for structured argumentation approaches.

A recent approach [21] to approximate reasoning with structured argumentation is based on sampling of arguments, instead of constructing all possible arguments. There, two parametrised algorithms are developed that solve the general problem of checking whether a certain proposition is acceptable wrt. a given knowledge base. Both algorithms rely on *sampling* arguments in order to avoid enumerating all arguments of a knowledge base. The first algorithm RAND$_I$ samples arguments *independently* by (1) selecting some rule from the knowledge base to be the top rule of the argument, and (2) recursively selecting rules where their conclusion appears in the body of a previously selected rule, until a valid argument is found. This process is repeated for a fixed number of arguments, yielding a set of arguments that is a subset of all possible arguments. The second algorithm RAND$_D$ samples arguments *directionally* by (1) sampling some argument that has the query as conclusion, and (2) recursively sampling counterarguments of previously sampled arguments.

References

1. Atkinson, K., et al.: Toward artificial argumentation. AI Mag. **38**(3), 25–36 (2017)
2. Besnard, P., Hunter, A.: Constructing argument graphs with deductive arguments: a tutorial. Argum. Comput. **5**(1), 5–30 (2014)
3. Biere, A., Heule, M., van Maaren, H., Walsh, T. (eds.): Handbook of Satisfiability. Frontiers in Artificial Intelligence and Applications, vol. 185. IOS Press, Amsterdam (2009)
4. Cerutti, F., Gaggl, S.A., Thimm, M., Wallner, J.P.: Foundations of implementations for formal argumentation. In: Baroni, P., Gabbay, D., Giacomin, M., van der Torre, L. (eds.) Handbook of Formal Argumentation, chap. 15. College Publications, February 2018. Also appears in IfCoLog J. Log. Appl. **4**(8), 2623–2706, October 2017
5. Cerutti, F., Giacomin, M., Vallati, M.: ArgSemSAT: solving argumentation problems using SAT. In: Computational Models of Argument - Proceedings of COMMA 2014, Atholl Palace Hotel, Scottish Highlands, UK, 9–12 September 2014, pp. 455–456 (2014)
6. Charwat, G., Dvořák, W., Gaggl, S.A., Wallner, J.P., Woltran, S.: Methods for solving reasoning problems in abstract argumentation - a survey. Artif. Intell. **220**, 28–63 (2015)
7. Dimopoulos, Y., Nebel, B., Toni, F.: On the computational complexity of assumption-based argumentation for default reasoning. Artif. Intell. **141**(1), 57–78 (2002)

---

[3] http://www.wietskevisser.nl/research/epr/.

8. Dung, P.M.: On the acceptability of arguments and its fundamental role in non-monotonic reasoning, logic programming and n-person games. Artif. Intell. **77**(2), 321–358 (1995)
9. Dvořák, W., Dunne, P.E.: Computational problems in formal argumentation and their complexity. In: Baroni, P., Gabbay, D., Giacomin, M., van der Torre, L. (eds.) Handbook of Formal Argumentation, chap. 14. College Publications, February 2018
10. Egly, U., Gaggl, S.A., Woltran, S.: Answer-set programming encodings for argumentation frameworks. Technical report DBAI-TR-2008-62, Technische Universität Wien (2008)
11. Gabbay, D., Rodrigues, O.: A self-correcting iteration schema for argumentation networks. In: Proceedings of the Fifth International Conference on Computational Models of Argumentation (COMMA 2014) (2014)
12. Gaggl, S.A., Manthey, N.: ASPARTIX-D: ASP argumentation reasoning tool - dresden. In: System Descriptions of the First International Competition on Computational Models of Argumentation (ICCMA 2015). ArXiv (2015)
13. García, A.J., Simari, G.R.: Defeasible logic programming: DeLP-servers, contextual queries, and explanations for answers. Argum. Comput. **5**(1), 63–88 (2014)
14. Gebser, M., Kaminski, R., Kaufmann, B., Schaub, T.: Answer Set Solving in Practice. Synthesis Lectures on Artificial Intelligence and Machine Learning. Morgan & Claypool Publishers, San Rafael (2012)
15. Geilen, N., Thimm, M.: Heureka: a general heuristic backtracking solver for abstract argumentation. In: Black, E., Modgil, S., Oren, N. (eds.) TAFA 2017. LNCS (LNAI), vol. 10757, pp. 143–149. Springer, Cham (2018). https://doi.org/10.1007/978-3-319-75553-3_10
16. Modgil, S., Prakken, H.: The ASPIC+ framework for structured argumentation: a tutorial. Argum. Comput. **5**, 31–62 (2014)
17. Nofal, S., Atkinson, K., Dunne, P.E.: Looking-ahead in backtracking algorithms for abstract argumentation. Int. J. Approx. Reason. **78**, 265–282 (2016)
18. Rodrigues, O.: A forward propagation algorithm for the computation of the semantics of argumentation frameworks. In: Black, E., Modgil, S., Oren, N. (eds.) TAFA 2017. LNCS (LNAI), vol. 10757, pp. 120–136. Springer, Cham (2018). https://doi.org/10.1007/978-3-319-75553-3_8
19. Snaith, M., Reed, C.: TOAST: online ASPIC+ implementation. In: Proceedings of the Fourth International Conference on Computational Models of Argument (COMMA 2012), pp. 509–510. IOS Press (2012)
20. Thimm, M.: Stochastic local search algorithms for abstract argumentation under stable semantics. In: Modgil, S., Budzynska, K., Lawrence, J. (eds.) Proceedings of the Seventh International Conference on Computational Models of Argumentation (COMMA 2018). Frontiers in Artificial Intelligence and Applications, Warsaw, Poland, vol. 305, pp. 169–180, September 2018
21. Thimm, M., Rienstra, T.: Approximate reasoning with ASPIC+ by argument sampling (2019, under review)
22. Toni, F.: A tutorial on assumption-based argumentation. Argum. Comput. **5**(1), 89–117 (2014)

Introduction

Flexible Querying and Analytics for Smart Cities and Smart Societies in the Age of Big Data: Overview of the FQAS 2019 International Conference

Alfredo Cuzzocrea[1(✉)] and Sergio Greco[2]

[1] DISPES Department, University of Calabria, Rende, Italy
alfredo.cuzzocrea@unical.it
[2] DIMES Department, University of Calabria, Rende, Italy
greco@dimes.unical.it

Abstract. This paper contains a brief overview on issues and challenges of the emerging topic recognized as *flexible querying and analytics for smart cities and smart societies*, which is strictly related to the actual *big data management and analytics* research trend, along with a brief overview of the FQAS 2019 international conference.

Keywords: Big data · Flexible query answering · Flexible analytics ·
Big data intelligence · Smart cities · Smart societies

1 Introduction

Nowadays, *big data management and analytics* is playing the major role in the academic and industrial research community (e.g., [1, 2]). In this context, several research challenges can be recognized, among which *effectively and efficiently supporting flexible querying and analytics* are major issues to be addressed (e.g., [3, 4]).

These topics become particularly critical when connected to systems and tools that fall in the broad application scenario represented by *smart cities and smart societies* (e.g., [5, 6]). Here, well-known big data features induct a plethora of research challenges, among which we recall: (*i*) heterogeneity of data types; (*ii*) streaming nature; (*iii*) data quality. These challenges can be reasonably intended as actual obstacles towards obtaining flexibility in query and analytics tools over big data repositories.

By looking into details, big data for smart cities and smart society includes rather a wide collection of emerging application domains, such as energy systems, transportation systems, building design systems, healthcare systems, environmental monitoring systems, and so forth. Indeed, this is actually a "hot-topic", even as demonstrated by a plethora of real-life smart city and smart society projects developed in cities like London, Amsterdam, Singapore, San Francisco, and so forth. The main idea here consists in improving the quality of life in these cities and societies, thanks to smart ICT technologies (among which big data management and analytics play the role of main enabling technologies), but also other scientific disciplines like physics, city planning, medicine, biology, electronics, cultural heritage, and so forth, by empowering the interdisciplinary nature of such projects.

A. Cuzzocrea et al. (Eds.): FQAS 2019, LNAI 11529, pp. 25–28, 2019.
https://doi.org/10.1007/978-3-030-27629-4_5

Within the so-delineated framework, in this paper we provide a brief overview on these research issues, along with a brief overview of the *13ᵗʰ International Conference on Flexible Query Answering* (FQAS 2019), held in Amantea, Italy, during July 2–5, 2019.

2 Flexible Querying and Analytics for Smart Cities and Smart Societies in the Age of Big Data: Issues and Challenges

As mentioned in Sect. 1, heterogeneity of data types, streaming nature, and data quality are actually the major research challenges for big data research, with particular regards to the emerging smart city and smart society application scenario.

Heterogeneity of data types in big data sources is a well-known issue of smart city and smart society applications and systems (e.g., [7]). Here, big data sources occur in different formats, including graph data (e.g., social networks), XML data (e.g., Web information systems), sensor data (e.g., environmental monitoring networks), relational data (e.g., legacy systems), and so forth. How to deal with such (big) data heterogeneity is still an open problem.

Streaming nature of big data is widely-accepted as an enabling feature of big data applications themselves (e.g., [8]). Indeed, almost all the popular big data sources are streaming sources, such as sensor networks, social networks, industrial plants in industry 4.0 settings, and so forth. As a consequence, supporting mining and analytics over such data sources exposes to several drawbacks. For instance, how to compute OLAP-based aggregations over streaming data? When the computation should be blocked? How to evaluate concept drifting (e.g., for classification purposes) over streaming data? When data for class induction should be considered completely observed? Questions like the latter are still open problems in actual literature.

Quality of big data is an emerging topic at now (e.g., [9]). Indeed, consumers of big data applications are used to process big data repositories but they do not really know about the origin of such (big) data. Therefore, there is not any external authority that can ensure about the quality of (processed) big data. This problem is recognized in literature as the so-called *big data provenance problem* (e.g., [10]), and it consists in detecting who/which-application has originated and pre-processed the target big data source, for quality of data assessment purposes.

By addressing research challenges like the ones discussed above, next-generation big data analytics tools will be prone to incorporate flexibility in query and analytics tools over big data repositories, for enhanced smart city and smart society applications and systems.

3 13ᵗʰ International Conference on Flexible Query Answering Systems (FQAS 2019): Overview

FQAS 2019 has been held in Amantea, Italy, during July 2–5, 2019. The conference focuses on the special theme *flexible querying and analytics for smart cities and smart societies*, whose fundamental research challenges have been highlighted in Sect. 1. The conference program has comprised three invited speeches, namely: (*i*) V.S. Subrah-manian, from Dartmouth College, NH, USA, *"Logic, Machine Learning, and Security"*; (*ii*) Josep Domingo-Ferrer, Universitat Rovira i Virgili, Spain, *"Personal Big Data, GDPR and Anonymization"*; (*iii*) Enrico Franconi, Free University of Bozen-Bolzano, Italy, *"Querying Databases with Ontologies: 17 Years Later"*. In addition to this, the conference program has also comprise two tutorials, namely: (*i*) Alejandro Moreo and Fabrizio Sebastiani, ISTI-CNR, Italy *"Supervised Learning for Prevalence Estimation"*; (*ii*) Matthias Thimm, Universitat Koblenz-Landau, Germany, *"Algorithmic Approaches to Computational Models of Argumentation"*.

FQAS 2019 has collected high-quality papers from Europe, North America, South America, Asia, and Africa. These papers focus the attention on different topics, including:

- *flexible database management and querying*;
- *ontologies and knowledge bases*;
- *argumentation-based query answering*;
- *data mining and knowledge discovery*;
- *advanced flexible query answering methodologies and techniques*;
- *flexible query answering methods and techniques*;
- *flexible intelligent information-oriented and network-oriented approaches*;
- *big data veracity and soft computing*;
- *flexibility in tools*;
- *systems and miscellanea*.

The positive news that one can derive from these contributions is that smart ICT technologies, and, particularly, big data management and analytics, can really provide a critical contribution to smart city and smart society applications and systems, thus improving the quality of life of people significantly.

We firmly believe that the conference has been a milestone in the exciting research road represented by the issue of effectively and efficiently supporting flexible query answering for smart cities and smart societies in the big data era.

4 Conclusions

This paper has provided a brief overview on issues and challenges of the emerging topic flexible querying and analytics for smart cities and smart societies, along with a brief overview of the FQAS 2019 international conference.

References

1. Zikopoulos, P., Eaton, C.: Understanding Big Data: Analytics for Enterprise Class Hadoop and Streaming Data, 1st edn. McGraw-Hill Osborne Media, Plano (2011)
2. LaValle, S.: Big data, analytics and the path from insights to value. MIT Sloan Manag. Rev. **52**, 21–32 (2011)

3. Zou, H., Yu, Y., Tang, W., Chen, H.-W.: Flex analytics: a flexible data analytics framework for big data applications with I/O performance improvement. Big Data Res. **1**, 4–13 (2014)
4. Zhao, D., Qiao, K., Zhou, Z., Li, T., Lu, Z., Xu, X.: Toward efficient and flexible metadata indexing of big data systems. IEEE Transact. Big Data **3**(1), 107–117 (2017)
5. Rani, S., Chauhdary, S.H.: A novel framework and enhanced QoS big data protocol for smart city applications. Sensors **18**(11), 3980 (2018)
6. Silva, B.N., et al.: Urban planning and smart city decision management empowered by real-time data processing using big data analytics. Sensors **18**(9), 2994 (2018)
7. Gal, A., Gunopulos, D., Panagiotou, N., Rivetti, N., Senderovich, A., Zygouras, N.: REMI: a framework of reusable elements for mining heterogeneous data with missing information - a tale of congestion in two smart cities. J. Intell. Inf. Syst. **51**(2), 367–388 (2018)
8. Rodríguez, J.Y.F., Álvarez-García, J.A., Arias-Fisteus, J., Luaces, M.R., Magaña, V.C.: Benchmarking real-time vehicle data streaming models for a smart city. Inf. Syst. **72**, 62–76 (2017)
9. Bertino, E., Jahanshahi, M.R.: Adaptive and cost-effective collection of high-quality data for critical infrastructure and emergency management in smart cities - framework and challenges. J. Data Inf. Q. **10**(1), 1 (2018)
10. Wu, D., Sakr, S., Zhu, L.: HDM: optimized big data processing with data provenance. In: Proceedings of EDBT 2017 (2017)

Flexible Database Management and Querying

Indexing for Skyline Computation
A Comparison Study

Markus Endres$^{(\boxtimes)}$ and Erich Glaser

Faculty of Computer Science and Mathematics, University of Passau,
Innstr. 33, 94032 Passau, Germany
markus.endres@uni-passau.de, erichglaser@gmail.com

Abstract. Skyline queries enable satisfying search results by delivering best matches, even if the filter criteria are conflictive. Skyline algorithms are often classified into *generic* and *index-based* approaches. While there are uncountable papers on the comparison on generic algorithms, there exists only a few publications on the effect of index-based Skyline computation. In this paper, we give an overview on the most recent index-based Skyline algorithms *BBS*, *ZSky*, and *SkyMap*. We conducted comprehensive experiments on different data sets and present some really interesting outcomes.

Keywords: Skyline · Pareto · Index · BBS · ZSky · SkyMap

1 Introduction

Preferences in databases are a well established framework to create personalized information systems [7]. Skyline queries [1] are the most prominent representatives of these queries; they model equally important preferences.

More detailed: Given a data set D, a Skyline query returns all objects that are not dominated by any other object in D. An object p is dominated by another object q, if q is at least as good as p on all dimensions and definitely better in at least one dimension. Thus, a Skyline query computes all Pareto-optimal objects w.r.t. to a preference or feature function and has many applications in multi-criteria optimization problems.

As an example consider Table 1. Imagine that the objects are *hotels* and the x and y coordinates in the 2-dim space correspond to the *price* and *distance to the beach*. The target is to find the *cheapest* hotels which are *close to the beach*. Then this query would identify the hotels $\{p_1, p_2, p_3, p_5, p_6\}$ as the *Skyline* result. All objects in this set are indifferent and dominate all other objects.

The main problem with Skyline queries is to efficiently find the set of non-dominated objects from a large data set, because Skyline processing is an expensive operation. Its cost is mainly constituted by *I/O costs* in accessing data from a secondary storage (e.g., disks) and CPU costs spent on *dominance tests*.

There exist several algorithms for Skyline processing which, in general, can be divided into *generic* and *index-based* techniques.

© Springer Nature Switzerland AG 2019
A. Cuzzocrea et al. (Eds.): FQAS 2019, LNAI 11529, pp. 31–42, 2019.
https://doi.org/10.1007/978-3-030-27629-4_6

Table 1. Sample data set for Skyline.

Object	p_1	p_2	p_3	p_4	p_5	p_6	p_7	p_8	p_9
x	3	1	2	3	5	7	6	4	6
y	3	6	4	7	2	1	2	4	6

Generic algorithms are often capable to evaluate each kind of preference (modeled as irreflexive and transitive order [4]) due to an object-to-object comparison approach. However, in a worst-case scenario the generic algorithms show a quadratic runtime $\mathcal{O}(n^2)$ in the size n of the input relation. On the other hand, index-based algorithms tend to be faster, but are less flexible – they are designed for quite static data, flat query structures and have a high maintenance overhead associated with database updates [6]. In general, they cannot deal with complex preference queries, where, e.g., intermediate relations are dynamically produced by a Cartesian product or a join.

As Skyline queries have been considered as an analytical tool in some commercial relational database systems [2,11], and the data sets to be processed in real-world applications are of considerable size, there is definitely the need for improved query performance. And indexing data is one natural choice to achieve this performance improvement. Also, Lee et al. [9] show that a wide variety of special Skyline queries (k-dominant Skylines, Skybands, Subspace Skylines, etc.) can be supported using a single index structure. While indexes can dramatically speed-up retrieval, they also introduce maintenance costs and tend to quickly degenerate on higher dimensional data.

In this paper, we compare the best known index algorithms for Skyline computation, namely *BBS* [12], *ZSky* [8,9], and *SkyMap* [14] w.r.t. their performance, since search efficiency is the most important performance criteria using this kind of queries. We will present comprehensive experiments on synthetic and real-world data to evaluate the behavior in different scenarios in order to find the best approach for one's field of application.

The rest of the paper is organized as follows: Sect. 2 presents background on Skylines and we introduce the index-based Skyline algorithms used in this paper in Sect. 3. Section 4 contains our comprehensive experiments and in Sect. 5 we give some final remarks.

2 Preliminaries

The aim of a Skyline query or Pareto preference is to find *the best matching objects* in a data set D, denoted by *Sky(D)* [3]. More formally:

Definition 1 (Dominance and Indifference). *Assume a set of vectors $D \subseteq \mathbb{R}^d$. Given $p = (p_1, ..., p_n), q = (q_1, ..., q_d) \in D$, p dominates q on D, denotes as $p \prec q$, if the following holds:*

$$p \prec q \Leftrightarrow \forall i \in \{1, ..., d\} : p_i \leq q_i \wedge \exists j \in \{1, ..., d\} : p_j < q_j \tag{1}$$

Note that following Definition 1, we consider a subset $D \subseteq \mathbb{R}^d$ in that we search for Skylines w.r.t. the natural order $\leq$ in each dimension. Characteristic properties of such a data set D are its dimensionality d, its cardinality n, and its Skyline size $|Sky(D)|$.

Definition 2 (Skyline Sky(D)). *The Skyline* Sky(D) *of D is defined by the maxima in D according to the ordering* $\prec$*, or explicitly by the set*

$$Sky(D) := \{p \in D \mid \nexists q \in D : q \prec p\} \tag{2}$$

In this sense, the minimal values in each domain are preferred and we write $p \prec q$ *if p is better than q.*

In the introductory example we have $Sky(D) = \{p_1, p_2, p_3, p_5, p_6\}$.

3   Algorithms

In this section we review the state-of-the-art index-based Skyline algorithms *BBS*, *ZSky*, and *SkyMap* as well as *BNL* as an object comparison approach.

3.1   BBS

BBS (Branch-and-Bound Skyline) [12,13] is based on a nearest neighbor (NN) search and uses R-trees for data partitioning. As an example consider Fig. 1a taken from [8]. The object p_1 is the first Skyline object, since it is the NN to the origin. The objects p_4, p_8, and p_9 fall into the *dominance region* of p_1 and therefore can be discarded. p_3 is the second NN (not worse than p_1) and hence is another Skyline object. The same idea applies to p_5 (which dominates p_7) and p_2 and p_6. All non-dominated objects build the Skyline.

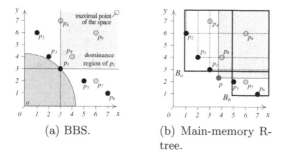

(a) BBS.   (b) Main-memory R-tree.

Fig. 1. The BBS algorithm, cp. [8].

BBS uses a *main-memory R-tree* to perform dominance tests on every examinee (i.e., data object or index node) by issuing an enclosure query. If an examinee is entirely enclosed by any Skyline candidate's dominance region, it is dominated and can be discarded. For example, in Fig. 1b, p_8 is compared with the minimum bounding rectangles (MBR) B_a and B_b. Since p_8 is in B_a, it is possibly dominated by some data objects enclosed by B_a. Hence, p_8 is compared with the dominance regions of all the data objects inside B_a and found to be dominated by p_1 and p_3.

3.2 ZSky

ZSky is a framework for Skyline computation using a Z-order space filling curve [9]. A Z-order curve maps multi-dimensional data objects to one-dimensional objects. Thereby each object is represented by a bit-string computed by interleaving the bits of its coordinate values, called *Z-address*, which then can be used for B-tree indexing. Through the Z-addresses the B-tree imposes a pre-sorting on the data, which can be exploited for dominance tests: No database item can dominate any item having a lower Z-address. These observations lead to the access order of the data objects arranged on a Z-order curve.

In Fig. 2a the data space is partitioned into four regions I to IV. Region I is not dominated by any other object, and all objects in region IV are dominated by region I. Region II and III are incomparable. These principles also apply to subregions and single coordinates. Using a Z-order curve, region I should be accessed first, followed by region II and III, and finally region IV. The access sequence therefore follows the mentioned Z-order curve as seen in Fig. 2b.

With effective region-based dominance tests, ZSky (more accurate *ZSearch*) can efficiently assert if a region of data objects is dominated by a single object or a region of Skyline objects. In each round, the region of a node is examined against the current Skyline candidate list. If its corresponding region is not dominated, the node is further explored.

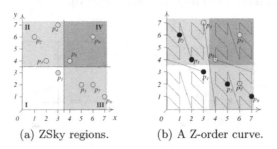

(a) ZSky regions.   (b) A Z-order curve.

Fig. 2. ZSky example, cp. [9].

Z-Sky can also be used with *bulkloading*. Bulkloading builds a ZB-tree in a bottom-up fashion. It sorts all data objects in an ascending order of their Z-addresses and forms leaf nodes based on every N data objects. It also puts every N leaf nodes together to form non-leaf nodes until the root of a ZB-tree is formed.

3.3 SkyMap

Selke and Balke [14] proposed *SkyMap* for Skyline query computation. In general, SkyMap is based on the idea of the Z-order curve, but relies on a *trie* (from re*trie*val) indexing structure instead on a ZB-tree. In a trie (also known as Prefix B-tree), internal nodes are solely used for navigational purposes, whereas the leaf nodes store the actual data. SkyMap is a multi-dimensional extension of binary tries, which additionally provides an efficient method for dominance checks. The SkyMap index has primarily been designed to resemble the recursive splitting process of Z-regions.

When traversing a SkyMap index while looking for objects q dominating an object p, one can skip any node (along with all its children) whose corresponding Z-region is worse than p w.r.t. at least one dimension. Navigation within the SkyMap index is particularly efficient by relying on inexpensive bitwise operations only. In this sense, SkyMap promises efficient navigation and index maintenance which should result in a higher performance in comparison to Z-Sky.

3.4 BNL

BNL (Block-Nested-Loop) was developed by Börzsönyi [1] in 2001. The idea of BNL is to scan over the input data set D and to maintain a *window* (or block) of objects in main memory containing the temporary Skyline elements w.r.t. the data read so far. When an object $p \in D$ is read from the input, p is compared to all objects of the window and, based on this comparison, p is either eliminated, or placed into the window. At the end of the algorithm the window contains *the Skyline*. The average case complexity is of the order $\mathcal{O}(n)$, where n counts the number of input objects. In the worst case the complexity is $\mathcal{O}(n^2)$ [1].

The major advantage of a BNL-style algorithm is its simplicity and suitability for computing the Skyline of arbitrary partial orders [4]. Note that BNL is *not* an index approach, but is used as a *baseline algorithm* in our experiments.

4 Experiments

In this section we show our comprehensive comparison study on index-based Skyline algorithms, i.e., **BBS, ZSky, ZSky-Bl** (ZSky with *bulkloading*), and **SkyMap**. As a base line algorithm we used the generic **BNL**. In all our experiments the data objects and index structures are held in main memory as has also been done by the original works [9,10,12] and [14]. All experiments were implemented in Java 1.8 and performed on a common PC (Intel i7 4.0 GHz CPU, 16 GB RAM) running Linux. We use a maximum of 4 GB RAM for the JVM.

Similar to most of the related work in the literature, we use *elapse time/runtime* as the main performance metric. Each measurement was based on 16 repetitions from which we neglected the four best and four worst runtimes. From the remaining 8 measurements we used the average runtime in our figures.

Four our synthetic data sets we used the data generator commonly used in Skyline research [1] and that one was also used by the original papers [9,12,14]. We generated *independent* (ind), *correlated* (cor), and *anti-correlated* (anti) data and varied the number of *dimensions* (d) and the number of *input objects* (n). For the experiments on real-data, we used the well-known *Zillow*, *House*, and *NBA* data sets which will be explained in detail later. Due to the restricted space in this paper we only present some characteristic results. More experiments and details can be found in our Technical Report [5].

4.1 Effect of Data Dimensionality

This section considers the influence of the *dimensions* d on the runtime of the algorithms. We varied $d \in \{4, 6, 8, 10, 15, 20, 25, 30\}$, where each dimension has the integer domain $[0, 1024)$, and used different data distributions. We fixed $n = 100K$, and plotted the elapsed time in log scale against dimensionality.

Independent Data. Figure 3 shows our results on synthetic *independent data*. Considering the index construction (on the top right, "Index"), BBS is worst and ZSky-Bl is best, because there are no special computations due to bulkloading. We also observe that the index construction time increases with growing dimensions. For the Skyline computation time (on the top left, "Skyline"), BNL outperforms some index algorithms, but has the highest runtime from 10 dimensions on. Note, that the size of the Skyline is nearly the size of the input data from 20 dimensions on and therefore the computation costs are nearly equal in these cases. In general, BBS is the slowest algorithm, whereas there is nearly no difference between ZSky and ZSky-Bl. Based on the incremental insert of objects, we only get slightly better Z-regions. In summary, BNL performs well for less number of dimensions, whereas SkyMap performs better with increasing dimensions.

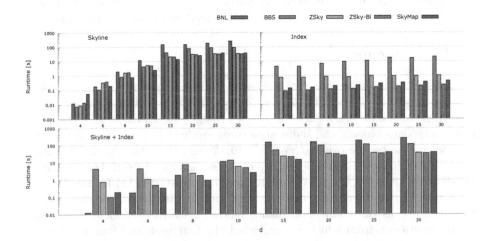

Fig. 3. Independent data. Runtime w.r.t. dimensionality.

Table 2(a) summarizes some statistics for the evaluation, e.g., the size of the Skyline, and the number of dominance tests. The dominance tests also include the comparison between regions to objects and other regions in BBS and ZSky. In particular, the number of dominance tests is very high for BNL and BBS, which are mainly based on object-to-object comparisons. On the other hand, ZSky and SkyMap are able to sort out leafs or inner nodes of the index structure, which leads to a etter performance and less comparisons.

Table 2. Dominance tests $\cdot 10^6$ w.r.t. dimensionality.

Dim	Skyline	BNL	BBS	ZSky	ZSky-Bl	SkyMap
4	246	0.472	0.211	0.199	0.258	0.229
6	2486	8	5	7	7	2
8	9671	88	51	32	31	9
10	25673	465	336	95	94	33
15	76944	3265	2967	411	409	168
20	97034	4794	4709	602	599	285
25	99806	4988	4980	649	647	315
30	99995	4999	4999	650	648	316

(a) Independent data.

Dim	Skyline	BNL	BBS	ZSky	ZSky-Bl	SkyMap
4	3465	17	76	31	34	16
6	14076	175	507	139	139	46
8	34278	823	1741	325	324	123
10	58508	2108	3346	612	610	415
15	94400	4603	5892	1066	1063	804
20	99669	4979	6295	1169	1166	876
25	99933	4995	6242	1193	1189	924
30	99978	4999	6187	1185	1182	921

(b) Anti-correlated data.

Anti-correlated Data. Figure 4 shows our results on *anti-correlated data*. Anti-correlated data is the worst-case for Skyline computation, because there are many indifferent objects and the result set is large. The costs for index creation and Skyline computation is very similar to independent data. Considering the total costs ("Skyline + Index"), BNL is better than all index-based approaches until 6 dimensions. In higher dimensions BBS, ZSky, and ZSky-Bl are nearly equally good and all are outperformed by SkyMap. Furthermore, SkyMap is much better than all other algorithms w.r.t. the pure Skyline computation. These results are also reflected by the numbers in Table 2(b). SkyMap uses the lowest number of dominance tests.

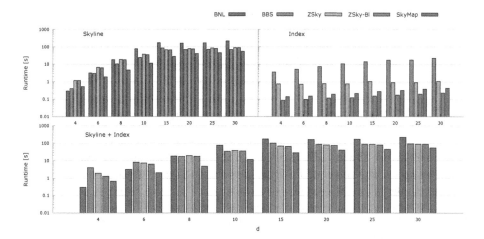

Fig. 4. Anti-correlated data. Runtime w.r.t. dimensionality.

4.2 Effect of Data Cardinality

In the next experiments we considered the influence of the *data input size* n using the following characteristics: Integer domain in $[0, 1024)$, $d = 8$ dimensions, input size $n \in \{10K, 100K, 500K, 1000K, 2000K\}$.

Independent Data. Figure 5 shows that ZSky and ZSky-Bl perform worse from $n = 500K$ objects on w.r.t. the Skyline computation. Even BNL as an object-to-object comparison algorithm is faster. This is based on the fact that the underlying ZB-tree constructs index nodes very fast, and due to less common prefixes this results in very large Z-regions which must be checked for dominance. SkyMap is definitely better than its competitors, because of its trie index structure. Also BBS is better than the ZSky approaches, although it is the oldest of all algorithms. On the other hand, BBS is really worse w.r.t. the index construction time because of the linear splits. The SkyMap sorting is a bit more costly than the filling of the ZB-trees via bulkloading.

Table 3(a) shows the number of dominance tests, where SkyMap clearly outperforms all other algorithms. It is notable that in ZSky the number of index nodes increase. Therefore, the algorithm builds larger Z-regions, which in the end lead to a higher runtime.

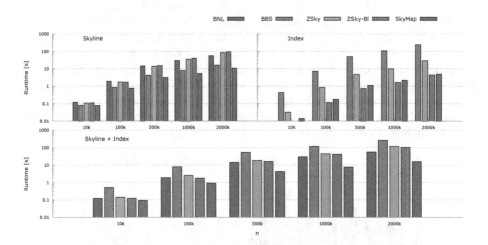

Fig. 5. Independent data. Runtime w.r.t. input size.

Anti-correlated Data. Figure 6 and Table 3(b) show our results on *anti-correlated data*. Anti-correlated data lead to many Skyline objects and therefore are more challenging for Skyline algorithms. Clearly, BNL shows a bad performance because of many object comparisons. BBS is quite good on less data objects but slows down with increasing number of objects. Even ZSky becomes worse because of larger Z-regions. The winner is definitely SkyMap, which outperforms all other algorithms by far.

Table 3. Dominance tests $\cdot 10^6$ w.r.t. input size.

n	Skyline	BNL	BBS	ZSky	ZSky-Bl	SkyMap
10k	2591	5.5	3.5	2.2	2.1	1.8
100k	9671	88	51	32	31	9
500k	22302	539	287	239	243	48
1000k	30332	1086	556	537	562	77
2000k	39301	2048	994	1215	1300	132

(a) Independent data.

n	Skyline	BNL	BBS	ZSky	ZSky-Bl	SkyMap
10k	5754	21.8	32.4	8.7	8.7	5.7
100k	34278	823	1741	325	324	123
500k	103719	21457	23265	2890	2877	1284
1000k	164304	21457	70307	7594	7569	3683
2000k	250442	53123	199088	1890	18829	10561

(b) Anti-correlated data.

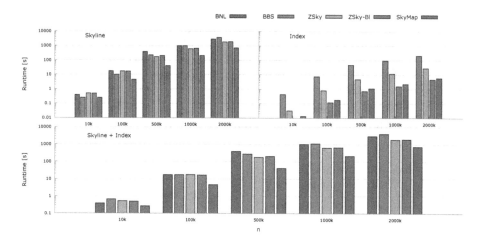

Fig. 6. Anti-correlated data. Runtime w.r.t. input size.

4.3 Effect of Domain Size

We now examine the influence of the domain size. Instead of considering domains in $[0, 1024)$, we utilize a domain size of $[0, \{2^5, 2^{10}, 2^{15}, 2^{20}, 2^{25}, 2^{30}\})$ for each dimension. In addition, we set $d = 5$, $n = 10^6$ and used independent data.

Figure 7 shows our results. It is notable that ZSky is highly efficient for $[0, 2^5)$, but worse for higher domains w.r.t. Skyline computation runtime. BBS and BNL are much better than ZSky and SkyMap for higher dimensions. This is due to the Z-addresses, which are stored as bits, and these bits are based on the domain values. That means, when using a maximal domain value of 2^5 on 5 dimensions we need 25 bits per Z-address, and 150 bits for 2^{30} values. This leads to the high computation costs. Therefore, algorithms using Z-addresses are mainly applicable for "low-cardinality" domains. On the other hand, the runtime of BNL and BBS are quite good, because they are based on an object comparison where a high or low cardinality domain does not matter. Considering the index constructions costs, BBS and ZSky are worse than ZSky-Bl and SkyMap.

Table 4 shows the number of dominance tests. SkyMap is better than its competitors in most cases w.r.t. the dominance tests, but performs worse w.r.t. the runtime.

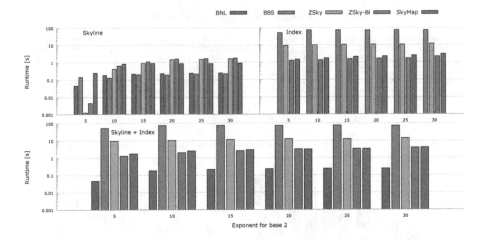

Fig. 7. Independent data. Runtime w.r.t. domain size.

Table 4. Independent data. Dominance tests $\cdot 10^6$ w.r.t. the domain size.

Domain size	Skyline	BNL	BBS	ZSky	ZSky-Bl	SkyMap
2^5	25	2.1	0.2	0.009	0.03	1.0
2^{10}	1277	9.2	5.3	8.5	11.3	2.8
2^{15}	1787	12.1	7.7	17.7	20.0	3.4
2^{20}	1842	12.3	7.5	27.8	28.6	3.5
2^{25}	1843	12.3	7.6	29.0	29.5	3.5
2^{30}	1843	12.3	7.6	29.0	29.5	3.5

Table 5. Real data. Dominance tests.

Data source	Zillow	House	NBA
n	1.288.684	127.931	17.265
dim	5	6	5
Skyline	1	5.762	493
Dominance tests $\cdot 10^3$			
BNL	1.289	24.945	412
BBS	36	23.669	765
ZSky	0.794	24.305	798
ZSky-Bulk	1.5	23.585	833
SkyMap	1.288	5.389	533

4.4 Real Data

For our experiments on real world data we used the well-known *Zillow* data set, which consists of 5 dimensions and 1.288.684 distinct objects. Zillow represents real estates in the United States and stores information about the number of rooms, base area, year of construction, and so on. The *House* data set is a 6-dimensional database of 127.931 objects and represents the average costs of a family in the USA for water, electricity, etc. Our third real data set is *NBA*, a 5-dimensional data with 17.265 entries about NBA players. For the sake of convenience, we search the objects with the lowest values, i.e., the smallest flat, the thrifty American and the worst basketball player. Note that ZSky is not able to deal with duplicates and hence we reduced all data sets to its essence.

Figure 8 shows that ZSky is best for the Zillow data set. This is obvious, because the Skyline only exists of 1 object. In contrast, the runtime of SkyMap, similar to our other tests, is quite high for small Skyline sets, i.e., Zillow and NBA, whereas it performs better for House. Considering the House data set, BBS and SkyMap perform best when considering the pure Skyline computation, even though BBS is much older than SkyMap. On the other hand, SkyMap produces lower index maintenance costs. In the NBA data set, BNL outperforms its competitors because the input data set is relatively small.

Table 5 presents the number of dominance tests used to find the Skyline. In particular, ZSky uses only a few dominance tests on the Zillow data set. This is due to the early rejection of Z-regions, which avoids many object-to-object comparisons.

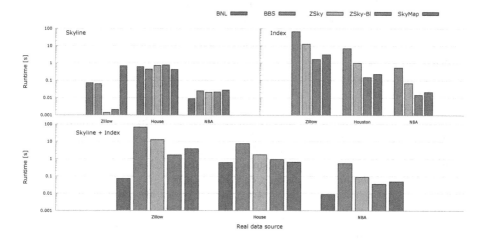

Fig. 8. Real data.

5   Summary and Conclusion

In this paper we briefly reviewed the well-known index-based Skyline algorithms BBS, ZSky, and SkyMap. In order to apply the most efficient index structure in database systems, we presented comprehensive experiments on synthetic and real-world data to evaluate the performance of the presented algorithms. As expected, none of the algorithms performs best for all experiments. The decision for an algorithm must be based on the application it should be used for.

BNL is quite good for a small number of dimensions, whereas SkyMap shows its advantages for higher dimensions. We have also seen that with increasing data dimensionality the performance of R-trees and hence of BBS deteriorates. On the other hand, BBS and SkyMap outperform the other algorithms with increasing input size, independently from the data distribution. When considering the domain size, BNL and BBS are better than their competitors and therefore should be preferred for high cardinality domains. The Z-Sky approaches do well in the case of real data. However, one of the drawbacks of Z-Sky is its restriction to total orders. Duplicates are not allowed. In addition, in the ZB-tree approach regions may overlap, which hampers effective pruning. Moreover, the maintenance of B-trees is rather expensive in case of frequent updates, in particular due to rebalancing operations caused by node underflows.

Based on these results, it will be necessary to develop a cost-based algorithm selection, which automatically decides which approach should be used. But this remains future work.

References

1. Börzsönyi, S., Kossmann, D., Stocker, K.: The skyline operator. In: Proceedings of ICDE 2001, pp. 421–430. IEEE, Washington (2001)
2. Chaudhuri, S., Dalvi, N., Kaushik, R.: Robust cardinality and cost estimation for skyline operator. In: Proceedings of ICDE 2006, p. 64. IEEE Computer Society, Washington (2006)
3. Chomicki, J., Ciaccia, P., Meneghetti, N.: Skyline queries, front and back. Proc. SIGMOD Rec. **42**(3), 6–18 (2013)
4. Endres, M.: The structure of preference orders. In: Morzy, T., Valduriez, P., Bellatreche, L. (eds.) ADBIS 2015. LNCS, vol. 9282, pp. 32–45. Springer, Cham (2015). https://doi.org/10.1007/978-3-319-23135-8_3
5. Endres, M., Glaser, E.: Evaluation of index-based skyline algorithms. Technical report 2019–01, University of Augsburg, Institute of Computer Science (2019). https://opus.bibliothek.uni-augsburg.de/opus4/49414
6. Endres, M., Weichmann, F.: Index structures for preference database queries. In: Christiansen, H., Jaudoin, H., Chountas, P., Andreasen, T., Legind Larsen, H. (eds.) FQAS 2017. LNCS (LNAI), vol. 10333, pp. 137–149. Springer, Cham (2017). https://doi.org/10.1007/978-3-319-59692-1_12
7. Kießling, W., Endres, M., Wenzel, F.: The preference SQL system - an overview. Bull. Tech. Commitee Data Eng. **34**(2), 11–18 (2011)
8. Lee, K., Zheng, B., Li, H., Lee, W.C.: Approaching the skyline in Z Order. In: Proceedings of VLDB 2007, pp. 279–290. VLDB Endowment (2007)
9. Lee, K.C.K., Lee, W.C., Zheng, B., Li, H., Tian, Y.: Z-SKY: an efficient skyline query processing framework based on Z-order. VLDB J. **19**(3), 333–362 (2009)
10. Liu, B., Chan, C.Y.: ZINC: efficient indexing for skyline computation. Proc. VLDB Endow. **4**(3), 197–207 (2010)
11. Mandl, S., Kozachuk, O., Endres, M., Kießling, W.: Preference analytics in EXA-Solution. In: Proceedings of BTW 2015 (2015)
12. Papadias, D., Tao, Y., Fu, G., Seeger, B.: An optimal and progressive algorithm for skyline queries. In: Proceedings of SIGMOD 2003, pp. 467–478. ACM (2003)
13. Papadias, D., Tao, Y., Fu, G., Seeger, B.: Progressive skyline computation in database systems. ACM TODS **30**(1), 41–82 (2005)
14. Selke, J., Balke, W.-T.: SkyMap: a trie-based index structure for high-performance skyline query processing. In: Hameurlain, A., Liddle, S.W., Schewe, K.-D., Zhou, X. (eds.) DEXA 2011. LNCS, vol. 6861, pp. 350–365. Springer, Heidelberg (2011). https://doi.org/10.1007/978-3-642-23091-2_30

A Simple Data Structure for Optimal Two-Sided 2D Orthogonal Range Queries

Alejandro Grez[1], Andrea Calí[2(✉)], and Martín Ugarte[1,3]

[1] Pontificia Universidad Católica de Chile, Santiago, Chile
[2] Birkbeck, University of London, London, UK
andrea@dcs.bbk.ac.uk
[3] Millenial Institute for Foundational Research on Data, Santiago, Chile

Abstract. Given an arbitrary set A of two-dimensional points over a totally-ordered domain, a two-sided planar range query consists on finding all points of A within an arbitrary quadrant. In this paper we present a novel data structure that uses linear space in $|A|$ while allowing for two-dimensional orthogonal range queries with logarithmic pre-processing and constant-delay enumeration.

1 Introduction and Preliminaries

Processing orthogonal range queries is a fundamental problem in computational geometry: in such queries, the interested points lie within a rectangle aligned with the axes. This problem also finds application in query processing, where a user is interested in all tuples satisfying two inequalities simultaneously [6].

Consider for example the following SQL query, which asks for all countries with less than twenty million inhabitants and a surface smaller than 500000 squared kilometers:

```
SELECT * FROM country
  WHERE population < 20000000
    AND surface < 500000
```

Figure 1 depicts a set of points representing countries, where the x axis represents the surface and the y axis the population. Answering the query then corresponds to reporting the set of filled dots (the dots inside the gray area).

Formally, let $\mathcal{N}$ be a totally ordered domain and let A be a finite subset of $\mathcal{N}^2$. A two-sided 2D orthogonal range query (from now on a 2D-ORQ) is simply a point $Q = (x_Q, y_Q)$ satisfying, and its evaluation over A consists on enumerating the set

$$Q(A) = \{(x, y) \in A \mid x \leq x_Q \wedge y \leq y_Q\}.$$

Contributions. In this paper we show how to construct, for any finite set $A \subseteq \mathcal{N}^2$, a data structure D_A satisfying the following:

© Springer Nature Switzerland AG 2019
A. Cuzzocrea et al. (Eds.): FQAS 2019, LNAI 11529, pp. 43–47, 2019.
https://doi.org/10.1007/978-3-030-27629-4_7

- D_A can be constructed in time $|A| \cdot \log(|A|)$.
- The memory required to store D_A is linear in $|A|$.
- Given a point $Q \in A$, D_A allows for constant delay enumeration of $Q(A)$ (without a pre-processing phase).

The third condition above is formalized by the existence of an algorithm enumerate(Q, D_A) that outputs all elements of the aforementioned set without repetitions [5], and can only spend a constant amount of time before the first output, between any two consecutive outputs, and after the last output.

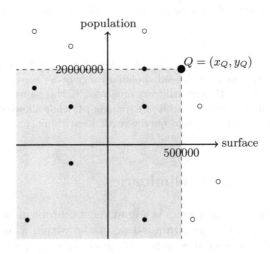

Fig. 1. A two-dimensional orthogonal range query $Q = ((x_0, y_0), (x_1, y_1))$ evaluated over an arbitrary set of points. The answer is the set of filled points.

2   The Data Structure

We now introduce our data structure for dealing with a 2D-ORQs. Let A be a set of points. For every point $Q = (x_Q, y_Q) \in A$, define the set A_Q as $\{(x, y) \in A \mid x \leq x_Q \text{ and } y \leq y_Q\}$. Our data structure D_A partitions the points of A in a number of *levels*. These levels are denoted $L_1, \ldots, L_m$, and satisfy the following two properties.

1. For each point $P \in L_i$, it is the case that $A_P \cap L_i = \{P\}$. In other words, for every $Q \in L_i$, if $Q \neq P$ then $Q \notin A_P$.
2. If P belongs to level L_i for $i > 1$, then $A_P \cap L_{i-1} \neq \emptyset$.

The data structure D_A connects the points in each level through a doubly-linked list ordered by the x-coordinate. Moreover, for every point $p \in L_i$ with $i > 1$, D_A stores a pointer from p to some $q \in A_p \cap L_{i-1}$. Figure 2 depicts D_A, where A is the set of points depicted in Fig. 1.

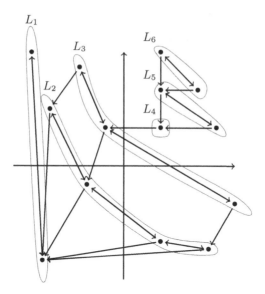

Fig. 2. The data structure D_A satisfying properties 1. and 2.

It is trivial to see that the space required to store D_A is linear in $|A|$, since every point has at most four pointers to other points. Note also that the levels are only an abstraction to simplify the explanation of D_A, but they are stored implicitly as doubly-linked lists.

Finally, we show how D_A is constructed from an arbitrary set A in Algorithm 1. This algorithm takes time $\mathcal{O}(n^2)$ and space $\mathcal{O}(n)$, where n is the cardinality of A. We stress that the structure could be constructed using the same space but in amortized time $\mathcal{O}(n \log n)$ by storing the array B of Algorithm 1 in a binary tree. For the ease of understanding, here we present a conceptually simple version of the algorithm.

3   Constant-Delay Enumeration

Now we describe how to enumerate A_p from D_A with constant-delay, for any point $p \in A$. To this end, assume that given a point p we have pointers $p.right$, $p.left$ and $p.child$. $p.right$ and $p.left$ point to the nodes at the same level of p that are immediately to the right and left of p, respectively. $p.child$ is the node in the previous level which p has a pointer to (as specified in Condition 2 of the previous section). Note that any of these pointers could be Null. Taking this information into account, Algorithm 2 enumerates A_p with constant delay.

Algorithm 1. GenD(A), $A = \{p_0, \ldots, p_{n-1}\}$ ordered lexicographically

---

1: B ← Array of n points initialized to `Null`
2: **for** i **from** 1 **to** n **do**
3:     j ← 0
4:     **while** B[j] != `Null` && p_i.y >= B[j].y **do**
5:         j++
6:     **if** B[j] != `Null` **then**
7:         B[j].right_sibling = p_i
8:         p_i.left_sibling = B[j]
9:     **if** j > 0 **then**
10:         p_i.child = B[j-1]
11:     B[j] = p_i

Algorithm 2. Enumerate($p \in A$)

1: currentp ← p
2: **while** currentp != `Null` **do**
3:     output(currentp)
4:     r ← currentp.right
5:     **while** r != `Null` && r.x <= p.x && r.y <= p.y **do**
6:         output(r)
7:         r ← r.right
8:     l ← currentp.left
9:     **while** l != `Null` && l.x <= p.x && l.y <= p.y **do**
10:         output(r)
11:         l ← l.left
12:     currentp ← currentp.child

---

4   Discussion

We have addressed the problem of efficiently processing two-sided 2D orthogonal range queries. The problem, which is relevant to many applications, has been studied for decades; see e.g. [1,3,4]; see e.g. [7] for a literature review and a study of applications to database theory.

Our data structure uses space linear in $|A|$, where A is the finite two-dimensional domain of the query points. We can perform constant-time enumeration of the answers to queries in A. This is possible thanks to a novel data structure that makes use of a partitioning into levels. While analogous asymptotic results have already been found [2,6], we believe that our approach provides a more nimble data structure and an algorithm that is easier to implement. Our next step will be the implementation and the testing of the techniques presented here.

References

1. Agarwal, P.K.: Range searching. In: Handbook of Discrete and Computational Geometry, 2nd edn, pp. 809–837. CRC Press (2004)

2. Chan, T.M., Larsen, K.G., Patrascu, M.: Orthogonal range searching on the ram, revisited. In: Proceedings of the 27th ACM Symposium on Computational Geometry, Paris, France, 13–15 June 2011, pp. 1–10 (2011)
3. Mehlhorn, K.: Data Structures and Algorithms: 3. Multidimensional Searching and Com-putational Geometry. Springer, Heidelberg (1994)
4. Preparata, F.P., Shamos, M.: Computational Geometry. Springer, Heidelberg (1985)
5. Segoufin, L.: Constant delay enumeration for conjunctive queries. SIGMOD Rec. **44**(1), 10–17 (2015)
6. Wilkinson, B.T.: Exploring the problem space of orthogonal range searching. Ph.D. thesis, Aarhus University (2015)
7. Willard, D.E.: Applications of range query theory to relational data base join and selection operations. J. Comput. Syst. Sci. **52**(1), 157–169 (1996)

Optimizing the Computation of Approximate Certain Query Answers over Incomplete Databases

Nicola Fiorentino, Cristian Molinaro$^{(\boxtimes)}$, and Irina Trubitsyna

DIMES, University of Calabria, Rende, Italy
{n.fiorentino,cmolinaro,trubitsyna}@dimes.unical.it

Abstract. In many database applications there is the need of extracting information from incomplete data. In such scenarios, certain answers are the most widely adopted semantics of query answering. Unfortunately, the computation of certain query answers is a coNP-hard problem. To make query answering feasible in practice, recent research has focused on developing polynomial time algorithms computing sound (but possibly incomplete) sets of certain answers. In this paper, we propose a novel technique that allows us to improve recently proposed approximation algorithms, obtaining a good balance between running time and quality of the results. We report experimental results confirming the effectiveness of the new technique.

1 Introduction

Incomplete information arises in many database applications, such as ontological reasoning [4,5], inconsistency management [2,3,11,16], data integration [7,17], and many others. A principled semantics of query answering over incomplete databases are *certain answers*, which are query answers that are obtained from all the complete databases represented by an incomplete database [6,18,19]. The following example illustrates the notion of a certain answer.

Example 1. Consider the database D consisting of the three unary relations P (Person), S (Student) and E (Employee) reported below, where $\perp$ is a null value.

P
john
mary

E
john
$\perp$

S
mary
bob

Under the missing value interpretation of nulls (i.e., a value for $\perp$ exists but is unknown), D represents all the databases obtained by replacing $\perp$ with an actual value. A certain answer to a query is a tuple that is an answer to the query for every database represented by D. For instance, consider the query asking for the people who are not employees and students, which can be expressed in relational algebra as $P - (E \cap S)$. The certain answers to the query are $\{\langle \text{john} \rangle\}$, because no matter how $\perp$ is replaced, $\langle \text{john} \rangle$ is always a query answer. $\square$

A. Cuzzocrea et al. (Eds.): FQAS 2019, LNAI 11529, pp. 48–60, 2019.
https://doi.org/10.1007/978-3-030-27629-4_8

For databases containing (labeled) nulls, certain answers to positive queries can be easily computed in polynomial time as follows: first a "standard" evaluation (that is, treating nulls as standard constants) is applied; then tuples with nulls in the result of the first step are discarded and the remaining tuples are the certain answers to the query. However, for more general queries with negation the problem of computing certain answers becomes coNP-hard.

To make query answering feasible in practice, one might resort to SQL's evaluation, but unfortunately, the way SQL behaves in the presence of nulls may result in wrong answers. As evidenced in [19], there are two ways in which certain answers and SQL's evaluation may differ: *(i)* SQL can miss some of the tuples that belong to certain answers, thus producing *false negatives*, or *(ii)* SQL can return some tuples that do not belong to certain answers, that is, *false positives*. While the first case can be seen as an under-approximation of certain answers (a sound but possibly incomplete set of certain answers is returned), the second scenario must be avoided, as the result might contain plain incorrect answers, that is, tuples that are not certain. The experimental analysis in [14] showed that false positive are a real problem for queries involving negation—they were always present and sometimes they constitute almost 100% of the answers.

Thus, on the one hand, SQL's evaluation is efficient but flawed, on the other hand, certain answers are a principled semantics but with high complexity. To deal with this issue, there has been work on developing algorithms that compute a sound but possibly incomplete set of certain answers [8,12–14,18,19]. Computing sound sets of *consistent* query answers over inconsistent databases has been addressed in [9], but databases are assumed to be complete, while in this paper we consider incomplete databases with no integrity constraints.

In this paper, we start with an experimental evaluation of the approach proposed in [8,12,13], where four algorithms have been proposed: *eager, semi-eager, lazy,* and *aware* (Sect. 3). Experimental results confirm what suggested from the theoretical analysis carried out in [13]: moving from the eager to the aware algorithm, running times increase, but this paid back by more certain answers being found. While we observe a mild increase of running times when moving from eager to semi-eager, and from semi-eager to lazy, there is a much higher difference between the running times of the lazy and aware evaluations.

This raised the question on whether we can devise a novel technique between lazy and aware, which achieves a good balance between running time and quality of the results. We answer this question positively by proposing a novel evaluation strategy, called $lazy^+$, which improves upon the lazy evaluation by drawing ideas of the aware evaluation, while keeping running times moderate (Sect. 4).

We then experimentally evaluate $lazy^+$ comparing it against the lazy and aware evaluations. Experimental results show the effectiveness of $lazy^+$: not only running times are much lower that those of the aware evaluation, but they are even lower than those of the lazy one, because of newly introduced optimizations. As for the quality of results, $lazy^+$ is placed between the lazy and aware algorithms, thereby achieving a good balance between computation time and quality of results.

2   Background

Basic Notations. We assume the existence of the following disjoint countably infinite sets: a set Const of *constants* and a set Null of *(labeled) nulls*. Nulls are denoted by the symbol $\perp$ subscripted. A *tuple* t of arity k is an element of $(\text{Const} \cup \text{Null})^k$, where k is a non-negative integer. The i-th element of t is denoted as $t[i]$, where $1 \leq i \leq k$. Given a possibly empty ordered sequence Z of integers $i_1, \ldots, i_h$ in the range $[1...k]$, we use $t[Z]$ to denote the tuple $\langle t[i_1], \ldots, t[i_h] \rangle$. For simplicity, a tuple $\langle u \rangle$ of arity 1 is simply written as u, where u is a constant or a null. A *relation* of arity k is a finite set of tuples of arity k. A *relational schema* is a set of *relation names*, each associated with a non-negative arity. A *database* D associates a relation R^D of arity k with each relation name R of arity k. A relation (resp. database) is *complete* if it does not contain nulls.

A *valuation* ν is a mapping from $\text{Const} \cup \text{Null}$ to Const s.t. $\nu(c) = c$ for every $c \in \text{Const}$. Valuations can be applied to tuples, relations, and databases in the obvious way. For instance, the result of applying ν to a database D, denoted $\nu(D)$, is the complete database obtained from D by replacing every null $\perp_i$ with $\nu(\perp_i)$. The semantics of a database D is given by the set of complete databases $poss(D) = \{\nu(D) \mid \nu \text{ is a valuation}\}$, which are also called *possible worlds*.

We consider queries expressed in relational algebra by means of the following operators: selection σ, projection π, Cartesian product $\times$, union $\cup$, intersection $\cap$, and difference $-$. The evaluation of a query Q on a database D, treating nulls as standard constants—i.e., every (labeled) null or constant is equal to itself and different from every other element of $\text{Const} \cup \text{Null}$—is denoted as $Q(D)$ and called *naive evaluation* [15]. A query Q returning k-tuples is said to be of arity k, and $ar(Q)$ denotes its arity.

The *certain answers* to a query Q on a database D are the tuples in $\bigcap \{Q(\nu(D)) \mid \nu \text{ is a valuation}\}$. Computing certain answers is coNP-hard (data complexity).

For query answering, in the rest of the paper we will use a more general notion first proposed in [20] and called *certain answers with nulls* in [19], which avoids some anomalies of certain answers. The *certain answers with nulls* to a query Q on a database D, denoted by $\text{cert}(Q, D)$, are all tuples t such that $\nu(t) \in Q(\nu(D))$ for every valuation ν.

Conditional Databases. Conditional tables [15] are relations possibly containing nulls extended by one additional special column (which cannot be used inside queries) containing logical formulae specifying under which conditions tuples are true. In this paper we consider the generalized version of conditional tables, where the set of conditions is extended with unknown and allows comparison operators $<, \leq, >, \geq$. Let $\mathcal{E}$ be the set of all expressions, called *conditions*, that can be built using the standard logical connectives $\wedge$, $\vee$, and $\neg$ with expressions of the form true, false, unknown, $(\alpha \star \beta)$, where $\alpha, \beta \in \text{Const} \cup \text{Null}$ and $\star \in \{=, \neq, <, \leq, >, \geq\}$. We say that a valuation ν *satisfies* a condition φ, denoted $\nu \models \varphi$, if its assignment of constants to nulls makes φ true. A *conditional tuple (c-tuple* for short) $\mathbf{t}$ of arity k ($k \geq 0$) is a pair $\langle t, \varphi \rangle$, where t is a tuple of arity k and $\varphi \in \mathcal{E}$. Notice that φ may involve nulls and constants not necessarily appearing in t—e.g., t is the tuple $\langle a, \perp_1 \rangle$ and φ is the condition $(\perp_2 = c) \wedge (\perp_1 \neq \perp_3)$. A *conditional table* (*c-table* for short) of arity k is a finite set of c-tuples of arity k. A *conditional database* C associates a c-table R^C of arity k with each relation name R of arity k. The result of applying a valuation ν to a conditional table T is $\nu(T) = \{\nu(t) \mid \langle t, \varphi \rangle \in T$ and $\nu \models \varphi\}$. Thus, $\nu(T)$ is the (complete) relation obtained from T by keeping only the c-tuples in T whose condition is satisfied by ν, and applying ν to such c-tuples. The set of complete relations represented by T is $rep(T) = \{\nu(T) \mid \nu$ is a valuation$\}$. Likewise, a conditional database $C = \{T_1, \ldots, T_m\}$ represents the set of complete databases $rep(C) = \{\{\nu(T_1), \ldots, \nu(T_m)\} \mid \nu$ is a valuation$\}$.

The *conditional evaluation* of a query over a conditional database [10,15] consists in evaluating relational algebra operators so that they can take c-tables as input and return a c-table as output. The conditional evaluation of a query is then obtained by applying the conditional evaluation of each operator.

Let T_1 and T_2 be c-tables of arity n and m, respectively. In the definitions below, for the union, intersection and difference operators it is assumed that $n = m$. For projection, Z is a possibly empty ordered sequence of integers in the range $[1..n]$. For selection, θ is a Boolean combination of expressions of the form $(\$i \star \$j)$, $(\$i \star c)$, where $1 \leq i, j \leq n$, and $c \in \mathsf{Const} \cup \mathsf{Null}$ and $\star \in \{=, \neq, <, \leq, >, \geq\}$. Given two tuples t_1 and t_2 of arity n, we use $(t_1 = t_2)$ as a shorthand for the condition $\bigwedge_{i \in [1..n]} (t_1[i] = t_2[i])$. The conditional evaluation of a relational algebra operator op is denoted as $\dot{op}$ and is defined as follows.

- *Projection:* $\dot{\pi}_Z(T_1) = \{\langle t[Z], \varphi \rangle \mid \langle t, \varphi \rangle \in T_1\}$.
- *Selection:* $\dot{\sigma}_\theta(T_1) = \{\langle t, \varphi' \rangle \mid \langle t, \varphi \rangle \in T_1$ and $\varphi' = \varphi \wedge \theta(t)\}$,
  where $\theta(t)$ is the condition obtained from θ by replacing every $\$i$ with $t[i]$.
- *Union:* $T_1 \dot{\cup} T_2 = \{\langle t, \varphi \rangle \mid \langle t, \varphi \rangle \in T_1$ or $\langle t, \varphi \rangle \in T_2\}$.
- *Intersection:* $T_1 \dot{\cap} T_2 = \{\langle t_1, \varphi' \rangle \mid \langle t_1, \varphi_1 \rangle \in T_1, \langle t_2, \varphi_2 \rangle \in T_2, \varphi' = \varphi_1 \wedge \varphi_2 \wedge (t_1 = t_2)\}$.
- *Difference:* $T_1 \dot{-} T_2 = \{\langle t_1, \varphi' \rangle \mid \langle t_1, \varphi_1 \rangle \in T_1$ and $\varphi' = \varphi_1 \wedge \varphi_{t_1, T_2}\}$,
  where $\varphi_{t_1, T_2} = \bigwedge_{\langle t_2, \varphi_2 \rangle \in T_2} \neg(\varphi_2 \wedge (t_1 = t_2))$.
- *Cartesian product:* $T_1 \dot{\times} T_2 = \{\langle t_1 \circ t_2, \varphi_1 \wedge \varphi_2 \rangle \mid \langle t_1, \varphi_1 \rangle \in T_1, \langle t_2, \varphi_2 \rangle \in T_2\}$,
  where $t_1 \circ t_2$ is the tuple obtained as the concatenation of t_1 and t_2.

The result of the conditional evaluation of a query Q over a conditional database C is denoted as $\dot{Q}(C)$. Notice that $\dot{Q}(C)$ is a c-table. For a fixed query Q and a conditional database C, $\dot{Q}(C)$ can be evaluated in polynomial time in the size of C (see [10]).

W.l.o.g., in the rest of the paper we assume that every selection condition is a conjunction of expressions of the form $(\$i \star \$j)$, $(\$i \star c)$, $(c < \$j)$, and $(c \leq \$i)$, where $\star \in \{=, \neq, <, \leq\}$.

Approximation Algorithms. Approximation algorithms computing sound sets of certain query answers have been recently proposed in [8,12,13]. These algorithms leverage conditional tables and the conditional evaluation of relational algebra. The conditional evaluation returns conditional tuples $\langle t, \varphi \rangle$, the expression φ says under which condition t can be derived. Conditions are valuable information that can be exploited to determine which tuples are certain answers. By condition evaluation we mean a way of associating φ with a truth value (*true*, *false*, or *unknown*). The aim is to ensure that if φ evaluates to *true*, then t is a certain answer. Tuples' conditions can be evaluated in different ways. The basic ideas of the strategies leading to algorithms presented in [8, 12, 13] are as follows:

- The *eager evaluation* evaluates tuples' conditions right after each relational algebra operator has been applied, using three-valued logic.
- The *semi-eager evaluation* behaves like the eager one, but it better exploits equalities in conditions (by propagating values into tuples and conditions) to provide more accurate results.
- The *lazy evaluation* improves upon the semi-eager one by postponing conditions' evaluation until the set difference operator is encountered in the query.
- The *aware evaluation* provides even more accurate results and behaves as follows: it performs the conditional evaluation of the entire query, then it uses a set of rewriting rules to "simplify" conditions, and eventually it evaluates (simplified) tuples' conditions.

With the same query and database, moving to more accurate strategie, that is, from the eager (resp. semi-eager, lazy) evaluation to the semi-eager (lazy, aware) one, we can obtain more certain answers, but running times might get higher. This aspect has been theoretically investigated in [13]. In the next section, we provide an experimental evaluation.

3   Experimental Evaluation of Approximation Algorithms

In this section, we report on an experimental evaluation we conducted to evaluate approximation algorithms in terms of efficiency and quality of the results.

We recall that there is a trade-off in choosing one of the algorithms: moving from the eager to the aware evaluation the complexity increases but more certain answers can be returned (still, all algorithms have polynomial time complexity).

The four evaluation strategies have been implemented in Java.

All experiments were run on an Intel i7 3770K 3.5 GHz, 64 GB of memory, running Linux Mint 17.1.

Datasets were generated using the DBGen tool of the TPC-H benchmark [1]. As the generated databases are complete, nulls were randomly inserted.

Semi-eager. In order to assess the benefits of the semi-eager evaluation, we measured the running time and the number of certain answers to the query $Q_{se} = R - \sigma_{\$2=c}(S)$, where c is a value randomly chosen from those in the second column of S. We considered datasets having 200–1000 tuples per relation in steps of 200. Notice that Q_{se} is a query where the propagation of the equality

Table 1. Runtime (msecs), number of certain answers to Q_{se} (10% of nulls).

	200		400		600		800		1000	
	Time	#T	Time	#T	Time	#T	Time	#T	Time	#T
Eager	27	136	101	291	230	437	380	587	623	741
Semi-eager	28	143	104	303	232	456	391	610	632	763
Lazy	29	143	106	303	237	456	395	610	636	763
Aware	220	143	837	303	2,522	456	4,166	610	6,743	763

Table 2. Runtime (msecs), number of certain answers to Q_{se} (10% of nulls).

	100		1000		10000	
	Time	#T	Time	#T	Time	#T
Eager	7	82	623	741	68,597	7,324
Semi-eager	7	86	632	763	68,963	7,610
Lazy	7	86	636	763	69,255	7,610
Aware	53	86	6,743	763	783,522	7,610

Table 3. Runtime (msecs), number of certain answers to Q_{se} (DB size: 1000).

	2% of nulls		4% of nulls		6% of nulls		8% of nulls		10% of nulls	
	Time	#T	Time	#T	Time	#T	Time	#T	Time	#T
Eager	503	758	539	755	593	743	606	740	623	741
Semi-eager	513	763	550	763	606	763	613	763	632	763
Lazy	535	763	562	763	612	763	625	763	636	763
Aware	6,135	763	6,467	763	6,585	763	6,708	763	6,743	763

in the selection condition can yield benefits, and thus it might be worth applying the semi-eager evaluation rather than the eager one (which is indeed the case, as shown by the experimental results below). Also, 10% of the values in the database are (randomly introduced) nulls. Experimental results are reported in Table 1.

As expected, running times increase as more powerful evaluation strategies are applied. We can see that the percentage of additional certain answers that the semi-eager evaluation yields w.r.t. to the eager one ranges from 3% to 5%. There is no benefit in applying evaluation strategies more accurate than the semi-eager one, as the structure of the query does not have features that can be exploited by them.

Table 2 reports results for databases having 100, 1000, and 10,000 tuples per relation. We can see a trend similar to the one previously discussed for Table 1—again, the percentage of additional certain answers that the semi-eager evaluation yields w.r.t. to the eager one ranges from 3% to 5%.

Table 4. Runtime (msecs), number of certain answers to Q_{lazy} (10% of nulls).

	200		400		600		800		1000	
	Time	#T	Time	#T	Time	#T	Time	#T	Time	#T
Eager	71	153	249	279	552	421	958	565	1,655	710
Semi-eager	76	153	293	279	640	421	1,095	565	1,736	710
Lazy	355	157	1,392	297	3,210	444	5,559	590	8,660	737
Aware	638	157	2,460	297	5,643	444	9,884	590	15,920	737

Table 5. Runtime (msecs), number of certain answers to Q_{lazy} (10% of nulls).

	100		1000		10000	
	Time	#T	Time	#T	Time	#T
Eager	18	63	1,655	710	150,881	7149
Semi-eager	19	63	1,736	710	170,491	7,149
Lazy	97	64	8,660	737	858,233	7,390
Aware	176	64	15,920	737	1,605,264	7,390

Table 6. Runtime (msecs), number of certain answers to Q_{lazy} (DB size: 1000).

	2% of nulls		4% of nulls		6% of nulls		8% of nulls		10% of nulls	
	Time	#T	Time	#T	Time	#T	Time	#T	Time	#T
Eager	1,310	734	1,421	721	1,481	723	1,550	714	1,655	710
Semi-eager	1,368	734	1,429	721	1,532	723	1,702	714	1,736	710
Lazy	7,221	737	7,569	737	7,741	737	8,238	737	8,660	737
Aware	12,395	737	13,166	737	13,657	737	14,292	737	15,920	737

We also ran experiments with databases having 1000 tuples per relation, varying the null rate from 2% to 10% in steps of 2, see Table 3. The advantage of the semi-eager evaluation w.r.t. the eager one (in terms of additional certain answers) ranges in 0.5–3%.

Lazy. In order to assess the benefits of the lazy evaluation, we measured the running time and the number of certain answers of the query $Q_{lazy} = P - (R \cap (\sigma_{\$2 \neq c}(S)))$, where c is a value randomly chosen from the second column of S. Once again, we considered datasets having 200–1000 tuples per relation in steps of 200 and 10% of nulls. Experimental results are reported in Table 4.

Running times increase as more accurate evaluation strategies are applied. The benefits of the lazy evaluation w.r.t. to the semi-eager one (in terms of additional certain answers) ranges from 2.5% to 6.45%. There is no benefit in applying the aware evaluation, as the structure of the query does not have features that can be exploited by it.

Table 7. Runtime (msecs), number of certain answers to Q_{aware} (10% of nulls).

	200		400		600		800		1000	
	Time	#T	Time	#T	Time	#T	Time	#T	Time	#T
Eager	100	13	374	41	826	66	1,472	84	2,632	100
Semi-eager	103	13	378	41	835	66	1,479	84	2,797	100
Lazy	401	13	1,489	41	3,334	66	5,803	84	12,645	100
Aware	39,306	36	334,604	93	1,053,816	143	2,311,524	192	5,589,977	231

Table 8. Runtime (msecs), number of certain answers to Q_{aware} (10% of nulls).

	100		1000		10000	
	Time	#T	Time	#T	Time	#T
Eager	26	15	2,632	100	238,100	1,269
Semi-eager	28	15	2,797	100	241,600	1,269
Lazy	107	15	12,645	100	1,187,733	1,269
Aware	3,263	25	5,589,977	231	Out of memory	Out of memory

Table 9. Runtime (msecs), number of certain answers to Q_{aware} (DB size: 1000).

	2% of nulls		4% of nulls		6% of nulls		8% of nulls		10% of nulls	
	Time	#T	Time	#T	Time	#T	Time	#T	Time	#T
Eager	1,761	252	1,956	217	2,148	180	2,285	153	2,632	100
Semi-eager	1,824	252	2,068	217	2,220	180	2,382	153	2,797	100
Lazy	8,646	252	9,705	217	10,412	180	11,110	153	12,645	100
Aware	4,018,252	307	4,629,472	288	5,285,823	280	5,794,665	267	6,663,986	231

Results for databases having 100, 1000, and 10,000 tuples per relation are shown in Table 5, exhibiting a similar behavior—here the lazy yields 1.5% to 3.8% more certain answers than the semi-eager (Table 6).

We also ran experiments with relations having 1000 tuples, varying the null rate from 2% to 10% in steps of 2. The advantage of the lazy evaluation w.r.t. the semi-eager one (in terms of additional certain answers) ranges in 0.4–4%.

Aware. Finally, to assess the benefits of the aware evaluation, we measured the running time and the number of certain answers to the query $Q_{aware} = P - (R - S)$ over datasets having 200–1000 tuples per relation. Also, 10% of the values in the database were (randomly introduced) nulls. Experimental results are reported in Table 7. The aware evaluation has the highest running times but it returns significantly more certain answers than the other algorithms, as the number of certain answer is always (at least) doubled.

Results for databases with 100, 1000, and 10,000 tuples per relations are shown in Table 8. While for the first two databases the trend is similar to the one previously discussed, for the largest database the aware evaluation ran out of memory. We also ran experiments with a database having 1000 tuples per relation, varying the null rate from 2% to 10% in steps of 2. Results are reported in Table 9. We can see that the aware evaluation is again the one returning the highest number of certain answers, but with much higher running time.

Discussion. The experimental evaluation has confirmed what we were expecting from the theory (cf. [13]), that is, moving to more powerful techniques we can get more certain query answers, but running times become higher. However, while the gaps in running time between eager and semi-eager and between semi-eager and lazy are somewhat mild, the gap between lazy and aware is significant. The reason is that the aware evaluation performs the conditional evaluation of the entire query and collapses conditions only after that. This means that long conditions need to be kept and manipulated, which makes the technique requiring more time and space than simpler ones. However, this has advantages in terms of quality of the results: longer conditions allows the aware algorithm to perform more refined analyses and thus return more certain query answers.

A natural question then arises: can we devise a technique with a behavior in the middle of the lazy and aware evaluations? Can we improve the lazy evaluation so as to return more certain query answers, drawing from the ideas that characterize aware, but without incurring in the high running times of the latter? We address these questions in the next section, where we propose a novel evaluation algorithm, called $lazy^+$, which indeed achieves a good trade-off between runtime and quality of the results.

4 Novel Approach

The two key features of the aware evaluation are postponing condition evaluation until the very end (i.e., after the conditional evaluation of the entire query), and applying a set of simplification rules to conditions.

In this section, we augment the lazy evaluation with a set of simplification rules (to better analyze conditions), which are applied when the difference operator is encountered. The atomic conditions involving only constants can be evaluated immediately, and substituted by the obtained result, which can be true or false. The set of simplification rules for conjunctions of simple conditions involving labelled nulls is reported next:

1. *Negation:* $\neg(\neg\varphi) \vdash \varphi$, $\neg(\varphi_1 = \varphi_2) \vdash (\varphi_1 \neq \varphi_2)$, $\neg(\varphi_1 \neq \varphi_2) \vdash (\varphi_1 = \varphi_2)$, $\neg(\beta < \alpha) \vdash \alpha \leq \beta$, $\neg(\beta \leq \alpha) \vdash \alpha < \beta$, $\neg$unknown $\vdash$ unknown, $\neg$true $\vdash$ false, and $\neg$false $\vdash$ true.
2. *Middle simplified:* $(\alpha \leq \beta) \wedge (\beta \leq \alpha) \vdash (\alpha = \beta)$;
3. *Contradiction:*
   (i) $(\alpha < \beta) \wedge (\beta \star \alpha) \vdash$ false, where $\star \in \{<, \leq, =\}$;
   (ii) $(\alpha = \beta) \wedge (\beta \neq \alpha) \vdash$ false;
   (iii) $(\alpha \star_1 \beta) \wedge (\beta' \star_2 \alpha) \vdash$ false, where $\beta, \beta' \in$ Const, $\beta < \beta'$, $\star_1, \star_2 \in \{<, \leq, =\}$;
   (iv) $(\alpha \star \beta) \wedge (\alpha = \beta') \vdash$ false, where $\beta, \beta' \in$ Const, $\beta < \beta'$ and $\star \in \{<, \leq, =\}$.
4. *And-simplification:* $\varphi \wedge \varphi \vdash \varphi$, $\varphi \wedge$ true $\vdash \varphi$, and $\varphi \wedge$ false $\vdash$ false.

5. *Equality:* $(\alpha = \alpha) \vdash$ true and $(\alpha \neq \alpha) \vdash$ false.

The result of applying a rule $\varphi' \vdash \varphi''$ to a condition φ is the condition obtained from φ by replacing every occurrence of φ' with φ''. We write $\varphi \overset{*}{\vdash} \varphi'$, where φ and φ' are conditions, if *(i)* φ' can be derived from φ by iteratively applying rules 1–5 along with the commutativity and associativity rules, and *(ii)* none of the rules 1–5 is applicable to any of the conditions in $[\varphi']$, where $[\varphi']$ is the set of all conditions that can be obtained from φ' by iteratively applying the commutativity and associativity rules zero or more times. If $\varphi \overset{*}{\vdash} \varphi'$, we say that φ' is a *minimal* condition for φ. Intuitively, a minimal condition φ' is obtained by iteratively applying rules 1–5 and the commutativity and associativity rules until none of the rules 1–5 can be applied to φ' or any other condition derivable from φ' by means of the commutativity and associativity rules.

There can be multiple minimal conditions of a condition φ, but they are all equivalent w.r.t. the commutativity and associativity rules (roughly speaking, they differ only w.r.t. the order of their terms), that is, if $\varphi \overset{*}{\vdash} \varphi'$ and $\varphi \overset{*}{\vdash} \varphi''$ then $\varphi' \in [\varphi'']$ and $\varphi'' \in [\varphi']$. Thus, we can talk about *the* minimal condition of φ, which we denote as minimal(φ).

The lazy$^+$ evaluation is defined as follows:

$$\mathsf{Eval}^{\ell^+}(R, D) = \overline{R^D}$$
$$\mathsf{Eval}^{\ell^+}(Q_1 \cup Q_2, D) = \mathsf{Eval}^{\ell^+}(Q_1, D) \;\dot{\cup}\; \mathsf{Eval}^{\ell^+}(Q_2, D)$$
$$\mathsf{Eval}^{\ell^+}(Q_1 \cap Q_2, D) = \mathsf{Eval}^{\ell^+}(Q_1, D) \;\dot{\cap}\; \mathsf{Eval}^{\ell^+}(Q_2, D)$$
$$\mathsf{Eval}^{\ell^+}(Q_1 - Q_2, D) = \mathsf{eval}^{\ell}(\mathsf{Eval}^{\ell^+}(Q_1, D) \;\dot{-}\; \mathsf{eval}^{\mathsf{s}}(\mathsf{minimal}(\mathsf{Eval}^{\ell^+}(Q_2, D))))$$
$$\mathsf{Eval}^{\ell^+}(Q_1 \times Q_2, D) = \mathsf{Eval}^{\ell^+}(Q_1, D) \;\dot{\times}\; \mathsf{Eval}^{\ell^+}(Q_2, D)$$
$$\mathsf{Eval}^{\ell^+}(\sigma_\theta(Q), D) = \dot{\sigma}_\theta(\mathsf{Eval}^{\ell^+}(Q, D))$$
$$\mathsf{Eval}^{\ell^+}(\pi_Z(Q), D) = \dot{\pi}_Z(\mathsf{Eval}^{\ell^+}(Q, D))$$

where $\mathsf{eval}^{\mathsf{s}}()$ and $\mathsf{eval}^{\ell}()$ are defined as in [13].

Given a query Q and a database D, we define

$$\mathsf{Eval}_t^{\ell^+}(Q, D) = \{t \mid \langle t, \mathsf{true} \rangle \in \mathsf{eval}^{\mathsf{s}}(\mathsf{Eval}^{\ell^+}(Q, D))\},$$

that is, the true answers are computed by *(i)* first, evaluating $\mathsf{Eval}^{\ell^+}(Q, D)$, yielding a c-table T, and *(ii)* then, evaluating $\mathsf{eval}^{\mathsf{s}}(T)$.

5   Experimental Evaluation of Lazy$^+$

In this section, we report an experimental evaluation of the lazy$^+$ algorithm.

We used a database consisting of the following three relations: *Person* (*person_id*), *Manager*(*manager_id*, *salary*), and *Employee*(*emp_id*, *salary*, *manager*), where *Person* and *Manager* are complete relations and *Employee* is an incomplete relation with null values occurring in the *salary* attribute.

Table 10. Runtime (msecs) and number of certain answers to Q_{lazy+} (10% of nulls).

	1000		2000		3000		4000		5000	
	Time	#T	Time	#T	Time	#T	Time	#T	Time	#T
Lazy	92	554	330	1,118	663	1,678	1,256	2,225	2,015	2,766
Lazy+	69	568	299	1,136	592	1,706	1,123	2,269	1,786	2,836
Aware	111	581	403	1,161	721	1,726	1,432	2,314	2,260	2,880

Table 11. Runtime (msecs) and number of certain answers to Q_{lazy+} (10% of nulls).

	10000		20000		30000		40000		50000	
	Time	#T	Time	#T	Time	#T	Time	#T	Time	#T
Lazy	8,202	5,586	44,606	11,114	104,412	16,766	180,375	22,343	382,442	27,896
Lazy+	7,871	5,710	32,369	11,334	81,819	17,077	158,252	22,742	247,352	28,385
Aware	8,758	5,795	41,996	11,542	121,299	17,370	254,284	23,112	391,270	28,908

Table 12. Runtime (msecs) and number of certain answers to Q_{lazy+} (DB size: 50,000).

	2% of nulls		4% of nulls		6% of nulls		8% of nulls		10% of nulls	
	Time	#T	Time	#T	Time	#T	Time	#T	Time	#T
Lazy	266,452	28,595	299,288	28,385	306,495	28,227	364,515	28,097	382,442	27,896
Lazy+	220,864	28,701	275,353	28,618	280,050	28,534	255,678	28,498	247,352	28,385
Aware	284,279	28,789	319,760	28,827	331,558	28,834	358,013	28,875	391,270	28,908

We used the following query:

$$Q_{lazy+} = Person \setminus \pi_{\$1}(\sigma_{\$1=\$2 \wedge \$2>\$5}(\sigma_{\$2<2000}(Employee) \times Manager).$$

The results of the experiments are shown in Tables 10, 11 and 12. As expected, given a certain database, the performances of the lazy+ evaluation, in terms of the number of certain answers, are placed, in each test, in the middle compared to those of the lazy and the aware approaches. What is surprising (positively) is that the execution times of the lazy+ approach not only outperforms those of the aware evaluation (as expected), but they are even better than those of the lazy evaluation. This highlights that the computational overhead introduced by the reduction of the logical expressions through the application of the aforementioned axioms, facilitates the calculation of evaluating the same expressions, leading, overall, to a reduction in execution times.

6   Conclusion

Certain answers are a principled manner to answer queries on incomplete databases. Since their computation is a coNP-hard problem, recent research has focused on developing polynomial time algorithms providing under-approximations.

We have provided an experimental evaluation of recently proposed approximation algorithms. Results have shown some limits of more powerful techniques in terms of efficiency. To cope with this issue, we have introduced a novel optimized evaluation strategy and experimentally evaluated it, showing that it achieves a good balance between running time and quality of the results.

References

1. Transaction processing performance council. TPC benchmark H standard specification, November 2014. Revision 2.17.1. (TPC-H)
2. Arenas, M., Bertossi, L.E., Chomicki, J.: Consistent query answers in inconsistent databases. In: Proceedings of the Symposium on Principles of Database Systems (PODS), pp. 68–79 (1999)
3. Bertossi, L.E.: Database Repairing and Consistent Query Answering. Synthesis Lectures on Data Management. Morgan & Claypool Publishers, San Rafael (2011)
4. Bienvenu, M., Ortiz, M.: Ontology-mediated query answering with data-tractable description logics. In: Faber, W., Paschke, A. (eds.) Reasoning Web 2015. LNCS, vol. 9203, pp. 218–307. Springer, Cham (2015). https://doi.org/10.1007/978-3-319-21768-0_9
5. Calì, A., Gottlob, G., Lukasiewicz, T.: A general datalog-based framework for tractable query answering over ontologies. J. Web Semant. **14**, 57–83 (2012)
6. Console, M., Guagliardo, P., Libkin, L.: Approximations and refinements of certain answers via many-valued logics. In: Proceedings of the International Conference on Principles of Knowledge Representation and Reasoning (KR), pp. 349–358 (2016)
7. De Giacomo, G., Lembo, D., Lenzerini, M., Rosati, R.: On reconciling data exchange, data integration, and peer data management. In: Proceedings of the Symposium on Principles of Database Systems (PODS), pp. 133–142 (2007)
8. Fiorentino, N., Greco, S., Molinaro, C., Trubitsyna, I.: ACID: a system for computing approximate certain query answers over incomplete databases. In: Proceedings of the International Conference on Management of Data (SIGMOD), pp. 1685–1688 (2018)
9. Furfaro, F., Greco, S., Molinaro, C.: A three-valued semantics for querying and repairing inconsistent databases. Ann. Math. Artif. Intell. **51**(2–4), 167–193 (2007)
10. Grahne, G. (ed.): The Problem of Incomplete Information in Relational Databases. LNCS, vol. 554. Springer, Heidelberg (1991). https://doi.org/10.1007/3-540-54919-6
11. Greco, S., Molinaro, C., Spezzano, F.: Incomplete Data and Data Dependencies in Relational Databases. Synthesis Lectures on Data Management. Morgan & Claypool Publishers, San Rafael (2012)
12. Greco, S., Molinaro, C., Trubitsyna, I.: Computing approximate certain answers over incomplete databases. In: Proceedings of the Alberto Mendelzon International Workshop on Foundations of Data Management and the Web (AMW) (2017)
13. Greco, S., Molinaro, C., Trubitsyna, I.: Approximation algorithms for querying incomplete databases. Inf. Syst. 1–54 (2019, to appear)
14. Guagliardo, P., Libkin, L.: Making SQL queries correct on incomplete databases: a feasibility study. In: Proceedings of the Symposium on Principles of Database Systems (PODS), pp. 211–223 (2016)

15. Imielinski, T., Lipski Jr., W.: Incomplete information in relational databases. J. ACM **31**(4), 761–791 (1984)
16. Koutris, P., Wijsen, J.: The data complexity of consistent query answering for self-join-free conjunctive queries under primary key constraints. In: Proceedings of the Symposium on Principles of Database Systems (PODS), pp. 17–29 (2015)
17. Lenzerini, M.: Data integration: a theoretical perspective. In: Proceedings of the Symposium on Principles of Database Systems (PODS), pp. 233–246 (2002)
18. Libkin, L.: How to define certain answers. In: Proceedings of the International Joint Conference on Artificial Intelligence (IJCAI), pp. 4282–4288 (2015)
19. Libkin, L.: Certain answers as objects and knowledge. Artif. Intell. **232**, 1–19 (2016)
20. Lipski, W.: On relational algebra with marked nulls. In: Proceedings of the Symposium on Principles of Database Systems (PODS), pp. 201–203 (1984)

Ontologies and Knowledge Bases

Leveraging Ontology to Enable Indoor Comfort Customization in the Smart Home

Daniele Spoladore$^{(\boxtimes)}$, Atieh Mahroo, and Marco Sacco

Institute of Intelligent Industrial Technologies and Systems for Advanced Manufacturing, (STIIMA), National Research Council of Italy (CNR), 23900 Lecco, Italy
{daniele.spoladore, atieh.mahroo, marco.sacco}@stiima.cnr.it

Abstract. This paper introduces the Future Home for Future Communities' Smart Home, a semantic-based framework for indoor comfort metrics customization inside a living environment. The Smart Home merges Ambient Intelligence, Ambient Assisted Living and Context Awareness perspectives to provide customized comfort experience to the dwellers, also leveraging on a ubiquitous interface. The smart home leverages ontological representations of inhabitants' health conditions, comfort metrics and available devices to provide dwellers with indoor temperature, humidity rate, CO_2 concentration and illuminance suitable for their health conditions and to the activities they want to perform inside the house. Dwellers interactions within the Smart Home are performed via the interface, while the ontologies composing the knowledge base are reasoned and hosted on a semantic repository. Two use cases depict the framework's functioning in two typical scenarios: adjusting indoor temperature and providing illuminance comfort while preparing a meal.

Keywords: Ontology · Indoor comfort customization · Ambient Intelligence · Ambient Assisted Living · Smart Home

1 Introduction

The Smart Home (SH) has emerged in recent decades as a promising paradigm to foster independent living among elderlies. This research field touches on Ambient Assisted Living (AAL) [1] and Ambient Intelligence (AmI) [2] and is aimed at enhancing the quality of life of elderlies and people with disabilities in order to foster their independent living. While most of the literature related to the SH focuses on its architecture [3], its functionalities [4] and the possibility to save energy [5], another branch of literature concentrates on the SH as a set of technologies able to help aging population to live independently and safely by proposing tailored services.

This idea of the SH requires the possibility to acquire information regarding the dwellers and their status, their activities, the contexts they live in, and their preferences. These pieces of information are even more important when considering dwellers afflicted by limitations and/or disabilities, a group of persons who could enormously benefit from tailored services while performing Activities of Daily Living (ADLs) [6].

© Springer Nature Switzerland AG 2019
A. Cuzzocrea et al. (Eds.): FQAS 2019, LNAI 11529, pp. 63–74, 2019.
https://doi.org/10.1007/978-3-030-27629-4_9

In this context, Semantic Web technologies can be a promising solution to tackle the knowledge representation of information coming from the above-mentioned domains [7]. Knowledge needs to be captured, processed, and interconnected to be considered as relevant. Thus, exploiting the ontology – i.e. a formal and explicit specification of shared conceptualizations [8] – to manage knowledge bases, and enriching these ontologies by deriving new facts using reasoning techniques, can be a robust solution.

This work introduces the Future Home for Future Communities (FHfFC) project's SH [9], an AAL system developed to help aging population and dwellers characterized by their impairments to live independently. FHfFC is an Italian research project aimed at creating the "house of the future", in which dwellers can rely on customized services to overcome some of their impairments while performing some ADLs. The proposed SH leverages on ontologies to represent relevant facts regarding the inhabitants and their health status, the devices deployed in the domestic environment (sensors, actuators, household appliances) and the comfort metrics that affect daily living (indoor temperature, humidity rate, illuminance, CO_2 concentration) with the aim of providing tailored comfort solutions to the SH's dwellers.

The remainder of this paper is organized as follow: Sect. 2 highlights some of the relevant works in the field of indoor comfort customization within a SH, focusing on solutions leveraging ontologies; Sect. 3 delves into the FHfFC's SH architecture, with a specific focus on the ontologies adopted to build the knowledge base; Sect. 4 depicts two use cases and highlights some of the SH features; finally, the Conclusions summarizes the main outcomes of this paper and sketch the future works.

2   Related Work

Comfort plays a pivotal role in SHs and several works can be traced in literature; however, most of these works focus on the possibility to produce energy saving and efficiency with regard to the indoor comfort metrics [10–12], thus neglecting the fact that indoor comfort is a necessary quality of the living environment – especially for elderlies and dwellers with disabilities. With regard to the issue of indoor comfort as a necessary quality for indoor environments, some works leveraged the use of ontologies to foster adaptation of indoor comfort metrics. Tila et al. [13] adopted ontologies to provide a description of indoor comfort metrics, domestic devices and context in an Internet of Things (IoT) framework queried with SPARQL [14] and SQL. Frešer et al. [15] exploited reasoning capabilities provided by semantic modeling to develop a decision support system to improve the quality of some indoor comfort metrics. Aeleke et al. [16] proposed an ontology for indoor air quality monitoring and control, formalizing some of the knowledge of the standard ISO 7730:2005. Stavropoulos et al. [17] developed BOnSAI, an ontology for smart buildings, encompassing some concepts related to comfort. More recently, ontologies have been adopted as a tool for representing knowledge related to the inhabitants inside a SH [18] with the aim of fostering the customization of comfort metrics. This approach is adopted also in [19], where the authors extend the semantic framework to the hotel industry – thus transforming a hotel room in a "smart" environment able to personalize indoor comfort metrics. Finally, ontologies for comfort customization have been adopted also in the field of ship cruise cabins [20], where the cabin environment fosters both energy saving and comfort personalization.

In the context of AmI and CA, the FHfFC's SH leverages ontological representation of the dwellers and their needs – exploiting an international health-related standard – to provide customization in several ADLs and daily-life activities. Moreover, the proposed SH hides its complexity to the dwellers, by adopting a simple interface that assists the dwellers in managing various aspects of the living environment.

3   The FHfFC Smart Home Architecture

This section describes the architecture of the FHfFC's SH framework and its modules in detail. As mentioned in Sect. 1, the possibility of enabling indoor environment responsiveness to the inhabitants' needs and comfort requirements plays a pivotal role in both AmI and AAL. With regard to these contexts, this work proposes a system that aims at providing customized comfort within the living environment; the system is also able to take into account diverse groups of people – including dwellers with disabilities. The proposed SH aims at adjusting the indoor comfort metrics according to the various activities the dwellers may be performing. In this regard, the first issue to be addressed is the physical environment and the set of smart devices deployed in it to ensure the inhabitants' comfort. The SH must be equipped with the necessary smart and ubiquitous devices to be prepared for exploitation by the framework. Thus, a solid network of sensors and actuators is needed to sense, measure, and exchange the data both from sensors to the application and from the application to the actuators. The FHfFC's SH leverages on the Home Interactive Controller (HIC) [21], a ubiquitous projected graphic user interface (GUI) providing the dwellers with a tool for controlling comfort metrics, appliances and systems within the SH. The SH also needs to "know" facts about the inhabitants, their needs and preferences, their activities, the comfort metrics (both indoor and outdoor); therefore, it requires a knowledge base to describe relevant facts and reasoning systems to provide tailored adjustments to the SH's services. The FHfFC's SH is composed of four different layers – as depicted in Fig. 1:

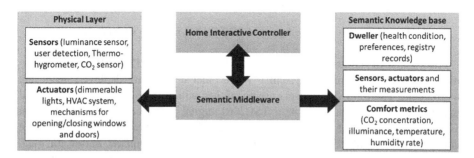

Fig. 1. The overall architecture of the FHfFC's SH and its four intercommunicating layers.

1. Physical living environment equipped with smart devices (sensors and actuators) to be connected to the HIC;
2. The HIC, a ubiquitous projectable GUI that can be used to control the indoor environment and provides assistance to the dwellers performing some ADLs;

3. The semantic knowledge base including the domain ontologies, hosted on a Stardog semantic repository [22] equipped with SL reasoner to run SPARQL Protocol and RDF Query Language (SPARQL) [14];
4. A middleware program to communicate between (b) and (c), translating the information from the HIC to the semantic repository (and vice versa), and also from the sensors and actuators to the semantic repository (and vice versa).

3.1 The Physical Layer

The FHfFC's SH is simulated within the Living Lab of Lecco (inside the CNR premises of Lecco, in Lombardy, Italy). The environment – which is a room of 4×6 m^2, as shown in Fig. 2 – is equipped with real kitchen furniture, while the household appliances are simulated using Augmented Reality.

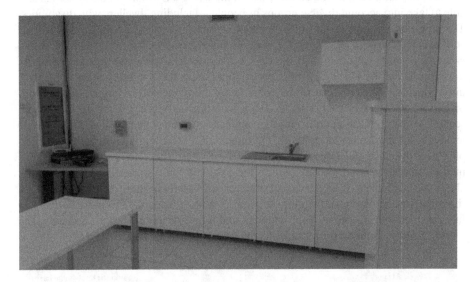

Fig. 2. A picture of the furnished FHfFC's SH in Lecco's Living Lab

Also, some of the actuators are simulated – such as the HVAC (Heating, Ventilation, and Air Conditioning) system – while other devices are deployed inside the environment. The following sensors are positioned within the SH: an AM2320 digital temperature and humidity sensor; a TSL2561 digital light sensor; a 3709 Adafruit SGP20 air quality sensor breakout. Sensors measuring the outdoor comfort metrics are simulated, such as illuminance, air quality and thermo-hygrometric sensor for measuring comfort metrics outside the SH. Due to restrictions in the possibility of actuating the real HVAC system installed in the premises and the inability of actuating real windows and doors, the following actuators have been simulated using Virtual Reality: the air conditioning system and the heating system, as part of the HVAC system; a window opener actuator. While, as a real actuator, the FHfFC's SH adopts two dimmable Philips HUE lights, which allows changing the intensity (i.e. the illuminance) and the color of the light. The process of data exchange takes place exploiting embedded ZigBee-based IoT gateways – such as XBee [23] – which is mounted on a Raspberry Pi device [24].

3.2 HIC: The Home Interface Controller

The FHfFC's SH leverages on a simple interface that allows the dwellers to manage domestic appliances, indoor comfort metrics, dweller's personal calendar and that can assist the inhabitants in performing some ADLs, such as the preparation of a meal – as described further in Sect. 4.2. HIC helps to hide from the end-users the complexity of the SH's architecture (especially when they are elders or afflicted by impairments) in order not to burden them; however, the interaction with the SH is fundamental to provide benefits to the dwellers.

The HIC acts as an interactive multi-touch surface that can be run on every plain surface of the house thanks to an interactive projector EPSON EB1430wi. This device allows the users to operate with multi-touch gestures (tapping, pinching, zooming, scrolling, dragging, rotating with two fingers) thanks to an infrared emitting laser unit able to detect touches in an area up to 100 in. In addition, HIC can also be used via tablet or smartphone, so that dwellers can use HIC as a "remote" for the whole SH in every room – even those not provided with a projector. HIC allows regulating and managing different activities and utilities within the living environment: (a) adjusting the lighting within the house; (b) regulating the indoor temperature and humidity rate; (c) providing visual assistance for meal preparation (as further described in Sect. 4.2); (d) activating the HVAC system according to dweller's preset preferences.

3.3 Knowledge Base and Semantic Repository

The semantic knowledge base acts as a "control center" – with special sets of rules and reasoning logic – between the sensors and the actuators. In other words, sensors measure the data about indoor comfort, send them to the semantic repository to be saved and reasoned over in the knowledge base, and finally decisions provided by reasoning process are sent back to the actuators to initiate the required action. The SH's knowledge base, its different domains' ontologies, semantic repository, and reasoner are stored on a private server to be available anytime while being protected. Thus, the third layer of the FHfFC's SH architecture consists of the following: (a) a set of domain ontologies describing the dwellers, their health conditions, their registry records and their comfort preferences, sensors and actuators; the ontologies are modeled with W3C-endorsed language Resource Description Framework (RDF) [25] and Ontology Web Language (OWL) [26]; (b) a set of rules defined in Semantic Web Rule Language (SWRL) [27] to infer new pieces of information; (c) a semantic repository to upload the ontologies on the server to allow querying, retrieving and reasoning over data to infer new triples; and (d) SPARQL to query over the semantic repository and allowing to insert, retrieve, and delete the information modeled in the ontologies.

The domain ontologies are modeled according to NeOn methodology [28], which ease the identification of existing resources to be re-used. The following subsections delve into the description of the FHfFC's SH domain ontologies.

Inhabitant's Model

The dwellers are described leveraging the Friend Of a Friend [29] vocabulary to annotate their registry records. With regard to inhabitants' health condition, the domain ontology leverages on the International Classification of Functioning, Disability and Health (ICF) [30], a World Health Organization standard developed as a common language to describe a person's functional impairment. ICF provides a set of codes, each indicating a specific impairment that can be completed with qualifiers in order to state the magnitude of the impairment (1st qualifier) and – only for impairments in body structures – the origin of the impairment (2nd qualifier) and its location in the body (3rd qualifier). Moreover, ICF has been translated into a widely-reused ontology [31]. The following Fig. 3 provides an example of dweller modeling.

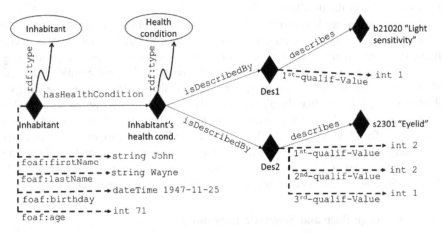

Fig. 3. An example of inhabitant's modeling. Diamonds represent individuals, circles represent concepts, arrows represent roles, dashed-line for datatype property, full-line for object properties.

Inhabitant's Comfort Preferences

For each inhabitant, comfort-related preferences can be saved in the ontology. Following the same ontology design pattern adopted for modeling health conditions, a dweller can specify his/her own preferences in terms of comfort metrics. The input of the preferences can be easily performed with the HIC and the result is the creation of an individual inside the semantic knowledge base. The compiling of the comfort preferences can be conducted by the dweller him/herself or – if he/she needs support due to some impairments – by the care-giver. If no customized preferences are set, the ontology relies on norms to provide the minimum amount of comfort. For visual comfort, it relies on the European norm EN 12464-1, which sets the minimum amount of illuminance to 200 lx (up to 500 lx when the dweller is working on the kitchen table, thus requiring more light); for indoor temperature and humidity rate, the ontology models the limits provided by the Italian law 74/2013 (which sets the maximum temperature for both winter and summer in a range between 20 °C and 22 °C). Similarly, the ISO 16000-26:2012 standard is adopted for indoor CO_2 concentration (which must be below 1000 ppm in living environments).

Sensors, Actuators and Appliances

Sensors and actuators are modeled relying on the W3C-endorsed Sensors, Observation, Sample and Actuator (SOSA) ontology [32], part of the Semantic Sensor Network (SSN) ontology [33]. SOSA is a lightweight and self-contained core ontology consisting of a set of classes and properties to describe sensors and actuators and their measurements (observations). For domestic appliances' description, the SH leverages on the Smart Appliances REFerence (SAREF) ontology [34], a model that provides concepts and properties to describe the functioning of devices and that shares many similarities with SSN [35]. The possibility of re-using SOSA enables the description of the measurements performed by the sensors, so that the measured values can be compared to the parameters defined by inhabitant's comfort preferences.

Set of SWRL Rules to Provide Tailored Comfort

A set of SWRL rules is developed to foster the actuation of tailored comfort metrics, constituting a rule-based system for the provision of tailored services within the SH. The rules can trigger the actuation of indoor lights and HVAC system. For example, referring to the user depicted in Fig. 3, who is afflicted by a vision-related problem, the SH can provide him with an adequate amount of illuminance by decreasing the amount of illuminance within the living environment; the actuation is supplied via HIC and triggered by an SWRL rule:

```
Dweller(?d), isInHealthCondition(?d, ?hc), HealthCondi-
tion (?hc), isDe-scribedBy (?hc, ?des),
HC_Descriptor(?des), involvesICFCode (?des, b21020),
LightSensitivity (b21020), hasBQual (?des, ?q), greater-
ThanOrEqual (?q, 2), isLocatedInRoom (?p, ?r), Room(?r),
Lighting device (?light), isDeployedIn (?light, ?r), In-
doorCustomizedIlluminance (?ill), ExternalIlluminance
(?exill), hasMeasurementValue(?exill, ?m), lessThan (?m,
250) -> setsLighting (?light, ?ill)
```

The triggering of this rule requires the SH to know the dweller's presence inside a specific room of the house (with an occupancy sensor), so that the provision of dweller's customized illuminance setting can be applied.

Middleware Program

The knowledge base, hosted on the Stardog semantic repository, is connected to the HIC with a middleware – a script designed and implemented in C#. The middleware gets an input JSON file containing the dweller's name as the user is detected within a room by sensors or as the dwellers declares his/her presence; the middleware generates a SPARQL query to retrieve the comfort preferences store in the repository and execute the query against the Stardog server, retrieving information to be sent back to the middleware via another JSON file – containing the required data retrieved from the knowledge base. In order to make this happen, a dynamic program has been written in C# language, to make the HIC application communicate and transmit data to/from semantic repository. The program receives a JSON file containing the inhabitant's name, as the user is detected, and generates a proper SPARQL query to retrieve the comfort preferences and health conditions of this specific inhabitant from the semantic repository. The program then run the Stardog server – the semantic based data repository where the knowledge base is stored there – and execute the SPARQL query made by the program. Then, the information retrieved as a result will be sent back to the program in another JSON file.

4 Use Cases Scenarios

This Section introduces two use cases highlighting how the FHfFC's SH can help the dwellers in providing them tailored comfort and assist them while performing ADLs.

4.1 Tailoring Indoor Temperature and Humidity Rate

The first use case illustrates how the SH recognizes the indoor temperature and humidity rate in summer are exceeding the customized comfort modeled in the knowledge base. The HIC then warns the dweller and asks him whether to activate the air conditioning system to restore the inhabitant's preferred comfort, as depicted in Fig. 4. Although it may seem a simple actuation, the SH helps elderlies and people with respiratory or temperature-related impairments to benefit of a constant thermo-hygrometric indoor comfort that suits the dweller's health condition. The SH does not substitute the dweller's will by automatically actuating the HVAC; automatic actuation can be set for inhabitants characterized by cognitive impairments, who may benefit from a non-intrusive and automatic actuation to guarantee indoor comfort.

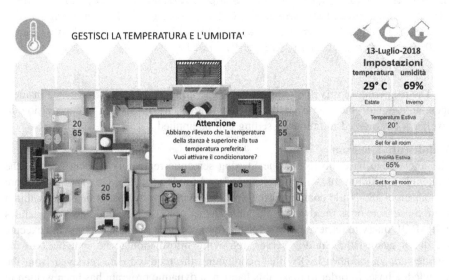

Fig. 4. A screenshot of the HIC warning the dweller that the indoor temperature and humidity rate have exceeded the comfort and asking him/her whether to activate the air conditioning to restore the tailored comfort.

4.2   Setting Illuminance According to the Activity

The second use case demonstrates how the SH can help the dweller in both providing tailored comfort and helping him/her in performing meal preparation, an instrumental ADL necessary for independent living. The dweller can, in fact, declare via the HIC that he/she wants to prepare a meal; therefore, the SH detects his/her presence inside the kitchen and sets the illuminance according to the preferences modeled in the semantic knowledge base. The inhabitants can then select a recipe using the HIC projected on the kitchen table and then the GUI guides the dweller in the preparation – as illustrated in Fig. 5.

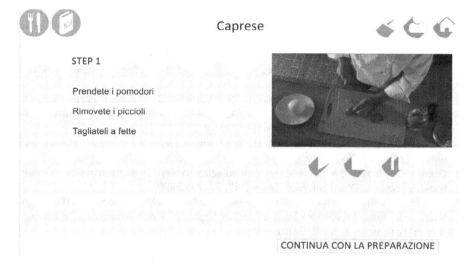

Fig. 5. A snapshot of the HIC illustrating the preparation of a recipe.

This feature allows, on the one hand, to perform an essential ADL (preparing a meal) relying on a cognitive support, while on the other hand, it ensures the most suitable comfort metrics to perform this activity. In fact, according to the EU norm EN 12464-1 it is of pivotal importance to provide an adequate illuminance on areas where the dwellers have to perform activities that require a certain amount of precision – such as cutting vegetables, reading labels of ingredients, etc.

5   Conclusion and Future Works

This work introduces the FHfFC's SH, a semantic-based framework aimed at enhancing indoor comfort for inhabitants. The framework relies on Context Awareness, Ambient Intelligence and Ambient Assisted Living paradigms to encompass also dwellers with disabilities' needs; semantic-based technologies provide a sharable and machine-understandable representation of dwellers' health condition and can trigger environmental actuation to help them in performing several activities. In addition, the proposed SH suggests a ubiquitous interface to ease the control of several domestic features. Future works foresee the validation of the SH framework and, in particular, the validation of the HIC using standard questionnaires and tests – such as the Mobile App Rating Scale (MARS) test [36], the Technology Acceptance Model 2 (TAM2) [37] and the System Usability Scale (SUS) [38]. It is indeed fundamental to evaluate the acceptance of these technologies among the target end-users (elderlies, people afflicted by mild cognitive impairment or specific impairments).

Acknowledgment. This work has been founded by "Convenzione Operativa No. 19365/RCC" in the framework of the project "Future Home for Future Communities".

References

1. Memon, M., Wagner, S.R., Pedersen, C.F., Beevi, F.H.A., Hansen, F.O.: Ambient assisted living healthcare frameworks, platforms, standards, and quality attributes. Sensors **14**, 4312–4341 (2014)
2. Remagnino, P., Hagras, H., Monekosso, N., Velastin, S.: Ambient intelligence. In: Remagnino, P., Foresti, G.L., Ellis, T. (eds.) Ambient Intelligence, pp. 1–14. Springer, New York (2005). https://doi.org/10.1007/0-387-22991-4_1
3. Alam, M.R., Reaz, M.B.I., Ali, M.A.M.: A review of smart homes—past, present, and future. IEEE Trans. Syst. Man Cybern. Part C (Appl. Rev.) **42**, 1190–1203 (2012)
4. Demiris, G., Hensel, B.K.: Technologies for an aging society: a systematic review of smart home applications. Yearbook Med. Inform. **17**, 33–40 (2008)
5. Jahn, M., Jentsch, M., Prause, C.R., Pramudianto, F., Al-Akkad, A., Reiners, R.: The energy aware smart home. In: 2010 5th International Conference on Future Information Technology (FutureTech), pp. 1–8. IEEE (2010)
6. Katz, S.: Assessing self-maintenance: activities of daily living, mobility, and instrumental activities of daily living. J. Am. Geriatr. Soc. **31**, 721–727 (1983)
7. Mahroo, A., Spoladore, D., Caldarola, E.G., Modoni, G.E., Sacco, M.: Enabling the smart home through a semantic-based context-aware system. In: 2018 IEEE International Conference on Pervasive Computing and Communications Workshops (PerCom Workshops), pp. 543–548. IEEE (2018)
8. Gruber, T.R.: A translation approach to portable ontology specifications. Knowl. Acquis. **5**, 199–220 (1993)
9. Future Home for Future Communities. Project Website. www.fhffc.it
10. Lee, D., Cheng, C.-C.: Energy savings by energy management systems: a review. Renew. Sustain. Energy Rev. **56**, 760–777 (2016)
11. Stojkoska, B.L.R., Trivodaliev, K.V.: A review of Internet of Things for smart home: challenges and solutions. J. Clean. Prod. **140**, 1454–1464 (2017)
12. Zhou, B., et al.: Smart home energy management systems: concept, configurations, and scheduling strategies. Renew. Sustain. Energy Rev. **61**, 30–40 (2016)
13. Tila, F., Kim, D.H.: Semantic IoT system for indoor environment control–a Sparql and SQL based hybrid model. Adv. Sci. Technol. Lett. **120**, 678–683 (2015)
14. Sirin, E., Parsia, B.: SPARQL-DL: SPARQL query for OWL-DL. In: OWLED. Citeseer (2007)

15. Frešer, M., Cvetkovi, B., Gradišek, A., Luštrek, M.: Anticipatory system for T–H–C dynamics in room with real and virtual sensors. In: Proceedings of the 2016 ACM International Joint Conference on Pervasive and Ubiquitous Computing: Adjunct, pp. 1267–1274. ACM (2016)

16. Adeleke, J.A., Moodley, D.: An ontology for proactive indoor environmental quality monitoring and control. In: Proceedings of the 2015 Annual Research Conference on South African Institute of Computer Scientists and Information Technologists, p. 2. ACM (2015)

17. Stavropoulos, T.G., Vrakas, D., Vlachava, D., Bassiliades, N.: BOnSAI: a smart building ontology for ambient intelligence. In: Proceedings of the 2nd International Conference on Web Intelligence, Mining and Semantics, p. 30. ACM (2012)

18. Spoladore, D., Arlati, S., Sacco, M.: Semantic and virtual reality-enhanced configuration of domestic environments: the smart home simulator. Mob. Inf. Syst. **2017**, Article ID 3185481, 15 p. (2017). https://www.hindawi.com/journals/misy/2017/3185481/. Accessed 14 Aug 2019

19. Spoladore, D., Arlati, S., Carciotti, S., Nolich, M., Sacco, M.: RoomFort: an ontology-based comfort management application for hotels. Electronics **7**, 345 (2018)

20. Nolich, M., Spoladore, D., Carciotti, S., Buqi, R., Sacco, M.: Cabin as a home: a novel comfort optimization framework for IoT equipped smart environments and applications on cruise ships. Sensors **19**, 1060 (2019)

21. Pizzagalli, S., Spoladore, D., Arlati, S., Sacco, M., Greci, L.: HIC: an interactive and ubiquitous home controller system for the smart home. In: 2018 IEEE 6th International Conference on Serious Games and Applications for Health (SeGAH), pp. 1–6. IEEE (2018)

22. Stardog 5-Knowledge Graph Platform. https://www.stardog.com/docs/

23. Busemann, C., et al.: Enabling the usage of sensor networks with service-oriented architectures. In: Proceedings of the 7th International Workshop on Middleware Tools, Services and Run-Time Support for Sensor Networks, p. 1. ACM (2012)

24. Richardson, M., Wallace, S.: Getting Started with Raspberry PI. O'Reilly Media Inc., Newton (2012)

25. Pan, J.Z.: Resource description framework. In: Staab, S., Studer, R. (eds.) Handbook on Ontologies. IHIS, pp. 71–90. Springer, Heidelberg (2009). https://doi.org/10.1007/978-3-540-92673-3_3

26. McGuinness, D.L., Van Harmelen, F., et al.: OWL web ontology language overview. W3C Recommendation **10** (2004)

27. Horrocks, I., et al.: SWRL: a semantic web rule language combining OWL and RuleML. W3C Member Submission **21**(79) (2004)

28. Suárez-Figueroa, M.C., Gómez-Pérez, A., Fernández-López, M.: The NeOn methodology for ontology engineering. In: Suárez-Figueroa, M.C., Gómez-Pérez, A., Motta, E., Gangemi, A. (eds.) Ontology Engineering in a Networked World, pp. 9–34. Springer, Heidelberg (2012). https://doi.org/10.1007/978-3-642-24794-1_2

29. Golbeck, J., Rothstein, M.: Linking social networks on the web with FOAF: a semantic web case study. In: AAAI, pp. 1138–1143 (2008)

30. World Health Organization: International Classification of Functioning, Disability and Health: ICF. Geneva: World Health Organization (2001)

31. Ontology of the International Classification of Functioning, Disability and Health. https://www.bioportal.bioontology.org/ontologies/ICF

32. Janowicz, K., Haller, A., Cox, S.J., Le Phuoc, D., Lefrançois, M.: SOSA: a lightweight ontology for sensors, observations, samples, and actuators. J. Web Semant. **56**, 1–10 (2018)

33. Compton, M., et al.: The SSN ontology of the W3C semantic sensor network incubator group. Web Semant.: Sci. Serv. Agents World Wide Web **17**, 25–32 (2012)

34. Daniele, L., den Hartog, F., Roes, J.: Created in close interaction with the industry: the smart appliances reference (SAREF) ontology. In: Cuel, R., Young, R. (eds.) FOMI 2015. LNBIP, vol. 225, pp. 100–112. Springer, Cham (2015). https://doi.org/10.1007/978-3-319-21545-7_9

35. Moreira, J., et al.: Towards IoT platforms' integration: semantic Translations between W3C SSN and ETSI SAREF. In: SIS-IoT: Semantic Interoperability and Standardization in the IoT Workshop at Semantics Conference (2017)

36. Stoyanov, S.R., Hides, L., Kavanagh, D.J., Zelenko, O., Tjondronegoro, D., Mani, M.: Mobile app rating scale: a new tool for assessing the quality of health mobile apps. JMIR mHealth uHealth **3**, e27 (2015)

37. Venkatesh, V., Davis, F.D.: A theoretical extension of the technology acceptance model: four longitudinal field studies. Manag. Sci. **46**, 186–204 (2000)

38. Brooke, J.: others: SUS-A quick and dirty usability scale. Usability Eval. Ind. **189**, 4–7 (1996)

Efficient Ontological Query Answering by Rewriting into Graph Queries

Mirko Michele Dimartino[1], Andrea Calì[1,2(✉)], Alexandra Poulovassilis[1], and Peter T. Wood[1]

[1] Knowledge Lab, Birkbeck, University of London, London, UK
{mirko,andrea,ap,ptw}@dcs.bbk.ac.uk
[2] Oxford-Man Institute of Quantitative Finance, University of Oxford, Oxford, UK

Abstract. The OWL 2 QL profile of the OWL 2 Web Ontology Language, based on the family of description logics called DL-Lite, allows for answering queries by rewriting, i.e. by reformulating a given query into another query that is then directly processed by a RDBMS system by pure querying, without materialising new data or updating existing data. In this paper we propose a new language whose expressive power goes beyond that of DL-Lite (in particular, our language extends both OWL 2 QL and linear $\mathcal{ELH}$, two well known DL ontology languages) while still allowing query answering via rewriting of queries into conjunctive two-way regular path queries (C2RPQs). Our language is identified by a syntactic property that can be efficiently checked. After defining our new language, we propose a novel rewriting technique for conjunctive queries (CQs) that makes use of nondeterministic finite state automata. CQ answering in our setting is NLogSpace-complete in data complexity and NP-complete in combined complexity; answering instance queries is NLogSpace-complete in data complexity and in PTime in combined complexity.

1 Introduction

Ontologies have been successfully employed in the conceptual modelling of data in several areas, particularly in Information Integration and the Semantic Web. An ontology is a formal specification of the domain of interest of an application, which allows for logical inference from the union of a data set and of an ontology. *Description Logics* (DLs) are a family of knowledge representation formalisms that are able to capture a wide range of ontological constructs [4]; DLs are based on *concepts* (unary predicates representing classes of individuals) and *roles* (binary predicates representing relations between classes). A DL knowledge base consists of a TBox (the *terminological* component) and an ABox (the *assertional* component). The former is a conceptual representation of the schema, while the latter is an instance of the schema. A common assumption in this context is the so-called *open-world* assumption, namely that the information in the ABox is sound but not complete; the TBox, in particular, specifies how the ABox can be expanded with additional information in order to answer queries. Answers

© Springer Nature Switzerland AG 2019
A. Cuzzocrea et al. (Eds.): FQAS 2019, LNAI 11529, pp. 75–84, 2019.
https://doi.org/10.1007/978-3-030-27629-4_10

to a query in this context are called *certain answers*, as they correspond to the answers that are true in all models of the theory constituted by the knowledge base [16]. The set of all models (which is not necessarily finite) is represented by the so-called *expansion* (or *chase*; see [8] for a relational version of the chase procedure) of an ABox $\mathcal{A}$ according to a TBox $\mathcal{T}$; this is illustrated in the following example.

Example 1. Consider the TBox $\mathcal{T}$ comprising the assertions $C \sqsubseteq A$ and $A \sqsubseteq \exists S.C$, where C and A are concepts. The concept $\exists S.C$ denotes the objects connected via the role S to some object belonging to the concept C; in other words, it contains all x such that $S(x, y)$ and $C(y)$ for some y. The first assertion means that every object in the class C is also in A; the second means that every object in the class A is also in the class represented by $\exists S.C$. Now suppose we have the ABox $\mathcal{A} = \{A(a)\}$; we can *expand* $\mathcal{A}$ according to the TBox $\mathcal{T}$ so as to add to it all atoms entailed by $(\mathcal{T}, \mathcal{A})$; we therefore add $S(a, z_0)$ and $C(z_0)$, where z_0 is a so-called *labelled null*, that is, a placeholder for an unknown value of which we know the existence (note that, with this approach, $\mathcal{A}$ can be expanded further). Given the query $\mathbf{q}$ defined as $q(x) \leftarrow S(x, y)$, the answer to $\mathbf{q}$ under $(\mathcal{T}, \mathcal{A})$ is $\{a\}$ because $S(a, z_0)$ is entailed by $(\mathcal{T}, \mathcal{A})$; in fact, the certain answers to $\mathbf{q}$ are obtained by evaluating $\mathbf{q}$ on the expansion and by considering answers that do not contain nulls. If we consider the query $\mathbf{q}_1$ defined as $q_1(x) \leftarrow C(x)$, the answer is empty because z_0, though known to exist, is not known.

Answers to queries over DL knowledge bases can be computed, for certain languages, by *query rewriting* [8]. In query rewriting, a new query $\mathbf{q}'$ is computed (rewritten) from the given query $\mathbf{q}$ according to the knowledge base $\mathcal{K} = (\mathcal{T}, \mathcal{A})$, such that the answers to $\mathbf{q}$ on $\mathcal{K}$ are obtained by evaluating $\mathbf{q}'$ on $\mathcal{A}$; it is said that $\mathbf{q}$ is *rewritten* into $\mathbf{q}'$ and that $\mathbf{q}'$ is the *perfect rewriting of* $\mathbf{q}$ *with respect to* $\mathcal{T}$. The language of $\mathbf{q}'$, called the *target language*, can be more expressive than that of $\mathbf{q}$. Query rewriting has been extensively employed in query answering under ontologies [13,17,18]. A common rewriting technique for DLs and other knowledge representation formalisms, inspired by resolution in Logic Programming, has as the target language *unions of conjunctive queries* [8].

Example 2. Let us consider again the knowledge base of Example 1. The perfect rewriting of query $\mathbf{q}$ is the query $\mathbf{q}'$ defined as $q(x) \leftarrow A(x) \cup S(x, y)$; intuitively, $\mathbf{q}'$ captures the fact that, to search for objects from which some other object is connected via the role S, we need also to consider objects in A, because the TBox might infer the former from the latter objects. The evaluation of $\mathbf{q}'$ on $\mathcal{A}$ returns the correct answer.

The OWL 2 QL profile of the OWL 2 Web Ontology Language—which is based on the family of description logics called DL-Lite$_\mathcal{R}$ [1]—is expressly designed so that query answering can be performed via query rewriting. Data (assertions) that are stored in a standard relational database can be queried through an ontology by rewriting the query into an SQL query that is then answered by the RDBMS, without any changes to the data (for example, a tractable rewriting was presented in [9]).

Extending the expressivity of DL-Lite$_\mathcal{R}$ may lead to the need for a more expressive target language than SQL, i.e. than first order (FO) queries. This occurs, for example, when *qualified existential quantification* is allowed on the left hand side (LHS) of axioms, i.e., formulae of the form $\exists R.D$ where R is a role and D a concept. In this case, we say that the language is not *FO-rewritable*. The following example illustrates this issue.

Example 3. Consider the TBox $\mathcal{T} = \{\exists R.A \sqsubseteq A\}$ and the query $\mathbf{q}$ defined as $q(x) \leftarrow A(x)$. Note that an expression of the form $\exists R.A$ is forbidden in DL-Lite$_\mathcal{R}$. It is easy to see that the query rewriting technique described earlier produces an infinite union of conjunctive queries: $q(x) \leftarrow A(x)$, $q(x) \leftarrow R(x,y), A(y)$ and all conjunctive queries of the form $q(x) \leftarrow R(x, y_1), \ldots, R(y_k, y_{k+1}), A(y_{k+1})$, with $k \geqslant 1$. This cannot be captured by an FO-rewriting.

However, by adopting the semantic web query language SPARQL 1.1 [14], database systems should be able to answer queries that are more expressive than FO queries since the *property paths* of SPARQL 1.1 are able to express navigational queries by defining regular expressions on predicates. In particular, every conjunctive two-way regular path query (C2RPQ) [6] can be translated to a SPARQL 1.1 query. Building on this, in this paper we propose a language that extends DL-Lite$_\mathcal{R}$ but still allows query answering via a simple rewriting mechanism, with C2RPQs instead of SQL queries as the target language. We allow qualified existential quantification on the LHS of axioms and identify a property of the resulting language that allows a rewriting into C2RPQs. The description logic resulting from this extension, which we call *harmless linear* $\mathcal{ELHI}$, denoted by $\mathcal{ELHI}_h^{\ell in}$, is a generalisation of both DL-Lite$_\mathcal{R}$ [1] and linear $\mathcal{ELH}$ [19].

Example 4. Recall the issue in the previous example, where a finite FO-rewriting was not feasible. In order to capture the infinite FO-rewriting, we can produce a rewriting into a C2RPQ $\mathbf{q}'$ defined as $q(x) \leftarrow R^*(x,y), A(y)$, where R^* is a regular expression denoting all finite compositions of R with itself.

Contributions. This paper extends our recent work [12] where we first proposed exploiting the capabilities of navigational queries in order to allow query rewriting of conjunctive queries into CRPQs (not C2RPQs) under a more restrictive DL, namely linear $\mathcal{ELH}$. The contributions of this paper are the following.

- We define $\mathcal{ELHI}_h^{\ell in}$ (harmless linear $\mathcal{ELHI}$), an ontology language that generalises both DL-Lite$_\mathcal{R}$ and linear $\mathcal{ELH}$.
- We propose an algorithm, based on non-deterministic finite-state automata, for rewriting *instance queries* (queries with a single atom in their body) into C2RPQs under $\mathcal{ELHI}_h^{\ell in}$ knowledge bases.
- From the above rewriting technique we devise a query rewriting algorithm for answering *conjunctive queries* (CQs), under $\mathcal{ELHI}_h^{\ell in}$ knowledge bases,

into C2RPQs. This algorithm significantly extends the *tree witness* rewriting of [12,15]. Since C2RPQs can be straightforwardly expressed in SPARQL 1.1 by means of property paths, our approach is therefore directly applicable to real-world querying settings.

The above techniques, for space reasons, are only sketched, and the reader is referred to [11] for a detailed exposition.

2 Preliminaries

In this section we present the formal notions that we will use in the rest of the paper.

Description Logics. Description Logics (DLs) [3] are a widely used family of knowledge representation languages; a DL uses a FO vocabulary containing only unary predicates (concept names), binary predicates (role names), and constants (individual names). The description logic $\mathcal{ELHI}^{\ell in}$ [18,20] is derived from the $\mathcal{EL}$ language (which is the core of the OWL 2 EL profile), extended with the additional features of inverse roles ($\mathcal{I}$) and role inclusion axioms ($\mathcal{H}$), but disallowing conjunction of concepts on the left-hand side of concept inclusion axioms. While we refer the reader to [20] for the details, we define syntax and semantics of the main DL constructs that we shall use in the following.

The alphabet contains three pairwise disjoint and countably infinite sets of *concept names* A, *role names* R, and *individual names* I. The alphabet also contains a set of *roles* P, such that each $P \in$ P is either a role name R or its *inverse*, denoted by R^-. Ontological assertions form what is called a TBox $\mathcal{T}$; data are constituted by an ABox $\mathcal{A}$, i.e. a finite set of *concept* and *role assertions* of the form $A(a)$ and $R(a,b)$, where $A \in$ A, $R \in$ R and $a, b \in$ I. Taken together, $\mathcal{T}$ and $\mathcal{A}$ constitute a *knowledge base* (or KB) $\mathcal{K} = (\mathcal{T}, \mathcal{A})$. An *interpretation* $\mathcal{I}$ [18,20] is a pair $(\Delta^{\mathcal{I}}, \cdot^{\mathcal{I}})$ that consists of a non-empty countable infinite *domain of interpretation* $\Delta^{\mathcal{I}}$ and an *interpretation function* $\cdot^{\mathcal{I}}$ which assigns *(i)* an element $a^{\mathcal{I}} \in \Delta^{\mathcal{I}}$ to each individual name a, *(ii)* a subset $A^{\mathcal{I}} \subseteq \Delta^{\mathcal{I}}$ to each concept name $A \in$ A and *(iii)* a binary relation $R^{\mathcal{I}} \subseteq \Delta^{\mathcal{I}} \times \Delta^{\mathcal{I}}$ to each role name $R \in$ R. We adopt the *unique name assumption* (UNA), so distinct individuals are assumed to be interpreted by distinct elements in $\Delta^{\mathcal{I}}$. The interpretation function $\cdot^{\mathcal{I}}$ is extended inductively to complex concepts, constructed from atomic ones, with the following definitions.

$$
\begin{aligned}
(R^-)^{\mathcal{I}} &= \{(v,u) \mid (u,v) \in R^{\mathcal{I}}\} \\
(\neg P)^{\mathcal{I}} &= (\Delta^{\mathcal{I}} \times \Delta^{\mathcal{I}}) \setminus P^{\mathcal{I}} \\
\top^{\mathcal{I}} &= \Delta^{\mathcal{I}} \\
(\exists P.\top)^{\mathcal{I}} &= \{u \mid \text{there is a } v \text{ such that } (u,v) \in P^{\mathcal{I}}\} \\
(\neg D)^{\mathcal{I}} &= \Delta^{\mathcal{I}} \setminus D^{\mathcal{I}} \\
(\exists P.C)^{\mathcal{I}} &= \{u \mid \text{there is a } v \in C^{\mathcal{I}} \text{ such that} \\
&\qquad (u,v) \in P^{\mathcal{I}}\}
\end{aligned}
$$

The satisfaction relation $\models$ for inclusions and assertions is defined as follows:

$$\mathcal{I} \models C \sqsubseteq D \text{ if and only if } C^{\mathcal{I}} \subseteq D^{\mathcal{I}},$$
$$\mathcal{I} \models P \sqsubseteq Q \text{ if and only if } P^{\mathcal{I}} \subseteq Q^{\mathcal{I}},$$
$$\mathcal{I} \models C(a) \text{ if and only if } a^{\mathcal{I}} \in C^{\mathcal{I}},$$
$$\mathcal{I} \models P(a, b) \text{ if and only if } (a^{\mathcal{I}}, b^{\mathcal{I}}) \in P^{\mathcal{I}}.$$

An interpretation $\mathcal{I}$ is a *model* of a knowledge base $\mathcal{K} = (\mathcal{T}, \mathcal{A})$, written $\mathcal{I} \models \mathcal{K}$, if it satisfies all concept and role inclusions of $\mathcal{T}$ and all concept and role assertions of $\mathcal{A}$.

Regular Languages and Conjunctive Regular Path Queries. A *non-deterministic finite state automaton* (NFA) over a set of symbols Σ is a tuple $\alpha = (Q, \Sigma, \delta, q_0, F)$, where Q is a finite set of *states*, $\delta \subseteq Q \times \Sigma \times Q$ is the *transition relation*, $q_0 \in Q$ is the *initial state*, and $F \subseteq Q$ is the set of *final states*. We use $L(\alpha)$ to denote the language defined by an NFA α, and Σ^* to denote the set of all strings over symbols in Σ, including the *empty string* ϵ. A language that is recognised by a NFA is also a *regular language* [5].

In order to define the queries below, it is assumed that there exists a countably infinite set of *variables* V and *individual names* I. A *term* t is an individual name in I or a variable in V. An *atom* is of the form $\alpha(t, t')$, where t, t' are terms, and α is an NFA or regular expression defining a regular language over $P \cup A$. A string $s \in (P \cup A)^*$ is a *path*.

A *conjunctive two-way regular path query* (C2RPQ) $\mathbf{q}$ of arity n has the form $q(\boldsymbol{x}) \leftarrow \gamma(\boldsymbol{x}, \boldsymbol{y})$, where $\boldsymbol{x} = x_1, \ldots, x_n$ and $\boldsymbol{y} = y_1, \ldots, y_m$ are tuples of variables, and $\gamma(\boldsymbol{x}, \boldsymbol{y})$ is a set of atoms with variables from $\boldsymbol{x}$ and $\boldsymbol{y}$. Atom $q(\boldsymbol{x})$ is the *head* of $\mathbf{q}$, denoted by $head(\mathbf{q})$, and $\gamma(\boldsymbol{x}, \boldsymbol{y})$ is the *body* of $\mathbf{q}$, denoted by $body(\mathbf{q})$. The variables in $\boldsymbol{x}$ are the *answer variables* of $\mathbf{q}$, while those in $\boldsymbol{y}$ are the *existentially quantified variables* of $\mathbf{q}$. A *conjunctive (one-way) regular path query* (CRPQ) is obtained by allowing only symbols from $R \cup A$ (i.e., disallowing role inverses) in atoms. A *Boolean C(2)RPQ* is a C(2)RPQ with no answer variables. A *two-way regular path query* (2RPQ) is a C2RPQ with a single atom in its body. A *regular path query* (RPQ) is a CRPQ with a single atom in its body. A *two-way path query* (2PQ) is a 2RPQ $head(\mathbf{q}) \leftarrow \alpha(x, y)$ such that $\alpha \in (P \cup A)^*$. A *path query* (PQ) is an RPQ $head(\mathbf{q}) \leftarrow \alpha(x, y)$ such that $\alpha \in (R \cup A)^*$. In both the latter cases, α is called the *path* of $\mathbf{q}$, denoted by $path(\mathbf{q})$.

We now define the semantics of C2RPQs. Given individual names a and b, an interpretation $\mathcal{I}$, and a regular language α over the alphabet $P \cup A$, we say that b α-*follows* a in $\mathcal{I}$, denoted by $\mathcal{I} \models a \xrightarrow{\alpha} b$, if and only if there is some $w = u_1 \ldots u_n \in L(\alpha)$ and some sequence $e_0, \ldots, e_n$ with $e_i \in \Delta^{\mathcal{I}}$, $0 \leqslant i \leqslant n$, such that $e_0 = a^{\mathcal{I}}$ and $e_n = b^{\mathcal{I}}$, and for all $1 \leqslant i \leqslant n$: (a) if $u_i = A \in A$, then $e_{i-1} = e_i \in A^{\mathcal{I}}$; (b) if $u_i = P \in P$, then $(e_{i-1}, e_i) \in P^{\mathcal{I}}$. A *match* for a Boolean C2RPQ $\mathbf{q}$ in an interpretation $\mathcal{I}$ is a mapping π from the terms in $body(\mathbf{q})$ to the elements in I such that:

(a) $\pi(c) = c$ if $c \in$ I;

(b) $\mathcal{I} \models \pi(t) \xrightarrow{\alpha} \pi(t')$ for each atom $\alpha(t, t')$ in $\mathbf{q}$.

To avoid notational clutter, we do not allow unary atoms in the body of the query, since each atom of the form $A(t)$, where $A \in \mathsf{A}$ and $t \in \mathsf{V} \cup \mathsf{I}$, can be always replaced by a binary atom $A(t, z)$, where z is a fresh variable (that is, freshly invented and not appearing elsewhere). However, we shall use unary atoms in this paper, whenever this improves the legibility. It is easy to see that the query with all binary atoms as above defined is equivalent to the original one, once we define suitable binary predicates to replace the unary ones; the proof of this equivalence is straightforward. We say that $\mathcal{I} \models \mathbf{q}$ if there is a match for $\mathbf{q}$ in $\mathcal{I}$, and that $\mathcal{K} \models \mathbf{q}$ if $\mathcal{I} \models \mathbf{q}$ for every model $\mathcal{I}$ of the KB $\mathcal{K}$. Also, we use the following notation: $\mathbf{q}^{\mathcal{I}} := \{t \mid \mathcal{I} \models \mathbf{q}(t)\}$ and $\mathbf{q}^{\mathcal{K}} := \{t \mid t \in \mathbf{q}^{\mathcal{I}} \text{ for every model } \mathcal{I} \text{ of } \mathcal{K}\}$. For brevity, given an ABox $\mathcal{A}$, we use $\mathcal{A} \models \mathbf{q}$ to refer to $(\varnothing, \mathcal{A}) \models \mathbf{q}$, where $(\varnothing, \mathcal{A})$ is a knowledge base with an empty TBox.

Given a C2RPQ $\mathbf{q}$ of arity n, a tuple of individual names $\boldsymbol{a} = (a_1, \ldots, a_n)$ is a *certain answer* for $\mathbf{q}$ with respect to a KB $\mathcal{K}$ if and only if $\mathcal{K} \models \mathbf{q}(\boldsymbol{a})$.

3   A Rewritable Ontology Language

In this section we present a DL language, called Harmless $\mathcal{ELHI}^{\ell in}$ Description Logic and denoted $\mathcal{ELHI}_h^{\ell in}$. Extending DL-lite$_{\mathcal{R}}$ with qualified existential quantification on the left-hand side of concept inclusion axioms is equivalent to allowing inverse roles in role inclusion axioms in $\mathcal{ELH}^{\ell in}$, resulting in $\mathcal{ELHI}^{\ell in}$. Allowing inverse roles in $\mathcal{ELH}^{\ell in}$ is shown in [19] to result in PTIME-completeness of CQ answering with respect to data complexity; therefore a rewriting in C2RPQs for this language is not feasible—if, as normally assumed, that NLOGSPACE is a proper subclass of PTIME—since the data complexity of answering C2RPQs is in NLOGSPACE. In fact, inverse roles allow the encoding of a conjunction of concepts on the left hand side of axioms (as shown in the example below), which is known to lead to PTIME-hardness ([19], Theorem 4.3).

We define our language $\mathcal{ELHI}_h^{\ell in}$ by enforcing a syntactic property that does not allow the above encoding of rules of the type $C_1 \sqcap C_2 \sqsubseteq C_3$, which are known to prevent the termination of rewriting [11]. We first convert $\mathcal{ELHI}^{\ell in}$ TBoxes to a normal form, similar to that of [2]; note that the transformation is always possible in linear time and that the result of it is equivalent to the original TBox.

Definition 1. *An $\mathcal{ELHI}^{\ell in}$ TBox is said to be in* normal form *if each of its concept inclusions and role inclusions is of one of the following forms:*

$$A_1 \sqsubseteq A_2, \ A_1 \sqsubseteq \neg A_2, \ \exists R.\top \sqsubseteq A, \ \exists R.A_1 \sqsubseteq A_2,$$
$$A \sqsubseteq \exists R.\top, \ R_1 \sqsubseteq R_2, \ R_1 \sqsubseteq \neg R_2, \ R_1 \sqsubseteq R_2^-,$$

where $A, A_1, A_2 \in \mathsf{A}$ and $R, R_1, R_2 \in \mathsf{R}$.

We now introduce some auxiliary definitions.

Definition 2. *Let R and R' be two role names appearing in an $\mathcal{ELHI}^{\ell in}$ TBox $\mathcal{L}$ that is in normal form. If R, R' are two roles in $\mathcal{L}$ and there exist $R_0, \ldots, R_n$*

such that (i) $R = R_0$, $R' = R_n$ and (ii) for $1 \leqslant i \leqslant n$ either $R_{i-1} \sqsubseteq R_i \in \mathcal{L}$ or $R_{i-1} \sqsubseteq R_i^- \in \mathcal{L}$, then: (a) if the number of inverse roles R_i^- is even, we write $R \rightarrow_{\mathcal{L}} R'$; (b) if the number is odd, we write $R \rightarrow_{\mathcal{L}} R'^-$.

We now define the *harmless* condition for two given roles appearing in an $\mathcal{ELHI}^{\ell in}$ TBox in normal form:

Definition 3. *Let R and R' be two role names appearing in an $\mathcal{ELHI}^{\ell in}$ TBox $\mathcal{L}$ in normal form. If neither $R \rightarrow_{\mathcal{L}} R'^-$ nor $R' \rightarrow_{\mathcal{L}} R^-$, then we say that R and R' are mutually harmless roles with respect to $\mathcal{L}$.*

We are now ready to define the class of *harmless* $\mathcal{ELHI}^{\ell in}$ TBoxes:

Definition 4. *Given an $\mathcal{ELHI}^{\ell in}$ TBox $\mathcal{L}$ in normal form, $A_1, A_2 \in \mathsf{A}$, $R_1, R_2 \in \mathsf{R}$, say that $\mathcal{L}$ is harmless if, whenever there is some $\exists R_2.A_2$ on the left-hand side of an axiom in $\mathcal{L}$, if there exists some axiom $\exists R_1.\top \sqsubseteq A_2$ or $\exists R_1.A_1 \sqsubseteq A_2$ in $\mathcal{L}$, then we have that R_1 and R_2 are mutually harmless roles with respect to $\mathcal{L}$. The language of all harmless $\mathcal{ELHI}^{\ell in}$ TBoxes is denoted by $\mathcal{ELHI}_h^{\ell in}$.*

In the next section we will show that the harmless property of the above definition allows the possibility of answering CQs by query rewritings into C2RPQs.

4   Rewriting

Rewriting conjunctive queries under ontologies is a topic that has been widely investigated and there exists a technique for query rewriting, widely adopted in the Knowledge Representation and Databases literature [7–9], that produces correct rewritings (the so-called *perfect* rewritings [10]) that compute exactly the set of certain answers to a given CQ when evaluated on the data. In our case such a technique produces infinite rewritings in general, but we are able to encode the possibly infinite steps of the aforementioned "classical" rewriting algorithm into NFAs, then captured by 2CRPQs. This is done initially for *instance* (atomic) queries composed by a single concept.

Definition 5. *Let $\mathcal{T}$ be an $\mathcal{ELHI}_h^{\ell in}$ TBox in normal form, Σ be the alphabet $\mathsf{P} \cup \mathsf{A}$, and A be a concept name appearing in $\mathcal{T}$. The NFA-rewriting of A with respect to $\mathcal{T}$, denoted by $\mathsf{NFA}_{A,\mathcal{T}}$, is the NFA $(Q, \Sigma, \delta, S_A, F)$ defined as follows:*

(1) states S_A, SF_A and $S_\top$ are in Q, SF_A and $S_\top$ are in F, and transition (S_A, A, SF_A) is in δ; S_A is the initial state;

(2) for each $B \in \mathsf{A}$ that appears in at least one concept or role inclusion axiom of $\mathcal{T}$, states S_B and SF_B are in Q, SF_B is in F, and transition (S_B, B, SF_B) is in δ;

(3) for each concept inclusion axiom $\rho \in \mathcal{T}$:

  (3.1) if ρ is of the form $B \sqsubseteq C$, where $B, C \in \mathsf{A}$, the transition (S_C, ϵ, S_B) is in δ;

(3.2) if ρ is of the form $B \sqsubseteq \exists R.\top$, where $B \in A$ and $R \in R$, for each transition $(S_X, R, S_\top) \in \delta$, the transition (S_X, ϵ, S_B) is in δ;

(3.3) if ρ is of the form $\exists R.\top \sqsubseteq B$, where $B \in A$ and $R \in R$, the transition $(S_B, R, S_\top)$ is in δ;

(3.4) if ρ is the form $\exists R.D \sqsubseteq C$, where $C, D \in A$ and $R \in R$, the transition (S_C, R, S_D) is in δ;

(4.1) for each role inclusion axiom $T \sqsubseteq S \in T$ and each transition of the form $(S_C, S, S_B) \in \delta$, the transition (S_C, T, S_B) is in δ.

(4.2) for each role inclusion axiom $T \sqsubseteq S^- \in T$ and each transition of the form $(S_C, S, S_B) \in \delta$ or $(S_C, S^-, S_B) \in \delta$, the transition (S_C, T^-, S_B) or (S_C, T, S_B) is in δ, respectively.

Example 5. Consider the TBox T defined by the following inclusion axioms: $\exists R.C \sqsubseteq \exists P.\top$, $\exists P.\top \sqsubseteq A$, $\exists P.\top \sqsubseteq B$, $\exists T.B \sqsubseteq C$, $\exists S.A \sqsubseteq A$ and $V \sqsubseteq T^-$, where P, R, S, T, V are role names and A, B, C are concept names. Consider now the query $\mathbf{q} = q(x) \leftarrow A(x, y)$. First, we transform T into normal form, T', by adding a fresh concept name X and by replacing $\exists R.C \sqsubseteq \exists P.\top$ by $\exists R.C \sqsubseteq X$ and $X \sqsubseteq \exists P.\top$. It is easy to see that the "classical" CQ-to-FO rewriting algorithm [9] would not terminate in this case.

Let us consider the NFA rewriting of A with respect to T'. We construct $\mathsf{NFA}^-_{A,T'}$ (shown in Fig. 1) as follows: by *(2)* in Definition 5 we have the transitions $(S_A, A, SF_A), (S_B, B, SF_B), (S_C, C, SF_C)$ and (S_X, X, SF_X); by *(3.3)* in Definition 5 and the inclusion assertions $\exists P.\top \sqsubseteq A$ and $\exists P.\top \sqsubseteq B$, we have the transitions $(S_A, P, S_\top)$ and $(S_B, P, S_\top)$; by *(3.2)* in Definition 5 and the inclusion assertion $X \sqsubseteq \exists P.\top$, we have the transitions (S_A, ϵ, S_X) and (S_B, ϵ, S_X); by *(3.4)* in Definition 5 and the inclusion assertions $\exists R.C \sqsubseteq X$, $\exists T.B \sqsubseteq C$ and $\exists S.A \sqsubseteq A$, we have the transitions (S_X, R, S_C), (S_C, T, S_B) and (S_A, S, S_A); finally, by *(4.2)* in Definition 5 and the inclusion assertion $V \sqsubseteq T^-$ we have the transition (S_C, V^-, S_B).

The language accepted by $\mathsf{NFA}^-_{A,T'}$ can be described by the following regular expression: $S^*((A|P|X)|(((R(T|V^-))^*(P|B|X|RC))))$. It is easy to see that all the infinite outputs of $\mathsf{Rewrite}(\mathbf{q}, T')$ are of the form $q(x) \leftarrow \mathsf{NFA}^-_{A,T'}(x, y)$. For instance, some rewritings of $\mathbf{q}$ follow.

$$q(x) \leftarrow S(x, z_1), S(z_1, z_2), P(z_2, y)$$
$$q(x) \leftarrow S(x, z_1), S(z_1, z_2), A(z_2, y)$$
$$q(x) \leftarrow R(x, z_1), T(z_1, z_2), R(z_2, z_3), C(z_3, y)$$
$$q(x) \leftarrow R(x, z_1), V(z_2, z_1), R(z_2, z_3), C(z_3, y)$$

At this point we can use the above NFA construction and, with a more general construction that we do not include here for space reasons, we are able to rewrite conjunctive queries into C2RPQs under $\mathcal{ELHI}^{\ell in}_h$ ontologies. More formally, given a conjunctive query q and an $\mathcal{ELHI}^{\ell in}_h$ TBox T, for every ABox A and any tuple a of individual names in A, we can compute a *rewriting* p of q, in the form of a C2RPQ, such that $(T, A) \models q$ if and only if $A \models p$.

Theorem 1. *The language of conjunctive queries is C2RPQ-rewritable under $\mathcal{ELHI}^{\ell in}_h$ knowledge bases.*

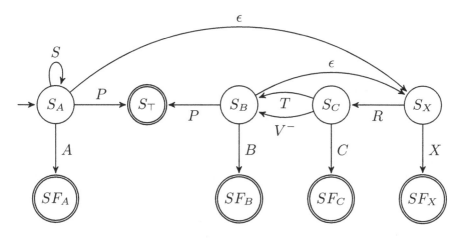

Fig. 1. NFA for Example 5.

5 Conclusions

In this paper we have introduced a new ontology language, named $\mathcal{ELHI}_h^{\ell in}$, which strictly extends the known ontology languages DL-Lite$_\mathcal{R}$ and linear $\mathcal{ELH}$. This novel language allows for a limited use of inverse roles in $\mathcal{ELHI}^{\ell in}$ while retaining C2RPQ-rewritability.

It is possible to show, starting from our rewriting algorithm from CQs to C2RPQs, that CQ answering under $\mathcal{ELHI}_h^{\ell in}$ ontologies is in NLogSpace in data complexity and in NP in combined complexity; we are also able to show that these bounds are tight. For a complete exposition of our techniques and more results, we refer the reader to [11]. Since DL-Lite$_\mathcal{R}$ and $\mathcal{ELH}$ are ontology languages that have been shown to be relevant to theory and practice, a fortiori our new language $\mathcal{ELHI}_h^{\ell in}$ is relevant and efficient at the same time.

Future work includes an empirical evaluation of our rewriting algorithms on real-world data sets, as well as an investigation of other ontology languages that may lie within the scope of rewritability of CQs into graph queries such as C2RPQs. In particular, it would be interesting to investigate more general ways of introducing inverse roles into our language.

References

1. Artale, A., Calvanese, D., Kontchakov, R., Zakharyaschev, M.: The DL-lite family and relations. J. Artif. Intell. Res. **36**(1), 1–69 (2009)
2. Baader, F., Brandt, S., Lutz, C.: Pushing the EL envelope. In: Proceedings of the 19th International Joint Conference on Artificial Intelligence, pp. 364–369 (2005)
3. Baader, F., Calvanese, D., McGuinness, D.L., Nardi, D., Patel-Schneider, P.F. (eds.): The Description Logic Handbook: Theory, Implementation, and Applications. Cambridge University Press, New York (2003)

4. Baader, F., Nutt, W.: Basic description logics. In: Description Logic Handbook, pp. 43–95 (2003)
5. Berry, G., Sethi, R.: From regular expressions to deterministic automata. Theor. Comput. Sci. **48**, 117–126 (1986)
6. Bienvenu, M., Ortiz, M., Simkus, M.: Conjunctive regular path queries in lightweight description logics. In: Proceedings of the 23rd International Joint Conference on Artificial Intelligence (2013)
7. Calì, A., Calvanese, D., De Giacomo, G., Lenzerini, M.: Accessing data integration systems through conceptual schemas. In: Kunii, H.S., Jajodia, S., Sølvberg, A. (eds.) ER 2001. LNCS, vol. 2224, pp. 270–284. Springer, Heidelberg (2001). https://doi.org/10.1007/3-540-45581-7_21
8. Calì, A., Lembo, D., Rosati, R.: Query rewriting and answering under constraints in data integration systems. In: Proceedings of the 18th International Joint Conference on Artificial Intelligence, pp. 16–21 (2003)
9. Calvanese, D., De Giacomo, G., Lembo, D., Lenzerini, M., Rosati, R.: Tractable reasoning and efficient query answering in description logics: the DL-lite family. J. Autom. Reasoning **39**(3), 385–429 (2007)
10. Calvanese, D., De Giacomo, G., Lenzerini, M., Vardi, M.Y.: What is view-based query rewriting? In: Proceedings of the 7th International Workshop on Knowledge Representation meets Databases, KRDB 2000, pp. 17–27 (2000)
11. Dimartino, M., Calí, A., Poulovassilis, A., Wood, P.T.: Efficient ontological query answering by rewriting into graph queries (2019). Manuscript; available from the authors
12. Dimartino, M.M., Calì, A., Poulovassilis, A., Wood, P.T.: Query rewriting under linear EL knowledge bases. In: 10th International Conference on Web Reasoning and Rule Systems, pp. 61–76 (2016)
13. Gottlob, G., Orsi, G., Pieris, A.: Ontological queries: rewriting and optimization. In: Proceedings of the 27th International Conference on Data Engineering, pp. 2–13 (2011)
14. Harris, S., Seaborne, A.: SPARQL 1.1 Query Language, W3C Recommendation 21 March 2013
15. Kontchakov, R., Zakharyaschev, M.: An introduction to description logics and query rewriting. In: Koubarakis, M., et al. (eds.) Reasoning Web 2014. LNCS, vol. 8714, pp. 195–244. Springer, Cham (2014). https://doi.org/10.1007/978-3-319-10587-1_5
16. Lenzerini, M.: Data integration: a theoretical perspective. In: Proceedings of the Twenty-First ACM SIGMOD-SIGACT-SIGART Symposium on Principles of Database Systems, PODS 2002, pp. 233–246. ACM, New York (2002)
17. Mosurovic, M., Krdzavac, N., Graves, H., Zakharyaschev, M.: A decidable extension of SROIQ with complex role chains and unions. J. Artif. Intell. Res. (JAIR) **47**, 809–851 (2013)
18. Pérez-Urbina, H., Horrocks, I., Motik, B.: Efficient query answering for OWL 2. In: Bernstein, A., et al. (eds.) ISWC 2009. LNCS, vol. 5823, pp. 489–504. Springer, Heidelberg (2009). https://doi.org/10.1007/978-3-642-04930-9_31
19. Pérez-Urbina, H., Motik, B., Horrocks, I.: Rewriting conjunctive queries over description logic knowledge bases. In: Schewe, K.-D., Thalheim, B. (eds.) SDKB 2008. LNCS, vol. 4925, pp. 199–214. Springer, Heidelberg (2008). https://doi.org/10.1007/978-3-540-88594-8_11
20. Rosati, R.: On conjunctive query answering in EL. In: 20th International Workshop on Description Logics (2007)

WeLink: A Named Entity Disambiguation Approach for a QAS over Knowledge Bases

Wissem Bouarroudj[1]([✉]), Zizette Boufaida[1]([✉]), and Ladjel Bellatreche[2]([✉])

[1] LIRE Laboratory, Université Abdelhamid Mehri Constantine 2,
Constantine, Algeria
{wissem.bouarroudj,zizette.boufaida}@univ-constantine2.dz
[2] LIAS/ISAE-ENSMA, Poitiers, France
bellatreche@ensma.fr

Abstract. Question Answering Systems (QASs) are usually built behind queries described by short texts. The explosion of knowledge graphs and Linked Open Data motivates researchers for constructing QASs over these rich data resources. The shortness nature of user questions contributes to complicate the problem of Entity Linking, widely studied for long texts. In this paper, we propose an approach, called WeLink, based on the context and types of entities of a given query. The context of an entity is described by synonyms of the words used in the question and the definition of the named entity, whereas the type describes the category of the entity. During the named entity recognition step, we first identify different entities, their types, and contexts (by the means of the Wordnet). The expanded query is then executed on the target knowledge base, where several candidates are obtained with their contexts and types. Similarity distances among these different contexts and types are computed in order to select the appropriate candidate. Finally, our system is evaluated on a dataset with 5000 questions and compared with some well-known Entity Linking systems.

Keywords: Entity Linking · Named entity · Disambiguation · Linked Data

1 Introduction

Nowadays, we assist to an explosion of public and enterprises knowledge bases (KBs) such as Freebase [1], Google Knowledge Graph, DBpedia [13], Amazon knowledge graph. These KBs have become immediately a candidate for building advanced data storage systems such as augmented data warehouses [12] and Question-Answering Systems (QAS). QAS has become a popular way for humans to access billion-scale KBs [3] due to their richness in terms of data and knowledge. The aim of QAS over a KB is to deliver more relevant and concise responses by understanding the intent and the context of the user's question [9,11]. QAS

© Springer Nature Switzerland AG 2019
A. Cuzzocrea et al. (Eds.): FQAS 2019, LNAI 11529, pp. 85–97, 2019.
https://doi.org/10.1007/978-3-030-27629-4_11

have been an active research area and are still dealing with a multitude of challenges. Among them, Named Entity Disambiguation or more commonly known as Entity Linking (EL). EL is the task of linking the identified named entities to the corresponding entries in a KB. Ambiguity happens when the entity mention can be linked to more than one KB entity. Thus, disambiguating the entity mention becomes a challenge. In general, the EL task consists of two phases: Candidates Generation which aims to generate a set of candidates containing the possible entities that the entity mention may refer to [18], and Candidates Disambiguation (Ranking) to filter out the set of candidates in order to select the most relevant ones.

EL can be performed on long texts (i.e. document). The used approaches are generally based on the similarity between the text surrounding the entity mention and the context of the entity candidate. However, for short texts (i.e. user question), the queries are composed of few ambiguous terms, thus the ambiguity may not be resolved because of the limited context [9].

To tackle this limit, we propose WeLink, a system to perform EL in question over a KB. To address the lack of textual description associated with the entity, our system expands the user question to enrich the context of the entity. Furthermore, while other systems do not exploit entity types or are limited to someone, such as People, Location and Organization, our system considers that an entity may be associated with multiple related types. For instance, Paris is a place, a city or a location. Overall, our system computes two scores of similarity: context similarity and types similarity, and thus selects the most relevant candidates. We evaluate our approach on a dataset with 5000 questions and compare it against the state-of-art systems.

This paper is organized as follows: First, we detail some well-known systems in Entity Linking in QAS in Sect. 2. So, we describe our approach in Sect. 3. Furthermore, we evaluate the quality of our approach and compare it with state-of-art systems in Sect. 4, and finally, we conclude in Sect. 5.

2   Related Works

A wide range of works has been done in the area of Entity Linking. We have selected some well-known in the Linked Data community.

DBpedia Spotlight [14] is a system for annotating documents with DBpedia. The approach works in four phases: It recognizes the entity mention using a list of surface forms. Then, for the candidate selection step, it generates candidate entities. Next, to disambiguate the entity mention, it uses the context around the entity to choose the correct DBpedia resource. The authors used a string matching algorithm with a weighted cosine similarity measure to recognize and disambiguate mentions.

Babelfy's approach [16] lies on random walks and the densest subgraph algorithm to tackle EL and the word sense disambiguation tasks. The author disambiguates both nominal and NE mentions occurring within a text by linking them to their corresponding resources from the KB.

TAGME [6] is a system for annotating short texts. First, the parsing step uses an anchor dictionary (extracted from Wikipedia) to spot the mention entities in the input text. These mentions are, next, disambiguated by selecting a pertinent sense drawn from the page catalog: a lucene index containing Wikipedia pages. To select the correct sense, a voting scheme is proposed to calculate a score for each pair of mention-entity as the sum of senses votes of all the mentions in the text. Finally, a pruning step eliminates irrelevant senses using a link probability and the coherence between the mention and other mentions of the text.

AIDA [10] is a graph-based approach for joint entity linking in a text. The approach defines mentions from the input text and candidate entities as a node set. It captures the context similarities based on weighted edges between mentions and entities, and coherence based on weighted edges among entities. The authors aim is to identify a dense subgraph that disambiguates a mention.

EARL [5] is a recent approach that jointly disambiguates entities and relations in the user query for QAS using a KB. The relations surrounding the entity are considered as the context of the ambiguous one. This approach uses two different strategies: The first is the Generalised Travelling Salesman Problem (GTSP) and the second strategy uses machine learning to exploit the connection density between nodes in the KG.

Table 1. Comparison of the related-works approachs

Systems	Approach		Input text		Features		
	Context based	Graph based	Long	Short	Joint EL	Query expansion	Types exploitation
DBpedia spotlight [14]	✓		✓		✓		✓
TAGME [6]	✓			✓	✓		
Babelfly [16]		✓		✓	✓		
AIDA [10]		✓		✓	✓		
EARL [5]		✓		✓	✓		
Our approach	✓			✓	✓	✓	✓

EL can be performed on long texts (i.e., documents), which has been widely studied for long texts where it is assumed that there is enough context for disambiguation. Recently, short texts draw attention and particularly EL in queries (ELQ). Queries consist of few terms which are generally considered as noisy. Consequently, the ambiguity may not be resolved because of the limited context [9].

The main contributions of this paper are the context expansion and types exploitation. To exploit a context-based disambiguation approach in short text, we expand the user's question by extracting definitions and synonyms from WorNet (Sect. 3.1) in order to measure context similarity. Contrary to [5,17] that treats entity types as a part of the relation linking task, we also exploit entity types, considering that each entity has multiple types, and measure the similarity between mention types and candidate types.

In Table 1, we detailed the main differences between the related-works approach and our approaches.

3   The WeLink Approach

The goal of an EL system is to link the identified named entities to their corresponding KB resources. An overview of the proposed system is depicted in Fig. 1.

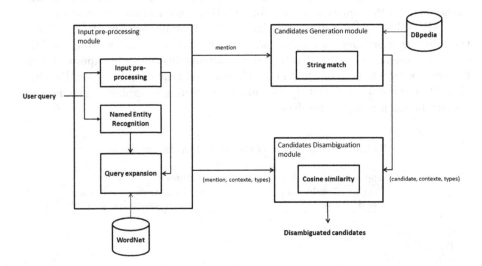

Fig. 1. WeLink approach

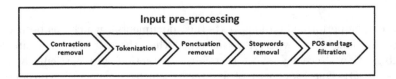

Fig. 2. Input pre-processing

3.1   Input Pre-processing

To identify keywords, the user query is analysed using different NLP techniques. The Fig. 2 describes the significant steps of the Input pre-processing. Firstly, contractions are converted to a full form ("don't" is converted to "do not"). Then, a Tokenizer is used to split the user's query into words. The next two steps help to remove commonly used word (like "the", "a", "in", etc.) and punctuation (like "?", ";", "."). A POS tagger and tags filtration are applied to only keep nouns, verbs and adjectives in order to get their synonyms.

Entity Mention Context: It is known that the context has an important role in any disambiguation process. We consider the context of the ambiguous NE as all the words that constitute the question. If the words used in a question mismatch the ones used in the KB, the lexical gap problem may happens [8]. Bridging this lexical gap is needed in every QAS to improve recall by using query expansion [11].

The concept of context differs from one approach to another. In Table 2 we detailed the entity mention context and the candidate context as defined in each approach.

Table 2. The definition of entity mention context and candidate context

Systems	Context	
	Mention	Candidate
EARL [5]	The keywords of the user question	Entities and relations surrounding the entity
Babelfly [16]	Named entities and concepts of the input text	Semantic signatures: related concepts and named entities
DBpedia spotlight [14]	Paragraphs around surface form	Wikilinks: anchor text, link target, and the paragraph representing the context of that wikilink occurrence
AIDA [10]	All words of the input text	Characteristic keyphrases or salient words from Wikipedia articles or similar sources
TAGME [6]	Mentions of the input text	Wikipedia pages
Our approach	All words of the user question, their synonyms and the NE definition	The dbo:abstract property value which is a short Wikipedia description of a resource

Usually, user queries are short and ambiguous, which make it difficult to retrieve relevant responses. A common solution is query expansion, that aims to extract related terms in order to better represent the user's intent. To expand the user's question and thus reduce the lexical gap between the user's question and the KB, we use Wordnet [15] to extract synonyms of the user's words. Synonymy is considered as the main relation among words in WordNet. Thus, Synsets are unordered sets of synonyms words that denote the same concept. A synset contains a brief definition, short sentences illustrating the synset. We utilized both, synonyms and synset definition to enrich the NE context in order to compare it to the candidates' context later. Figure 3 describes the steps used to reach our goal.

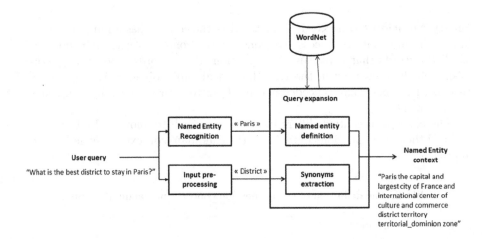

Fig. 3. Query expansion

Entity Mention Types: A Named Entity Recognition (NER) step is used to identify the entity mention and associate it to its type (also called category) for instance Person, Organization, Location, etc.

An entity may be classified into multiple types. For example, Paris is a place, a city or a location. We consider those types as different but related in meaning. Based on that, we choose to exploit multiple types for a given entity mention. In our previous work [2], we showed the importance of entity type in the disambiguation process. Using the entity types helped us to reduce ambiguity. We concluded that the more the type is precise the better the results.

We used Spacy[1], an open source library, for the NER step to extract the named entities and their types, for instance : PERSON, GPE, ORG. We also exploit their description. We explained some types and their descriptions[2] in Table 3.

We use the types given by the NER step and their descriptions like it is illustrated in Fig. 4.

---

[1] https://spacy.io.

[2] https://spacy.io/api/annotation.

Table 3. Spacy types description

Type	Description
PERSON	People, including fictional
ORG	Companies, agencies, institutions, etc.
GPE	Countries, cities, states

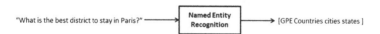

Fig. 4. Named entity recognition

3.2 Candidate Generation

The Candidate Generation step is as important as the Candidate Disambiguation step. It is considered to be critical for the whole EL process [7,18]. We used SPARQL to query Dbpedia [13] in order to generate a set of candidates. The following characteristics are used:

String Match: We followed the features used in [4]. We used the KB properties to extract different surface form of the ambiguous entity mention. For a **partial match**, We utilized *Disambiguation* and *Redirects* properties that regroup URIs of resources that have different names but refer to the same entity.

Table 4. The used DBpedia properties

Properties	Definition
rdfs:label	Wikipedia page titles
foaf:name	Indicate the name of a person (string)
dbo:wikiPageRedirects	URIs of synonyms, acronyms and misspellings
dbo:wikiPageDisambiguates	Regrouped URIs of resources considered to be ambiguous

For the **exact match**, we used *Label* and *Name* properties to extract URIs of resources having the same title or the same name. The used properties are defined in Table 4.

Candidate Types: For each candidate, the types are extracted using the rdf:type property. This property states that a resource is an instance of a class. It generally has multiple values which are URIs identifying classes. We construct a list that contains all the types as illustrated in Fig. 5.

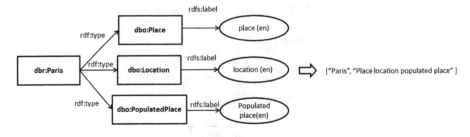

Fig. 5. Candidate types

Candidate Context: In context similarity approach, the context varies from one work to another as detailed in Table 2. Each DBpedia's resource has a short description contained in the value of the dbo :abstract property. In our work, we considered this description as the context of the candidate.

The following SQARQL query is used to generate candidates based on the mentioned features :

```
PREFIX dbr  :  <http ://dbpedia.org/resource/>
PREFIX rdf  :  <http ://www.w3.org/1999/02/22-rdf-syntax-ns#>
PREFIX rdfs :  <http ://www.w3.org/2000/01/rdf-schema#>
PREFIX dbo  :  <http ://dbpedia.org/ontology/>
PREFIX foaf :  <http ://xmlns.com/foaf/0.1/>

SELECT DISTINCT
?y ?s (concat(group_concat(distinct ?lt;separator=' ')) as ?t) ?na
WHERE {
{<dbr :+normalized_entity+> dbo :wikiPageDisambiguates ?y}
UNION
{<dbr :+normalized_entity+_(disambiguation)> dbo :wikiPageDisambiguates ?y}
UNION
{?y rdfs :label '+entity +'@en.}
UNION
{<dbr :+normalized_entity+> dbo :wikiPageRedirects ?y }
UNION
{<dbr :+entity+> foaf :name ?y }
?y dbo :abstract ?s FILTER (lang(?s) = "en").
?y rdf :type ?t.
OPTIONAL {?t rdfs :label ?lt FILTER (lang(?lt) = "en").}
OPTIONAL {?y rdfs :label ?na FILTER (lang(?na) = "en").}
}
 group by ?y ?s ?na
```

3.3   Candidate Disambiguation

Selection Measures: TFIDF (Term Frequency−Inverse Document Frequency) is a numerical statistic measure used in information retrieval for measuring the importance of a word w to a document d in a collection C. This measure is used as a ranking function for search engines and is was also used in in document classification and clustering.

$$tfidf(w, d, c) = tf(w, d) * idf(w, C)$$

- **TF** (Term Frequency) is the number of times that a term t occurs in a document d compared to the total number of words in that document.
- **IDF** (Inverse document frequency) measure the weight of rare words across all documents in the corpus. The words that occur rarely have a high IDF score. It illustrates the importance of the word in the collection.

  By applying this theoretical definitions to our approach, we consider a document as each context of a candidate. The collection of documents is then all the candidate contexts.
- **Vector Space Model** For each candidate context, we derive a term vector weighted by TF*ICF.
- **Cosine Similarity** Cosine similarity is a measure of similarity between two non-negative vectors. If v_1 and v_2 are tf-idf vectors, then:

$$cosine\theta = \frac{v_1.v_2}{||v_1||\ ||v_2||}$$

  where θ is the angle between the vectors. As θ ranges from 0 to 90°, because tf-idf vectors are non-negative, cosine θ ranges from 1 to 0. Two vectors with the same orientation have a cosine similarity of 1 [19].

Selection Process of the Best Candidate: To select the best candidate, we rely on two scores of similarity. First, we use the Cosine to measure the similarity between the entity mention m context vector and each candidate c context vector. Second, we compute the Cosine similarity between the entity mention types vector and each candidate types vector.

Then, we attribute a global score for each candidate composed of the addition of the two scores of similarities and the best candidate is then selected as follow:

$$Max(Cosine(m\_context, c\_context) + Cosine(m\_types, c\_types))$$

Details of our WeLink's procedure are described in the Algorithm 1.

Algorithm 1. Named Entities Disambiguation

```
 1: Input : List NE of named entities m
 2: Output : DBpedia resource corresponding to each input NE
 3: begin
 4:      C ← EmptyList[]
 5:      candidates ← EmptyList[]
 6:      for m in NE do :
 7:          C ← StringMatch(ne);
 8:          for c in C do :
 9:              CosineContext ← CosineSimilarity(m.context, c.context)
10:              CosineTypes ← CosineSimilarity(m.types, c.types);
11:              T ← CosineContext + CosineTypes
12:              candidates.append(c, T)
13:          BestCandidate ← candidates[0]
14:          for(int i = 0;  i < candidates.lenght; i + +) :
15:              if candidates[i].T > BestCandidate.T
16:                  BestCandidate = candidates[i]
17:      return BestCandidate
18: end.
```

4 Experiments and Results

4.1 Dataset

LC-QuAD is the largest existing dataset for question answering over knowlege graphs. The dataset are natural language questions. It contains 5000 questions. Example "What are shows whose theme music composer's home town is New York?" [20]. We have used the annotated LC-QuAD dataset made by [5].

4.2 Metrics

To evaluate our approach we use precision, recall, and F1 measure as defined in [18]. The precision is computed as the correctly linked entity mentions out of all the linked mentions generated by the system. It provides how correct the results are.

$$precision = \frac{|\{correctly\ linked\ entity\ mentions\}|}{|\{linked\ mentions\ generated\ by\ system\}|}$$

The recall is number of correctly linked entity mentions divided by the number entity mentions that should be linked. It states how much information was found.

$$recall = \frac{|\{correctly\ linked\ entity\ mentions\}|}{|\{entity\ mentions\ that\ should\ be\ linked\}|}$$

The F measure is the weighted average of Precision and Recall. The F-measure is the harmonic mean of precision and recall. F measure describes the quality of the results. It is calculated as follow:

$$F1 = \frac{2 \; . \; precision \; . \; recall}{precision \; + \; recall}$$

4.3 Results

We compared our approach to the related-works systems using the LC-QuAD dataset. The results of these systems have been reported from [17].

Table 5. Performance of related-works EL systems and our system on LC-QuAD

Dataset	Author	Precision	Recall	F-measure
LC-QuAD	Babelfly [16]	0.43	0.50	0.44
	AIDA [10]	0.50	0.45	0.47
	EARL [5]	0.53	0.55	0.53
	WeLink	0.59	0.58	0.58
	DBpedia spotlight [14]	0.60	0.65	0.61
	TAGME [6]	0.65	0.77	0.68

We reported macro precision, macro recall, and macro F-measure in Table 5. We obtained the third best performance. Our system performs better results than the Babelfly, AIDA and EARL.

4.4 Discussion

By analyzing the results, we observed that 12% of named entities were not detected, and 4% were not correctly detected for instance, in the question "Count the number of actors in Lucy Sullivan Is Getting Married." the NER system returns "Lucy Sullivan" and not "Lucy Sullivan Is Getting Married". We will consider these cases by focusing on the Entity Recognition step to improve results in our future work.

5   Conclusion

In this paper, we proposed a system called WeLink for Entity Linking in Question-Answering Systems over knowledge bases that have become a serious candidate for end users due to their knowledge abundance. To well develop our system, we first, we detailed the expansion of the user question in order to enrich the entity mention context. Second, we suggested the exploitation of multiple entity types to add a disambiguation score. We finally compute similarities between the context and types of the entity mention and the entity candidate. We have evaluated our system over 5000 questions dataset using DBpedia. We then compared our results to related-works systems. Our system outperforms some well-known systems.

Our work opens several directions that we currently dealing with: (i) the exploitation of the relations between entities to increase the quality of WeLink results and (ii) Deployment of Welink as a Web Service.

References

1. Bollacker, K.D., Evans, C., Paritosh, P., Sturge, T., Taylor, J.: Freebase: a collaboratively created graph database for structuring human knowledge. In: ACM SIGMOD, pp. 1247–1250 (2008)
2. Bouarroudj, W., Boufaida, Z.: A candidate generation algorithm for named entities disambiguation using DBpedia. In: Rocha, Á., Adeli, H., Reis, L.P., Costanzo, S. (eds.) WorldCIST'18 2018. AISC, vol. 745, pp. 712–721. Springer, Cham (2018). https://doi.org/10.1007/978-3-319-77703-0_71
3. Cui, W., Xiao, Y., Wang, H., Song, Y., Hwang, S., Wang, W.: KBQA: learning question answering over QA corpora and knowledge bases. PVLDB **10**(5), 565–576 (2017)
4. Dredze, M., McNamee, P., Rao, D., Gerber, A., Finin, T.: Entity disambiguation for knowledge base population. In: Proceedings of the 23rd International Conference on Computational Linguistics, pp. 277–285. Association for Computational Linguistics (2010)
5. Dubey, M., Banerjee, D., Chaudhuri, D., Lehmann, J.: Earl: Joint entity and relation linking for question answering over knowledge graphs. arXiv preprint arXiv:1801.03825 (2018)
6. Ferragina, P., Scaiella, U.: Fast and accurate annotation of short texts with wikipedia pages. IEEE Softw. **29**(1), 70–75 (2012)
7. Hachey, B., Radford, W., Nothman, J., Honnibal, M., Curran, J.R.: Evaluating entity linking with wikipedia. Artif. Intell. **194**, 130–150 (2013)
8. Hakimov, S., Unger, C., Walter, S., Cimiano, P.: Applying semantic parsing to question answering over linked data: addressing the lexical gap. In: Biemann, C., Handschuh, S., Freitas, A., Meziane, F., Métais, E. (eds.) NLDB 2015. LNCS, vol. 9103, pp. 103–109. Springer, Cham (2015). https://doi.org/10.1007/978-3-319-19581-0_8
9. Hasibi, F., Balog, K., Bratsberg, S.E.: Entity linking in queries: efficiency vs. effectiveness. In: Jose, J.M., et al. (eds.) ECIR 2017. LNCS, vol. 10193, pp. 40–53. Springer, Cham (2017). https://doi.org/10.1007/978-3-319-56608-5_4
10. Hoffart, J., et al.: Robust disambiguation of named entities in text. In: Proceedings of the Conference on Empirical Methods in Natural Language Processing, pp. 782–792. Association for Computational Linguistics (2011)
11. Höffner, K., Walter, S., Marx, E., Usbeck, R., Lehmann, J., Ngonga Ngomo, A.C.: Survey on challenges of question answering in the semantic web. Seman. Web **8**(6), 895–920 (2017)
12. Khouri, S., Bellatreche, L.: LOD for data warehouses: managing the ecosystem co-evolution. Information **9**(7), 17493 (2018)
13. Lehmann, J., et al.: Dbpedia-a large-scale, multilingual knowledge base extracted from wikipedia. Seman. Web **6**(2), 167–195 (2015)

14. Mendes, P.N., Jakob, M., García-Silva, A., Bizer, C.: DBpedia spotlight: shedding light on the web of documents. In: Proceedings of the 7th international conference on semantic systems, pp. 1–8. ACM (2011)
15. Miller, G.A.: Wordnet: a lexical database for english. Commun. ACM **38**(11), 39–41 (1995)
16. Moro, A., Raganato, A., Navigli, R.: Entity linking meets word sense disambiguation: a unified approach. Transact. Assoc. Comput. Linguist. **2**, 231–244 (2014)
17. Sakor, A., et al.: Old is gold: linguistic driven approach for entity and relation linking of short text. In: Proceedings of the NAACL HLT (2019)
18. Shen, W., Wang, J., Han, J.: Entity linking with a knowledge base: Issues, techniques, and solutions. IEEE Transact. Knowl. Data Eng. **27**(2), 443–460 (2015)
19. Sidorov, G., Gelbukh, A., Gómez-Adorno, H., Pinto, D.: Soft similarity and soft cosine measure: Similarity of features in vector space model. Computación y Sistemas **18**(3), 491–504 (2014)
20. Trivedi, P., Maheshwari, G., Dubey, M., Lehmann, J.: LC-QuAD: a corpus for complex question answering over knowledge graphs. In: d'Amato, C., et al. (eds.) ISWC 2017. LNCS, vol. 10588, pp. 210–218. Springer, Cham (2017). https://doi.org/10.1007/978-3-319-68204-4_22

Argumentation-Based Query Answering

A Heuristic Pruning Technique for Dialectical Trees on Argumentation-Based Query-Answering Systems

Andrea Cohen[✉], Sebastian Gottifredi, and Alejandro J. García

Institute for Computer Science and Engineering,
CONICET-UNS Department of Computer Science and Engineering,
Universidad Nacional del Sur, San Andrés 800,
Bahía Blanca, Buenos Aires, Argentina
{ac,sg,ajg}@cs.uns.edu.ar

Abstract. Arguments in argumentation-based query-answering systems can be associated with a set of evidence required for their construction. This evidence might have to be retrieved from external sources such as databases or the web, and each attempt of retrieving a piece of evidence comes with an associated cost. Moreover, a piece of evidence may be available at one moment but not at others, and this is not known beforehand. As a result, the set of active arguments (whose entire set of evidence is available) that can be used by the argumentation machinery of the system may vary from one scenario to another. In this work we propose a heuristic pruning technique for building dialectical trees in argumentation-based query-answering systems, with the aim of minimizing the cost of retrieving the pieces of evidence associated with the arguments that need to be accounted for in the reasoning process.

1 Introduction

Argumentation is a form of reasoning that has proved to be useful in different domains, such as logic-based environments [7,16], decision making and negotiation [8,15], AI & Law [2,21], and has led to the development of argumentation-based recommender and decision support systems [5,9,17]. Briefly, it is a form of reasoning where a piece of information (claim) is accepted or rejected after considering the reasons (arguments) for and against that acceptance, providing a reasoning mechanism able to handle contradictory, incomplete and/or uncertain information. There exists a variety of approaches to argumentation-based reasoning, among which we can distinguish abstract (with the work by Dung [14] being the most widely known) and structured ones (see [6] for an overview).

Given its query-answering nature, a structured argumentation system like DeLP [16] can be effectively used to implement decision-support or recommender

Funded by PGI-UNS (grants 24/N046 and 24/ZN32) and EU H2020 research and innovation programme (Marie Sklodowska-Curie grant agreement No. 69074: MIREL project).

© Springer Nature Switzerland AG 2019
A. Cuzzocrea et al. (Eds.): FQAS 2019, LNAI 11529, pp. 101–113, 2019.
https://doi.org/10.1007/978-3-030-27629-4_12

systems (*e.g.,* [9]). In such systems, the knowledge used for building arguments is encoded through rules of the form premises-conclusion. However, the rules used for building the arguments involved in the system's reasoning process may not be applicable at every moment. Rather, the system will only be able to use a rule when it is capable of retrieving every piece of information (from hereon referred to as *evidence*) corresponding to the rule's premises. Taking this into account, it could be the case that a piece of evidence required for building an argument is available from one source at a given time, but not from others, or not even from the same source at a different time. As a result, it could be the case that one argument can be built at one moment (because all its associated evidence is available, in which case we say it is *active*) but not at others; thus, there is an inherently dynamic component in the argumentative process.

Regarding the pieces of evidence associated to arguments, they could correspond to information mined from an external source such as a database [12] or, more generally, the web [20]. Then, the process of building an argument comes with an additional associated cost, which may be the financial cost of accessing a particular database, the time for resolving a query, etc. As a result, if we account for the cost of building an argument, as well as the dynamic nature mentioned above, a reasonable approach for determining the acceptance status of an argument $\mathcal{A}$ would try to minimize the associated cost, while accounting for the fact that arguments may not be active.

In this work we propose an approach for determining the acceptance status of arguments that have an associated set of evidence, based on the construction and pruning of dialectical trees [7,16]. We will work with a simplified version of the Dynamic Argumentation Framework (DAF) proposed in [22], where arguments have an associated set of evidence and might be active or inactive. Then, by accounting for the arguments in a DAF (regardless their activation status), we will consider the construction of potential dialectical trees. Based on those trees, we will propose a heuristic measure to guide the construction of the active dialectical trees, while trying to minimize the cost of retrieving the evidence associated with the arguments in those trees. Furthermore, this measure will be helpful for pruning branches of the active trees that do not affect the acceptance status of the argument in the tree's root.

The rest of this paper is organized as follows. Section 2 introduces the theoretical basis for our approach, including the formalization of a simple Dynamic Argumentation Framework and a characterization of dialectical trees. In Sect. 3 we propose a heuristic measure to be used for guiding the construction of dialectical trees in active scenarios. Section 4 describes the algorithm implementing the construction of pruned active dialectical trees, showing how the heuristic measure is effectively used for that purpose. Finally, in Sect. 5 we comment on related works, discuss initial findings from empirically testing our approach, and provide some concluding remarks.

2   Theoretical Basis

We begin by introducing a modified version of the *Dynamic Argumentation Framework* (DAF) presented in [22], which provides the basis for the development of our approach. This version of the DAF consists of a universal set of *potential arguments*, holding every conceivable argument, and the attack relation among them. Each potential argument will be associated with a set of *evidence*, which will have to be retrieved for the argument to be active at a given state of the world. In particular, different states of the world will be represented through *sessions*, and they will be identified with natural numbers ($\mathbb{N}$).

Active arguments are the only ones that can be used by the argumentation machinery to make inferences and compute the acceptance status of arguments at a given session. Notwithstanding this, active arguments in one session could become inactive in later sessions (*e.g.*, when some of their associated evidence becomes unavailable) and, analogously, inactive arguments may also become active later. For this purpose, we will augment the DAF with a function able to retrieve the pieces of evidence that are available in a given session (thus, allowing to determine the active arguments in that session). Moreover, since retrieving a piece of evidence comes with an associated cost, and this cost may vary from one piece to another, we will equip the DAF with a function to determine the evidence retrieval cost (expressed in natural numbers) in a given session.

Definition 1 (Dynamic Argumentation Framework). *A* Dynamic Argumentation Framework (DAF) *is a tuple* $\langle \mathbb{U}, \hookrightarrow, \mathbb{E}, \Theta, \Gamma, \mathfrak{ev} \rangle$, *where* $\mathbb{U}$ *is the universal set of arguments,* $\hookrightarrow \, \subseteq \mathbb{U} \times \mathbb{U}$ *is an attack relation,* $\mathbb{E}$ *is the universal set of evidence,* $\Theta : \mathbb{E} \times \mathbb{N} \mapsto \{\top, \bot\}$ *is the evidence retrieval function,* $\Gamma : \mathbb{E} \mapsto \mathbb{N}$ *is the evidence cost function, and* $\mathfrak{ev} : \mathbb{U} \mapsto 2^{\mathbb{E}}$ *is a function determining the evidence required by each argument.*

Definition 2 (Active Arguments). *Let* $\langle \mathbb{U}, \hookrightarrow, \mathbb{E}, \Theta, \Gamma, \mathfrak{ev} \rangle$ *be a DAF,* $\mathcal{A} \in \mathbb{U}$ *and* $\mathbf{s}$ *a session. We say that* $\mathcal{A}$ *is* active *in* $\mathbf{s}$ *iff* $\forall \epsilon \in \mathfrak{ev}(\mathcal{A}) : \Theta(\epsilon, \mathbf{s}) = \top$. *The set of active arguments in a session* $\mathbf{s}$ *is denoted* $\mathbb{A}_{\mathbf{s}} \subseteq \mathbb{U}$.

To determine whether an argument is active in a given session, we need to be able to retrieve all its evidence in that session. As discussed before, it may be the case that some piece of evidence ϵ is available in a session $\mathbf{s}$ but another piece ϵ' is not. Since every attempt of retrieving a piece of evidence through the Θ function comes with an associated cost (as determined by the Γ function), we want to minimize the use of Θ. Hence, to be able to keep track of the evidence that has been attempted to be retrieved so far in a session (both successfully and unsuccessfully), we define the notion of *session state* as follows.

Definition 3 (Session State). *Let* $\langle \mathbb{U}, \hookrightarrow, \mathbb{E}, \Theta, \Gamma, \mathfrak{ev} \rangle$ *be a DAF and* $\mathbf{s}$ *a session. A* session state *is a tuple* $\sigma = (\mathbf{s}, \mathsf{CE}, \mathsf{ME})$, *where* $\mathsf{CE}, \mathsf{ME} \subseteq \mathbb{E}$, $\forall \epsilon \in \mathsf{CE} : \Theta(\epsilon, \mathbf{s}) = \top$, *and* $\forall \epsilon' \in \mathsf{ME} : \Theta(\epsilon', \mathbf{s}) = \bot$.

A session state identifies the set of evidence that has already been collected in the session (current evidence), and the set of evidence that has been attempted to be retrieved and found missing in that session (missing evidence). Therefore, when using the Θ function to try to retrieve a piece of evidence ϵ in a session state $\sigma = (\mathsf{s}, \mathsf{CE}, \mathsf{ME})$, a new session state will be obtained depending on its outcome. That is, if $\Theta(\epsilon, \mathsf{s}) = \top$, then the new session state will be $\sigma' = (\mathsf{s}, \mathsf{CE} \cup \{\epsilon\}, \mathsf{ME})$; otherwise, the new session state will be $\sigma'' = (\mathsf{s}, \mathsf{CE}, \mathsf{ME} \cup \{\epsilon\})$.

The DAF yields a graph of arguments connected by the attack relation. Given a session, an *active subgraph* could be considered, containing only active arguments. In argumentation, the challenge consists in finding out which arguments prevail after all things considered (*i.e.,* those arguments that are accepted under some criterion). In this paper we will adopt an approach that consists on resolving queries about arguments by building tree structures for determining their acceptance status, considering only the arguments that may attack or defend them according to the attack relation [7,16].

We define a *potential dialectical tree* as a tree structure where every node is associated with an argument, and the children of each node correspond to attackers of the associated argument. Also, no argument can be considered more than once within the same branch, and each branch of the tree should be exhaustive in the consideration of attackers.

Definition 4 (Potential Dialectical Tree). *Let $\tau = \langle \mathbb{U}, \hookrightarrow, \mathbb{E}, \Theta, \Gamma, \mathfrak{ev} \rangle$ be a DAF and $\mathcal{A} \in \mathbb{U}$. The potential dialectical tree $TP(\mathcal{A})$ for $\mathcal{A}$ is a tree structure where:*

1. *The root of $TP(\mathcal{A})$ is labeled with argument $\mathcal{A}$.*
2. *Given a node N labeled with $\mathcal{B}$ in $TP(\mathcal{A})$, $\forall \mathcal{C} \in \mathbb{U}$ such that $(\mathcal{C}, \mathcal{B}) \in \hookrightarrow$, if there is no ancestor of N in $TP(\mathcal{A})$ labeled with $\mathcal{C}$, then there exists a node N' in $TP(\mathcal{A})$ such that N' is labeled with $\mathcal{C}$ and N' is a child of N.*

Note that there will be a single potential tree for each argument in $\mathbb{U}$. We refer to the tree as "potential" since it accounts for every argument in the universal set and thus, for every attack in the attack relation. However, since arguments (thus, the attacks involving them) may be active or not depending on the session, to determine the acceptance status of an argument $\mathcal{A}$ we just need to account for the active arguments in that session. The notion of *active dialectical tree* aims at capturing this intuition.

Definition 5 (Active Dialectical Tree). *Let $\tau = \langle \mathbb{U}, \hookrightarrow, \mathbb{E}, \Theta, \Gamma, \mathfrak{ev} \rangle$ be a DAF, s a session, $\mathbb{A}_\mathsf{s}$ the set of active arguments in s, and $\mathcal{A} \in \mathbb{A}_\mathsf{s}$. The active dialectical tree $T_\mathsf{s}(\mathcal{A})$ for $\mathcal{A}$ in s is a tree satisfying clauses 1 and 2 from Definition 4, where every node in $T_\mathsf{s}(\mathcal{A})$ is labeled with an active argument $\mathcal{A}' \in \mathbb{A}_\mathsf{s}$.*

To determine the acceptance status of an argument $\mathcal{A}$ in a session s, the following marking criterion is applied over $T_\mathsf{s}(\mathcal{A})$: leaves are marked **U** (undefeated); a non-leaf node is marked **D** (defeated) iff it has at least one child marked **U**, otherwise, it is marked **D**. Finally, a query for an argument $\mathcal{A}$ in a session s is resolved in terms of the marking of its active dialectical tree: if the root of $T_\mathsf{s}(\mathcal{A})$ is marked **U**, argument $\mathcal{A}$ is accepted in session s; otherwise, $\mathcal{A}$ is rejected in that session.

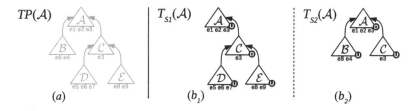

Fig. 1. (a) The potential dialectical tree $TP(\mathcal{A})$ for argument $\mathcal{A}$, and two active dialectical trees for $\mathcal{A}$: (b_1) $T_{S1}(\mathcal{A})$ in session S_1 and (b_2) $T_{S2}(\mathcal{A})$ in session S_2.

Definition 6 (Query and Answer). *Let $\tau = \langle \mathbb{U}, \hookrightarrow, \mathbb{E}, \Theta, \Gamma, \mathfrak{ev} \rangle$ be a DAF, s a session, $\mathbb{A}_s$ the set of active arguments in s, and $\mathcal{A} \in \mathbb{U}$. The answer for a query about argument $\mathcal{A}$ in session s is **accepted** iff the root of $T_s(\mathcal{A})$ is marked* **U**, *and **rejected** iff $\mathcal{A} \notin \mathbb{A}_s$ or the root of $T_s(\mathcal{A})$ is marked* **D**.

Example 1. Consider $TP(\mathcal{A})$, the potential dialectical tree for an argument $\mathcal{A}$, depicted in Fig. 1(a). Each node in the tree is depicted as a triangle; the argument labeling the node is inside the triangle, and the pieces of evidence associated with the argument are depicted below the triangle. Suppose that Θ is such that the every piece of evidence, except from e_4, can be retrieved in session S_1. Similarly, suppose that the only pieces of evidence that cannot be retrieved in session S_2 are e_6 and e_9. Then, Figs. 1(b_1) and (b_2), respectively illustrate the active dialectical tree for $\mathcal{A}$ in session S_1 and S_2. Given the difference in the set of active arguments in sessions S_1 and S_2, the answer for a query about $\mathcal{A}$ is: *accepted* in session S_1 (the root of $T_{S1}(\mathcal{A})$ is marked **U**) and *rejected* in session S_2 (the root of $T_{S2}(\mathcal{A})$ is marked **D**).

The marking criterion introduced above can be optimized, so that the children of a node N are considered only up to the point where we find a children N' marked as **U**. In order to capture this behavior, we introduce the notion of *pruned active dialectical tree*, following the *and-or* pruning technique of [11].

Definition 7 (Pruned Active Dialectical Tree). *Let $T_s(\mathcal{A})$ be the active dialectical tree for $\mathcal{A}$ in a session s, N the set of nodes in $T_s(\mathcal{A})$, and E the set of edges in $T_s(\mathcal{A})$. A pruned active dialectical tree $P_s(\mathcal{A})$ for $\mathcal{A}$ in session s is a tree rooted in $\mathcal{A}$ with a set of nodes $N_p \subseteq N$ and a set of edges $E_p \subseteq E$, such that $\forall N \in N_p$: if N has a child N' marked* **U** *in $T_s(\mathcal{A})$, then N has exactly one child marked* **U** *in $P_s(\mathcal{A})$.*

Given an active dialectical tree, different pruned versions of it can be obtained, depending on the order in which attackers are considered. To illustrate this, let us consider the following example.

Example 2. Consider the active dialectical trees $T_{S1}(\mathcal{A})$ and $T_{S2}(\mathcal{A})$ from Example 1. On the one hand, $P_{S1}(\mathcal{A})_1$, depicted in Fig. 2(a), is the pruned version of $T_{S1}(\mathcal{A})$ obtained by considering the child $\mathcal{D}$ of $\mathcal{C}$ before $\mathcal{E}$. Alternatively, if $\mathcal{E}$ is chosen before $\mathcal{D}$, we obtain the pruned active dialectical tree $P_{S1}(\mathcal{A})_2$

shown in Fig. 2(b). On the other hand, for $T_{S2}(\mathcal{A})$, if the child $\mathcal{C}$ of $\mathcal{A}$ is chosen before $\mathcal{B}$, we obtain $P_{S2}(\mathcal{A})_1$ as depicted in Fig. 2(c). In contrast, by choosing $\mathcal{B}$ before $\mathcal{C}$, we obtain the tree $P_{S2}(\mathcal{A})_2$ illustrated in Fig. 2(d).

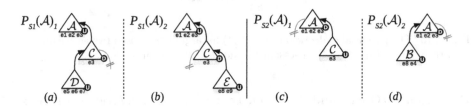

(a)   (b)   (c)   (d)

Fig. 2. Two pruned active dialectical trees for $T_{S1}(\mathcal{A})$ and $T_{S2}(\mathcal{A})$ from Example 1.

As mentioned in the introduction, in this work we will propose a technique for building dialectical trees for determining the acceptance status of arguments to resolve queries, while trying to minimize the evidence retrieval costs for obtaining them. Driven by this goal, in the next section we propose a heuristic measure that can be used for guiding the construction of pruned active dialectical trees.

3   Related Evidence and Heuristic Measure

Here, we will propose a heuristic measure for guiding the construction of active dialectical trees in order to prune those subtrees with the highest evidence retrieval cost. For that purpose, given a node N labeled with an argument $\mathcal{A}$ in a potential dialectical tree, we will first determine the set of evidence related to that argument, which includes every piece of evidence required to build the potential subtree rooted in it. Then, the cost associated with the related evidence set will account for the costs of attempting to retrieve each piece of evidence in the set, as specified by the Γ function.

Note that, given the possibility of pruning active dialectical trees, an argument located in a deep level of a potential tree is less likely to be constructed in an active scenario than another argument located in a higher level of the tree. In general, the probability of trying to retrieve a piece of evidence in an active scenario decreases as the depth of the argument requiring that piece of evidence increases. Hence, when determining the related evidence of an argument in a potential tree, we estimate its cost accounting for these issues.

Definition 8 (Related Evidence and Cost). *Let N be a node labeled with argument $\mathcal{A}$ in a potential dialectical tree TP and $\mathsf{CIF} \in (0, 1]$ a constant representing the cost impact factor of a piece of evidence. We define the set of related evidence of N in TP and its cost as:*

$$RelEv(N, TP) = \{(\epsilon, \Gamma(\epsilon) * \mathsf{CIF}^L) \mid \epsilon \in \mathit{ev}(Arg), Arg \in (\{\mathcal{A}\} \cup \mathsf{desc}(N, TP))\}$$

where $L = \mathsf{minLevel}(\epsilon, \mathsf{subTree}(TP, N))$ is the lowest level of a node in the subtree of TP rooted in $\mathcal{A}$ that is labeled with an argument requiring the piece of evidence ϵ^1; and $\mathsf{desc}(N, TP)$ returns the set of arguments that label the descendants of N in the potential tree TP.

The related evidence cost given in Definition 8 provides an estimation of the actual cost of building an active dialectical tree. In particular, the reduction by CIF aims at adjusting the impact the cost of a piece of evidence has in the final cost, depending on its location on the tree. Finally, the reason why we consider the lowest level, is that it corresponds to the level of the argument requiring that piece of evidence that is more likely to be constructed.

Example 3. Consider the potential dialectical tree $TP(\mathcal{A})$ from Example 1. Let us assume that $\mathsf{CIF} = 0.5$, and $\Gamma(e_1) = 8$, $\Gamma(e_2) = 7$, $\Gamma(e_3) = 2$, $\Gamma(e_4) = 20$, $\Gamma(e_5) = 9$, $\Gamma(e_6) = 3$, $\Gamma(e_7) = 1$, $\Gamma(e_8) = 6$, $\Gamma(e_9) = 4$. The related evidence and cost for the different argument nodes in $TP(\mathcal{A})$ is:

$$RelEv(\mathcal{A}, TP(\mathcal{A})) = \{(e_1, 8 * 0.5^0), (e_2, 7 * 0.5^0), (e_3, 2 * 0.5^0), (e_8, 6 * 0.5^1),$$
$$(e_4, 10 * 0.5^1), (e_5, 9 * 0.5^2), (e_6, 3 * 0.5^2), (e_7, 1 * 0.5^2),$$
$$(e_9, 4 * 0.5^2)\} = \{(e_1, 8), (e_2, 7), (e_3, 2), (e_8, 3), (e_4, 5),$$
$$(e_5, 2.25), (e_6, 0.75), (e_7, 0.25), (e_9, 1)\}$$

$$RelEv(\mathcal{B}, TP(\mathcal{A})) = \{(e_8, 6 * 0.5^0), (e_4, 10 * 0.5^0)\} = \{(e_8, 6), (e_4, 10)\}$$

$$RelEv(\mathcal{C}, TP(\mathcal{A})) = \{(e_3, 2 * 0.5^0), (e_5, 9 * 0.5^1), (e_6, 3 * 0.5^1), (e_7, 1 * 0.5^1),$$
$$(e_8, 6 * 0.5^1), (e_9, 4 * 0.5^1)\} = \{(e_3, 2), (e_5, 4.5), (e_6, 1.5),$$
$$(e_7, 0.5), (e_8, 3), (e_9, 2)\}$$

$$RelEv(\mathcal{D}, TP(\mathcal{A})) = \{(e_5, 9 * 0.5^0), (e_6, 3 * 0.5^0), (e_7, 1 * 0.5^0)\} = \{(e_5, 9), (e_6, 3),$$
$$(e_7, 1)\}$$

$$RelEv(\mathcal{E}, TP(\mathcal{A})) = \{(e_8, 6 * 0.5^0), (e_9, 4 * 0.5^0)\} = \{(e_8, 6), (e_9, 4)\}$$

Note that the calculus of the related evidence and cost only uses information from potential dialectical trees; specifically, it accounts for the pieces of evidence required by the arguments labeling the nodes and the level of such nodes. As a result, for every node in every potential tree, it is possible to determine its related evidence and cost during precompilation, avoiding any runtime cost during the system's query-answering process in an active scenario.

Next, using the information about the related evidence and cost for a given argument node in a potential dialectical tree we define the *heuristic evidence cost* for that node. This measure will be used for guiding the construction of the active dialectical tree in a particular session, with the aim of minimizing the evidence retrieval cost for building it.

Definition 9 (Heuristic Evidence Cost). *Let N be a node in a potential dialectical tree TP and $\sigma = (\mathsf{s}, \mathsf{CE}, \mathsf{ME})$ a session state. The heuristic evidence cost of N in σ is:*

---

[1] We consider that the root of a tree is in level 0, its children are in level 1, and so on.

$$HeurEvCost(N, TP, \sigma) = \sum c$$
$$(\epsilon, c) \in RelEv(N, TP) \land \epsilon \notin \mathsf{CE}$$

Example 4. Continuing with our example, let $\sigma = (S_1, \{e_1, e_2, e_3\}, \emptyset)$ be the session state after building argument node $\mathcal{A}$ in session S_1. Then, we have $HeurEvCost(\mathcal{B}, TP(\mathcal{A}), \sigma) = 16$; $HeurEvCost(\mathcal{C}, TP(\mathcal{A}), \sigma) = 11.5$ (note that e_3 is in the current evidence set, so its associated cost is disregarded); $HeurEvCost(\mathcal{D}, TP(\mathcal{A}), \sigma) = 13$; and $HeurEvCost(\mathcal{E}, TP(\mathcal{A}), \sigma) = 10$.

Differently from the calculus of the related evidence and cost, the heuristic evidence cost requires the consideration of information from the session state and thus, cannot be obtained during precompilation time. However, since the biggest part of the calculus involves determining the related evidence and its cost, the computation during execution time simply reduces to sum up the cost of the pieces of related evidence (determined during precompilation) that are not in the set of current evidence from the given session state.

4   Building Pruned Active Dialectical Trees Through the Consideration of Heuristic Evidence Cost

In this section we propose an approach for using the heuristic measure introduced in Sect. 3 to guide the construction of dialectical trees in an active scenario. This measure will help to decide which branch of a tree should be explored at each time (thus which arguments are to be built next). Also, the tree building process will exploit the possibility of pruning branches that can be dismissed in order to determine the acceptance status of the root argument.

The process for building active dialectical trees is shown in Algorithm 1. Since the construction of an active tree involves the construction of its subtrees (following a Depth-First Search strategy), the algorithm is designed for building the subtree rooted in an argument, given its ancestors. In particular, given an argument $\mathcal{A}$, if $\mathcal{A}$ is established as the root and we consider an empty set of ancestors, the algorithm will in turn build the active dialectical tree rooted in $\mathcal{A}$. The structure of a node in Algorithm 1 contains an argument, its marking and a set of child nodes, therefore, a tree is represented directly by the node corresponding to its root argument.

It should be noted that the active tree returned by Algorithm 1 is a pruned tree. That is, once an argument node has been marked as **U** in the active tree, its unexplored siblings from the corresponding potential tree are dismissed. As a result, by guiding the selection of argument nodes through their heuristic evidential cost, the final cost of building the active pruned trees is reduced. Also, even though Algorithm 1 does not make explicit reference to a session, information from the session state is used by the canBeBuilt and the heuristicSort functions (which are in turn used by Algorithm 1 and are discussed below).

The construction of a single argument in a session state is handled by the function canBeBuilt. Given the abstract nature of arguments in our approach,

---

Algorithm 1. Builds the pruned active subtree of a given argument

---

Function: prunedActiveSubTree($\mathcal{A}$, *Root*, *Ancestors*)

Input: an argument $\mathcal{A}$, the root argument *Root* of an active dialectical tree, and a set of arguments *Ancestors* representing the ancestors of argument node $\mathcal{A}$ in the active tree rooted in *Root*

Global : A DAF $\langle \mathbb{U}, \hookrightarrow, \mathbb{E}, \Theta, \Gamma, \mathfrak{ev} \rangle$

Result: A Pruned (sub)Tree

1   $NodeA \leftarrow$ createNode($\mathcal{A}$, **U**);
2   $Attackers \leftarrow \{\mathcal{B} \mid (\mathcal{B}, \mathcal{A}) \in \hookrightarrow\}$;
3   $OrderedAttackers \leftarrow$ heuristicSort($Attackers$, $Root$);
4   **while** $OrderedAttackers \neq \emptyset$ **do**
5      $\mathcal{B} \leftarrow$ getFirst($OrderedAttackers$);
6   **if** $\mathcal{B} \notin Ancestors$ **then**
7   **if** canBeBuilt($\mathcal{B}$) **then**
8            $NodeB \leftarrow$ prunedActiveSubTree($\mathcal{B}$, $Root$, $Ancestors \cup \{\mathcal{A}\}$);
9            $NodeA \leftarrow$ addChild($NodeA$, $NodeB$);
10   **if** mark($NodeB$) = **U then**
11              $NodeA \leftarrow$ setMark($NodeA$, **D**);
12   **return** $NodeA$;
13     $OrderedAttackers \leftarrow$ remove($\mathcal{B}$, $OrderedAttackers$);
14     $OrderedAttackers \leftarrow$ heuristicSort($OrderedAttackers$);
15 $NodeA \leftarrow$ setMark($NodeA$, **U**);
16 **return** $NodeA$;

---

this task reduces to determining whether the argument is active or not. In other words, we simply have to find out whether we can successfully gather all its evidence in the given session. Furthermore, since attempting to retrieve a piece of evidence through the use of the Θ function comes with an associated cost (as specified by the Γ function), to determine whether an argument can be built we will try to use the Θ function as little as possible. Therefore, our strategy will reutilize every piece of evidence that was already fetched during the session, avoiding to pay the retrieval cost more than once. On the other hand, when attempting to build an argument that has a piece of evidence already found to be missing in the session, such argument will be immediately discarded. Finally, every time the Θ function is used to attempt to retrieve a piece of evidence (paying the corresponding cost), the sets of current and missing evidence are updated, leading to a new session state.

Once an argument node N is built (initially, the root argument), we need to account for the children of N in the potential tree and then decide which subtree we will attempt to build next. For this purpose, the function heuristicSort is used for sorting a set of attackers from lowest to highest value using our proposed heuristic measure. In particular, as mentioned in Sect. 3, to calculate an argument's heuristic evidence cost, the function makes use of the current session state, more specifically, of the set of current evidence.

Example 5. Let us consider the resolution of a query about argument $\mathcal{A}$ through the construction of its pruned active dialectical tree in session S_1. After building the argument node $\mathcal{A}$ we obtain the session state $\sigma = (S_1, \{e_1, e_2, e_3\}, \emptyset\})$ and we have the empty set of ancestors. We establish $\{\mathcal{B}, \mathcal{C}\}$ as the set of attackers of $\mathcal{A}$ and obtain a list sorted by their heuristic evidence cost (lines 2 and 3 in Algorithm 1). As shown in Example 4, $HeurEvCost(\mathcal{B}, TP(\mathcal{A}), \sigma) = 16$ and $HeurEvCost(\mathcal{C}, TP(\mathcal{A}), \sigma) = 11.5$. As a result, the sorted list returned by heuristicSort is $[\mathcal{C}, \mathcal{B}]$ and $\mathcal{C}$ is chosen next (Algorithm 1, line 5). Then, since argument $\mathcal{C}$ is not in the set of ancestors and is buildable in σ (because e_3, the only piece of evidence it requires, is in the current evidence set), we proceed to build the pruned dialectical subtree rooted in $\mathcal{C}$ (Algorithm 1, line 8). The process of building the subtree for $\mathcal{C}$ is then analogous, by considering the set of ancestors $\{\mathcal{A}\}$ and the new session state; however, since the only piece of evidence required by $\mathcal{C}$ was already in the current evidence set, the session state obtained after building $\mathcal{C}$ continues to be σ. The set of attackers of $\mathcal{C}$ is $\{\mathcal{D}, \mathcal{E}\}$ and, by Example 4, we have $HeurEvCost(\mathcal{D}, TP(\mathcal{A}), \sigma) = 13$ and $HeurEvCost(\mathcal{E}, TP(\mathcal{A}), \sigma) = 10$. So, the ordered list of attackers is $[\mathcal{E}, \mathcal{D}]$ and argument $\mathcal{E}$ is chosen next. We are then able to build argument $\mathcal{E}$ (because its pieces of evidence e_8 and e_9 are available in session S_1) and, since it has no attackers to be considered, it is marked as **U**. Consequently, $\mathcal{C}$ can be marked as **D**, pruning the branch corresponding to the argument node $\mathcal{D}$. As a result, we go back to the construction of the tree rooted in $\mathcal{A}$ and consider the remaining attacker $\mathcal{B}$. Then, since the piece of evidence e_4 cannot be retrieved in session S_1, argument $\mathcal{B}$ is not buildable. Finally, since $\mathcal{A}$ has no other attackers, we come up with the pruned dialectical active tree $P_{S1}(\mathcal{A})_2$, depicted in Fig. 2(b), whose root is marked **U** meaning that argument $\mathcal{A}$ is *accepted* in session S_1.

5   Related Work and Conclusions

In this paper we proposed a heuristic measure used for building pruned dialectical trees in argumentation-based query-answering systems, with the aim of minimizing the cost of retrieving the evidence associated with arguments in a given active scenario. Since the same piece of evidence may be available or unavailable in different scenarios (thus, leading to different sets of active arguments in each case), our approach inherently deals with a dynamic component.

Recently, there has been an increasing interesting in studying the dynamic nature of argumentation [13], and this has also become evident with the inclusion of a dedicated track in the latest edition of the *International Competition of Computational Models of Argumentation (ICCMA)* [1]. In particular, approaches like [3,4,19] address the incremental recomputation of extensions of a Dung's abstract argumentation framework after some updates have been performed. Our approach aligns with these works in the sense that, in order to determine the acceptance status of a given argument, we only seek to account for those arguments (also, the interactions) that affect it. However, since those works are aimed at identifying sets of extensions of a given framework (hence, the acceptance status of *every* argument), to determine the acceptance status of an argument $\mathcal{A}$ they may also require to consider (thus, attempt to build) arguments whose acceptance status is affected by $\mathcal{A}$, but which do not affect the acceptance status of $\mathcal{A}$; consequently, they may incur in unnecessary costs.

Another difference between our proposal and the above mentioned works is that, in their approaches, after the updates have been performed the entire set of arguments of the framework is known to be active. In contrast, in our approach, the dynamic component is the available evidence. Then, since the changes on the set of evidence are not known beforehand, we still have to attempt to retrieve the evidence associated to the arguments, not knowing whether they will be active or not. As a result, our proposal relates to works like [10] and [22] that put more focus on the way in which the set of active arguments changes. In particular, our work is most closely related to [22], since we considered the variation of available evidence, determining the active arguments at each time.

A preliminary empirical testing of our approach, the heuristic evidence cost-guided pruned active tree building process (**CGPT**), showed promising results. We tested it against a non-guided process for building pruned active dialectical trees (**NGPT**), which does not sort the set of attackers of a node but randomly selects one attacker from the set as the next node to be considered.

We ran a simulation involving the generation of DAFs and potential dialectical trees, with two parameters: `TreeNodeCount` (amount of nodes in the potential dialectical tree, with values ranging between 100 and 900) and `DeactCuota` (% of missing/deactivated evidence in a given session, with values ranging between 1 and 30). For each combination of values we built 500 DAFs and performed 100 evidence deactivations (with the corresponding % of `DeactCuota`) per DAF, each of which was considered for building a potential dialectical tree (*i.e.*, 500 potential trees were built, each of which was considered under 100 scenarios with different sets of available evidence). Then, for each of these potential trees and scenarios, we built the pruned active dialectical trees following the **CGPT** and **NGPT** approaches. Finally, for each combination of parameters, we obtained the average cost of building an active tree under each approach (referred to as `TreeEvidCost`), where the cost associated with the construction of an active tree is determined by adding up the cost of the retrieved pieces of evidence and the cost the pieces of evidence found missing.

The results showed that **CGPT** significantly reduces the `TreeEvidCost` in all cases. In general, the cost reduction obtained with **CGPT** over **NGPT** increases with the tree size, going from 30% to 70%. Furthermore, the deactivation cuota also affected the results, with smaller percentages of missing evidence leading to obtaining greater cost reductions; specifically, the cost reduction goes from 20% to 50% as the amount of available evidence increases. Finally, as part of future work, we plan to test our method against other approaches like [18], which defines a heuristic measure for building pruned active dialectical trees based on the notion of argument strength.

References

1. International Competition on Computational Models of Argumentation. http://argumentationcompetition.org
2. Al-Abdulkarim, L., Atkinson, K., Bench-Capon, T.J.M.: Abstract dialectical frameworks for legal reasoning. In: Proceedings of JURIX, pp. 61–70 (2014)
3. Alfano, G., Greco, S., Parisi, F.: Efficient computation of extensions for dynamic abstract argumentation frameworks: an incremental approach. In: Proceedings of IJCAI, pp. 49–55 (2017)
4. Baroni, P., Giacomin, M., Liao, B.: On topology-related properties of abstract argumentation semantics. A correction and extension to dynamics of argumentation systems: a division-based method. Artif. Intell. **212**, 104–115 (2014)
5. Bedi, P., Vashisth, P.B.: Empowering recommender systems using trust and argumentation. Inf. Sci. **279**, 569–586 (2014)
6. Besnard, P., García, A.J., Hunter, A., Modgil, S., Prakken, H., Simari, G.R., Toni, F.: Introduction to structured argumentation. Argum. Comput. **5**(1), 1–4 (2014)
7. Besnard, P., Hunter, A.: A logic-based theory of deductive arguments. Artif. Intell. **128**(1–2), 203–235 (2001)
8. Black, E., Hunter, A.: An inquiry dialogue system. Auton. Agent. Multi-Agent Syst. **19**(2), 173–209 (2009)
9. Briguez, C.E., Budán, M.C.D., Deagustini, C.A.D., Maguitman, A.G., Capobianco, M., Simari, G.R.: Argument-based mixed recommenders and their application to movie suggestion. Expert Syst. Appl. **41**(14), 6467–6482 (2014)
10. Capobianco, M., Chesñevar, C.I., Simari, G.R.: Argumentation and the dynamics of warranted beliefs in changing environments. Auton. Agent. Multi-Agent Syst. **11**(2), 127–151 (2005)
11. Chesñevar, C.I., Simari, G.R., García, A.J.: Pruning search space in defeasible argumentation. In: Proceedings of ATAI, pp. 46–55 (2000)
12. Deagustini, C.A.D., Dalibón, S.E.F., Gottifredi, S., Falappa, M.A., Chesñevar, C.I., Simari, G.R.: Defeasible argumentation over relational databases. Argum. Comput. **8**(1), 35–59 (2017)
13. Doutre, S., Mailly, J.: Constraints and changes: a survey of abstract argumentation dynamics. Argum. Comput. **9**(3), 223–248 (2018). https://doi.org/10.3233/AAC-180425
14. Dung, P.M.: On the acceptability of arguments and its fundamental role in non-monotonic reasoning, logic programming and n-person games. Artif. Intell. **77**(2), 321–358 (1995)
15. Ferretti, E., Tamargo, L.H., García, A.J., Errecalde, M.L., Simari, G.R.: An approach to decision making based on dynamic argumentation systems. Artif. Intell. **242**, 107–131 (2017)
16. García, A.J., Simari, G.R.: Defeasible logic programming: an argumentative approach. TPLP **4**(1–2), 95–138 (2004)
17. Gómez, S.A., Goron, A., Groza, A., Letia, I.A.: Assuring safety in air traffic control systems with argumentation and model checking. Expert Syst. Appl. **44**, 367–385 (2016)
18. Gottifredi, S., Rotstein, N.D., García, A.J., Simari, G.R.: Using argument strength for building dialectical bonsai. Ann. Math. Artif. Intell. **69**(1), 103–129 (2013). https://doi.org/10.1007/s10472-013-9338-x
19. Liao, B., Jin, L., Koons, R.C.: Dynamics of argumentation systems: a division-based method. Artif. Intell. **175**(11), 1790–1814 (2011)

20. Lippi, M., Torroni, P.: Argumentation mining: state of the art and emerging trends. ACM Trans. Internet Technol. **16**(2), 10:1–10:25 (2016). https://doi.org/10.1145/2850417
21. Prakken, H., Sartor, G.: Law and logic: a review from an argumentation perspective. Artif. Intell. **227**, 214–245 (2015)
22. Rotstein, N.D., Moguillansky, M.O., García, A.J., Simari, G.R.: A dynamic argumentation framework. In: Proceedings of COMMA, pp. 427–438 (2010)

A Method for Efficient Argument-Based Inquiry

Bas Testerink[1(✉)], Daphne Odekerken[1,2], and Floris Bex[2]

[1] Police Lab AI, Netherlands National Police, Driebergen, The Netherlands
{bas.testerink,daphne.odekerken}@politie.nl
[2] Police Lab AI, Utrecht University, Utrecht, The Netherlands
f.j.bex@uu.nl

Abstract. In this paper we describe a method for efficient argument-based inquiry. In this method, an agent creates arguments for and against a particular topic by matching argumentation rules with observations gathered by querying the environment. To avoid making superfluous queries, the agent needs to determine if the acceptability status of the topic can change given more information. We define a notion of stability, where a structured argumentation setup is *stable* if no new arguments can be added, or if adding new arguments will not change the status of the topic. Because determining stability requires hypothesizing over all future argumentation setups, which is computationally very expensive, we define a less complex approximation algorithm and show that this is a sound approximation of stability. Finally, we show how stability (or our approximation of it) can be used in determining an optimal inquiry policy, and discuss how this policy can be used to, for example, determine a strategy in an argument-based inquiry dialogue.

Keywords: Computational argumentation · Inquiry

1 Introduction

When performing inquiry or information seeking, an agent gathers information from the environment such that it can form an opinion on a particular topic. There are different strategies that one can consider for an agent [3,7,11]. We propose a method for capturing agent inquiry policies in a way that is efficient – both computationally and in terms of the length of the inquiry process. The knowledge of the agent is modelled as a structured argumentation setup similar to ASPIC$^+$ [8]. A set of possible queryable literals (observations which can be made in the future) is also defined as part of the argumentation setup. Given these queryable literals and the arguments that follow from the current observations, it can then be determined whether the topic is an acceptable conclusion [4], and which future observations (i.e. answers to queries) could conceivably change the acceptability of this conclusion.

© Springer Nature Switzerland AG 2019
A. Cuzzocrea et al. (Eds.): FQAS 2019, LNAI 11529, pp. 114–125, 2019.
https://doi.org/10.1007/978-3-030-27629-4_13

In order to avoid making superfluous queries we define a notion of *stability*: an argumentation setup is stable if given the possible queries no new arguments can be added or adding new arguments will not change the acceptability of the topic. Concretely: does an argument for the topic exist, is this argument in the grounded extension [4], and can future answers to available queries change these facts? It is computationally complex to generate all arguments given the current observations and then calculate the grounded extension. Extra complexity is added for inquiry because one has to hypothesize on the possible results of future queries. We therefore we propose a considerably less complex *approximation algorithm* for determining stability. We also show that this algorithm provides a sound approximation of stability: if the approximation algorithm, for example, determines that the topic is acceptable, it is guaranteed that the topic is in the grounded extension and further observations cannot change this.

The proposed inquiry method is currently applied in practice for crime investigation. As an example throughout the paper, we use a simplified version of the domain of internet trade fraud (e.g. scammers on eBay or fake online stores), and specifically the situation where a complainant files an official complaint with the police. Structured argumentation is an obvious way to model the practical and legal rules concerning a crime [10]. Crime investigation should also be performed efficiently, as investigative actions (questioning the complainant, requesting the counterparty's bank details) inevitably come with a cost. Furthermore, investigation is a stochastic process, as investigative actions are not guaranteed to yield new information – the complainant might, for instance, not know the requested information. Our method takes these aspects into account. The method shows how the argumentation setup can be used to construct a Markov-decision process that represents the inquiry task. Any suitable technique can be used to approximate the optimal policy given the MDP (e.g. dynamic programming or reinforcement learning). Roughly speaking, the argumentation aspect of the method determines what kind of information is still relevant, and the policy learning aspect determines which relevant information to inquire about next.

Due to limited space we had to abbreviate examples and proofs. For the interested reader we provide extended examples and full proofs[1]. The rest of this paper is structured as follows. In Sect. 2 we discuss our base argumentation formalism. In Sect. 3 we then describe stability, that is, how to hypothesize over possible future observations, and an algorithm that approximates stability, and give soundness and complexity results for the approximation algorithm. Section 4 discusses our inquiry policy. Section 5 discusses related work and Sect. 6 concludes the paper.

2   Base Formalism

The base formalism for argumentation draws upon ASPIC$^+$ [8] for structured argumentation and Dung's grounded semantics [4] for abstract argumentation.

---

[1] Extended examples and proofs: https://preview.tinyurl.com/y656r3ek.

From ASPIC$^+$ the concepts of a topic language, knowledge base and defeasible rules are used. The concepts of queryable literals and a topic are added to these. The queryable literals are those literals in the topic language of which an observation might be made. The topic is a special literal of interest for which the agent aims to get a stable opinion. Together, these components are referred to as an argumentation setup as defined below. For notation convenience we use $-l$ to negate a literal l, i.e.: $-l = p$ if $l = \neg p$ and $-l = \neg p$ if $l = p$, for some propositional atom p.

Definition 1 (Argumentation Setup, AS). *An argumentation setup AS is a tuple $AS = (\mathcal{L}, \mathcal{R}, \mathcal{Q}, \mathcal{K}, \tau)$ where:*

- *$\mathcal{L}$ is a logical language consisting of propositional literals, such that if $l \in \mathcal{L}$ then also $-l \in \mathcal{L}$.*
- *$\mathcal{R}$ is a set of defeasible rules $p_1...p_m \Rightarrow q$ s.t. $p_1, ..., p_m, q \in \mathcal{L}$. $p_1...p_m$ are called the antecedents of a rule and q the consequent. The antecedents of a rule are unordered. We refer to a rule $p_1...p_m \Rightarrow q$ as 'a rule for q'.*
- *$\mathcal{Q} \subseteq \{l \in \mathcal{L} | l \neq \neg p\}$ is a set of non-negated queryable literals.*
- *$\mathcal{K} \subseteq \mathcal{L}$, such that $\forall l \in \mathcal{K} : (-)l \in \mathcal{Q} \wedge -l \notin \mathcal{K}$, is a knowledge base of observations which is a consistent set of literals.*
- *$\tau \in \mathcal{L}$ is a topic.*

Example 1. As an example, let $AS = (\mathcal{L}, \mathcal{R}, \mathcal{Q}, \mathcal{K}, \tau)$ be an argumentation setup for a simplified fraud scenario. Figure 1 depicts the topic language and rules. We abbreviate in formal examples the literals in the graph to the parenthesized literals. In this example $\mathcal{L}$ consists of literals made of the atoms f, cp, c, p, s and w, where 'f' stands for 'this is a case of fraud', 'c' for 'the complainant delivered', 'cp' for 'the counterparty delivered', 'p' for 'the complainant paid', 's' for 'the complainant sent a product' and 'w' for 'the wrong product was delivered'. The rules are given by $\mathcal{R} = \{p \Rightarrow c, s \Rightarrow c, (\neg cp, c) \Rightarrow f, w \Rightarrow cp, w \Rightarrow \neg f\}$. In the graph we represent a rule with an '&' that points to its consequent and is undirectionally connected to its antecedents. The idea behind the rules is that if the complainant delivered in the trade but the counterparty did not, then defeasibly the setup is a case of fraud. If a wrong product was delivered, then it is defeasibly not a case of fraud. Finally, if a wrong product was delivered then arguably the counterparty delivered in the trade, but this could be overruled by the fact that the complainant considers the ordered product to not have been delivered. The queryable literals are given by $\mathcal{Q} = \{p, s, w, cp\}$. This means that for instance the complainant can be queried for whether he/she paid. As the topic we take $\tau = f$. We will consider different knowledge bases throughout the examples.

As per ASPIC$^+$'s formalism, an argument is an inference tree that is constructed through the application of rules. The starting points for constructing an argument are the observations in the knowledge base. They are arguments themselves and on top of them new arguments can be made. Cyclic arguments are forbidden to avoid an infinite number of arguments. This is enforced by requiring that the conclusion of an argument cannot occur in any of its subarguments. The inference function that gives the arguments for a given argumentation setup is defined next.

Definition 2 (Inference, I). *Let $AS = (\mathcal{L}, \mathcal{R}, \mathcal{Q}, \mathcal{K}, \tau)$ be an argumentation setup. An argument is an inference $A_1...A_m \mapsto c$ such that $A_1...A_m$ is an unordered set of arguments called its premises and $c \in \mathcal{L}$ is its conclusion. We refer to $A_1...A_m \mapsto c$ as 'an argument for c'. The arguments of AS are given by $I(AS)$:*

- *$\emptyset \mapsto c \in I(AS)$ iff $c \in \mathcal{K}$.*
- *$A_1...A_m \mapsto c \in I(AS)$ iff $A_1...A_m$ are in $I(AS)$ and their conclusions are $c_1...c_m$, and there is a rule $c_1...c_m \Rightarrow c \in \mathcal{R}$, and c does not occur in any of the arguments $A_1...A_m$.*

Example 2. Consider the previously defined argumentation setup and let the knowledge base be $\mathcal{K} = \{p, \neg cp\}$ (the complainant paid but the counterparty did not deliver). For this example $I(AS) = \{A_1 = (\emptyset \mapsto p), A_2 = (\emptyset \mapsto \neg cp), A_3 = (A_1 \mapsto c), A_4 = (A_2, A_3 \mapsto f)\}$. Hence, given this knowledge there is an argument for fraud.

Arguments may attack and/or defend each other. An argument A attacks an another argument B if A's conclusion negates some conclusion of a subargument of B (a premise attack) or B's own conclusion (a rebut). In the first case, the attack is one-sided (from A to B), in the other case it is two-sided. There is one exception; an argument cannot be attacked on a premise or its conclusion if that premise/conclusion is an observation. The reasoning behind this is that an observation is a low-level directly observed piece of evidence and not defeasibly inferred. An argument A can defend another argument B if A attacks attackers for B. The notion of attack and defense are defined next.

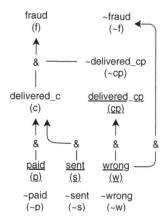

Fig. 1. A graphical representation of the example topic language and rules. Queryable literals are underlined.

Definition 3 (Attack, Defense). *Let $AS = (\mathcal{L}, \mathcal{R}, \mathcal{Q}, \mathcal{K}, \tau)$ be an argumentation setup. For two arguments $A, B \in I(AS)$ we say that A attacks B iff A's conclusion is c and $-c$ occurs in B and $-c \notin \mathcal{K}$. A set of arguments $X \subseteq I(AS)$ defends an argument $A \in I(AS)$ iff for each $B \in I(AS)$ that attacks A there is a $C \in X$ that attacks B.*

The acceptability of arguments is determined by Dung's grounded semantics for abstract argumentation [4].

Definition 4 (Grounded Extension, G). *Let $AS = (\mathcal{L}, \mathcal{R}, \mathcal{Q}, \mathcal{K}, \tau)$ be an argumentation setup. The grounded extension $G \subseteq I(AS)$ of AS is the smallest set of arguments (w.r.t. set inclusion) such that:*

- *There is no pair $A, B \in G$ such that A attacks B (conflict-free), and*
- *$G = \{A \in I(AS) | G$ defends $A\}$ (complete)*

Example 3. Consider the previously defined argumentation setup and let the knowledge base be $\mathcal{K} = \{p, \neg cp, w\}$ (the complainant paid and the counterparty delivered the wrong product). For this example $I(AS)$ are the arguments in Fig. 2. The attack relation is also shown in Fig. 2. The grounded extension for this example is $\{A_1, A_2, A_3, A_5\}$. Note that without the observation w, as in the previous example, the argument A_4 for fraud would be in the grounded extension. Hence, extra observations may change whether or not an argument is in the grounded extension.

3   Hypothesizing over Future Observations

An inquiry agent tries to form a stable opinion on its topic literal. An argument for a literal can be non-existent, in the grounded extension, or outside the grounded extension. In the latter case, the argument might be attacked from within the grounded extension or otherwise from outside the grounded extension. These four cases indicate different belief-statuses. If the status of the topic cannot change by executing more queries, then the argumentation setup is called stable. The possible future argumentation setups are all those setups where the queryable literals are put in a current knowledge base as either positive or negative. Stability of an argumentation setup is defined below.

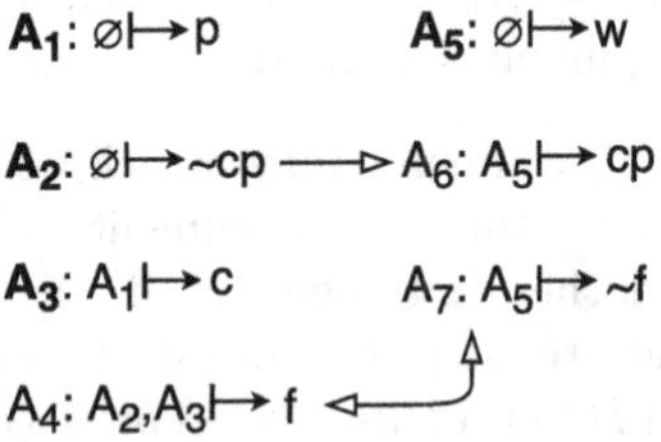

A_1: $\varnothing \mapsto p$ A_5: $\varnothing \mapsto w$

A_2: $\varnothing \mapsto \sim cp \longrightarrow A_6$: $A_5 \mapsto cp$

A_3: $A_1 \mapsto c$ A_7: $A_5 \mapsto \sim f$

A_4: $A_2, A_3 \mapsto f \longleftarrow$

Fig. 2. A graphical representation arguments and their attack relation (the arrows). Boldface arguments are in the grounded extension.

Definition 5 (Future setups, Stability, F). *Let $AS = (\mathcal{L}, \mathcal{R}, \mathcal{Q}, \mathcal{K}, \tau)$ be an argumentation setup. The set of all future setups $F(AS)$ consists of all setups $(\mathcal{L}, \mathcal{R}, \mathcal{Q}, \mathcal{K}', \tau)$ such that $\mathcal{K} \subseteq \mathcal{K}'$. AS is stable iff any of the following holds:*

- ***Unsatisfiable:*** *For each $AS' \in F(AS)$ there is no argument for τ in $I(AS')$*
- ***Defended:*** *For each $AS' \in F(AS)$ there is an argument for τ in the grounded extension of AS'*
- ***Out:*** *For each $AS' \in F(AS)$ there is an argument for τ in $I(AS')$ but all arguments for τ are attacked by an argument in the grounded extension of AS'*
- ***Blocked:*** *For each $AS' \in F(AS)$ there is an argument for τ in $I(AS')$ but not in the grounded extension of AS' and at least one argument for τ is not attacked by an argument from the grounded extension of AS'*

Example 4. Let us consider the previous example again where $\mathcal{K} = \{p, \neg cp, w\}$ and the arguments and attack relation are shown in Fig. 2. The **blocked** case applies because there exist arguments for f and $\neg f$ (A_4 and A_7) and they are both outside the grounded extension. Furthermore, the only queryable literal that is left is s, which cannot influence this situation if s or $\neg s$ is observed. Consider also the setup where $\mathcal{K} = \{cp\}$. For this setup no argument can possibly exist for f because all potential arguments require $\neg cp$. Therefore, in that setup the **unsatisfiable** case applies. If s, $\neg w$ and $\neg cp$ are observed, then there exists an argument for f in the grounded extension and no further observations (i.e. p or $\neg p$) can change this. Therefore in that case the **defended** case applies. Finally, in this example the **out** case can only apply for the literal $\neg cp$. This happens when w and cp are observed. In that case w is a basis for an argument for cp whilst $\neg cp$'s observation unilaterally attacks that argument.

A brute-force method for determining stability would be to calculate all possible future setups and then for each setup calculate the grounded extension to see whether the topic is stable. This results in possibly $3^{|\mathcal{Q}|}$ different setups to calculate the grounded extension for. The number of arguments in the grounded extension given $n = |\mathcal{L}|$ is maximally $n \cdot g(n), g(n) = (1 + g(n))^{n-1}$. The runtime complexity of this approach would be unpractical. Therefore a less complex approach to this task is preferable. The following labelling is an approximation of the task. The idea behind it is that rules and literals are labelled, where labels relate to the cases of stability. The labelling is defined as follows. After the definition and an example we discuss the soundness and complexity of the labelling.

Definition 6 (Labelling, L). *Let $AS = (\mathcal{L}, \mathcal{R}, \mathcal{Q}, \mathcal{K}, \tau)$ be an argumentation setup. A labelling L is a partial function that assigns a label from $\{U, D, O, B\}$ to literals and rules. Literals that are in $\mathcal{Q}$ but not observed ($l, -l \notin \mathcal{K}$) are not labelled. For the other literals and the rules the labelling is defined as follows:*

> ***Case U literal:*** *$l \in \mathcal{L}$ is labelled U iff either: (A) No rule exists for l and if $(-)l \in \mathcal{Q}$ then $-l \in \mathcal{K}$. (B) There are rules for l and they are labelled U and $l \notin \mathcal{K}$.*
> ***Case U rule:*** *$r \in \mathcal{R}$ is labelled U iff any of its antecedents is labelled U.*
> ***Case D literal:*** *$l \in \mathcal{L}$ is labelled D iff either: (A) $l \in \mathcal{K}$. (B) There is a rule for l labelled D, $-l \notin \mathcal{K}$ and there is no rule for $-l$. (C) There is a rule for l labelled D, $-l \notin \mathcal{K}$ and there are rules for $-l$ but they are all labelled U or O.*
> ***Case D rule:*** *$r \in \mathcal{R}$ is labelled D iff all its antecedents are labelled D.*
> ***Case O literal:*** *$l \in \mathcal{L}$ is labelled O iff either: (A) There exists a rule for l labelled D, O or B and $-l$ is labelled D. (B) There are rules for l of which at least one is labelled O and the rest is either labelled O or U.*
> ***Case O rule:*** *$r \in \mathcal{R}$ is labelled O iff at least one antecedent is labelled O and the rest is labeled D, B or O.*
> ***Case B literal:*** *$l \in \mathcal{L}$ is labelled B iff $l, -l \notin \mathcal{Q}$ and either: (A) A rule for l and a rule for $-l$ is labelled D or B. (B) There are rules for l of which one is labelled B and the rest is either labelled U, O or B.*

Case B rule: *$r \in \mathcal{R}$ is labelled B iff at least one antecedent is labelled B and the rest is labeled B or D.*

Example 5. Figure 3 shows the labelling for the example argumentation setup where $\mathcal{K} = \{p, \neg cp, w\}$. As expected given the previous example, the f literal is labelled B. Consider also the setup where $\mathcal{K} = \{cp\}$. The labelling for that setup labels $\neg cp$ U due to case 'U **literal** A'. Consequently, the rule $c, \neg cp \Rightarrow f$ is labelled U due to case 'U rule'. Finally f is labelled U because of case 'U **literal** B'. Hence, as discussed in the previous example, for the example argumentation setup where $\mathcal{K} = \{cp\}$ the topic f is unsatisfiable. In the 'extended examples and proofs' document we discuss more examples.

Note that alongside possible future observations, other literals can also be unlabelled. In particular, as long as the topic remains unlabelled it means that more information is required. The labelling of an argumentation setup is a sound approximation of stability. This means that if the topic is labelled, then the argumentation setup is stable. The following two propositions together show this. As the method is an approximation there are cases where a literal might be stable but unlabelled. The proof for Proposition 2 in the 'extended examples and proofs' document[2] contains such an example.

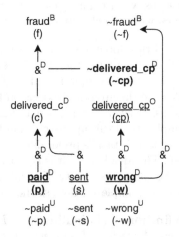

Fig. 3. Labelling of Fig. 2 given $\mathcal{K} = \{p, w, \neg cp\}$. Boldface literals are in $\mathcal{K}$ and underlined literals are queryable.

Proposition 1. *Let L be the labelling of an argumentation setup $AS = (\mathcal{L}, \mathcal{R}, \mathcal{Q}, \mathcal{K}, \tau)$. If for a rule $r = (p_1...p_m \Rightarrow c) \in \mathcal{R}$: $L(r) \in \{D, B, O\}$ then there exists an argument for c in $I(AS)$.*

Proof Sketch: By following the labels D, B and O from literals to rules we must end up in observed literals. Hence, if a rule is labelled D, B or O then we can follow the labelling until we end up with a set of observed literals. The observed literals, and the rules that were passed by following the labelling, can be used to construct the argument for c.

Proposition 2. *Let $AS = (\mathcal{L}, \mathcal{R}, \mathcal{Q}, \mathcal{K}, \tau)$ be an argumentation setup and L be its labelling. If $L(\tau) = U, D, O$ or B then AS is stable because of the **unsatisfiable**, **defended**, **out**, or **blocked** case of Definition 5, respectively.*

Proof Sketch: The different labels are 'introduced' under the stated property and their propagation through the rules to other literals preserves this property. U is introduced if a literal l has no rules for it and is unobservable (possibly due to

---

[2] Extended examples and proofs: https://preview.tinyurl.com/y656r3ek.

$-l$ being observed). Hence, no argument could exist for l. D is introduced for observed literals and hence for such literals an argument is guaranteed to exist that is in the grounded extension. O is introduced if a rule for a literal l can be applied to make an argument but $-l$ is observed. Hence every argument for l is unilaterally attacked by an argument in the grounded extension. B is introduced if for l and $-l$ there exists at least one argument that is not attacked by an argument from the grounded extension.

U is propagated through rules if for a rule at least one premise is labelled U. This indicates that the rule cannot be applied to construct an argument for its conclusion. If a literal has only U-labelled rules then therefore no rule can be applied to construct an argument for that literal. D is propagated if for a rule all premises are labelled D. This indicates that if the conclusion cannot have a rebutter, then this rule can be applied to construct an argument for in the grounded extension. So an unobservable literal becomes D if this holds. O is propagated if for a rule all premises are not unsatisfiable (so arguments can be made) but at least one is O, indicating that there will always be a unilateral premise attack from the grounded extension to arguments based on this rule. Which is why literals with only O-applicable rules are labelled O. B is propagated if for a rule if at least one of its premises is labelled B and the others are D or B-labelled. This indicates that every argument based on this rule will have a unilateral attacker on one of its premises. However, this attacker has a bi-lateral attacker that rebuts it. Hence arguments based on this rule will be attacked but not by arguments in the grounded extension. Therefore if a literal has only rules that are labelled U, O or B then the labelled becomes B.

Finally, we aim to improve upon the complexity of the brute-force method of determining stability. The following proposition discusses the big-Oh complexity of labelling an argumentation setup.

Proposition 3. Let $AS = (\mathcal{L}, \mathcal{R}, \mathcal{Q}, \mathcal{K}, \tau)$ be an argumentation setup. The labelling L of AS can be constructed in $O((|\mathcal{L}| + |\mathcal{R}|)^2)$.

Proof Sketch: A simple algorithm for the labelling works as follows. We can start with the set $\mathcal{L} \cup \mathcal{R}$ minus the literals from $\mathcal{L}$ that might be observed in the future. Then, we iterate through the cases of Definition 6 until no case applies anymore. Any time a case applies for a literal or rule, we remove it from the set. Worst-case, the set shrinks one-by-one until the empty set is reached (every literal/rule has a label) in which case a quadratic number of passes through the cases has been executed $(0.5 * (|\mathcal{L}| \cdot |\mathcal{R}|)^2)$.

4   Optimizing Inquiry Policies

An inquiry policy returns a query to execute given an argumentation setup and available queries. In the following, we show how to model the inquiry setting as a Markov Decision Process (MDP) for which the optimal policy can be obtained by standard methods. An MDP consists of actions, states, a transition function and a reward function. For the actions we take the queries that are available. A query can be executed once during a dialogue.[3] A state in the MDP is a pair of an argumentation setup and a set of available queries. After executing a query it is removed from the available queries and the setup may change because new observations might be added to the knowledge base.

The transition function tells us what the probability of a transition from one state to the next is when executing some query. For example, observing that a wrong product was received increases the probability of observing in the future that the complainant paid. We cancel out illegal transitions by setting their probability to zero. As for the reward function; we generate positive reward when a stable argumentation setup is reached from an unstable setup. Any transitions among unstable setups are negative because a query was executed. The transitions among stable setups are considered neutral. The labelling of Sect. 3 is applied to approximate stability. Finally, the optimal policy immediately follows from the MDP. The best action to execute give a state is the query which maximizes the expected reward. By maximizing reward, the policy will minimize the expected number of executed queries before reaching a stable setup.

Definition 7 (Argumentation MDP, policy, M, π). *Let $AS = (\mathcal{L}, \mathcal{R}, \mathcal{Q}, \mathcal{K}, \tau)$ be an argumentation setup and $F(AS)$ be all its possible future setups. An argumentation MDP M for AS is a tuple (Q, S, δ, r), where:*

- *Q is a set of queries*
- *$S = F(AS) \times 2^Q$ is the state space*
- *$\delta : S \times Q \times S \rightarrow [0, 1]$ is the transition function which returns the probability of the next state being $s_2 \in S$ given some state $s_1 \in S$ and query $q \in Q$. Furthermore, $\delta(s_1, q, s_2) = 0$ if the knowledge base of AS_1 is not a subset of that of AS_2, or if q is not available ($q \notin Q_1$), or if $Q_2 \neq Q_1 \setminus \{q\}$.*
- *$r : S \times S \rightarrow \mathbb{I}$ is the reward for transitioning from $s_1 = (AS_1, Q_1) \in S$ to $s_2 = (AS_2, Q_2) \in S$ and is given by: $r(s_1, s_2) = |Q_1|$ if τ is labelled in the labelling of AS_2 but not AS_1, $r(s_1, s_2) = 0$ if τ was already labelled in the labelling of AS_1, else $r(s_1, s_2) = -1$.*

The policy $\pi : S \rightarrow Q$ is given by:
$$\forall s_1 = (AS_1, Q_1) \in S : \pi(s_1) = argmax_{q \in Q_1} \Sigma_{s_2 \in S} \delta(s_1, q, s_2)(r(s_1, s_2) + V(s_2))$$
where: $V(s_2) = \Sigma_{s_3 \in S} \delta(s_2, \pi(s_2), s_3)(r(s_2, s_3) + V(s_3))$.

Example 6. Consider a policy for the MDP that belongs to the argumentation setup of the previous examples. A query can be any action that potentially leads to some observations. For this example we take Boolean queries that only have single queryable literal for which they may lead to an observation. Let the queries be $Q = \{p?, s?, w?, cp?\}$. For a query $x?$ assume that its execution results in x or $-x$ being added to the knowledge base. The policy may then look like the one that is shown in Fig. 4. Note that for simplicity's sake, we assume

---

[3] Note that, if desired, the same query can be 'copied' multiple times in the formal model to allow for repeated execution.

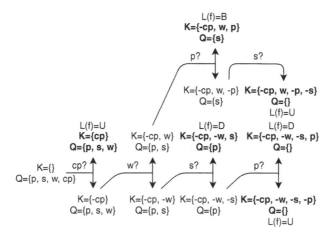

Fig. 4. Part of the example policy. These are the reachable states/actions from the empty observation set (i.e., zero probability transitions are omitted). States with stable setups are boldface and the label of the topic f is shown as well for such states.

some (implicit) probabilities for the transitions. From the policy it can be read that first it queried whether the counterpary delivered (partially) upon his/her promise. If not, then it is queried whether a wrong product was delivered. If so, then it is queried whether the complainant paid, or otherwise whether the complainant sent a product. In both situations, if the answer is negative, then the last query is executed. Note that in the example policy, after the user answered negative to 'cp?' and positive to 'w?', that the label for fraud cannot be D in the future. It depends on an application whether this might be a reason to halt the execution. Formally, the system still executes queries because the reason why the label is not 'D' is still unstable.

Roughly speaking, for our real-world applications the argumentation system provides information on what queries are relevant and the policy then chooses among the relevant queries. We apply various techniques to make the policy such as dynamic programming and q-learning. The policy itself can also be used in different ways. In one of our applications it guides a dialogue with the user and in another it prioritizes database queries. Similarly, the argumentation setup has different applications. It can be used to determine what information is relevant but also provide argumentation-based explanations for the agent's decisions.

5   Related Work

A typical argument-based inquiry is a so-called *inquiry dialogue* [3, 7], in which arguing agents collaborate to answer some question the answer to which is not known by the individual agents. Our setting is different in that the information source of our agent is not necessarily another arguing agent: a query can be implemented as an utterance in an argumentation dialogue, but it can also for instance be a query on a database. Thus, our optimal query policy can be used to determine an efficient strategy for inquiry dialogues, but it can also be used outside such dialogues. Furthermore, as already discussed in Sect. 3, in our setting the agent can only query observations, whereas in an argument inquiry dialogue the other agent (i.e. the agents that "answers" the query) can also provide an argument, making these dialogues slightly more flexible. However, in the existing work on inquiry dialogue strategies [3,11] only exhaustive strategies are defined, which simply perform all queries, that is, the agent keeps asking questions even if it already has an argument for its topic, or if adding new arguments cannot change the status of the topic. Such exhaustive strategies are both inefficient (in terms of the length of the inquiry process) and computationally very expensive. While there is work on developing more optimal policies or strategies for argumentation dialogues (see [9] for a fairly recent overview), some of which shows some similarities with our work in their use of (in their case partially observable) MDPs for defining policies [6], this existing work all focuses on strategies for so-called persuasion dialogue, in which the agent tries to convince an opponent of some conclusion. Furthermore, this existing work is all based on abstract argumentation frameworks [4], in which only arguments as single entities (propositions, nodes) and their attacks are considered, and there is no argument structure that includes inferences based on a knowledge base. Work on inquiry that does not explicitly use arguments is [5], in which the authors propose a four-valued logic with the truth values true, false, inconsistent and unknown, which, broadly speaking, are similar to the current paper's Defended, Out, Blocked and Unsatisfiable stability cases. Like [3], the strategies for inquiry discussed in this paper are all exhaustive and hence not efficient.

With respect to the idea of stability, much of the work on argumentation is more concerned with the static situation: given the knowledge we have now, what are the acceptable arguments. A notable exception is by Ballnat and Gordon [1]. This work looks at determining which possible future additions to a knowledge base might change the acceptability of a conclusion. They do not use their basic ideas for determining optimal policies, however, nor do they discuss the complexity and approximation results we provide in this paper. The idea of stability also has clear links to what is called the enforcing problem [2]: given a set of arguments, can we modify this set by adding or removing arguments and conflicts so that some argument from the original set becomes acceptable? The work that exists on this topic, however, again only deals with abstract argumentation frameworks.

6   Conclusion and Future Work

In this paper we have described a policy for efficient argument-based inquiry – that is, a policy that minimizes the expected number of queries required to reach a stable setup in which the acceptability of some conclusion cannot change any more given a stochastic environment. Our approach is efficient in a number of ways, computationally as well as with respect to the inquiry process itself.

- By rewarding an agent that reasons towards a stable argumentation as quickly as possible we ensure that only the minimum required number of queries is executed to draw a stable conclusion.
- By approximating the notion of stability we make determining or learning the policy feasible in terms of computational complexity.
- Finally, by defining the policy by means of an MDP we allow the agent to avoid executing queries that are likely to be unsuccessful.

As for future work we want to further explore the notion of stability in structured argumentation, taking into account the possibility of rules, preferences and attacks being added through queries. We also intend to see how we can further embed the policy in argument dialogues between agents. Finally, our implementations of this method are leading to best-practices (e.g. to deal with noisy observations) which we aim to publish publicly.

References

1. Ballnat, S., Gordon, T.F.: Goal selection in argumentation processes. In: Computational models of argument: Proceedings of COMMA 2010. Frontiers in Artificial Intelligence and Applications, vol. 216, pp. 51–62. IOS Press (2010)
2. Baumann, R.: What does it take to enforce an argument? Minimal change in abstract argumentation. In: Proceedings of the 20th European Conference on Artificial Intelligence. Frontiers in Artificial Intelligence and Applications, pp. 127–132, no. 242. IOS Press (2012)
3. Black, E., Hunter, A.: An inquiry dialogue system. Auton. Agent. Multi-Agent Syst. **19**(2), 173–209 (2009)
4. Dung, P.M.: On the acceptability of arguments and its fundamental role in non-monotonic reasoning, logic programming and n-person games. Artif. Intell. **77**(2), 321–357 (1995)
5. Dunin-Keplicz, B., Strachocka, A.: Tractable inquiry in information-rich environments. In: Proceedings of the Twenty-Fourth International Joint Conference on Artificial Intelligence (IJCAI 2015), pp. 53–60. AAAI publishing (2015)
6. Hadoux, E., Beynier, A., Maudet, N., Weng, P., Hunter, A.: Optimization of probabilistic argumentation with Markov decision models. In: Proceedings of the Twenty-Fourth International Joint Conference on Artificial Intelligence (IJCAI 2015), pp. 2004–2010. AAAI publishing (2015)
7. Parsons, S., McBurney, P., Wooldridge, M.: The mechanics of some formal inter-agent dialogues. In: Dignum, F. (ed.) ACL 2003. LNCS (LNAI), vol. 2922, pp. 329–348. Springer, Heidelberg (2004). https://doi.org/10.1007/978-3-540-24608-4_19
8. Prakken, H.: An abstract framework for argumentation with structured arguments. Argum. Comput. **1**(2), 93–124 (2010)
9. Thimm, M.: Strategic argumentation in multi-agent systems. KI-Künstl. Intell. **28**(3), 159–168 (2014)
10. Verheij, B.: Dialectical argumentation with argumentation schemes: an approach to legal logic. Artif. Intell. Law **11**(2–3), 167–195 (2003)
11. Yan, C., Lindgren, H., Nieves, J.C.: A dialogue-based approach for dealing with uncertain and conflicting information in medical diagnosis. Auton. Agent. Multi-Agent Syst. **32**(6), 861–885 (2018)

DAQAP: Defeasible Argumentation Query Answering Platform

Mario A. Leiva, Gerardo I. Simari$^{(\boxtimes)}$, Sebastian Gottifredi,
Alejandro J. García, and Guillermo R. Simari

Depto. de Cs. e Ing. de la Comp., Inst. de Cs. e Ing. de la Comp.
(ICIC UNS–CONICET), Universidad Nacional del Sur (UNS),
Bahía Blanca, Argentina
{mario.leiva,gis,sg,ajg,grs}@cs.uns.edu.ar

Abstract. In this paper we present the DAQAP, a Web platform for *Defeasible Argumentation Query Answering*, which offers a visual interface that facilitates the analysis of the argumentative process defined in the Defeasible Logic Programming (DeLP) formalism. The tool presents graphs that show the interaction of the arguments generated from a DeLP program; this is done in two different ways: the first focuses on the structures obtained from the DeLP program, while the second presents the defeat relationships from the point of view of abstract argumentation frameworks, with the possibility of calculating the extensions using Dung's semantics. Using all this data, the platform provides support for answering queries regarding the states of literals of the input program.

Keywords: Defeasible Argumentation ·
Abstract argumentation frameworks ·
Argumentation-based query answering

1 Introduction

In structured argumentation, we assume a formal language for representing knowledge, as well as specifying how arguments and counterarguments can be constructed from that knowledge. This allow to describe arguments, attacks, and defeats [2]. The research community has recently developed new tools for argumentation that are useful for analyzing the structure of different kinds of reasoning. It is often claimed that structuring and visualizing arguments in graphs is beneficial and provides faster learning, since the visualization of arguments and relationships between them can be seen more clearly compared to plain text [4]. Apart from the tools focused on the visualization, there also exist *automated reasoning systems* and *argument assistance systems*. The first automatically performs reasoning on the basis of the information in the knowledge base, while the second assists one or more users in the formulation, organization, and presentation of arguments [21]. The main difference between them is that, while

© Springer Nature Switzerland AG 2019
A. Cuzzocrea et al. (Eds.): FQAS 2019, LNAI 11529, pp. 126–138, 2019.
https://doi.org/10.1007/978-3-030-27629-4_14

automated reasoning systems can do reasoning tasks for the user, argument assistance systems do not reason themselves; the goal of assistance systems is not to *replace* the user's reasoning, but to *assist* the user in their reasoning process.

In this paper we present a Web platform called *DAQAP* (Defeasible Argumentation Query Answering) that offers a visual interface that facilitates the analysis of the argumentative process defined in the DeLP formalism [8]. This platform has the characteristics of both an argument assistance and automatic reasoning system, since on the one hand it allows the automatic construction of arguments and an argumentative process based on a knowledge base, and on the other hand it presents this information through graphs in a clear way to the user, allowing them to analyze the argumentative process. Furthermore, it is possible to calculate and display the extensions for Dung's semantics (grounded, stable, preferred, and semistable) for the graph, as well as different *intersections* of such corresponding extensions.

This paper is organized as follows. In Sect. 2 we discuss work related to visualization tools for argumentation. Section 3 presents the basic concepts of Defeasible Logic Programming and Abstract Argumentation Frameworks, which are central to the platform. Then, Sect. 4, presents the platform's features, architecture, and functionalities. Finally, Sect. 7 discusses some aspects of the interface and future work, along with our conclusions.

2 Related Work

It is often claimed that structuring and visualization of arguments is a powerful method to analyze and evaluate arguments, as well as to offer faster learning. Since this task is laborious, researchers have turned to develop software tools that support the construction and visualization of arguments and argumentative structures in various representation formats, such as graphs or tables [4]. As a result, there are several argument visualization tools [11], such as *Araucaria* [15], *Athena* [13], *Convince Me* [17], *Belvedere* [19], *Reason!Able* [20], and *Grafix* [5]. Typically, some of these tools produce "box and arrow" diagrams in which premises and conclusions are formulated as statements. These are represented by nodes that can be joined by lines to display inferences, and arrows are used to indicate their direction.

Some of these tools (*Belvedere, Convince Me, and Reason!Able*) have in common that they are education-oriented and designed to teach critical thinking or discussion skills, and are tested in an educational setting. However, important discrepancies exist between them; for example, *Belvedere* and *Reason!Able* are entirely designed to assist argument construction and analysis, while *Convince Me* produces causal networks. *Reason!Able* [20] is an educational software that supports argument mapping to teach reasoning skills. The argument trees constructed by this tool contain claims, reasons, and objections. Reasons and objections are complex objects that can be unfolded to show the full set of premises and helping premises that are underlying them.

Another tool is *Araucaria* [15], a software for analyzing arguments that helps users to reconstruct and diagram a given argument using a point-and-click interface. The user moves the text of discourse containing an argument as a text file into a box in a windows of interface, and then highlights each statement (premises and conclusions). Each highlighted statement appears as a text box in another window, and the user can then draw an arrow representing each inference from a set of premises to a conclusion. The outcome is an argumentation chain that appears as an argument diagram. Once the argument has been fully diagrammed, it can be saved for further use in a format called *AML* (Argument Markup Language). Araucaria was the first argument visualization tool to incorporate the use of argumentation schemes.

More recent tools to work with argumentation with visualization features include OVA+, OpMAP, and AVIZE. OVA+ [16] (Online Visualization of Argument) is an interface for the analysis of arguments online and is accessible from any Web browser. The tool was built as a response to the Argument Interchange Format (AIF) [14] – it is a tool allowing what the AIF has advocated for, *i.e.* the representation of arguments and the possibility to exchange, share, and reuse the argument maps. The most interesting feature is the possibility of saving the analyses in the AIF format either locally or to AIFdb [12] and add them to a dedicated corpus (created beforehand) in the AIFdb Corpora. OpMAP [3] is a tool for visualizing large scale, multi-dimensional opinion spaces as geographic maps. It uses probabilistic degrees of justification and Bayesian coherence measures to calculate how strongly any two opinions cohere with each other. The opinion sample is, accordingly, represented as a weighted graph – a so-called *opinion graph* – with opinion vectors serving as nodes and coherence values as edge weights. Finally, AVIZE (Argument Visualization and Evaluation) [10] is an argument diagramming tool. Its goal is to aid users in the construction and self-evaluation of real-world arguments in the domain of international politics. AVIZE provides a set of argument schemes as cognitive building blocks for constructing argument diagrams.

3   Background

An *argumentation framework* is defined as a pair composed of a set of arguments and a binary relation representing the attack relationship between arguments. Here, an argument is an abstract entity whose role is solely determined by its relations to other arguments [7]. To determine which argument are able to survive the conflict, a well-defined systematic method is needed; such formal methods to identify conflict outcomes for any argumentation framework are called *argumentation semantics*. Two main approaches to the definition of argumentation semantics are available in the literature: the *labelling-based* approach and the *extension-based* approach [1].

The idea underlying the *labelling*-based approach is to give each argument a *label*. A sensible choice for the set of labels is: *in*, *out*, and *undec*, where the label *in* means the argument is *accepted*, *out* means the argument is *rejected*, and *undec* means that whether the argument is accepted or rejected is a matter of opinion. The idea underlying the *extension*-based approach is to identify sets of arguments, called *extensions*, which can survive the conflict together and thus represent collectively a reasonable position an autonomous reasoner might take.

If we want a more detailed formalization of arguments than is available with abstract argumentation, we can turn to *structured* argumentation. In the literature there are several formalisms that are based on this idea; some of them are ABA, ASPIC+, *Defeasible Logic Programming* (DeLP), and *deductive argumentation* [2]. In particular, DeLP offers a computational reasoning system that uses an argumentation-based mechanism to obtain answers from a knowledge base represented using an extended logic programming language with defeasible rules. This combination generates a computationally effective system together with a reasoning model similar to the one used by humans that facilities its use in real-world applications. The tool we present in this work is based on *DeLP* and we focus on the *extension*-based approach to calculate the extensions for Dung graphs generated from DeLP programs in the Web tool.

3.1 Defeasible Logic Programming

Defeasible Logic Programming (DeLP) combines results of Logic Programming and Defeasible Argumentation. A DeLP program $\mathcal{P}$ is a set of facts, strict rules, and defeasible rules. *Facts* are ground literals representing atomic information or the negation of atomic information using strong negation "$\sim$". *Strict Rules* represent non-defeasible information noted as $\alpha \leftarrow \beta_1, \ldots, \beta_n$, where α is a ground literal and $\beta_{i>0}$ is a set of ground literals. *Defeasible Rules* represent tentative information noted as $\alpha \prec \beta_1, \ldots, \beta_n$, where α is a ground literal and $\beta_{i>0}$ is a set of ground literals. When required, $\mathcal{P}$ will be denoted (Π, Δ) distinguishing the subset Π of facts and string rules, and the subset Δ of defeasible rules. From a program (Π, Δ), contradictory literals could be derived; nevertheless, the set Π must possess certain internal coherence – no pair of contradictory literals can be derived from Π. Strong negation can be used in the head of a rule, as well as in any literal in its body. In DeLP, literals can be derived from rules as in logic programming; a *defeasible derivation* is one that uses at least one defeasible rule.

The dialectical process used in deciding which information prevails as *warranted* involves the construction and evaluation of arguments that either support or interfere with the query under analysis. In DeLP, an *argument* $\mathcal{A}$ is a minimal set of defeasible rules that, along with the set of strict rules and facts, is not contradictory, and derives a certain conclusion α; this is noted as $\langle \mathcal{A}, \alpha \rangle$. Those arguments supporting the answer for a given query can be organized using *dialectical trees*. A query is issued to a defeasible logic program (Π, Δ) in the form of a ground literal α.

A literal α is *warranted* if there exists a non-defeated argument $\mathcal{A}$ supporting α. To establish if $\langle \mathcal{A}, \alpha \rangle$ is a non-defeated argument, *defeaters* for $\langle \mathcal{A}, \alpha \rangle$ are considered, *i.e.*, *counter-argument* that by some criterion are preferred to $\langle \mathcal{A}, \alpha \rangle$. An argument $\mathcal{A}_1$ is a counter-argument for $\mathcal{A}_2$ *iff* $\mathcal{A}_1 \cup \mathcal{A}_2 \cup \Pi$ is contradictory. Given a preference criterion, and an argument $\mathcal{A}_1$ that is a *defeater* for $\mathcal{A}_2$, $\mathcal{A}_1$ is called a *proper defeater* if it's preferred to $\mathcal{A}_2$, or a *blocking defeater* if is equally preferred or is incomparable with $\mathcal{A}_2$.

In DeLP, the comparison criterion is modular, *i.e.*, one can define its own criterion. Two criterion that are commonly used are *generalized specificity* [18] and *priority between rules*. Since defeaters are arguments, there may exist defeaters for them, and defeaters for these defeaters, and so on. Thus, a sequence of arguments called *argumentation line* is constructed, where each argument defeats its predecessor. To avoid undesirable sequences that may represent circular of fallacious argumentation lines, in DeLP an argumentation line must be *acceptable*, that is, it has to be finite, arguments cannot appear twice, and supporting (resp., interfering) arguments must be non-contradictory.

Clearly, there might be more than one defeater for a particular argument. Therefore, many acceptable argumentation lines could arise from one argument, leading to a tree structure. This is called a *dialectical tree* because it represents an exhaustive dialectical analysis for the argument in its root. In a dialectical tree, every node (except the root) represents a defeater of its parent, and leaves correspond to non-defeated arguments. Each path from the root to a leaf corresponds to a different acceptable argumentation line. A dialectical tree provides a structure for considering all the possible acceptable argumentation lines that can be generated for deciding whether an argument is defeated.

Given a literal α and an argument $\langle \mathcal{A}, \alpha \rangle$ from a program $\mathcal{P}$, to decide whether α is warranted, every node in the tree is recursively marked as "D" (*defeated*) or "U" (*undefeated*), obtaining a marked dialectical tree $\mathcal{T}_{\mathcal{P}}(\mathcal{A})$: (1) all leaves in $\mathcal{T}_{\mathcal{P}}(\mathcal{A})$ are marked as "U"s; and (2) let $\mathcal{B}$ be an inner node of $\mathcal{T}_{\mathcal{P}}(\mathcal{A})$, then $\mathcal{B}$ will be marked as "U" *iff* every child of $\mathcal{B}$ is marked as "D". Thus, the node $\mathcal{B}$ will be marked as "D" *iff* it has at least one child marked as "U". Given an argument $\langle \mathcal{A}, \alpha \rangle$ obtained from $\mathcal{P}$, if the root of $\mathcal{T}_{\mathcal{P}}(\mathcal{A})$: is marked as "U", then we say that $\mathcal{T}_{\mathcal{P}}(\mathcal{A})$: *warrants* α and that α is *warranted* from $\mathcal{P}$. In this way, the DeLP interpreter takes a program $\mathcal{P}$, and a DeLP-query L as input, and returns one of the following four possible answers: YES, if L is warranted from $\mathcal{P}$; NO, if the complement of L is warranted from $\mathcal{P}$; UNDECIDED, if neither L nor its complements are warranted from $\mathcal{P}$; or UNKNOWN, if L is not in the language of the program $\mathcal{P}$.

4   Defeasible Argumentation-Based Query Answering

The Web platform that we present here consists of an interface to visualize via graphs the interaction of the arguments generated from an input DeLP program. We distinguish two sections: the first is dedicated to the analysis of the structures obtained from DeLP (arguments and defeats) and its interactions; the second analyzes those defeat relationships in a Dung graph environment. In the following we present a summary of the platform's architecture, and we then focus on the DeLP and Dung analysis in turn.

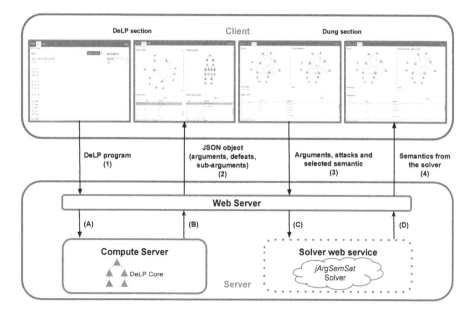

Fig. 1. The DAQAP platform architecture.

4.1 Architecture

The DAQAP platform is based on a client-server architecture. The client sends the input DeLP program to be processed by the DeLP core hosted on a compute server; the DeLP core is responsible for generating the arguments, the relationships between them (sub-argument and defeat), and determining the status of each argument, for which it generates and analyzes the dialectic trees. The resulting data is then sent in JSON format to the client, where it is graphically presented. Figure 1 presents a general outline of this architecture.

DAQAP Workflow (Fig. 1). The user enters the DeLP program to be analyzed along with a preference criterion (*rule priority* or *specificity*). A syntactical analysis is performed and if the program does not contain errors it is sent to the Web server (1). Then, the Web server sends the program and the instruction to be executed by the DeLP Core hosted on the compute server (A). The DeLP Core module is responsible for generating the arguments and the relations between them (sub-arguments and defeats), and for returning the data in JSON format to the Web server (B) so that, after verifying the response, it can be sent to the client so that the data can be presented (2). This corresponds to the DeLP analysis, in which it is possible to obtain all arguments generated and the dialectical trees constructed during the argumentative process. With respect to the Dung graph analysis, the first part of the flow is analogous to that of DeLP, the main difference is that after (2), the client sends the identifiers of the arguments, the attacks, and the semantics to be calculated (3); in the Web server a JSON is built to perform a query to a solver through a Web service (C) and then, once a

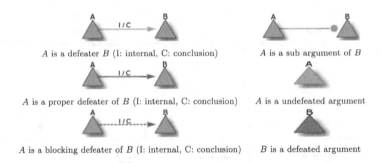

Fig. 2. Elements of a DeLP graph.

solver response is obtained, the Web server verifies the response (D) and sends it to the client (4).

5   DeLP Analysis

As mentioned above, the analysis for DeLP programs is handled by the DeLP core module, which takes a DeLP program $\mathcal{P}$ and a preference criterion as inputs and return a JSON object that contains information about all arguments that can be constructed from $\mathcal{P}$, the defeat relationships, the set of warranted literals as its correspond labeled tree, and the sub-argument relationships between arguments. From this data, a DeLP graph is drawn to show all arguments, sub-arguments, defeat relationships, and status of each argument. The elements used to represent the data in the graph can be seen in Fig. 2; in the graph, the arguments are represented as triangles with the conclusion of the argument at the top and an identifier in its body. In addition to the graph, two tables are created, one with the information for each argument (conclusion and extended argument [9]) and the other with the warranted literals and the arguments that provide the warrant for them. It is also possible to visualize the dialectical tree generated for each argument and configure different views for the DeLP graph.

Regarding the DeLP program to be analyzed, the facts in set Π must be specified as follows: $fact \leftarrow true$. In addition to the program itself, it is optional to specify the preference criterion to be used, which can be either *generalized specificity* (entering the statement *"use_criterion(more_specific)"*) or *priority between rules* (entering *"use_criterion(rule_priorities)"*, along with statements indicating the priorities between rules as follows: *"has_priority(R1, R2)"*, to specify that rule $R1$ has priority over rule $R2$).

We now show these features with an example, starting with a simple graph; consider the following DeLP program $\mathcal{P} = (\Pi, \Delta)$, where $\Pi = (t \leftarrow true, z \leftarrow true, p \leftarrow t)$ and $\Delta = (\sim a \prec y, y \prec x, x \prec z, y \prec p, a \prec w, w \prec y, \sim w \prec t, \sim x \prec t, x \prec p)$, and suppose we use the *generalized specificity* criterion. In Fig. 3 we show the graph generated for this DeLP program with the default view (all setting panel options enabled). Note that one can

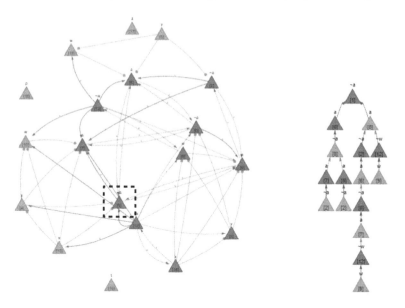

Fig. 3. DeLP graph of $\mathcal{P}_1$ **Fig. 4.** Dialectical tree

see the arguments created, each with its identifier and conclusion that it supports, its warrant statuses, and the defeat relationships. From the DeLP graph it is possible to analyze the structures and relationships that are generated from the input program. In order to see the set of rules that make up a particular argument, the user can hover the mouse pointer over the argument in the graph and it will be show (in a tooltip window) the set of rules that comprise it. As detailed above, it is also possible to visualize the dialectical tree associated with each argument. In Fig. 4 we present the dialectical tree of the argument with id 1 (marked with a square), here it is also possible to distinguish between the proper and blocking defeat relationships. Furthermore, it is possible to see the tables with information for each argument and the warranted literals, which allows for better readability and avoids visually saturating the graph.

We now move on to a discussion of the different views that the user can leverage in order to obtain a clearer visualization of the DeLP graph.

Views. The interface is capable of showing all arguments generated from the DeLP program, the defeat and sub-argument relationships, and the status of each argument in a single graph called the *DeLP graph*. By default, all of this data is draw; however, since for larger programs this can generate very saturated graphs that are difficult to analyze, we developed a set of different views that can be configured through the "Settings" panel. These views allow to hide certain information, reducing the connections or hiding the final status of the arguments, so the user can focus on the aspect that is most important to them. There are four views defined; next we will present each of them and the effect produced for some of them on the graph generated for the program depicted in Fig. 3.

Fig. 5. DeLP graph of $\mathcal{P} = (\Pi, \Delta)$ *Left*: Without the sub-argument relationship arcs. *Center*: Without conclusion attacks and sub-argument arcs. *Right*: Without conclusion attack type, sub-argument relationship, and status of arguments.

1. *Arguments and sub-argument relationship*: This view allows to show or hide the sub-argument relationships, *i.e.*, the arcs with circle in their ends that represent that an argument is a sub-argument of another (see Fig. 5 (left)).
2. *Types of defeat*: Allows to distinguish between types of defeat (proper or blocking), *i.e.*, shows all arcs with arrows in their ends of the same form.
3. *Attack type*: With this view it is possible to show or hide the attack type (specified by arcs) of a defeat relation.
   The result of hiding the *conclusion* attack type and the sub-argument relationship in the graph of the DeLP program $\mathcal{P}$ is shown in Fig. 5 (center).
4. *Status of each argument*: This view allows to show the status of each argument in the graph.
   The result of hiding the status of the arguments, sub-argument relationships, and conclusion type attack in the graph of the DeLP program $\mathcal{P}$ is shown in Fig. 5 (right).

One of the "cleanest" configurations to analyze DeLP programs that generate many defeats is achieved by hiding the internal attack type (disabling the option *Show internal attacks*) and enabling the option *Show the sub-argument relationship* in the "Settings" panel. With this view, it is possible to appreciate the relationships without overloading the graph as it will only show the defeats to the conclusions; naturally, this clarity is obtained since the arcs that represent defeats to internal conclusions are eliminated. This allows to concentrate on conflicts in a more direct way without losing information, since the eliminated arcs are presented in an "implicit" way by the sub-argument relationship. Finally, it is also possible to combine all of these views.

6   Dung Graph Analysis

As was mentioned above, DAQAP also allows to analyze the generated DeLP graph by considering it as an abstract argumentation frameworks, which is essentially a directed graph in which the arguments are represented by the nodes and the attack relation is represented by the arcs. It is also possible to calculate and display different semantics (*grounded, stable, preferred* and *semistable*) for the graph, as well as different *intersections* of calculated extensions, in support of cautious query answering approaches.

This functionality is provided since, given the abstract argumentation framework, one can then examine the question of which set(s) of arguments should be accepted through *argumentation semantics*. Recall that two main approaches to the definition of argumentation semantics are available in the literature; it is important to note that, even when a *labelling-based* or an *extension-based* approach is used, the "final answer" regarding argument justification is not easily determined. In fact, several choices are available as to the derivation of justification status from a set of labellings or extensions. At a basic level, two very simple alternatives for the notion of justification can be considered: *skeptical (or cautious)* justification requires that an argument is accepted in *all* extensions (or labellings), while *credulous* justification requires that an argument is accepted in *at least one* extension (or labelling) [1]. Intuitively, a skeptical attitude tends to make less committed choices about the justification of the arguments; in other words, a skeptical behavior tends to leave arguments in an "undecided" justification state and to accept (or reject) the least amount of arguments possible, while a less skeptical (or more credulous) behavior corresponds to more extensive acceptance (or rejection) of arguments – clearly skeptical justification implies credulous justification. Moreover, a third justification can be derived: an argument is *not justified* (or *rejected*) if it is not credulously justified (and hence also not skeptically justified). It is also important to note that in any unique-status semantics the skeptical and credulous approaches coincide, so that an argument can only be accepted or rejected.

DAQAP allows to work with both approaches to analyze which set(s) of arguments can be accepted. Next we show how to calculate the semantics for the input DeLP program.

Calculation of Semantics and Skepticism. In DeLP, an attack only succeeds as a defeat if the attacked argument is not preferred to the attacking argument. Then, it is this defeat relation that is used as the binary relation in the Dung framework. Here, to create the graph the classical component is used, *i.e.*, the arguments are represented by nodes (dots) and the attack relations are represented by arcs. From the generated Dung graph, the following semantics can be calculated: *grounded, preferred, stable and semistable*; and the calculated extensions are plotted in another graph to the right of the Dung framework. The calculation of these semantics is done through the *jArgSemSAT* [6] solver, which is provided as a Web service.

Under the generated Dung graph, the semantics that can be calculated are shown; when selecting any one of them, the query is made to the *jArgSemSAT* Web service and the result is shown in another graph to the right of the first one. In the second graph, the nodes that represent the argument that belongs to some extension of the calculated semantics are colored green. All calculated extensions are listed below the second graph. In Figs. 6 and 7 we show some examples of semantics calculated from the DeLP program $\mathcal{P} = (\Pi, \Delta)$.

Fig. 6. DeLP semantics. (Color figure online)

Fig. 7. Extension of the stable semantics. (Color figure online)

In the same way, it is possible to calculate and show the *intersections* of the extensions yielded (option "All semantics" of the list of semantics that can be calculated). Once the intersections have been calculated, a menu is enabled in order to select which semantics (intersections of its extensions) the user wishes to display in the second graph. Also, by means of this menu, it is possible to calculate the *intersection of the intersections* of the calculated semantics and display them in the second graph, which yields an even "more cautious" answer.

7   Conclusions and Future Work

We begin our final discussion by noting that the development of tools to work with argumentation theories is still mainly in an experimental phase. There is a much to learn and experiment about the way arguments and relationships between them can be sensibly and clearly presented to the users. DAQAP is therefore very much a work in progress, both in terms of functionality and user experience. An important point to address in this regard is that the amount of information to be displayed can be quite overwhelming, and it is critical to define precisely what information should be presented to the user, as well as how it should be delivered. In this respect, we are currently continuing to experiment with different configurations to achieve a more efficient distribution.

Therefore, an important part of current and future work in this research line involves improving the tool and adding functionality, such as: (1) exporting graphs in AIF format, (2) design a graphical interface to introduce preference criteria, (3) design a better graphical interface to work with the calculation of semantics, and (4) design an external library to support distribution and allow DAQAP to be imported by other tools. Finally, it is essential to offer the option of storing, printing, and exporting the generated graphs in different formats.

Acknowledgments. This work was partially supported by funds provided by CONICET, Universidad Nacional del Sur (UNS), and by the EU H2020 research and innovation programme under the Marie Sklodowska-Curie grant agreement 690974 for the project "MIREL: MIning and REasoning with Legal texts".

References

1. Baroni, P., Caminada, M., Giacomin, M.: An introduction to argumentation semantics. Knowl. Eng. Rev. **26**(4), 365–410 (2011)
2. Besnard, P., et al.: Introduction to structured argumentation. Arg. Comput. **5**(1), 1–4 (2014)
3. Betz, G., Hamann, M., Mchedlidze, T., von Schmettow, S.: Applying argumentation to structure and visualize multi-dimensional opinion spaces. Arg. Comput. 1–18 (2018, preprint)
4. Van den Braak, S.W., Oostendorp, H.V., Prakken, H., Vreeswijk, G.A.: A critical review of argument visualization tools: do users become better reasoners? In: Proceedings of CMNA, pp. 67–75 (2008)
5. Cayrol, C., Doutre, S., Lagasquie-Schiex, M.C.: GRAFIX: a tool for abstract argumentation (2014)
6. Cerutti, F., Vallati, M., Giacomin, M.: jArgSemSAT: an efficient off-the-shelf solver for abstract argumentation frameworks. In: Proceedings of KR (2016)
7. Dung, P.M.: On the acceptability of arguments and its fundamental role in non-monotonic reasoning, logic programming and n-person games. Artif. Intell. **77**(2), 321–357 (1995)
8. García, A.J., Simari, G.R.: Defeasible logic programming: DeLP-servers, contextual queries, and explanations for answers. Arg. Comput. **5**(1), 63–88 (2014)
9. García, A.J.: La programación en lógica rebatible: su definición teórica y computacional. Master's thesis. Departamento de Ciencias de la Computación, Universidad Nacional del Sur (UNS) (1997)
10. Green, N.L., Branon, M., Roosje, L.: Argument schemes and visualization software for critical thinking about international politics. Arg. Comput. **10**(1), 41–53 (2019)
11. Kirschner, P.A., Buckingham-Shum, S.J., Carr, C.S.: Visualizing Argumentation: Software Tools for Collaborative and Educational Sense-Making. Springer, London (2012)
12. Lawrence, J., Bex, F., Reed, C., Snaith, M.: AIFdb: infrastructure for the argument web. In: COMMA, pp. 515–516 (2012)
13. Magnusson, C., Rolf, B.: Developing the art of argumentation-a software approach. In: International Conference on Argumentation (2002)
14. Modgil, S., Rahawan, I., Reed, C., Chesñevar, C., McGinnis, J., et al.: Towards an argument interchange format. KER **21**(4), 293–316 (2006)
15. Reed, C., Rowe, G.: Araucaria: software for argument analysis, diagramming and representation. Int. J. Artif. Intell. Tools **13**(04), 961–979 (2004)
16. Janier, M., Lawrence, J., Reed, C.: OVA+: an argument analysis interface. In: Computational Models of Argument: Proceedings of COMMA, vol. 266, p. 463 (2014)
17. Schank, P., Ranney, M.: Improved reasoning with convince me. In: Conference Companion on Human Factors in Computing Systems, pp. 276–277. ACM (1995)
18. Stolzenburg, F., García, A.J., Chesnevar, C.I., Simari, G.R.: Computing generalized specificity. J. Appl. Non-Class. Log. **13**(1), 87–113 (2003)

19. Suthers, D., Weiner, A., Connelly, J., Paolucci, M.: Belvedere: engaging students in critical discussion of science and public policy issues. In: Proceedings of WCAIE, Washington, DC, pp. 266–273 (1995)
20. Van Gelder, T.: Argument mapping with Reason!Able. Am. Philos. Assoc. Newsl. Philos. Comput. **2**(1), 85–90 (2002)
21. Verheij, B.: Artificial argument assistants for defeasible argumentation. Artif. Intell. **150**(1–2), 291–324 (2003)

An Efficient Algorithm for Computing the Set of Semi-stable Extensions

Gianvincenzo Alfano$^{(\boxtimes)}$

Department of Informatics, Modeling, Electronics and System Engineering,
University of Calabria, Rende, Italy
g.alfano@dimes.unical.it

Abstract. Argumentation is one of the most relevant fields in the sphere of Artificial Intelligence. In particular, Dung's abstract argumentation framework (AF) has received much attention in the last twenty years, and many computational issues have been investigated for different argumentation semantics. Specifically, enumerating the sets of arguments prescribed by an argumentation semantics (i.e., *extensions*) is arguably one of the most challenging problems for AFs, and this is the case also for the well-known *semi-stable* semantics.

In this paper, we propose an algorithm for efficiently computing the set of semi-stable extensions of a given AF. Our technique relies on exploiting the computation of grounded extension to snip some arguments in order to obtain a smaller framework (called cut-AF) over which state-of-the-art solvers for enumerating the semi-stable extensions are called, as needed to return the extensions of the input AF.

We experimentally evaluated our technique and found that our approach is orders of magnitude faster than the computation over the whole AF.

Keywords: Abstract argumentation · Semi-stable semantics · Enumeration of semi-stable extensions

1 Introduction

Abstract argumentation has emerged as one of the major fields in Artificial Intelligence [10,15,41,44].

The capability to handle incompatible and conflicting information make argumentation applicable to several real-world scenarios as, for example, building arguments by retrieving information from relational databases [20] (within different context applications), such that a query corresponds to determine from a skeptical viewpoint the truth of such arguments.

In particular, abstract argumentation frameworks (AFs) [21] are a simple, yet powerful formalism for modelling disputes between two or more agents. The formal meaning of an AF is given in terms of argumentation semantics, which intuitively tell us the sets of arguments (called *extensions*) that can collectively be used to support a point of view in a discussion.

© Springer Nature Switzerland AG 2019
A. Cuzzocrea et al. (Eds.): FQAS 2019, LNAI 11529, pp. 139–151, 2019.
https://doi.org/10.1007/978-3-030-27629-4_15

Although the idea underlying AFs is very simple and intuitive, most of the argumentation semantics proposed so far suffer from a high computational complexity [22,24,26–28]. In particular, the enumeration problem of AFs (i.e., the problem of computing all extensions according to some semantics) is intractable for several argumentation semantics [23,35], including the *semi-stable* semantics, one of the more recent semantics introduced in [18] to avoid a problem the stable semantics has. In fact, although stable semantics is one of the oldest way to determine which argument can be accepted [30], it is not always true that, given an argumentation framework, a stable extension for it exists. Complexity bounds and evaluation algorithms for AFs have been deeply investigated in the literature, and the International Competition on Computational Models of Argumentation (ICCMA)[1] has been established for promoting research and development of efficient algorithms for computational models of AFs. A challenging computational tasks of ICCMA is EE-sst, that is, enumerating all the extensions of a given AF under the semi-stable semantics.

In this paper, we propose an approach for scaling up the computation of the EE-sst problem.

Contributions. The main contributions of the paper are as follows:

– We propose the concept of *cut-AF* that allows us to compute all the semi-stable extensions by focusing only on a smaller portion of the initial AF. Particularly, the cut-AF is built by removing from the whole AF all those relationships and arguments belonging to the grounded extension, which is a proper set of arguments contained in every semi-stable extensions [18].
– We come up with an efficient algorithm for computing the set of all semi-stable extensions. The algorithm enables the computation of the semi-stable extensions by focusing only on the cut-AFs and using state-of-the-art AF solvers.
– An experimental analysis to show the relevance of our approach is presented. It is carried out by comparing our technique with other state-of-the-art solvers able to solve both the enumeration problem of semi-stable semantics and computation of grounded semantics, and show that our technique is at least 400 times faster than the computation from scratch.

2   Preliminaries

We assume the existence of a set Arg of *arguments*. An *(abstract) argumentation framework* [21] *(AF)* is a pair $\langle A, \Sigma \rangle$, where $A \subseteq Arg$ is a finite set of *arguments*, and $\Sigma \subseteq A \times A$ is a binary relation over A whose elements are called *attacks*. Thus, an AF can be viewed as a directed graph where nodes correspond to arguments and edges correspond to attacks.

Example 1 (Running example). The pair $\mathcal{A}_0 = \langle A_0, \Sigma_0 \rangle$ where $A_0 = \langle \{a, b, c, d, e, f, g, h\}$ and $\Sigma_0 = \{(a, b), (b, c), (c, d), (d, a), (f, e), (g, h), (e, a), (h, a)\} \rangle$ is an AF, and the corresponding graph is shown in Fig. 1(a).

---

[1] http://argumentationcompetition.org.

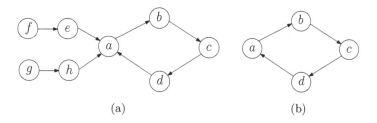

Fig. 1. (a) AF $\mathcal{A}_0$, (b) AF $\mathit{Cut}(\mathcal{A}_0)$.

Given an AF $\langle A, \Sigma \rangle$ and arguments $a, b \in A$, we say that a *attacks* b iff $(a, b) \in \Sigma$, and that a set $S \subseteq A$ attacks b iff there is $a \in S$ attacking b. We use $S^+ = \{b \mid \exists a \in S : (a, b) \in \Sigma\}$ to denote the set of arguments attacked by S. For instance, in our running example, we have that $\{b, d\}^+ = \{c, a\}$.

Moreover, we say that $S \subseteq A$ *defends* a iff $\forall b \in A$ such that b *attacks* a, there is $c \in S$ such that c *attacks* b. In our running example, we have that $\{b, d\}$ defends both b and d, as b defends d from the attack of c, and d defends b from the attack of a.

A set $S \subseteq A$ of arguments is said to be:

(*i*) *conflict-free*, if there are no $a, b \in S$ such that a *attacks* b;
(*ii*) *admissible*, if it is conflict-free and it defends all its arguments.

For instance, in our example, $\{b, d\}$ is conflict-free and thus it is admissible since, as said earlier, it defends all of its arguments.

An argumentation semantics specifies the criteria for identifying a set of arguments that can be considered "reasonable" together, called *extension*.

A *complete extension* (co) is an admissible set that contains all the arguments that it defends. It is easy to see that, the complete extensions of the AF in Fig. 1(a) are $\{f, g\}, \{a, c, f, g\}, \{b, d, f, g\}$.

A complete extension S is said to be:

- *grounded (gr)* iff it is minimal (w.r.t. $\subseteq$);
- *semi-stable (sst)* iff $S \cup S^+$ is maximal (w.r.t. $\subseteq$).

Given an AF $\mathcal{A}$ and a semantics $\mathcal{S} \in \{\text{co}, \text{gr}, \text{sst}\}$, we use $\mathcal{E}_\mathcal{S}(\mathcal{A})$ to denote the set of $\mathcal{S}$-extensions for $\mathcal{A}$, i.e., the set of extensions for $\mathcal{A}$ prescribed by semantics $\mathcal{S}$.

All the above-mentioned semantics admit at least one extension, while the grounded admits exactly one extension [21]. The grounded semantics is called *deterministic* or *unique status* as $|\mathcal{E}_{\text{gr}}(\mathcal{A})| = 1$, whereas the semi-stable semantics is called *nondeterministic* or *multiple status* since $|\mathcal{E}_{\text{sst}}(\mathcal{A})| \geq 1$.

Example 2. Continuing with our example, we have that the grounded extension of $\mathcal{A}_0$ is $E_{gr} = \{f, g\}$ (i.e., $\mathcal{E}_{\text{gr}}(\mathcal{A}_0) = \{\{f, g\}\}$). Moreover, the set of semi-stable extensions is $\mathcal{E}_{\text{sst}}(\mathcal{A}_0) = \{\{a, c, f, g\}, \{b, d, f, g\}\}$.

It is well-known that, for any AF $\mathcal{A}$ and semantics $\mathcal{S} \in \{\text{gr}, \text{sst}\}$, it is the case that $\mathcal{E}_{\mathcal{S}}(\mathcal{A}) \subseteq \mathcal{E}_{co}(\mathcal{A})$, and let E_{gr} and E_{sst} be the grounded and semi-stable extensions, for every $E \in \mathcal{E}_{\text{sst}}(\mathcal{A})$, it holds that $E_{gr} \subseteq E$. Indeed, in the example above, we have that $E_{gr} = \{f, g\} \subseteq E_{sst} = \{a, c, f, g\} \subseteq E_{co} = \{a, c, f, g\}$ and $E_{gr} = \{f, g\} \subseteq E_{sst} = \{b, d, f, g\} \subseteq E_{co} = \{b, d, f, g\}$.

3   Enumerating Semi-stable Extensions

In this section, we provide an approach for efficiently enumerating all the semi-stable extensions of a given AF. Our approach relies on first computing the grounded extension and then using it to define a smaller AF, called cut-AF, to be used as the starting point for enumerating the semi-stable extensions.

Definition 1. Let $\mathcal{A} = \langle A, \Sigma \rangle$ be an AF, and E_{gr} the grounded extension for $\mathcal{A}$. The cut-AF for $\mathcal{A}$ is $Cut(\mathcal{A}) = \langle A_{cut}, \Sigma_{cut} \rangle$ where:

- $A_{cut} = A \setminus (E_{gr} \cup E_{gr}^{+})$;
- $\Sigma_{cut} = \Sigma \setminus \{(a, b) \mid a \in (E_{gr} \cup E_{gr}^{+}) \text{ or } b \in (E_{gr} \cup E_{gr}^{+})\}$.

Thus, the cut-AF is obtained by removing from the initial AF all the arguments belonging to the grounded extension as well as the arguments attacked by some argument in the grounded extension. Consistently with this, all the attacks towards or from the arguments removed are deleted as well.

Example 3. Continuing with our example, since $E_{gr} = \{f, g\}$, we have that $Cut(\mathcal{A}_0) = \langle A_{cut}, \Sigma_{cut} \rangle$ where:

- $A_{cut} = A_0 \setminus (\{f, g\} \cup \{h, e\}) = \{a, b, c, d\}$, and
- $\Sigma_{cut} = \Sigma_0 \setminus \{(f, e), (e, a), (g, h), (h, a), \} = \{(a, b), (b, c), (c, d), (d, a)\}$.

The graph corresponding to the cut-AF is shown in Fig. 1(b).

Observe that computing the cut-AF con be accomplished in polynomial time w.r.t. the size (i.e., number of arguments/attacks) of the initial AF.

The following theorem states that every semi-stable extension E of an AF $\mathcal{A}$ one-to-one corresponds to a semi-stable extension of the AF $Cut(\mathcal{A})$, and we can obtain a semi-stable extension of the whole AF by joining a semi-stable extension of the cut-AF with the grounded extension of $\mathcal{A}$.

Theorem 1. Let $\mathcal{A} = \langle A, \Sigma \rangle$ be an AF, E_{gr} the grounded extension for $\mathcal{A}$, and $Cut(\mathcal{A}) = \langle A_{cut}, \Sigma_{cut} \rangle$ the cut-AF for $\mathcal{A}$. Then, $E \in \mathcal{E}_{sst}(\mathcal{A})$ iff $E = E_{gr} \cup E_{cut}$ where $E_{cut} \in \mathcal{E}_{sst}(Cut(\mathcal{A}))$.

Example 4. Continuing from Example 3, the set of semi-stable extensions of the cut-AF is $\mathcal{E}_{sst}(Cut(\mathcal{A})) = \{\{a, c\}, \{b, d\}\}$. Using the result of Theorem 1, we obtain that $\mathcal{E}_{sst}(\mathcal{A}) = \{\{a, c\} \cup E_{gr}, \{b, d\} \cup E_{gr}\}$, where $E_{gr} = \{f, g\}$. Thus, we obtain the semi-stable extensions $\{f, g, a, c\}$ and $\{f, g, b, d\}$ (c.f. Example 2).

3.1 Algorithm

The pseudo-code of our algorithm for computing the set of semi-stable extensions of an AF is shown in Algorithm 1. It takes as input an AF $\mathcal{A}$, and a percentage value p that is a parameter used for deciding when the computation should be carried out by using the cut-AF or not. In fact, in some cases, such as when the grounded extension of the input AF is empty, the overhead of computing the cut-AF does not pay off because it will correspond to be the whole initial framework, and so, computing the semi-stable extensions over the cut-AF would cost the same as computing the extension on the initial AF plus the overhead of computing the cut-AF.

Thus, we use parameter p to decide when computing or not the cut-AF. In particular, if the grounded extension of the given AF is larger than $p\%$ of the number of arguments in the AF, then the cut-AF is computed; otherwise, the semi-stable extensions are directly computed w.r.t. the whole AF from scratch. Here, computing the grounded extension is polynomial-time (while computing the semi-stable extension is hard), and this suggests that the overhead of computing the grounded extension of the input AF is likely to pay off—in Sect. 4 we thoroughly discuss the results of experiments where different values of p are considered, including $p = 0\%$ which means forcing the algorithm to compute the cut-AF in any case.

Algorithm 1 works as follows. It first computes the grounded extension of the given AF $\mathcal{A}$ (Line 1), and then it checks if the size of the grounded extension is bigger than or equal to $p\%$ of the number of the arguments of $\mathcal{A}$ (Line 2). If this holds, the algorithm proceeds by computing the cut-AF (Line 3). Next, an external AF-solver SST-Solver is called for enumerating the set of extensions of the cut-AF (Line 4), from which the extensions of the whole AF are finally computed at Line 5 using the result of Theorem 1. However, if at Line 2 the size of the grounded extension is smaller than $p\%$ of the number of the arguments of $\mathcal{A}$, then the set of extensions of $\mathcal{A}$ is computed from scratch by calling the external solver SST-Solver with input the whole AF (Line 7). Finally, the set of extensions $\mathcal{E}_{\mathrm{sst}}(\mathcal{A})$ computed by using the cut-AF (Lines 3–5) or not (Line 7) is returned.

Example 5. Continuing with our running example, if $p = 0\%$ then the condition at Line 2 trivially holds since $|E_{gr}| \geq 0$ for every AF. Therefore, the cut-AF $\mathcal{A}_{cut} = Cut(\mathcal{A}) = \langle\{a, b, c, d\}, \{(a, b), (b, c), (c, d), (d, a)\}\rangle$ is computed at Line 3. Next, the set of all semi-stable extensions $\mathcal{E}_{\mathrm{sst}}(\mathcal{A}_{cut}) = \{\{a, c\}, \{b, d\}\}$ of the cut-AF is computed (Line 4), and the set of semi-stable extensions of the whole AF is computed at Line 5 by combining the arguments in the grounded extension with those in the semi-stable extensions of the cut-AF. Therefore, the output of the algorithm is obtained as follows: $\mathcal{E}_{\mathrm{sst}}(\mathcal{A}) = \{\{\{f, g\}\cup\{a, c\}\}, \{\{f, g\}\cup\{b, d\}\}\} = \{\{f, g, a, c\}, \{f, g, b, d\}\}$.

Considering now the case that $p = 5\%$, we have again that $|E_{gr}| \geq p{\cdot}|A|$ (since $2 \geq 0.05 \cdot 8 = 0.4$), and thus the execution of Algorithm 1 is again as above.

Finally, consider the case that $p = 30\%$ for which we have that $|E_{gr}| \not\geq p \cdot |A|$ (since $2 \not\geq 0.3 \cdot 8 = 2.4$). Thus Algorithm 1 directly computes the set

---

Algorithm 1. CutSST($\mathcal{A}, p$)

Input: AF $\mathcal{A} = \langle A, \Sigma \rangle$,
      A percentage value p.
Output: Set $\mathcal{E}_{sst}(\mathcal{A})$ of semi-stable extensions of $\mathcal{A}$.
begin
1: $E_{gr} = $ GR-Solver($\mathcal{A}$)
2: **if** $|E_{gr}| \geq p \cdot |A|$ **then**
3:     $\mathcal{A}_{cut} = Cut(\mathcal{A})$
4:     $\mathcal{E}_{sst}(\mathcal{A}_{cut}) = $ SST-Solver($\mathcal{A}_{cut}$)
5:     $\mathcal{E}_{sst}(\mathcal{A}) = \{E \mid E = E_{gr} \cup E_{cut}, \text{ where } E_{cut} \in \mathcal{E}_{sst}(\mathcal{A}_{cut})\}$
6: **else**
7:     $\mathcal{E}_{sst}(\mathcal{A}) = $ SST-Solver($\mathcal{A}$)
8: **return** $\mathcal{E}_{sst}(\mathcal{A})$

$\mathcal{E}_{sst}(\mathcal{A})$ of semi-stable extensions by calling the solver SST-Solver with input the whole AF (Line 7).

The following theorems states that Algorithm 1 is sound and complete, provided that the external solvers return the correct results.

Theorem 2. *Given an AF $\mathcal{A}$, if GR-Solver and SST-Solver are sound and complete, then Algorithm 1 returns the set $\mathcal{E}_{sst}(\mathcal{A})$ of semi-stable extensions of $\mathcal{A}$.*

4   Implementation and Experiments

We implemented a C++ prototype to evaluate our technique over benchmark AFs taken from the EE-**sst** track of ICCMA'17, which consists in determining all the semi-stable extensions of a given AF. Specifically, we used the AFs in the datasets named $E2$ and $E3$ having more than one semi-stable extension.

Particularly, dataset $E2$ (resp. $E3$) consists of 19 (resp. 41) AFs, and a number of arguments contained in AFs of dataset $E2$ (resp. $E3$) that varies from a minimum value of 61 (resp. 40) to a maximum of $1.2K$ (resp. $1.9K$). Furthermore, the range of the number of attacks in the AFs of dataset $E2$ (resp. $E3$) varies from a minimum of 97 (resp. 72) to a maximum of $10.3K$ (resp. $218K$).

Methodology. For every AF $\mathcal{A}$ in each dataset, we first computed the set of all semi-stable extensions of $\mathcal{A}$ by calling Algorithm 1, where as external grounded solver (GR- Solver) is used CoQuiAAS [36], able to resolve the ICCMA'17 track for computing the grounded extension, as well as for computing all the semi-stable extensions (SST-Solver) we used *ArgSemSAT* [19]. Then, the amount of time required by Algorithm 1 was compared with that required by *ArgSemSAT* to compute all semi-stable extension over the given AF $\mathcal{A}$ from scratch.

All experiments were carried out on an Intel Core i7-3770K CPU 3.5 GHz with 12 GB RAM running Ubuntu 16.04.

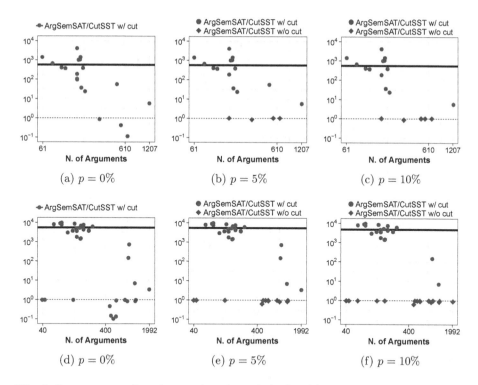

Fig. 2. Improvement (i.e. the running time of *ArgSemSAT* over the running time of Algorithm 1) for $p = 0\%$ (a and d), $p = 5\%$ (b and e), and $p = 10\%$ (c and f), over the datasets $E2$ (first row) and $E3$ (second row). Circle-shaped data points (coloured blue) represent AFs having a grounded extension larger than or equal to $p\%$ of the number of the arguments, and thus the cut-AF is computed by executing Lines 3–5 of Algorithm 1. Diamond-shaped data points (coloured red) represent AFs having a grounded extension smaller than $p\%$ of the number of arguments, and thus the cut-AF is *not* computed (Line 7 of Algorithm 1 is executed). (Color figure online)

Results. Figure 2 reports the average improvement (log scale) obtained by our algorithm over the computation from scratch for the AFs in the datasets $E2$ (first row), and $E3$ (second row), and for $p = 0\%$ (first column), $p = 5\%$ (second column), $p = 10\%$ (third column).

Specifically, given an AF $\mathcal{A}$ and a percentage value p, we measured the improvement as follows:

$$impr(\mathcal{A}, p) = \frac{\text{running time of } \textit{ArgSemSAT} \text{ with input } \mathcal{A}}{\text{running time of } CutSST(\mathcal{A}, p)}$$

In Fig. 2, circle-shaped data points (coloured blue) correspond to AFs having a grounded extension larger than or equal to $p\%$ of the number of the arguments. In these cases, the cut-AF is computed by executing Lines 3–5 of Algorithm 1. Diamond-shaped data points (coloured red) represent AFs having a grounded extension smaller than $p\%$ of the number of the arguments, and in this case, both the cut-AF is *not* computed and Line 7 of Algorithm 1 is executed.

For each plot in Fig. 2, a solid black line representing the average improvement obtained for the considered dataset and value of p is reported. Moreover, to easy readability, we also report a dashed grey line corresponding to average improvement equal to 1. Clearly, an improvement strict less than 1 means that the overall overhead of computing the grounded extension, and eventually the cut-AF, does not pay off. However, when the improvement is close to 1, the overhead is negligible.

From the results in Fig. 2, we can draw the following conclusions:

- Our algorithm significantly outperforms the competitor that computes the semi-stable extensions from scratch. In fact, the average improvement is greater than 410 and 2100 over the datasets $E2$ and $E3$, respectively, meaning that Algorithm 1 is on average at least 410 and 2100 times faster than *ArgSemSAT*.
- The smaller the number of arguments of the AFs, the bigger the (average) improvement obtained. In particular, for the datasets $E2$ and $E3$, this implies that the amount of time required decreases from dozens of minutes (computation from scratch) to a few seconds (our algorithm).
- The average improvement remains high for $p = 0\%$, that is, when computing both the grounded extension and the cut-AF irrespectively of the size of the grounded extension. However, the number of AFs for which the improvement is too lower than 1 decreases if $p > 0\%$. In particular, for the datasets $E2$ and $E3$, using $p = 5\%$ is enough for avoiding all the cases for which the improvement is significantly lower than 1. Thus, using p greater than zero allows us to reduce the overhead due to the computation of the grounded extension plus the cut-AF.
- Although increasing the value of p avoids cases where our approach may work worse than the computation from scratch, using too high values of p deteriorates performances on average because the cut-AF is not built even when it would be helpful. In fact, for the datasets $E2$ and $E3$, using $p = 10\%$ entails that the cut-AF is not built in vain for the AFs whose improvements are shown as blue data points in Fig. 2 for $p = 5\%$ and become colored red when passing to $p = 10\%$ (since increasing p entails that cut-AF is no longer computed).
- All in all, the best trade-off between paying the cost of computing the grounded extension along with the cut-AF and risking to have the overhead of the computation of the cut-AF seems to be choosing p greater than zero but no more than 10%.

5   Related Work

Overviews of key concepts in argumentation theory and of formal models of argumentation in the field of Artificial Intelligence can be found in [9,15,16,44].

Further discussion regarding uses of computational argumentation as an Agreement Technology can be found in [42]. Several computational problems of AFs have been studied such as skeptical and credulous reasoning [5], existence of a non-empty extension, and verifying if a set of arguments is an extension under different argumentation semantics [22,24–26]. The complexity of the problem of computing all extensions according to some semantics for AFs has been recently investigated in [35], where it was shown that the enumeration problem is intractable under the semi-stable semantics, and, in particular, it is not in *OutputP* ("output-polynomial time", also known as *TotalP* "total polynomial time" [34]) even for bipartite AFs.

An approach to deal with the problem of enumerating the semi-stable extensions is proposed in [17], where a new algorithm for computing semi-stable semantics using dynamic programming on tree decompositions that runs in linear time on AFs of bounded treewidth is presented. However, this kind of approaches provide advantages only in case of bounded treewidth, noting that that algorithm should not be seen as general solvers that outperform standard techniques on average. This is not case of our technique which performances are not related to the size of treewidth.

Approaches for dividing AFs into subgraphs have been explored also in the context of dynamic AFs—AFs which are updated by adding/removing (set of) attacks/arguments—for which the set of extensions evolves. The division-based method, proposed by [37] and then refined by [12], divides the updated framework into two parts: *affected* and *unaffected*, where only the status of affected arguments is recomputed after updates. Using the results in [37,39] investigated the efficient evaluation of the justification status of a subset of arguments in an AF (instead of the whole set of arguments), and proposed an approach based on answer-set programming for *local* computation. In [38], an AF is decomposed into a set of strongly connected components, yielding sub-AFs located in layers, which are then used for incrementally computing the semantics of the given AF by proceeding layer by layer. Focusing on unique-status semantics, the concept of *influenced set* was introduced in [31–33] to further restrict the set of affected arguments defined in [37], while [2] provided an incremental technique for computing *some* extension of dynamic AFs under multiple-extensions semantics. [13] proposed an approach exploiting the concept of *splitting* of logic programs to deal with dynamic argumentation. [14] investigated whether and how it is possible to modify a given AF so that a desired set of arguments becomes an extension, whereas [43] studied equivalence between two AFs when further information (another AF) is added to both AFs.

Dung's abstract argumentation framework has been extended along several dimensions (e.g. [11,40,45]), and techniques for the efficient computation in dynamic extended AFs were proposed [1,3,4] that, similarly to [32], rely on identifying portions of the AFs that change after performing updates. Finally, the approaches recently proposed in [7,8] focused on the efficient computation of the status of *structured* arguments in dynamic DeLP-programs [29].

The above-cited approaches are related to ours because of the idea of reducing the computation effort by trying to consider a smaller portion of the input AF. However, our technique relies on the novel idea of using cut-AFs through the grounded extension and enabling the modular use of external AF-solvers to compute the set of the semi-stable extensions.

6   Conclusion and Future Work

We introduced a technique for efficiently enumerating the semi-stable extensions of abstract argumentation frameworks. Our approach is modular with respect to the solvers used for computing the grounded extensions, as well as the solver used for the enumeration of semi-stable extensions on the cut-AF—any solver addressing one of these tasks could be plugged-in and exploited for addressing the enumeration problem under the semi-stable semantics. A similar approach is proposed in [6] for enumerating the set of preferred extensions.

We have experimentally investigated the behavior of our technique, and analyzed the conditions under which building the cut-AF is convenient for computing the semi-stable extensions. It turned out that it is worth paying the cost of building the cut-AF after looking at the size of the grounded extension as the computation of the semi-stable extensions over the cut-AF yields significant improvements over the computation from scratch.

Future work will be devoted to extending our technique to the enumeration problem in the presence of other argumentation semantics, such as the *stable* semantics [21]. In fact, a stable extension is a complete extension which attacks all the arguments outside the extension, and the set of stable extensions are a subset of the set of semi-stable extensions; thus, similarly to the semi-stable semantics, the grounded extension is contained in every stable extension. For instance, in our running example the set of the stable extensions coincides with that of the semi-stable extensions, both considering the cut-AF and the whole initial one. However, extending the technique to deal with the stable semantics requires to face up with the fact that a stable extension may not exists for an AF, and checking this is computationally hard [24].

References

1. Alfano, G., Greco, S., Parisi, F.: Computing stable and preferred extensions of dynamic bipolar argumentation frameworks. In: Proceedings of the 1st Workshop on Advances in Argumentation in AI Co-located with AI*IA, pp. 28–42 (2017)
2. Alfano, G., Greco, S., Parisi, F.: Efficient computation of extensions for dynamic abstract argumentation frameworks: an incremental approach. In: Proceedings of IJCAI, pp. 49–55 (2017)
3. Alfano, G., Greco, S., Parisi, F.: Computing extensions of dynamic abstract argumentation frameworks with second-order attacks. In: Proceedings of IDEAS, pp. 183–192 (2018)

4. Alfano, G., Greco, S., Parisi, F.: A meta-argumentation approach for the efficient computation of stable and preferred extensions in dynamic bipolar argumentation frameworks. Intelligenza Artificiale **12**(2), 193–211 (2018)
5. Alfano, G., Greco, S., Parisi, F.: An efficient algorithm for skeptical preferred acceptance in dynamic argumentation frameworks. In: Proceedings of IJCAI (2019, to appear)
6. Alfano, G., Greco, S., Parisi, F.: On scaling the enumeration of the preferred extensions of abstract argumentation frameworks. In: Proceedings of ACM/SIGAPP SAC, pp. 1147–1153 (2019)
7. Alfano, G., Greco, S., Parisi, F., Simari, G.I., Simari, G.R.: An incremental approach to structured argumentation over dynamic knowledge bases. In: Proceeding of KR, pp. 78–87 (2018)
8. Alfano, G., Greco, S., Parisi, F., Simari, G.I., Simari, G.R.: Incremental computation of warranted arguments in dynamic defeasible argumentation: the rule addition case. In: Proceedings of ACM/SIGAPP SAC, pp. 911–917 (2018)
9. Atkinson, K., et al.: Towards artificial argumentation. Artif. Intell. Mag. **38**(3), 25–36 (2017)
10. Baroni, P., Caminada, M., Giacomin, M.: An introduction to argumentation semantics. Knowl. Eng. Rev. **26**(4), 365–410 (2011)
11. Baroni, P., Cerutti, F., Giacomin, M., Guida, G.: Encompassing attacks to attacks in abstract argumentation frameworks. In: Sossai, C., Chemello, G. (eds.) ECSQARU 2009. LNCS, vol. 5590, pp. 83–94. Springer, Heidelberg (2009). https://doi.org/10.1007/978-3-642-02906-6_9
12. Baroni, P., Giacomin, M., Liao, B.: On topology-related properties of abstract argumentation semantics. A correction and extension to dynamics of argumentation systems: a division-based method. Artif. Intell. **212**, 104–115 (2014)
13. Baumann, R.: Splitting an Argumentation Framework. In: Delgrande, J.P., Faber, W. (eds.) LPNMR 2011. LNCS, vol. 6645, pp. 40–53. Springer, Heidelberg (2011). https://doi.org/10.1007/978-3-642-20895-9_6
14. Baumann, R., Brewka, G.: Expanding argumentation frameworks: enforcing and monotonicity results. In: Proceedings of COMMA, pp. 75–86 (2010)
15. Bench-Capon, T.J.M., Dunne, P.E.: Argumentation in artificial intelligence. Artif. Intell. **171**(10–15), 619–641 (2007)
16. Besnard, P., Hunter, A.: Elements of Argumentation. MIT Press, Cambridge (2008)
17. Bliem, B., Hecher, M., Woltran, S.: On efficiently enumerating semi-stable extensions via dynamic programming on tree decompositions. In: Proceedings of COMMA, pp. 107–118 (2016)
18. Caminada, M.: Semi-stable semantics. In: Proceedings of COMMA, pp. 121–130 (2006)
19. Cerutti, F., Giacomin, M., Vallati, M.: ArgSemSAT: solving argumentation problems using SAT. In: Proceedings of COMMA, pp. 455–456 (2014)
20. Deagustini, C.A.D., Dalibón, S.E.F., Gottifredi, S., Falappa, M.A., Chesñevar, C.I., Simari, G.R.: Defeasible argumentation over relational databases. Argument Comput. **8**(1), 35–59 (2017)
21. Dung, P.M.: On the acceptability of arguments and its fundamental role in nonmonotonic reasoning, logic programming and n-person games. Artif. Intell. **77**(2), 321–358 (1995)
22. Dunne, P.E.: The computational complexity of ideal semantics. Artif. Intell. **173**(18), 1559–1591 (2009)

23. Dunne, P.E., Caminada, M.: Computational complexity of semi-stable semantics in abstract argumentation frameworks. In: Hölldobler, S., Lutz, C., Wansing, H. (eds.) JELIA 2008. LNCS, vol. 5293, pp. 153–165. Springer, Heidelberg (2008). https://doi.org/10.1007/978-3-540-87803-2_14

24. Dunne, P.E., Wooldridge, M.: Complexity of abstract argumentation. In: Simari, G., Rahwan, I. (eds.) Argumentation in Artificial Intelligence, pp. 85–104. Springer, Boston (2009). https://doi.org/10.1007/978-0-387-98197-0_5

25. Dvořák, W., Pichler, R., Woltran, S.: Towards fixed-parameter tractable algorithms for argumentation. In: Proceedings of KR (2010)

26. Dvořák, W., Woltran, S.: Complexity of semi-stable and stage semantics in argumentation frameworks. Inf. Process. Lett. **110**(11), 425–430 (2010)

27. Fazzinga, B., Flesca, S., Parisi, F.: On the complexity of probabilistic abstract argumentation frameworks. ACM Trans. Comput. Log. **16**(3), 22 (2015)

28. Fazzinga, B., Flesca, S., Parisi, F.: On efficiently estimating the probability of extensions in abstract argumentation frameworks. IJAR **69**, 106–132 (2016)

29. García, A.J., Simari, G.R.: Defeasible logic programming: an argumentative approach. Theory Pract. Log. Program. (TPLP) **4**(1–2), 95–138 (2004)

30. Gelfond, M., Lifschitz, V.: The stable model semantics for logic programming. In: Logic Programming, vol. 2, pp. 1070–1080 (1988)

31. Greco, S., Parisi, F.: Efficient computation of deterministic extensions for dynamic abstract argumentation frameworks. In: Proceedings of ECAI, pp. 1668–1669 (2016)

32. Greco, S., Parisi, F.: Incremental computation of deterministic extensions for dynamic argumentation frameworks. In: Michael, L., Kakas, A. (eds.) JELIA 2016. LNCS, vol. 10021, pp. 288–304. Springer, Cham (2016). https://doi.org/10.1007/978-3-319-48758-8_19

33. Greco, S., Parisi, F.: Incremental computation of grounded semantics for dynamic abstract argumentation frameworks. In: Aydoğan, R., Baarslag, T., Gerding, E., Jonker, C.M., Julian, V., Sanchez-Anguix, V. (eds.) COREDEMA 2016. LNCS, vol. 10238, pp. 66–81. Springer, Cham (2017). https://doi.org/10.1007/978-3-319-57285-7_5

34. Johnson, D.S., Papadimitriou, C.H., Yannakakis, M.: On generating all maximal independent sets. Inf. Process. Lett. **27**(3), 119–123 (1988)

35. Kröll, M., Pichler, R., Woltran, S.: On the complexity of enumerating the extensions of abstract argumentation frameworks. In: Proceedings of IJCAI, pp. 1145–1152 (2017)

36. Lagniez, J., Lonca, E., Mailly, J.: CoQuiAAS: a constraint-based quick abstract argumentation solver. In: Proceeding of IEEE International Conference on Tools with Artificial Intelligence (ICTAI), pp. 928–935 (2015)

37. Liao, B.S., Jin, L., Koons, R.C.: Dynamics of argumentation systems: a division-based method. Artif. Intell. **175**(11), 1790–1814 (2011)

38. Liao, B.: Toward incremental computation of argumentation semantics: a decomposition-based approach. Ann. Math. Artif. Intell. **67**(3–4), 319–358 (2013)

39. Liao, B., Huang, H.: Partial semantics of argumentation: basic properties and empirical results. J. Log. Comput. **23**(3), 541–562 (2013)

40. Modgil, S.: Reasoning about preferences in argumentation frameworks. Artif. Intell. **173**(9–10), 901–934 (2009)

41. Modgil, S., Prakken, H.: Revisiting preferences and argumentation. In: Proceedings of IJCAI, pp. 1021–1026 (2011)

42. Modgil, S., et al.: The added value of argumentation: examples and challenges. In: Ossowski, S. (ed.) Agreement Technologies. LGTS, vol. 8, pp. 357–404. Springer, New York (2013). https://doi.org/10.1007/978-94-007-5583-3_21
43. Oikarinen, E., Woltran, S.: Characterizing strong equivalence for argumentation frameworks. Artif. Intell. **175**(14–15), 1985–2009 (2011)
44. Rahwan, I., Simari, G.R.: Argumentation in Artificial Intelligence, 1st edn. Springer, Heidelberg (2009). https://doi.org/10.1007/978-0-387-98197-0
45. Villata, S., Boella, G., Gabbay, D.M., van der Torre, L.W.N.: Modelling defeasible and prioritized support in bipolar argumentation. Ann. Math. Artif. Intell. **66**(1–4), 163–197 (2012)

Data Mining and Knowledge Discovery

Using Word Embeddings and Deep Learning for Supervised Topic Detection in Social Networks

Karel Gutiérrez-Batista$^{(\boxtimes)}$ ⓘ, Jesús R. Campaña ⓘ, Maria-Amparo Vila ⓘ, and Maria J. Martin-Bautista ⓘ

Department of Computer Science and Artificial Intelligence, ETSIIT, University of Granada, 18071 Granada, Spain
{karel,jesuscg,vila,mbautis}@decsai.ugr.es

Abstract. In this paper we show how word embeddings can be used to evaluate semantically the topic detection process in social networks. We propose to create and train a word embeddings with word2vec model to be used for text classification process. Then when the documents are classified, we use a pre-trained word embeddings and two similarity measures for semantic evaluation of the classification process. In particular, we perform experiments with two datasets of Twitter, using both bag-of-words with conventional classification algorithms and word embeddings with deep learning-based classification algorithms. Finally, we perform a benchmark and make some inferences about results.

Keywords: Topic detection · Word embeddings · Deep learning

1 Introduction

Topic detection allows organizing or grouping a collection of documents by topics. The advantage of having texts grouped by theme is that it facilitates many tasks related to Natural Language Processing (NLP) such as sentiment analysis, recommender systems, etc. There are many techniques used in the topic detection process, both from the supervised point of view (Support Vector Machines (SVM) [1], Naive Bayes [2], deep learning-based classification algorithms, etc.) and unsupervised (Latent Dirichlet Allocation (LDA) [3], Non Negative Matrix Factorization (NMF) [4], Hierarchical Clustering Algorithm, etc.).

One of the challenges to take into account during the topic detection process is the representation of the documents. Traditionally, documents are represented as bag-of-words. The main disadvantage of this approach, is that each text is represented by a vector of fixed length, where vector's dimension is equal to the size of the vocabulary, resulting in a sparse and high-dimensional document representation.

Nowadays, it is an incontestable fact that the use of deep learning techniques in tasks related to NLP such as entity recognition [5], part-of-speech tagging [6],

© Springer Nature Switzerland AG 2019
A. Cuzzocrea et al. (Eds.): FQAS 2019, LNAI 11529, pp. 155–165, 2019.
https://doi.org/10.1007/978-3-030-27629-4_16

sentiment analysis [7], text classification [8], etc., allows to improve the baseline results. Through the use of word embeddings, a word can be represented by a low-dimensional vector, which allows to capture syntactic and semantic characteristics of the language from a collection of documents. The main idea behind word embeddings, is that words that appear in the same context, are represented by vectors that are sufficiently close.

In literature we can find several proposals to address the problem of document categorization. The use of classification algorithms for text classification allows to obtain good results, these results can be improved with the use of word embeddings and deep learning-based algorithms. At this point, it is of great interest to check whether the results of the classification process are correct from the semantic point of view.

This paper presents a proposal to semantically evaluate the classification of social network texts with supervised techniques. For a better understanding of our proposal, we have divided our work into three main tasks: (1) to create a word embeddings from a set of documents using the word2vec model [9], (2) once the word embeddings have been created and trained, supervised techniques to classify the documents have been used and (3) finally, we use a pre-trained word embeddings to semantically evaluate the main topics obtained from the classification process. To evaluate our proposal, we have selected two datasets from Twitter.

The rest of the paper is structured as follows: In Sect. 2, a review of related works for topic detection process is presented. Section 3 describes the techniques and methods used in our proposal for semantic evaluation of topics detection. Section 4 presents and discusses the experimental results. Finally, in Sect. 5 the conclusions derived from the analysis are presented.

2   Related Work

Topic modeling has been addressed from unsupervised and supervised point of view. Within the unsupervised algorithms the most used in literature are LDA and Hierarchical Clustering Algorithms. While from the supervised point of view, the most widely used are Naive Bayes, SVM and deep learning-based algorithms. For a better understanding, first we will see a set of works related to unsupervised topic detection, and lastly, we will present the works that address topic detection through supervised techniques.

An example of the use of hierarchical clustering algorithms for topic detection can be found in [10], where authors present a multilingual and ontology-based approach for the automatic topic detection in textual data. On the other hand, there are several papers presenting a combination of certain topic detection model like LDA and its extensions, that take advantage of word embeddings [11–13].

Naive Bayes and SVM are supervised classification algorithms that are widely used for text classification. In [14,15], authors propose different models based in Naive Bayes Algorithm. Similarly, techniques based in SVM are presented in

[16–18] to address text classification problem. In both cases, the obtained results outperform the state-of-the-art results at that moment.

In the same way in [8,19] we can find the use of deep learning-based classification algorithms leveraging word embeddings for NLP tasks. Specifically, in [8] authors take advantage of word order for text classification with Convolutional Neural Networks. Meanwhile, authors in [19] use word embeddings for sentiment analysis.

3   Techniques and Methods

In this section, we discuss the different techniques and methods used to semantically evaluate the topics discovered during the classification process.

3.1   Word Embeddings

Word Embeddings are the texts converted into numerical representations and there may be different numerical representations of the same text. Word embeddings try to map a word to a vector using a dictionary.

For example in the sentence *"Orange is a fruit"*, we can define a dictionary with the list of all unique words in the sentence [*'Orange', 'is', 'a', 'fruit'*]. One of the different representations of a word in a vector may be a one-hot encoded vector where 1 stands for the position where the word is present and 0 everywhere else. The vector representation of *'fruit'* in this format is [0,0,0,1]. There are many pre-trained word embeddings (Google News, Wikipedia, Twitter, among others) using different models (word2vec [9], GloVe [20], fastText [21], etc.

Word2vec is a particularly computationally-efficient predictive model for learning word embeddings from raw text. It comes in two flavors, the Continuous Bag-of-Words model (CBOW) and the Skip-Gram model [9]. From algorithmic point of view, both models are similar, except that CBOW predicts target words from source context words, while the skip-gram performs the inverse process and is able to predict source context-words from the target words.

Word2vec's applications extend beyond parsing sentences. For example word2vec can be applied in the following scenarios: (1) sentiment analysis, (2) text classification, (3) word sense desambiguation (WSD) and (4) named entity recognition (NER), etc.

Glove is an unsupervised learning algorithm for obtaining vector representations for words. Training is performed on aggregated global word-word co-occurrence statistics from a corpus, and the resulting representations showcase interesting linear substructures of the word vector space [20]. Like in the word2vec model, the resulting word vectors representation try to encapsulate the semantic associated.

3.2 Deep Learning Techniques for Texts Classification

For over a decade, machine-learning approaches such as Naive Bayes or SVM led tasks related to NLP. Models based on neural networks have been used mostly to solve problems related to image recognition. Over last few years, neural networks models have become in a powerful tool in NLP tasks.

For this reason, in the present work we have selected a set of algorithms based on neural network models for text classification. We will use the following algorithms: Simple Neural Networks, Long Short-Term Memory (LSTM) [22], Gated Recurrent Unit (GRU) [23] and Convolutional Neural Networks (CNN) [24]. The use of this models yield the state-of-the-art results in process related to NLP.

3.3 Semantic Topic Evaluation Using Word Embeddings

As we have previously mentioned, classification algorithms provide excellent results in tasks related to NLP. But we want to verify whether the classification results make sense from the semantic point of view. In other words, it is convenient to verify that documents classified in the same class share the same topics.

In Fig. 1 our proposal to semantically evaluate the classification process is shown. Below, we have brief details of each of the stages that make up our approach. It should be noted that the stage where the word embeddings are created and the stage to evaluate the classification results from the semantic point of view are explained in more detail in the following sections.

First of all, the documents are syntactically preprocessed. In this stage stop words and frequently used terms are eliminated, because they do not provide relevant information for text classification process. In addition, spelling errors are corrected.

Once the texts have been preprocessed syntactically, they can be used directly in conventional classification algorithms or create a word embeddings from the documents to be analyzed and then use the embeddings in deep learning algorithms. Finally, the semantic associated with the topic or topics found in the classification process is evaluated.

Learning Word Embeddings from Textual Data. In this work to create the word embeddings, we have used the word2vec model. The parameters used to construct the word embeddings are the following:

- **Architecture** Skip-Gram,
- **Number of dimensions** 100, and
- **Window size** 10.

Semantic Topic Evaluation Using Pre-trained Word Embeddings. As mentioned in Sect. 3.1, there are many pre-trained word embeddings, which

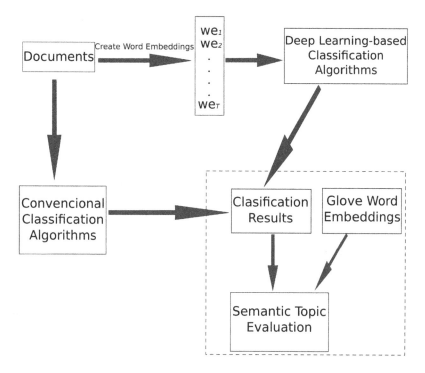

Fig. 1. Proposal for semantic topic evaluation using word embeddings

among other aims, are meant to save data scientists time. Suppose we work with data that does not correspond to any specific domain, a good choice would be to select one of the pre-trained models obtained from generic documents such as Google News, Wikipedia or Twitter.

In our case, we decided to use the Twitter model created by the GloVe architecture, with 100 dimensions and from 27B corpus. This model has been chosen because the texts used for experimentation belong to this social network.

The semantic evaluation process consists in:

1. once the documents have been classified, for each target class the most relevant terms in the documents are obtained (in our case the 10 most relevant according to the frequency),
2. the terms obtained in the previous step, are transformed by their representation in the pre-trained word embeddings of Twitter,
3. making use of the pre-trained word embeddings of Twitter, we get the 10 most similar terms of the labels representing the classes (e.g for class *"politics"* the most similar terms according the Twitter pre-trained word embeddings are *'political'*, *'government'*, *'policy'*, *'democracy'*, *'politicians'*, *'culture'*, *'education'*, *'society'*, *'journalism'* and *'congress'*),
4. then, the similarity (using (1) or (2)) is determined for each class between the most relevant terms of the documents classified in a given class and the

most similar terms to the label representing that class (according to the word embeddings used)

5. finally, the classification average is obtained.

$$cos(d_1, d_2) = \frac{\sum d_1 \cdot d_2}{\sqrt{\sum d_1^2}\sqrt{\sum d_2^2}} \tag{1}$$

$$distance\_matrix\_sum(d_1, d_2) = \frac{1}{n^2}\sum_i^n\sum_j^n cos(w_{1i}, w_{2j}) \tag{2}$$

Where w_{1i} and w_{2j} are word representations in a low-dimensional space (word embeddings) and d_1 and d_2 are a set of word embeddings of the same dimension ($d_1 = \{w_{1_1}, w_{1_2}, ..., w_{1_n}\}$, $d_2 = \{w_{2_1}, w_{2_2}, ..., w_{2_n}\}$ and $dim(d_1) = dim(d_2)$).

4 Experiments

In this section, we have performed a set of experiments to illustrate the objective of our approach. First we describe the datasets that have been used, then explain in detail the experimentation carried out. Finally, we analyze the results obtained.

4.1 Dataset

Two datasets with Twitter documents have been used, one in English and the other in Spanish. All documents were crawled using the Twitter Search API. Were selected tweets related to topics about *"politics"*, *"contamination"* and *"airline"* for tweets in English, while for tweets in Spanish were selected tweets related to *"política"*, *"Deporte"* and *"tecnología"*. In Table 1 the main characteristics of each dataset are exposed.

Table 1. Datasets description

Dataset	Tweets	Classes	Vocabulary size	Language
Dataset 1	3055	3	8269	English
Dataset 2	5060	3	17197	Spanish

4.2 Evaluation

The details of the experimentation are exposed below.

Dataset splitting. The used datasets have been split into training and test. The training dataset contains 80% of the data, while the test dataset contains 20%.

Algorithms. Six classification algorithms have been selected. Two of them are classical classification algorithms (Naive Bayes and SVM) and the other ones are deep learning-based classification algorithms NN, LSTM, GRU and CNN. Naive Bayes and SVM have been included since they have great performance for text classification.

Hyperparameters. The hyperparameters used for each algorithm are shown in Table 2.

Word representation. Two forms of word representation have been used. In addition to use the word embeddings with deep learning-based algorithms, we will also take into account the representation of the words according to the *tf-idf* measure and we will use it in Naive Bayes, SVM and for a simple neural network.

Measures. As we are addressing the topic detection process from the point of view of a supervised problem, the accuracy measure has been used. In addition, as we wish to evaluate the semantic correspondence of the classification process, we have also used the measures proposed in the Sect. 3.3 ((1) and (2)).

Table 2. Hyperparameters

Algotithm	Optimizer	Layers	Loss function	Epochs	Trainable params
NN (tf-idf)	Adam	3	Categorical crossentropy	50	2569653
NN (WE)	Adam	5	Categorical crossentropy	50	25503
LSTM (WE)	Adam	5	Categorical crossentropy	50	173703
GRU (WE)	Adam	5	Categorical crossentropy	50	136053
CNN (WE)	Adam	7	Categorical crossentropy	50	45703

4.3   Results and Discussion

In Table 3 the accuracy measure related to the classification process for each dataset is shown. As we can appreciate, for Dataset 1 the best results are obtained with LSTM and GRU, while for Dataset 2 the algorithm that provides the best result is simple NN with the *tf-idf* measure. It should be noted that for both datasets, the algorithm with the worst performance is SVM.

In this case, we can see that the accuracy results obtained are really good if we take into account that these are real texts from Twitter. In addition, deep learning-based algorithms outperform the standard machine learning approach for Dataset 1, but they do not improve for Dataset 2. This is due to the fact that these algorithms obtain better performance when a large volume of data is available. This is a challenge when dealing with the problem of classification of texts with supervised techniques, since it is very difficult to find a corpus labeled by topics.

Table 3. Measures of classification process

Algotithm	Accuracy (Dataset 1)	Accuracy (Dataset 2)
Naive Bayes	98,82	80,13
SVM	38,91	43,82
NN (TF-IDF)	98,80	**83,79**
NN (WE)	99,02	78,45
LSTM (WE)	**99,61**	81,13
GRU (WE)	**99,61**	78,84
CNN (WE)	99,41	78,66

Table 4. Semantic measures of classification process

Algotithm	Cosine dataset 1	Cosine dataset 2	Distance matrix sum dataset 1	Distance matrix sum dataset 2
Naive Bayes	0,54	0,63	0,27	0,34
SVM	0,13	0,19	0,07	0,09
NN (TF-IDF)	0,56	**0,68**	**0,29**	**0,36**
NN (WE)	**0,57**	0,67	**0,29**	0,34
LSTM (WE)	0,53	**0,68**	0,28	0,34
GRU (WE)	0,53	0,65	0,28	0,34
CNN (WE)	0,55	0,67	**0,29**	0,34

As the main goal of our work is to evaluate the classification from the semantic point of view, in Table 4 the semantic measures (1) and (2) related to the classification process for each dataset are shown. In this case, the best results are obtained for deep learning-based algorithms for both datasets. As the previous discussion, we can consider that results are good, considering that we are working with real texts from Twitter.

Lastly, in Table 5, we show the detected topics for each algorithm. Although the detected topics do not match syntactically with the topics of the class labels, they have a strong semantic relationship. In addition, it should be mentioned that the detected topics by the algorithms are more specific, so it would be interesting to use a measure based on the use of an ontology such as Wikipedia to obtain a better understanding of the topics.

Table 5. Topics for Dataset 1

Topic/Algorithm	WE Topics	Naive Bayes	SVM	NN (TF-IDF)	NN (WE)	LSTM (WE)	GRU (WE)	CNN (WE)
Politic	political	debate		debate	debate	debate	debate	debate
	government	gop		gop	gop	gop	gop	gop
	policy	trump		trump	trump	trump	trump	trump
	democracy	last		donald	real	real	real	real
	politicians	kelly		last	donald	donald	donald	donald
	culture	donald		real	kelly	kelly	kelly	last
	education	night		kelly	last	last	last	kelly
	society	megyn		megyn	night	night	night	night
	journalism	real		night	megyn	megyn	megyn	megyn
	congress	foxnews		like	women	like	like	like
Contamination	contaminated	link		link	link	link	link	link
	groundwater	climate		climate	climate	change	change	climate
	listeria	change		change	change	climate	climate	change
	aspartame	global		global	global	global	global	global
	pollution	warming		warming	warming	warming	warming	warming
	outbreak	allergies		report	fight	allergies	allergies	fight
	displacement	fight		fight	allergies	report	report	allergies
	fukushima	environmental		may	report	fight	fight	report
	leakage	carbon		green	carbon	help	help	carbon
	spillage	ocean		volcanic	air	air	air	air
Arline	airlines	virgin	debate	united	virgin	virgin	virgin	virgin
	qantas	america	gop	virgin	united	united	united	united
	airways	united	america	america	america	america	america	america
	easyjet	flight	virgin	flight	flight	flight	flight	flight
	flights	help	link	thanks	need	need	need	need
	aircraft	time	united	customer	help	help	help	help
	passengers	thanks	change	website	flights	thanks	thanks	thanks
	flight	need	climate	service	thanks	bag	bag	bag
	plane	one	global	cancelled	bag	flights	flights	flights
	transportation	cancelled	warming	airline	customer	customer	customer	customer

5   Conclusions

In this paper, a proposal for semantic evaluation of classification algorithms for text classification is presented. For such purpose, we used standard machine learning approach and deep learning-based algorithm with *tf-idf* measure and word embeddings as word representation. We evaluated the results using two semantic measures based on pre-trained word embeddings (cosine and sum of matrix distance).

The idea presented in this paper represents a starting point, as there are several challenges related to our approach to be faced in the future. For example, it would be interesting to extend our proposal to textual data of different sources. Also, we should consider the use of an external knowledge base to assess the semantic relationship between the true topics and the predicted topics.

Acknowledgements. This research paper is part of the COPKIT project, which has received funding from the European Union's Horizon 2020 research and innovation programme under grant agreement No. 786687.

References

1. Cortes, C., Vapnik, V.: Support-vector networks. Mach. Learn. **20**(3), 273–297 (1995)
2. Friedman, N., Geiger, D., Goldszmidt, M.: Bayesian network classifiers. Mach. Learn. **29**(2–3), 131–163 (1997)
3. Blei, D.M., Ng, A.Y., Jordan, M.I.: Latent dirichlet allocation. J. Mach. Learn. Res. **3**, 993–1022 (2003)
4. Lee, D.D., Seung, H.S.: Learning the parts of objects by non-negative matrix factorization. Nature **401**(6755), 788 (1999)
5. Melamud, O., McClosky, D., Patwardhan, S., Bansal, M.: The role of context types and dimensionality in learning word embeddings. In: HLT-NAACL (2016)
6. Plank, B., Søgaard, A., Goldberg, Y.: Multilingual part-of-speech tagging with bidirectional long short-term memory models and auxiliary loss. In: Proceedings of the 54th Annual Meeting of the Association for Computational Linguistics (Volume 2: Short Papers), pp. 412–418. Association for Computational Linguistics (2016)
7. Ruder, S., Ghaffari, P., Breslin, J.G.: A hierarchical model of reviews for aspect-based sentiment analysis. In: Proceedings of the 2016 Conference on Empirical Methods in Natural Language Processing, Austin, Texas, pp. 999–1005. Association for Computational Linguistics, November 2016
8. Johnson, R., Zhang, T.: Effective use of word order for text categorization with convolutional neural networks. In: NAACL HLT 2015, The 2015 Conference of the North American Chapter of the Association for Computational Linguistics: Human Language Technologies, Denver, Colorado, USA, May 31 - June 5 2015, pp. 103–112 (2015)
9. Mikolov, T., Chen, K., Corrado, G., Dean, J.: Efficient estimation of word representations in vector space. In: 1st International Conference on Learning Representations, ICLR 2013, Scottsdale, Arizona, USA, 2–4 May 2013, Workshop Track Proceedings (2013)

10. Gutiérrez-Batista, K., Campaña, J.R., Vila, M.A., Martin-Bautista, M.J.: An ontology-based framework for automatic topic detection in multilingual environments. Int. J. Intell. Syst. **33**(7), 1459–1475 (2018)
11. Esposito, F., Corazza, A., Cutugno, F.: Topic modelling with word embeddings, December 2016
12. Xun, G., Gopalakrishnan, V., Ma, F., Li, Y., Gao, J., Zhang, A.: Topic discovery for short texts using word embeddings. In: 2016 IEEE 16th International Conference on Data Mining (ICDM), pp. 1299–1304, December 2016)
13. Li, C., Wang, H., Zhang, Z., Sun, A., Ma, Z.: Topic modeling for short texts with auxiliary word embeddings. In: Proceedings of the 39th International ACM SIGIR Conference on Research and Development in Information Retrieval, SIGIR 2016, pp. 165–174. ACM, New York (2016)
14. Kim, S.B., Han, K.S., Rim, H.C., Myaeng, S.H.: Some effective techniques for naive bayes text classification. IEEE Trans. Knowl. Data Eng. **18**(11), 1457–1466 (2006)
15. McCallum, A., Nigam, K.: A comparison of event models for naive Bayes text classification. In: Learning for Text Categorization: Papers from the 1998 AAAI Workshop, pp. 41–48 (1998)
16. Forman, G.: BNS feature scaling: an improved representation over TF-IDF for SVM text classification. In: Proceedings of the 17th ACM Conference on Information and Knowledge Management, CIKM 2008, pp. 263–270. ACM, New York (2008)
17. Fan, R.E., Chang, K.W., Hsieh, C.J., Wang, X.R., Lin, C.J.: LIBLINEAR: a library for large linear classification. J. Mach. Learn. Res. **9**, 1871–1874 (2008)
18. Sun, A., Lim, E.P., Liu, Y.: On strategies for imbalanced text classification using SVM: a comparative study. Decis. Support Syst. **48**(1), 191–201 (2009). Information product markets
19. Rudkowsky, E., Haselmayer, M., Wastian, M., Jenny, M., Emrich, Å., Sedlmair, M.: More than bags of words: Sentiment analysis with word embeddings. Commun. Methods Measures **12**, 140–157 (2018)
20. Pennington, J., Socher, R., Manning, C.D.: GloVe: global vectors for word representation. In: EMNLP vol. 14, pp. 1532–1543 (2014)
21. Bojanowski, P., Grave, E., Joulin, A., Mikolov, T.: Enriching word vectors with subword information. Trans. Assoc. Comput. Linguist. **5**, 135–146 (2017)
22. Hochreiter, S., Schmidhuber, J.: Long short-term memory. Neural Comput. **9**(8), 1735–1780 (1997)
23. Chung, J., Gulcehre, C., Cho, K., Bengio, Y.: Empirical evaluation of gated recurrent neural networks on sequence modeling. In: NIPS 2014 Workshop on Deep Learning, December 2014 (2014)
24. Lecun, Y., Bottou, L., Bengio, Y., Haffner, P.: Gradient-based learning applied to document recognition. Proc. IEEE **86**(11), 2278–2324 (1998)

Generalized Association Rules for Sentiment Analysis in Twitter

J. Angel Diaz-Garcia$^{(\boxtimes)}$, M. Dolores Ruiz, and Maria J. Martin-Bautista

Department of Computer Science and A.I., University of Granada,
Daniel Saucedo Aranda, s/n, 18014 Granada, Spain
joseangeldiazg@ugr.es, {mdruiz,mbautis}@decsai.ugr.es

Abstract. Association rules have been widely applied in a variety of
fields over the last few years, given their potential for descriptive problems. One of the areas where the association rules have been most prominent in recent years is social media mining. In this paper, we propose
the use of association rules and a novel generalization of these based on
emotions to analyze data from the social network Twitter. With this, it
is possible to summarize a great set of tweets in rules based on 8 basic
emotions. These rules can be used to categorize the feelings of the social
network according to, for example, a specific character.

Keywords: Association rules · Sentiment analysis ·
Social media mining · Generalized association rules

1 Introduction

Social media mining is defined as a branch of data mining that encompasses
all those techniques that are used to extract valuable knowledge from a social
network. It uses techniques such as text mining, natural language processing,
unsupervised and supervised learning. Recently, social media mining has taken
a great relevance in the current world, since it allows automatic systems to obtain
information about products, brands, services or people that can be transformed
into competitive advantages. Among the most used techniques in social media
mining we can find, association rules and sentiment analysis. These techniques
have been analysed in numerous studies where the value of association rules
to summarize and discover knowledge from large data sets has been verified
[14], also as the great importance of sentiment analysis [11,15] for completing
subjective analysis of problems or domains where these techniques are applied.

In this paper we propose a social media mining system based on generalized
association rules capable of summarizing a large set of tweets into a reduced
set of rules. This set of rules can serve, among other things, to categorize the
feelings associated with a certain character, place or product at a certain time.
The novelty of the system, is in a mixed approach that uses association rules
and sentiments analysis. The fusion of both techniques is carried out through

A. Cuzzocrea et al. (Eds.): FQAS 2019, LNAI 11529, pp. 166–175, 2019.
https://doi.org/10.1007/978-3-030-27629-4_17

the generalized association rules. To this end, the terms associated to each association rule are swapped for its associated feeling, allowing to obtain strong and cohesive rules.

To validate the correct functioning of the proposed system, two well-known US politicians, Bernie Sanders and Hillary Clinton, have been chosen. Choosing these characters, among all of the people that the system discovered as relevant in the social network Twitter, is that we can contrast the results, according to the events that occurred during the US electoral campaing.

The paper is structured as follows: Sect. 2 reviews some of the related theoretical concepts that allow us to understand perfectly the following sections and also describes the related works. Section 3 explains our proposal and finally in Sect. 4 we explain the experimentation carried out. The paper concludes with an analysis of the proposed approach and the future lines that this work opens.

2   Preliminar Concepts and Related Work

In this section, we will see the basic concepts related to association rules and generalized association rules. We will also study previous related works following the scope of generalized association rules and the use of association rules with sentiment analysis in the field of social media mining.

2.1   Association Rules

Association rules belong to Automatic Learning and Data Mining fields. One of the first references to them dates back to 1993 [1]. They are used to obtain relevant knowledge from large databases and their representation is given by the form $X \rightarrow Y$ where X is an itemset that represents the antecedent and Y an item or itemset called consequent. As a result, we can conclude that consequent items have a co-occurrence relationship with antecedent items. Therefore, association rules can be used as a method for extracting apparently hidden relationships. The classical way of measuring the goodness of association rules is with two measures: support and confidence. In the following definitions we will see how these measures can be defined.

Definition 1. *Support of a itemset is represented as supp (X), and is the proportion of transactions containing item X out of the total amount of transactions of the dataset (D). The equation to define the support of an itemset is:*

$$supp(X) = \frac{||t \in D : X \subseteq t||}{|D|} \tag{1}$$

Definition 2. *Support of an association rule is represented as supp(X → Y), consequently, is the total amount of transactions containing both items X and Y, as defined in the following equation:*

$$supp(X \rightarrow Y) = supp(X \cup Y) \tag{2}$$

Definition 3. *Confidence is represented as conf (X→ Y) and represents the proportion of transactions containing item Y out of the transactions containing item X. The equation is:*

$$conf(X \to Y) = \frac{supp(X \to Y)}{supp(X)} \tag{3}$$

If we focus on how to obtain the rules, they can be approached from two perspectives, brute force solution (prohibitive) or from a two-step approach. The first of these stages is the generation of frequent itemsets, from which, in the second stage, the association rules are obtained. It is in this last approach where we find the most famous algorithms for mining association rules. Among these, the most famous is the Apriori proposed by Agrawal and Srikant [2], an exhaustive algorithm (gets all the rules), compared to for example the FP-Growth algorithm proposed by Han et al. [10] a very fast and appropriate for Big Data problems but not exhaustive.

2.2   Generalized Association Rules

Association rules can be interpreted and studied in different ways. One of the multiple, along with the analysis of negative association rules [18] or association rules with absent items [6], is the use of generalized association rules. This technique was introduced by Srikant and Agrawal [17] in 1995. Also knows as multilevel association rules, they propose that the rule {*Strawberries, Oranges*} → {*Milk*} could be replaced by {*Fruit*} → {*Milk*}. This hierarchical point of view allows a higher level of abstraction that offers us the possibility of obtaining even more information from our data. They also allow us to summarize the data in a very important way, which for Big Data environments can be of vital importance. Finally, it should be noted that the rules obtained with this interpretation tend to be very strong.

2.3   Related Work

Since they were defined by Agrawal, association rules have been widely used in various problems. One of the main studies in the field of association rules is the one proposed in 2000 by Silverstein et al. [16], where they are used for the well-known problem of shopping baskets. If we look at the problem of social media mining, we can find studies such as the one proposed by Cagliero and Fiori [4] or the one proposed by Erlandsson et al. [7]. In the first study, the authors use dynamic association rules where confidence and support measures change over time, in order to obtain data on user habits and behaviours on Twitter. In the latter, an analysis based on association rules to find influencers on Twitter is put forward.

The use of association rules in conjunction with sentiment analysis, has been less studied, so it represents an incipient problem in which we can find some studies such as Hai et al. [9] where an approach based on association rules, co-occurrence of words and clustering is applied to obtain the most common characteristics regarding certain groups of words that represent an opinion and its polarization.

If we focus on generalized association rules, they have been used in diverse approaches. For example, to improve visualization of the rules, summarizing the set of rules to be visualized [8] and have also been used in other applications such as a data mining application applied to library recommendations [12]. It is necessary to mention, their most famous use, to obtain stronger rules and better interpretation in shopping baskets problems [3]. As far as we know, the only application of generalized association rules to the field of social media mining is the work of Cagliero and Fiori [5]. In this paper, the authors propose obtaining generalized association rules through a taxonomy created by twitter topics and contexts. This work is related to ours, but in ours we use the emotions related to each word as taxonomy when extracting generalized association rules. This, offers us a powerful way to apply sentiment analysis to the Twitter environment, instead of a summary of them as the previous work does.

According to the foregoing, our work differs from all the others in that it proposes a novel mixed technique that combines the use of generalized association rules, the sentiment analysis and applies it to the field of social media mining, more specifically the microblogging platform, Twitter, although it could be extended to other fields.

3   Our Proposal

In this section we will see in detail the proposal introduced in the previous sections. We can find a graphic summary of our proposal in the Fig. 1.

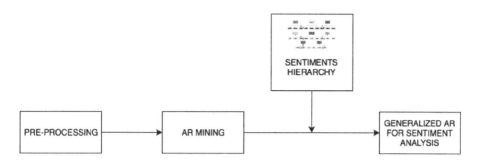

Fig. 1. Methodology followed.

3.1   Pre-processing

The data obtained from Twitter are very noisy so it is necessary a pre-processing step before working with them. The techniques used have been:

- Elimination of empty words in English.
- Removal of links, removal of punctuation marks, non-alphanumeric characters, and missing values (empty tweets).
- Identification and removal of unusual terms.
- Named-Entity Recognition to get those tuits that talk about people.
- Content transformation to lower case letters.
- Union of compound names.

At this point, we have a set of clean tuits on which we can apply the association rules mining techniques.

3.2   Generalized Association Rules for Sentiment Analysis

The first step of our proposal is based on obtaining the feelings associated with each word present in the data set. For this, we used the dictionary with the same name of the package, Syuzhet, created by the Nebraska Literature Laboratory. This approach takes into account the 8 basic emotions proposed by the psychologist Plutchik [13]. These emotions are *trust, anger, anticipation, disgust, fear, joy, sadness* and *surprise*. We can find an example of the emotions associated with certain words in the Fig. 2.

Fig. 2. Words associated to emotions.

The next step is to obtain association rules about our data set. To do this, we have use the Apriori algorithm with minimum support threshold of 0.001 and minimum confidence threshold of 0.7. The last step of the proposal is to combine the last two steps. For this, we will use the sentiments associated to the terms to substitute these terms (some examples can be see in the Fig. 3) in the antecedents of the generated association rules, as long as these are not a proper name. To choose the sentiment, a majority vote is used. Finally, we will obtain association rules involving people who are talked about on Twitter and their associated sentiments.

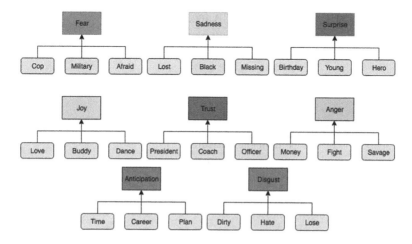

Fig. 3. Example of generalization of words based on emotions.

At this point we find the major contribution of this article to the state-of-the-art of using association rules for social media mining, demonstrating that generalized association rules by feelings, generates strong rules that can categorize, for example, a character. These affirmations will be demonstrated with two real examples in the process of experimentation.

4   Experimentation

The purpose of the experimentation is to categorize by means of association rules generalized by feelings, a certain character. On the one hand, this categorization will be the reflection of the feelings that this character raises in the social network. On the other hand, this will allow us to contrast the result obtained by our proposal. For this, we should have a sample large enough to be determined randomly.

The restrictions of the Twitter API do not allow to get a large number of tweets, which is why a crawler was developed that obtains English-speaking data, tweet in the United States during the first 6 months of 2016. The final data set is comprised of 1.7M tweets in total, and 140000 after the NER process. It is on these 140000 tuits that we will focus. For the general data mining processes, the computer whose specifications can be seen in the Table 1 has been used. For the NER process, a processing cluster was used whose specifications can be seen in the Table 2.

Table 1. Computer specifications.

Component	Features
CPU	2,6 GHz Intel Core i5
RAM	8 GB 1600 MHz DDR3
Hard Disk	SATA SSD de 120 GB

Table 2. Cluster specifications.

Component	Features
CPU	Intel Xeon E5-2665
RAM	32 GB
Cores	8

4.1 Results

After applying the Apriori algorithm to our dataset, we get 34.119 rules with minimum support threshold of 0.001. Once these rules have been obtained, the terms have been swapped for their associated emotion as seen in Sect. 3.2. In this way, we obtain for each proper name present in the dataset a set of 8 very cohesive and strong rules that can be contrasted with reality. In this case we demonstrate the system with the candidates of the primary elections of the Democratic Party of the United States in the last elections.

Use Case: Hillary Clinton and Bernie Sanders. After generalizing the rules, the results the system found for Hillary Clinton are those that can be seen in the Table 3. On the other hand, for Bernie Sanders we can see them in the Table 4. Thus, the system has obtained an ordered list of the emotions that a certain character awakens in Twitter. According to emotions, there are interesting cases such as the emotion of fear, placed in the same position according to their values of support in both politicians. This shows that the American society, tweeted words of fear according to these two candidates equally, which it can be translated into a fear sentiment towards the Democratic Party, something that was contrasted with the victory of the Republican Party. In this way of interpretation also comes the similarity of the emotion anger. In this last emotion, Hillary Clinton stands out. One interpretation that can be shelled is that there were many angry tweets about this character, knowing that he would be the candidate of the Democratic Party and that most Americans preferred a change of party. Again, this was corroborated by Donald Trump's victory.

Table 3. Rules based on feelings about Hillary Clinton.

Antedecent	Consequent	Supp	Conf
{*trust*}	=>{*hillary-clinton*}	0.93968872	1
{*anger*}	=>{*hillary-clinton*}	0.49221790	1
{*anticipation*}	=>{*hillary-clinton*}	0.48638132	1
{*fear*}	=>{*hillary-clinton*}	0.29961089	1
{*surprise*}	=>{*hillary-clinton*}	0.20038911	1
{*joy*}	=>{*hillary-clinton*}	0.14591440	1
{*sadness*}	=>{*hillary-clinton*}	0.07976654	1
{*disgust*}	=>{*hillary-clinton*}	0.07782101	1

Table 4. Rules based on feelings about Bernie Sanders.

Antedecent	Consequent	Supp	Conf
{*trust*}	=>{*bernie-sanders*}	0.97297297	1
{*anticipation*}	=>{*bernie-sanders*}	0.52432432	1
{*anger*}	=>{*bernie-sanders*}	0.47027027	1
{*fear*}	=>{*bernie-sandersn*}	0.22162162	1
{*joy*}	=>{*bernie-sanders*}	0.21351351	1
{*surprise*}	=>{*bernie-sandersn*}	0.19459459	1
{*disgust*}	=>{*bernie-sanders*}	0.09459459	1
{*sadness*}	=>{*bernie-sanders*}	0.08378378	1

5   Conclusions and Future Work

The proposed system based on Generalized Association Rules has shown with a concrete case, that it can be used to analyze the social network Twitter. The power of association rules for problems of the social media mining type has been demonstrated. For the Twitter data, it should be mentioned that it is complicated its treatment due to the noise they offer. If we look at future avenues of work, it would be interesting to apply Fuzzy Association Rules in the mining process and compare with the work done in this study. Also, it would be interesting to contrast the application with other characters from the social network.

Acknowledgment. This research paper is part of the COPKIT project, which has received funding from the European Union's Horizon 2020 research and innovation programme under grant agreement No 786687.

References

1. Agrawal, R., Imieliński, T., Swami, A.: Mining association rules between sets of items in large databases. In: ACM sigmod record, vol. 22, pp. 207–216. ACM (1993)
2. Agrawal, R., Srikant, R., et al.: Fast algorithms for mining association rules. In: Proceedings of 20th International Conference on Very Large Databases, VLDB, vol. 1215, pp. 487–499 (1994)
3. Boztuğ, Y., Reutterer, T.: A combined approach for segment-specific market basket analysis. Eur. J. Oper. Res. **187**(1), 294–312 (2008)
4. Cagliero, L., Fiori, A.: Analyzing twitter user behaviors and topic trends by exploiting dynamic rules. In: Cao, L., Yu, P. (eds.) Behavior Computing. Springer, London (2012). https://doi.org/10.1007/978-1-4471-2969-1_17
5. Cagliero, L., Fiori, A.: Discovering generalized association rules from Twitter. Intell. Data Anal. **17**(4), 627–648 (2013)
6. Delgado, M., Ruiz, M.D., Sanchez, D., Serrano, J.M.: A fuzzy rule mining approach involving absent items. In: Proceedings of the 7th Conference of the European Society for Fuzzy Logic and Technology, pp. 275–282. Atlantis Press (2011)
7. Erlandsson, F., Bródka, P., Borg, A., Johnson, H.: Finding influential users in social media using association rule learning. Entropy **18**(5), 164 (2016)
8. Hahsler, M., Karpienko, R.: Visualizing association rules in hierarchical groups. J. Bus. Econ. **87**(3), 317–335 (2017)
9. Hai, Z., Chang, K., Kim, J.: Implicit feature identification via co-occurrence association rule mining. In: Gelbukh, A.F. (ed.) CICLing 2011. LNCS, vol. 6608, pp. 393–404. Springer, Heidelberg (2011). https://doi.org/10.1007/978-3-642-19400-9_31
10. Han, J., Pei, J., Yin, Y.: Mining frequent patterns without candidate generation. In: ACM sigmod record, vol. 29, pp. 1–12. ACM (2000)
11. Kwon, K., Jeon, Y., Cho, C., Seo, J., Chung, I.J., Park, H.: Sentiment trend analysis in social web environments. In: 2017 IEEE International Conference on Big Data and Smart Computing (BigComp), pp. 261–268. IEEE (2017)
12. Michail, A.: Data mining library reuse patterns using generalized association rules. In: Proceedings of the 22nd International Conference on Software Engineering, pp. 167–176. ACM (2000)
13. Plutchik, R.: The nature of emotions: human emotions have deep evolutionary roots, a fact that may explain their complexity and provide tools for clinical practice. Am. Sci. **89**(4), 344–350 (2001)
14. Ruiz, M.D., Gómez-Romero, J., Molina-Solana, M., Campaña, J.R., Martín-Bautista, M.J.: Meta-association rules for mining interesting associations in multiple datasets. Appl. Soft Comput. **49**, 212–223 (2016)

15. Salas-Zárate, M.P., Medina-Moreira, J., Lagos-Ortiz, K., Luna-Aveiga, H., Rodriguez-Garcia, M.A., Valencia-García, R.: Sentiment analysis on tweets about diabetes: an aspect-level approach. Computational and mathematical methods in medicine 2017 (2017)
16. Silverstein, C., Brin, S., Motwani, R., Ullman, J.: Scalable techniques for mining causal structures. Data Min. Knowl. Disc. 4(2–3), 163–192 (2000)
17. Srikant, R., Agrawal, R.: Mining generalized association rules. Future Gener. Comput. Syst. 13(2–3), 161–180 (1997)
18. Yuan, X., Buckles, B.P., Yuan, Z., Zhang, J.: Mining negative association rules. In: Proceedings of Seventh International Symposium on Computers and Communications, ISCC 2002, pp. 623–628. IEEE (2002)

Data Exploration in the HIFUN Language

Nicolas Spyratos[1,2] and Tsuyoshi Sugibuchi[1,2](✉)

[1] Laboratoire de Recherche en Informatique,
Université Paris-Sud 11, Orsay, France
Nicolas.Spyratos@lri.fr
[2] Allianz France, Paris, France
tsuyoshi.sugibuchi@allianz.fr

Abstract. When big data sets are stored in databases and data ware-houses data exploration usually involves ad hoc querying and data visualization to identify potential relationships or insights that may be hidden in the data. The objective of this work is to provide support for these activities in the context of HIFUN, a high level functional language of analytic queries proposed recently by the authors [5]. Our contributions are: (a) we show that HIFUN queries can be partially ordered and this allows the analyst to drill down or roll up from a given query during data exploration, and (b) we introduce a visualization algebra that allows the analyst to specify desirable visualizations of query results.

1 Introduction

Today the volume of data accumulated by modern applications increases in unprecedented rates. Striking examples from the business world include Facebook, which handles more than 40 billion photos from its user base; and Walmart, which handles more than 1 million customer transactions every hour, imported into databases estimated to contain more than 2.5 petabytes of data.

The processing of such big volumes of data is usually preceded by so called "data exploration" aimed at creating a clear mental model and understanding of the data in the mind of the analyst, and defining basic metadata (statistics, structure, relationships) for the data set that can be used in further analysis [2].

Once this initial understanding of the data is had, the data can be pruned or refined by removing unusable parts of the data, correcting poorly formatted elements and defining relevant relationships across data sets [3]. This process is also known as determining data quality.

When the data sets are stored in databases and data warehouses data exploration usually involves ad hoc querying and visualization of data to identify potential relationships or insights that may be hidden in the data.

The objective of this work is to provide support to the data analyst during these activities. We do so in the context of HIFUN, a high level functional language of analytic queries proposed recently by the authors [5].

N. Spyratos—Work conducted while the first author was visiting at FORTH Institute of Computer Science, Crete, Greece (https://www.ics.forth.gr/).

© Springer Nature Switzerland AG 2019
A. Cuzzocrea et al. (Eds.): FQAS 2019, LNAI 11529, pp. 176–187, 2019.
https://doi.org/10.1007/978-3-030-27629-4_18

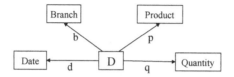

Fig. 1. Running example

Our contributions are: (a) we show that HIFUN queries can be partially ordered and this provides support to the analyst for drilling down or rolling up from a given query during data exploration, and (b) we introduce a visualization algebra that allows the analyst to specify desirable visualizations of query results.

In what follows, in Sect. 2, we recall briefly the basic definitions of the HIFUN language using examples; in Sect. 3 we define a partial ordering between HIFUN queries; in Sect. 4 we introduce a visualization algebra that allows the analyst to create desirable visualizations of query results; and in Sect. 5 we offer concluding remarks and discuss perspectives for further research.

2   The HIFUN Language

The basic notion used in defining HIFUN is that of *attribute* of a data set. In HIFUN, each attribute is seen as a function from the data set to some domain of values. For example, if the data set D is a set of tweets, then the attribute "character count" (denoted as cc) is seen as a function $cc : D \rightarrow Count$ such that, for each tweet t, $cc(t)$ is the number of characters in t.

Let us see an example to motivate the definition of a HIFUN query. We shall use this example as our running example throughout the paper.

Consider a distribution center (e.g. Walmart) which delivers products of various types in a number of branches and suppose D is the set of all delivery invoices collected over a year. Each delivery invoice has an identifier (e.g. an integer) and shows the date of delivery, the branch in which the delivery took place, the type of product delivered (e.g. *CocaLight*) and the quantity (i.e. the number of units delivered of that type of product). There is a separate invoice for each type of product delivered; and the data on all invoices during the year are stored in a data warehouse for analysis purposes.

The information provided by each invoice would most likely be represented as a record with the following fields: Invoice number, Date, Branch, Product, Quantity. In the HIFUN approach, this information is seen as a set of four functions, namely d, b, p and q, as shown in Fig. 1, where D stands for the set of all invoice numbers and the arrows represent attributes of D. Following this view, given an invoice number, the function d returns a date, the function b a branch, the function p a product type and the function q a quantity (i.e. the number of units of that product type).

Suppose now that we want to know the total quantity delivered to each branch (during the year); call this query Q. Its evaluation needs the extensions

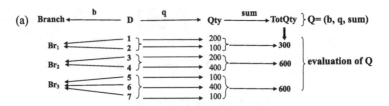

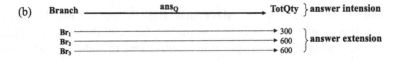

Fig. 2. An analytic query and its answer

of only two among the four functions, namely b and q. Figure 2(a) shows a toy example, where the data set D consists of seven invoices, numbered 1 to 7. It also shows the values of the functions b and q, for example, $b(1) = Br_1, b(2) = Br_1, b(3) = Br_2$ and so on; and $q(1) = 200, q(2) = 100, q(3) = 200$ and so on.

In order to find the answer to query Q, for each branch Br_i, we proceed in three steps as follows:

Grouping group together all invoices j of D such that $b(j) = Br_i$;
Measuring apply q to each invoice j of the Br_i-group to find the corresponding quantity $q(j)$;
Aggregation sum up the $q(j)'s$ thus obtained to get a single value v_i.

The value v_i is defined to be the answer of Q on Br_i, that is $ans_Q(Br_i) = v_i$. Therefore the answer to Q is a function $ans_Q : Branch \to Tot$ such that:

$$ans_Q(Br_1) = 300, ans_Q(Br_2) = 600, ans_Q(Br - 3) = 600$$

This function is shown in Fig. 2(a). We view the ordered triple $Q = (b, q, sum)$ as a query, the function ans_Q as the answer to Q, and the computations described above as the query evaluation process.

The function b that appears first in the triple (b, q, sum) and is used in the grouping step is called the *grouping function*; the function q that appears second in the triple is called the *measuring function*; and the function sum that appears third in the triple is called the *reduction operation* or the *aggregate operation*.

To see another example of query, suppose that T is a set of tweets accumulated over a year; dd is the function associating each tweet t with the date $dd(t)$ in which the tweet was published; and cc the function associating t with its character count, $cc(t)$. To find the average number of characters in a tweet by date, we follow the same steps as in the delivery invoices example: first group the tweets by date (using function dd); then find the number of characters per tweet (using function cc); and finally take the average of the character counts in each group (using "average" as the aggregate operation). The appropriate query formulation in this case is the triple (dd, cc, avg).

Conceptually, all one needs in order to perform the three-step query evaluation described above is the ability to extract attribute values from the data set D. Now, the method used to extract these attribute values depends on the structure of the data set. For example, if the data set resides in a relational database then one can use SQL in order to extract attribute values, whereas if the data is unstructured then one needs specialized algorithms to do the extraction (as in Hadoop).

Analysis Context

Now, the attributes d, b, p and q of our running example are "factual", or "direct" attributes of D in the sense that their values appear on the delivery invoices.

However, apart from these attributes, analysts might be interested in attributes that are not direct but can be "derived" from the direct attributes. Figure 3 shows the direct attributes of Fig. 1 together with several derived attributes: attribute r can be derived from attribute b based on geographical information on the location of each branch; and attribute h can be derived from attribute s based on geographical information on the location of each supplier's headquarters; and attributes s and c can be derived from a product master table.

The set of all attributes (direct and derived) that are of interest to a group of analysts is called an *analysis context* (or simply a context).

Actually, as we shall see shortly, the context is the interface between the analyst and the data set, in the sense that the analyst uses attributes of the context in order to formulate queries (in the form of triples, as seen earlier).

In [5] a context C is defined to be an acyclic directed labelled graph with possibly parallel paths; two paths being parallel if they have the same source and the same target (like the two paths from node D to node *Region* in Fig. 3).

Moreover, each node A of a context is associated with a set of values called the *domain* of A and denoted by $dom(A)$.

At any moment t in time, each node A of a context is associated with a subset $\delta_t(A)$ of its domain, and each edge $f : A \to B$ is associated with a total function $\delta_t(f) : \delta_t(A) \to \delta_t(B)$.

Roughly speaking, a context C can be seen as a database schema and the assignment δ_t as a database over C at time t (the "current" database).

However, hereafter, in order to simplify our discussion, we shall confuse the syntactic objects (i.e. nodes and edges) with their associated sets of values when no ambiguity can arise.

The HIFUN Language

The users of a context can combine attributes to form complex grouping functions. For example, in the context of Fig. 3, in order to ask for the total quantities by region, we need to use the composition $r \circ b$ as grouping function in order to express the query: $(r \circ b, q, sum)$.

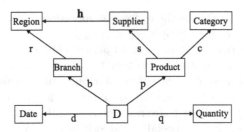

Fig. 3. A context with parallel paths

In HIFUN one can form complex grouping or measuring functions using the following four operations on functions: *composition, pairing, restriction* and *Cartesian product projection*. These operations form what is called *functional algebra* (as in [4]). We note that these operations are well known, elementary operations except probably for pairing, which is defined as follows.

Definition 1 (Pairing). *Let $f : X \rightarrow Y$ and $g : X \rightarrow Z$ be two functions with common source X. The pairing of f and g, denoted $f \wedge g$ is a function from X to $Y \times Z$ defined by: $f \wedge g(x) = (f(x), g(x))$, for all x in X*

Now, using the operations of the functional algebra we can form not only complex grouping functions but also complex conditions when defining restrictions. For example, in Fig. 3), we can ask for the total quantities by region only for product $P1$, using the following query:

$$((r \circ b)/E, q, sum), \text{ where } E = \{i|i \in D \text{ and } p(i) = P1\}$$

Here, $(r \circ b)/E$ means restriction of the function $(r \circ b)$ to the subset E of its domain of definition (which is D).

In general, a query over a context can use functional expressions instead of just functions. A functional expression over a context is defined to be a well formed expression whose operands are edges and whose operations are those of the functional algebra.

We note that if we evaluate a functional expression we obtain a function. Therefore every functional expression e can be associated with a source and a target, defined recursively based on the notions of source and target of an edge. For example, if $e_1 = r \circ b$ then $source(e_1) = D$ and $target(e_1) = Region$; similarly, if $e_2 = (r \circ b) \wedge p$ then $source(e_2) = D$ and $target(e_2) = Region \times Product$.

Functional expressions should be regarded as complex attributes that are derived from other attributes using operations of the functional algebra.

Definition 2 (The HIFUN Language). *Let C be a context. A query over C is a triple (e, e', op) such that e and e' have a common source and op is an operation over the target of e'. The set of all queries over C is called the HIFUN language of C.*

We end this section by mentioning two distinctive features of the HIFUN language. First, each HIFUN query can be mapped either as a SQL group-by query or as a Map-Reduce job. Second, HIFUN possesses a powerful rewriting rule that can be used for defining and optimizing query execution plans as well as for studying semantic caching (see [5] for more details).

3   Ordering HIFUN Queries

As mentioned in the introduction, data exploration requires ad hoc querying and data visualization. Ad hoc querying can greatly benefit if queries are partially ordered so that the analyst can "drill down" from a (current) query to a finer query or "roll up" to a coarser or "summary" query.

For example if the current query is "totals by branch" the analyst might want to also see the result of "totals by branch and product", or the result of "totals by region".

When asking these queries what actually changes is the grouping function while the measuring function and the aggregate operation remain the same. Of course, at some point, the analyst might also want to restrict (or "filter") the current query to some subset X of the data set D and/or to change the measuring function or the aggregate operation. So let's see how we can order HIFUN queries over a given analysis context in a way that covers all the above cases.

Let C be an analysis context over a data set D and let $\mathcal{Q}$ be the set of all queries over C. Let X be a subset of D and let $\mathcal{Q}_X$ be the set of all queries over over C and X (i.e. all queries in $\mathcal{Q}$ whose grouping function is restricted to X).

Clearly, if X and Y are different subsets of D then the sets $\mathcal{Q}_X$ and $\mathcal{Q}_Y$ are disjoint and therefore the family:

$$\Pi_X = \{\mathcal{Q}_X / X \subseteq D\} \text{ is a partition of } \mathcal{Q}.$$

In what follows we show how the queries of each $\mathcal{Q}_X$ can be ordered.

We begin by considering queries in which the only part that changes is the grouping function. Such queries can be ordered by comparing their grouping functions.

Definition 3 (Comparing Grouping Functions). *Let X be a subset of the data set D and let f and g be two functions on X. We shall say that f is less than or equal to g, denoted $f \leq g$ if for all x, x' in X, $f(x) = f(x')$ implies $g(x) = g(x')$; or equivalently, if $\pi_f \sqsubseteq \pi_g$ (i.e. if the partition of X induced by f is less than or equal to the partition of X induced by g in the usual partition ordering [1]).*

Clearly, the relation "$\leq$" between functions on X is a pre-ordering (i.e. it is reflexive and transitive but not necessarily anti-symmetric). However, it can become a partial ordering up to equivalence if we define equivalence between functions f and g on X as follows:

$$f \equiv g, \text{if } f \leq g \text{ and } g \leq f \text{ (i.e. if } \pi_f = \pi_g)$$

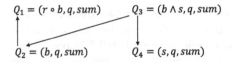

Fig. 4. Examples of query orderings

This definition can be extended to functional expressions in the obvious way (recall that a functional expression always evaluates to a function).

Now, two queries having equivalent grouping functions, the same measuring function and the same aggregate operation are equivalent queries in the sense that they always return the same answer. This follows from the fact that equivalent grouping functions induce the same partition on their common source.

Definition 4 (Comparing Queries). *Let X be a subset of the data set D and let $Q_X(m, op)$ denote the set of all queries in Q_X with measuring function m and operation op (i.e. the only thing that changes is the grouping function). We shall say that $Q = (g, m, op)$ is less than or equal to $Q' = (g', m, op)$, denoted by $Q \leq Q'$, if $g \leq g'$, for all Q, Q' in $Q_X(m, op)$. If $Q \leq Q'$ then we shall also say that Q is finer or more informative that Q', and that Q' is coarser or less informative than Q. Finally, we shall say that Q is equivalent to Q', denoted by $Q \equiv Q'$ if $Q \leq Q'$ and $Q' \leq Q$*

The following facts are immediate consequences of the above definitions: (a) the family of all sets $Q_X(m, op)$ partitions the set Q_X and (b) the queries of each $Q_X(m, op)$ are partially ordered by $\leq$ up to equivalence.

Note that for convenience of notation (and without ambiguity) we use the same symbol $\leq$ for the ordering of grouping functions and for the ordering of queries. Therefore the set of all queries on a given analysis context is partially ordered by the relation $\leq$ defined above.

Consider now an analyst who has evaluated a query Q (call it the *current query*) and wants to evaluate one or more queries finer or coarser than Q. Then the question is: how such queries can be specified using the analysis context? The answer is based on the following proposition.

Proposition 1 (Refinement Specification). *(1) Let $Q = (h, m, op)$ be a query such that $h = g \circ f$. Then the query $Q' = (f, m, op)$ is finer than Q (2) Let $Q_1 = (f, m, op)$ and $Q_2 = (g, m, op)$ be two queries such that f and g have common source. Then the query $Q = (f \wedge g, m, op)$ is finer than each of Q_1 and Q_2.*

The proof follows directly from the definition of $\leq$ (Definition 3) and is omitted here.

For example, if the current query is $Q = (r \circ b, q, sum)$ (i.e. totals by region) then the query $Q' = (b, q, sum)$ (i.e. totals by branch) is finer than Q since $b \leq r \circ b$. Similarly, if the current query is $Q = (b, q, sum)$ (totals by branch) then the query $Q' = (b \wedge p, q, sum)$ (totals by branch and product) is finer than Q. Figure 4 shows examples of query orderings.

As these examples show, given a query $Q = (g, m, op)$, if one replaces g with a sub-path of g with the same source as g then the resulting query is finer than Q (here, we view g as the path of functions whose composition defines g). We shall call such a sub-path a *refinement* of g; and by consequence, if one replaces g with a super-path of g with the same source as g then the resulting query is coarser than Q. We shall call such a super-path a *coarsening* of g.

Therefore, given a query $Q = (g, m, op)$, one can specify a query finer than Q by replacing g with a refinement of g; and one can specify a query coarser than Q by replacing g with a coarsening of g. Hence the following definitions and notation:

– if ρ is a refinement of g then $refine(Q, \rho) = (\rho, m, op)$
– if κ is a coarsening of Q then $coarsen(Q, \rho) = (\kappa, m, op)$

For example, referring to Fig. 3, if $Q = (s \circ p, q, sum)$ then we have:

– $refine(Q, p) = (p, q, sum)$
– $coarsen(Q, h) = (h \circ s \circ p, q, sum)$

Clearly, given a query Q, there can be zero, one or more queries that are finer or coarser than Q. Therefore we extend the above definitions as follows:

– if $\rho_1, ..., \rho_n$ are refinements of g then $refine(Q, \rho_1, ..., \rho_n) = \{(\rho_1, m, op), ..., (\rho_n, m, op)\}$
– if $\kappa_1, ..., \kappa_n$ are coarsenings of g then $coarsen(Q, \kappa_1, ..., \kappa_n) = \{(\kappa_1, m, op), ..., (\kappa_n, m, op)\}$

We note that all the above also hold if we replace g by any g' equivalent to g. For example, $r = proj_{Branch} \circ (r \wedge p)$ (this follows immediately from the definition of pairing). Therefore the function $proj_{Branch} \circ (r \wedge p)$ can replace r in finding refinements or coarsenings of r.

In the next section we use the HIFUN algebra together with query refinement to propose a visualization algebra for specifying desired visualizations of query results.

4   Visual Data Exploration

Data visualization refers to the techniques used to communicate data or information by encoding it as visual objects (e.g. points, lines or bars) contained in graphics. The goal is to communicate information clearly and efficiently to users. Overall there are many types of graphs to visualize data, and such types of graphs are usually referred to as "visualization templates".

Our objective in this section is *not* to propose yet another visualization template but rather to provide formal tools for specifying complex visualizations with clear semantics.

Our approach to visual data exploration is motivated by the basic fact that a query result in HIFUN is a function. This implies that (a) a HIFUN query result

Table 1. Queries, answers and examples of applicable visualizations

Query	$Q = (p, q, sum)$	$Q = (p \wedge b, q, sum)$	
Answer	$Prod \to Tot$	$Prod \times Br \to Tot$	$Br \to (Prod \to Tot)$
Visualization	Bar chart	Cross tabulation	Table of charts

can be visualized using any available template for visualizing functions and (b) all operations of the HIFUN algebra apply to query results as well.

Therefore we define a *visualization algebra* to be the HIFUN algebra augmented with two additional operations: the operation of query refinement that we saw in the previous section and the operation of *currying* that we introduce below.

Currying is the mathematical technique of translating the evaluation of a functionthat takes multipleargumentsinto evaluating a sequence of functions, each with a single argument [6]. For example:

Proposition 2 (Currying). *Consider a function $A \times B \to C$ where A, B, C are any sets and $(B \to C)$ denotes the set of all functions from B to C. Then we have:*

$$A \times B \to C \equiv A \to (B \to C)$$

Here, equivalence is meant in the sense that there is a 1-1 correspondence between tuples of the form $((a, b), c)$ and tuples of the form $(a, (b, c))$. This correspondence is rather obvious: the second type of tuple can be obtained from the first by a different parenthesizing. However, the formal proof is long and tedious so we omit it here.

For example the query result $Branch \times Prod \to Tot$ (totals by branch and product) can be transformed as follows:

$$Branch \times Prod \to Tot \equiv Branch \to (Prod \to Tot))$$

Table 1 shows the visualizations of these two different but equivalent functions using bar chart as visualization template for functions.

Note that, in the equivalent transformation above, $Branch$ can be seen as a "parameter" whose values index the functions of the set $(Prod \to Tot)$.

Also note that the above proposition holds for more than two factors on the left. For example:

$$A \times B \times C \to D \equiv A \to (B \to (C \to D))$$

Finally, note that the above proposition can be generalized in the way indicated by the following example:

$$A \times B \times C \to D \equiv A \times B \to (C \to D)$$

As a concrete example consider the following query result:

$Region \times Prod \times Branch \rightarrow Tot$ (totals by region, product and branch)

Applying currying on region and product we have:

$$Region \times Prod \rightarrow (Branch \rightarrow Tot)$$

This last function can be visualized as a two-dimensional matrix that we can call a "visualization matrix". Its rows are labelled by $Region$, its columns are labeled by $Prod$, and each cell (region, product) contains the visualization of the corresponding function $Branch \rightarrow Tot$. This matrix is shown schematically in Fig. 5.

In what follows we describe transformation techniques involving pairing, refinement and currying and demonstrating how our visualization algebra can be used for transforming query results (and therefore their visualizations).

Currying and Pairing

In general, applying currying, one can produce several different but equivalent visualizations of a query result. The goal here is that by switching between different visualizations the analyst can discover in one of them a fact that he might have missed in another.

However, these different visualizations concern a *single* query result and the question is: can we combine visualizations of *different* query results in a single, higher order visualization in which the analyst can compare different but related query results? The answer is yes if we use pairing in conjunction with currying. As a concrete example consider the following query results:

$$Region \times Prod \rightarrow Tot \text{ (totals by region and product)}$$
$$Region \times Branch \rightarrow Tot \text{ (totals by region and branch)}$$

Applying currying on the results of these queries we have:

$$Region \rightarrow (Prod \rightarrow Tot)$$
$$Region \rightarrow (Branch \rightarrow Tot)$$

As the above two functions have $Region$ as common source, we can apply pairing to obtain the following function:

$$Region \rightarrow (Prod \rightarrow Tot) \times (Branch \rightarrow Tot)$$

This pairing combines (or "integrates") the two query results into a single higher order function that can be visualized based on any template for visualizing functions. Figure 6 shows one possible visualization of this pairing based on bar charts.

Note that, as the two query results have $Region$ in common the above process can be seen as "factoring out" $Region$.

Refining and Currying

This technique is used when we want to visualize two query results through a common refinement. For example, consider the following two query results:

$$Branch \rightarrow Tot \text{ (totals by branch)}$$
$$Prod \rightarrow Tot \text{ (totals by product)}$$

We can refine these results by "multiplying" their domains of definition with a common factor, say by *Supplier*, to obtain the following query results:

$$Supplier \times Branch \rightarrow Tot \text{ (totals by supplier and branch)}$$
$$Supplier \times Prod \rightarrow Tot \text{ (totals by supplier and product)}$$

We can now apply the previous technique of Currying and Pairing to "factor out" *Supplier* obtaining the following function:

$$Supplier \rightarrow (Branch \rightarrow Tot) \times (Prod \rightarrow Tot)$$

As seen from these examples, the specification of a desired visualization is just a functional expression of the visualization algebra. However, the functional expression doesn't tell you how to create a visualization (i.e. how to select templates for visualizing individual components of the expression and how to arrange component visualizations to communicate information clearly and efficiently to the user).

Summarizing our discussion in this and the previous section we can say that visual data exploration in our approach proceeds as follows:

1. The analyst defines a subset X of the data set D and an initial query on X. Then the analyst rolls up or drills down from the current query to new queries (based on the ordering of $\mathcal{Q}_X$); and at each moment the analyst can use one of the techniques of the visualization algebra to specify the visualization of one or more (current) query results in a desirable way.
2. At any moment in time, the analyst can choose to move to a new subset Y of D and then continue visual data exploration as above.

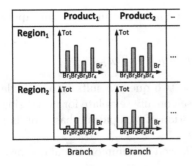

Fig. 5. Currying

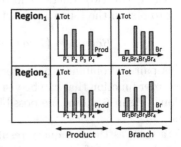

Fig. 6. Currying and pairing

5   Concluding Remarks

Today visual data exploration is an important activity in the context of big data management and several techniques for visualizing the results of analytic queries are being developed.

In this paper we have used the HIFUN language as the basis for defining a visualization algebra for visual data exploration. The advantages of using HIFUN are the following:

1. The result of a HIFUN query is a function and therefore it can be visualized by any available template for visualizing functions.
2. HIFUN is a high level functional query language in which queries can be partially ordered.
3. The HIFUN model provides a "good fit" between the data model and data visualization in the sense that the techniques used for data visualization are derived from the HIFUN model (in contrast to the relational model where sophisticated visualization techniques such as nested structures have no counterpart in the relational model).

In this paper, we have seen just two techniques for transforming HIFUN query results demonstrating the expressive power of our visualization algebra. A complete formal account is left to a forthcoming paper.

We are currently investigating two practical issues: (a) how our approach can be implemented in SQL-based systems and in MapReduce-based platforms (given that, as shown in [5], each HIFUN query can be mapped either as a SQL group-by query or as a MapReduce job and (b) how can we use our approach to visualize JSON data which is a data model very commonly used today.

References

1. Davey, B.A., Priestley, H.A.: Introduction to Lattices and Order, 2nd edn. Cambridge University Press, Cambridge (2002)
2. Idreos, S., Papaemmanouil, O., Chaudhuri, S.: Overview of data exploration techniques. In: Proceedings of the 2015 ACM SIGMOD International Conference on Management of Data, pp. 277–281. ACM (2015)
3. Kandel, S., Paepcke, A., Hellerstein, J.M., Heer, J.: Enterprise data analysis and visualization: an interview study. IEEE Trans. Visual. Comput. Graph. **18**(12), 2917–2926 (2012)
4. Spyratos, N.: A functional model for data analysis. In: Larsen, H.L., Pasi, G., Ortiz-Arroyo, D., Andreasen, T., Christiansen, H. (eds.) FQAS 2006. LNCS (LNAI), vol. 4027, pp. 51–64. Springer, Heidelberg (2006). https://doi.org/10.1007/11766254_5
5. Spyratos, N., Sugibuchi, T.: HIFUN - a high level functional query language for big data analytics. J. Intell. Inf. Syst. **51**(3), 529–555 (2018)
6. Strachey, C.: Fundamental concepts in programming languages. High. Order Symb. Comput. **13**(1–2), 11–49 (2000)

Advanced Flexible Query Answering Methodologies and Techniques

Reducing Skyline Query Results: An Approach Based on Fuzzy Satisfaction of Concepts

Mohamed Haddache[1,2,3], Allel Hadjali[2(✉)], and Hamid Azzoune[3]

[1] DIF-FS/UMBB, Boumerdes, Algeria
m.haddache@univ-boumerdes.dz
[2] LIAS/ENSMA, Poitiers, France
allel.hadjali@ensma.fr
[3] LRIA/USTHB, Algers, Algeria
hazzoune@usthb.dz

Abstract. Querying databases to search for the best objects matching user's preferences is a fundamental problem in multi-criteria databases. The skyline queries are an important tool for solving such problems. Based on the concept of Pareto dominance, the skyline process extracts the most interesting (not dominated in Pareto sense) objects from a set of data. However, this process may lead to a huge skyline problem as the size of the results of skyline grows with the number of criteria (dimensions). In this case, the skyline is less informative for the end-users. In this paper, we propose an efficient approach to refine the skyline and reduce its size, using some advanced techniques borrowed from the formal concepts analysis. The basic idea is to build the fuzzy lattice of skyline objects based on the satisfaction rate of concepts. Then, the refined skyline is given by the concept that contains k objects (where k is a user-defined parameter) and has the great satisfaction rate w.r.t. the target concept. Experimental study shows the efficiency and the effectiveness of our approach compared to the naive approach.

Keywords: Skyline queries · Pareto dominance ·
Fuzzy formal concepts analysis · Refining the skyline

1 Introduction

Nowadays an overwhelming flow of data have been generated by public internet applications (social networks, E-commerce ...) or even professional applications (sensors networks, business intelligence applications, geographical information systems, ...). This makes extracting relevant objects that best match users' preferences a very arduous operation. In order to solve this problem and avoid flooding the users with unmanageable large query results a new kind of queries, called preference queries have been introduced. They retrieve not necessarily all answers to queries but rather the best, most preferred answers. Skyline

A. Cuzzocrea et al. (Eds.): FQAS 2019, LNAI 11529, pp. 191–202, 2019.
https://doi.org/10.1007/978-3-030-27629-4_19

queries introduced by [4], are a popular example of preference queries. They rely on Pareto dominance relationship and they have been shown to be a powerful means in multi-criteria decision-making like decision support, multi-criteria decision making application, services selection . The skyline comprises the objects that are not dominated (in Pareto sense) by any other object. Given a set of database objects, defined on a set of attributes, an object p dominates (in sense of Pareto) another object q iff p is better than or equal to q in all dimensions and strictly better than q in at least one dimension. Many variations of algorithms have been proposed to compute skyline [7,9,11,15]. However, querying a d-dimensional data sets using a skyline operator gives often a huge number of objects, which is very difficult for the user to select the best elements that coincide with his preferences. To solve this problem and reduce the size of skyline, several works have been proposed [2,5,10,14,16,18,20,22]. In this paper, we address the problem of refining skyline and we return the most interesting objects. In particular, we develop an efficient approach exploiting a lattice of fuzzy concepts. The basic idea consists in building a particular lattice for skyline objects based on the satisfaction rate of a defined target concept by each concept. The refined skyline S_{ref} is given by the concept that has the maximal satisfaction rate w.r.t target concept and contains k objects (k is a user-defined parameter). Furthermore, an algorithm to compute the refined skyline, called FLASR is provided. In summary, the main contributions of this paper are the following:

- First, we provide the foundations of an approach to refine efficiently the skyline.
- Second, we develop an algorithm called $FLASR$ to compute S_{ref} efficiently.
- Third, we conduct an experimental evaluation of our algorithm and we compare its performance with the naive algorithm.

The rest of this paper is structured as follows. In Sect. 2, we define some necessary notions and concepts about the skyline and the formal concept analysis then, we report some works related to the skyline refinement. In Sect. 3, we present our approach and describe the $FLASR$ algorithm that computes the refined skyline S_{ref}. Section 4 is dedicated to the experimental study and Sect. 5 concludes the paper and outlines some perspectives for future work.

2   Background and Related Work

2.1   Skyline Queries

Skyline queries [4] are example of preference queries that can help users to make intelligent decisions in the presence of multidimensional data where different and often conflicting criteria must be taken. They rely on Pareto dominance principle which can be defined as follows:

Definition 1. *Let D be a set of d-dimensional data points (objects) and u_i and u_j two points (objects) of D. u_i is said to dominate, in Pareto sense, u_j*

(denoted $u_i \succ u_j$) iff u_i is better than or equal to u_j in all dimensions (property) and strictly better than u_j in at least one dimension(property).

Formally, we write:

$$u_i \succ u_j \Leftrightarrow (\forall k \in \{1, ..., d\}, u_i[k] \geq u_j[k]) \wedge (\exists l \in \{1, .., d\}, u_i[l] > u_j[l]) \quad (1)$$

where each tuple (object) $u_i = (u_i[1], u_i[2], \cdots, u_i[d])$ with $u_i[k]$ stands for the value of the tuple u_i for the attribute A_k.

In Eq. (1), without loss of generality, we assume that the largest value, the better.

Definition 2. *The skyline of D, denoted by S, is the set of objects which are not dominated by any other object.*

Example 1. To illustrate the concept of the skyline, let us consider a database containing information on candidates as shown in Table 1. The list of candidates includes the following information: code, the marks of mathematics (MM), the marks of physics (MP) and the age of candidate. Ideally, we look for a candidate having a good (large) marks in mathematics (MM) and physics (MP) ignoring the other pieces of information. Applying the traditional skyline on the candidates list, shown in Table 1, returns the following skyline candidates: $S = \{M_1, M_2, M_4, M_7\}$, see Fig. 1.

Table 1. List of candidates

Code	Mathematics (MM)	Physics (MP)	Age
M_1	17	10	25
M_2	18	6	24
M_3	10	7.5	32
M_4	15	15	23
M_5	5	10	27
M_6	4	4	28
M_7	20	5	22

2.2 Formal Concept Analysis with Fuzzy Attributes

Formal Concept analysis (FCA) was introduced in the early by Rudolf Wille in 1982 [21], it provides means to analyze data that describe objects, attributes, and their relationship. The data can be represented by a triplet $\mathcal{K} = (O, P, R)$ which is called formal context, where O is a set of objects, P is a set of properties (attributes) and R is a binary relation in the basic setting introduced by Wille

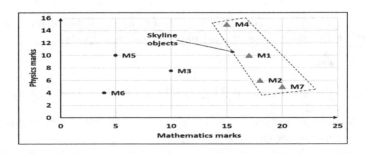

Fig. 1. Skyline of candidates

[21]. The correspondences between O and P are called a Galois derivation operator denoted by $\triangle$. But in many applications attributes are fuzzy rather than crisp. In order to take into account relations allowing a gradual satisfaction of a property by an object, a fuzzy FCA was proposed by belohlávek et al. in [3]. In this case, the notion of satisfaction can be expressed by a degree in $[0, 1]$. A fuzzy formal context is a tuple (L, O, P, R), where $R : O \times P \longrightarrow L$ is fuzzy relation. It assigns for each object $o \in O$ and each property $p \in P$, the degree $R(o, p)$ for which the object o has the property p. In general $L = [0, 1]$. Belohlávek et al. [3] generalize the Galois derivation operator to the fuzzy settings a follows. For a set $A \in L^{O}$ and a set $B \in L^{P}$, $A^{\triangle}$ and $B^{\triangle}$ are defined by

$$A^{\triangle}(p) = \bigwedge_{o \in O} (A(o) \rightarrow R(o, p)) \tag{2}$$

$$B^{\triangle}(o) = \bigwedge_{p \in P} (B(p) \rightarrow R(o, p)) \tag{3}$$

$A^{\triangle}(p)$: is the truth degree of "p is shared by all objects from A" and $B^{\triangle}(o)$ is the truth degree of "o has all attributes from B". Every pair (A, B) for which $A^{\triangle} = B$ and $B^{\triangle} = A$ is called a fuzzy formal concept of the fuzzy formal context $\mathcal{K}$. A and B are respectively called extent and intent of the formal concept (A, B). The set of all formal concepts is equipped with a partial order denoted $\preceq$ defined by: $(A_1, B_1) \preceq (A_2, B_2)$ iff $A_1 \subseteq A_2$ or $B_2 \subseteq B_1$. The set of all formal concepts ordered by $\preceq$ forms a fuzzy formal lattice of the fuzzy formal context $\mathcal{K}$ denoted by $\mathcal{L}(\mathcal{K})$.

Definition 3. *Let A, B be two fuzzy subsets. The degree of inclusion $\mathcal{S}(A, B)$ of A in B is given by [19]*

$$\mathcal{S}(A, B) = A \rightarrow B \tag{4}$$

Definition 4. *Let be $O = \{o_1, o_2, \cdots, o_n\}$ be a set of crisp objects, $intent(o_i)$ the fuzzy intent of the object o_i and B a fuzzy intent, the satisfaction rate of B by O is given by [19]*

$$sat\_rate(B, O) = \frac{\sum_{i=1}^{n}(\mathcal{S}(B, intent(o_i)))}{|O|} \tag{5}$$

In all equations above $\bigwedge$ is a min conjunction operator and $\rightarrow$ is a fuzzy impli-cation that verifies $(0 \rightarrow 0 = 0 \rightarrow 1 = 1 \rightarrow 1 = 1$ and $1 \rightarrow 0 = 0)$.

Example 2. To illustrate the computation of fuzzy formal concepts, let us con-sider a database containing information about hotels shown in Table 2. The set of objects O is composed by different hotels $\{h_1, h_2\}$, the set of properties P contains the properties Expensive and Near the beach (denoted respectively by E, Nb), i.e., $P = \{E, Nb\}$. $R(o_i, p_j)$ represents the degree for witch the object o_i satisfies the property p_j, for example $R(h_2, E) = 0.7$ means that the hotel h_2 satisfies the property Expensive with degree 0.7. Let us consider the sets of objects $A_1 = \{h_1, h_2\} = \{h_1^1, h_2^1\}$, $A_2 = \{h_1\} = \{h_1^1\}$ and the set of properties $B_1 = \{E^{0.5}, Nb^{0.5}\}$. Now, we explain how to compute $(A_1)^\triangle$, $(A_2)^\triangle$ and $(B_1)^\triangle$. For $(A_1)^\triangle$ and $(A_2)^\triangle$, we use Eq. (2) and the implication of Gödel defined by

$$p \longrightarrow q = 1 \ if \ p \leq q \ q \ else \tag{6}$$

$(A_1)^\triangle(E) = \wedge(1 \rightarrow 0.5, 1 \rightarrow 0.7) = \wedge(0.5, 0.7) = 0.5$ $(A_1)^\triangle(Nb) = \wedge(1 \rightarrow 0.5, 1 \rightarrow 0.8) = \wedge(0.5, 0.8) = 0.5$ $(A_1)^\triangle = \{E^{0.5}, Nb^{0.5}\} = B_1$
Similarly, we obtain $(A_2)^\triangle = \{Ch^{0.5}, Nb^{0.5}\} = B_1$.
To compute $(B_1)^\triangle$, we use Eq. (3) and the implication of Rescher Gaines defined by

$$p \longrightarrow q = 1 \ if \ p \leq q \ 0 \ else \tag{7}$$

$(B_1)^\triangle(h1) = \wedge(0.5 \rightarrow 0.5, 0.5 \rightarrow 0.5) = \wedge(1, 1) = 1$ $(B_1)^\triangle(h2) = \wedge(0.5 \rightarrow 0.7, 0.5 \rightarrow 0.8) = \wedge(1, 1) = 1$ $(B_1)^\triangle = \{h_1^1, h_2^1\} = \{h_1, h_2\} = A_1$. We have $(A_1)^\triangle = B_1$ and $(B_1)^\triangle = A_1$, this means that (A_1, B_1) forms a fuzzy formal concept, A_1 is its extent and B_1 its intent, on the other hand $(A_2)^\triangle = B_1$ but $(B_1)^\triangle = \{h_1, h_2\} \neq A_2$ then, (A_2, B_1) is not a fuzzy formal concept.

Table 2. List of hotels

Hotel	Expensive (E)	Near the beach (Nb)
h_1	0.5	0.5
h_2	0.7	0.8

2.3 Related Work

The work proposed by Borzsonyi et al. in [4] is the first work that addresses the issue of skyline queries in the database field. Later many algorithms have been developed to compute skyline [6,7,9,11,15]. The skyline computation often leads to a huge skyline. Several works have been developed to reduce the size of the skyline using additional mechanisms. In [2,10,14,16–18,20] ranking functions are used to refine the skyline. The idea of these approaches is to combine the skyline operator with the top-k operator. For each tuple in the skyline, one joins a related score, which is computed by the means of a ranking function F. We note that F must be monotonic on all its arguments. Skyline tuples are ordered according to their scores, and the top-k tuples will be returned. In [8], authors propose the notion of fuzzy skyline queries, which replaces the standard comparison operators $(=, <, >, \leq, \geq)$ with fuzzy comparison operators defined by user. While in [12], Hadjali et al. have proposed some ideas to introduce an order between the skyline points in order to single out the most interesting ones. In [1], a new definition of dominance relationship based on the fuzzy quantifier "almost all" is introduced to refine the skyline, while in [13] authors introduce a strong dominance relationship that relies on the relation called "*much preferred*". This leads to a new extension of skyline, called MPS (Must Preferred Skyline), to find the most interesting skyline tuples. Recently in [22] Yin et al. propose ϵ-distance to select the points that have ϵ-distance w.r.t given query point q.

At the end, and for comparison purpose, we review the naive approach [5] to rank-order the skyline objects. It relies on two steps: (*i*) first, it computes for each skyline objects p, the number of objects dominated by p denoted by $num(p)$, (*ii*) then, the skyline objects are sorted according to $num(p)$ in order to choose the $top - k$.

3   Our Approach to Skyline Refinement

Let $O = \{o_1, o_2, \cdots, o_n\}$ be a database formed by n objects, $P = \{p_1, p_2, \cdots, p_m\}$ a set of m properties (dimensions or attributes), $f(o_j, p_j)$ the value of the object o_j w.r.t property p_j and $R(o_i, p_j)$ the degree for which the object o_j maximizes the property p_j. Let S be the skyline of O and S_{ref} the refined skyline returned by our approach. In summary, our approach is based on the following steps:

– First, we calculate the skyline using the Basic Nested Loop algorithm (BNL) for more details see [4].
– Compute the refined skyline using the Algorithm 1 as follows:
  1. Algorithm $FLASR$ computes for each object skyline o_j the degree $R(o_i, p_j)$.
  2. It computes the target intent (intent that maximizes the degree of the properties chosen by the user).
  3. Then, it builds the fuzzy lattice of the skyline objects by starting computing the formal concept whose intent minimizes the degree of properties chosen by the user.
  4. For each new concept, it computes his satisfaction rate w.r.t the target intent using the Eq. (5). Then, $FLASR$ selects the concept that gives the highest satisfaction rate and computes the size of its extent.
  • If the size equals k the process stops and the refined skyline is given by the objects of this extent.
  • If the size is greater than k, the algorithm started from the step 4.

Algorithm 1. FLASR

Input: A Skyline S,k: the number of objects chosen by the user
Output: A refined skyline S_{ref}
1 $S_{ref} \leftarrow \emptyset$; $stop \leftarrow false$;
2 $Compute\_degre\_skyline(S)$;
3 $Target\_intent = Compute\_target\_Intent()$; /* compute the target intent*/
   $Intent\_min = Compute\_Intent\_Min()$; $Intent \leftarrow Intent\_min$;
4 **while** $stop == false$ **do**
5 $\quad$ $Intent1 \leftarrow Next\_intent(Intent\_min, 1)$; /*compute the first following
   $\quad$ $extent1 \leftarrow Compute\_Extent(Intent1)$; intent and its extent */
   $\quad$ $Sat1 \leftarrow Compute\_sat(extent1, Intent\_target)$;
6 $\quad$ **for** $i := 2$ **to** nb_d **do**
7 $\quad\quad$ $Intent2 \leftarrow Next\_intent(Intent\_min, i)$;/*compute the others
   $\quad\quad$ $extent2 \leftarrow Compute\_Extent(Intent2)$; intents of the intent and their
   $\quad\quad$ extents */ $Sat2 \leftarrow Compute\_sat(extent2, Intent_target)$;
   $\quad\quad$ **if** $Sat2 > Sat1$ **then**
8 $\quad\quad\quad$ $extent1 \leftarrow extent2$; $Sat1 \leftarrow Sat2$;
9 $\quad\quad\quad$ $Intent1 \leftarrow Intent2$;
10 $\quad\quad$ **end**
11 $\quad$ **end**
12 $\quad$ $Intent \leftarrow Intent1$;
13 $\quad$ **if** $extent1.size() = k$ **then**
14 $\quad\quad$ $stop \leftarrow true$; $S_{ref} \leftarrow extent1$;
15 $\quad$ **end**
16 **end**
17 **return** S_{ref};

Algorithm $FLASR$ makes use of the following functions:

- **Compute_degre_skyline(S)** computes for each object skyline, the degree $R(o_i, p_j)$.
- **Compute_target_Intent()**, **Compute_Intent_Min()** computes the intent that maximizes (resp. minimizes) the degrees of properties chosen by user.

Example 3. To illustrate our approach, let us come back to the skyline calculated in Example 1 presented in Sect. 2.1. As a reminder, we use two properties MM and MP. Furthermore, we assume that the maximal value, the better. **BNL** algorithm returns as skyline the following candidates: $\{M_1, M_2, M_4, M_7\}$, see Table 3.

First, we compute for each candidate skyline M_i the degrees $R(M_i, MM)$ and $R(M_i, MP)$. To do this we divide each value of skyline by the maximum value of the same property as follows: $R(M_i, MM) = f(M_j, MM)/20$, $R(M_i, MP) = f(M_j, MP)/15$, see Table 3. Then, we compute the target intent w.r.t properties MM and MP. From Table 3, we have $Target\_Intent = \{1, 1\}$.

Secondly, we build the lattice of skyline objects. To do this, we start by computing the minimal intent w.r.t properties MM and MP. Using data from

Table 3 and Algorithm 1, one can observe that $Intent\_min = \{0.75, 0.34\}$. Then, we compute the following intents of $Intent\_min$: $Intent_1 = \{0.85, 0.34\}$ and $Intent_2 = \{0.75, 0.4\}$. After $FLASR$ computes the extent of each intent using Eq. (3) and the implication given by the Eq. (7). So, $extent_1 = \{M_1, M_2, M_7\}$ and $extent_2 = \{M_1, M_2, M_4\}$. The algorithm $FLASR$ computes the satisfaction rate of $Target\_Intent$ by each extent using Eq. (5).

$sat\_rate(\{1,1\}, extent_1) = \frac{(S(\{1,1\}, intent(M_1)) + S(\{1,1\}, intent(M_2)) + S(\{1,1\}, intent(M_7)))}{3}$

Using data from Table 3, Eq. (4) and implication given by Eq. (6), we have

$S(\{1,1\}, intent(M_1)) = S(\{1,1\}, \{0.85, 0.67\}) = \wedge(1 \rightarrow 0.85, 1 \rightarrow 0.67) = 0.67$

$S(\{1,1\}, intent(M_2)) = S(\{1,1\}, \{0.9, 0.4\}) = \wedge(1 \rightarrow 0.9, 1 \rightarrow 0.4) = 0.4$

$S(\{1,1\}, intent(M_7)) = S(\{1,1\}, \{1, 0.34\}) = \wedge(1 \rightarrow 1, 1 \rightarrow 0.34) = 0.34$

$sat\_rate((1,1), extent_1) = (0.67 + 0.4 + 0.34)/3 = 0.47$

Similarly, we obtain $sat\_rate((1,1), extent_2) = 0.61$.

We have $sat\_rate(\{1,1\}, extent_2) > sat\_rate(\{1,1\}, extent_1)$, so if $k = 3$, the process stops and $S_{ref} = extent_2 = \{M_1, M_2, M_4\}$. If $k < 3$, we select the intent $\{0.75, 0.4\}$ (because his extent has the greatest satisfaction rate) then, we compute its following intents and the process continues as shown in Fig. 2. From Fig. 2, we can see that if $k = 2$, $S_{ref} = \{M_1, M_4\}$ and for $k = 1$, $S_{ref} = \{M_4\}$.

Table 3. Classic skyline and the degree of each object

Classic skyline				The degrees of objects	
Candidate	Mathematics (MM)	Physics (MP)	Age	$R(M_i, MM)$	$R(M_i, MP)$
M_1	17	10	25	0.85	0.67
M_2	18	6	24	0.9	0.4
M_4	15	15	23	0.75	1
M_7	20	5	22	1	0.34

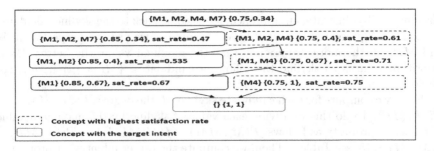

Fig. 2. Lattice of skyline objects based on satisfaction rate

4   Experimental Study

In this section, we present the experimental study that we have conducted. The goal of this studys is to demonstrate the effectiveness of our algorithm and its ability to refine the huge skyline and compare its relevance to the naive method. All experiments were performed under Windows OS, on a machine with an Intel core i7 2,90 GHz processor, a main memory of 8 GB and 250 GB of disk. All algorithms were implemented with Java. Dataset benchmark is generated using the method described in [4]. The test parameters used are distribution dataset [DIS] (correlated, anti-correlated and independent), the dataset size [D] (100K, 250K, 500K, 1000K, 2000K, 4000K) and the number of dimensions [d] (2, 4, 6, 10, 15). To interpret the results we define the following refinement rate (ref_rate):

$$ref\_rate = \frac{(ntcs - ntrs)}{(ntcs)} \tag{8}$$

where $ntcs$ is the number of tuples of the regular skyline and $ntrs$ is the number of tuples for the refined skyline.

Impact of [DIS]. In this case, we use a dataset with $|D| = 50K$, $d = 6$. Figure 3 shows that the efficiency of the two algorithms to refine the skyline is very high for all types of data. In the case of correlated data the refinement rate equals $= (60 - 5)/60 = 0.91$ and 0.99 $((1991 - 5)/1991 = (9880 - 5)/9880 = 0.99)$ in the case of independent and anti-correlated distribution respectively. Figure 3 shows also that the execution time of the two algorithms for anti-correlated data is high compared to that of the correlated or independent data. This is due to the important number of objects to refine (9880 objects for anti-correlated data, 1991 and 60 objects for independent and correlated data). Figure 3 shows also that our algorithm $FLASR$ has the best execution time compared to the naive algorithm (0.007 s for $FLASR$ and 0.34 s for the naive algorithm in the case of correlated data, 17.76 s for $FLASR$ and 25.57 s for the naive algorithm in the case of anti-correlated data, where in the case of independent data the execution time equals to 9.29 s for $FLASR$ and 15.92 s for naive algorithm).

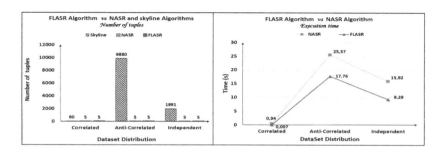

Fig. 3. Impact of [DIS]

Impact of the Number of Dimensions [d]. In this case, we study the impact of varying the number of skyline dimensions in the process of computing S_{ref}. We use an anti-correlated distribution data with $|D| = 10K$. Figure 4 shows that on the one hand, the size of the classic skyline increases with the evolution of the number of the skyline dimensions (from 138 tuples for $d = 2$ to 9999 tuples for $d = 15$). On the other hand the number of objects remains almost equals 5 when the number of dimensions increases from 2 to 15 for $FLASR$ and the naive algorithms. The refinement rate remains very high and varies between 0.96 to 0.99 for the two algorithms. Figure 4 shows also that the execution time increases with the number of dimensions (from 0.0009 s for $d = 2$ to 12.19 s when $d = 15$ for the $FLASR$ algorithm, between 0.06 s and 19.8 s when d varies from 2 to 15 for naive algorithm). This indicates that our algorithm gives the best execution time compared to naive algorithm.

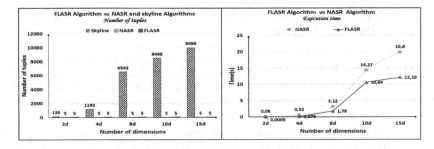

Fig. 4. Impact of [d]

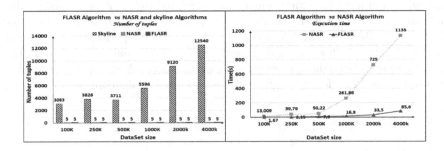

Fig. 5. Impact of [D]

Impact of the Size of the Dataset [D]. In this case, we study the impact of the size of the database on the execution time of the refined skyline and the refinement rate for the two algorithms. To do this, we use an anti-correlated database with $d = 4$ and we consider six different sizes (100k, 250k, 500k, 1000k, 2000k, 4000k). Figure 5 shows that the size of the regular skyline evolves proportionally with the size of the dataset. The refining rate shows that the ability of the two algorithms to compute S_{ref} is independent of the dataset size, it equals 0.99 for the two algorithms. Figure 5 shows also that the execution time increases with the size of dataset, but the execution time of our algorithm ($FLASR$) remains the best compared to that of the naive algorithm (the execution time varies from 1.67 s to 85.6 s when the dataset size increases from 100K to 4000K for $FLASR$ and from 13.009 s to 1135 s for the naive).

5   Conclusion and Perspectives

In this paper, we addressed the problem of refining the skyline, especially a huge skyline and we proposed a new approach to reduce its size. The basic idea of this approach is to build the fuzzy lattice of the skyline objects based on the satisfaction rate of the target intent by each concept, the refined skyline is given by the concept that contains k objects (k is user-defined parameter) and has the highest satisfaction rate w.r.t target concept. Our approach is illustrated by an example that details the different steps to compute S_{ref}. An algorithm called $FLASR$ to compute the refined skyline is proposed. In addition, we implemented the naive algorithm to compare its performances to that of our algorithm. The experimental study we have done showed that, our approach is a good alternative to reduce the size of the regular skyline (the refinement rate reached 99%) also, the execution time of our algorithm is the best compared to the naive algorithm. As for future work, we will compare our approach to others approaches of refinement and implement this algorithm to refine group skyline.

References

1. Abbaci, K., Hadjali, A., Lietard, L., Rocacher, D.: A linguistic quantifier-based approach for skyline refinement. In: Joint IFSA World Congress and NAFIPS Annual Meeting, IFSA/NAFIPS, Edmonton, Alberta, Canada, 24–28 June, pp. 321–326 (2013)
2. Balke, W., Güntzer, U., Lofi, C.: User interaction support for incremental refinement of preference-based queries. In: Proceedings of the First International Conference on Research Challenges in Information Science (RCIS), Ouarzazate, Morocco, 23–26 April, pp. 209–220 (2007)
3. Belohlávek, R.: Fuzzy Galois connections. Math. Log. Q. **45**, 497–504 (1999)
4. Börzsönyi, S., Kossmann, D., Stocker, K.: The skyline operator. In: Proceedings of the 17th International Conference on Data Engineering, Heidelberg, Germany, 2–6 April, pp. 421–430 (2001)
5. Chan, C.Y., Jagadish, H.V., Tan, K., Tung, A.K.H., Zhang, Z.: Finding k-dominant skylines in high dimensional space. In: Proceedings of the International Conference on Management of Data (ACM SIGMOD), Chicago, Illinois, USA, 27–29 June, pp. 503–514 (2006)
6. Chomicki, J., Ciaccia, P., Meneghetti, N.: Skyline queries, front and back. SIGMOD Rec. **42**(3), 6–18 (2013)
7. Endres, M., Kießling, W.: Parallel skyline computation exploiting the lattice structure. J. Database Manag. **26**(4), 18–43 (2015)

8. Goncalves, M., Tineo, L.: Fuzzy dominance skyline queries. In: Wagner, R., Revell, N., Pernul, G. (eds.) DEXA 2007. LNCS, vol. 4653, pp. 469–478. Springer, Heidelberg (2007). https://doi.org/10.1007/978-3-540-74469-6_46

9. Gulzar, Y., Alwan, A.A., Salleh, N., Shaikhli, I.F.A.: Processing skyline queries in incomplete database: issues, challenges and future trends. JCS **13**(11), 647–658 (2017)

10. Haddache, M., Belkasmi, D., Hadjali, A., Azzoune, H.: An outranking-based approach for skyline refinement. In: 8th IEEE International Conference on Intelligent Systems, IS 2016, Sofia, Bulgaria, 4–6 September 2016, pp. 333–344 (2016)

11. Hadjali, A., Pivert, O., Prade, H.: Possibilistic contextual skylines with incomplete preferences. In: Second International Conference of Soft Computing and Pattern Recognition, (SoCPaR), Cergy Pontoise/Paris, France, 7–10 December, pp. 57–62 (2010)

12. Hadjali, A., Pivert, O., Prade, H.: On different types of fuzzy skylines. In: Kryszkiewicz, M., Rybinski, H., Skowron, A., Raś, Z.W. (eds.) ISMIS 2011. LNCS (LNAI), vol. 6804, pp. 581–591. Springer, Heidelberg (2011). https://doi.org/10.1007/978-3-642-21916-0_62

13. Mahmoud, H., Habiba, D., Hadjali, A.: A strong-dominance-based approach for refining the skyline. In: Proceedings of the 12th International Symposium on Programming and Systems (ISPS), Algiers, Algeria, 28–30 April, pp. 1–8 (2015)

14. Koltun, V., Papadimitriou, C.H.: Approximately dominating representatives. In: Eiter, T., Libkin, L. (eds.) ICDT 2005. LNCS, vol. 3363, pp. 204–214. Springer, Heidelberg (2004). https://doi.org/10.1007/978-3-540-30570-5_14

15. Lee, J., Hwang, S.: Scalable skyline computation using a balanced pivot selection technique. Inf. Syst. **39**, 1–21 (2014)

16. Lee, J., You, G., Hwang, S.: Telescope: zooming to interesting skylines. In: Kotagiri, R., Krishna, P.R., Mohania, M., Nantajeewarawat, E. (eds.) DASFAA 2007. LNCS, vol. 4443, pp. 539–550. Springer, Heidelberg (2007). https://doi.org/10.1007/978-3-540-71703-4_46

17. Loyer, Y., Sadoun, I., Zeitouni, K.: Personalized progressive filtering of skyline queries in high dimensional spaces. In: Proceedings of the 17th International Conference on Database Engineering & Applications Symposium (IDEAS), Barcelona, Spain, 9–11 October, pp. 186–191 (2013)

18. Papadias, D., Tao, Y., Fu, G., Seeger, B.: An optimal and progressive algorithm for skyline queries. In Proceedings of the International Conference on Management of Data (ACM SIGMOD), San Diego, California, USA, 9–12 June, pp. 467–478 (2003)

19. Raja, H., Djouadi, Y.: Projection extensionnelle pour la reduction d'un treillis de concepts formels flous. In: 22emes rencontres francophones sur la Logique Floue et ses Applications, LFA 2013, Reims, France, 10–11 octobre 2013 (2013)

20. Sarma, A.D., Lall, A., Nanongkai, D., Lipton, R.J., Xu, J.: Representative skylines using threshold-based preference distributions. In: Proceedings of the 27th International Conference on Data Engineering (ICDE), Hannover, Germany, 11–16 April, pp. 387–398 (2011)

21. Wille, R.: Restructuring lattice theory: an approach based on hierarchies of concepts. In: Rival, I. (ed.) Ordered Sets. AISC, vol. 83, pp. 445–470. Springer, Dordrecht (1982). https://doi.org/10.1007/978-94-009-7798-3_15

22. Yin, B., Wei, X., Liu, Y.: Finding the informative and concise set through approximate skyline queries. Expert Syst. Appl. **119**, 289–310 (2019)

23. Yiu, M.L., Mamoulis, N.: Efficient processing of top-k dominating queries on multidimensional data. In: Proceedings of the 33rd International Conference on Very Large Data Bases (VLDB), University of Vienna, Austria, 23–27 September, pp. 483–494 (2007)

Quantify the Variability
of Time Series of Imprecise Data

Zied Ben Othmane[1,2], Cyril de Runz[1], Amine Aït Younes[1(✉)],
and Vincent Mercelot[2]

[1] CReSTIC, University of Reims Champagne-Ardenne,
Chemin des Rouliers CS30012, 51687 Reims Cedex 2, France
`zied.ben-othmane@etudiant.univ-reims.fr`,
{`cyril.de-runz,amine.ait-younes`}`@univ-reims.fr`
[2] Kantar Media Company, Advertising Intelligence,
2 Rue Franis Pèdron, Chambourcy, France
{`zied.benothmane,vincent.mercelot`}`@kantarmedia.com`
`https://crestic.univ-reims.fr/en/equipe/modeco`, `https://kantarmedia.com`

Abstract. In order to analyze the quality of web data harvest, it is important to consider the variability of the volumes of data harvested over time. However, these volumes of data collected over time form more trend information than accurate information due to the non-exhaustiveness of the harvests and the temporal evolution of the strategies. They form imprecise time series data. Therefore, due to the characteristics of the data, the variability of a particular series must be considered in relation to the other series. The purpose of this paper is to propose a fuzzy approach to measure the variability of time series of imprecise data represented by intervals. Our approach is based (1) on the construction of fuzzy clusters on all data at each time-stamp (2) on the difference in the positioning of data in clusters at each time-stamp.

Keywords: Variability index · Fuzzy model · Imprecise time series · Position index

1 Introduction

In order to study advertising placements on the Internet, Kantar deploys robots on the web to collect log data on the ads displayed in the banners on the various sites used. The data collected by the robots are logs with at least a time label, the web page on which the ad was displayed, and information about the ad displayed (product name, brand name). An important thing is the volume of acquired data over time periods, e.g. number of ad displays for a web page. Volume data over time form time series.

In order to previous bad data interpretation/analysis, it is important to study their quality. Between the several quality indicators, the variability, that characterizes the volatility of the data over time, is on major concern in our context.

© Springer Nature Switzerland AG 2019
A. Cuzzocrea et al. (Eds.): FQAS 2019, LNAI 11529, pp. 203–214, 2019.
https://doi.org/10.1007/978-3-030-27629-4_20

However, given the continuous increase in data harvested from the Internet, and given the dynamics of the web pages on which they can be published, it is not realistic to ensure full monitoring. In fact, the harvested data are more trend indicators or estimations than a complete reflection of the reality of advertising placements. Moreover, the harvest strategy may evolves over time. Therefore, it is important to consider the dynamics of the different time series not according to only them but according to the others. Therefore, traditional techniques evaluating their quality are inconvenient in this context.

This paper aims to quantify the variability of our data in accordance to their imperfection (imprecision, incompleteness) and to their position in the set of harvested data at each time. Our approach models imprecise values as intervals, null values (no recorded data) in a specific way according to the total ignorance principle. According to this first modeling, it proposes a new variability index based on grouping data at each time into fuzzy sets, then positioning them. The variability index is then computed in order to quantify the variation between the data positions.

This paper is structured as follows. Section 2 presents the related work and their limits. Section 3 is devoted to the data modeling with respect to their imprecision. Section 4 introduces our 3-step approach for quantifying the variability over our data. Section 5 exposes the experimentation we made. Section 6 concludes this study.

2   Related Work

To improve the value of the information, Capiello et al. [3] discussed the necessity to measure its veracity. Many indicators, such as stability, variability, etc., can highlight the potential problems and find hidden knowledge. Tasks can be more complex when the system handles imperfect data [11]. In this issue, many techniques and approaches deal with imprecision in data. The most-used approaches aim to surround the imprecision with special sets [13], affecting the intervals for measurement. Other approaches use temporal parametric systems to continuously compute a convenient simulation. In this regard, Coelho et al. [5] proposed studying the variability of the data-income flow.

In statistics, variability refers to the nature of data distribution with the aim to describe how much datasets vary. In data-mining approaches, as for instance [5], the variability is defined as the volatility of the variation of measurements over time. It is used to determine the extreme events in a time series by adopting quantile ranges. In an other context, the variability, in [7], is defined to measure the robustness of the quality of a system that deals with failure detection.

In fuzzy approaches, the variability computation differs from one paper to another, but it is still stingy. It can be considered as the aggregation of fuzzy variance over fuzzy sets over time. In [8], from a scalar variance of each element, a fuzzy model is built and models a unified incomplete knowledge about that element. This fuzzy set represents its imprecision or vague knowledge. In this way, the variability is the assignment of value's element to classes that may take over such a variable of study. Kruse and Meyer [10] chose a possibilistic interpretation of these fuzzy sets, and they consider that the membership degree of each real number x belonging to the novel fuzzy set $\tilde{X}$ should represent the degree of the assertion computed relevant to a weight $\omega(x)$. The aggregation of this derived variability is a crisp set of potentially attainable variances that reflect the imprecision pervading the observation of the outcome [6]. It only determines the variability of the outcome imprecision.

Those approaches are mainly considering variability of a time series according to only itself but not according to the other data harvested at the same period. Therefore, global variation on data harvest strategies, such as in our industrial context, may impact the variability of each time series. In our context, there is a need of defining a variability index of a time series according to other time series. In this context, Ben Othmane et al. [2] define the concept of external variability as the variability of a time series in accordance with the position of each data, at a time t, in the set of data collected at the same time t. Data position is defined, in this approach, as the projection of the data into their quantile. Therefore, the evaluation is done on a unique grid. This approach does not take into consideration the real variation into the data distribution at each time.

The following presents a kind of combination of [2] and fuzzy approaches.

3   Data Modeling

In our approach, the term 'variability' of temporal data is specific. It refers to the method of providing measurement to temporal data x^t in a domain $\mathcal{D}^T$ along T. In [2], it is called the external variability (i.e. the relative variability to the temporal data towards the rest of the data). Moreover, x^T is considered very variable if and only if its movements during T are very volatile in view of the behaviours of the rest of the elements. Otherwise, it is less variable if and only if the data have almost the same range as the rest of them along T.

In this paper, in order to deal with data imprecision, each data x^t is assigned to an appropriate interval. The idea behind these choices is that data vary over T by the σ parameter, which determines its imprecision rate, and this parameter differs from time to time. The data position is changeable, and sometimes no value is recorded. This could happen according to external factors. Apart from the huge volume and the temporally it may have, data suffer from the lack of veracity towards the recorded values. Thus, we opt to sort the data in specific groups. This allows referencing data in each timestamp.

We handle n data crawled by n sensors at each timestamp t_i. Each sensor s_j ensures a recording of only one measure at each t_i.

In the case of the impossibility to crawl data using s_j, a null value is attributed. This null value could be used due to the inexistence of the data or displaying an error. In this case, we apply the epistemic state to this possible value (i.e. we assign 0 as the unique value to reflect to the belief of any contingent outcome) [14].

Let X_j^T be the vector of the crawled data over m periods of time by s_j. Let $x_j^{t_i}$ be the value crawled by the sensor s_j in that timestamp t_i.

We propose to treat, as in [15], the imprecision by associating a relevant interval $I_{x_j^{t_i}}$ to each $x_j^{t_i}$ according to σ_{x_j}. σ_{x_j}, the first system parameter, characterizes the imprecision that surround $x_j^{t_i}$. $I_{x_j^{t_i}}$ is bounded by $\underline{I}_{x_j^{t_i}}$ and $\overline{I}_{x_j^{t_i}}$ for the lower and upper bounds, and are defined in Eq. 1.

$$\underline{I}_{x_j^{t_i}} = x_j^{t_i} - \sigma_{x_j}$$
$$\overline{I}_{x_j^{t_i}} = x_j^{t_i} + \sigma_{x_j} \tag{1}$$

To surround the imprecision, the parameter σ_{x_j} can take several formats (e.g. standard deviation, % of the value) of the vector X_j^T.

Therefore, data are now modeled in accordance with their imprecision.

4   Variability Computation Approach

As previously said, the variability index we propose is based on the idea to consider both the data imprecision, the data position into groups of the data set acquired at the same time, and the variation on those position.

In order to consider each value, harvested at a time t_i, within the set of values at the same time, we first opt to group data.

4.1   Grouping Data

To study the behaviour of sensor's recordings and spotting the range variability of each value at a specific time-stamp, we propose to group data.

At a specific time t_i, we increasingly order $x_j^{t_i}$ for all s_j. Let $x_k^{t_i}$ be the value at the k rank into the set of $x_j^{t_i}$, $j \in [1, n]$.

Let d be a static and unique value over T, representing the desired distance between groups. It is a density based approach. If $|x_k^{t_i} - x_{k+1}^{t_i}| \geq d$ then, $x_k^{t_i}$ and $x_{k+1}^{t_i}$ belong to two different groups. The group determination is calculated on the basis of $x_k^{t_i}$ and not on the associated intervals of its elements.

Let C^{t_i} be the set of the p groups $\{C_l^{t_i}, \ldots, c_p^{t_i}\}$ we obtain at t_i. $C_l^{t_i}$, $l \in [1, p]$, is the set of values between $[x_{l_1}^{t_i}$ and $x_{l_c}^{t_i}]$, where c_l is the number of elements of $C_l^{t_i}$. By construction, $(x_{(l+1)_1}^{t_i} - x_{l_c}^{t_i}) \geq d$.

As each $x_k^{t_i}$ is associated to an interval $I_{x_k^{t_i}}$, therefore, each $C_l^{t_i}$ ($l \in [1, p]$) may be dynamically surrounded by ϕ_l interval (see Eq. 2).

$$\underline{\phi}_l^{t_i} = \underline{I}_{x_{l_1}^{t_i}} = x_{l_1}^{t_i} - \sigma_{x_{l_1}}$$
$$\overline{\phi}_l^{t_i} = \overline{I}_{x_{l_c}^{t_i}} = x_{l_c}^{t_i} + \sigma_{x_{l_1}} \tag{2}$$

where $x_{l_1}^{t_i}$ and $x_{l_c}^{t_i}$ represent respectively the lowest and highest recorded values belonging to $C_l^{t_i}$.

According to the used values for d and σ, overlaps may occur between different *phi*.

The Fig. 1 illustrates the previous treatments.

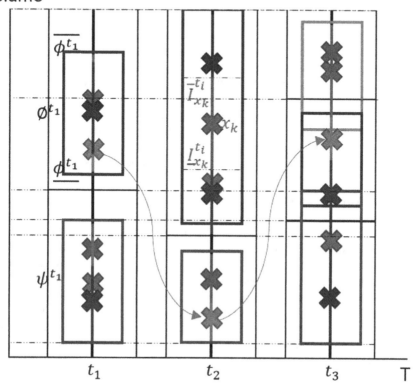

Fig. 1. Principle for grouping imprecise data into imprecise time series according $S_{d,\sigma}$

Let $S_{d,\sigma}^{T}(X)$ be the parametric system, that computes values over a period T using two parameters d and σ. According to the previous steps, these parameters allow defining groups and the surrounding imprecision in the crawled data, respectively. Furthermore, $S_{d,\sigma}^{T}(X)$ is responsible for rearranging n data at each time-stamp, even if no record is held.

4.2   Fuzzy Cluster

The parametric system $S_{d,\sigma}^{T}(X)$ defines particular groups to spot data positions over T. These groups are defined according to the system parameters d and σ that determine the number of elements they contain and their border limits. Our system may generate overlap sets (ϕ_l and ϕ_{l+1} may overlap).

In order to positioning data according to their membership to the groups, we choose to transform each ϕ into a fuzzy set. This transformation is based on cooperation principle [4] and reverse application principle [11].

In this section, we define these principles and show how this allows computing through fuzzy reasoning. This is important to handle overlapping between groups and determining metrics of the temporal flow variability.

Cooperation Principle. Let there be a group of n elements $\{x_1, x_2, ..., x_n\}$ in ϕ. These sets cooperate in $\mathcal{D}(\phi)$ within certain rules noted as $\mathcal{R}_\phi$. In the cooperation principle, rules are axioms in the associated algebra $\mathcal{A}$, noted as $\mathcal{R}_\phi \rightarrow\, <\mathcal{A}, \{f^{\mathcal{R}_\phi}\}>$ and refer to all possible relations between the ϕ element. The ϕ elements vote the rules that must be considered (i.e. a set of $\mathcal{R}_\phi$). These voted rules, denoted as ρ_ϕ, characterise the ϕ set and give it new features.

The aim of this method is to determine the precision domain of the set (i.e. where most elements coincide). This gives a determination of areas that have the most elements since these ends are imprecise and extensible.

Reverse Application. The term refers to newly characterising a set with respect to certain rules voted by the elements (i.e. before the i set elements are gathered into one group, giving some characterisation of it) [1]. Then, they define certain rules $\mathcal{R}_\phi$. These rules newly define the group. Finally, each element obtains new specifications (e.g. its degree of imprecision is characterised due to belonging to ϕ, its position takes the position of $\phi \in \Phi$, etc.).

Consequently, voters adopt new parameters according to the vote of all ϕ elements. This principle is important when we study element behaviour during T. It allows giving parameters to new arrivals, determining a plan of possible element circuits, etc. The Fig. 2 simulates an example of k data belonging to a specific ϕ, showing how they newly define their belonging scores and set parameters through reverse application.

The new belonging score of each element x_k, called the degree of precision, is done due to ρ_ϕ and denoted by $Pres(x_k^t|\rho_\phi)$. As an example, this degree can be expressed as a table of imprecise rates given by the Eq. 3.

$$Pres(x_k^t|\rho_\phi) = \frac{1}{k} \sum_{j=1}^{k} x_k^t * \omega_j \forall j \in I_{x_{k^t}} \tag{3}$$

These rates measure the membership degree of each element to its group. Additionally, even new income will follow the equation. These rates allow fuzzy computation since the ϕ^t belonging score could be normalised, which ensures computing the degree of membership in the overlapped mode.

Fuzzification. In this work, we have chosen to touch upon fuzzy reasoning to model element positioning over time and then deduce the variability scores.

In the literature, many works adopt fuzzy reasoning to formulate imprecision in data. In [6], Dubois and Prade advocated that classes can be intentionally

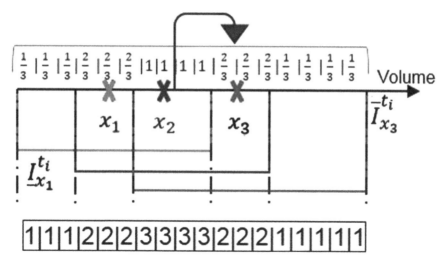

Fig. 2. Nested intervals of $\{x_1, x_2, x_3\}$ define $\mathcal{D}(\phi^t)$ given belonging scores as in the table below. Then, they adopt certain ρ_ϕ rules given new scores as marked in the table above.

described in terms of attributes that are distinguished between the range of allowed values and the range of typical values. The degree of inclusion between a class C_1 and a subclass C_2 is computed by comparing the typical ranges of C_1 with the typical ranges of C_2.

This paper propose to transform the different ϕ sets to a convenient fuzzy model. This allows studying relations between imprecise temporal data and the data positioned over T.

Let Φ be a nonempty set. Each $\phi \in \Phi$ admits a fuzzy set presenter A_ϕ in Φ, which is characterised by its membership function $\mu_{A_\phi}(x)$ (see Eq. 4).

$$\mu_{A_\phi} : \Phi \rightarrow [0, 1] \qquad (4)$$

This is interpreted as the degree of membership of each x in the fuzzy set A_ϕ (i.e. $\forall x \in \{Pres(x_k^t | \rho_\phi)\}$). The transformation is done due to the belonging score of each element x_i in ϕ^t and is relevant to the effective rules $\mathcal{R}$ between them.

In some cases, when $\mathcal{R}$ is not well defined, the modelled fuzzy set can be partitioned and can appear inconsistent. This is just an appearance caused by the system parameters. For example, this could happen for two consecutive elements x_i^t and x_{i+1}^t in ϕ^t given $dist(|x_i^t - x_{i+1}^t|) > d$. In this particular case, one could normalise the computation and then cover parts to form an ordinal fuzzy set. Even more, the system is still robust in view of the application of the same $\mathcal{R}$ by whole sets.

After transforming all ϕ sets to fuzzy representation, we then proceed to determine the membership function when one element A_x belongs to two consecutive imprecise sets $\{\phi_l \cap \phi_{l+1}\}$, effectively when nested sets are present [12].

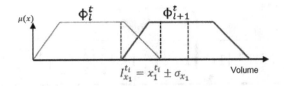

Fig. 3. The element $x_1^{t_1}$ belong to 2 consecutive fuzzy sets $A_{\phi_l}^{t_1}$ and $A_{\phi_{l+1}}^{t_1}$ respectively

In this case, many approaches give answers to compute the membership function of an element belonging to two consecutive overlapped sets, such as ϕ_l and ϕ_{l+1}, respectively (see Fig. 3). Hence, in this article, we simply follow the Zadeh t-norm (Eq. 5) and t-co-norm (Eq. 6).

$$\mu_{A_{\phi_l} \cap A_{\phi_{l+1}}}(x) = min(\mu_{A_{\phi_l}}, \mu_{A_{\phi_{l+1}}}) \tag{5}$$

$$\mu_{A_{\phi_l} \cup A_{\phi_{l+1}}}(x) = max(\mu_{A_{\phi_l}}, \mu_{A_{\phi_{l+1}}}) \tag{6}$$

The membership degree of each element is calculated relevant to the proposition. By illustrating its belonging to all sets of the domain, it represents the degree of truth as a valuable extension to all possible values in $\mathcal{D}(\varPhi)$.

4.3   Position Index

Since x_j^t represents the data captured by the sensor s_j in one timestamp t (i.e. in $\mathcal{D}(\varPhi^t)$), then we can consider $\mu_A(x)$ a score of its fuzzy positioning over $\mathcal{D}(\varPhi^t)$. These measures allow obtaining a value that represents x_j^t toward the rest of the set domain. This positioning score allows an assessment of the data passage through time-stamps. Consequently, we propose measuring the variability of its movement over the period T.

The positioning indice of x_j^t at a specific time-stamp t is defined in Eq. 7,

$$\mathcal{P}_{x_j}^t = \sum_{\phi_l=1}^{p} \mu_{A_{\phi_l}}(x_j^t) * \frac{rank(maxOf(\mathcal{D}(\phi_l^t)))}{|\varPhi^t|} \tag{7}$$

where $rank$ represents the rank of ϕ_l in the domain of $\mathcal{D}(\varPhi)$ following an ascendant order.

4.4   Variability

As data position change temporally, for a period of time T for each x_j, a vector $\mathcal{VP}_{x_j}^T$ composed with the position index values $\mathcal{P}_{x_j}^{t_i}$ ($\forall t_i \in T$) may be built.

In fact, we see the variability as 'the way to provide a measurement to a temporal data of an element by a specified system and in a determined temporal domain'.

The mean position can be computed (Eq. 8).

$$\mathcal{M}^T_{x_j} = mean(\mathcal{VP}^T_{x_j}) = \frac{\sum_{t_i \in T} \mathcal{P}^{t_i}_{x_j}}{|T|} \qquad (8)$$

The variability can therefore be obtained considering several metrics on the vector. In the following, we choose the variance (Eq. 9).

$$\mathcal{V}^T_{x_j} = \sigma^2(\mathcal{VP}^T_{x_j}) = \frac{\sum_{t_i \in T}(x_j{}^{t_j} - \mathcal{M}^T_{x_j})^2}{|T|} \qquad (9)$$

However, our aim is to verify the variability of the harvest and determine its effectiveness to generate valuable information.

4.5   Example

To illustrate the position index calculation, please refer to the example shown in the Fig. 4. In this example, we provide insight to determine the variability score of the red element (γ) over time.

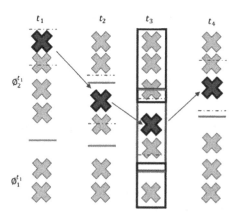

Fig. 4. γ behaviour over a time period T

Table 1 presents the example results of γ position index values.

Table 1. (a) γ^T Matrix's of fuzzy membership degrees of γ to fuzzy clusters over time. (b) γ^T Vector's of position index values of γ over time.

t_1	t_2	t_3	t_4
0	0.2	0.1	1
1	0.8	0.9	0
	0	0	

T	t_1	t_2	t_3	t_4
$\mathcal{P}if^t_\gamma$	1	0.73	0.55	1

For instance, the position index value for t_2 is calculated as follows:

$$\mathcal{P}_\gamma^{t_2} = 0 * \frac{2}{6} + 0.8 * \frac{4}{6} + 0.2 * \frac{6}{6} \approx 0.73$$

According those positions, we can compute the mean and the variability:

$$\mathcal{M}_\gamma^T \approx 0.82$$

$$\mathcal{V}_\gamma^T \approx 0.22$$

This approach brought relative scores to measure the external movement of the data (i.e. the volatility of data movement respects the normality of the rest of the sets belonging to the same domain). The generated scores provide the detection of hidden and significant data behaviour. Merging the temporal position index values of an element (e.g. by the variance) provides a level of collection, which represents singular movements. This gives novel information about detecting potential defective sensors.

5   Experimentation

To present results using the proposed approach, we tested it on the basis of 708 sensors crawling data over $T = 180$ harvesting days. Indicators were computed by month. The values given into the following are the mean of the indicators for the 708 sensors by month.

We compare the present proposal with the approach from [2]. We empirically chose $d = 50$ as the distance between cluster and the standard deviation into each stream as σ for the present approach. For the approach of [2], the number of quantile has been define as 4 and therefore data are projected into quartiles.

Generally, the computation of the variability type by the two approaches follows the same trajectory and has almost the same trend. The correlation score is 0.6697942 on this dataset. By adjusting the parameters, the two curves become closer (i.e. the correlation can be close to 1).

Table 2 compares real values between diverse approaches in terms of variability measurement on one sample sensor. The studied approaches have the same logic, while handling the variability with the presented approach (i.e. they always study the variability of one sensor towards the rest).

To test whether the computation mechanism always follows the majority in the cited approach in the table, the dispersion of the output variability scores, i.e. the density, is studied in Fig. 5.

The dispersion of most of these approaches generally has the same form as the Felber statistical approach [9] and the presented one (computed by the mean). The general central tendency is around 0.7. However, with parameter adjustment, the approach can be closer to 1. On this side, we verified that the variability scores given by this approach are consistent and that the system has solid features that allow judging the dynamic volatility of the imperfect data.

Table 2. Variability scores by divers approaches. var and Mean refer to the present approach by computation method respectively

t_i	t_1	t_2	t_3	t_4	t_5	t_6
Quant [2]	0.0700	0.1200	0.5200	0.44827	0.4666	0.6551
$\mathcal{V}$ (I-app)	0.0481	0.0988	0.1566	0.04469	0.0911	0.1146
$\mathcal{M}$ (I-app2)	0.7855	0.8511	0.6394	0.8574	0.7962	0.6428
Fuzzy [8]	0.0105	0.0111	0.0177	0.0051	0.0102	0.0129
Stat [9]	7.133	28.7142	56.966	65.300	90.600	28.710

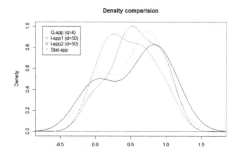

Fig. 5. Density similarity between variability approaches

6   Conclusion

This paper defines a variability index to determine a significant score regarding the temporal volatility of an element against the rest, giving a significant consistency score concerning its crawled manner. The variability of a sensor harvest is considered towards the positions of the data in a temporal series.

The presented approach works on the basis of imperfect recorded values. It highlights the embedded mechanism to provide variability scores that are relevant to each sensor.

The results seem to show that this method can detect hidden knowledge and provide valuable information. The approach allows the detection of irregular temporal patterns by measuring the position index of an element in its class. We have seen that it can be considered as a complement to the quantile-based approach to obtain deeper insight to judge the variability of a harvest.

References

1. Bagui, S., Mink, D., Cash, P.: Data mining techniques to study voting patterns in the US. Data Sci. J. **6**, 46–63 (2007)
2. Ben Othmane, Z., Bodenes, D., de Runz, C., Aït Younes, A.: A multi-sensor visualization tool for harvested web information: insights on data quality. In: IV, pp. 110–116. IEEE Computer Society (2018)

3. Cappiello, C.: On the role of data quality in improving web information value. In: Proceedings of the 24th International Conference on World Wide Web, WWW 2015 Companion, pp. 1433–1433. ACM, New York (2015)

4. Charkhabi, M., Dhot, T., Mojarad, S.A.: Cluster ensembles, majority vote, voter eligibility and privileged voters. Int. J. Mach. Learn. Comput. **4**(3), 275 (2014)

5. Coelho, C., Ferro, C., Stephenson, D., Steinskog, D.: Methods for exploring spatial and temporal variability of extreme events in climate data. J. Clim. **21**(10), 2072–2092 (2008)

6. Couso, I., Dubois, D.: On the variability of the concept of variance for fuzzy random variables. IEEE Trans. Fuzzy Syst. **17**(5), 1070–1080 (2009). https://doi.org/10.1109/TFUZZ.2009.2021617

7. Dedeke, A.: Building quality into information supply chains: robust information supply chains. In: Information Quality, pp. 99–110. Routledge (2014)

8. Dubois, D., Hadjali, A., Prade, H.: Fuzziness and uncertainty in temporal reasoning. J. UCS **9**, 1168 (2003)

9. Felber, D.: Order statistics and variability in data streams. Ph.D. thesis, UCLA (2015)

10. Kruse, R., Meyer, K.D.: Statistics with Vague Data, vol. 6. Springer, Heidelberg (2012)

11. McSherry, D.: Precision and recall in interactive case-based reasoning. In: Aha, D.W., Watson, I. (eds.) ICCBR 2001. LNCS (LNAI), vol. 2080, pp. 392–406. Springer, Heidelberg (2001). https://doi.org/10.1007/3-540-44593-5_28

12. Nguyen, H.T., Kreinovich, V.: Nested intervals and sets: concepts, relations to fuzzy sets, and applications. In: Kearfott, R.B., Kreinovich, V. (eds.) Applications of Interval Computations. APOP, vol. 3, pp. 245–290. Springer, Boston (1996). https://doi.org/10.1007/978-1-4613-3440-8_11

13. Nikolaidis, E., Chen, S., Cudney, H., Haftka, R.T., Rosca, R.: Comparison of probability and possibility for design against catastrophic failure under uncertainty. J. Mech. Des. **126**(3), 386–394 (2003). https://doi.org/10.1115/1.1701878

14. Smets, P.: Probability, possibility, belief: which and where? In: Smets, P. (ed.) Quantified Representation of Uncertainty and Imprecision. HDRUMS, vol. 1, pp. 1–24. Springer, Dordrecht (1998). https://doi.org/10.1007/978-94-017-1735-9_1

15. Yao, Y.Y., Wong, S.K.M.: Interval approaches for uncertain reasoning. In: Raś, Z.W., Skowron, A. (eds.) ISMIS 1997. LNCS, vol. 1325, pp. 381–390. Springer, Heidelberg (1997). https://doi.org/10.1007/3-540-63614-5_37

Semantic Understanding of Natural Language Stories for Near Human Question Answering

Hasan M. Jamil[✉] [ID] and Joel Oduro-Afriyie [ID]

Department of Computer Science, University of Idaho, Moscow, ID, USA
jamil@uidaho.edu, odur8117@vandals.uidaho.edu

Abstract. Machine understanding of natural language stories is complex, and automated question answering based on them requires careful knowledge engineering involving knowledge representation, deduction, context recognition and sentiment analysis. In this paper, we present an approach to near human question answering based on natural language stories. We show that translating stories into knowledge graphs in RDF, and then restating the natural language questions into SPARQL to answer queries can be successful if the RDF graph is augmented with an ontology and an inference engine. By leveraging existing knowledge processing engines such as FRED and NLQuery, we propose the contours of an open-ended and online flexible query answering system, called *Omniscient*, that is able to accept a natural language user story and respond to questions also framed in natural language. The novelty of Omniscient is in its ability to recognize context and respond deductively that most current knowledge processing systems are unable to do.

Keywords: Knowledge graphs · Contextual inference ·
Natural language processing · Story understanding · RDF · SPARQL ·
Data Science

1 Introduction

Knowledge contained in texts are often nuanced, and represent intricate relationships among the entities and their properties. Contexts often also flow from one sentence to the next and relationships can be interpreted unambiguously without explicit mentions. For example, in the two sentences below,

> *"John is a boy, and his girlfriend Alice is about five feet tall. He is one foot taller than her."*

it is easy for us to interpret *John*'s height. Therefore, the questions

1. "How tall is John?"
2. "Who is shorter than him?"

© Springer Nature Switzerland AG 2019
A. Cuzzocrea et al. (Eds.): FQAS 2019, LNAI 11529, pp. 215–227, 2019.
https://doi.org/10.1007/978-3-030-27629-4_21

should be answerable by a rational human and answer "Six feet" and "Alice" respectively as responses. More nuanced and thus complex questions are,

3. "Is Alice a boy?" or
4. "What is Alice's gender?"

to which our answers should be (under conventional customs) respectively "No" and "Girl". We, however, often respond to such questions with a bit of dressing and finesse such as – "No, Alice is a girl." or "She is a girl.", respectively. The interesting question is, can a knowledge processing system understand natural language (NL) stories and respond to questions in such near human fashion?

In this paper, we present a novel story understanding and query answering system called *Omniscient* that is able to generate near human responses most of the time against "simple stories." By simple story we mean sentences that do not include deep context embeddings or ambiguities, which in turn will require transitive context translation or recognition. For example, the sentences below include ambiguities that are difficult to parse,

> *"John is a boy from Idaho and Pedro is from Argentina. He fell in love with Alice and did not enjoy her going out with Pedro."*

and even harder to analyze when asked

5. "Who did not enjoy Alice going out?"

for which the obvious answer is "John" as will be interpreted by a rational human. The complexities, however, include the fact that we did not explicitly state that *Pedro* is a boy too, and *Alice* is a girl. We also did not state who fell in love with her, and given that there are apparently two boys, either one could do so. But given that one of them did not enjoy her outings with *Pedro*, it must be *John* who did not enjoy it. A couple of more complex questions are

6. "Is Alice shorter than John?"
7. "Whose feelings were hurt?"

which can only be answered by determining *John*'s height and knowing that five feet is less than six, and thus shorter. Arguably, answering the last question is one of the hardest tasks for several obvious reasons. While interesting, Omniscient currently does not address such extensive and complex context recognition and disambiguation. We have plans to address such queries in a future release.

2   Background and Motivation

The recent interests in knowledge graphs is fueled by the need for gleaning information embedded in non-traditional data sources in unstructured texts such as legal documents, micro-blogs, social networks, technical documents, internet contents, etc. Even more recent emergence of Data Science as a distinct discipline calls for convenient ways of extracting useful information from a vast repository of diverse data which potentially cannot be efficiently and effectively analyzed by developing applications to meet each unique information need. Thus, the most abstract and convenient ways we can request information is in natural language using conceptual terms, and require that the system understands our needs, identify appropriate information sources and analytics to construct and furnish the information. One such specific application calls for orchestrating computer programs from NL specifications of an abstract algorithm. Since the steps in the algorithm are related, understanding the contexts and relationships among them are essential. The steps in story understanding closely parallel the technologies needed for knowledge graph querying in NL.

3   Related Research

Constructing knowledge graphs from texts have been an active area of research for a while, and so is research into NL interface for such knowledgebases [18, 20]. Knowledge graphs are distinct from both traditional relational and graph structured data – in relations, the network of implicit relationships are inferred through joins while in general graphs and knowledge graphs, relationships are explicit. In knowledge graphs, however, the entities and their relationships are elementary but in general graphs, they can be arbitrarily complex. The popular representation used in knowledge graphs is W3C RDF that essentially is a set of triples of subjects, predicates and objects, called statements, representing an arbitrarily complex but simple structured networks. Once in this format, several querying and inferencing systems can be used to decipher the embedded knowledge including SPARQL, and Jena.

One exciting way NL questions were mapped to knowledge graph queries is based on recurrent neural network (RNN) [11]. In this approach, a RNN model is trained to learn mappings from a sequence of English keywords (queries) to graph query sentence templates. But machine learning based systems such as RNN require substantial amount of training data and are highly dependent on application's domain and the types of queries asked. Other approaches often involve mapping semantic intent of queries to underlying graph structures in the knowledgebase [8, 20]. One of the interesting approaches involve two complementary mapping processes – one that maps NL texts to RDF graphs [5, 6, 10], and the other that generates knowledge queries in SPARQL [14, 15, 17] over RDF databases. Another prong of research that completes the loop of interactive and dialogue based knowledge graph querying is generating NL responses from RDF data [3, 7]. In this paper, our goal is to assemble an online system that leverages these three complementary approaches to build a NL interface for near human question answering in natural English. Following its popularity in knowledge modeling, we chose RDF as the platform for representing the knowledge graphs, and SPARQL to query the generated knowledge graph. Finally, we have used Apache Jena to reason about the base knowledge and what it entailed.

4   Architecture of Omniscient

An ideal NL system aims to create a 'black box' with which humans can freely interact and precludes the use of restraining key words or phrases. In Omniscient, we seek to design a system to which we can speak naturally, ask questions in NL, and get back a response in NL. We also require that this system be able to understand and process arbitrary NL content in any application domain. One of the biggest hurdles in realizing this goal is that there exists a gap between humans and computers in ways they communicate, understand and process information. The discussion in Sect. 1 highlights this gap and points to human's ability to gather contexts, infer and correlate with both explicit and implicit knowledge that computers cannot without help. The overall principle and the three essential functional components of Omniscient black box model is shown in Fig. 1.

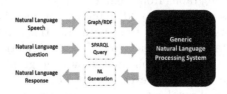

Fig. 1. A black-box model of a knowledge graph query processing system using NL.

4.1   Natural Language Story to Knowledge Graph Conversion

In Omniscient, we take a minimalist's approach and scavenge open source components that can be easily pieced together. Thus, for our NL to RDF conversion component in Fig. 1, we have used the FRED API [5] which supports mapping to various graph formats. FRED applies a number of linguistic and ontology analysis tools to produce structured data from unstructured text. The generated data is then enriched using named entity recognition and word-sense disambiguation. Users have a choice of a number of output data formats including graphical, RDF (XML or JSON), and Turtle. We choose to work with an RDF/XML output format purely as a matter of convenience. Schematically this component of Omniscient looks like the structure in Fig. 2.

Fig. 2. NL to RDF conversion.

4.2 Translating Natural Language Questions to SPARQL Queries

Generating a relevant SPARQL query from a NL query is technically involved. This is mainly because the queries are asked in the context of articulated stories which essentially requires the translation system to be aware of the underlying knowledge graph, and its logical implications. Since its inception, DBPedia [2] ontology has emerged as one of the comprehensive knowledge sources for Wikipedia, which potentially provides the context needed to understand a user story. Translating NL questions into SPARQL queries using DBpedia thus became an active and vibrant area of research. Among them, Steinmetz et al. [17] (SAS), interQA [14] and D2RQ [15] approaches are recent and aptly address this issue in unique ways. While interQA is primarily focused on DBpedia's QALD[1] data sets for factoid (a ground truth or fact such as a tuple in a relation) question answering, SAS and D2RQ tends to address question answering over open domain data sets. Since our goal is to go beyond factoid question answering over domain independent data repositories, and directly from texts, these systems though interesting do not apply as is.

We therefore look at NLQuery[2] for NL query to SPARQL translation that relies on Stanford CoreNLP Engine[3]. NLQuery works well for primarily factoid query answering over WikiData [1] using DBpedia ontology similar to interQA. But due to its reliance on CoreNLP parser, we are able to adapt it to answer inferential and contextual questions. In particular, NLQuery's pipeline includes context analysis using Lango that converts the grammar parse tree to context parameters by matching the parse trees with the corresponding symbols in the Lango rules, which facilitates construction of SPARQL queries based on the underlying knowledge graphs. We have significantly modified and enhanced these rules to make NLQuery to understand context, and perform limited inferencing.

A further customization involves adjusting NLQuery's reliance on WikiData and focus its SPARQL generation on FRED generated RDF graphs, but still leverage the DBpedia ontology assuming that it covers a large corpus of concepts to be able to annotate arbitrary user stories. This choice has several obvious advantages and a minor disadvantage – the major advantage is that we do not need to develop a universal ontology to rely on for knowledge modeling, and the disadvantage is that it is possible that some stories may involve terms that are

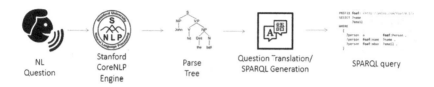

| NL
Question | Stanford
CoreNLP
Engine | Parse
Tree | Question Translation/
SPARQL Generation | SPARQL query |

Fig. 3. NL to SPARQL query translation.

[1] https://qald.sebastianwalter.org/index.php?x=home&q=home.

[2] https://blog.ayoungprogrammer.com/2016/10/natural-lang-query-engine.html/.

[3] http://nlp.stanford.edu:8080/corenlp/.

not covered by DBpedia and hence will not be very effective, i.e., as we point out in Sect. 5 when we discuss Omniscient's effectiveness. The NL to SPARQL query translation pipeline of Omniscient is shown in Fig. 3.

4.3   Deduction Enabled Knowledge-Rich Responses

As it stands, NLQuery can only answer factoid questions of a specific class of queries - entity identification. For example, it answer's the question "*Who is the CEO of Google?*" with the response "Eric Schmidt, Larry Page, Sundar Pichai," but it fails to answer the question "*Who is the current CEO of Google?*." Similarly, once asked "*Who is Obama?*, it responds by saying "44th President of the United States." But if asked subsequently "*Who is his wife?*", it fails to answer even though when asked "*Who did Obama marry?*" or "*Who is Obama's wife?*", it can correctly answer "Michelle Obama." In other words, it fails to interpret or deduce context from the texts – WikiData created from Wikipedia.

In Omniscient, we overcome some of these limitations by introducing context rules, and enhanced knowledge modeling and enriched query formulation. But to answer questions similar to 2 through 6 in Sect. 1, Omniscient demands substantial capabilities requiring extensive knowledge engineering and remains outside the scope of its current edition. However, given the story below,

> "*Bob and his friend Alice went ice fishing in the nearby lake. It was frozen solid. They drilled a hole to lower a line with a hook. The lake was near a forest which had no trees with leaves except on a few evergreen trees. A hawk was watching from atop one of the bare trees. Bob caught a few trout and left them on the ice. When his friend went to light a fire to grill the fish, the hawk snatched one of the fish and flew away. Just around lunch time, they both enjoyed a couple of nicely grilled fish on the ice and spent some time chatting. They talked about their life and their work. They returned home after a warm cup of coffee Bob made.*"

Omniscient is capable of responding to interesting questions as shown in Fig. 4, that are not possible in NLQuery.

4.4   Humanoid-Like Response Generation in Natural Language

In general, NLQuery does a great job at responding naturally in a human-like fashion. For example, it responds "44th President of the United States" when asked "*Who is Obama?*", and "American actress and activist" when asked "*Who is Susan Sarandon?*" But, such constructions in NLQuery are also factoids. In Omniscient, we plan to actually enrich the raw factoid data to construct a natural response beyond what is stored in the database. For example, currently Omniscient responds to the question "*Who caught the fish?*" by saying "Bob." We would like to improve this response by perhaps saying "Bob caught a few trouts." To this end, we are re-purposing Natural Language Generation from Graphs (NLGG) [4] primarily because it is designed for RDF/XML graphs which is exactly what we use. Figure 5 shows the Omniscient pipeline for raw data or factoid to natural English response generation.

Omni*scient*

Input

Bob and his friend Alice went ice fishing in the nearby lake. It was frozen solid. They drilled a hole to lower a line with a hook. The lake was near a forest which had no trees with leaves except on a few evergreen trees. A hawk was watching from atop one of the bare trees. Bob caught a few trout and left them on the ice. When Bob's friend went to light a fire to grill the fish, the hawk snatched one of the fish and flew away. Just around lunch time, they both enjoyed a couple of nicely grilled fish on the ice and spent some time chatting. They talked about their life and their work. They returned home after a warm cup of coffee Bob made.

Read

Who made coffee?
>> **Bob**

Who snatched the fish?
>> **hawk**

Who caught the trout?
>> **Bob**

What was frozen?
>> **No results**

Who ate the fish?
>> **No results**

Who ate the grilled trout?
>> **No results**

Who lit the fire?
>> **Alice**

Who was near the forest?
>> **No results**

Who snatched the fish?
>> **hawk**

Who caught the fish?
>> **Bob**

Fig. 4. A sample Omniscient session over a story.

SPARQL
Query
Result

NLGG

NL
Response

Fig. 5. SPARQL/RDF to natural language response generation.

4.5 Omniscient Architecture

The complete system architecture is shown in Fig. 6 in which we identify the deductive capability we have introduced in NLQuery pipeline discussed in Sect. 4.3. Omniscient is implemented in Python and its web interface is implemented in Flask using Apache Jena TDB2 with Fuseki2 as its back-end storage.

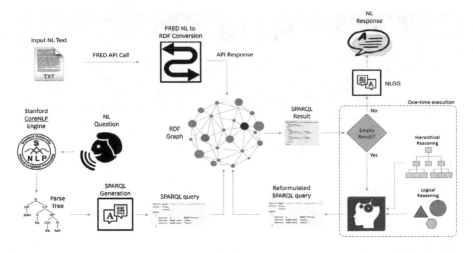

Fig. 6. Overall Omniscient system architecture.

5   Experimental Set-Up, Evaluation and Comparison

Given the fact that Omniscient is not a factoid only question answering system, and more in line with research such as [13,16], a toe to toe comparison with NLQuery (or similar factoid based systems) is not too expository. The closest system that attempts to understand texts for question answering using knowledge graphs is Kernel Entity Salience Model [19] currently under development. We therefore proceed to qualitatively evaluate Omniscient as follows.

5.1   Query Classes

For the purpose of evaluation of Omniscient, we identify six broad classes of queries – *factoid, co-actor, contextual, entity disambiguation, inferential,* and *generalization* queries. These queries are defined and exemplified below largely in the context of the story in Sect. 4.3. Formal definitions for these queries are deferred until a more technical exposition of Omniscient.

Factoid Queries [F]. Factoid queries can be answered from base data explicitly stored in the database and are fundamentally binary in nature – either the answer exists or it does not in ground form. For example, *"Who is the 44th president of the United States?"* answer to which is "President Barrack Obama." Query *"Who is Susan Sarandon?"* is also a factoid query, i.e., can be answered directly from the database using an SPJ (select-project-join) query.

Co-Actor Queries [A]. In our story, the question *"Who went fishing?"* is a co-actor query as opposed to a set query involving two factoids. Co-actor queries recognize that both Bob and Alice went fishing together, not just went fishing. In

NLQuery, they are treated as separate facts. Such as *"Who were the Governors of Michigan?"* returns a set of names. Interestingly, when asked *"Who are the Governors of Michigan?"* or *"Governors of Michigan?"*, NLQuery returns empty responses. However, it returns the same set of names when asked *"Who is the Governor of Michigan?"* indicating NLQuery just treats them as individual facts and requires a proper interrogative sentence.

Contextual Queries [C]. In our story, the sentence *"It was frozen solid."* is a continuation of the previous sentence. And thus the context is the lake, and the pronoun "it" is used in place of the noun – lake. Therefore, the query *"What was frozen?"* is a contextual query and should be answered as "The lake." Similarly, *"Who lit the fire?"* is a contextual question.

Entity Disambiguation Queries [E]. The fragment *"... they both enjoyed a couple of nicely grilled fish ..."* implies both Bob and Alice ate fish for lunch. But the question *"Who ate grilled fish?"* is ambiguous and very difficult to parse. This is because it is uttered right after the fragment *"... the hawk snatched one of the fish and flew away."* and thus the context could potentially include the hawk. Thus a context disambiguation becomes essential to exclude the hawk.

Generalization Queries [G]. More often than not, questions are asked using generalization. For example, it is never mentioned in our story that trouts are fish. But, they are and given the facts that they went ice fishing, lowered a hook in the lake through the hole they dug, caught a few trouts and then they grilled the fish, amply imply that trouts are fish. The simplest way they can be recognized as such and answer the question *"Who caught the fish?"* is by creating ontologies that capture such class relationships.

Inferential Queries [I]. Questions 3, 5 or 6 in Sect. 1 are inferential queries, simply because they cannot be answered by any fact alone, context resolution or disambiguation. In particular the questions *"Where were the trouts left?"* or *"Was Alice near the forest?"* can only be answered after active and transitive affirmations using deductions. Furthermore, the query *"Who is Alice's friend?"* or *"Is Bob Alice's friend?"* requires the knowledge that friendship is reciprocal, and can be computed using symmetricity rules.

5.2   Evaluation of Omniscient

While our goal remains to compare Omniscient with other question answering systems of similar kinds, in this section we investigate how it performs in terms of the six query classes on any given story, and roughly estimate its precision and recall. We also note that the most common queries are the FACE queries, and that the GI queries are knowledge queries [9] not addressed by most contemporary query answering systems. In Table 1, we show the NL questions in

Table 1. Sample questions and Omniscient responses.

Q#	Class	NL question	Omniscient response	Correct answer
Q1	F	Who made coffee?	Bob	Bob
Q2	F	Who snatched the fish?	Hawk	Hawk
Q3	F	Who caught the trouts?	Bob	Bob
Q4	C	What was frozen?	No answer	Lake
Q4	E	Who ate the fish?	No answer	Bob, Alice
Q6	E	Who ate the grilled trouts?	No answer	Bob, Alice
Q7	I	Who lit the fire?	Alice	Alice
Q8	I	Who was near the forest?	No answer	Bob, Alice, hawk
Q9	A	Who went fishing?	Bob, Alice	Bob, Alice
Q10	G	Who caught the fish?	Bob	Bob

different query classes, their corresponding expected responses and the Omniscient responses as computed. We then compute the precision and recall values on this small set of test questions as a preliminary performance indicator.

While the test data sets are not extensive and the experimental setup is small, Omniscient shows a precision of ≈100% and recall of ≈60%, which is encouraging. In this context, several observations are worth discussing. In our story, we stated that "... *his friend [referring to Bob] went to light a fire...*", and Omniscient was able to infer first of all that "his" refers to Bob, and that "his friend" is a placeholder for "Bob's friend". It is then able to deduce that this friend is Alice. This is possible because of the relationship information represented in the RDF graph, and the context resolution process of the system.

Furthermore, Bob catching trout has been explicitly mentioned and no mention was made that trout is a fish. Intuitively, we know that trout refers to fish. It is interesting to note that when asked, "*Who caught the fish?*", the system correctly answers "Bob". This particular behavior is a result of natural language processing (NLP) employed within Omniscient empowering the system with some form of generalization of the information in the text. After searching the graph and not finding a match for anyone catching fish, currently common NLP technique is employed to enable the system to search for occurrences within the graph that refer to fish. In this way, the system can "learn" new information that it did not previously have because it was not explicitly stated.

6   Discussion and Future Research

The current edition of Omniscient serves as a prototype to demonstrate that the architecture depicted in Fig. 6 for general purpose and open ended question answering based on unstructured texts and stories are possible. More importantly, its performance attests to the fact that research has matured enough to seriously consider an open-ended question answering system for arbitrary texts based on semantic storytelling and story understanding.

The other observation is that the investment in DBpedia ontology can be successfully leveraged to build a generic text to knowledge graph translation system which can be coupled with NL query to knowledge query translation over the knowledge graphs. As the reader may have observed that the human-like response generation from the computed and raw RDF/XML views still require significant research. In the case of Omniscient, we did not yet fully decide how to implement this component. Mainly because it is still under investigation when such human-like responses are warranted. For example, is it truly needed that we respond by saying "Bob's friend Alice lit the fire." when we ask *"Who lit the fire?"*, or is just "Alice" enough? In this context, it is perhaps interesting to note that in a conversational system, such a humanoid response is more appealing. In such a system, ambiguity resolution can be attempted by the system asking clarifying questions.

The Omniscient reasoning and inference engine discussed in Sect. 4.3 is also under development. This is because such a general purpose engine calls for significant investments and knowledge engineering. One interesting approach can be similar to DBpedia type community effort and curation system to collect general and common knowledge in ways similar to [12]. We are currently developing a seed knowledge base in Apache Jena to be able to seamlessly reason over the RDF knowledge graphs and deductive rules. We are also investigating a possible rule learning module to incrementally improve the body of general and common knowledge to better handle inferential and generalization queries, which the current edition does not handle well.

Finally to understand how well Omniscient handles open-ended stories, we have also experimented with the following story (also used by other researchers).

Rensselaer Polytechnic Institute, or RPI, is a private research university located in Troy, New York, with two additional campuses in Hartford and Groton, Connecticut. It was founded in 1824 by Stephen van Rensselaer and Amos Eaton for the "application of science to the common purposes of life" and is described as the oldest technological university in the English-speaking world. Built on a hillside, RPI's 265 acre campus overlooks the city of Troy and the Hudson River and is a blend of traditional and modern architecture. The institute operates an on-campus business incubator and the 1,250 acre Rensselaer Technology Park. Numerous American colleges or departments of applied sciences were modeled after Rensselaer. The university is one among a small group of polytechnic universities in the United States which tend to be primarily devoted to the instruction of technical arts and applied sciences.

While it could answer questions such as *"Where is RPI?"*, or *"Who founded RPI?"*, it could not respond to questions such as *"Who founded it?"* or *"Where was RPI built?"* resulting in low precision and recall, and indicating generalization of Omniscient requires more involved knowledge engineering.

7   Conclusion

In the age of Apple's Siri, Amazon's Alexa and IBM's Watson, there is ample motivation to be able to understand texts better than we currently do and respond intelligently to questions based on the embedded knowledge. To this end, we have developed the outlines of a general purpose text understanding system called *Omniscient* that is able to convert texts (interrelated sentences) into a general knowledge graph in RDF and then interrogate the graph using a network query language such as SPARQL. We have demonstrated the architecture we have proposed is a feasible and viable alternative to much expensive machine learning based approaches and that its performances are encouraging. It is our thesis that once we complete the prototype presented here to include a full blown general knowledgebase and reasoning system in it, Omniscient will be more effective and precise than many of the open domain contemporary question answering systems that rely on user stories.

References

1. A natural language query engine on wikidata. https://github.com/ayoungprogrammer/nlquery. Accessed 23 Apr 2019
2. Auer, S., Bizer, C., Kobilarov, G., Lehmann, J., Cyganiak, R., Ives, Z.: DBpedia: a nucleus for a web of open data. In: Aberer, K., et al. (eds.) ASWC/ISWC -2007. LNCS, vol. 4825, pp. 722–735. Springer, Heidelberg (2007). https://doi.org/10.1007/978-3-540-76298-0_52
3. Cimiano, P., Lüker, J., Nagel, D., Unger, C.: Exploiting ontology lexica for generating natural language texts from RDF data. In: ENLG, Sofia, Bulgaria, pp. 10–19 (2013)
4. Dong, N.T., Holder, L.B.: Natural language generation from graphs. Int. J. Semant. Comput. **8**(3), 335 (2014)
5. Draicchio, F., Gangemi, A., Presutti, V., Nuzzolese, A.G.: FRED: from natural language text to RDF and OWL in one click. In: Cimiano, P., Fernández, M., Lopez, V., Schlobach, S., Völker, J. (eds.) ESWC 2013. LNCS, vol. 7955, pp. 263–267. Springer, Heidelberg (2013). https://doi.org/10.1007/978-3-642-41242-4_36
6. Exner, P., Nugues, P.: Entity extraction: from unstructured text to DBpedia RDF triples. In: Web of Linked Entities Workshop, Boston, USA, pp. 58–69 (2012)
7. Gardent, C., Shimorina, A., Narayan, S., Perez-Beltrachini, L.: The WebNLG challenge: generating text from RDF data. In: INLG, Santiago de Compostela, Spain, pp. 124–133 (2017)
8. Hu, S., Zou, L., Yu, J.X., Wang, H., Zhao, D.: Answering natural language questions by subgraph matching over knowledge graphs. IEEE TKDE **30**(5), 824–837 (2018)
9. Jamil, H.M.: Knowledge rich natural language queries over structured biological databases. In: ACM BCB, Boston, MA, USA, pp. 352–361 (2017)
10. Kertkeidkachorn, N., Ichise, R.: An automatic knowledge graph creation framework from natural language text. IEICE Trans. **101**-D(1), 90–98 (2018)
11. Khapra, M.M., Raghu, D., Joshi, S., Reddy, S.: Generating natural language question-answer pairs from a knowledge graph using a RNN based question generation model. In: EACL, Valencia, Spain, vol. 1, pp. 376–385 (2017)

12. Patelli, A., et al.: An architecture for the autonomic curation of crowdsourced knowledge. Cluster Comput. **20**(3), 2031–2046 (2017)
13. Rehm, G., Zaczynska, K., Moreno, J.: Semantic storytelling: towards identifying storylines in large amounts of text content. In: Text2Story Workshop @ECIR, Cologne, Germany, pp. 63–70 (2019)
14. Rico, M., Unger, C., Cimiano, P.: Sorry, I only speak natural language: a pattern-based, data-driven and guided approach to mapping natural language queries to SPARQL. In: IESD co-located with ISWC, Bethlehem, Pennsylvania, USA (2015)
15. Sander, M., Waltinger, U., Roshchin, M., Runkler, T.A.: Ontology-based translation of natural language queries to SPARQL. In: AAAI Fall Symposia, Arlington, Virginia, USA (2014)
16. Shi, Q., Wang, Y., Sun, J., Fu, A.: Short text understanding based on conceptual and semantic enrichment. In: Gan, G., Li, B., Li, X., Wang, S. (eds.) ADMA 2018. LNCS (LNAI), vol. 11323, pp. 329–338. Springer, Cham (2018). https://doi.org/10.1007/978-3-030-05090-0_28
17. Steinmetz, N., Arning, A., Sattler, K.: From natural language questions to SPARQL queries: a pattern-based approach. In: (BTW), (DBIS), März, Rostock, Germany, pp. 289–308 (2019)
18. Wang, R., Wang, M., Liu, J., Chen, W., Cochez, M., Decker, S.: Leveraging knowledge graph embeddings for natural language question answering. In: Li, G., Yang, J., Gama, J., Natwichai, J., Tong, Y. (eds.) DASFAA 2019. LNCS, vol. 11446, pp. 659–675. Springer, Cham (2019). https://doi.org/10.1007/978-3-030-18576-3_39
19. Xiong, C.: Text representation, retrieval, and understanding with knowledge graphs. SIGIR Forum **52**(2), 180–181 (2018)
20. Zheng, W., Cheng, H., Yu, J.X., Zou, L., Zhao, K.: Interactive natural language question answering over knowledge graphs. Inf. Sci. **481**, 141–159 (2019)

Flexible Query Answering Methods and Techniques

Deductive Querying of Natural Logic Bases

Troels Andreasen[1]([✉]), Henrik Bulskov[1], Per Anker Jensen[2],
and Jørgen Fischer Nilsson[3]

[1] Computer Science, Roskilde University, Roskilde, Denmark
{troels,bulskov}@ruc.dk
[2] Management, Society and Communication, Copenhagen Business School,
Frederiksberg, Denmark
paj.msc@cbs.dk
[3] Mathematics and Computer Science, Technical University of Denmark,
Lyngby, Denmark
jfni@dtu.dk

Abstract. We introduce a dedicated form of natural logic intended for representation of sentences in a knowledge base. Natural logic is a version of formal logic whose sentences cover a stylized fragment of natural language. Thus, the sentences in the knowledge base can be read and understood directly by a domain expert, unlike, say, predicate logic and description logic. The paper describes the inference rules enabling deductive querying of the knowledge base. The natural logic sentences and the inference rules are represented in DATALOG providing a convenient graph form. As such, the natural logic knowledge base may be viewed as an enriched formal ontology structure. We describe various query facilities including pathway finding accommodated by this setup.

Keywords: Natural logic · Knowledge bases · Deductive querying · Formal ontology

1 Introduction

This paper briefly introduces a form of natural logic (Sánchez Valencia 1991; van Benthem 1986; Klíma 2010) intended for ontology-structured knowledge bases. After having introduced a natural logic dubbed NATURALOG, the second half of the paper focuses on deductive querying of natural logic knowledge bases. Basically the natural logic states quantified relationships between classes. As such, NATURALOG generalizes the inclusion relationships in formal ontologies by admitting arbitrary relations in addition to class inclusion. In addition, the present version of NATURALOG offers complex class terms reflecting the phrase structures of natural language according to the principles of generative ontologies, cf. (Andreasen and Nilsson 2004). Furthermore, NATURALOG bears some affinity to description logic as discussed in (Andreasen et al. 2018). However, as

© Springer Nature Switzerland AG 2019
A. Cuzzocrea et al. (Eds.): FQAS 2019, LNAI 11529, pp. 231–241, 2019.
https://doi.org/10.1007/978-3-030-27629-4_22

one noteworthy difference, NATURALOG abandons forced use of copula sentences in favor of sentences with free choice of transitive verbs from the considered knowledge base domain.

We explain how NATURALOG sentences can be encoded as propositions in DATALOG, that is definite clauses without function symbols. Moreover, the inference rules used for deductive querying are also expressed in DATALOG extended, where relevant, with negation as non-provability as known from logic programming. Representing the sentences and the inference rules in DATALOG ensures decidability and tractability of the deductive querying.

In Sects. 2 and 3 we explain the elementary forms of NATURALOG sentences and the encoding of NATURALOG as propositions. We proceed in Sect. 4 by explaining the relevant inference rules for the purpose of deductive querying as DATALOG clauses. Thereafter, in Sect. 5 we extend NATURALOG to comprise recursively structured noun phrases and verbs endowed with adverbial forms. This extension calls for decomposition of the compound phrases in the DATALOG Encoding. Section 6 explains the concept of materialization and Sect. 7 demonstrates various different query facilities. Finally, we conclude in Sect. 8.

The present paper focuses on query functionalities for NATURALOG knowledge bases and follows up on our former publications on the application of natural logic in (Andreasen et al. 2017a, 2015, 2017b; Nilsson 2015). The details of the syntax and the formal semantics of the NATURALOG logic are elaborated in the coming paper (Andreasen et al. 2018) that also specifies NATURALOG in terms of predicate logic and introduces the concomitant graph conception of NATURALOG knowledge bases.

2   Elementary NATURALOG Sentence Forms

NATURALOG elementary sentences primarily take the form
            [every] *Cnoun Verb* [some] *Cnoun*
where *Cnoun* is a common noun and *Verb* is a transitive verb (i.e. a verb taking a linguistic object), or *Verb* may be the copula *is* written isa as common in formal ontologies. In the natural logic, we ignore inflections, using singular forms of common nouns.

With the indicated defaults for the determiners (quantifiers), as an example there is
            betacell produce insulin
for
            every betacell produce some insulin
As another example one may state the inclusion
            insulin isa hormone
for
            every insulin is-equal-to some hormone
understood modelling-wise as claiming that every portion of insulin is-equal-to some portion of hormone. A knowledge base consists of a finite number of affirmative NATURALOG sentences. A NATURALOG knowledge base may be conceived

as a class-inclusion ontology extended with more general sentence forms containing transitive verbs stating relations between classes. The determiner *no* yielding denials is not admitted in knowledge base sentences. It appears only in deduced sentences by way of the closed world assumption.

In (Andreasen et al. 2018) we discuss alternative quantifiers to the given defaults

$$(\text{every}|\text{some}|\text{no})\ Cnoun\ Verb\ (\text{some}|\text{every})\ Cnoun$$

3   Encoding of NATURALOG as Propositions

We now describe the encoding of NATURALOG sentences in DATALOG since this is crucial for deductive querying. Recall that DATALOG restricts clauses to being definite logical clauses without compound terms, so that predicate arguments are either implicitly universally quantified variables or constants. Logically, NATURALOG sentences represent relationships between two relata classes or concepts with the inclusion relation as a common case in formal ontologies, cf. (Smith and Rosse 2004; Moss 2010).

The above elementary NATURALOG sentences are encoded as what we refer to as propositions in DATALOG factual atomic sentences of the form

p(*Det, Noun, Verb, Noun*)

with a predicate **p** at this metalogical level, and where *Det* is either every or some. At the DATALOG metalogical level *Noun* and *Verb* appear as constants as in the sample

p(every, betacell, produce, insulin)

In the propositions at the metalogical level nouns are conceived of as concepts C (one-argument predicates) and verbs as relations R. For the default case of the determiner being every, we introduce a variant form of the predicate **p** through the pair of defining clauses

p(C, R, D) ↔ **p**(every, C, R, D)

In the setup of the knowledge base nouns and verbs are declared by additional metalevel predicates as in the sample

concept(betacell), **concept**(insulin), **relation**(produce), **relation**(isa)

or indirectly by

concept(C) ← **p**(Q, C, R, D)
concept(D) ← **p**(Q, C, R, D)
relation(R) ← **p**(Q, C, R, D)

For a full predicate logical construal of NATURALOG we refer to (Andreasen et al. 2018).

We appeal to the principle of existential import, implying that there is no explicit presence of an empty concept, cf. (Andreasen et al. 2017a; Nilsson 2015). In Sect. 4, we explain how this doctrine may handle the case of disjoint concepts, that is, concepts having an empty overlapping concept. This principle means that all concepts appearing in a knowledge base proposition are assumed to be non-empty through presence of a hypothetical anonymous entity. By contrast, concepts that do not appear anywhere in the knowledge base are assumed to be empty in the deductive querying process.

4   Inference Rules

The universally quantified variables appearing in the following DATALOG clauses effectively range over encoded concepts C, D etc. and relations R in NATURALOG propositions.

Reflexivity
>**p**(C, isa, C)

Monotonicity
>**p**(C', R, D) ← **p**(C', isa, C) ∧ **p**(C, R, D)
>**p**(C, R, D') ← **p**(C, R, D) ∧ **p**(D, isa, D')

Transitivity
>**p**(C, R, D) ← **trans**(R) ∧ **p**(C, R, CD) ∧ **p**(CD, R, D)

Inversion (passive voice formation)
>**p**(some, D, Rinv, C) ← **inv**(R, Rinv) ∧ **p**(some, C, R, D)

Weakening of quantifiers
>**p**(some, C, R, D) ← **p**(C, R, D)

Denials
>**p**(no, C, R, D) ← ⊬ **p**(some, C, R, D)

Disjointness
>**p**(no, C, isa, D) ← ⊬ **common**(C, D)
>**common**(C, D) ← **p**(CD, isa, C) ∧ **p**(CD, isa, D)

The auxiliary predicate **inv** lists pairs of inverse relations such as **inv**(promote, promoted_by).

The above inference rules serve logical purposes being justified eventually by the underlying logical construal of NATURALOG. In addition, one may introduce ad hoc rules such as transitivity for causality and parthood relations.

5   Restrictive Modifiers

We now extend the elementary NATURALOG sentences by incorporation of recursive phrase structures acting as restrictive modifiers. When adjoined to nouns modifiers provide subconcepts (specialization) of the concept denoted by the noun. Similarly, when adjoined to verbs as adverbials they yield subrelations (specialized relations).

This paper focusses on adnominal modifiers, assuming in the logical treatment that they linguistically take the form of restrictive relative clauses as in the sample noun phrase

>cell that produce hormone

A more comprehensive treatment of the linguistic variants would include also adnominal PPs and restrictive adjectives.

Restrictive modifiers give rise to formation of auxiliary concepts that are subconcepts of the head noun concept. These auxiliary concepts may be thought to come about by synonymity as if instituted by the pair

>cell-that-produce-hormone isa cell that produce hormone
>cell that produce hormone isa cell-that-produce-hormone

However, these prospective sentences are shown for explanatory reasons only, as they are going to be dealt with in a dedicated manner: At the metalogical level of propositions modifiers are handled by means of definitions complementing the propositions **p** and being of the factual clausal form

$\quad$ **d**$(Caux, C, R, C')$

with the additional predicate **d** (for definition) and where $Caux$ is a new concept coming about by modification of the concept C with the modifier that $R\ C'$, as in that produce hormone. As a special case, R may be isa. The new concept $Caux$ is generated as a constant in the metalogical representation as in the sample

$\quad$ **d**(cell-that-produce-hormone, cell, produce, hormone)

Such a definition is made to act as two propositions through

$\quad$ **p**(CRC, isa, C) ← **d**(CRC,C,R,C')
$\quad$ **p**(CRC, R, C') ← **d**(CRC,C,R,C')

The definition **d**(CRC',C,R,C') can be visualized as in Fig. 1, where by convention unlabelled arcs represent isa.

With the stated inference rules and adding a rule covering subsumption,

$\quad$ **p**(X, isa, CRC') ← **d**(CRC', C, R, C') ∧
$\quad\quad\quad$ **p**(X, isa, C) ∧ **p**(X, R, C')

and assuming **p**(X,isa,C) and **p**(X,R,C') for any concept X, one gets the inferred proposition as indicated by the dashed arrow in Fig. 2(a). The subsumption rule is to be activated in a compilation phase in order to ensure that all inclusion relationships are made explicit prior to querying.

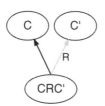

Fig. 1. Definition of the concept CRC'

For definitions, the defining edges share origins as shown for CRC' in Fig. 1.

As an example consider the definition **d**(cell-that-produce-insulin, cell, produce, insulin). From this the two propositions **p**(cell-that-produce-insulin, isa, cell) and **p**(cell-that-produce-insulin, produce, insulin) follows. Now given **p**(betacell,produce,insulin) and **p**(betacell, isa, cell), it follows by subsumption that **p**(betacell, isa, cell-that-produce-insulin), as indicated in Fig. 2(b).

The syntactic class of noun phrases with restrictive modifiers further comprises conjunctions as shown schematically in

$\quad$ C that $R1\ C1$ and $\ C$ that $R2\ C2$

giving rise to

$\quad\quad$ **d**(C-that-$R1$-$C1$, C, $R1\ C1$)
$\quad\quad$ **d**(C-that-$R2$-$C2$, C, $R2\ C2$)

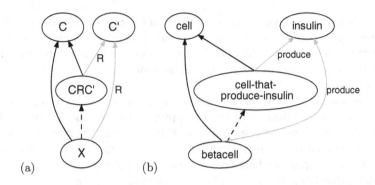

Fig. 2. Propositions inferred by subsumption (dashed edges)

and in turn
       d(C-that-$R1$-$C1$-and-C-that-$R2$-$C2$, C-that-$R1$-$C1$,isa, C-that-$R2$-$C2$)
       Example: cell that produce hormone and cell that in thyroid_gland
This should not to be confused with the recursively nested form in
       production of hormone in thyroid_gland

6   Materialization of Concepts in the Knowledge Base

We advance the following subsumption materialization principle:

Besides those concepts that are mentioned in the deconstructed knowledge
base propositions, all conceivable concepts that subsume those concepts
are to be materialized in the knowledge base. Moreover, these materialized
concepts are furnished with their pertinent isa relations (less, generally, isa
relations following by transitivity) and coalesced into the knowledge base.

In other words, the ontology logically inherent in the knowledge base by
virtue of isa-relationships is to be completed upwards by adding the necessary,

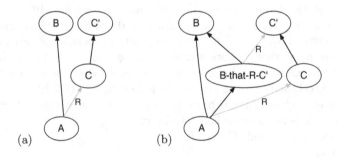

Fig. 3. Materialization of a new concept B-that-R-C' from a defined concept A

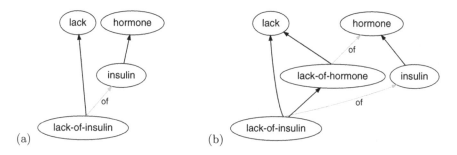

Fig. 4. Materialization of a new concept lack-of-hormone from a defined concept lack-of-insulin

finite number of additional concepts like B-that-R-C' in Fig. 3 or lack-of-hormone in Fig. 4.

As a corollary to this principle, all non-empty concepts, that is, all concepts possibly contributing to query answers, are made explicit in the knowledge base in advance by a compilation of the entire knowledge base. Thus, the subsumption materialization principle ensures that concepts that may appear as query answers are explicitly present in the knowledge base as an integral part of the ontological structure. The original individual propositions remain unaffected by this compilation. Inference rules for dynamically creating these new concepts and fitting them into the ontology are described in our (Andreasen et al. 2018).

7   Querying

In this section, we discuss some of the query functionalities for NATURALOG. Given that the NATURALOG knowledge base consists of propositions encoded as DATALOG atomic clauses supported by the stated clausal inference rules in DATALOG, querying can now be explained and carried out as deduction initiated by an appropriate query clause as known from logic programming.

7.1   Concept Querying

The primary query case is a NATURALOG sentence containing a variable as in

  X isa c_{query}

being encoded as $\mathbf{p}(X, \text{isa}, c_{query})$, where X is a DATALOG variable ranging over all concept terms, and where the constituent symbols of c_{query} are assumed to be present in the knowledge base. For instance, considering the knowledge base fragment in Fig. 2, the term c_{query} could be the concept cell that produce insulin with the expected deduced answer being betacell, while, considering Fig. 6, an answer to a query hormone would be insulin.

Assuming that the term c_{query} is actually present in the knowledge base, it is to provide as answers all concept terms immediately subsumed by c_{query}, that is, residing just below c_{query}. Effectively, then, the answer is trivial if the term c_{query} itself is the only one available due to the reflexivity of isa.

7.2   Relaxed Concept Querying

Now, let us turn to the case where c_{query} is absent from the knowledge base. Then, logically the answer is empty in the closed world assumption setting. However, in order to achieve a more flexible query functionality, we devise a relaxation principle transcending deduction in DATALOG amounting to ascending step by step in the ontological structure from where the concept c_{query} would have been be placed. As an example, take the query concept

cell that reside_in brain and that produce insulin

In a first ascending step, given that brain isa organ and insulin isa hormone, this would relax to

cell that reside_in organ and that produce insulin

as well as to

cell that reside_in brain and that produce hormone

both potentially subsuming concepts in the knowledge base, thereby providing useful answers by subsumption (Fig. 5).

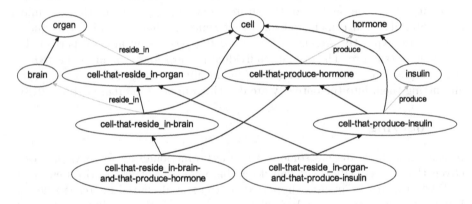

Fig. 5. Relaxed query where the query term is absent from the knowledge base

In outline, the relaxation algorithm works as follows: Without essential loss of generality, assume that c_{query} is of the form c-that-r_1-c_1-and-that-r_2-c_2 with the two restrictive modifiers that-r_1-c_1 and that-r_2-c_2. Then consider the three concept terms formed by generalization

c^{sup}-that-r_1-c_1-and-that-r_2-c_2

c-that-r_1-c_1^{sup}-and-that-r_2-c_2

c-that-r_1-c_1-and-that-r_2-c_2^{sup}

where c^{sup}, c_1^{sup} and c_2^{sup} are the corresponding concept terms one step up ontologically (assuming here for simplicity that they are unique). If either of these is present in the knowledge base, then those ones are engaged for deducing the query answers as shown in Sect. 7.1. Otherwise the relaxation step is iterated one step up again.

7.3   Pathway Querying

The entire knowledge base graph forms a road map between all the applied concepts. The introduction of a universal concept at the top of the ontology ensures that all concepts are connected. This concept map can be queried by means of rules searching pathways in the graph between two stated concepts as sketched here:

path(C, D) ← **p**(Q, C, R, CD) ∧ **path**(CD, D)
path(C, D) ← **p**(Q, C, R, D)

In our setup, the knowledge base may be conceived as a bidirectional graph: by applying the inversion and the weakening rules and leaving the quantifiers Q unspecified, the predicate **path** may exploit the inverse relation paths. The interesting pathways are obviously the shortest ones, employing appropriate distance weights to the various relations.

Below we consider a few examples of pathway queries with reference to the knowledge base fragment shown in Fig. 6, loosely based on (Kehler 1988; Weston et al. 1997).

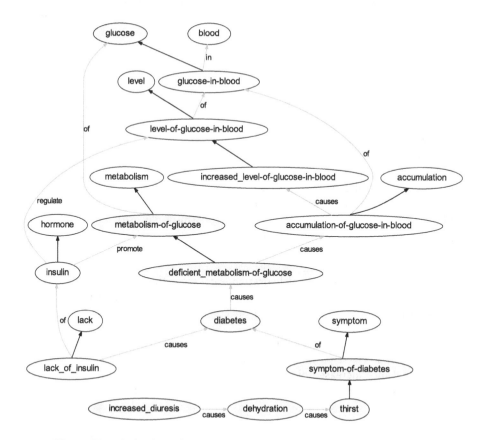

Fig. 6. Knowledge base fragment exemplifying a pathway (greyed nodes)

The pathway query (diabetes, accumulation) requesting a path connecting the two concepts. This would correspond to the edges traversed by evaluation of **path**(diabetes, accumulation), that is, the following propositions

p(diabetes, causes, deficient_metabolism-of-glucose),

p(deficient_metabolism-of-glucose, causes, accumulation-of-glucose-in-blood),

p(accumulation-of-glucose-in-blood, isa, accumulation)

thus, a path connecting diabetes and accumulation is

diabetes − causes − deficient_metabolism-of-glucose − causes −
accumulation-of-glucose-in-blood − isa − accumulation

An example of a pathway query exploiting inverse relation paths is (deficient_metabolism-of-glucose, insulin). One possible answer path would involve the following propositions

p(deficient_metabolism-of-glucose, isa, metabolism-of-glucose),

p(some, metabolism-of-glucose, promoted_by, insulin)

Notice that the latter proposition traverses an edge in the opposite direction by applying the weakening rule leading to **p**(some, insulin, promote, metabolism-of-glucose) and then the inversion inference rule assuming the fact inv(promote, promoted_by). Thus, the connecting path in this case is

deficient_metabolism-of-glucose − isa −
metabolism-of-glucose − promoted_by − insulin

As a final example consider the query (increased_diuresis, glucose). One path connecting the two query concepts would be based on the following propositions

p(increased_diuresis, causes, dehydration),

p(dehydration, causes, thirst),

p(thirst, isa, symptom-of-diabetes),

p(symptom-of-diabetes, of, diabetes),

p(diabetes, causes, deficient_metabolism-of-glucose),

p(deficient_metabolism-of-glucose, isa, metabolism-of-glucose),

p(metabolism-of-glucose, of, glucose),

and thus traverse

increased_diuresis − causes − dehydration − causes − thirst − isa − symptom-of-diabetes − of − diabetes − causes − deficient_metabolism-of-glucose − isa − metabolism-of-glucose − of − glucose,

The corresponding path is indicated in Fig. 6 by the greyed nodes.

Notice that derived paths can be reduced by applying again the inference rules. For instance increased_diuresis − causes − dehydration − causes − thirst can be reduced to increased_diuresis − causes − thirst assuming **trans**(causes).

8   Conclusion and Perspectives

We have described a deductive knowledge base setup for a natural logic based on the DATALOG decidable logic used as metalogic.

In addition to the query forms described in this paper, we envisage query facilities such as spreading activation traversing near concepts in the graph, commonality querying deducing common properties of two concepts and analogy queries, where, given a, b and c, an analogy query is to deduce an X such that $X\ R\ c$ whenever we have $a\ R\ b$.

References

Andreasen, T., Bulskov, H., Nilsson, J.F., Jensen, P.A.: A system for conceptual pathway finding and deductive querying. In: Andreasen, T., et al. (eds.) Flexible Query Answering Systems 2015. AISC, vol. 400, pp. 461–472. Springer, Cham (2016). https://doi.org/10.1007/978-3-319-26154-6_35

Andreasen, T., Bulskov, H., Jensen, P.A., Nilsson, J.F. A natural logic for natural-language knowledge bases. In: Partiality, Underspecification, and Natural Language Processing. Cambridge Scholars (2017a)

Andreasen, T., Bulskov, H., Jensen, P.A., Nilsson, J.F.: Pathway computation in models derived from bio-science text sources. In: Kryszkiewicz, M., Appice, A., Ślęzak, D., Rybinski, H., Skowron, A., Raś, Z.W. (eds.) ISMIS 2017. LNCS (LNAI), vol. 10352, pp. 424–434. Springer, Cham (2017b). https://doi.org/10.1007/978-3-319-60438-1_42

Andreasen, T., Bulskov, H., Jensen, P.A., Nilsson, J.F.: Natural logic knowledge bases and their graph form. Submitted to Journal, 34 p. (2018, under review)

Andreasen, T., Nilsson, J.F.: Grammatical specification of domain ontologies. Data Knowl. Eng. **48**(2), 221–230 (2004)

Kehler, A.: Anatomi og Fysologi I og II. Arnold Busk (1988)

Klíma, G.: Natural logic, medieval logic and formal semantics. Logic Lang. Math. 2 (2010)

Moss, L.S.: Syllogistic logics with verbs. J. Log. Comput. **20**(4), 947–967 (2010)

Nilsson, J.F.: In pursuit of natural logics for ontology-structured knowledge bases. In: The Seventh International Conference on Advanced Cognitive Technologies and Applications (2015)

Sánchez Valencia, V.M.: Studies on Natural Logic and Categorial Grammar. Categorial grammar. Universiteit van Amsterdam, Amsterdam, Holland (1991)

Smith, B., Rosse, C.: The role of foundational relations in the alignment of biomedical ontologies. Medinfo **11**(Pt 1), 444–448 (2004)

van Benthem, J.: Essays in Logical Semantics. Studies in Linguistics and Philosophy, vol. 29. D. Reidel, Dordrecht (1986)

Weston, T., Horton, C., Weston, T.: Atlas of Atonomy. Marshall Cavendish (1997)

Clustering of Intercriteria Analysis Data Using a Health-Related Quality of Life Data

Sotir Sotirov[1]($\boxtimes$), Desislava Vankova[2], Valentin Vasilev[1],
and Evdokia Sotirova[1]

[1] Prof. Assen Zlatarov University, 1 Prof. Yakimov str., 8010 Burgas, Bulgaria
{ssotirov, esotirova}@btu.bg, vailvasilev@mail.bg
[2] Medical University "Prof. Dr. Paraskev Stoyanov", 55 Prof. Marin Drinov str.,
9002 Varna, Bulgaria
vanko07@gmail.com

Abstract. Determination of Inter Criteria Analysis (ICA) dependence very often uses large amounts of data. In this paper, the large amount of data is reduced using the Self Organizing Map Neural Networks to use only the cluster representative vector. The data used are intuitionistic fuzzy estimations of quality of life. To obtain the data, a population study on health-related quality of life is used.

Keywords: Intuitionistic fuzzy set · Health-related quality of life · Clustering · Neural networks

1 Introduction

Using ICA, dependencies of parameters (or objects) are derived based on their data. Very often, the parameters and the resulting dependencies are many to be used in real-life applications. The proposed report suggests that ICA-derived intuitionist fuzzy values should be clustered with one of the commonly used methods - Self Organizing Map Neural Networks (SOM). This allows a large number of data to be combined into one vector of each cluster. SOM is trained using unsupervised learning to produce low dimensional representation of the training samples while preserving the topological properties of the input space. This makes SOM reasonable for visualizing low-dimensional views of high-dimensional data, akin to multidimensional scaling. This reduces the amount of information without losing its importance. The obtained vector can be used for real purposes. For example, we used data on health-related quality of life measured in a cross-sectional survey conducted in Bourgas, Bulgaria. In previous articles [16, 19], Feed Forward Neural Network and ICA were used.

2 Health-Related Quality of Life

Health-related quality of life (HrQoL) has been used in medicine and public health as a reliable outcome measure and a needs assessment frame [1, 11, 17]. The importance of standardized HrQoL-instruments is growing because we need to evaluate and

© Springer Nature Switzerland AG 2019
A. Cuzzocrea et al. (Eds.): FQAS 2019, LNAI 11529, pp. 242–249, 2019.
https://doi.org/10.1007/978-3-030-27629-4_23

internationally compare the impact of the socially important diseases [22]. The terms HrQoL, quality of life, functional status, self-assessed health, subjective health and health status are often used interchangeably.

Measuring HrQoL is a way to "hear the voice" of the patient or of the person and to analyze the determinants that could influence the health status of every individual. Researching HrQoL at a community level could be an alternative or complementary approach in understanding health inequalities [21].

The data used in the current analysis is extracted from a cross-sectional population study which measures the HrQoL in the Burgas community, Bulgaria. Further, the influence of socio-economic, demographic, and behavioral determinants on HrQoL are assessed [18]. The relationship between HrQoL and social capital (SC) is analyzed through a network-based approach [14].

The HrQoL is assessed through the standardized generic EQ-5D-3L instrument which defines health in five dimensions including mobility, self-care, usual activities (work, study, housework, family, or leisure), pain or discomfort, and anxiety or depression. Each dimension has three levels ranging from "no problem", then "some problem", and to "extreme problem". EQ-5D-3L tool consists of two components. The first part is the descriptive element with the five dimensions. Respondents rating their health status are asked to select the level of dimension which describes at best their "health today". The second part is the Visual Analogue Scale (VAS – "Thermometer" type) in which respondents record their self-rating of health "100- denoting as best imaginable health state" and "0 - denoting as worst imaginable health state".

The influence of the following demographic and socio-economic determinants on HrQoL is investigated: age; sex; marital status (married, unmarried, divorced, partnership, widowed); numbers of children in the family (none, one, two, three, more); ethnicity (Bulgarians, Turks, Roma, other); religious (yes, no, no identification); literacy – reading and writing (yes, no); educational level (no education, basic, primary, secondary, Bachelor, Master, PhD); employment (employed, what exactly; pensioner related to age; pensioner related to disability; working at home; unemployed); regular monthly income in the household per person (8 levels starting with the mean minimum income). The influence of the following behaviorial determinants on HrQoL is investigated: smoking (smoker, non-smoker, ex-smoker); regular physical activity/sport- twice weekly (yes/no); hobby or regular leisure activity (yes/no). The SC as a determinant of HrQoL is investigated through a membership in 2 types of organizations [14, 20] which are: Putnamesque type (voluntary): club of interest, retirement club and non-governmental or charity foundation; or Olsonian type –professional organization, e political party or students' organization.

3   Intercriteria Analysis

As we mentioned above, the ICA-method [6, 8, 9] is based on two main concepts: intuitionistic fuzzy sets and index matrices. A brief description is offered below for completeness.

Let I be a fixed set of indices and let R be the set of the real numbers. An index matrix (IM) with sets of indices K and L ($K, L \subset I$) is defined by [4]

$$[K, L, \{a_{k_i,l_j}\}] \equiv \begin{array}{c|cccc} & l_1 & l_2 & \cdots & l_n \\ \hline k_1 & a_{k_1,l_1} & a_{k_1,l_2} & \cdots & a_{k_1,l_n} \\ k_2 & a_{k_2,l_1} & a_{k_2,l_2} & \cdots & a_{k_2,l_n} \\ \vdots & \vdots & \vdots & \ddots & \vdots \\ k_m & a_{k_m,l_1} & a_{k_m,l_2} & \cdots & a_{k_m,l_n} \end{array},$$

where $K = \{k_1, k_2, ..., k_m\}$, $L = \{l_1, l_2, ..., l_n\}$, for $1 \leq i \leq m$, and $1 \leq j \leq n : a_{k_i,l_j} \in R$.

For any two IMs, a series of relations, operations, and operators have been defined. The theory behind the IMs is described in a more detail fashion in [15].

Here, following the description of the ICA approach, given by [4], we will start with the IM M with index sets with m rows $\{O_1, ..., O_m\}$ and n columns $\{C_1, ..., C_n\}$, where for every p, q $(1 \leq p \leq m, 1 \leq q \leq n)$, O_p in an evaluated object, C_q is an evaluation criterion, and e_{O_p,C_q} is the evaluation of the p-th object against the q-th criterion, defined as a real number or another object that is comparable according to relation R with all the rest elements of the IM M.

$$M = \begin{array}{c|cccccccc} & C_1 & \cdots & C_k & \cdots & C_l & \cdots & C_n \\ \hline O_1 & e_{O_1,C_1} & \cdots & e_{O_1,C_k} & \cdots & e_{O_1,C_l} & \cdots & e_{O_1,C_n} \\ \vdots & \vdots & \ddots & \vdots & \ddots & \vdots & \ddots & \vdots \\ O_i & e_{O_i,C_1} & \cdots & e_{O_i,C_k} & \cdots & e_{O_i,C_l} & \cdots & e_{O_i,C_n} \\ \vdots & \vdots & \ddots & \vdots & \ddots & \vdots & \ddots & \vdots \\ O_j & e_{O_j,C_1} & \cdots & e_{O_j,C_k} & \cdots & e_{O_j,C_l} & \cdots & e_{O_j,C_n} \\ \vdots & \vdots & \ddots & \vdots & \ddots & \vdots & \ddots & \vdots \\ O_m & e_{O_m,C_1} & \cdots & e_{O_m,C_j} & \cdots & e_{O_m,C_l} & \cdots & e_{O_m,C_n} \end{array},$$

From the requirement for comparability above, it follows that for each i, j, k it holds the relation $R(e_{O_i,C_k}, e_{O_j,C_k})$. The relation R has a dual relation $\bar{R}$, which is true in the cases when the relation R is false, and vice versa.

For the requirements of the proposed method, pairwise comparisons between every two different criteria are made along all evaluated objects. During the comparison, a counter is maintained for the number of times when the relation R holds, and another counter – for the dual relation.

Let $S_{k,l}^\mu$ be the number of cases in which the relations $R(e_{O_i,C_k}, e_{O_j,C_k})$ and $R(e_{O_i,C_l}, e_{O_j,C_l})$ are simultaneously satisfied. Let also $S_{k,l}^\nu$ be the number of cases in which the relations $R(e_{O_i,C_k}, e_{O_j,C_k})$ and its dual $\bar{R} = (e_{O_i,C_l}, e_{O_j,C_l})$ are simultaneously satisfied. As the total number of pairwise comparisons between the objects is given by $m(m-1)/2$, it can be verified that the following inequalities hold:

$$0 \leq S_{k,l}^{\mu} + S_{k,l}^{\nu} \leq \frac{m(m-1)}{2}.$$

For every k, l, such that $1 \leq k \leq l \leq n$, and for $m \geq 2$ two numbers are defined:

$$\mu_{C_k,C_l} = 2\frac{S_{k,l}^{\mu}}{m(m-1)}, \nu_{C_k,C_l} = 2\frac{S_{k,l}^{\nu}}{m(m-1)}$$

The pair constructed from these two numbers plays the role of the intuitionistic fuzzy evaluation [2, 3, 5, 7] as an extension of the concept of reflection of sets defined by Zadde [23] of the relations that can be established between any two criteria C_k and C_l. In this way, the IM M that relates evaluated objects with evaluating criteria can be transformed to another IM M^* that gives the relations detected among the criteria, where stronger correlation exists where the first component μ_{C_k,C_l} is higher while the second component ν_{C_k,C_l} is lower.

$$M^* = \frac{\begin{array}{c|ccc} & C_1 & \cdots & C_n \end{array}}{\begin{array}{c|ccc} C_1 & \langle \mu_{C_1,C_1}, \nu_{C_1,C_1} \rangle & \cdots & \langle \mu_{C_1,C_n}, \nu_{C_1,C_n} \rangle \\ \cdots & \cdots & \cdots & \cdots \\ C_n & \langle \mu_{C_n,C_1}, \nu_{C_n,C_1} \rangle & \cdots & \langle \mu_{C_n,C_n}, \nu_{C_n,C_n} \rangle \end{array}}$$

From practical considerations, it has been more flexible to work with two IMs M^{μ} and M^{ν}, rather than with the IM M^* of IF pairs. IM M^{μ} contains as elements the first components of the IFPs of M^*, while M^{ν} - the second components of the IFPs of M^*.

4 Self Organizing Map Neural Networks

Self-learning self-organizing maps are a kind of artificial neural networks [10, 12, 13, 15]. The purpose of self-organizing maps (SOM) is to transform the input model (signal) of a certain size into n-dimensional dimension and to transform it adaptively into a topological mode. The SOM neurons are located in a m-grid, each of the inlets being fed to the entrance of each of the neurons. The figure shows Self Organizing Map Neural Networks with $n = 2$ (Fig. 1). This network is a single-layer straight structure of neurons located in lines and columns. This network is a single-layer straight structure of neurons located in lines and columns. The training of the neural network is based on the principle of competitive training, with only one winner after the SOM training (Fig. 2).

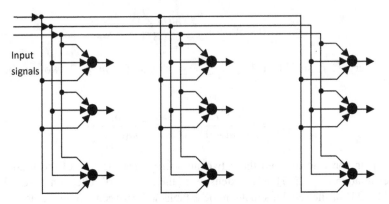

Fig. 1. Two dimension SOM neural network.

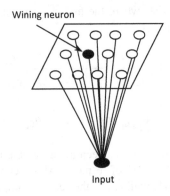

Fig. 2. Wining neuron of the SOM.

5 Discussion

For the preparation we use MATLAB and SOM neural network structure 3:9 (3 inputs, 9 neurons of the output) (Fig. 3). These 9 output neurons show that we will have 9 clusters that will contain the input data. For the inputs data we use intuitionistic fuzzy estimations from the data taken from quantitative EQ-5D-data taken from the presented above cross-sectional study [18, 21], (in this case we use 230).

For the learning vector we use the data from ICA quantitative data analysis EQ-5D-data. The data contain values of the degree of affiliations μ, non-affiliations v and degree of the uncertainty π. The obtained information, are represented by ordered triples $\langle \mu, v, \pi \rangle$ of real numbers from the set $[0, 1] \times [0, 1] \times [0, 1]$ as a $\pi = 1 - \mu - v$.

For the learning of the neural network the data with 230×3 values were used.

For the test we use 230 vectors. We train the SOM neural network with 1000 epochs. The structure of the neural network is shown at Fig. 3: The neural network structure. After the learning process weight coefficients are shown at the Fig. 4: The weight positions, where the green spots are the training vectors and the black points are weight coefficients (Fig. 5).

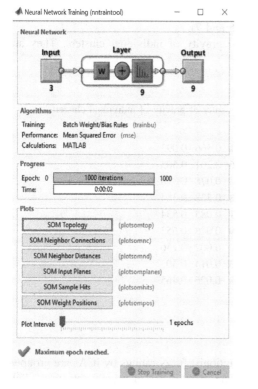

Fig. 3. The neural network structure.

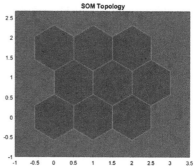

Fig. 4. The neural network topology.

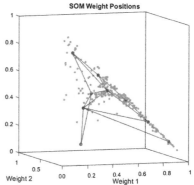

Fig. 5. The weight positions.

For the testing of the neural network all 230 vectors were used. The hits of the neural network are shown on the figure below (Fig. 6: The hits in the clusters).

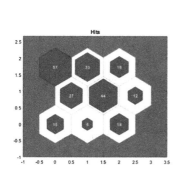

Fig. 6. The hits in the clusters.

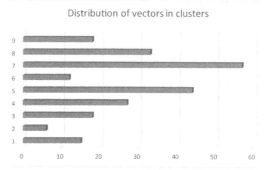

Fig. 7. Distribution of vectors in clusters.

After the training of the neural network, you can see the number of input vectors that belong to the different clusters (Figs. 6 and 7).

Weight coefficients form the center of gravity of individual clusters. They are shown in the Table 1.

Table 1. Weight coefficients form the center of gravity of individual clusters.

	μ	ν	π
Cluster 1	0.341	0.566	0.093
Cluster 2	0.296	0.201	0.503
Cluster 3	0.104	0.078	0.818
Cluster 4	0.278	0.338	0.384
Cluster 5	0.381	0.085	0.534
Cluster 6	0.299	0.048	0.653
Cluster 7	0.842	0.002	0.156
Cluster 8	0.683	0.014	0.303
Cluster 9	0.509	0.026	0.465

6   Conclusion

The article proposes a method in which intuitionist fuzzy ratings by ICAs are grouped into clusters. To get the clusters we used one of the types of neuron networks - Self organizing map. In addition to clustering from the neural network, representative vectors can be obtained and can be used to replace the values of the vectors of the respective cluster. For testing and applying the method, we used data on health-related quality of life measures from a study conducted in Burgas, Bulgaria.

Acknowledgments. The authors are grateful for the support provided by the project DN-02-10/2016 "New Instruments for Knowledge Discovery from Data, and their Modelling", funded by the National Science Fund, Bulgarian Ministry of Education, Youth and Science.

The authors declare that there is no conflict of interest regarding the publication of this paper.

References

1. Atanasov, A., et al.: Evaluation of the quality of life in patients with various abdominal anastomoses in case of colon carcinoma. In: Regional Scientific Conference, Svilengrad, vol. 17, pp. 110–112, 19 November 2011. ISBN 978 -954-397-023-0
2. Atanassov, K.T.: Intuitionistic fuzzy relations (IFRs). In: Atanassov, K.T. (ed.) On Intuitionistic Fuzzy Sets Theory. STUDFUZZ, vol. 283, pp. 147–193. Springer, Heidelberg (2012). https://doi.org/10.1007/978-3-642-29127-2_8
3. Atanassov, K.T.: Intuitionistic fuzzy sets. Fuzzy Sets Syst. **20**(1), 87–96 (1986)
4. Atanassov, K.T.: Index Matrices: towards an Augmented Matrix Calculus. Studies in Computational Intelligence, vol. 573. Springer, Cham (2014). https://doi.org/10.1007/978-3-319-10945-9

5. Atanassov, K.: Intuitionistic Fuzzy Sets: Theory and Applications. Physica-Verlag, Heidelberg (1999)
6. Atanassov, K., et al.: Intercriteria analysis over normalized data. In: 2016 IEEE 8th International Conference on Intelligent Systems (IS), pp. 564–566. IEEE (2016). https://doi.org/10.1109/is.2016.7737480
7. Atanassov, K.: Intuitionistic Fuzzy Sets. Springer, Heidelberg (1999). https://doi.org/10.1007/978-3-642-29127-2
8. Atanassov, K., Mavrov, D., Atanassova, V.: Intercriteria decision making: a new approach for multicriteria decision making, based on index matrices and intuitionistic fuzzy sets. Issues IFSs GNs **11**, 1–8 (2014)
9. Atanassova, V., Mavrov, D., Doukovska, L., Atanassov, K.: Discussion on the threshold values in the InterCriteria Decision Making approach. Int. J. Notes Intuitionistic Fuzzy Sets **20**(2), 94–99 (2014). ISSN 1310-4926
10. Bishop, C.M.: Neural Networks for Pattern Recognition. Oxford University Press, Oxford (2000). ISBN 0 19 853864 2
11. Ducheva, D., Paskaleva, R., Popov, I.: The role of kinesiotherapy in improving motor activity and quality of life in elderly people, 65 years Medical College - Stara Zagora, Collection of Papers, pp. 57–63, October 2012. ISBN 978-954-9443-63-9
12. Hagan, M.T., Demuth, H.B., Beale, M.: Neural Network Design. PWS Publishing Company, Boston (1996)
13. Haykin, S.: Neural Networks: A Comprehensive Foundation. Prentice Hall, Upper Saddle River (1999)
14. Knack, S., Keefer, P.: Does social capital have an economic payoff? a cross-country investigation. Q. J. Econ. **112**(4), 1251–1288 (1997)
15. Kohonen, T.: Exploration of very large databases by self-organizing maps. In: Proceedings of International Conference on Neural Networks, ICNN 1997, vol. 1. IEEE (1997)
16. Vankova, D., Sotirov, S., Doukovska, L.: An application of neural network to health-related quality of life process with intuitionistic fuzzy estimation. In: Atanassov, K.T., et al. (eds.) IWIFSGN 2016. AISC, vol. 559, pp. 183–189. Springer, Cham (2018). https://doi.org/10.1007/978-3-319-65545-1_17
17. Vankova, D., Kerekovska, A., Kostadinova, T., Usheva, N.: Health-related quality of life in the community. Assessing the socio-economic, demographic and behavioural impact on health-related quality of life at a community level: evidence from Bulgaria. In: Proceedings database (2013). http://www.euroqol.org/uploads/media/EQ12-P05.pdf
18. Vankova, D.: Community-cantered research in Bulgaria, a mixed-methods approach to health-related quality of life. Eur. J. Public Health **25**(3), 291 (2015). https://doi.org/10.1093/eurpub/ckv175.046. 8th European Public Health Conference: Proceedings, ckv175.046 First published online: 6 October 2015
19. Vankova, D., Sotirova, E., Bureva, V.: An application of the InterCriteria analysis approach to health-related quality of life. Notes on Intuitionistic Fuzzy Sets **21**(5), 40–48 (2015). 11th International Workshop on IFSs, Banská Bystrica, Slovakia, 30 Oct. 2015
20. Vankova, D., Kerekovska, A., Kostadinova, T., Feschieva, N.: Health-related quality of life and social capital at a community level – a review and research. Trakia J. Sci. Vol. **10**(3), 5–12 (2012)
21. Vankova, D., Kerekovska, A., Kostadinova, T., Todorova, L.: Researching health-related quality of life at a community level: survey results from Burgas, Bulgaria. Health Promot. Int. **31**, 1–8 (2015). https://doi.org/10.1093/heapro/dav016
22. Vazelov, E., Popov, I.: Socially important diseases as a national and international health problem. Med. Art Mag. **2**, 66–68 (2013). ISSN 1312 - 9384
23. Zadeh, L.A.: Fuzzy sets. Inf. Control **8**(3), 338–353 (1965)

A Flexible Query Answering System for Movie Analytics

Carson K. Leung[1]([✉]) [iD], Lucas B. Eckhardt[1],
Amanjyot Singh Sainbhi[1], Cong Thanh Kevin Tran[1], Qi Wen[1],
and Wookey Lee[2]

[1] University of Manitoba, Winnipeg, MB, Canada
kleung@cs.umanitoba.ca
[2] Inha University, Incheon, South Korea

Abstract. With advances in technologies, huge volumes of a wide variety of valuable data—which may be of different levels of veracity—are easily generated or collected at a high velocity from a homogenous data source or various heterogeneous data sources in numerous real-life applications. Embedded in these big data are rich sources of information and knowledge. This calls for data science solutions to mine and analyze various types of big data for useful information and valuable knowledge. Movies are examples of big data. In this paper, we present a flexible query answering system (FQAS) for movie analytics. To elaborate, nowadays, data about movies are easy accessible. Movie analytics help to give insights about useful revenues, trends, marketing related to movies. In particular, we analyze movie datasets from data sources like Internet Movie Database (IMDb). Our FQAS makes use of our candidate matching process to generate a prediction of a movie IMDb rating as a response to user query on movie. Users also have flexibility to tune querying parameters. Evaluation results show the effectiveness of our data science approach—in particular, our FQAS—for movie analytics.

Keywords: Data science · Data mining · Data analytics · Predictive analytics · Movie analytics · Movie · Movie rating · Information retrieval

1 Introduction

As we are living in the era of big data [1–3], data are everywhere. With advances in technologies, huge volumes of a wide variety of valuable data—which may be of different levels of veracity (e.g., precise data, imprecise and uncertain data)—can be easily generated or collected at a high velocity. They can be originated from a single homogenous data source or a wide variety of heterogeneous data sources in various real-life applications. These include online games [4], board games like Go [5], sports [6], bioinformatics like DNA sequence analysis [7], multimedia data like YouTube videos [8] and movies [9, 10].

With more and more movie ideas being pitched every year, it is a concern for production companies to decide which movies they should choose to produce or invest in. The *key contribution* of this paper is our data science solution—specifically, our

© Springer Nature Switzerland AG 2019
A. Cuzzocrea et al. (Eds.): FQAS 2019, LNAI 11529, pp. 250–261, 2019.
https://doi.org/10.1007/978-3-030-27629-4_24

flexible query answering system (FQAS)—for movie analytics in examining different aspects of a movie and predicts how well it will do in terms of Internet Movie DataBase (IMDb) rating based on similar historical data.

Here, we mine movie data from IMDb as it is a popular source for movie, TV and celebrity content. It provides movie information platform that allows audiences and professional movie critics to rate and review movies based on their personal and professional opinions. Studies have shown that there is a very solid relationship between the success (or quality of a movie) and its IMDb rating [11]. Our data science solution—namely, our FQAS—predicts a movie success by looking at *similar* movies from the past and their performance. Similarity is determined by clustering or unsupervised learning techniques. By using data from historical movies as an indicator (or predictor) of how well a new movie will perform, our FQAS generates a list of similar movies in the dataset based on cast, directors, production companies, etc. with respect to the given data of a new movie that we need to predict. With these similar past movies and their performance information our algorithm will come up with a predicted IMDb rating.

The remainder of this paper is organized as follows. Next section discusses related works. Section 3 describes our data science solution (i.e., our FQAS) for movie analytics. Evaluation and conclusions are given in Sects. 4 and 5, respectively.

2 Related Works

Numerous studies have been conducted on various aspects of movie analytics [10]. For example, Haughton et al. [10] visualized the co-starring social networks, analyzed movie attendance and trends, and predicted Oscar from Twitter and movie review data. Krauss et al. [12] applied both sentiment analysis and social network analysis to predict movie success. Ahmad et al. [13] used a mathematical model with data mining techniques for predicting the success and failure of movies. Meenakshi et al. [14] also used data mining but for Bollywood films. Mundra et al. [15] conducted sentiment analysis of tweets, together with random forests, in predicting movie success. Trabelsi and Pasi [16] used a hidden Markov model to recommend movie ratings.

In contrast, our data science solution (i.e., FQAS) first uses a clustering approach to group movies that are similar in combinations of attributes like the running length, budget, cast, director, genres, and the production company. Based on the clustering results, our data science solution then predicts the popularity rating and revenues of similar movies. This data science solution (i.e., FQAS) is our key contribution of this paper.

3 Our Flexible Query Answering System for Predictive Analytics

Our data science solution—i.e., our flexible query answering system (FQAS)—first groups movies that are similar combination of attributes or criteria. For a given movie, our solution then searches through all possible candidate movies in a group of similar

dataset to find the N best matches based on the combination of attributes or criteria. These attributes or criteria including the following:

1. Running time (in minutes)
2. Budget
3. Genres
4. Cast
5. Director
6. Production company.

3.1   Calculating the Matching Score

For each of the above matching criteria, we compute a *matching score*. It ranges between 0–100, where 100 being the best match. It is calculated for each of the attributes at a time for every candidate. Here, we calculate the match based in the form of a logarithmic equation:

$$\text{Match} = \frac{100}{\log(X)}\log((X+1) - Y) \tag{1}$$

where X is the number of intervals required, and Y is the selected interval.

Calculating the Matching Score for Running Time. *Running time* of a feature movie is its length or duration. It is usually expressed in minutes. Typical running time of a movie is around 90–100 min. To calculate the matching score between the running times of two movies M1 and M2, we first compute the absolute value of the difference in running times (in minutes):

$$\text{RunningTimeDiff} = |\text{RunningTime}(M1) - \text{RunningTime}(M2)| \tag{2}$$

where M1 is a new movie to be predicted for its rating, and M2 is an old movie in the dataset. Dividing these running time differences into multiple bins of a 5-min interval (e.g., a difference of less than 5 min, of 5–10 min, of 10–15 min, etc.) seems to be a logical way to partition the time differences. As such, each running time difference is then hashed into one of the 7 bins (i.e., Intervals) for running time match. Specifically, based on the absolute difference in running times computed by Eq. (2), we compute their corresponding running time match:

$$\text{RunningTimeMatch} = \frac{100}{\log(7)}\log(8 - \text{Interval}) \tag{3}$$

The resulting running time match is captured by Table 1. Note that, although we use 7 intervals in Eq. (3) as a logical choice, *our FQAS gives users flexibility to reset the number of intervals (or bins).*

Example 1. Let running times of movies M1 and M2 be 120 min and 127 min, respectively. Then, by Eq. (2), RunningTimeDiff = 7 min (i.e., Interval 2 on Table 1). By a quick look up from the table, we obtain the matching score on running times between the two movies, i.e., RunningTimeMatch = 92.1. Similarly, let running times of movies M1 and M2 be 120 min and 89 min, respectively. Then, Eq. (2) gives RunningTimeDiff = 31 min (i.e., Interval 7 on Table 1), which leads to RunningTimeMatch = 0.0.

Table 1. Computation of RunningTimeMatch based on Eq. (3)

RunningTimeDiff	Interval	RunningTimeMatch
$X \leq 5$	1	100.0
$5 < X \leq 10$	2	92.1
$10 < X \leq 15$	3	82.7
$15 < X \leq 20$	4	71.2
$20 < X \leq 25$	5	56.5
$25 < X \leq 30$	6	35.6
$30 < X$	7	0.0

Calculating the Matching Score for Budget. *Budget* of a movie usually accounts for costs associated with the story rights, screenplay (by screenwriter and script doctors), film and executive producers, director, production costs (e.g., crew wages, accommodation, catering, costumes, hotel stay, live set and studio costs, production design, transportation, travel, etc.), computer-generated imagery and other visual effects, as well as music. To calculate the matching score between the budgets of two movies M1 and M2, we first compute the absolute percentage of the difference in budget:

$$BudgetDiff = \left| \frac{Budget(M1) - Budget(M2)}{Budget(M1)} \times 100\% \right| \qquad (4)$$

where M1 is a new movie to be predicted for its rating, and M2 is an old movie in the dataset. Dividing these budget percentage differences into multiple bins of a 5% range (e.g., a difference of less than 5%, of 5–10%, of 10%–15%, etc.) seems to be a logical way to partition the budget percentage differences. As such, each budget percentage difference is then hashed into one of the 6 bins (i.e., Intervals) for budget match. Again, *our FQAS gives users flexibility to reset the number of intervals (or bins)*. Then, based on the absolute percentage difference in budget computed by Eq. (4), we compute their corresponding budget match:

$$BudgetMatch = \frac{100}{\log(6)} \log(7 - Interval) \qquad (5)$$

The resulting budget match is captured by Table 2.

Example 2. Let budgets of movies M1 and M2 be $250 million and $310 million, respectively. Then, by Eq. (4), BudgetDiff= 24% (i.e., Interval 5 on Table 2). By a quick look up from the table, we obtain the matching score on budgets between the two movies, i.e., BudgetMatch < 38.7. Similarly, let budgets of movies M1 and M2 be $250 million and $350 million, respectively. Then, Eq. (4) gives BudgetDiff = 40% (i.e., Interval 6 on Table 2), which leads to BudgetMatch = 0.0.

Table 2. Computation of BudgetMatch based on Eq. (5)

BudgetDiff	Interval	BudgetMatch
X ≤ 5%	1	100.0
5% < X ≤ 10%	2	89.8
10% < X ≤ 15%	3	77.4
15% < X ≤ 20%	4	61.3
20% < X ≤ 25%	5	38.7
25% < X	6	0.0

Calculating the Matching Score for Genre. *Genres* are categories of artistic composition in movie. They are usually characterized by similarities in form, style, or subject matter. Common genres include: action, adventure, animation, comedy, crime, drama, fantasy, horror, mystery, romance, science fiction (sci-fi), superhero, and thriller. As such, it is not uncommon for a movie to be categorized into multiple genres. We compute the genre match by counting the common genres in the genres of two movies M1 and M2:

$$\text{GenreMatch} = \frac{\#\text{common genres in M1 and M2}}{\#\text{genres in M1}} \times 100\% \tag{6}$$

where M1 is a new movie to be predicted for its rating, and M2 is an old movie in the dataset.

Example 3. Consider the four genres of movie M1 (action, drama, horror, and thriller) and the three genres of movie M2 (action, drama, and romance). Here, there are two common genres: action and drama. By Eq. (6), GenreMatch = 2/4 = 50%. Similarly, consider the two genres of movie M1 (action and horror) and the five genres of movie M2 (action, drama, fantasy, horror, and romance). Here, there are two common genres: action and horror. By Eq. (6), GenreMatch = 2/2 = 100%.

Calculating the Matching Score for Cast. For most movies, there are multiple *cast members* (*actors and actresses*). We compute the genre match by counting the common cast in two movies M1 and M2. The number of common cast is then hashed into one of the 6 bins for cast match. Specifically, based on the number of common cast in M1 and M2, we compute their corresponding cast match:

$$\text{CastMatch} = \frac{100}{\log(6)} \log(\#\text{CommonCast}(M1, M2) + 1) \tag{7}$$

where M1 is a new movie to be predicted for its rating, and M2 is an old movie in the dataset. The resulting cast match is captured by Table 3.

Example 4. Consider two movies M1 and M2, in which there are three common cast members. Then, by a quick look up from Table 3, we obtain the matching score on common cast between the two movies, i.e., CastMatch = 77.4. Similarly, consider two movies M1 and M2, in which there is no common cast member. Then, by a quick look up from Table 3, we obtain the matching score on common cast between the two movies, i.e., CastMatch = 0.0.

Table 3. Computation of CastMatch based on Eq. (7)

#CommonCast	CastMatch
X ≥ 5	100.0
X = 4	89.8
X = 3	77.4
X = 2	61.3
X = 1	38.7
X = 0	0.0

Calculating the Matching Score for Director. A *movie director* usually directs the making of a movie, controls artistic and dramatic aspects of the movie, and visualizes the screenplay while guiding the technical crew and actors in the fulfilment and realization of that vision. The director plays a key role in choosing the cast members, production design, and the creative aspects of filmmaking. For most movies, there is only one director. So, if the director of two movies M1 and M2 is the same, the corresponding director match is expected to be 100; otherwise, it is 0. However, it is possible—though not too common—to have multiple directors for a single movie (e.g., the 1989 movie titled "New York Stories" was directed by three directors—namely, Woody Allen, Francis Ford Coppola, and Martin Scorsese). Hence, we generalize the computation of director match to become the following: If there are common directors between two movies M1 and M2, the corresponding director match is 100; otherwise, it is 0:

$$\text{DirectorMatch} = \begin{cases} 100 & \text{if } \#\text{CommonDirectors}(M1, M2) \geq 0 \\ 0 & \text{if } \#\text{CommonDirectors}(M1, M2) = 0 \end{cases} \tag{8}$$

where M1 is a new movie to be predicted for its rating, and M2 is an old movie in the dataset.

Calculating the Matching Score for Production Companies. *Production companies* generally consist of groups of technical staff to provide the physical basis for works in the realms of the movies. Many of the movies are produced by multiple production companies. We compute the production company match by counting the common production companies in two movies M1 and M2. It is tempting to apply exact sub-string matching on the name of production companies because it is easy to perform exact string matching of the names of the production company. However, due to human clerical error, it is not uncommon to mistype or use short form (e.g., "Avi Arad" instead of "Avi Arad Productions"). Hence, we apply similar-substring matching on the name of production companies when counting the number of *common production companies* between movies M1 and M2. The number of common production companies is then hashed into one of the 4 bins for production company match. Specifically, based on the number of common production companies in M1 and M2, we compute their corresponding *production company match*:

$$\text{ProdComMatch} = \frac{100}{\log(4)} \log(\#\text{CommonProdCom}(M1, M2) + 1) \qquad (9)$$

where M1 is a new movie to be predicted for its rating, and M2 is an old movie in the dataset. The resulting production company match is captured by Table 4.

Table 4. Computation of ProdComMatch based on Eq. (9)

#CommonProdCom	ProdComMatch
$X \geq 3$	100.0
$X = 2$	79.2
$X = 1$	50.0
$X = 0$	0.0

Example 5. Consider production companies of movies M1 (Avi Arad Productions, Columbia Pictures, and Marvel Studios) and M2 (Avi Arad Productions, Columbia Pictures, Marvel Studios, and Matt Tolmach Productions), in which there are three common production companies. Then, by a quick look up from Table 4, we obtain the matching score on common production companies between the two movies, i.e., ProdComMatch = 100.0. Similarly, consider production companies of movies M1 (Avi Arad, and Marvel Studios) and M2 (Avi Arad Productions, Columbia Pictures, and Marvel Studios). Here, we apply similar-substring matching to determine that the production company "Avi Arad" for movie M1 is the same as the production company "Avi Arad Productions" for movie M2. Consequently, we determine that there are two common production companies, which leads to ProductionCompanyMatch = 79.2.

Combining the Matching Scores. After computing the matching scores for the movie running time, budget, genres, cast, director, and production company, the next logical step is the combine them to compute a weighted average of these matching scores:

$$\text{MatchScore} = w_{RT}\,\text{RTM} + w_B\,\text{BM} + w_G\,\text{GM} + w_C\,\text{CM} + w_D\,\text{DM} + w_{PC}\,\text{PCM} \quad (10)$$

where w_{RT}, w_B, w_G, w_C, w_D and w_{PC} are use-specified weights for the RunningTimeMatch (RTM), BudgetMatch (BM), GenreMatch (GM), CastMatch (CM), DirectorMatch (DM) and ProdComMatch (PCM), respectively. The sum of these weights adds up to 1. The matches can be computed by Eqs. (3), (5) (6)–(9). Here, *our FQAS gives users the flexibility to specify the weights of these six aspects/attributes depending on the user preference.*

For any given movie M1 to be predicted, we compute the weighted combined matching scores (as in Eq. (10)) and obtain a list of its N closest candidates (which are ranked in descending order of the matching score). Our solution can easily find the top-N new movies with the highest matching score (i.e., closer than 100). For any new movie M1 having a high matching score, it means that it is very similar (in terms of running time, budget, genres, cast, director, and production company) to an old movie M2 in the dataset. As such, our solution can make predictions on related aspects of M1 based on the prior knowledge about M2.

Example 6. Consider a movie M1 with RTM = 100 (i.e., with a running time within 5 min of that of an old movie M2 in the dataset), BM = 77.4 (i.e., with a budget within 10%–15% of that of M2), GM = 50 (i.e., with 50% of its genres match those of M2), CM = 38.7 (i.e., having only 1 common cast with M2), DM = 100 (i.e., having the same director ass M2) and PCM = 79.2 (i.e., with 2 common production companies as M2). When setting w_{RT} = 5%, w_B = 10%, w_G = 5%, w_C = 50%, w_D = 20% and w_{PC} = 10% (i.e., by putting more emphasize on cast than director than other attributes like budget & production company, and putting the least emphasize on running time and genres), the resulting matching score is 62.51.

3.2 Predicting the Cast Popularity

Based on the weighted combined matching score, we can find all the old movies that are very similar to the new movie M1. As such, our solution can make predictions on a specific aspect (say, cast popularity) of M1 based on the cast popularity about any old movie M2 in the same cluster as M1.

Specifically, for each of the common cast members in both movies M1 and M2, we obtain their popularity points. Then, we sum up their popularity points. If a cast member is common but does not have a popularity ranking, a base value of 5 points will be returned. Afterwards, our solution assigns the cast popularity score based on these cast popularity points. See Table 5.

Table 5. Computation of CastPopularityScore

CastPoints	CastPopularityScore
Top-10	100
20,000 < CastPoints ≤ 50,000	85
10,000 < CastPoints ≤ 20,000	70
5,000 < CastPoints ≤ 10,000	50
2,000 < CastPoints ≤ 5,000	30
1,000 < CastPoints ≤ 2,000	15
0 < CastPoints ≤ 1,000	10
0	5

Example 6. Consider two movies M1 and M2, in which there are two common top-10 cast members. Then, by a quick lookup at Table 5, we know that each of the top-10 casts scores a cast popularity score of 100. Hence, the corresponding cast popularity score for two of these cast members is 200.

3.3 Predicting the Director Popularity

Similar to cast popularity, based on the weighted combined matching score, we can find all the old movies that are very similar to the new movie M1. As such, our solution can then make predictions on a specific aspect (say, director popularity) of M1 based on the director popularity about any old movie M2 in the same cluster as M1. Here, our solution assigns the director popularity score based on director popularity points. See Table 6.

Table 6. Computation of DirectorPopularityScore

DirectorPoints	DirectorPopularityScore
Top-10	100
$50,000 \leq$ DirectorPoints, but not top-10	85
$20,000 \leq$ DirectorPoints $< 50,000$	70
$10,000 \leq$ DirectorPoints $< 20,000$	50
$5,000 \leq$ DirectorPoints $< 10,000$	30
$0 <$ DirectorPoints $< 5,000$	10
0	5

Example 7. Consider two movies M1 and M2, in which the director points are 25,000. Then, by a quick lookup at Table 6, we obtain the corresponding director popularity score of 70.

3.4 Predicting the Movie Rating

After computing the weighted combined matching scores in Sect. 3.1, the cast popularity in Sect. 3.2 and the director popularity in Sect. 3.3, the next step is the combine them for predicting movie rating based on the top-N similar old movies:

$$\text{PredictedRating} = \frac{\sum_{i=1}^{N} cs_i \times rating_i}{\sum_{i=1}^{N} cs_i} \qquad (11)$$

where

$$\text{CombinedScore } cs_i = w_{MS} \text{ MS} + w_{CP} \text{ CPS} + w_{DP} \text{ DPS} \qquad (12)$$

such that w_{MS}, w_{CP} and w_{DP} are use-specified weights for the MatchingScore (MS), CastPopularityScore (CPS) and DirectorPopularityScore (DPS), respectively. These matches can be computed by Eq. (10) and looked up from Tables 5 and 6 described earlier. Here, our solution gives users the flexibility to specify the weights of these three aspects/attributes depending on the user preference.

Example 13. Consider predicting the rating of a new movie M1 based on N = 3 similar old movies (M2, M3 and M4), where

- MS(M2) = 95, CPS(M2) = 100, DPS(M2) = 100, and rating(M2) = 7.8;
- MS(M3) = 100, CPS(M3) = 85, DPS(M3) = 0, and rating(M2) = 6.0; and
- MS(M4) = 70, CPS(M4) = 70, DPS(M4) = 100, and rating(M2) = 8.0.

Then, when setting $w_{MS} = 3$, $w_{CP} = 2$ and $w_{DP} = 1$, we obtain cs(M2) = 755, cs (M3) = 475 and cs(M4) = 520. Hence, the PredictedRating = (755 × 7.8 + 475 × 6.0 + 520 × 8.0) ÷ (755 + 475 + 520) = 7.37, which is the rating of M1 predicted by our FQAS.

4 Evaluation

We evaluated predictive analytics of our solution (FQAS) by applying it to real-life IMDb movie data. As of May 2019, IMDb contains about 5.98 million titles (e.g., movies, TV, videos) and captures information for about 126 thousands movies[1]. For evaluation, we *randomly* selected about 11 thousands movies as old movie (M2) in the dataset and another 110 recent movies as new movies to be predicted (M1) for ratings. Please note that, although we selected a subset of movie data from IMDb, *our FQAS is designed to handle big data and is thus capable of handling larger portion, if not all, data from IMDb.*

The evaluation results show the accuracy of our solution. Although we only showed a small sample (say, top-7) of the results in Table 7, the results are positive. For instance, in term of accuracy, all of the results shown in Table 7 our predicted ratings fall within 5% range of the actual ratings. Among all tested movies, more than half of our predicted ratings fall within 10% range of the actual ratings.

Table 7. Evaluation results

Movie title	Predicted rating	Actual rating	Difference
Now You See Me 2 (2016)	6.55	6.5	−0.81%
Fantastic Beasts and Where to Find Them (2016)	7.40	7.3	−1.32%
Black Panther (2018)	7.56	7.4	−2.12%
Wonder Woman (2017)	7.67	7.5	−2.25%
A Ghost Story (2017)	6.58	6.8	+3.23%
Halloween (2018)	6.77	7.1	+4.63%
Deadpool 2 (2018)	7.36	7.8	+5.59%

---

[1] https://www.imdb.com/pressroom/stats/.

5 Conclusions

In the paper, we presented a data science solution for movie analytics. Specifically, our flexible query answering system (FQAS) first groups similar movies into the same cluster based on parameters like their running time, budget, genres, cast, director, and production company. Here, we allow users or analysts the flexibility to adjust granularities of these parameters. Moreover, we also allow users or analysts the flexibility to express their preference on the weights of these different parameters representing different aspects of the movies. By comparing these different aspects of a new movie with an old movie in the dataset, if they are similar, their corresponding matching score would be high. After clustering similar/matching movies, FQAS then predicts ratings for any new movies. It does so by (i) incorporating additional information such as cast and director popularity and (ii) making predictions based on the combination of matching score and these popularity scores of top-N similar movies within the same cluster of the new movie to be predicted. Evaluation on real-life IMDb movie data shows the effectiveness of our FQAS in predicting the movie ratings.

As ongoing and future work, we would also like to extend our evaluation on other classification techniques and further comparisons with related works. Moreover, we are exploring different settings of weights to see if they would significantly affect the prediction accuracy. We are also incorporating additional information—such as popularity of genres and of the production company, as well as the number of online votes or ratings for each movie—so as to further enhance our prediction accuracy. In addition, we are also extending our predictive analytics solution to predict revenues in addition to movie ratings. Along this direction, we would like to incorporate additional information on any other external factors (e.g., holiday or not, competitive movies) that may affect the movie rating, movie revenue, and/or other prediction results.

Acknowledgements. This project is partially supported by (i) Natural Sciences and Engineering Research Council of Canada (NSERC) and (ii) University of Manitoba.

References

1. Braun, P., Cuzzocrea, A., Leung, C.K., Pazdor, A.G.M., Souza, J.: Item-centric mining of frequent patterns from big uncertain data. Proc. Comput. Sci. **126**, 1875–1884 (2016)
2. Leung, C.K.: Big data analysis and mining. In: Advanced Methodologies and Technologies in Network Architecture, Mobile Computing, and Data Analytics, pp. 15–27 (2019)
3. Prabhu, C.S.R.: Fog Computing, Deep Learning and Big Data Analytics-Research Directions. Springer, Singapore (2019). https://doi.org/10.1007/978-981-13-3209-8
4. Braun, P., Cuzzocrea, A., Keding, T.D., Leung, C.K., Pazdor, A.G.M., Sayson, D.: Game data mining: clustering and visualization of online game data in cyber-physical worlds. Proc. Comput. Sci. **112**, 2259–2268 (2017)
5. Leung, C.K., Kanke, F., Cuzzocrea, A.: Data analytics on the board game Go for the discovery of interesting sequences of moves in joseki. Proc. Comput. Sci. **126**, 831–840 (2018)
6. Leung, C.K., Joseph, K.W.: Sports data mining: predicting results for the college football games. Proc. Comput. Sci. **35**, 710–719 (2014)

7. Sarumi, O.A., Leung, C.K., Adetunmbi, A.O.: Spark-based data analytics of sequence motifs in large omics data. Proc. Comput. Sci. **126**, 596–605 (2018)
8. Braun, P., et al.: Enhanced prediction of user-preferred YouTube videos based on cleaned viewing pattern history. Proc. Comput. Sci. **112**, 2230–2239 (2017)
9. Choudhery, D., Leung, C.K.: Social media mining: prediction of box office revenue. In: IDEAS 2017, pp. 20–29 (2017)
10. Haughton, D., McLaughlin, M., Mentzer, K., Zhang, C.: Movie Analytics: A Hollywood Introduction to Big Data. Springer, Cham (2015). https://doi.org/10.1007/978-3-319-09426-7
11. Wasserman, M., Mukherjee, S., Scott, K., Zeng, X., Radicchi, F., Amaral, L.: Correlations between user voting data, budget, and box office for films in the internet movie database. J. Assoc. Inf. Sci. Technol. **66**(4), 858–868 (2014)
12. Krauss, J., Nann, S., Simon, D., Gloor, P.A., Fischbach, K.: Predicting movie success and academy awards through sentiment and social network analysis. In: ECIS 2008, pp. 2026–2037 (2008)
13. Ahmad, J., Duraisamy, P., Yousef, A., Buckles, B.: Movie success prediction using data mining. In: ICCCNT 2017, pp. 1573–1576 (2017)
14. Meenakshi, K., Maragatham, G., Agarwal, N., Ghosh, I.: A data mining technique for analyzing and predicting the success of movie. In: NCMTA 2018 (2018)
15. Mundra, S., Dhingra, A., Kapur, A., Joshi, D.: Prediction of a movie's success using data mining techniques. In: Satapathy, S.C., Joshi, A. (eds.) Information and Communication Technology for Intelligent Systems. SIST, vol. 106, pp. 219–227. Springer, Singapore (2019). https://doi.org/10.1007/978-981-13-1742-2_22
16. Trabelsi, C., Pasi, G.: MRRA: a new approach for movie rating recommendation. In: Christiansen, H., Jaudoin, H., Chountas, P., Andreasen, T., Legind Larsen, H. (eds.) FQAS 2017. LNCS, vol. 10333, pp. 84–95. Springer, Cham (2017). https://doi.org/10.1007/978-3-319-59692-1_8

Flexible Intelligent Information-Oriented and Network-Oriented Approaches

Can BlockChain Technology Provide Information Systems with Trusted Database? The Case of HyperLedger Fabric

Pablo Garcia Bringas[1], Iker Pastor[1], and Giuseppe Psaila[2(✉)]

[1] University of Deusto, Avenida de l'Universidad, 24,
48007 Bilbao, Spain
pablo.garcia.bringas@deusto.es, iker.pastor@deusto.es
[2] University of Bergamo, viale Marconi, 5, Bergamo, Italy
giuseppe.psaila@unibg.it
https://www.deusto.es/cs/Satellite/deusto/en/university-deusto,
http://www.unibg.it

Abstract. *BlockChain* technology has imposed a new perspective in the area of data management, i.e., the possibility of realizing immutable and distributed ledgers. Furthermore, the introduction of the concept of smart contract has further extended the potential applicability of this potentially disruptive technology. Although *BlockChain* was developed to support virtual currencies and is usually associated with them, novel platforms are under development, that are not at all related to the original application context.

An example is *HyperLedger Fabric*. Developed by the Linux Foundation, it is aimed to provide information systems with distributed databases where the transaction log is immutable. This should ensure trusted cooperation among many parties. In this paper, we briefly present main concepts and functionalities provided by HyperLedger Fabric. We then discuss its potential applicability and current limitations.

Keywords: BlockChain technology ·
BlockChain beyond virtual currencies · HyperLedger Fabric ·
Distributed information systems

1 Introduction

In 2008 Nakamoto described [17] a system to support a new virtual currency, named *bitcoin*. The novelty of this virtual currency was the absence of any authority having the responsibility of validating transactions (that exchange money). This role was, instead, played by a peer-to-peer network, that (1) validates transactions (avoiding the so called *double spending* of money) and (2) stores transactions into an immutable and distributed ledger. The platform that

© Springer Nature Switzerland AG 2019
A. Cuzzocrea et al. (Eds.): FQAS 2019, LNAI 11529, pp. 265–277, 2019.
https://doi.org/10.1007/978-3-030-27629-4_25

supports this peer-to-peer network was called *Bitcoin* [17]: it is the first ledger implemented as a *BlockChain*, i.e., a chain of blocks of data.

After the birth of *bitcoin* (the virtual currency) and *Bitcoin* (the *BlockChain* platform), many other virtual currencies and related *BlockChain* platforms have been proposed: in this sense, the most popular competitor of *bitcoin* is named *Ether*, that is supported by the *Ethereum (BlockChain)* platform [24].

After a shy beginning, the interest in *bitcoin* and, more in general, in virtual currencies has exploded. Private people and financial operators are operating with them. To understand in depth the dynamics of this phenomenon, the interested reader can refer to [7,9]: they are two surveys that studied the dynamics of virtual currency markets. Furthermore, the introduction of the concept of *smart contract*, i.e., a contract that is automatically executed (possibly) within the *BlockChain* platform, has further increased the interest in virtual currencies.

Consequently, people usually associate *BlockChain* technology with virtual currencies. However, the concept of distributed ledger can, in principle, be applied to any human activity, that needs to rely on a ledger. The most intuitive one is the sale of real estate: a notary registers the event on a ledger and maintains it for decades. A *BlockChain* platform does the same, but does not need a notary: the peer-to-peer network maintains many distributed copies of the ledger, in order to guarantee that the ledger cannot be changed (neither erroneously nor maliciously). In this respect, the idea of adopting *BlockChain* technology beyond virtual currencies does make sense, in particular to support the integration of information systems. In fact, in the globalized economy, companies have to strictly cooperate; to do so, they have to integrate their information systems. If there were a unique version of shared data, with shared business logic rules that are executed in a central point, this would strongly help the integration; furthermore, if there were not a central party, i.e. a party that provides the central information system (thus, other parties have to trust it) but a shared distributed system in its place, all parties would increase their level of trust in the integration.

HyperLedger Fabric is the first result of the *HyperLedger* project [12] by Linux Foundation. Precisely, it is a *BlockChain* platform beyond virtual currencies. It is designed to be a distributed database, that guarantees immutable history of transactions. It plays the role of central database for many information systems connected in a peer-to-peer network; furthermore, procedures working on data are executed directly within the platform. Thus, it promises to push the adoption of *BlockChain* technology to integrate information systems. In this paper, we present the main features of *HyperLedger Fabric*, by discussing its potential application through an illustrating example.

The paper is organized as follows. Section 2 presents the necessary background concerning *BlockChain* technology, to understand the different types of platforms. Section 3 introduces *HyperLedger Fabric*. Section 4 presents the illustrating example. Finally, Sect. 5 draws the conclusions.

2   Background About *BlockChain*

In this section, we provide a short background about *BlockChain* technology. Section 2.1 introduces the execution mechanism implemented within *Bitcoin*. Section 2.2 presents some points of view that are useful to characterize platforms.

2.1   Execution Mechanism in *Bitcoin* and *Proof of Work*

We illustrate the execution mechanism implemented in *Bitcoin*, the first *BlockChain* platform. This will help readers understand the different approach proposed by *HyperLedger Fabric* (see Sect. 3). Figure 1 depicts the process.

1. The mechanism starts when a user issues a transaction; some of its fields are the issuer, the receiver, and the exchanged amount.
2. The transaction is included in a block, together with other transactions that occurred within a given time interval. The block becomes the fundamental unit of information representation and management. For example, in the left-hand side of Fig. 1, five transactions (T_1, T_2, T_3, T_4 and T_5) are sent and grouped into one block. Notice that, possibly, other blocks are simultaneously built by other nodes in the network.
3. The block is sent to all peers (nodes) of the *BlockChain* network.
4. Each pear in the network is responsible for verifying that transactions in the block are *valid*, i.e., it has to verify that the issuer of a transaction is truly the owner of the transacted *bitcoin* item. Records in the local copy of the chain are traced (the history of transactions is followed backward) searching for records concerning the issuer of the transaction to validate, so as to prove the current possession of the transacted item.
5. If all transactions are valid, the block is now eligible to be added to the chain. However, this can happen only if it is not in conflict with other blocks generated by other peers. The network has to give the consensus by means of a *Proof of Work* mechanism [3].

In practice, the network has to guarantee that a block is inserted into the chain if and only if the chronological order of transactions is respected.

Second, the immutability of the chain is guaranteed by the adoption of hash codes: a block points to the hash code of the next block, and its hash code has been generated by moving from this. This way, a change in the content of blocks is almost impossible, because it could not be possible to do that without regenerating (an unaffordable amount of) hash codes.

The Proof of Work Mechanism. Referring to step 5, the key problem is to generate a hash code that cannot be attacked and guarantees that the block is attached to the more recent block in the chain. This task is performed by specialized nodes called *miners*: because they have to find a hash code that respects some given characteristics imposed by the platform. The process is conducted as follows (refer again to Fig. 1).

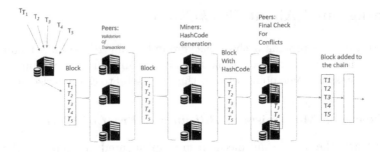

Fig. 1. The *Proof of Work* consensus.

- When a miner receives a block, it begins a loop of attempts. In each iteration, a casual *nonce* is generated.
- By means of the nonce, data from the block are hashed together, including the hash code of the block that is supposed to be the most recent one.
- When the miner finds a hash code that satisfies the desired property, it sends the block to peers in the network, with the generated hash code.
- Peers easily verify that the provided hash code actually meets the desired property and actually derives from the block; not only, they verify that the hash of the previous block is actually the hash of the most recent block in the chain. If so, the block can be added; otherwise, it is refused and transactions are validated again: this way, a double spending transaction (considered as valid in the first attempt) is no longer valid (because the *bitcoin* item has been already spent) and the transaction is refused.

The rationale behind the mechanism is the following. Due to the difficulty that the hash mechanisms introduce in producing intentional outputs, the probability that a specific miner has for its result to be a valid hash is very low. At the same time, due to the high number of miners in the network, the probability that at least one miner finds the wanted hash code is high. This way it becomes impossible to predict (and attack) which miner will find the hash code.

Furthermore, this mechanism ensures correct order and avoids double spending: if two transactions asking to spend the same *bitcoin* item are simultaneously managed by the network and are put in two different blocks, in order to respect the chronological order they should be attached to the same most recent block in the chain. But this violates the chronological order of blocks, so one of the two blocks cannot be appended to the chain and the double spending transaction in it is refused.

2.2   Short Classification of *BlockChain* Platforms

The initial design of *BlockChain* addressed a scenario in which *nobody trusts anybody* (typical when virtual money must be exchanged). However, the subsequent emergence of scenarios in which there is a partial trust among many parties, has led to the definition of two families of *BlockChain* platforms:

– *Permissionless* platforms. This family encompasses classical *BlockChain* technology, devoted to support virtual currencies. A new peer is totally free to enter the network, provided that it behaves as imposed by general rules that govern the platform. In fact, a very large number of nodes guarantees resiliency to attacks (so, new nodes are encouraged to enter).
– *Permissioned* platforms. This family encompasses platforms such that new peers cannot freely enter the network; they must be authorized by an administrator. This family is good for supporting cooperation of a (relatively) small number of parties, for specific activities.

Smart Contracts. Originally, this concept was introduced in [21], "to describe agreements between two or more parties, that can be automatically enforced without a trusted intermediary." (from [14]). Thus, we can figure out that a contract has a state and some procedures/actions that determine how the state can change; thus a transaction consists in asking to change the contract state by means of a given action.

The potentiality of this concept is incredible: once two parties have agreed to start the contract, its behavior can become automatic, no need for a third party that handles the contract is necessary.

This behavior can be summarized by the following sentence taken from [8]: "A smart contract is an automatable and enforceable agreement. Automatable by computer, although some parts may require human input and control. Enforceable either by legal enforcement of rights and obligations or via tamper-proof execution of computer code."

Anyway, smart contracts are supported by *BlockChain* platforms in different ways. Hereafter, we analyze where the code (of procedures/actions) is executed.

– *In-platform code.* This approach to smart contracts is characterized by the fact that action code is shared within the *BlockChain* platform, ready to be used when necessary. Furthermore, it is also executed within the platform.
– *External Code.* This category encompasses smart contracts whose business logic is not within the *BlockChain* platform. This is the case of *Bitcoin*: it has not been designed to host smart contracts; nevertheless, it is used for many applications based on smart contracts (see [14]), This is made possible by implementing protocols based on cryptographic-message exchange: involved parties are the only able to read them and, consequently, act.
Clearly, the business logic of smart contracts is handled outside the *BlockChain* platform: each party must implement its version of the business logic (they have to hope that all versions behave properly).

3   HyperLedger Fabric

HyperLedger Fabric is a *permissioned* platform (see Sect. 2.2): only authorized peers can enter the peer-to-peer network. The code of procedures/actions is stored and executed within the platform. Usually, it is classified as supporting smart contracts, but it is not exactly true: in fact, it is closer to the concept of

Stored Procedure in relational databases, than to the idea of smart contract. In fact, when the application is designed, both data structure and procedure code are developed; transactions are invocations of the code, that can possibly act on many items stored within the database. In fact, it is designed to provide a distributed database supported by an immutable ledger of all issued transactions (that guarantees the reliability of data).

Hereafter, we give an overview of basic concepts that characterize *Hyper-Ledger Fabric*. A detailed presentation of technical features is in [2].

- *Channel.* A *BlockChain* platform involves a number of peers, that not necessarily coincide with parties involved in an application/business. Since many different applications can be supported by an installation of *HyperLedger Fabric*, each of them is managed as a *channel*. Thus, parties are authorized by a channel administrator to participate; the channel stores data and business logic of the application; it is isolated from the other channels, i.e., data are not shared among channels and transactions are processed only by peers involved in the channel.
- *State Database.* *HyperLedger Fabric* provides a database view of data which the business logic of the application operates on. Thus, it maintains the *state database*, where data are stored and can be accessed by querying the database. The database also maintains the history of data items: in fact, when a state is changed, the old state becomes invalid and the new state is the valid one; the full history of states can be obtained.
- *Ledger.* The counterpart of the state database is the *ledger*: it stores in an immutable way all state changes; this way, the state of a data items is *certified* by the identifier of the transaction that generated it (this way, the state database could be, theoretically, rebuilt from scratch, if necessary).
- *Transactions.* Clients (applications used by parties to participate to the business logic) invoke the execution of some procedures that change states of data items. Since the execution of these changes must be atomic (all the changes must be performed or nothing) and isolated, they are called *transactions* (thus, we are very close to the concept of transactions typical of Relational Databases [13]: a transaction is an atomic and isolated update of the sate of one or more data items).

  However, when a client issues a transaction, it is not ensured that it occurs: in fact, it sends a *transaction proposal*, that activates the execution mechanism, whose goal is to ensure that the transaction is valid; if it is valid, its effects become persistent as the new state of affected data items, otherwise it is refused.
- *Chaincode.* The business logic is executed by procedural code that the channel makes available to participant parties. This procedural code is called *chaincode* (we will describe more in Sect. 3.2).

3.1   The *Byzantine Fault-Tolerant* Consensus Mechanism

The concepts described above ask for a suitable execution mechanism. *Hyper-Ledger Fabric* does not rely on *Bitcoin's Proof of Work* approach (see Sect. 2.1) to validate transactions; in contrast, it relies on the consensus about ordering of transactions, called *Byzantine Fault-Tolerant (BFT) Ordering* [20].

BFT manages transaction proposals in three phases, depicted in Fig. 2:

– *Execution.* When a client submits a *transaction proposal* T, the execution of the transaction is performed by some *endorsing peers* (they are chosen on the basis of specific endorsement policies [20]), also called *Executors*. They actually execute the invoked chaincode and generate the new states of data items, that are not still visible in the state database.

  In practice, each executor endorses the transaction: first of all, it verifies if the required action is legal; then, it builds the *read set*, that contains the objects states that become invalid; finally, it generates the *write set*, that contains the new object states to write into the state database. Input arguments, read set and write set constitute the *payload* of the transaction.

  In practice, if an endorsing peer is able to terminate this process, it approves (endorses) the transaction proposal and sends its endorsement (denoted as E_i in Fig. 2) to the client.

– *Ordering.* The client collects endorsements by executors, including the transaction payloads. Then, it broadcasts transaction payloads to the *ordering service*, that tries to create a total order among read sets and write sets, in order to generate a new *block* to add to the chain (i.e., the ledger), as reported in the center of Fig. 2. For each transaction, the block contains the whole payload. In this step, consensus is reached among ordering services only as far as ordering of transactions is concerned. Conflicting transactions are inserted in the block and properly marked (see next point).

– *Validation.* Since blocks can contain faulty transactions or the order can be faulty, it is necessary to validate the block.

  The validation phase is performed by nodes called *Validators* (see the right-hand side of Fig. 2), that check for read-write conflicts: when faulty transactions are found, they are marked as invalid (in Fig. 2, this is exemplified by the red transaction T_3 in the right-hand side block), but they still remain in the block (for audit purposes). When the validation phase is concluded, the block is added to the chain and the state database is updated with write sets produced by valid transactions.

Notice the separation between consensus about the order of transactions and validity of transactions. If an ordering peer tries to maliciously force a wrong transaction ordering, the BFT protocol [20] resists and refuses the malicious attempt because the other peers disagree. Instead, if many clients concurrently issue conflicting transactions, i.e., transactions that try to change the state of the same data items at the same time, it is responsibility of the validation phase to check for this type of conflicts.

3.2   Chaincode

In *Hyperlegdger Fabric*, the execution of smart contracts is performed by *Chaincode*, i.e., a code that handles state changes of data in the database. This is

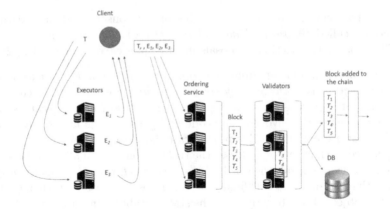

Fig. 2. The *Byzantine Fault-Tolerant* consensus.

a very different approach with respect to *Bitcoin*, that is a public *BlockChain* platform: in *HyperLedger Fabric*, a *channel* is a *permissioned BlockChain*, i.e., only authorized peers can participate; consequently, only parties involved in the channel can see data managed through that channel. From the organizational point of view, this means that parties are permitted to participate if and only if they previously agreed with rules in the cooperation/integration contract (not a smart contract, but a regular contract signed by parties to start cooperating).

Currently, *HyperLedger Fabric* allows for using three different programming languages to write chaincode: *Java*, *JavaScript* (powered with the *Node.js* framework [22]) and *Go* [18] (the novel programming language by *Google*). The chaincode is executed within a protected environment, so that it is not possible to interfere with the system.

The general structure of a chaincode procedure that can be invoked by clients is reported (as pseudo-code) in Fig. 3. Hereafter, we describe it.

- The procedure name is the name which the action is invoked with by clients.
- The procedure receives two parameters: a *stub* to the channel and an array *args* of arguments provided in the REST invocation sent by clients.
- The procedure (Line 1) extracts data from array *args*: typically they are keys of data items to update or to create.
- The *stub* is a place-holder for the channel and gives the chaincode indirect access to the database: data items can be obtained (Lines 2 to 4) by exploiting keys $okey_1, \ldots, okey_n$ of data items to update (possibly extracted from within array *args*). Old states are assigned to variables, that we denote as $o_1, \ldots, o_n$.
- New states are generated (Line 5) by processing the request.
- New states are sent to the database (Lines 6 to 8): note that method *putStatae* of object *stub* receives two parameters, i.e., the key $nkey_j$ of the new state and the new state n_j.
- The procedure terminates by sending back the REST response to the client (Line 9), to indicate success or failure of the action.

Procedure *name*(*stub*, *args*)
Begin
1. extraction of REST arguments from array *args* (including keys $okey_1, \ldots, okey_n$)
2. $o_1 = stub.getState(okey_1)$;
3. $\ldots$
4. $o_n = stub.getState(okey_n)$;

5. generation of new states $n_1, \ldots, n_m$
6. $stub.putState(nkey_1, n_1)$;
7. $\ldots$
8. $stub.putState(nkey_m, n_m)$;

9. $SendResponse(\ldots)$;
End Procedure

Fig. 3. Structure of a chaincode procedure.

So, the structure of the procedure is not difficult. Of course, there is no direct access to data, neither for reading nor for writing; in this latter case, this choice is obvious, because the update must be validated by the BFT protocol. Consequently, object *stub* generates read sets and write sets.

Finally, notice that the database is seen as a map, i.e., a collection of pairs $(key, value)$. Probably, this is because the first DBMS chosen by developers was *GoLevelDB* [16,23], that is based on this model. The alternative choice is *CouchDB* [1,15]: it is a NoSQL DBMS that stores JSON objects in a native way; it is a more professional solution, that provides a query language (*GoLevelDB* does not), so it appears to be more suitable for engaging contexts.

4   Illustrating Example

In order to illustrate how *HyperLedger Fabric* could be adopted, we propose an illustrating example.

Consider the context of large-scale distribution. Often, several companies cooperate, by creating a common fidelity card. Through this fidelity card, customers can gain points when they buy products or services. Once customers accumulate enough points (independently of the company which they made the purchase from), they can use points to get free products or discount vouchers.

Usually, each involved company has its own information system and its own database. Which one of the companies should provide the service of trusted repository to the overall pool of companies? Why should the other companies trust that one?

HyperLedger Fabric offers a different approach.

– It can be used to realize a *distributed database*, cooperatively maintained by each involved party.

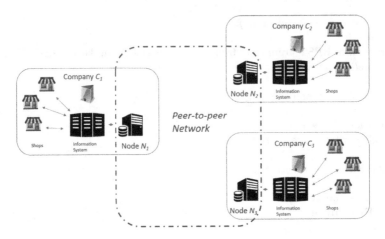

Fig. 4. Application Scenario: companies cooperating for managing points gained by customers.

- Chaincode, deployed within the platform, provides a unique version of business logic and maintains correctness of data.

Figure 4 illustrates this application scenario. Suppose we have a pool of three companies, for simplicity denoted as C_1, C_2 and C_3. Each company has its own information system.

The cooperation starts by agreeing on business rules concerning how customers can gain and use points. This preliminary step is essential, because these rules will be implemented as chaincode within the platform. Specifically, the companies agree that they want to share information concerning *customers* and *wallets* (of points); a customer can have multiple wallets and can transfer points from one wallet to another. When a customer performs a purchase in a shop of one of the cooperating companies, new points are charged to one of the owned wallet (associated with a fidelity card); then, points are spent to get discount vouchers. After that, the technical part of the process begins.

- Company C_1 sets up the first node of the chain, named N_1. The channel is created and companies C_2 and C_3 are allowed to enter.
- Companies C_2 and C_3 create their nodes, named N_2 and N_3, respectively, and enter the chain. The peer-to-peer network is, so far created. From now on, every change in the channel will be represented in all the three nodes.
- The three companies are in charge for specific parts of the development process: for example, C_1 could develop chaincode dealing with customers; C_2 could develop chaincode dealing with wallets; C_3 can perform testing and assessment activities.
- At this point, each company can autonomously modify its own information system, in order to provide shops with functionalities concerning managements of wallets. Each information system interacts with only one node of the peer-to-peer network, i.e., the one owned by the company.

This approach provides many tangible advantages, if compared with a classical and centralized approach.

- *Local copy of the database.* Each node has a local copy of the distributed database. This way, each information system sends queries to its associated node; only one node is involved in processing queries issued by a given information system.
- No other parties, except the ones that agreed to cooperate, are involved in the process. The consequences are:
  - transactions are validated by a reduced number of nodes, i.e., the ones involved in the channel. This provides high efficiency;
  - data are not shared on unknown nodes: they are stored only in databases managed by the specific channel.
- Since transactions are performed by chaincode deployed within the platform, incorrect states of data due to errors in programs within one specific information system do not risk to put data into incorrect states.
- The distributed validation of transactions provides high robustness to attacks (for example, an intruder could try to force unpermitted transactions).
- Finally, if a new party agrees to enter the chain, its database is automatically built from scratch: in fact, the instance of the platform installed onn the new node automatically re-executes all state changes stored in the ledger, obtaining the last state in its local database.

5   Conclusions

In this paper, we presented the main features provided by *HyperLedger Fabric*, the first of a novel generation of *BlockChain* platforms, that operate beyond virtual currencies. Specifically, *HyperLedger Fabric* is a permissioned platform, that provides a distributed database that guarantees immutable recording of transactions. Since procedures (chaincode) are executed within the platform, it is a powerful tool to easy integrate information systems of many cooperating parties that have to share data and transform them in a robust way (as we showed through the illustrating example in Sect. 4).

Anyway, the reader should not think that every problem concerning its adoption is solved. Unfortunately, scalability is still the main obstacle to its wide diffusion. From the study reported in [19], it clearly appears that *HyperLedger Fabric* is much faster in processing transactions than permissionless platforms: this is due to the fact that it does not rely on the *Proof of Work* consensus strategy, as well as by the fact that only peers involved in a *channel* actually participate to computation. Compared with *Ethereum*, *HyperLedger Fabric* obtains better throughput and smaller latency. However, there can be applications contexts in which it is not possible to wait for 34 s (as reported by [19]) to complete transactions.

As a future work, many activities can be performed, by studying many aspects concerned with the adoption of *HyperLedger Fabric* in various application contexts (improving performance provided by the platform is a matter of developers working on it). A first topic to study is the effect of choosing *CouchDB* in place of *GoLevelDB*: is it really better? why? is it less performing?

Another topic to study is concerned with design of data structures. In fact, the data model is quite simple and not structured; however, giving structure to data through a conceptual design phase is always a good practice. Is it possible to reuse models such as Entity-Relationships? How to manage constraints within the platform?

The IoT (Internet of Things) world asks for solutions able to deal with (billions of) devices in an effective and efficient way. Could *HyperLedger Fabric* be used in this context? Finally, we can consider the area of Open Data and Big Data. Typically, they are represented as JSON data sets, possibly geo-referenced. Many questions arise in this respect: can Big Data management be supported by exploiting *HyperLedger Fabric*? could it be considered as a source for Big Data analysis activities? Could it improve the level of confidence in Big Data? Could geo-referenced queries be performed on its state database?

As the reader can see, many research activities can be conducted in the next years concerning the adoption of this platform. Many of the above-mentioned questions originate from previous work on querying geo-referenced JSON data sets [4,5], as well as on analysis of (geo-referenced) Big Data describing social-media users [6,10,11].

References

1. Anderson, J.C., Lehnardt, J., Slater, N.: CouchDB: The Definitive Guide: Time to Relax. O'Reilly Media, Inc., Newton (2010)
2. Androulaki, E., et al.: Hyperledger fabric: a distributed operating system for permissioned blockchains. In: Proceedings of the Thirteenth EuroSys Conference, p. 30. ACM (2018)
3. Andrychowicz, M., Dziembowski, S., Malinowski, D., Mazurek, Ł.: Modeling bitcoin contracts by timed automata. In: Legay, A., Bozga, M. (eds.) FORMATS 2014. LNCS, vol. 8711, pp. 7–22. Springer, Cham (2014). https://doi.org/10.1007/978-3-319-10512-3_2
4. Bordogna, G., Capelli, S., Ciriello, D.E., Psaila, G.: A cross-analysis framework for multi-source volunteered, crowdsourced, and authoritative geographic information: the case study of volunteered personal traces analysis against transport network data. Geo-Spat. Inf. Sci. **21**(3), 257–271 (2018)
5. Bordogna, G., Capelli, S., Psaila, G.: A big geo data query framework to correlate open data with social network geotagged posts. In: Bregt, A., Sarjakoski, T., van Lammeren, R., Rip, F. (eds.) GIScience 2017. LNGC, pp. 185–203. Springer, Cham (2017). https://doi.org/10.1007/978-3-319-56759-4_11
6. Bordogna, G., Frigerio, L., Cuzzocrea, A., Psaila, G.: Clustering geo-tagged tweets for advanced big data analytics. In: 2016 IEEE International Congress on Big Data (BigData Congress), pp. 42–51. IEEE (2016)
7. Bouri, E., Gupta, R., Roubaud, D.: Herding behaviour in cryptocurrencies. Finance Res. Lett. **29**, 216–221 (2018)
8. Clack, C.D., Bakshi, V.A., Braine, L.: Smart contract templates: foundations, design landscape and research directions. arXiv preprint arXiv:1608.00771 (2016)

9. Corbet, S., Meegan, A., Larkin, C., Lucey, B., Yarovaya, L.: Exploring the dynamic relationships between cryptocurrencies and other financial assets. Econ. Lett. **165**, 28–34 (2018)

10. Cuzzocrea, A., Psaila, G., Toccu, M.: Knowledge discovery from geo-located tweets for supporting advanced big data analytics: a real-life experience. In: Bellatreche, L., Manolopoulos, Y. (eds.) MEDI 2015. LNCS, vol. 9344, pp. 285–294. Springer, Cham (2015). https://doi.org/10.1007/978-3-319-23781-7_23

11. Cuzzocrea, A., Psaila, G., Toccu, M.: An innovative framework for effectively and efficiently supporting big data analytics over geo-located mobile social media. In: Proceedings of the 20th International Database Engineering and Applications Symposium, pp. 62–69. ACM (2016)

12. Dhillon, V., Metcalf, D., Hooper, M.: The hyperledger project. In: Dhillon, V., Metcalf, D., Hooper, M. (eds.) Blockchain Enabled Applications, pp. 139–149. Apress, Berkeley (2017). https://doi.org/10.1007/978-1-4842-3081-7_10

13. Garcia-Molina, H.: Database Systems: The Complete Book. Pearson Education, New Delhi (2008)

14. Atzei, N., Bartoletti, M., Cimoli, T., Lande, S., Zunino, R.: SoK: unraveling bitcoin smart contracts. In: Bauer, L., Küsters, R. (eds.) POST 2018. LNCS, vol. 10804, pp. 217–242. Springer, Cham (2018). https://doi.org/10.1007/978-3-319-89722-6_9

15. Manyam, G., Payton, M.A., Roth, J.A., Abruzzo, L.V., Coombes, K.R.: Relax with CouchDB–into the non-relational DBMS era of bioinformatics. Genomics **100**(1), 1–7 (2012)

16. Minglani, M., et al.: Kinetic action: performance analysis of integrated key-value storage devices vs. LevelDB servers. In: 2017 IEEE 23rd International Conference on Parallel and Distributed Systems (ICPADS), pp. 501–510. IEEE (2017)

17. Nakamoto, S.: Bitcoin: a peer-to-peer electronic cash system. Working Paper (2008)

18. Pike, R.: The go programming language. Talk given at Google's Tech Talks (2009)

19. Pongnumkul, S., Siripanpornchana, C., Thajchayapong, S.: Performance analysis of private blockchain platforms in varying workloads. In: 2017 26th International Conference on Computer Communication and Networks (ICCCN), pp. 1–6. IEEE (2017)

20. Sousa, J., Bessani, A., Vukolic, M.: A byzantine fault-tolerant ordering service for the hyperledger fabric blockchain platform. In: 2018 48th Annual IEEE/IFIP International Conference on Dependable Systems and Networks (DSN), pp. 51–58. IEEE (2018)

21. Szabo, N.: Formalizing and securing relationships on public networks. First Monday **2**(9) (1997)

22. Tilkov, S., Vinoski, S.: Node.js: using Javascript to build high-performance network programs. IEEE Internet Comput. **14**(6), 80–83 (2010)

23. Wang, L., Ding, G., Zhao, Y., Wu, D., He, C.: Optimization of LevelDB by separating key and value. In: 2017 18th International Conference on Parallel and Distributed Computing, Applications and Technologies (PDCAT), pp. 421–428. IEEE (2017)

24. Wood, G.: Ethereum: a secure decentralised generalised transaction ledger. Ethereum project yellow paper 151, 1–32 (2014)

Anticipating Depression Based on Online Social Media Behaviour

Esteban A. Ríssola[✉], Seyed Ali Bahrainian, and Fabio Crestani

Faculty of Informatics, Università Della Svizzera Italiana, Lugano, Switzerland
{esteban.andres.rissola,bahres,fabio.crestani}@usi.ch

Abstract. Mental disorders are major concerns in societies all over the world, and in spite of the improved diagnosis rates of such disorders in recent years, many cases still go undetected. The popularity of online social media websites has resulted in new opportunities for innovative methods of detecting such mental disorders.

In this paper, we present our research towards developing a cutting-edge automatic screening assistant based on social media textual posts for detecting depression. Specifically, we envision an automatic prognosis tool that can anticipate when an individual is developing depression, thus offering low-cost unobtrusive mechanisms for large-scale early screening. Our experimental results on a real-world dataset reveals evidence that developing such systems is viable and can produce promising results. Moreover, we show the results of a case study on real users revealing signs that a person is vulnerable to depression.

1 Introduction

According to the World Health Organisation (WHO), out of every four individuals worldwide, one is likely to experience a mental disorder at some point in one's life. A study has revealed that in the past year, around 83 million people (ageing between 18–65) have been subject to one or more mental disorder(s) in the European Economic Area (EEA) countries[1]. The lack of an appropriate treatment can lead to psychotic episodes, thoughts of self-harm and at its worst, suicide. For this reason, it is important to identify the onset of these kinds of mental disorders at early stages in order to avoid undesirable consequences.

Many useful cues about an individual's mental state as well as personality, social and emotional conditions can be discovered by examining the patterns of language use [7]. Previous research shows that language attributes can be indicators of current mental state [25], personality [21] and even personal values [5]. That is because such latent mental-related variables are manifested in the words that individuals express.

Online social media websites, such as Twitter, Reddit and Facebook have become increasingly popular and more people are using these platforms to share

---

[1] See: http://www.euro.who.int/en/health-topics/noncommunicable-diseases/mental-health/data-and-statistics.

© Springer Nature Switzerland AG 2019
A. Cuzzocrea et al. (Eds.): FQAS 2019, LNAI 11529, pp. 278–290, 2019.
https://doi.org/10.1007/978-3-030-27629-4_26

their thoughts, feelings and moods on a daily basis. Thus, these sites have become a promising source of data for detecting different mental disorders [8], such as depression [6]. Although to date, detection of mental disorders via the content shared on social media websites has been limited, such sources of data can enable a preliminary screening process to automatically identify and help people who might be struggling with psychological disorders. In this paper we propose and compare various models for detection of depression in textual posts.

However, manual collection of large amounts of labelled data for automatic depression detection is usually a complex and time-consuming endeavour. To address this issue we follow a weak-supervision framework for collecting such data. As a result, design of data-driven solutions to this problem becomes feasible. To the best of our knowledge, this is the first step towards developing a depression post-classifier following a data-driven approach.

The main contributions of this paper are as follows: (1) We build a depression post-classifier using automatically gathered data. We present a range of models for this purpose. (2) Based on the developed models and the gathered data, we present a case study showing the potential of this research to identify users at risk of depression.

The remainder of the paper is organised as follows: Sect. 2 summarises the related work; Sect. 3 details the methodology followed to automatically select the post providing evidences of depression necessary to build the depression post-classifier; Sect. 5 describes the collection used to conduct the experiments and the results analysis; Sect. 6 presents a case study of depression using time-series analysis to demonstrate the potential use that the depression post-classifier could have; Sect. 7 concludes and outlines future work.

2   Related Work

De Choudhury et al. [6] presented an early work on automatic depression detection by using crowd-sourcing to collect assessments from several Twitter users who reported being diagnosed with depression. They a built a depression lexicon containing words that are associated with depression and its symptoms. We use this lexicon as one of the tools for automatically gathering posts expressing depression.

Jamil et al. [14] previously attempted to build a depression post-classifier using a small set of manually annotated posts. As a result of the small dataset, their model showed a weak performance. In this paper we re-visit developing a depression post-classification model with the difference that we used a large automatically gathered training dataset and adopted a very different model to build an effective depression classifier.

The study of sentiment through lexical analysis has been previously applied in different psychology-related tasks, such as memorability [2], and particularly in the domain of automatic depression detection [6,14,23]. Based on these findings we define a criteria to automatically select relevant depression sample posts. In addition, we consider the success that topic models have shown two extract meaningful features to detect depression [26].

Moreno et al. [20] sought for traces of depression from publicly available Facebook profiles. They recruited manual coders to review the history of profile updates according to established clinical criteria. Here, we adopt a similar procedure for labelling a set of posts using human annotators for evaluating our proposed models.

The Computational Linguistics and Clinical Psychology (CLPsych) [9] as well as the Early Risk Prediction on the Internet (eRisk) [15,16] workshops were the first to propose benchmarks to bring together many researchers to address the automatic detection of mental disorders in online social media. The nature of these tasks is different than ours, in that we are trying to design a depression post-classifier as a first step to analyse users' posts and then interpret the evolution of a user's mental state over time and understand the patterns of depression. The workshops' tasks, however, merely aim at identifying depressed users. We use the eRisk dataset to evaluate our methodology and to conduct a user study showing patterns of depressed users against the control users.

3   Automatic Data Gathering

Our main objective is to develop a robust model to extract evidences from each message posted by a tracked user in order to anticipate the onset of depression. For this purpose, we propose novel methods for assigning depression scores to each post written by the user. Based on these scores, time-series models are designed to capture the dynamics involved in the user's mental state evolution. Such evolution can be seen as a temporal signal, where at each point in time its strength and trend can be assessed to determine the development of a mental disorder in the user.

Bearing this in mind, we introduce a methodology to automatically gather depression and non-depression post samples and then use such samples to train a classification model. Such model can determine whether a message is conveying signs of depression. Moreover, this methodology can be utilised to generate large datasets of depression and non-depression posts. We hypothesise that given a set of users which we have definitive knowledge that they are depressed and their history of textual posts, we can define features to characterise depression signs and use this information to automatically select posts for building a training set. In the following section we explain the steps taken to gather the dataset and build our proposed models.

3.1   Training Set Generation

Our initial goal is to distinguish posts that show signs of depression from those that do not. In order to build a depression post-classifier a key requirement is to collect a relevant training dataset for the task. To this end, the positive samples (D^+), that are the social media posts containing evidence of depression, are retrieved from a set of users who have already publicly disclosed their mental disorder. However, not all the posts in the users' posting history might be useful for our purposes. To filter out those irrelevant posts, we consider two different strategies: (1) Selecting posts with negative sentiment polarity score; (2) Selecting posts with high semantic similarity with respect to a *depression topic*.

Negative samples (D^-), that are the control posts (*i.e.*, those not conveying depression), are randomly sampled from a group of users which are not affected by the disorder. It is noteworthy that the posts, comprising the training set we intend to automatically gather, are drawn from a group of individuals who have already been labelled by a human annotator as depressed. This is the reason why we consider this setting as being weakly-supervised. In the next two subsections we describe the two strategies mentioned above.

3.2   Selecting Posts with Negative Sentiment

Sentiment analysis constitutes the computational study of opinions, feelings and subjectivity in text [22]. Since the sentiment polarity of a message can be linked with the emotions evoked by a text [22], we consider that when this value is negative (*i.e.*, below zero) it can be a good indicator of distress or unhappiness, especially when the posts come from users that are already experiencing depression. Using TextBlob[2] python library we compute the polarity score of the posts in D^+ and sort them in ascending order. The polarity score is calculated using a lexicon-based approach and ranges from -1 to $+1$.

However, simply considering the expression of sentiment is not a sufficient criteria since some *noisy* posts will be included in the training samples set (*e.g.*, the message "That's the worst name I ever heard" shows also a low polarity score). To address this issue we filter such noisy posts by requiring the presence of words related with specific emotions. According to the *Diagnostic and Statistical Manual of Mental Disorders* [1] (DSM)[3] depressive moods are characterised by the predominance of *sadness* and *disgust*. To be included in the training set, a post should have at least one word associated with either sadness or disgust according to the entries in the emotion lexicon developed by Saif et al. [19]. Each word in this dictionary is associated with the emotions it evokes.

As a stronger complement, we are using the affect-intensity lexicon created by Saif [18] which associates words with real-valued scores of intensity for different emotions. Given a word and an emotion, the scores range from 0 to 1, where a score of 1 means that the word conveys the highest intensity of that emotion. Using this information we calculated for each message what we defined as the *depression score*. This score is the average of the intensities found in the post with respect to "sadness". The rationale behind employing this second dictionary is to twofold: Firstly, we want to be more strict with the words we are considering to represent sadness, since we are using them to filter noisy posts. Secondly, in addition to common English words, the affect-intensity lexicon includes words

---

[2] See: https://textblob.readthedocs.io/en/dev/index.html.

[3] The DSM determines a common vocabulary and standard criteria to group and characterise the different mental disorders. Its three main components are: the diagnostic classification, the diagnostic criteria sets and the descriptive text.

that are more prominent in social media platforms, which the emotion lexicon does not.

Hence, to consider a post as a valid sample it should contain at least one word related with either sadness or disgust plus a depression score higher than a threshold. We decide to use threshold of 0.1 as we want to omit words marginally related with depression without being too stringent. A more thorough analysis on the best threshold is left as a future work.

3.3   Selecting Posts with Topical Relevance to Depression

As previously stated, our second strategy to automatically select posts for training a depression post-classifier is topical relevance to depression. Since we would like to obtain a ranked list of the documents according to their similarity with terms related to depression, we first formulate a so-called *depression topic*. As a starting point for building this topic we use the dictionary released by Choudhury et al. [6]. In addition, we extend this set by collecting all possible online vocabularies with concepts and terms commonly related to depression. The goal is to select from all these words those that are considered closely associated with this mental disorder and define a compact but accurate list. For instance, generic terms present in the dictionary such as *relationship* or *family* might introduce significant noise as they are in general very frequent terms in any context and not only when writing about depression-related themes. On the other hand, terms like *grief* and *sorrow* are normally used with higher frequency by individuals suffering from this mental disorder. With the aid of a clinical psychologist we select a subset of the words obtaining a list of 78 depression-related words.

Topic models are hierarchical Bayesian models of discrete data, where each topic is a set of words drawn from a fixed vocabulary representing a high level concept. The Latent Dirichlet Allocation [3] (LDA) is a topic model that discovers latent topics present in a given text collection. LDA represents each topic as a probability distribution over words in the documents. For each document, a multinomial distribution θ over topics is randomly sampled from a Dirichlet function with parameter α (which influences the shape of the distribution).

Using LDA gensim's[4] implementation we obtain the topics that emerged from the posts in D^+ and compute the cosine similarity between each post and the depression topic. This gives us a ranked list where the documents at the top of the list are the ones with the higher topical relevance to depression and are selected as the training data.

Given that the number of topics (K) is an unknown parameter in the LDA model, we follow a similar method to the one proposed by Griffiths et al. [13]. Basically, it consists in keeping the LDA parameters (commonly known as α and η) fixed, while assigning different values to K and run the LDA model each time. We selected the model that minimise $log P(W|K)$, where W contains all the words in the vocabulary. This procedure is performed until the optimal number

---

[4] See: https://radimrehurek.com/gensim/models/ldamodel.html.

of topics has been obtained. In our case, we train the LDA model with K equals to 50 up to 200 at steps of 50, where optimal value is 200.

Following the strategies defined in Sects. 3.2 and 3.3 we select the top 3500 posts according to each method in order to obtain the positive samples (D^+). The same number of posts is randomly picked from a group of users which are not affected by depression to obtain the negative samples (D^-).

4   Proposed Model

Once we have collected the set of depression and non-depression post samples, we proceed to build a depression post-classifier and evaluate various features. We considered two sets of features, bag-of-words and word embeddings. In the first case, each post is represented with the raw frequency of the unigrams extracted from the textual content of the posts (named Unigrams in Table 2). We decide to keep the stop-words since many words such as pronouns, articles and prepositions reveal part of people's emotional state, personality, thinking style and connection with others. As a matter of fact, such words called *function words*, account for less than one-tenth of one percent of an individual's vocabulary but constitute almost 60 percent of the words a person employs [7]. Additionally, we also include a model variant where the unigrams are extended with four extra features, the word count, the polarity score, the sadness score (Sect. 3) and the happiness score [11] of the post (named Unigrams++ in Table 2).

To produce an embedding representation of the posts, we use the words embeddings obtained from the eRisk training set, using word2vec [17] (named W2V in Table 2) and fastText [4] (named FTT in Table 2) methods. Furthermore, GloVe [24] pre-trained word embeddings are also considered (named GloVe in Table 2). The embedding representation of the words found in each post are averaged column-wised to obtain a k-dimensional representation of it. For the sake of comparison, we set the number of dimensions of W2V and FTT word embeddings to 200 as that is the largest number available for GloVe.

The different features sets are used to train various Logistic Regression (denoted as LR in Table 2) classifiers. Let π be the probability that the response variable equals the case in which a post is a reference of depression given some linear combination of the predictor variables ($x_1, \ldots, x_p$), for instance the frequency of the unigrams extracted. The g *logit* function is expressed as:

$$g(x_1, ..., x_p) = \ln(\pi/(1 - \pi)) = \beta_0 + \beta_1 x_1 + \cdots + \beta_p x_p$$

This allows to model the response probabilities and estimates the parameters ($\beta_0, \beta_1, \ldots, \beta_p$) by solving a regression problem. We choose this learning method since it has state-of-the-art effectiveness on a range of text categorisation tasks [12].

5   Evaluation

Dataset Description: To evaluate our methodology we use the eRisk 2018 dataset [16]. This publicly available test corpus consists of a set of documents posted by users of the popular social website Reddit and includes two groups of users namely depressed and non-depressed. Following the methodology proposed by Coppersmith et al. [8], users of the positive class (*i.e.*, depression) were gathered by retrieving self-expressions of depression diagnoses (*e.g.*, the sentence "I was diagnosed with depression") and verifying if they truly contained a statement of diagnosis. Non-depressed users were collected by randomly sampling from the large set of available users in the platform.

For each user, up to their most recent 2,000 submissions were retrieved and included in the corpus. In order to make the corpus more realistic, users who were active on the "depression subreddit"[5] but had no depression were included in the non-depressed class. These were mostly people concerned about depression because they had a close relative suffering from the disorder. The resulting corpus comprised of 1,076,582 submissions from 1,707 unique users. A summary of the dataset, including the train/test splits provided by the workshop organisers, is shown in Table 1.

Despite the limitation of the eRisk dataset which is the fact that some of the individuals in the non-depressed set of users may also be experiencing depression even though they have not publicly expressed it, we are sampling individual posts. Subsequently, the chances of collecting a considerable amount of misleading posts is very low.

Table 1. Summary of eRisk 2018 dataset.

	Train		Test	
	Positive	Control	Positive	Control
# of Subjects	135	752	79	741
# of Documents	49,557	481,837	40,665	504,523
Avg. # of Documents/Subject	367.1	640.7	514.7	680.9
Avg. # of Words/Document	27.4	21.8	27.6	23.7
Avg. Activity Period (days)	586.43	625	786.9	702.5

To asses the quality of the automatically gathered samples and the depression post-classifier, we developed a test set of manually annotated posts. To this end, we have randomly sampled 200 posts from each class in the eRisk dataset and ask four human annotators to label them. We have followed a similar procedure to that defined by Moreno et al. [20] as annotators were requested to label the posts following the criteria extracted from the DSM. More precisely, they were asked

---

[5] Titled forums on Reddit are denominated *subreddits*.

to determine which posts can be considered as a reference to depression. Each post was assigned with one of the following labels: (1) No depression reference is expressed; (2) One or more depression references are expressed; (3) Unable to make a judgement. The four annotators achieved a pairwise Cohen's Kappa score ranging between 0.577 and 0.7492. Reaching a high inter-rater agreement can be a difficult endeavour since in some cases taking a decision upon a message is complex without any additional information. The final set was comprised of 55 positive posts (*i.e.*, references to depression) and 93 negative posts.

Baselines: As it was stated in Sect. 3, sentiment analysis refers to the study of positive and negative feelings expressed in a piece of text. Determining whether a post contains an evidence of depression or not, can be thought as a specific case of sentiment analysis given that it involves the analysis of the emotions and mood communicated by the post. For this reason, we consider a baseline that is commonly used for sentiment analysis [22]. As we define two strategies to automatically select the relevant posts to train a depression post-classifier, we train two different classifiers using each set. Two separate classifiers are trained on each corresponding set using only unigram binary features and a Support Vector Machine as the baselines (named SVM_Unigrams_B in Table 2).

Experimental Results: Since the task we intend to perform is a binary classification problem, classic metrics such as Precision, Recall, F_1, and Area Under the Curve ROC (AUC) are applicable. The results obtained by the depression post-classifier trained on the automatically gathered training sets are presented in Table 2.

The highest precision is achieved by the unigram-based features. In the case of the posts gathered based on the negative sentiment there is an improvement of 6% over the baseline. Overall, the use of word embeddings increases the recall, F_1 and the AUC performance. Particularly, the use of GloVe pre-trained embeddings as well as task-specific word2vec embeddings provide an improvement over the baseline of more than 18% in Recall and 5% in both F_1 and AUC, for both automatically derived training sets. Regarding the quality of the training sets gathered, overall the topical relevance allows to achieve a better effectiveness.

6   A Case Study of Depression Using Time-Series Analysis

In this section we show an important application of our depression post-classifier by conducting a case study for analysing users' posts over time. To accomplish this, we randomly chose eight users from the eRisk test dataset, such that four belong to the positive class (*i.e.*, depressed) and the other four belong to the control class (*i.e.*, non-depressed). This case study can reveal how the moods of depressed and non-depressed people evolve over time.

Table 2. Overall effectiveness achieved by the depression post-classifier trained on the two automatically derived training sets and using various features.

	Precision (%)	Recall (%)	F_1 (%)	AUC (%)
Negative_Sentiment				
SVM_Unigrams_B (Baseline)	72.72	72.72	72.72	78.29
LR_Unigrams	**78.94**	81.81	80.35	84.45
LR_Unigrams++	75.92	74.54	75.22	80.28
LR_W2V	62.33	87.27	72.72	78.04
LR_FTT	68.05	89.09	77.16	82.17
LR_Glove	71.62	**96.36**	**82.17**	**86.89**
Topical_Relevance				
SVM_Unigrams_B (Baseline)	80.76	76.36	78.50	82.80
LR_Unigrams	80.39	74.54	77.35	81.89
LR_Unigrams++	**83.33**	72.72	77.66	82.06
LR_W2V	75.36	**94.54**	**83.87**	**88.13**
LR_FTT	69.86	92.72	79.68	84.53
LR_Glove	67.94	96.36	79.69	84.74

Figures 1 and 2 illustrate the results of this case study by showing the smoothed signal of depression/non-depression (obtained from the confidence scores that our classifier assigned to each post) of the four positive subjects and the four control subjects, respectively. In particular, we use the model trained on the posts selected based on the negative sentiment and unigram features to conduct this user study. The signals generated by the confidence score produced by the classifier are smoothed by computing the moving average of the series with a window equal to the 10% of the user posts. The horizontal line (dotted) represents the decision threshold which separates the depressed from the non-depressed posts for each user. We observe in the two figures that the behaviour of the positive and negative users is very distinctive. In particular, the signals corresponding to the positive users are most of the time above the 0 decision threshold, except for the last individual. In this particular case, the individual show in the beginning what can be defined as a "normal" behaviour until a turning point where signs of depression becomes evident. This could mean that the user has developed depression over time. Conversely, the signals corresponding to the negative users always remain by far below the 0 decision threshold.

Another feature that is clear in the positive group is a much higher mood swing as compared with the control class. Such analysis is useful to anticipate the point where a user is developing depression and as we have observed can distinguish between depressed and non-depressed effectively.

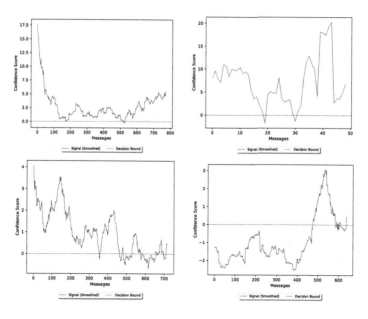

Fig. 1. Smoothed signal generated for users in the positive class (Depressed)

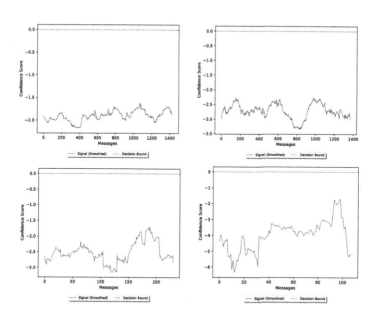

Fig. 2. Smoothed signal generated for users in the control class (Non-depressed)

7 Conclusions and Future Work

Identifying mental health disorders has been a challenge worldwide and the proliferation of online social media platforms is changing its dynamics. Online social media has created the opportunity of detecting potential mental disorder patients and proactively assisting them as soon as possible.

In this paper we introduced a methodology to automatically gather post samples of depression and non-depression and used the data to train models which are able to determine whether a post is conveying an evidence of depression. Our results showed that this methodology is very effective for gathering data. Furthermore, we observed that our LR_W2V (Topical_Relevance) model outperformed all other proposed models as well as the baseline in terms of F_1 and AUC. Moreover, we showed the potential of our models in identifying latent depression patterns via a case study using time-series analysis.

An important issue is the practical use of these technologies (*e.g.*, how to intervene). As argued by De Choudhury [10], design considerations in this space need to ensure that the benefits obtained by intervening exceed the risks. This can be achieved by communicating the risks to either the individuals, or to trusted social contacts or clinicians. Some social media websites are already offering basic intervention services to support vulnerable people. However, such services could be studied and analysed further to ensure their efficacy.

As future work, we would like to investigate other signs (*e.g.*, neuroticism level or various psychometric attributes) that can be potentially adopted to improve our proposed post-classifier. Additionally, we would like to explore means of leveraging the information provided by the post-classifier in order to improve the early detection of users with possible depression. Furthermore, we plan to extend our proposed model to other mental disorders.

Acknowledgements. We thank the reviewers for the constructive suggestions. This work was supported in part by the Swiss Government Excellence Scholarships and Hasler Foundation.

References

1. Association, A.P.: Diagnostic and Statistical Manual of Mental Disorders, 5th edn. American Psychiatric Publishing, Washington (2013)
2. Bahrainian, S.A., Crestani, F.: Towards the next generation of personal assistants: systems that know when you forget. In: Proceedings of the ACM SIGIR International Conference on Theory of Information Retrieval, ICTIR 2017, Amsterdam, The Netherlands, pp. 169–176 (2017)
3. Blei, D.M., Ng, A.Y., Jordan, M.I.: Latent Dirichlet allocation. J. Mach. Learn. Res. **3**, 993–1022 (2003)
4. Bojanowski, P., Grave, E., Joulin, A., Mikolov, T.: Enriching word vectors with subword information. Trans. Assoc. Comput. Linguist. **5**, 135–146 (2017)
5. Boyd, R.L., Wilson, S.R., Pennebaker, J.W., Kosinski, M., Stillwell, D.J., Mihalcea, R.: Values in words: using language to evaluate and understand personal values. In: Proceedings of the Ninth International Conference on Web and Social Media, ICWSM 2015, Oxford, UK, pp. 31–40 (2015)

6. Choudhury, M.D., Gamon, M., Counts, S., Horvitz, E.: Predicting depression via social media. In: Proceedings of the Seventh International Conference on Weblogs and Social Media, ICWSM 2013, Cambridge, USA (2013)
7. Chung, C., Pennebaker, J.: The psychological functions of function words. In: Social Communication. Frontiers of Social Psychology (2007)
8. Coppersmith, G., Dredze, M., Harman, C.: Quantifying mental health signals in Twitter. In: Proceedings of the Workshop on Computational Linguistics and Clinical Psychology: From Linguistic Signal to Clinical Reality, Baltimore, USA (2014)
9. Coppersmith, G., Dredze, M., Harman, C., Hollingshead, K., Mitchell, M.: CLPsych 2015 shared task: Depression and PTSD on Twitter. In: Proceedings of the 2nd Workshop on Computational Linguistics and Clinical Psychology: From Linguistic Signal to Clinical Reality, Denver, USA (2015)
10. De Choudhury, M.: Anorexia on tumblr: a characterization study. In: Proceedings of the 5th International Conference on Digital Health 2015, DH 2015, Florence, Italy, pp. 43–50 (2015)
11. Dodds, P.S., Harris, K.D., Kloumann, I.M., Bliss, C.A., Danforth, C.M.: Temporal patterns of happiness and information in a global social network: hedonometrics and Twitter. PloS One (2011)
12. Genkin, A., Lewis, D.D., Madigan, D.: Large-scale Bayesian logistic regression for text categorization. Technometrics **49**, 291–304 (2007)
13. Griffiths, T.L., Steyvers, M.: Finding scientific topics. Proc. Nat. Acad. Sci. **101**, 5228–5235 (2004)
14. Jamil, Z., Inkpen, D., Buddhitha, P., White, K.: Monitoring tweets for depression to detect at-risk users. In: Proceedings of the Fourth Workshop on Computational Linguistics and Clinical Psychology - From Linguistic Signal to Clinical Reality, Vancouver, Canada (2017)
15. Losada, D.E., Crestani, F., Parapar, J.: CLEF 2017 eRISK overview: early risk prediction on the internet: experimental foundations. In: Conference and Labs of the Evaluation Forum. CEUR-WS.org (2017)
16. Losada, D.E., Crestani, F., Parapar, J.: Overview of eRISK early risk prediction on the internet. In: Conference and Labs of the Evaluation Forum. CEUR-WS.org (2018)
17. Mikolov, T., Sutskever, I., Chen, K., Corrado, G., Dean, J.: Distributed representations of words and phrases and their compositionality. In: Proceedings of the 26th International Conference on Neural Information Processing Systems, NIPS 2013, Lake Tahoe, USA, pp. 3111–3119 (2013)
18. Mohammad, S.: Word affect intensities. In: Proceedings of the Eleventh International Conference on Language Resources and Evaluation, LREC 2018, Miyazaki, Japan (2018)
19. Mohammad, S., Turney, P.D.: Crowdsourcing a word-emotion association lexicon. Comput. Intell. **29**, 436–465 (2013)
20. Moreno, M.A., et al.: Feeling bad on Facebook: depression disclosures by college students on a social networking site. Depress. Anxiety **28**, 447–455 (2011)
21. Neuman, Y.: Computational Personality Analysis: Introduction, Practical Applications and Novel Directions. Springer, Cham (2016). https://doi.org/10.1007/978-3-319-42460-6
22. Pang, B., Lee, L.: Opinion mining and sentiment analysis. Found. Trends Inf. Retr. **2**, 1–135 (2008)
23. Park, M., Cha, C., Cha, M.: Depressive moods of users portrayed in Twitter. In: Proceedings of the ACM SIGKDD Workshop On Healthcare Informatics (2012)

24. Pennington, J., Socher, R., Manning, C.D.: Glove: global vectors for word representation. In: Proceedings of the 2014 Conference on Empirical Methods in Natural Language Processing, EMNLP 2014, Doha, Qatar, pp. 1532–1543 (2014)
25. Preoţiuc-Pietro, D., et al.: The role of personality, age and gender in tweeting about mental illnesses. In: Proceedings of the 2nd Workshop on Computational Linguistics and Clinical Psychology: From Linguistic Signal to Clinical Reality (2015)
26. Resnik, P., Garron, A., Resnik, R.: Using topic modeling to improve prediction of neuroticism and depression in college students. In: Proceedings of the 2013 Conference on Empirical Methods in Natural Language Processing, Seattle, USA (2013)

Method for Modeling and Simulation of Parallel Data Integration Processes in Wireless Sensor Networks

Alexander Alexandrov$^{(\boxtimes)}$ (ID), Rumen Andreev, D. Batchvarov, A. Boneva,
L. Ilchev, S. Ivanov, and J. Doshev

Department of Communication Systems and Services,
Institute of Information and Communication Technologies,
Bulgarian Academy of Sciences, Sofia, Bulgaria
akalexandrov@iit.bas.bg
http://www.iit.bas.bg

Abstract. The parallel sensor data integration local processing in Wireless Sensor Networks (WSNs) is one of the possible solutions to reduce the neighbor sensor node's communication and to save energy. At the same time, the process of local sensor node integration needs an additional processor and energy resources. Therefore the development of a realistic and reliable model of data integration processes in WSNs is critical in many aspects. The proposed GN based method and the related modeling process covers most of the aspects of the parallel sensor data integration in the WSN's, based on 802.15.4 protocols. For simulation and analysis tool is used the WSNet simulator and some additional software libraries.

The article presents a new method for modeling and simulation of sensor data integration parallel processing in WSNs. The proposed method uses modeling based on the Generalized Nets (GN) approach which is a new and an advanced way of parallel data processing analysis of Wireless Sensor Systems (WSS).

Keywords: Generalized Nets · Sensor data integration · WSN ·
Kalman filter · Fraser-Potter · Cluster topology · Simulation ·
Modeling · WSNet

1 Introduction

1.1 Parallel Sensor Data Integration Process in WSN with Cluster Topology

The proposed process is designed to redundant the data from different sensors that observe the same environment, to improve the signal/noise level, and to then to generate more reliable information.

This paper is supported by the National Scientific Program "Information and Communication Technologies for a Single Digital Market in Science, Education and Security (ICTinSES)", financed by the Ministry of Education and Science.

A. Cuzzocrea et al. (Eds.): FQAS 2019, LNAI 11529, pp. 291–301, 2019.
https://doi.org/10.1007/978-3-030-27629-4_27

The sensors of the WSN are grouped into clusters. Every cluster has own Cluster Head (CH). The sensors which belong to a specific cluster integrates their data simultaneously and send the integrated data directly to its CH (Fig. 1).

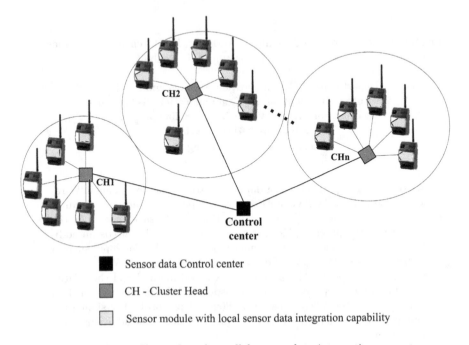

Fig. 1. Cluster based parallel sensor data integration

The sensor local data integration process is going in parallel in the sensor nodes and is based on the Kalman filter and consists of 2 basic stages - prediction and correction as is shown in Fig. 2.

As is described in details in [11,12] the prediction stage starts with initial estimation of $\hat{x}_{k-1}$ and covariance vector P_{k-1} and proceed with

$$\hat{x}_k = A\hat{x}_{k-1} + Bu_k + Cw_k \tag{1}$$

$$z_k = H_k x_k + D_k v_k \tag{2}$$

where $\hat{x}_k$ in our case is the sensor measurement estimated value, A is the transition state matrix of the integration process, B is the input data matrix, C is the noise state transition matrix, u_k is the known input value, w_k is the noise, z_k is the observation vector, v_k is a variable describing observation noise, and H_k is the matrix of the observed sensor value z_k, and D_k is a indexed matrix describing the level of noise to the measured observation. The correction stage tune the sensor data estimate by an actual measurement at that time. The current article, is focused mainly on the sensor data measurement update algorithm.

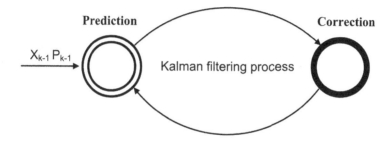

Fig. 2. Sensor data integration local process

Based on the papers above [11,12] we accept that the final Kalman filter measurement update equations are formulated as follows:

$$G_k = (P_k H_k)/(H_k P_k H_k^t + R_k) \tag{3}$$

$$\hat{x}_k = \hat{x}_k + G_k(z_k - H_k.\hat{x}_k) \tag{4}$$

$$P_k = (1 - G_k H_k).P_k \tag{5}$$

where G_k is the Kalman gain, P_k is error covariance vector, H_k is as described above the matrix of the observed value vector z_k and R_k is the covariance matrix.

The initial step during the measurement update is to calculate the Kalman gain G_k (3). The next step is to measure the process to accept, and then to calculate a posteriori state estimate by adding the correction based on the measurement and estimation as in (4). The last step is to receive an a posteriori error covariance estimate via (5). After each measurement update pair, the process is repeated with the previous a posteriori estimates used to project. This principle can be realized by a recursive function and is one of the important benefits of the Kalman filter – the software implementation is very simple and fast.

By this way the Kalman filter generates recursively the conditions of the current estimate based on past measurements [12]. In the equation above of the filter, each measurement error covariance matrix R_k can be obtained before the execution of the Kalman filter process. In the case of the measurement error covariance R_k especially this is important because the need to measure the process. It is possible to be realized some sample measurements to determine the variance of the measurement error.

In both cases, we have a good basis for choosing the parameters. Very often superior filter performance (statistically speaking) can be obtained by changing of the filter parameter R_k. The modification is usually performed offline. Finally, under condition where R_k is constant, both the estimation error covariance P_k and the Kalman gain G_k can be stabilized very fast and then remain constant. If we have a constant value, the R_k parameter can be calculated by running the filter off-line. The process of the local sensor data integration in the Cluster Head is shown on Fig. 3.

Every sensor of the WSN during the process of the sensor network forming process is assigned to a specific cluster. As part of the group of sensors organized in the cluster, every sensor node collects data from his environment for a fixed period of time, integrates locally the collected data using the Kalman filtering method and sends the integrated data to the CH. The CH starts a second level integration by implementation shown on a Fig. 3 Fraser-Potter equation combined by Central Limit Theorem (CLT) based algorithm and sends the integrated data to the control center.

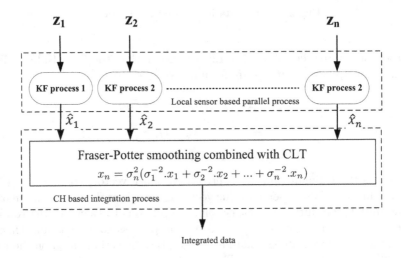

Fig. 3. CH based sensor data parallel data integration process

The criterion

$$x_n = \sigma_n^2(\sigma_1^{-2}.x_1 + \sigma_2^{-2}.x_2 + \ldots\ldots + \sigma_n^{-2}.x_n) \tag{6}$$

is based on the Central Limit Theorem and the Fraser-Potter fixed interval smoother, where $\sigma_n^2 = (\sigma_1^{-2} + \sigma_2^{-2} + \ldots\ldots + \sigma_n^{-2}$ is the variance of the combined estimate.

The clustered sensor data integration process is repeating in fixed time periods which depend on the specific WSN's architecture and embedded routing protocols.

1.2 Generalized Nets Based Parallel Processes Modeling

The Generalized Nets (GNs, [1–5]) appears as extensions of the regular Petri Nets (PNs) and all their modifications. In principle, the GNs are different from the ways of defining the other types of PNs. The components in the typical GN-definition provide more and better modeling capabilities and therefore determine the GNs among the separate types of PNs. Similarly to the PNs, GNs contain places, transitions, and tokens, but their transitions have a much more complex structure.

Based on [1] in GNs every transition is described by a three-tuple:

$$Z = \langle L', L'', r \rangle, \tag{7}$$

where L' and L'' are non-empty sets of places (the transition's input and output places, respectively); for the transition Z these are:

$L' = \{l'_1, l'_2 \ldots \ldots l'_i\}$ and $L'' = \{l''_{i+1}, l''_{i+2} \ldots \ldots l''_j\}$

r is the transition's condition determining which tokens will pass (or transfer) from the transition's inputs to its outputs; it has the form of an Index Matrix (IM):

The GN-tokens enter the network with initial predefined parameters. After the move to the new place, the GN-tokens can change their parameters or save the initial ones. The biggest difference between Petri Nets and the Predicate-Transition Nets is that the GN-tokens can keep all their own characteristics during the process. Later they can be used for evaluation of the transition condition predicates. The second big difference to the remaining types of Petri Nets is that the GNs contain a global temporal scale (Fig. 4).

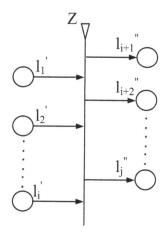

Fig. 4. GN transition example

The GNs can have more than 20 conservative extensions (i.e., extensions for which their functioning and the results of their work can be represented by an ordinary GN). Some of them are: GNs with global memory; GNs with optimization components; GNs with complex transition type; GNs with characteristic functions of the places and arcs.

In the current paper, we will be focused on the GNs with Global Memory as the most appropriate to the data parallel processing in the LSWSN. Based on [1,2] the ordered 4-tuple

$$E^* = \langle \langle A, \rangle, \langle K \rangle, \langle T \rangle, \langle B, X, \Phi, b \rangle \rangle \tag{8}$$

is called a Generalized Net with Global Memory where:

- A is the set of transitions;
- K is the set of the GN's tokens;
- T is the time moment when GN starts to function;
- B is the Global Memory component which is list of variables assigning values depend of the GN model execution stage;
- X is the set of all initial characteristics which the tokens can obtain on entering the net;
- Φ is the characteristic function that assigns new characteristics to every token when it makes the transfer from an input to an output place of a given transition.
- b is a function which specifies the maximal number of the token's characteristics.

2   GN Model of Cluster-Based Sensor Data Parallel Integration Processes in WSN

A new GN model of the sensor data clustered parallel integration process is presented in Fig. 5. The proposed new model is related to WSN's with cluster topology. In the model the inputs $l_{11} - l_{i1}$ represent the measured data input parameters needed for the integration clustering process described in details in [1–3].

The token α enters GN in place l_{i1} with characteristic "C_i -measured sensor data where $i \in N$". N is the number of sensor nodes in the cluster.

The token β enters GN in place l_{i2} with characteristic "$S_{measure}$ - maximum number of sensor data measurements".

$$Z_{i1} = <\{l_{i1}, l_{i2}\}, \{l_{i2}, l_{i3}\}, r_{i,1}> \quad i \in N \tag{9}$$

$$r_{i,1} = \begin{array}{c|cc} & l_{i,2} & l_{i,3} \\ \hline l_{i,1} & true & true, \wedge(l_{i1}, l_{i2}) \\ l_{i,2} & true & W_{i2,i3}, \wedge l_{i3} \end{array} \tag{10}$$

Where $W_{i2,i3}$ is "finished number of measurements P_i" The transitions $Z_{11} - Z_{i1}$ in Fig. 5 represent the initial process of sensor measurements and sensor data collection of the sensor nodes in the WSN's cluster.

$$Z_2 = <\{l_{1,3}.....l_{i,3}, l_8 \quad i \in N\}, \{l_4, l_5\}, r_2> \tag{11}$$

$$r_2 = \begin{array}{c|cc} & l_4 & l_5 \\ \hline l_{1,3} & true & true \\ . & . & . \\ . & . & . \\ . & . & . \\ l_{i,3} & true & W_{4,5} \\ l_{10} & true & W_{4,8} \end{array} \tag{12}$$

Where $W_{4,5}$ is "finished data measurement process" and $W_{4,8}$ represents the "sensor data measurement cycle in fixed time periods".

The transition Z_3 represents the execution stage of the Cluster Head sensor data integration process based on Central Limit Theorem and Fraser-Potter equation.

$$Z_3 = <\{l_5, l_6\}, \{l_6, l_7, l_8\}, r_3> \tag{13}$$

$$r_3 = \begin{array}{c|ccc} & l_6 & l_7 & l_8 \\ \hline l_5 & true & W_{6,7} & true \\ l_6 & true & true & W_{6,8} \end{array} \tag{14}$$

As is shown on Fig. 5 the transition Z_4 and output l_9 represents the process of saving the process configuration in the Global Memory.

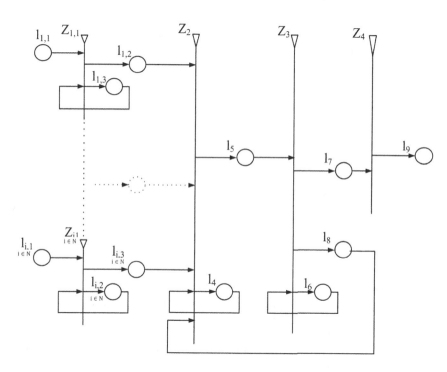

Fig. 5. GN model of parallel sensor data integration in clustered WSNs

3 Performance Simulation of the Sensor Data Integration Parallel Processing

Based on the developed model shown on Fig. 5 is created a performance simulation of the parallel data integration process in a cluster consisting of 10 wireless sensor nodes. The main task of the simulation was to get information about two critical sensor data integration performance parameters:

- Integration data parallel process delay in the function of the number of the sensor nodes in the cluster.
- Integration data parallel process delay in the function of the distance between the sensor nodes and CH.

For the needs of the simulation are accepted the following assumptions (Table 1):

Table 1. WSN simulation WSNet based prerequisites

Sensor node parameter description	Parameter
Number of clusters	1
Number of sensor nodes	10 pcs
Field size	$1000\,\text{m}^2$
Max. transmission range	100 m
Packet length	128 bit/64 bit
Relay hop	1
Duty cycle	50 ms
Data rate	256 KB/s

The simulation process was implemented in the WSNet simulator and is divided into the following stages:

Initialize variables - in this stage are assigned the values of the variables based on the required scenario, such as the number of sensor nodes, field size, transmission, range and relay hop and etc.

Generate and deploy sensor nodes - in this stage, the sensor nodes are deployed depending on the size of the field size using the embedded in the WSNet random number generator.

Constructing the Routing path between the sensor nodes and the Cluster Head (CH) - in our simulation is used a star topology and every sensor node is connected to the CH directly.

Selecting Data Gathering Scheme - for the current simulation we use a randomly generated sensor data with different size stored in the database.

The developed simulation in WSNet simulator is executed to ensure a relatively realistic environment with the respective performance benchmark of the sensor data parallel processing in the modeled Wireless Sensor Network. The main benefits of the proposed method for modeling and simulation are:

- generation an adequate and reliable model of sensor data parallel processes in WSNs using the Generalized Nets approach. Compared with those of the existing simulators for WSNs, for instance, the execution time with the increasing number of nodes in comparison with other simulators.
- generation of reliable simulation results which can be used during the WSN architecture design.

As a result of the simulation, we got information shown on Tables 2 and 3, about two critical sensor data parameters related to the parallel processing - delay in milliseconds in the dependence of a number of the nodes in the cluster and the delay in milliseconds in the dependency of the distance between sensor nodes.

Table 2. 64/128 bits packet size delay

Number of nodes	1	2	3	4	5	6	7	8	9	10
64 bits packet size - delay in ms	2,75	2,77	2, 85	2,95	2,83	2,69	2,78	2,98	3,12	3,46
128 bits packet size - delay in ms	3,65	4,02	4,34	5,15	5,53	5,92	6,35	7,05	7,92	8,12

These dependencies are shown on the Figs. 6 and 7.

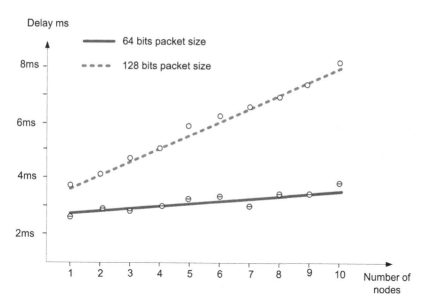

Fig. 6. Integration data parallel process delay in function of the number of the sensor nodes in the cluster

Table 3. 64/128 bits packet size delay

Distance in m	10	20	30	40	50	60
64 bits packet size - delay in ms	2,75	2,79	2,91	3,05	3,12	3,19
128 bits packet size - delay in ms	4,25	4,92	5,24	5,65	6,73	7,09

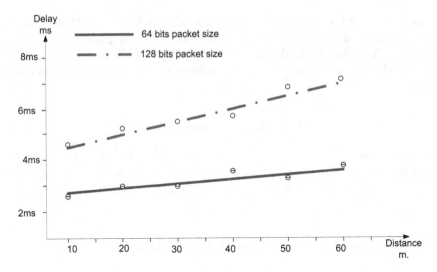

Fig. 7. Integration data parallel process delay in function of the distance between the sensor nodes and CH.

4   Conclusion

The paper presents a new method for modeling, based on Generalized Nets (GNs) and Kalman filtering as a relatively new and very power modeling approach for generating a reliable and flexible model of parallel processes. As it was shown above the GNs main benefit is that they are designed to focus on parallel processing. The simulation using WSNet simulator of the described sensor data integration processes in WSNs confirms that the GN approach has sensitively better flexibility and reliability compared to regular Petri Nets and Markov models. The advantages of the new concept are:

- the proposed GN model is a very good start point for WSN's parallel data integration processes analysis and simulation and can reduce sensitively the cost of the WSN's system architecture design.
- the information, collected during the chosen model generation process (GNs with Global Memory) can be stored and can be used for parametrization and adaptive dynamic data change during the simulation of the sensor data parallel integration processes.
- the implemented in the proposed method Kalman Filter with a combination of Central Limit Theorem and the Fraser-Potter equations reduces the data noise and fluctuations, not related to the main process.

The future step will be to apply the proposed new concept in the area of real WSN's design with a focus on multivariate optimized sensor data integration.

References

1. Atanassov, K.: Generalized Nets. World Scientific, Singapore (1991)
2. Fidanova, S., Atanasov, K., Marinov, P.: Generalized Nets and Ant Colony Optimization. Prof. Marin Drinov Academic Publishing House, Sofia (2011). ISBN 978-954-322-473-9
3. Sotirov, S., Atanasov, K.: Generalized Nets and Supervised Neural Networks. Prof. Marin Drinov Academic Publishing House, Sofia (2011). ISBN 978-954-322-623-8
4. Doukovska, L., Atanassova, V., Shahpazov, G., Sotirova, E.: Generalized net model of the creditworthiness financial support mechanism for the SMEs. Int. J. Comput. Inform. (2016). ISSN 1335–9150
5. Balabanov, T., Sevova, J., Kolev, K.: Optimization of string rewriting operations for 3D fractal generation with genetic algorithms. In: Nikolov, G., Kolkovska, N., Georgiev, K. (eds.) NMA 2018. LNCS, vol. 11189, pp. 48–54. Springer, Cham (2019). https://doi.org/10.1007/978-3-030-10692-8_5
6. Alexandrov, A., Monov, V.: Method for adaptive node clustering in AD HOC wireless sensor networks. In: Vishnevskiy, V.M., Kozyrev, D.V. (eds.) DCCN 2018. CCIS, vol. 919, pp. 257–263. Springer, Cham (2018). https://doi.org/10.1007/978-3-319-99447-5_22
7. Hall, D.L., Llinas, J.: An introduction to multisensor data fusion. Proc. IEEE 85(1), 6–23 (1997)
8. Durrant-Whyte, H.F., Stevens, M.: Data fusion in decentralized sensing networks. In: Proceedings of the 4th International Conference on Information Fusion, Montreal, Canada, pp. 302–307 (2001)
9. Tcheshmedjiev, P.: Synchronizing parallel processes using generalized nets, NT. J. "Bioautom." 14(1), 69–74 (2010)
10. Atanasova T.: Modelling of complex objects in distance learning systems. In: Proceedings of the First International Conference - "Innovative Teaching Methodology", Tbilisi, Georgia, 25–26 October 2014, pp. 180–190 (2014). ISBN 978-9941-9348-7-2
11. Alexandrov, A.: Ad-hoc Kalman filter based fusion algorithm for real-time wireless sensor data integration. In: Andreasen, T., et al. (eds.) Flexible Query Answering Systems 2015. AISC, vol. 400, pp. 151–159. Springer, Cham (2016). https://doi.org/10.1007/978-3-319-26154-6_12
12. Luo, R.C., Yih, C.-C., Su, K.L.: Multisensor fusion and integration: approaches, applications, and future research directions. IEEE Sens. J. 2(2), 107–119 (2002)

Find the Right Peers: Building and Querying Multi-IoT Networks Based on Contexts

Claudia Diamantini[1], Antonino Nocera[2], Domenico Potena[1(✉)], Emanuele Storti[1], and Domenico Ursino[1]

[1] DII, Polytechnic University of Marche, Ancona, Italy
d.potena@univpm.it
[2] DIII, University of Pavia, Pavia, Italy

Abstract. With the evolution of the features smart devices are equipped with, the IoT realm is becoming more and more intertwined with people daily-life activities. This has, of course, impacts in the way objects are used, causing a strong increase in both the dynamism of their contexts and the diversification of their objectives. This results in an evolution of the IoT towards a more complex environment composed of multiple overlapping networks, called Multi-IoTs (MIoT). The low applicability of classical cooperation mechanisms among objects leads to the necessity of developing more complex and refined strategies that take the peculiarity of such a new environment into consideration. In this paper, we address this problem by proposing a new model for devices and their contexts following a knowledge representation approach. It borrows ideas from OLAP systems and leverages a multidimensional perspective by defining dimension hierarchies. In this way, it enables roll-up and drill-down operations on the values of the considered dimensions. This allows for the design of more compact object networks and the definition of new strategies for the retrieval of relevant devices.

1 Introduction

In the Internet of Things (IoT) [1] and its recent Multi-IoT (MIoT) extension [3], the development of techniques for the retrieval of relevant devices and data conveyed by them is of crucial importance. In the literature, some approaches propose simple criteria to decide about the creation of the network [2]: *(i) proximity* (devices connect to each other if they are spatially close for a sufficiently long time interval); *(ii) homogeneity* (devices belonging to the same brand and of the same kind, e.g. Samsung community); *(iii) ownership* (devices belonging to the same user); *(iv) friendship* (devices belonging to users that are connected to each other in some social networks).

When it is necessary to decide the actual usefulness of the contact, these criteria do not take into account the similarity of contexts in which devices are used. As a consequence, information exchanged is likely to be less relevant for

© Springer Nature Switzerland AG 2019
A. Cuzzocrea et al. (Eds.): FQAS 2019, LNAI 11529, pp. 302–313, 2019.
https://doi.org/10.1007/978-3-030-27629-4_28

the peers. For instance, consider the following situation: Laura likes to keep fit and make outdoor workout, in particular running in the countryside. Several devices can be used for this purpose: smart phone, smart watch, fitband, ipod, smart speedform (smart running shoes, like Altra Torin IQ), running sensor (e.g. Lumo Run Sensor), smart coach (e.g. LifeBeam), neuropriming smart device (e.g. Halo Sport), sportcam. These devices are very diverse from the point of view of available sensors. Laura typically uses its smart phone application to record her running activity. She also checks outdoor conditions (temperature, humidity, cloud coverage or raining) before going to her preferred sites in the neighborhood, because her health status requires specific weather conditions. This may be done by querying her network of devices, asking for quantities (measures) that can be typically obtained by sensors embedded in smart devices, such as *(i)* Position, *(ii)* Temperature, and *(iii)* Brightness.

Let us now suppose that Laura enters a bus where other 50 persons have a smart device. Traditional proximity criteria would lead to connect Laura's devices to any other device nearby. However, it turns out that most of people in the bus are children coming back from school, who spend most of their time at home. It is clear that, by using proximity as a criterion, the probability to obtain relevant information about temperature or brightness from the new contacts is trivially related to the increased number of new contacts.

Since only a limited number of contacts can be managed by devices, having a mechanism to form the network based on the similarity of the device context of use would be a benefit. On the other hand, even an identity of contexts would be of little use if the two devices are not able to communicate each other, for instance because they do not belong to the same brand, or because of incompatible measures. Hence, device properties and capabilities must also be taken into account.

In the past literature, several approaches for the definition of contexts in IoT have been developed. This task has been often intertwined with that of empowering the IoT of social features. Indeed, the idea of studying device contexts has risen from the need of improving the quality of the interactions among them. For instance, [13] is the first work in which the idea of filtering contacts based on context proximity has been developed. The authors of this work actually suggest to combine the classical notion of proximity with other metrics, such as movement patterns, thus defining a context proximity notion. Several other studies have, then, completed this attempt by bringing the notions of context and context matching under the spotlight as a mean to confer social features to devices in the IoT [6,11].

This paper aims at providing a contribution in this setting. Indeed, it proposes a context-based approach to identifying and querying relevant devices within a MIoT. To this end, first it proposes a model to represent devices properties, contexts and context dimensions. As usually done in the framework of IoT research, contexts and properties are defined as a set of couples (p, v), where p is a property name, and v represents a corresponding admissible value. Differently from other approaches, context properties are organized in *dimensions*, a notion borrowed from the multi-dimensional model, each with its own hierarchy of admissible values. This allows us to introduce different types of relationship among contexts, namely identity, inclusion (similar to the notion of roll-up among the members of each context dimension) and a fuzzier relationship of compatibility.

As a second contribution, our paper uses the proposed model to define a flexible querying mechanism to determine the subset of devices that are more likely to provide relevant answers to a user's query. In this way, it produces a projection (or view) of the original overall network that can be actually exploited for the goal at hand. Finally, it defines a measure scoring the utility for a given device to add another one in its list of contacts, in such a way as to build a compact and more homogeneous network.

Context modeling has been extensively investigated in the knowledge representation literature [4,15] with the aim of accurately describing complex entities, relationships, and constraints [12] forming a context. Much work adopts logical languages and ontologies [7,8,16,19]; however, the expressiveness of ontologies has complexity as a shortcoming, which can be critical for applications like IoT, where computing abilities are limited [4]. Furthermore, none of the cited models considers a hierarchical organization of context properties. The Context Dimension Tree, implemented in the PerLa context language for designing and managing wireless sensor network applications [17], considers a tree structure where a *dimension* node is the parent of a set of *concept* nodes. Nesting of more than one dimension level is possible, allowing the representation of structured concepts (namely admissible values). In contrast, the model proposed in this paper adopts dimension hierarchies in the multidimensional perspective, typical of OLAP systems, representing roll-up relationships between admissible values of the dimensions.

The above literature focuses on "how" context information can be represented. Another issue is related to "which" information should be included in context. This greatly varies from application to application. In [5], the authors recognize a limit inherent in the adoption of knowledge representation methodologies for context modelling, namely the difficulty for a limited group of people to enumerate all the possible concepts and relationships that may be used in a practical mobile or desktop context-aware application. We believe that the multidimensional perspective proposed in this paper helps to overcome this limit. Indeed, if a dimension is not relevant for a given application, we model it as if any possible admissible value was acceptable, which corresponds to selecting the highest level of the hierarchy of values (also termed the "all" value).

A device's network(s) is analogous to a person's list of contacts in a social network. This analogy is strongly supported by the research community and, indeed, a number of works have tried to adopt the paradigm of social network in the IoT realm and to combine these worlds, thus improving their usability and the offered services [2,10,14,18]. In [11], the authors propose a social infrastructure allowing access to both humans and devices. In this system, humans can interact with each other offering services through their own devices; furthermore, they can interact directly with devices by using the infrastructure as a communication channel. An important step towards the definition of a unified framework for including things in the virtual human communities is described in [2]. This paper provides contribution in both the definition of policies managing the social interaction among devices, so that the result is an accessible and usable social network, and the formalization of an architecture for the IoT, so that devices include all the features needed for an easy and effective integration in existing social sites. As a result of this study the authors propose a new paradigm called Social Internet of Things (SIoT).

Very recently, other studies have focused on the social factors that foster the rise of new and stable communication in the IoT. For instance, the work described in [10] first proposes a study on which the social aspect improves the quality of device-to-device communication. Afterwards, it provides insights on how to include those aspects in a new framework for creating an IoT-only social community.

Differently from social networks, where peers are not classified according to their profile, or only very naïve manual classification in a predefined set of categories can be done, the model proposed in this paper allows a very rich and flexible definition of contexts, and a graded association of profiles to contexts. Furthermore, interaction mechanisms in social networks are typically limited to information sharing by broadcasting (posting information that reaches all the contacts of a node) or to one-to-one messaging (directly contacting a node via its name/address).

The rest of this paper is structured as follows: Sect. 2 presents our model for device contexts in a Multi-IoT scenario. Our supervised algorithm for device retrieval is, then, illustrated in Sect. 3, whereas Sect. 4 discusses factors taken into account in network creation. Experiments to assess the effectiveness of our approach are reported in Sect. 5. Finally, Sect. 6 ends the paper.

2   A Model for Devices in a Multi-IoT Network

This section is devoted to introduce the model used to represent the devices and their relations in a multi-IoT environment. We define a device Δ_i as a set of sensors $\Delta_i = \{S_1, \ldots, S_n\}$. A set $P(i)$ of properties is associated with a device, each represented as a pair (p, v), where p is the property name and v is the corresponding value. Properties describe device's metadata like *owner*, *brand*, *model*, as well as device's capabilities, namely the set of *measure(s)* provided by its component sensors. For instance, if the device is endowed with a GPS sensor and a clock, its capabilities will be expressed as (measure, Position), (measure, Time). While metadata are basically static, the actual data measured by sensors varies over time, and is exploited to define a device's context according to the model introduced in the following subsection.

In order to specify a context, we organize sensor data according to a set of dimensions $\mathcal{D} = \{D_1, \ldots, D_m\}$, which are to be intended as the dimensions in the multidimensional model. Following the previous example, we can consider *Position* and *Time* as dimensions. It is also worth considering a dimension representing the *Goal* for which the device is used (e.g., running). In the present paper we do not delve into the issue of how to define goals starting from sensor data. We just note that some devices are already endowed with this kind of capability (e.g., step counters can classify the activity as "walking" or "running", depending on step frequency).

Analogously to the multidimensional model, given a dimension $D_j \in \mathcal{D}$, it is possible to define a hierarchy of levels $L_j = \{l_{j_1}, \ldots, l_{j_m}\}$ such that $l_{j_1} \rightarrow l_{j_2} \rightarrow \cdots \rightarrow l_{j_m}$. The notation $l_{j_p} \rightarrow l_{j_q}$ implies that a functional dependency exists from l_{j_p} to l_{j_q}. To make an example, given the dimension *Position*, the following relation holds: *street* $\rightarrow$ *district* $\rightarrow$ *city* $\rightarrow \cdots \rightarrow$ *country*. Each level l_{j_i} of a dimension D_j has a set of instances $\{\iota_{j_1}, \ldots, \iota_{j_i}\}$; for example, the level *city* can include *Rome, Venice, Milan* as its instances.

Given a dimension $D_j \in \mathcal{D}$, let $\iota_{j_p}, \iota_{j_q} \in D_j$ be two instances of D_j. The following relations are defined between ι_{j_p} and ι_{j_q}:

- $id(\iota_{j_p}, \iota_{j_q})$: it means that ι_{j_p} and ι_{j_q} are identical instances, e.g. $id(Montecitorio\ square, Montecitorio\ Sq.)$.
- $inc(\iota_{j_p}, \iota_{j_q})$: it means that ι_{j_p} is included in ι_{j_q}, e.g. $inc(Montecitorio\ square, Rome)$. In order for this property to hold, it must be true that *square* $\rightarrow$ *city* and *Montecitorio square* is in Rome. Moreover, given that *square* $\rightarrow$ *city* and, in turn, *city* $\rightarrow$ *nation*, it also holds that $inc(Montecitorio\ square, Italy)$.
- $dist(\iota_{j_p}, \iota_{j_q})$: it is the distance between ι_{j_p} and ι_{j_q}, that is the number of steps in the dimensional hierarchy necessary to move from the former to the latter.
- $cpt(\iota_{j_p}, \iota_{j_q})$: it means that $inc(\iota_{j_p}, \iota_{j_r})$, $inc(\iota_{j_q}, \iota_{j_r})$, where $l_{j_p} \rightarrow l_{j_r}, l_{j_q} \rightarrow l_{j_r}$ and l_{j_p} (resp., l_{j_q}, l_{j_r}) represents the level of ι_{j_p} (resp., ι_{j_q}, ι_{j_r}). This means that ι_{j_p} and ι_{j_p} are siblings, e.g. $cpt(Rome, Milan)$, $cpt(Italy, France)$, whereas it does not hold that $cpt(Rome, Paris)$.

We are now ready to define the notions of context schema and context instance. Specifically, the schema of a context C for a device is defined as a set of dimensions $\mathcal{D}$. In turn, a context instance $c \in C$ is a tuple $c = (\iota_1, \iota_2, \cdots, \iota_m)$, where, to ease the notation, we refer to ι_j as any instance of any level of the dimension D_j. To make an example, considering the dimensional schema $\{Position, Time, Goal\}$, a possible instance is: $\iota_{Position} = Amantea$, $\iota_{Time} = July\ 2^{nd}\ 2019,\ 11:00-12:00$, $\iota_{Goal} = Running$. Another example is $\iota_{Position} = Calabria$, $\iota_{Time} = July\ 2019$, $\iota_{Goal} = Running$.

Based on the relationships between dimension instances defined before, the following relationships between two context instances $c = (\iota_1, \iota_2, \cdots, \iota_m)$ and $c' = (\iota'_1, \iota'_2, \cdots, \iota'_m)$ can be defined:

- $id_C(c, c')$, if $id(\iota_i, \iota'_i), 1 \leq i \leq m$; for instance $c = (Montecitorio\ square, [10:00-11:00],\ Running)$ $c' = (Montecitorio\ sq., [10:00-11:00],\ Running)$.
- $inc_C(c, c')$, if $id(\iota_i, \iota'_i)$ or if $inc(\iota_i, \iota'_i), 1 \leq i \leq m$ and $id_C(c, c')$ does not hold; for instance $c = (Montecitorio\ square, [10:00-11:00],\ Running)$, $c' = (Montecitorio\ sq., Morning,\ Running)$. We define $dist(c, c')$ as a measure of distance between c and c', measured as $\sum_{i=1}^{m} dist(\iota_i, \iota'_i)$, where $dist(\iota_i, \iota'_i) = 0$ if $id(\iota_i, \iota'_i)$.

- $cpt_C(c, c')$, if either $id(\iota_i, \iota_i')$ or $inc(\iota_i, \iota_i')$ or $cpt(\iota_i, \iota_i'), 1 \le i \le m$ and neither $id_C(c, c')$ nor $inc_C(c, c')$ holds; for instance, $c = (Montecitorio\ square, [09:00–10:00], Running)$ $c = (Montecitorio\ square, [10:00–11:00], Running)$.

These are very important relationships because they will allow us to develop our techniques for device retrieval and network construction.

3   Retrieval of Devices in a Multi-IoT Network

Given a user and its network, this section presents an algorithm aimed to retrieve the subset of devices satisfying some requirements. Since these last are expressed through a user query, this algorithm performs the search in a *supervised* way[1], where a query q is represented as $q = \langle c, Z \rangle$, with c being the context of interest and $Z = \{(p_1, v_1), (p_2, v_2), \cdots, (p_n, v_n)\}$ being the set of properties, and their values, which the devices must satisfy.

To provide an answer to a query $q = (c, Z)$, the algorithm executes a SEARCH function, checking whether there are devices whose contexts are identical (id_C) to or included (inc_C) in c. If this does not happen, the function searches for devices with contexts that are compatible (cpt_C) with c. The retrieved devices are ranked according to how their properties are similar of Z. On the other hand, in case there is no answer from the previous step, the algorithm *rewrites* the query q as a new query $q' = (c', Z)$, where c' is a context more general than c (i.e. such that c is included in c': $inc_C(c, c')$). This allows an increase of recall even if this is coupled with a decrease of precision. The algorithm is, then, recursively called with q'.

The whole procedure iterates until to: *(i)* a solution is found, *(ii)* the number of rewritings is greater than a defined threshold (e.g., the function *dist* discussed in Sect. 2 can be used), or *(iii)* the query cannot be further rewritten. The pseudocode for the SEARCH function is reported in Algorithm 1. Specifically:

1. The Algorithm searches for devices whose contexts are identical to or included in c, by calling the corresponding function (line 4). For each retrieved device Δ_i, its properties $P(i)$ are matched against the vector Z of properties in such a way as to rank its ability to satisfy the user query (line 6). Any suitable metric can be adopted to this end. In Algorithm 1 and in our experiments, we considered the Jaccard metric J. Finally, the device is added to the output list Δ_O together with its rank value (line 7).
2. In case no device is found at the previous step, the algorithm searches for devices having a context compatible with c, through the corresponding function. Similarly to the previous case, for each retrieved device, a rank r is computed and the pair $\langle device, rank \rangle$ is added to the output list Δ_O (line 14).

---

[1] An unsupervised retrieval of devices will be subject of future work.

To take into account that these devices have contexts that are compatible, but neither identical to nor included in c, the rank is weighted by a parameter $\alpha_{cpt} < 1$.

Finally, the list Δ_O is returned as output (line 18).

Algorithm 1. Pseudocode for the SEARCH function

Input:
    The set Δ of devices in the user net.
    A query q=$\langle c, Z \rangle$ over Δ, where $c \in C$ is a context and $Z = \{(p_1, v_1), (p_2, v_2), \cdots, (p_n, v_n)\}$ is a set of pairs (property value)
Output:
    a ranked set of devices $\Delta_O = \{\langle \Delta_1, r_1 \rangle, \ldots, \langle \Delta_n, r_n \rangle\}$, where $\Delta_i \in \Delta$ and $r_i \in [0, 1]$

```
 1: function SEARCH(q)
 2:     Δ_O ← []
 3:     Δ' ← FIND_DEVICES_ID(c,Δ)
 4:     if Δ' ≠ ∅ then
 5:         for each Δ_i ∈ Δ' do
 6:             r ← J(Z, P(i))
 7:             Δ_O ← ⟨Δ_i, r⟩
 8:         end for
 9:     else
10:         Δ' ← FIND_DEVICES_CPT(c,Δ)
11:         if Δ' ≠ ∅ then
12:             for each Δ_i ∈ Δ' do
13:                 r ← α_cpt * J(Z, P(i))
14:                 Δ_O ← ⟨Δ_i, r⟩
15:             end for
16:         end if
17:     end if
18:     return Δ_O
19: end function

20: function FIND_DEVICES_ID(c, Δ)
21:     C' ← {c' ∈ C | id_C(c, c') ∨ inc_C(c', c)}
22:     Δ' ← {Δ_i ∈ Δ | c_i ∈ C'}
23:     return Δ'
24: end function

25: function FIND_DEVICES_CPT(c, Δ)
26:     C' ← {c' ∈ C | cpt_C(c, c')}
27:     Δ' ← {Δ_i ∈ Δ | c_i ∈ C'}
28:     return Δ'
29: end function
```

In the next section, we show how we can optimize the creation of the IoT to cope with the peculiarities of our model and of the associated information retrieval strategy.

4   Building the Internet of Things

According to the scientific literature, the IoT creation is usually triggered by considering devices' dynamics as a fundamental aspect. Typically, this is encoded in factors directly related to devices but also to their owners. Specifically, as pointed out in the introduction, the main factors are: *(i)* proximity, *(ii)* homogeneity, *(iii)* ownership, and *(iv)* friendship. However, these classical factors do not allow for filtering contacts based on the real use of the information provided by its neighbors.

Following this reasoning, in this section, we introduce a metric leveraging two contributions when analyzing a potential new contact in the IoT realm: *(i)* a direct factor F^d related to the factors discussed above, and *(ii)* an indirect factor F^i measuring the advantage in the device's capability of answering queries brought about by the addition of a new contact.

Given two devices Δ_x and Δ_y, F^d consists of the following sub-factors: *(i)* the proximity $P_{x,y}$, *(ii)* the homogeneity $O_{x,y}$, *(iii)* the ownership $OW_{x,y}$ representing both the case in which the devices belong to the same user or to users that are friends each other in a virtual community.

The proximity can be computed as: $P_{x,y} = \frac{\sum_{e_i \in EN_{x,y}} t_{e_i}}{|EN_{x,y}|}$, where $EN_{x,y}$ represents the set of the events e_i in which the devices have been in proximity, whereas t_{e_i} is the duration of such an event. The homogeneity, instead, can assume the following values: 1 if both the brand and the typology of Δ_x and Δ_y are the same; 0.5 if either the brand or the typology is the same; 0 otherwise. Similarly, the ownership can be: 1 if the devices belong to the same owner; 0.5 if the owner of Δ_x and Δ_y are reciprocal contacts/friends; 0 otherwise. Therefore, F^d can be computed as: $F^d_{x,y} = \frac{\delta P_{x,y} + \iota O_{x,y} + \gamma OW_{x,y}}{\delta + \iota + \gamma}$, where $\delta, \iota, \gamma \in [0,1]$ are three parameters stating the importance of each of the corresponding sub-factors.

As for the indirect component F^i, it is directly proportional to the gain in the capacity of a device to retrieve the needed information due to the presence of a new contact. In order to define this component, we refer to a set of queries $Q^x = \{q_1^x, q_2^x, \cdots, q_k^x\}$ of interest for a device Δ_x, where $q_i^x = (c_i^x, Z_i^x)$.

Let $QC^x = \{c_1^x, c_2^x, \cdots, c_n^x\}$ be the set of the contexts in Q^x. Given a device Δ_y and a set of contexts QC^y, its rank for id_C can be computed as: $r_{\Delta_y}^{id_C} = \alpha_{id} \cdot \sum_{c_i^x | \exists c_i^y \in QC^y, id_C(c_i^x, c_i^y)}(J(Z_i^x, P(y)))$. We recall that $P(y)$ denotes the set of properties of Δ_y and J is the Jaccard metric.

Analogously, we can define ranks $r_{\Delta_y}^{inc_C}$ and $r_{\Delta_y}^{cpt_C}$ for the inc_C and cpt_C relations, respectively, where $0 < \alpha_{cpt} < \alpha_{inc} < \alpha_{id} = 1$.

The direct gain brought about by a device in the query answering capability of another device can be estimated as:

$$\hat{G}_{x,y} = \frac{\hat{G}_{x,y}^{id_C} + \hat{G}_{x,y}^{inc_C} + \hat{G}_{x,y}^{cpt_C}}{\alpha + \alpha_{inc} + \alpha_{cpt}},$$

where:

$$\hat{G}_{x,y}^{id_C} = \frac{r_{\Delta_y}^{id_C}}{|QC^x|}, \hat{G}_{x,y}^{inc_C} = \frac{r_{\Delta_y}^{inc_C}}{|QC^x|}, \hat{G}_{x,y}^{cpt_C} = \frac{r_{\Delta_y}^{cpt_C}}{|QC^x|}.$$

Actually, when a new contact is added, it offers its contact list as a mean to build new useful paths toward information sources. Therefore, F^i coincides with the *global* gain considering both the direct gain and the contribution from the neighborhood of the newly added contact. It can be formalized as: $F^i_{x,y} = (1-\beta)\hat{G}_{x,y} + \beta\frac{\sum_{z\in\Gamma(y)}\hat{G}_{x,z}}{|\Gamma(y)|}$.

In this formula, β is a parameter that tunes the importance of the neighborhood and $\Gamma(y)$ represents the contact list (neighborhood) of the device Δ_y.

Finally, a device Δ_x will add Δ_y as a new contact if: $\mathcal{F}(F^d_{x,y}, F^i_{x,y}) \geq \theta$, where θ is a suitable threshold and $\mathcal{F}$ is a function that properly combines F^d and F^i.

5   Experiments

The supervised algorithm discussed in Sect. 3 has been evaluated and compared with two baseline algorithms:

- *Baseline₁* (no contexts): this approach does not consider contexts. Therefore, the query is expressed only as $q = \langle \emptyset, Z \rangle$.
- *Baseline₂* (only identical): this approach considers contexts but it does not include a knowledge base. Therefore, the supervised approach can only match identical contexts but no reasoning on inclusion or compatibility can be done.

First, we introduce the dataset, the knowledge base and the experimental settings. Then, we present our results aimed to evaluate three different measures, namely: *(i)* the probability to obtain an answer from a query, *(ii)* how the query rewriting approach discussed in Sect. 3 affects the retrieval task, and *(iii)* how it affects the precision of the supervised algorithm. Hereby, we refer to the precision as the ratio $\frac{relevant contexts}{retrieved contexts}$, where *retrieved contexts* stands for the contexts belonging to the retrieved sensors, whereas *relevant contexts* refer to those contexts that are relevant to the query.

Dataset and Setup. In this set of experiments, we refer to a dataset that includes 5000 devices, each with a single sensor. Each device belongs to one or more IoTs, the largest of which includes 500 devices. These are described in terms of their properties, although, in these tests, for the sake of simplicity, we consider a single property, namely the "measure" retrieved by the device (e.g., temperature, humidity or pressure). The model taken into consideration for these tests includes 3 dimensions, 3 hierarchical levels for each dimension and a branching factor of the dimensional tree equal to 3. In particular, the dimensional tree includes 1 root element at level 1, 3 elements at level 2 and 9 elements at level 3 (i.e., 13 elements in total). The overall number of possible contexts is, therefore, given by all the possible combinations of elements for each dimension, e.g. $|C| = 13^3 = 2197$. Specific compatibility relationships among members are established for each dimension. In our experimental setting, each member is defined to be compatible with 5% of the other members at the same level (e.g., given the level "street" of the dimension *Position*, each specific member will have 5% of the chances to be defined as compatible with any other street). The initialization includes the following steps:

- *Device initialization*: a device is picked from the dataset, and the set S of all the devices belonging to its net are extracted. In our test, the following procedure is repeated with 5 devices belonging to nets with sizes $S_1, \ldots, S_5$ from $|S_1| = 100$ to $|S_5| = 500$.
- *For each device $\Delta_i \in S_j$ a context c is randomly assigned to Δ_i*. The assignment strategy follows a power law. Specifically, we randomly assign a context instance from a small subset of C (i.e., 20% its size) to the large majority of devices (i.e., 80% in our tests), which hereafter we name C_s. In this way, we aim to model the most plausible context similarity of devices belonging to the same network. The procedure assigns a random context from the remaining set $C - C_s$ (i.e., in this case corresponding to the remaining 80% of C) to the rest (i.e., the remaining 20% of devices).
- A query $q = \langle c, Z \rangle$ is defined by assigning a context c from C_s and a property value from the list of possible property values seen in the database.
- The query q is launched on the network.

The procedure has been repeated for a number of queries equal to $|C|$, in order to perform a comprehensive evaluation. Results are, then, averaged.

Results. Results are summarized in Fig. 1. Figure 1(a) shows the performances of the supervised algorithm with increasing net sizes, in terms of percentage of queries with an answer. Figure 1(b) shows how the number of rewritings affects precision and recall in terms of the increase in the percentage of queries answered when one or more rewritings occur (see Sect. 3).

The most relevant insights are summarized as follows: the increase in the number of devices in a net has a positive impact, on average, on results. In particular, the larger the size, the greater the ratio of queries with an answer. By rewriting a query c as a query c' (which includes the former), the likelihood of obtaining an answer increases as the number of contexts included or compatible in c' is obviously larger. A single rewriting is enough to significantly increase the chance to find at least one solution to the query. However, this is achieved at the price of a relaxation of the original query specification and, as a consequence, of a decrease of the precision of results.

A direct comparison with $Baseline_1$ is straightforward, as the number of retrieved devices is only based on property information. Therefore, with $Baseline_1$ the result set is always larger, but the whole set of sensors in the network must be analysed and matched against the properties, with no guarantee on the correctness of the results. In other terms, recall is not higher, whereas precision is much lower. On the other hand, by comparing these results with $Baseline_2$, it is possible to conclude that our approach allows the retrieval of a much larger number of relevant results. In this respect, $Baseline_2$ is equivalent to the evaluation of only identical contexts. Therefore, precision is high, whereas recall is typically much lower. On the other hand, by exploiting the knowledge base, and specifically inclusion relations among contexts, more contexts can be obtained. Furthermore, compatible contexts are added to the result with a lower rank, meaning that their relevance is lower than the others, even if it can be still useful, depending on the specific application case. Finally, by exploiting inclusion relationships and the notion of rewriting, our approach can optionally lower precision in order to increase the probability to answer a query.

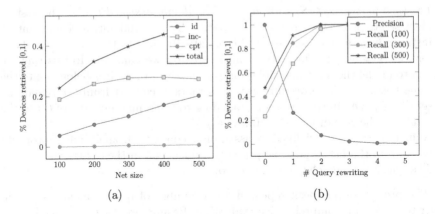

Fig. 1. (a) Percentage of retrieved devices with networks of difference size, (b) precision and recall against the number of query rewritings.

6   Conclusion

This paper presented an approach to model the context of a device through a multidimensional representation taking user interest and behavior into account. On this top, we introduce a supervised algorithm to retrieve the best set of nodes that can be queried according to given information needs or preferences and contexts, experimentally evaluating its effectiveness. Finally, we propose a measure to establish the utility for a given device to add another device to its network. We are currently working on: *(i)* extending the model with more expressive relationships between dimensions members to enable more advanced analysis (e.g. [9]), *(ii)* developing an unsupervised algorithm capable of automatically generating queries based on its current context and device's properties, and *(iii)* carrying out a more comprehensive experimentation.

References

1. Atzori, L., Iera, A., Morabito, G.: The Internet of Things: a survey. Comput. Netw. **54**(15), 2787–2805 (2010)
2. Atzori, L., Iera, A., Morabito, G., Nitti, M.: The social internet of things (SIoT)-when social networks meet the Internet of Things: concept, architecture and network characterization. Comput. Netw. **56**(16), 3594–3608 (2012)
3. Baldassarre, G., Lo Giudice, P., Musarella, L., Ursino, D.: The MIoT paradigm: main features and an "ad-hoc" crawler. Future Gener. Comput. Syst. **92**, 29–42 (2019)

4. Bettini, C., et al.: A survey of context modelling and reasoning techniques. Pervasive Mob. Comput. **6**(2), 161–180 (2010)
5. Bhargava, P., Krishnamoorthy, S., Agrawala, A.: RoCoMo: a generic ontology for context modeling, representation and reasoning in a context-aware middleware. In: Proceedings of the 2012 ACM Conference on Ubiquitous Computing, UbiComp 2012, pp. 584–585. ACM (2012)
6. Bleecker. J.: A manifesto for networked objects—cohabiting with pigeons, arphids and aibos in the Internet of Things. Technical report. University of Southern California (2006)
7. Cabrera, O., Franch, X., Marco, J.: Ontology-based context modeling in service-oriented computing: a systematic mapping. Data Knowl. Eng. **110**, 24–53 (2017)
8. Chen, H., Finin, T., Joshi, A.: SOUPA: standard ontology for ubiquitous and pervasive applications. In: The First Annual International Conference on Mobile and Ubiquitous Systems: Networking and Services, MOBIQUITOUS 2004 (2004)
9. Diamantini, C., Potena, D., Storti, E., Zhang, H.: An ontology-based data exploration tool for key performance indicators. In: Meersman, R., et al. (eds.) OTM 2014. LNCS, vol. 8841, pp. 727–744. Springer, Heidelberg (2014). https://doi.org/10.1007/978-3-662-45563-0_45
10. Du, Q., Song, H., Zhu, X.: Social-feature enabled communications among devices toward the smart IoT community. IEEE Commun. Mag. **57**(1), 130–137 (2019)
11. Guinard, D., Fischer, M., Trifa, V.: Sharing using social networks in a composable Web of Things. In: 2010 8th IEEE International Conference on Pervasive Computing and Communications Workshops (PERCOM Workshops), pp. 702–707. IEEE (2010)
12. Henricksen, K., Indulska, J.: Developing context-aware pervasive computing applications: models and approach. Pervasive Mob. Comput. **2**(1), 37–64 (2006)
13. Holmquist, L.E., Mattern, F., Schiele, B., Alahuhta, P., Beigl, M., Gellersen, H.-W.: Smart-its friends: a technique for users to easily establish connections between smart artefacts. In: Abowd, G.D., Brumitt, B., Shafer, S. (eds.) UbiComp 2001. LNCS, vol. 2201, pp. 116–122. Springer, Heidelberg (2001). https://doi.org/10.1007/3-540-45427-6_10
14. Ning, H., Wang, Z.: Future Internet of Things architecture: like mankind neural system or social organization framework? IEEE Commun. Lett. **15**(4), 461–463 (2011)
15. Perera, C., Zaslavsky, A., Christen, P., Georgakopoulos, D.: Context aware computing for the Internet of Things: a survey. IEEE Commun. Surv. Tutor. **16**(1), 414–454 (2014)
16. Ranganathan, A., McGrath, R.E., Campbell, R.H., Mickunas, M.D.: Use of ontologies in a pervasive computing environment. Knowl. Eng. Rev. **18**(3), 209–220 (2003)
17. Schreiber, F.A., Tanca, L., Camplani, R., Viganò, D.: Pushing context-awareness down to the core: more flexibility for the PerLa language. In: Electronic Proceedings of PersDB 2012 Workshop (Co-located with VLDB 2012), pp. 1–6 (2012)
18. Dingand, L., Shi, P., Liu, B.: The clustering of internet, Internet of Things and social network. In: 2010 Third International Symposium on Knowledge Acquisition and Modeling, pp. 417–420. IEEE (2010)
19. Strang, T., Linnhoff-Popien, C., Frank, K.: CoOL: a context ontology language to enable contextual interoperability. In: Stefani, J.-B., Demeure, I., Hagimont, D. (eds.) DAIS 2003. LNCS, vol. 2893, pp. 236–247. Springer, Heidelberg (2003). https://doi.org/10.1007/978-3-540-40010-3_21

Big Data Veracity and Soft Computing

Handling Veracity of Nominal Data in Big Data: A Multipolar Approach

Guy De Tré[1(✉)] , Toon Boeckling[1], Yoram Timmerman[1], and Sławomir Zadrożny[2]

[1] Department of Telecommunications and Information Processing, Ghent University, St.-Pietersnieuwstraat 41, B9000 Ghent, Belgium
{Guy.DeTre,Toon.Boeckling,Yoram.Timmerman}@UGent.be
[2] Systems Research Institute, Polish Academy of Science, ul. Newelska 6, 01-447 Warsaw, Poland
zadrozny@ibspan.waw.pl

Abstract. With this paper we aim to contribute to the proper handling of veracity, which is generally recognized as one of the main problems related to 'Big' data. Veracity refers to the extent to which the used data adequately reflect real world information and hence can be trusted. More specifically we describe a novel computational intelligence technique for handling veracity aspects of nominal data, which are often encountered when users have to select one or more items from a list. First, we discuss the use of fuzzy sets for modelling nominal data and specifying search criteria on nominal data. Second, we introduce the novel concept of a multipolar satisfaction degree as a tool to handle criteria evaluation. Third, we discuss aggregation of multipolar satisfaction degrees. Finally, we demonstrate the proposed technique and discuss its benefits using a film genre example.

Keywords: Big data · Veracity · Nominal data · Computational intelligence · Multipolarity

1 Introduction

Data science [8], advanced telecommunication infrastructure and technological developments in IT brought frameworks for handling tremendous 'Big' data volumes at our disposal. Among others, social media and e-commerce applications feed these volumes with new (kinds of) data, new opportunities and new challenges [2]. Four important kinds of problems that can manifest themselves in this new way of data usage have been identified and are related to Volume (Big data), Variety (Varied data), Velocity (Fast data) and Veracity (Bad data). Considering data(base) management, the volume, variety and velocity problems have been quite successfully tackled by NoSQL and NewSQL database management systems that support distributed data storage and databases that do not have to fit a fixed database schema. The adequate handling of the data veracity problem

© Springer Nature Switzerland AG 2019
A. Cuzzocrea et al. (Eds.): FQAS 2019, LNAI 11529, pp. 317–328, 2019.
https://doi.org/10.1007/978-3-030-27629-4_29

is more difficult and is still subject to further research [11]. 'Bad' data can have serious consequences on the results of data processing and data analyses [14]. Hence the importance and relevance of research on data quality issues and the proper handling of 'bad' data.

With this paper we aim to contribute to the handling of veracity problems by studying the specific case of the management of nominal data. Nominal data often occur from cases where a predefined list of items is used to handle selection or labelling options in applications. Examples are the sentiment emoticons denoting 'like', 'love', 'laugh', 'surprise', 'sad' and 'angry' in social media and labels like 'comedy', 'horror', 'drama', 'sci-fi', 'fantasy', 'animation', 'western' and 'war' to categorize films based on their genre. Often when nominal data from different sources have to be integrated and processed, data quality becomes an important issue. Moreover, there are cases where multiple labels apply (to some extent) or where data imperfection leads to ambiguous interpretations. Adequately handling veracity in such cases is important in view of correct data processing and correctly informing users.

In this work we apply computational intelligence techniques, more specifically fuzzy set theory and fuzzy logic [19], to improve the handling of veracity in nominal data. This is especially relevant for the handling of 'Big' data, as it should help preventing and improving bad data. Our aim and motivation is to better reflect what users know when providing nominal data and prefer when working with nominal data. The proposed approach is inspired by our previous work on bipolarity in criteria evaluation [12] where 'positive' and 'negative' can be seen as a nominal case with two labels. The contributions of this paper are (1) a discussion on the use of conjunctive fuzzy sets for modelling nominal data and specifying search criteria on nominal data; (2) the introduction of the novel concept of a multipolar satisfaction degree as a tool to handle criteria evaluation on nominal data; and (3) the proposal of an aggregation framework for multipolar satisfaction degrees.

Multipolar satisfaction degrees are obtained as generalizations of bipolar satisfaction degrees, which we proposed in [3,12]. A bipolar satisfaction degree is, among others, used for expressing criterion satisfaction in the bipolar case where a pool of positive and a pool of negative criteria are considered. Considering a given object that is subject to evaluation, satisfaction of a positive criterion contributes to the global evaluation label 'positive' and hence the acceptance of the object, whereas satisfaction of a negative criterion contributes to a global evaluation label 'negative' and hence the rejection of the object. Bipolarity has also been studied distinguishing a pool of mandatory criteria and a pool of optional criteria [5,6,9]. In this context, a generalization to multipolarity has been proposed by further distinguishing different preference levels for poles of optional criteria [10]. This manifestation of multipolarity differs from the multipolarity studied in this paper as it has different underlying semantics.

The structure of the remainder of the paper is as follows. In Sect. 2 we give some preliminaries on veracity handling and the human-centric modelling of nominal data. Next, we discuss how computational intelligence techniques can be used for the human-centric modelling of nominal data. The novel concept of multipolar satisfaction degree is proposed in Sect. 3. Herewith we introduce the definition and some basic operators. A canonical aggregation structure for transforming a multipolar satisfaction degree into a (bipolar) satisfaction degree is proposed and discussed in Sect. 4. In Sect. 5 an illustrative example is given. Finally, in Sect. 6 our conclusions with some ideas for future work are presented.

2   Computational Intelligence Techniques

A considerable part of research in computational intelligence has been devoted to studying the modelling and handling of information in a human-centric way [4], involving techniques that are close to the human way of reasoning.

2.1   Veracity Handling

Veracity handling is a complex, but important issue for an information system. This is simply due to the fact that, if the data that go in are of inadequate quality, the outcome of the data processing or data analysis will also be of inadequate quality. Research on data quality stressed its multi-dimensionality [13, 16]. Measuring data quality using computational intelligence techniques is believed to be an important step in view of proper veracity handling [1]. With this paper we aim to contribute to the development of such measurement techniques by proposing a multipolar approach that can explicitly cope with hesitation. The existence of hesitation is herewith considered as a manifestation of a decrease of data quality.

2.2   Human-Centric Modelling of Nominal Data

In this paper we focus on veracity handling of nominal data [15]. Nominal data are often generated when users have to select an item from an item list (e.g. a film genre from a predefined list of genres). This task is not always easy because multiple items might apply to a different extent, often depending on the point of view and context of the user. Depending on the point of view, James Cameron's movie 'Titanic' can be considered by a user as 'historic', 'drama', 'disaster', or even 'romantic'.

Fuzzy set theory [18] permits to adequately model what users know in such cases, herewith limiting information loss and hence contributing to the veracity of the data. Considering the list L of labels corresponding to all the different items under consideration, a veristic fuzzy set

$$V = \{(x, \mu_V(x)) | x \in L \wedge 0 < \mu_V(x) \le 1\} \tag{1}$$

can be used to adequately express the nominal information users have. The membership grades $0 \le \mu_V(x) \le 1$, $x \in L$ are interpreted as degrees of truth, denoting to which extent it is true that label x applies. Moreover, the semantics of a veristic fuzzy set is conjunctive, which means that all elements x with membership grade $\mu_V(x) > 0$ apply.

For example, considering

$$L = [crime, drama, disaster, historic, horror, scifi, romantic, war],$$

the veristic fuzzy set

$$V_{Titanic} = \{(historic, 0.8), (drama, 1), (disaster, 1), (romantic, 0.5)\}$$

expresses that 'Titanic' is fully considered to be a drama and disaster movie, to a lesser extent to be historic and to an even lesser extent considered to be romantic.

Depending on the application and context, the membership grades might also be subject to constraints. Such constraints might, e.g., express that

- at least one item should be selected, i.e. $\max_{x \in L} \mu_V(x) > 0$, or
- that some items (e.g. historic and scifi) cannot be selected together, i.e. $(\mu_V(historic) > 0 \Rightarrow \mu_V(scifi) = 0) \wedge (\mu_V(scifi) > 0 \Rightarrow \mu_V(historic) = 0)$.

Another possibility is to impose a consistency condition like $\sum_{x \in L} \mu_V(x) \leq 1$. In such a case the difference $h = 1 - \sum_{x \in L} \mu_V(x)$ can be interpreted as reflecting the overall hesitation a user might have while making a selection.

In what follows, we assume that nominal data is modelled using veristic fuzzy sets, as this permits to better reflect reality.

3   Multipolar Satisfaction Degrees

If we want to apply veristic fuzzy sets to handle veracity problems, it is needed to develop evaluation techniques that adequately handle veristic fuzzy sets and closely reflect human reasoning. Assume that a user is looking for a historic movie with drama and romantic scenes. In such a case, the user's preferences can also be modelled by means of a veristic fuzzy set, e.g.,

$$P = \{(historic, 1), (drama, 0.8), (romantic, 0.8)\}.$$

The membership grades of a veristic fuzzy set expressing user preferences might also be subject to constraints as described in the previous section. The question is then to find out to what extent the movie Titanic with genres modelled by the veristic fuzzy set $V_{Titanic}$ (dis)satisfies the user's preferences P.

In order to evaluate situations as this in a human-centric way, we propose a framework of multipolar satisfaction degrees.

3.1   Definition

Consider nominal data represented by the $n \in \mathbb{N}$ labels l_i, $i = 1, \ldots, n$ of a list L, i.e., $|L| = n$.

A *multipolar satisfaction degree* (MSD) expressing evaluation results on L is defined by an n-tuple consisting of n satisfaction degrees $s_i \in [0,1]$, $i = 1, \ldots, n$, i.e.

$$[s_1, \ldots, s_n]_L. \tag{2}$$

Each satisfaction degree s_i uniquely corresponds to a label $l_i \in L$. The first satisfaction degree corresponds to the first label in L, the second satisfaction degree to the second label in L, and so on.

Evaluating if nominal data V satisfies user preferences P (both being defined on L), can for example be done by checking for each element x in P, whether its membership grade $\mu_V(x)$ in V – what is given – is better ($\geq$) than its membership grade $\mu_P(x)$ in P –what is preferred–. A residual implicator like

$$R : [0,1]^2 \to [0,1]$$
$$(x, y) \mapsto \begin{cases} 1 & \text{if } x \leq y \\ y & \text{otherwise} \end{cases} \tag{3}$$

can be used for this purpose. Labels that are not an element of P are not considered in the evaluation as these are not preferred by the user and we only want to check whether preferred labels apply for a movie under consideration. This results in an MSD

$$[R(\mu_P(l_1), \mu_V(l_1)), \ldots, R(\mu_P(l_m), \mu_V(l_m))]_{supp(P)} \tag{4}$$

where m is the number of elements in the support of P, i.e.

$$m = |\{x \in L | \mu_P(x) > 0\}|.$$

Hence, evaluating a movie for preferences P results in an MSD that is defined over the support $supp(P)$ of P.

For the running example of evaluating the genres of the movie 'Titanic' this yields the MSD

$$[s_{drama} = 1, s_{historic} = 0.8, s_{romantic} = 0.5]_{supp(P)}.$$

Other evaluation functions can be used, which is subject for further research.

Considering the list $L = [True, False]$, we obtain bipolar satisfaction degrees (BSD) as a special case. Indeed, the second satisfaction degree s_2 in the MSD $[s_1, s_2]_L$ can then be interpreted as dissatisfaction degree d, such that a BSD (s, d) as in [3] is obtained.

3.2   Basic Operators

Basic conjunction, disjunction and negation on MSDs are defined using the following rules. Consider two MSDs $s_L^1 = [s_1^1, \ldots, s_n^1]_L$ and $s_L^2 = [s_1^2, \ldots, s_n^2]_L$ expressing evaluation results for the *same* nominal data L.

- *Conjunction.*
$$s_L^1 \wedge s_L^2 = [i(s_1^1, s_1^2), \ldots, i(s_n^1, s_n^2)]_L. \tag{5}$$

- *Disjunction.*
$$s_L^1 \vee s_L^2 = [u(s_1^1, s_1^2), \ldots, u(s_n^1, s_n^2)]_L. \tag{6}$$

- *Negation.*
$$\neg(s_L^1) = [1 - s_1^1, \ldots, 1 - s_n^1]_L. \tag{7}$$

Herewith, i (resp. u) is a t-norm (resp. t-conorm), e.g., $i = \min$ and $u = \max$.

4   Aggregation

An MSD $s_L = [s_1, \ldots, s_n]_L$ is in essence a list of satisfaction degrees. Each of these expresses a part of the result of an evaluation of nominal data. More specifically, the ith, $i = 1, \ldots, n$ satisfaction degree s_i expresses the result of evaluating the ith element in the list.

When performing evaluations, humans usually expect a single satisfaction degree s, denoting how well given nominal data satisfy their preferences. Such a single satisfaction degree also better fits as a component in evaluation schemes of more complex evaluations (as for example described in [7]). Alternatively, an MSD can also be transformed into a single BSD (s, d). In the next two subsections we handle both alternatives.

4.1   Transforming an MSD into a Satisfaction Degree

In this paper we use the aggregation function $owa_{w_1, \ldots, w_n}(.)$ to aggregate the n satisfaction degrees $s_1, \ldots, s_n$ of an MSD $s_L = [s_1, \ldots, s_n]_L$ to an overall satisfaction degree s. This aggregation function uses an ordered weighted averaging (OWA) aggregator [17] and is preconfigured with n weights $w_i \in [0, 1]$, $i = 1, \ldots, n$, $\sum_{i=1}^n w_i = 1$, determining its logical behaviour. Its definition is as follows.

$$owa_{w_1, \ldots, w_n} : [0, 1]^n \to [0, 1]$$
$$[s_1, \ldots, s_n] \mapsto \sum_{j=1}^n w_j s_j' \tag{8}$$

where s_j' is the jth largest of the s_i.

In this paper we consider that all satisfaction degrees contribute to an equal extent to the computation of s. For that purpose we choose $w_i = 1/n$, $i = 1, \ldots, n$. Other weights, modelling other linguistically expressed aggregation operations, can be used. This supports human-centric computing and is our main motivation for using the OWA aggregator.

4.2   Transforming an MSD into a Bipolar Satisfaction Degree

An MSD $[s_1,\ldots,s_n]_L$ can also be transformed into a single BSD (s,d). The semantic richer concept of a BSD allows to model satisfaction, dissatisfaction and hesitation, which permits to avoid information loss in the cases were consistency constraints are applied. The canonical aggregation structure we propose, is shown in Fig. 1 and discussed below.

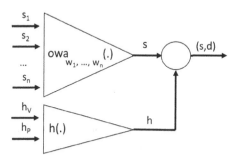

Fig. 1. A canonical aggregation structure for transforming an MSD into a BSD.

The inputs for the proposed aggregation structure are the n satisfaction degrees of an MSD and two hesitation degrees h_V and h_P originating from the veristic fuzzy sets V and P involved in the evaluation. If a consistency condition $\sum_{x \in L} \mu_V(x) \leq 1$ holds for V, then h_V can be computed by

$$h_V = 1 - \sum_{x \in L} \mu_V(x). \tag{9}$$

Otherwise, h_V can be considered to be zero. Likewise, if a consistency condition $\sum_{x \in L} \mu_P(x) \leq 1$ holds for P, then

$$h_P = 1 - \sum_{x \in L} \mu_P(x). \tag{10}$$

Otherwise, h_P can be considered to be zero.

The aggregation function $owa_{w_1,\ldots,w_n}(.)$ is used to aggregate the n satisfaction degrees $s_1,\ldots,s_n$ of the MSD as described in the previous subsection. The so-called *hesitation function* $h(.)$ is used to compute the overall hesitation h from h_V and h_P. Because both V and P are involved in the evaluation, we consider that both can influence the hesitation about the evaluation results. Therefore, $h(.)$ can be implemented by a t-conorm, e.g.

$$h : [0,1]^2 \to [0,1]$$
$$(h_V, h_P) \mapsto \max(h_V, h_P). \tag{11}$$

Applying the aggregator $owa_{w_1,...,w_n}(.)$ results in an overall satisfaction degree s, whereas applying the hesitation function $h(.)$ yields a measure h for hesitation. Both s and h are finally used to construct the resulting BSD. A basic approximation is

$$(s, d) = (s, 1 - s - \min(h, 1 - s)).$$ (12)

This BSD reflects how V satisfies and dissatisfies the preferences P and additionally gives information on the hesitation about the data involved in the evaluation process. By subtracting $\min(h, 1 - s)$ (instead of h) it is assured that $d \in [0, 1]$ and assumed that the impact of hesitation on the computation of d cannot be larger than $1 - s$. The explicit consideration of hesitation and the facility to fine-tune the aggregation makes the proposed method more human-centric than conventional approaches.

5   Illustrative Example

The benefits of the proposed approach are demonstrated using an extension of our running film genre example. Reconsider the list

$$L = [crime, drama, disaster, historic, horror, scifi, romantic, war]$$

of selectable film genres and consider the extract of a movie description database given in Table 1. The nominal genre data are represented by veristic fuzzy sets. A consistency condition $\sum_{x \in L} \mu_V(x) \leq 1$ is imposed on each veristic fuzzy set V. The hesitation h_V computed by Eq. (9) is shown in the fourth column of the table.

Table 1. Film genres extracted from a movie database.

ID	Title	Genres	h_V
1	The Shawshank Redemption (1994)	$\{(crime, 0.2), (drama, 0.8)\}$	0
2	The Godfather (1972)	$\{(crime, 0.7), (drama, 0.3)\}$	0
3	The Dark Knight (2008)	$\{(crime, 0.3), (drama, 0.2), (scifi, 0.5)\}$	0
4	12 Angry Men (1957)	$\{(crime, 0.2), (drama, 0.6)\}$	0.2
5	Pulp Fiction (1994)	$\{(crime, 0.3), (drama, 0.2)\}$	0.5
6	Forrest Gump (1994)	$\{(drama, 0.5), (romantic, 0.2), (war, 0.1)\}$	0.2
7	Gladiator (2000)	$\{(historic, 0.6), (drama, 0.1), (war, 0.3)\}$	0
8	Interstellar (2014)	$\{(scifi, 0.8)\}$	0.2
9	A Bridge Too Far (1977)	$\{(historic, 0.3), (drama, 0.1), (war, 0.6)\}$	0

For this data set, we consider the user preferences $P_1 = \{(historic, 0.6)\}$, $P_2 = \{(crime, 0.2), (horror, 0.8)\}$ and $P_3 = \{(drama, 0.6), (war, 0.4)\}$. It is assumed that the same consistency condition should hold for each user preference. Using Eq. (10) we obtain that the hesitation inherent to these preferences is resp. $h_{P_1} = 0.4$, $h_{P_2} = 0$ and $h_{P_3} = 0$.

The evaluation of the preferences P_1, P_2 and P_3 considering the movies $1, \ldots, 9$ using Eq. (4) yields the MPDs with respective formats $[s_{historic}]_{supp(P_1)}$, $[s_{crime}, s_{horror}]_{supp(P_2)}$ and $[s_{drama}, s_{war}]_{supp(P_3)}$, presented in Table 2.

Table 2. Evaluation results.

ID	$\{(historic, 0.6)\}$	$\{(crime, 0.2), (horror, 0.8)\}$	$\{(drama, 0.6), (war, 0.4)\}$
1	$[0]_{supp(P_1)}$	$[1, 0]_{supp(P_2)}$	$[1, 0]_{supp(P_3)}$
2	$[0]_{supp(P_1)}$	$[1, 0]_{supp(P_2)}$	$[0.3, 0]_{supp(P_3)}$
3	$[0]_{supp(P_1)}$	$[1, 0]_{supp(P_2)}$	$[0.2, 0]_{supp(P_3)}$
4	$[0]_{supp(P_1)}$	$[1, 0]_{supp(P_2)}$	$[1, 0]_{supp(P_3)}$
5	$[0]_{supp(P_1)}$	$[1, 0]_{supp(P_2)}$	$[0.2, 0]_{supp(P_3)}$
6	$[0]_{supp(P_1)}$	$[0, 0]_{supp(P_2)}$	$[0.5, 0.1]_{supp(P_3)}$
7	$[1]_{supp(P_1)}$	$[0, 0]_{supp(P_2)}$	$[0.1, 0.3]_{supp(P_3)}$
8	$[0]_{supp(P_1)}$	$[0, 0]_{supp(P_2)}$	$[0, 0]_{supp(P_3)}$
9	$[0.3]_{supp(P_1)}$	$[0, 0]_{supp(P_2)}$	$[0.1, 1]_{supp(P_3)}$

The further processing results of MPDs are given in Table 3. The overall satisfaction degrees s are obtained from Eq. (8), the hesitation on the evaluation h is computed using Eq. (11) and the BSDs result from Eq. (12).

Table 3. Evaluation results (continued).

ID	$\{(historic, 0.6)\}$			$\{(crime, 0.2), (horror, 0.8)\}$			$\{(drama, 0.6), (war, 0.4)\}$		
	s	h	BSD	s	h	BSD	s	h	BSD
1	0	0.4	$(0, 0.6)$	0.5	0	$(0.5, 0.5)$	0.5	0	$(0.5, 0.5)$
2	0	0.4	$(0, 0.6)$	0.5	0	$(0.5, 0.5)$	0.15	0	$(0.15, 0.85)$
3	0	0.4	$(0, 0.6)$	0.5	0	$(0.5, 0.5)$	0.1	0	$(0.1, 0.9)$
4	0	0.4	$(0, 0.6)$	0.5	0.2	$(0.5, 0.3)$	0.5	0.2	$(0.5, 0.3)$
5	0	0.5	$(0, 0.5)$	0.5	0.5	$(0.5, 0)$	0.1	0.5	$(0.1, 0.4)$
6	0	0.4	$(0, 0.6)$	0	0.2	$(0, 0.8)$	0.3	0.2	$(0.3, 0.5)$
7	1	0.4	$(1, 0)$	0	0	$(0, 1)$	0.2	0	$(0.2, 0.8)$
8	0	0.4	$(0, 0.6)$	0	0.2	$(0, 0.8)$	0	0.2	$(0, 0.8)$
9	0.3	0.4	$(0.3, 0.3)$	0	0	$(0, 1)$	0.55	0	$(0.55, 0.45)$

The evaluation of the database entries with preferences $P_1 = \{(historic, 0.6)\}$ yields the movie set presented in Table 4. Only 'Gladiator' fully satisfies the preferences, 'A Bridge Too Far' partially satisfies the preferences, whereas all the other movies have a satisfaction degree zero. For these movies however, hesitation in the preferences and movie classifaction lowers their dissatisfaction degree, reflecting the hesitation about their dissatisfaction. In the case of 'Gladiator' the match is strong enough to discard the hesitation in the preferences.

Table 4. Evaluation results for $P_1 = \{(historic, 0.6)\}$.

ID	Title	Genres	BSD
1	The Shawshank Redemption	$\{(crime, 0.2), (drama, 0.8)\}$	$(0, 0.6)$
2	The Godfather	$\{(crime, 0.7), (drama, 0.3)\}$	$(0, 0.6)$
3	The Dark Knight	$\{(crime, 0.3), (drama, 0.2), (scifi, 0.5)\}$	$(0, 0.6)$
4	12 Angry Men	$\{(crime, 0.2), (drama, 0.6)\}$	$(0, 0.6)$
5	Pulp Fiction	$\{(crime, 0.3), (drama, 0.2)\}$	$(0, 0.5)$
6	Forrest Gump	$\{(drama, 0.5), (romantic, 0.2), (war, 0.1)\}$	$(0, 0.6)$
7	Gladiator	$\{(historic, 0.6), (drama, 0.1), (war, 0.3)\}$	$(1, 0)$
8	Interstellar	$\{(scifi, 0.8)\}$	$(0, 0.6)$
9	A Bridge Too Far	$\{(historic, 0.3), (drama, 0.1), (war, 0.6)\}$	$(0.3, 0.3)$

With preferences $P_2 = \{(crime, 0.2), (horror, 0.8)\}$, the evaluation yields the movie set presented in Table 5. Movies 1 to 5 partially satisfy the preferences (that are now not subject to hesitation). This is because the genre 'crime'. For '12 Angry Men' and 'Pulp Fiction' the hesitation in the movie classification lowers the dissatisfaction degree. Movies 6 to 9 do not satisfy the preferences at all (neither 'crime' nor 'horror' are in their genre specification). There is hesitation in the movie classification for 'Forrest Gump' and 'Interstellar', this hesitation is also reflected by a lower dissatisfaction degree. For 'Gladiator' and 'A Bridge Too Far' there is no hesitation. These movies have to be removed from the result set, but are included for the sake of illustration.

Table 5. Evaluation results for $P_2 = \{(crime, 0.2), (horror, 0.8)\}$.

ID	Title	Genres	BSD
1	The Shawshank Redemption	$\{(crime, 0.2), (drama, 0.8)\}$	$(0.5, 0.5)$
2	The Godfather	$\{(crime, 0.7), (drama, 0.3)\}$	$(0.5, 0.5)$
3	The Dark Knight	$\{(crime, 0.3), (drama, 0.2), (scifi, 0.5)\}$	$(0.5, 0.5)$
4	12 Angry Men	$\{(crime, 0.2), (drama, 0.6)\}$	$(0.5, 0.3)$
5	Pulp Fiction	$\{(crime, 0.3), (drama, 0.2)\}$	$(0.5, 0)$
6	Forrest Gump	$\{(drama, 0.5), (romantic, 0.2), (war, 0.1)\}$	$(0, 0.8)$
7	Gladiator	$\{(historic, 0.6), (drama, 0.1), (war, 0.3)\}$	$(0, 1)$
8	Interstellar	$\{(scifi, 0.8)\}$	$(0, 0.8)$
9	A Bridge Too Far	$\{(historic, 0.3), (drama, 0.1), (war, 0.6)\}$	$(0, 1)$

The evaluation result for $P_3 = \{(drama, 0.6), (war, 0.4)\}$ are given in Table 6. Movies 1, 2, 3, 7 and 9 only partially satisfy the preferences and no hesitation is present. For '12 Angry Men', 'Pulp Fiction' and 'Forrest Gump' there is partial satisfaction but also hesitation on their classification, which is reflected by a lower dissatisfaction degree. 'Interstellar' is not satisfying the preferences, but hesitation on its classification lowers its dissatisfaction degree.

Table 6. Evaluation results for $P_3 = \{(drama, 0.6), (war, 0.4)\}$.

ID	Title	Genres	BSD
1	The Shawshank Redemption	$\{(crime, 0.2), (drama, 0.8)\}$	$(0.5, 0.5)$
2	The Godfather	$\{(crime, 0.7), (drama, 0.3)\}$	$(0.15, 0.85)$
3	The Dark Knight	$\{(crime, 0.3), (drama, 0.2), (scifi, 0.5)\}$	$(0.1, 0.9)$
4	12 Angry Men	$\{(crime, 0.2), (drama, 0.6)\}$	$(0.5, 0.3)$
5	Pulp Fiction	$\{(crime, 0.3), (drama, 0.2)\}$	$(0.1, 0.4)$
6	Forrest Gump	$\{(drama, 0.5), (romantic, 0.2), (war, 0.1)\}$	$(0.3, 0.5)$
7	Gladiator	$\{(historic, 0.6), (drama, 0.1), (war, 0.3)\}$	$(0.2, 0.8)$
8	Interstellar	$\{(scifi, 0.8)\}$	$(0, 0.8)$
9	A Bridge Too Far	$\{(historic, 0.3), (drama, 0.1), (war, 0.6)\}$	$(0.55, 0.45)$

6 Conclusions and Future Work

In this paper we presented a novel approach for handling veracity of nominal data and introduced the concept of a multipolar satisfaction degree. Multipolar satisfaction degrees are generalizations of satisfaction degrees and bipolar satisfaction degrees. These allow to evaluate criteria on nominal data in a more flexible, configurable way. The presented approach is especially useful in cases of big data, which are often subject to hesitation, e.g., originating from data integration or data imperfections. Its ability to explicitly cope with hesitation and its facilities to handle gradual membership in nominal data makes the approach more human-centric than conventional approaches. We illustrated the added value and potentials of the approach with a movie database sample for which data modelling and preference evaluation are discussed.

Besides that, we presented a basic evaluation technique for nominal data and basic aggregators for multipolar satisfaction degrees. In our future work we aim to further investigate evaluation and aggregation. Another topic for future research is the inclusion of more advanced (consistency) constraints for nominal data and user preferences. Multipolar satisfaction degrees are also believed to play an important role in the study of multipolarity as a generalization of bipolarity.

References

1. Bronselaer, A., De Mol, R., De Tré, G.: A measure-theoretic foundation for data quality. IEEE Trans. Fuzzy Syst. **26**(2), 627–639 (2018)
2. De Mauro, A., Greco, M., Grimaldi, M.: A formal definition of big data based on its essential features. Library Rev. **65**, 122–135 (2016)
3. De Tré, G., Zadrożny, S., Matthé, T., Kacprzyk, J., Bronselaer, A.: Dealing with positive and negative query criteria in fuzzy database querying. In: Andreasen, T., Yager, R.R., Bulskov, H., Christiansen, H., Larsen, H.L. (eds.) FQAS 2009. LNCS (LNAI), vol. 5822, pp. 593–604. Springer, Heidelberg (2009). https://doi.org/10.1007/978-3-642-04957-6_51
4. De Tré, G., Kacprzyk, J., Pasi, G., Zadrożny, S., Bronselaer, A. (eds.): International Journal of Intelligent Systems, Special Issue on Human Centric Data Management, vol. 33, no. 10 (2018)
5. Dubois, D., Prade, H.: Handling bipolar queries in Fuzzy Information Processing. In: Galindo, J. (ed.) Handbook of Research on Fuzzy Information Processing in Databases, pp. 97–114. IGI Global, New York (2008)
6. Dubois, D., Prade, H.: An introduction to bipolar representations of information and preference. Int. J. Intell. Syst. **23**, 866–877 (2008)
7. Dujmović, J.J.: Soft Computing Evaluation Logic: The LSP Decision Method and Its Applications. Wiley-Blackwell, Hoboken (2018)
8. Hayashi, C.: What is data science? Fundamental concepts and a heuristic example. In: Hayashi, C., Yajima, K., Bock, H.H., Ohsumi, N., Ohsumi, Y., Baba, Y. (eds.) Data Science, Classification, and Related Methods. STUDIES CLASS, pp. 40–51. Springer, Tokyo (1998). https://doi.org/10.1007/978-4-431-65950-1_3
9. Lacroix, M., Lavency, P.: Preferences: putting more knowledge into queries. In: Proceedings of the 13 International Conference on Very Large Databases, Brighton, UK, pp. 217–225 (1987)
10. Liétard, L., Hadjali, A., Rocacher, D.: Towards a gradual QCL model for database querying. In: Laurent, A., Strauss, O., Bouchon-Meunier, B., Yager, R.R. (eds.) IPMU 2014. CCIS, vol. 444, pp. 130–139. Springer, Cham (2014). https://doi.org/10.1007/978-3-319-08852-5_14
11. Lukoianova, T., Rubin, V.L.: Veracity roadmap: is big data objective, truthful and credible? Adv. Classif. Res. Online **24**(1), 4–15 (2014)
12. Matthé, T., De Tré, G., Zadrożny, S., Kacprzyk, J., Bronselaer, A.: Bipolar database querying using bipolar satisfaction degrees. Int. J. Intell. Syst. **26**(10), 890–910 (2011)
13. Redman, T.: Data Quality for the Information Age. Artech-House, Norwood (1996)
14. Saha, B., Srivastava, D.: Data quality: the other face of big data. In: Proceedings of the 2014 IEEE 30th International Conference on Data Engineering, Chicago, USA, pp. 1294–1297 (2014)
15. Stevens, S.S.: On the theory of scales of measurement. Science **103**(2684), 677–680 (1946)
16. Wang, R., Strong, D.: Beyond accuracy: what data quality means to data consumers. J. Manag. Inf. Syst. **12**(4), 5–34 (1996)
17. Yager, R.R.: On ordered weighted averaging aggregation operators in multi-criteria decision making. IEEE Trans. Syst. Man Cybern. **18**, 183–190 (1988)
18. Zadeh, L.A.: Fuzzy sets. Inf. Control **8**(3), 338–353 (1965)
19. Zadeh, L.A.: Soft computing and fuzzy logic. In: Advances in Fuzzy Systems - Applications and Theory, vol. 6, pp. 796–804 (1996)

InterCriteria Analysis with Interval-Valued Intuitionistic Fuzzy Evaluations

Krassimir Atanassov[1]($\boxtimes$) (iD), Pencho Marinov[2] (iD), and Vassia Atanassova[1]($\boxtimes$) (iD)

[1] Department of Bioinformatics and Mathematical Modelling,
Institute of Biophysics and Biomedical Engineering,
Bulgarian Academy of Sciences,
105 Acad. G. Bonchev Street, 1113 Sofia, Bulgaria
`krat@bas.bg`, `vassia.atanassova@gmail.com`
[2] Institute of Information and Communication Technologies,
Bulgarian Academy of Sciences,
25A Acad. G. Bonchev Street, 1113 Sofia, Bulgaria
`pencho@parallel.bas.bg`

Abstract. The Intercriteria Analysis (ICA) is a new tool for decision making similar, but different from the correlation analyses. In the present paper, a new form of ICA, based over interval-valued intuitionistic fuzzy evaluations is described for a first time.

Keywords: InterCriteria Analysis · Intuitionistic fuzzy sets · Interval-valued intuitionistic fuzzy sets

1 Introduction

During the last five years, the idea of Intercriteria Analysis (ICA) has been developed (see, e.g., [5,7] and a lot of its applications were described in industry [28,29], economics [10,11,13,15], education [12,16,27], medical and biotechnological processes [17,20,24], genetic algorithms and metaheuristics [14,19–23], neural networks [25,26].

The ICA was based on the theories of Index Matrices (IMs; see [1,4]) and Intuitionistic Fuzzy Sets (IFSs, see [3]).

In the present paper, for the first time, a variant of ICA will be proposed, based on one of the IFS-extensions, called Interval-Valued IFSs (IVIFSs, see [2,6]) and Interval-Valued Intuitionistic Fuzzy Pairs (IVIFPs, see [9]).

The IMs are essentially new and not well-known mathematical objects, that are extensions of the ordinary matrices. They are discussed in Sect. 2.

A. Cuzzocrea et al. (Eds.): FQAS 2019, LNAI 11529, pp. 329–338, 2019.
https://doi.org/10.1007/978-3-030-27629-4_30

In the paper we use also the concept of Intuitionistic Fuzzy Pair (IFP, see [8]) and IVIFP, that will be described in Sect. 3.

In Sect. 4 we describe ICA with Interval-Valued Intuitionistic Fuzzy Evaluations (ICA-IVIFE) in which the IM has a symmetric form.

2 Short Remarks on Index Matrices

Let I be a fixed set of indices and $\mathcal{R}$ be the set of the real numbers. By IM with index sets K and L ($K, L \subset I$), we will denote the object:

$$[K, L, \{a_{k_i, l_j}\}] \equiv \begin{array}{c|cccc} & l_1 & l_2 & \cdots & l_n \\ \hline k_1 & a_{k_1, l_1} & a_{k_1, l_2} & \cdots & a_{k_1, l_n} \\ k_2 & a_{k_2, l_1} & a_{k_2, l_2} & \cdots & a_{k_2, l_n} \\ \vdots & \vdots & \vdots & \ddots & \vdots \\ k_m & a_{k_m, l_1} & a_{k_m, l_2} & \cdots & a_{k_m, l_n} \end{array} ,$$

where $K = \{k_1, k_2, \ldots, k_m\}$, $L = \{l_1, l_2, \ldots, l_n\}$, for $1 \le i \le m$, and $1 \le j \le n : a_{k_i, l_j} \in \mathcal{R}$.

3 Short Remarks on Interval-Valued Intuitionistic Fuzzy Pairs

The Interval-Valued Intuitionistic Fuzzy Pair (IVIFP) is an object with the form $\langle M, N \rangle$, where $M, N \subseteq [0, 1]$ are closed intervals, $M = [\inf M, \sup M]$, $N = [\inf N, \sup N]$ and $\sup M + \sup N \le 1$, that is used as an evaluation of some object or process and which components (M and N) are interpreted as intervals of degrees of membership and non-membership, or intervals of degrees of validity and non-validity, or intervals of degree of correctness and non-correctness, etc.

Let us have two IVIFPs $x = \langle M, N \rangle$ and $y = \langle P, Q \rangle$. We define the relations

$$
\begin{aligned}
x <_\square y \quad &\text{iff} \quad \inf M < \inf P \text{ and } \sup M < \sup P \\
x <_\Diamond y \quad &\text{iff} \quad \inf N > \inf Q \text{ and } \sup N > \sup Q \\
x < y \quad &\text{iff} \quad \inf M < \inf P \text{ and } \sup M < \sup P \\
&\qquad \text{and } \inf N > \inf Q \text{ and } \sup N > \sup Q \\
x \le y \quad &\text{iff} \quad \inf M \le \inf P \text{ and } \sup M \le \sup P \\
&\qquad \text{and } \inf N \ge \inf Q \text{ and } \sup N \ge \sup Q \\
x = y \quad &\text{iff} \quad \inf M = \inf P \text{ and } \sup M = \sup P \\
&\qquad \text{and } \inf N = \inf Q \text{ and } \sup N = \sup Q
\end{aligned}
$$

One of the basic geometrical interpretations of an IVIFP is the following

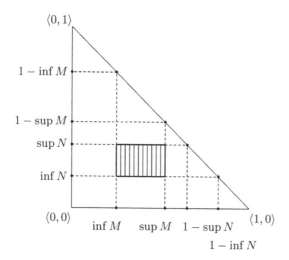

4 The New Form of the Intercriteria Analysis

Let us have an IM

$$
A = \begin{array}{c|ccccccc}
 & O_1 & \cdots & O_i & \cdots & O_j & \cdots & O_n \\
\hline
C_1 & a_{C_1,O_1} & \cdots & a_{C_1,O_i} & \cdots & a_{C_1,O_j} & \cdots & a_{C_1,O_n} \\
\vdots & \vdots & \ddots & \vdots & \ddots & \vdots & \ddots & \vdots \\
C_k & a_{C_k,O_1} & \cdots & a_{C_k,O_i} & \cdots & a_{C_k,O_j} & \cdots & a_{C_k,O_n} \\
\vdots & \vdots & \ddots & \vdots & \ddots & \vdots & \ddots & \vdots \\
C_l & a_{C_l,O_1} & \cdots & a_{C_l,O_i} & \cdots & a_{C_l,O_j} & \cdots & a_{C_l,O_n} \\
\vdots & \vdots & \ddots & \vdots & \ddots & \vdots & \ddots & \vdots \\
C_m & a_{C_m,O_1} & \cdots & a_{C_m,O_i} & \cdots & a_{C_m,O_j} & \cdots & a_{C_m,O_n} \\
\end{array},
$$

where for every p, q, $(1 \leq p \leq m, 1 \leq q \leq n)$:

- C_p is a criterion,
- O_q is an object,
- a_{C_p,O_q} is a real number or another object, including the empty place in the matrix, marked by $\perp$, that is comparable about relation R with the other a-objects, so that for each i, j, k: $R(a_{C_k,O_i}, a_{C_k,O_j})$ is defined. Let $\overline{R}$ be the dual relation of R in the sense that if R is satisfied, then $\overline{R}$ is not satisfied and vice versa. For example, if "R" is the relation "$<$", then $\overline{R}$ is the relation "$>$", and vice versa.

In the research by the moment we discuss the case when the relation between two objects a_{C_k,O_i} and a_{C_k,O_j}, evaluated by real numbers, was a relation of equality ($=$) with the degree of uncertainty. The reason was that if we work by the first digit after decimal point and if both objects are evaluated, e.g., as 2.1, then we can adopt them as equal, but if we work with two digits after decimal point and if the first object has an estimation 2.15, then the probability the second object to have the same estimation is only 10%.

We must note that if we have real numbers in fixed-point format, i.e. precision of k digits after the decimal point, we can multiply all numbers by 10^k and then all a-arguments will be integers. In the general case for the real numbers in floating-point format we may assume some precision ε and two numbers c_1 and c_2 are coincident if $|c_1 - c_2| \leq \varepsilon$.

When the evaluations of the ICA-procedure is based on the apparatus of the IFSs, we must have *all* evaluations of the objects. If there are omitted values (denoted by $\perp$), then we must: (a) ignore the row with the omitted evaluation, or (b) ignore the column with the omitted evaluation, or (c) work with these objects as in the case of equality.

Let the real numbers $\alpha_L^o, \alpha_R^o, \beta_L^o, \beta_R^o, \alpha_L^\perp, \alpha_R^\perp, \beta_L^\perp, \beta_R^\perp$ be fixed and let them satisfy the inequalities

$$0 \leq \alpha_L^o \leq \alpha_R^o \leq 1, \qquad 0 \leq \beta_L^o \leq \beta_R^o \leq 1,$$

$$0 \leq \alpha_L^\perp \leq \alpha_R^\perp \leq 1, \qquad 0 \leq \beta_L^\perp \leq \beta_R^\perp \leq 1,$$

$$0 \leq \alpha_L^o + \alpha_R^o + \beta_L^o + \beta_R^o \leq 1,$$

$$0 \leq \alpha_L^\perp + \alpha_R^\perp + \beta_L^\perp + \beta_R^\perp \leq 1.$$

There are several ICA-algorithms with respect to the type of a-elements. We will discuss them sequentially.

We start with the *general case*.

Let

- S_{C_k,C_l}^μ be the number of cases in which $R(a_{C_k,O_i}, a_{C_k,O_j})$ and $R(a_{C_l,O_i}, a_{C_l,O_j})$ are simultaneously satisfied and the a-arguments are different from $\perp$.
- S_{C_k,C_l}^ν be the number of cases in which $R(a_{C_k,O_i}, a_{C_k,O_j})$ and $\overline{R}(a_{C_l,O_i}, a_{C_l,O_j})$ are simultaneously satisfied and the a-arguments are different from $\perp$.
- $S_{C_k,C_l}^\perp$ be the number of cases in which none of the relations $R(a_{C_k,O_i}, a_{C_k,O_j})$ and $\overline{R}(a_{C_k,O_i}, a_{C_k,O_j})$ or none of the relations $R(a_{C_l,O_i}, a_{C_l,O_j})$ or $\overline{R}(a_{C_l,O_i}, a_{C_l,O_j})$ is satisfied, because at least one of the elements a_{C_k,O_i} and a_{C_k,O_j} or a_{C_l,O_i} and a_{C_l,O_j} is empty ($\perp$).
- S_{C_k,C_l}^o be the number of cases in which

$$a_{C_k,O_i} = a_{C_k,O_j},$$

or

$$a_{C_l,O_i} = a_{C_l,O_j},$$

and all a-arguments are different from $\perp$.

Let

$$S_{C_k,C_l}^{\pi} = S_{C_k,C_l}^{\perp} + S_{C_k,C_l}^{o}$$

$$N_p = \frac{n(n-1)}{2}.$$

Obviously,

$$S_{C_k,C_l}^{\mu} + S_{k,l}^{\nu} + S_{k,l}^{\pi} = \frac{n(n-1)}{2} = N_p.$$

Let us assume everywhere below that each interval X has the form $[\inf X, \sup X]$. Now, for every k, l, such that $1 \le k < l \le m$ and for $n \ge 2$, we define

$$\inf M_{C_k,C_l} = \frac{S_{C_k,C_l}^{\mu} + \alpha_L^o S_{C_k,C_l}^o + \alpha_L^{\perp} S_{C_k,C_l}^{\perp}}{N_p}, \tag{1}$$

$$\sup M_{C_k,C_l} = \frac{S_{C_k,C_l}^{\mu} + \alpha_R^o S_{C_k,C_l}^o + \alpha_R^{\perp} S_{C_k,C_l}^{\perp}}{N_p}, \tag{2}$$

$$\inf N_{C_k,C_l} = \frac{S_{C_k,C_l}^{\nu} + \beta_L^o S_{C_k,C_l}^o + \beta_L^{\perp} S_{C_k,C_l}^{\perp}}{N_p}, \tag{3}$$

$$\sup N_{C_k,C_l} = \frac{S_{C_k,C_l}^{\nu} + \beta_R^o S_{C_k,C_l}^o + \beta_R^{\perp} S_{C_k,C_l}^{\perp}}{N_p}. \tag{4}$$

Hence, we can construct the intervals

$$M_{C_k,C_l} = [\inf M_{C_k,C_l}, \sup M_{C_k,C_l}] \tag{5}$$

and

$$N_{C_k,C_l} = [\inf N_{C_k,C_l}, \sup N_{C_k,C_l}], \tag{6}$$

so that

$$\sup M_{C_k,C_l} + \sup N_{C_k,C_l}$$

$$= \frac{S_{C_k,C_l}^{\mu} + \alpha_R^o S_{C_k,C_l}^o + \alpha_R^{\perp} S_{C_k,C_l}^{\perp}}{N_p}$$

$$+ \frac{S_{C_k,C_l}^{\nu} + \beta_R^o S_{C_k,C_l}^o + \beta_R^{\perp} S_{C_k,C_l}^{\perp}}{N_p}$$

$$= \frac{1}{N_p}(S_{C_k,C_l}^{\mu} + S_{C_k,C_l}^{\nu} + (\alpha_R^o + \beta_R^o)S_{C_k,C_l}^o$$

$$+ (\alpha_R^{\perp} + \beta_R^{\perp})S_{C_k,C_l}^{\perp})$$

$$\leq \frac{S^{\mu}_{C_k,C_l} + S^{\nu}_{C_k,C_l} + S^{o}_{C_k,C_l} + S^{\perp}_{C_k,C_l}}{N_p} \leq 1.$$

Now, we construct the interval

$$P_{C_k,C_l} = [\inf P_{C_k,C_l}, \sup P_{C_k,C_l}]$$
$$= [1 - \sup M_{C_k,C_l} - \sup N_{C_k,C_l},$$
$$1 - \inf M_{C_k,C_l} - \inf N_{C_k,C_l}].$$

(7)

The *simplest case*, in which there are no intervals, is obtained for

$$\alpha^{o}_L = \alpha^{o}_R = \beta^{o}_L = \beta^{o}_R = \alpha^{\perp}_L = \alpha^{\perp}_R = \beta^{\perp}_L = \beta^{\perp}_R = 0.$$

In the *simple form of the optimistic approach* the α- and β-constants are

$$\alpha^{o}_L = \alpha^{o}_R = \frac{1}{2}, \qquad \alpha^{\perp}_L = 0, \qquad \alpha^{\perp}_R = \frac{1}{2},$$

$$\beta^{o}_L = \beta^{o}_R = 0, \qquad \beta^{\perp}_L = 0, \qquad \beta^{\perp}_R = \frac{1}{2}.$$

Then

$$\inf M_{C_k,C_l} = \frac{S^{\mu}_{C_k,C_l} + \frac{1}{2}S^{o}_{C_k,C_l}}{N_p},$$

$$\sup M_{C_k,C_l} = \frac{S^{\mu}_{C_k,C_l} + \frac{1}{2}S^{o}_{C_k,C_l} + \frac{1}{2}S^{\perp}_{C_k,C_l}}{N_p},$$

$$\inf N_{C_k,C_l} = \frac{S^{\nu}_{C_k,C_l}}{N_p},$$

$$\sup N_{C_k,C_l} = \frac{S^{\nu}_{C_k,C_l} + \frac{1}{2}S^{\perp}_{C_k,C_l}}{N_p}.$$

In the *simple form of the pessimistic approach* the α- and β-constants are

$$\alpha^{o}_L = \alpha^{o}_R = 0, \qquad \alpha^{\perp}_L = 0, \qquad \alpha^{\perp}_R = \frac{1}{2},$$

$$\beta^{o}_L = \beta^{o}_R = \frac{1}{2}, \qquad \beta^{\perp}_L = 0, \qquad \beta^{\perp}_R = \frac{1}{2}.$$

Then

$$\inf M_{C_k,C_l} = \frac{S^{\mu}_{C_k,C_l}}{N_p},$$

$$\sup M_{C_k,C_l} = \frac{S^{\mu}_{C_k,C_l} + \frac{1}{2}S^{\perp}_{C_k,C_l}}{N_p},$$

$$\inf N_{C_k,C_l} = \frac{S^{\nu}_{C_k,C_l} + \frac{1}{2}S^{o}_{C_k,C_l}}{N_p},$$

$$\sup N_{C_k,C_l} = \frac{S^{\nu}_{C_k,C_l} + \frac{1}{2}S^{o}_{C_k,C_l} + \frac{1}{2}S^{\perp}_{C_k,C_l}}{N_p}.$$

The general case has two forms: standard and uniform.

For the *standard* $(\alpha - \beta)$-*approach,* let $\alpha, \beta \in [0,1]$ be two fixed numbers, so that $\alpha + \beta \leq 1$ and let

$$\alpha^{o}_{L} = \alpha^{o}_{R} = \alpha \qquad \alpha^{\perp}_{L} = 0, \quad \alpha^{\perp}_{R} = \frac{1}{2}$$

$$\beta^{o}_{L} = \beta^{o}_{R} = \beta, \qquad \beta^{\perp}_{L} = 0, \quad \beta^{\perp}_{R} = \frac{1}{2}$$

Then

$$\inf M_{C_k,C_l} = \frac{S^{\mu}_{C_k,C_l} + \alpha S^{o}_{C_k,C_l}}{N_p},$$

$$\sup M_{C_k,C_l} = \frac{S^{\mu}_{C_k,C_l} + \alpha S^{o}_{C_k,C_l} + \frac{1}{2}S^{\perp}_{C_k,C_l}}{N_p},$$

$$\inf N_{C_k,C_l} = \frac{S^{\nu}_{C_k,C_l} + \beta S^{o}_{C_k,C_l}}{N_p},$$

$$\sup N_{C_k,C_l} = \frac{S^{\nu}_{C_k,C_l} + \beta S^{o}_{C_k,C_l} + \frac{1}{2}S^{\perp}_{C_k,C_l}}{N_p}.$$

For the *uniform* $(\alpha - \beta)$-*approach,* let $\alpha, \beta \in \left[0, \frac{1}{4}\right]$ be two fixed numbers, so that $\alpha + \beta \leq \frac{1}{2}$ and let

$$\alpha^{o}_{L} = \beta^{o}_{L} = \alpha^{\perp}_{L} = \beta^{\perp}_{L} = \alpha,$$

$$\alpha^{o}_{R} = \beta^{o}_{R} = \alpha^{\perp}_{R} = \beta^{\perp}_{R} = \beta.$$

Then

$$\inf M_{C_k,C_l} = \frac{S^{\mu}_{C_k,C_l} + \alpha S^{o}_{C_k,C_l} + \alpha S^{\perp}_{C_k,C_l}}{N_p},$$

$$\sup M_{C_k,C_l} = \frac{S^{\mu}_{C_k,C_l} + \beta S^{o}_{C_k,C_l} + \beta S^{\perp}_{C_k,C_l}}{N_p},$$

$$\inf N_{C_k,C_l} = \frac{S^{\nu}_{C_k,C_l} + \alpha S^{o}_{C_k,C_l} + \alpha S^{\perp}_{C_k,C_l}}{N_p},$$

$$\sup N_{C_k,C_l} = \frac{S^{\nu}_{C_k,C_l} + \beta S^{o}_{C_k,C_l} + \beta S^{\perp}_{C_k,C_l}}{N_p}.$$

Using the above values for pairs $\langle M_{C_k,C_l}, N_{C_k,C_l} \rangle$, we can construct the final form of the IM that determines the degrees of correspondence between criteria $C_1, ..., C_m$:

	C_1	$\cdots$	C_m
C_1	$\langle M_{C_1,C_1}, N_{C_1,C_1} \rangle$	$\cdots$	$\langle M_{C_1,C_m}, N_{C_1,C_m} \rangle$
$\vdots$	$\vdots$	$\ddots$	$\vdots$
C_m	$\langle M_{C_m,C_1}, N_{C_m,C_1} \rangle$	$\cdots$	$\langle M_{C_m,C_m}, N_{C_m,C_m} \rangle$

If we know which criteria are more complex, or that their evaluation is more expensive, or it needs longer time, then we can omit these criteria keeping the simpler, cheaper or those requiring less time.

5   Procedure for Simplifying the Index Matrix that Determines the Degrees of Correspondence Between the Criteria

Let $\gamma, \delta \in [0,1]$ be given, so that $\gamma + \delta \leq 1$. We call that criteria C_k and C_l are in

- strong (γ, δ)-positive consonance, if

$$\inf M_{C_k, C_l} > \gamma \text{ and } \sup N_{C_k, C_l} < \delta;$$

- weak (γ, δ)-positive consonance, if

$$\sup M_{C_k, C_l} > \gamma \text{ and } \inf N_{C_k, C_l} < \delta;$$

- strong (γ, δ)-negative consonance, if

$$\sup M_{C_k, C_l} < \gamma \text{ and } \inf N_{C_k, C_l} > \delta;$$

- weak (γ, δ)-negative consonance, if

$$\inf M_{C_k, C_l} < \gamma \text{ and } \sup N_{C_k, C_l} > \delta;$$

- (γ, δ)-dissonance, otherwise.

Similarly, we can compare the objects, determining which of them are in strong (γ, δ)-positive, weak (γ, δ)-positive, strong (γ, δ)-negative, weak (γ, δ)-negative consonance, or in (γ, δ)-dissonance.

6   Conclusion

In a next research, we will describe an intercriteria analysis with interval-valued intuitionistic fuzzy evaluations in which the IM has an asymmetric form.

In future, the two forms of the new method will be applied in different areas.

The results over intercriteria analysis show that in its standard form it is a suitable Data Mining instrument. In near future, we will show that the new variant of this analysis, discussed in the present paper, is also a suitable instrument. It will be extended with the new ideas developed in the theory of interval-valued IFSs.

Acknowledgment. This research has been supported by the Bulgarian National Science Fund under Grant Ref. No. KP-06-N22/1/2018 "Theoretical research and applications of InterCriteria Analysis".

References

1. Atanassov, K.: Generalized index matrices. In: Comptes rendus de l'Academie Bulgare des Sciences, vol. 40, no. 11, pp. 15–18 (1987)
2. Atanassov, K.: Intuitionistic Fuzzy Sets. Springer, Heidelberg (1999)
3. Atanassov, K.: On Intuitionistic Fuzzy Sets Theory. Springer, Berlin (2012). https://doi.org/10.1007/978-3-642-29127-2
4. Atanassov, K.: Index Matrices: Towards an Augmented Matrix Calculus. Springer, Cham (2014). https://doi.org/10.1007/978-3-319-10945-9
5. Atanassov, K., Atanassova, V., Gluhchev, G.: Intercriteria analysis: ideas and problems. Notes Intuitionistic Fuzzy Sets **21**(1), 81–88 (2015)
6. Atanassov, K., Gargov, G.: Interval valued intuitionistic fuzzy sets. Fuzzy Sets Syst. **31**(3), 343–349 (1989)
7. Atanassov, K., Mavrov, D., Atanassova, V.: Intercriteria decision making: a new approach for multicriteria decision making, based on index matrices and intuitionistic fuzzy sets. Issues Intuitionistic Fuzzy Sets Generalized Nets **11**, 1–8 (2014)
8. Atanassov, K., Szmidt, E., Kacprzyk, J.: On intuitionistic fuzzy pairs. Notes Intuitionistic Fuzzy Sets **19**(3), 1–13 (2013)
9. Atanassov, K., Vassilev, P., Kacprzyk, J., Szmidt, E.: On interval valued intuitionistic fuzzy pairs. J. Univers. Math. **1**(3), 261–268 (2018)
10. Atanassova, V., Doukovska, L., de Tre, G., Radeva, I.: Intercriteria analysis and comparison of innovation-driven and efficiency-to-innovation driven economies in the European Union. Notes Intuitionistic Fuzzy Sets **23**(3), 54–68 (2017)
11. Atanassova, V., Doukovska, L., Kacprzyk, A., Sotirova, E., Radeva, I., Vassilev, P.: InterCriteria analysis of the global competitiveness reports: from efficiency- to innovation-driven economies. J. Multiple-Valued Logic Soft Comput. **31**(5–6), 469–494 (2018)
12. Bureva, V., Sotirova, E., Sotirov, S., Mavrov, D.: Application of the InterCriteria decision making method to Bulgarian universities ranking. Notes Intuitionistic Fuzzy Sets **21**(2), 111–117 (2015)
13. Doukovska, L., Atanassova, V., Shahpazov, G., Capkovic, F.: InterCriteria analysis applied to variuos EU Enterprises. In: Proceedings of the Fifth International Symposium on Business Modeling and Software Design, Milan, Italy, pp. 284–291 (2015)
14. Fidanova, S., Roeva, O.: Comparison of different metaheuristic algorithms based on intercriteria analysis. J. Comput. Appl. Math. **340**, 615–628 (2018)
15. Kacprzyk, A., Sotirov, S., Sotirova, E., Shopova, D., Georgiev, P.: Application of intercriteria analysis in the finance and accountancy positions. Notes Intuitionistic Fuzzy Sets **23**(4), 84–90 (2017)
16. Krawczak, M., Bureva, V., Sotirova, E., Szmidt, E.: Application of the intercriteria decision making method to universities ranking. In: Atanassov, K.T., et al. (eds.) Novel Developments in Uncertainty Representation and Processing. AISC, vol. 401, pp. 365–372. Springer, Cham (2016). https://doi.org/10.1007/978-3-319-26211-6_31
17. Krumova, S., et al.: Intercriteria analysis of calorimetric data of blood serum proteome. Biochim. et Biophys. Acta - Gen. Subj. **2017**, 409–417 (1861)
18. Marinov, P., Fidanova, S.: Intercriteria and correlation analyses: similarities, differences and simultaneous use. Ann. "Inform." Sect. Union Sci. Bulgaria **8**, 45–53 (2016)

19. Pencheva, T., Angelova, M.: InterCriteria analysis of simple genetic algorithms performance. In: Georgiev, K., Todorov, M., Georgiev, I. (eds.) Advanced Computing in Industrial Mathematics. SCI, vol. 681, pp. 147–159. Springer, Cham (2017). https://doi.org/10.1007/978-3-319-49544-6_13

20. Pencheva, T., Angelova, M., Vassilev, P., Roeva, O.: InterCriteria analysis approach to parameter identification of a fermentation process model. In: Atanassov, K.T., et al. (eds.) Novel Developments in Uncertainty Representation and Processing. AISC, vol. 401, pp. 385–397. Springer, Cham (2016). https://doi.org/10.1007/978-3-319-26211-6_33

21. Pencheva, T., Roeva, O., Angelova, M.: Investigation of genetic algorithm performance based on different algorithms for intercriteria relations calculation. In: Lirkov, I., Margenov, S. (eds.) LSSC 2017. LNCS, vol. 10665, pp. 390–398. Springer, Cham (2018). https://doi.org/10.1007/978-3-319-73441-5_42

22. Roeva, O., Pencheva, T., Angelova, M., Vassilev, P.: InterCriteria analysis by pairs and triples of genetic algorithms application for models identification. In: Fidanova, S. (ed.) Recent Advances in Computational Optimization. SCI, vol. 655, pp. 193–218. Springer, Cham (2016). https://doi.org/10.1007/978-3-319-40132-4_12

23. Roeva, O., Vassilev, P.: InterCriteria analysis of generation gap influence on genetic algorithms performance. In: Atanassov, K.T., et al. (eds.) Novel Developments in Uncertainty Representation and Processing. AISC, vol. 401, pp. 301–313. Springer, Cham (2016). https://doi.org/10.1007/978-3-319-26211-6_26

24. Roeva, O., Vassilev, P., Angelova, M., Pencheva, T.: InterCriteria analysis of parameters relations in fermentation processes models. In: Núñez, M., Nguyen, N.T., Camacho, D., Trawiński, B. (eds.) ICCCI 2015. LNCS (LNAI), vol. 9330, pp. 171–181. Springer, Cham (2015). https://doi.org/10.1007/978-3-319-24306-1_17

25. Sotirov, S.: Opportunities for application of the intercriteria analysis method to neural network preprocessing procedures. Notes Intuitionistic Fuzzy Sets **21**(4), 143–152 (2015)

26. Sotirov, S., et al.: Application of the intuitionistic fuzzy intercriteria analysis method with triples to a neural network preprocessing procedure. Comput. Intell. Neurosci. Hindawi 2017 (2017). Article ID 2157852

27. Sotirova, E., Bureva, V., Sotirov, S.: A generalized net model for evaluation process using intercriteria analysis method in the university. In: Angelov, P., Sotirov, S. (eds.) Imprecision and Uncertainty in Information Representation and Processing. SFSC, vol. 332, pp. 389–399. Springer, Cham (2016). https://doi.org/10.1007/978-3-319-26302-1_23

28. Stratiev, D., et al.: Dependence of visbroken residue viscosity and vacuum residue conversion in a commercial visbreaker unit on feedstock quality. Fuel Process. Technol. **138**, 595–604 (2015)

29. Stratiev, D., et al.: Investigation of relationships between bulk properties and fraction properties of crude oils by application of the intercriteria analysis. Pet. Sci. Technol. **34**(13), 1113–1120 (2015)

Business Dynamism and Innovation Capability in the European Union Member States in 2018 Through the Prism of InterCriteria Analysis

Vassia Atanassova[1(✉)] and Lyubka Doukovska[2]

[1] Institute of Biophysics and Biomedical Engineering, Bulgarian Academy of Sciences, 105 Acad. Georgi Bonchev Street, Sofia, Bulgaria
vassia.atanassova@gmail.com
[2] Institute of Information and Communication Technologies,
Bulgarian Academy of Sciences, Acad. Georgi Bonchev Street 2, Sofia, Bulgaria
doukovska@iit.bas.bg

Abstract. Here we apply the intuitionistic fuzzy sets-based InterCriteria Analysis on the data from the Global Competitiveness Index of 2018, about the two best correlating pillars of competitiveness '11 Business Dynamism' and '12 Innovation Capability' based on the data of the 28 European Union Member States. We get a deeper look on how the eight subindicators of the countries' business dynamism and the ten subindicators of their innovation capability correlate in between and among each other.

Keywords: InterCriteria analysis · Global Competitiveness Index ·
Business dynamism · Innovation capability · Intuitionistic fuzzy sets

1 Introduction

In the end of 2018, the World Economic Forum (WEF) restructured the methodology of its annual Global Competitiveness Index (GCI), now labeled "4.0" [15], preserving some of their traditional twelve pillars of competitiveness, while changing others, not only nominally, but also in terms of their sub-indicators, derived from the databases of various international organizations and WEF itself. After a series of research on both European and global level, using the instrumentarium of the intuitionistic fuzzy sets-based intercriteria analysis and data from the annual WEF's Global Competitiveness Reports from 2007 to 2017, we have observed that two of the twelve pillars of competitiveness specifically tend to correlate more strongly than any other pair of criteria, namely Pillar 11 'Business Sophistication' and Pillar 12 'Innovation'. Now, we are challenged to research the intercriteria performance of the corresponding two new set of pillars, namely Pillar 11 'Business Dynamism' and Pillar 12 'Innovation Capability', and specifically get a deeper look in the relations between their eight and ten subindicators, respectively.

© Springer Nature Switzerland AG 2019
A. Cuzzocrea et al. (Eds.): FQAS 2019, LNAI 11529, pp. 339–349, 2019.
https://doi.org/10.1007/978-3-030-27629-4_31

2 Presentation of the Method

InterCriteria Analysis (ICA), originally introduced in 2014, is a method based on intuitionistic fuzzy sets [2] which receives as input datasets of the evaluations of multiple objects against multiple criteria and returns as output a table of detected dependencies in the form of intuitionistic fuzzy pairs [3] between each pair of criteria. These dependencies are interpreted as presence of pairwise correlation (termed positive consonance), lack of correlation (or, negative consonance), and uncertainty (i.e., dissonance). In the original problem formulation that leads to the idea of ICA, measuring against some of the criteria is slower or more expensive than measuring against others, and the decision maker's aim is to accelerate or lower the cost of the overall decision making process by eliminating the costly criteria on the basis of these existing correlations. The use of intuitionistic fuzzy pairs requires the introduction of two thresholds, respectively, for the membership and the non-membership part of the IFP [10], which is to ensure that the precision of the decision taken is not compromised by uncertainty. A detailed presentation of the method is given in [1, 2], and of the various ways of defining these thresholds are presented in [9].

3 Presentation of the Input Data

In the 2018 GCI, two of the twelve pillars of competitiveness form the countries' innovation ecosystem: Pillar 11 'Business Dynamism' and Pillar 12 'Innovation Capability'. Each of them is formed from a number of subindicators, as given in the Table 1 below.

We notice that between the pillars 11 and 12 from the previous GCI methodology (until 2018) and those from the new methodology (as of 2018), there are not only nominal differences, but also differences in the selected subindicators that form the pillars. For instance, Pillar 11 'Business dynamism' with 8 subindicators replaces the previous Pillar 11 'Business sophistication with nine subindicators, and only one of these remained in the new methodology, 11.06 'Willingness to delegate authority', and another subindicator 12.02 'State of cluster development' was moved from the old pillar 11 to the new Pillar 12. In Pillar 12, it is noticed that the two old subindicators related to research and development – 'Company spending on R&D' and 'University-industry collaboration in R&D' now are combined in the new subindicator 12.07 'R&D expenditures', and the subindicator 'Quality of scientific research institutions' now reads 12.08 'Quality of research institutions'. On this basis we cannot draw significant comparisons and conclusions related to the performance of the pair of pillars before and after 2018, but we notice in [9] that under the new GCI methodology, the two 'Innovation Ecosystem' pillars again correlate most strongly as their respective predecessors from the previous GCI, collectively called 'Innovation and Sophistication Factors', like [5, 7], as identified with the InterCriteria Analysis.

Table 1. Pillars 11 and 12 (the innovation ecosystem) from the 2018 GCI report.

Pillar /subindicator	Measure
Pillar 11: Business dynamism	*0–100 (best)*
11.01 Cost of starting a business	% GNI per capita
11.02 Time to start a business	days
11.03 Insolvency recovery rate	Cents/$
11.04 Insolvency regulatory framework	0–16 (best)
11.05 Attitudes toward entrepreneurial risk	1–7 (best)
11.06 Willingness to delegate authority	1–7 (best)
11.07 Growth of innovative companies	1–7 (best)
11.08 Companies embracing disruptive	1–7 (best)
Pillar 12: Innovation capability	*0–100 (best)*
12.01 Diversity of workforce	1–7 (best)
12.02 State of cluster development	1–7 (best)
12.03 International co-inventions	Applications/million pop
12.04 Multi-stakeholder collaboration	1–7 (best)
12.05 Scientific publications	H Index
12.06 Patent applications	Applications/million pop
12.07 R&D expenditures	% GDP
12.08 Quality of research institutions	Index
12.09 Buyer sophistication	1–7 (best)
12.10 Trademark applications	Applications/million pop

4   Main Results

The input data from Table 2 was analysed with the software for ICA, developed by D. Mavrov [12, 13], freely available from http://intercriteria.net, [16]. The output represents two tables, for the membership and the non-membership parts of the intuitionistic fuzzy pairs that stand collectively for the intuitionistic fuzzy consonance/dissonance between each pair of criteria. While the input is objects (in this case 28 countries) against criteria (here, a total of 2 competitiveness indicators and a total of 18 subindicators), the output is two 20×20 matrices. They are both symmetrical according to the main diagonal, as in the ICA method the intercriteria consonance between criteria C_i and C_j is identical with the intercriteria consonance between C_j and C_i. Also, along the main diagonal all the elements are the IFPs $\langle 0, 1 \rangle$, which represents the perfect 'truth'.

Here on Table 3 we present the ICA results showing the membership (a) and the non-membership (b) parts of the intercriteria pairwise correlations. As the reader will see from Fig. 1, the intercriteria pairs are depicted by points on the intuitionistic fuzzy interpretational triangle [4, 8, 11] very close to or on the hypotenuse, meaning very low uncertainty, hence the non-membership values are almost everywhere complementary to 1 to the respective memberships ones. We will discuss in details the three segments of the table, first, in Subsect. 4.1, the intercriteria correlations in between the

Table 2. InterCriteria analysis input with data for the European union member states in 2018 (objects) against Pillar '11 business dynamism' and Pillar '12 innovation capability' (criteria).

	Austria	Belgium	Bulgaria	Croatia	Cyprus	Czech Republic	Denmark	Estonia	Finland	France	Germany	Greece	Hungary	Ireland	Italy	Latvia	Lithuania	Luxembourg	Malta	Netherlands	Poland	Portugal	Romania	Slovak Republic	Slovenia	Spain	Sweden	United Kingdom
Pillar 11	69.9	73.8	60.3	55.7	66.9	70.2	79.1	69.3	78.3	69.4	81.6	58	57.2	76.9	65.4	64.3	64.5	65.8	59.2	80.3	61.5	69.7	60.1	64.5	70.3	66.3	79.8	79
11.01	97.5	97.2	99.4	96.4	93.8	99.9	99.9	99.4	99.5	99.7	99.1	98.9	97.3	99.9	93.2	99.1	99.7	99.2	96.4	97.8	94	99	99.8	99.5	100	97.6	99.8	100
11.02	79.4	96.5	77.4	93.5	94.5	91.5	97	97	86.4	97	89.9	87.9	93.5	95.5	94	95	95	83.9	84.3	97	63.3	95.5	88.4	87.9	93.5	87.4	93.5	96
11.03	86.1	91.1	38.8	35.2	78.8	72.1	94.8	43.7	95	79.1	86.8	36.2	47	92.4	69.5	43.2	48.8	47.1	41.8	96.6	67.9	68.7	38.3	50.9	95.5	82.5	84.1	91.7
11.04	68.8	71.9	81.3	75	78.1	81.3	75	87.5	90.6	68.8	93.8	75	62.5	65.6	84.4	75	50	43.8	34.4	71.9	87.5	90.6	81.3	81.3	71.9	75	75	68.8
11.05	45.5	46.1	45.4	32.1	54.8	47.3	55.7	50.6	53.1	46.2	67.5	45.6	33.4	64.7	49.6	44.3	51.5	52.3	57.5	66.6	46.7	46.7	38.5	43.6	42.5	46	66	68.5
11.06	71.9	75.7	48.8	42.7	51.9	66.2	84.9	66.2	79.5	63.2	76.3	48.6	51.2	76.5	48.1	58.7	63.8	74.7	61.3	79.7	51	54.2	47.4	57.2	58.4	56.4	83.8	75.3
11.07	62.2	59.2	48.5	38.2	42.9	55.8	64.7	59.5	64.9	54.7	72.9	38.4	41.6	66.1	47.8	53.5	57.7	68.5	52.3	71.5	46	56.3	47.8	54	58.9	48	74.1	69.4
11.08	47.5	53	43.2	32.4	40.1	47.7	61.1	50.3	57.3	46.7	66.5	33.1	31.5	54.8	36.6	45.7	49.7	56.9	45.9	61.3	35.5	46.7	39	41.9	41.7	37.2	62.5	62.1
Pillar 12	74.3	73.4	43.9	37.7	44.7	57.3	75.4	52.5	76.3	76.1	87.5	45	48	67	65.8	42	47.4	68.2	51	77.5	48.7	53.1	39.6	46.6	57.9	62.9	79.8	79.2
12.01	59	62.7	53.4	38.9	52.3	55.4	65.3	41.4	59.9	57.4	71.9	45.8	29.7	69.8	34.4	51.6	64.9	77.7	62.2	72.7	38.9	63	66.2	48.6	56.4	52.1	73.2	76.6
12.02	66.7	64.9	46.8	30.4	46.3	50.5	63.9	45.6	64.9	63.2	75.4	32.3	46.8	60.8	74.5	46	41.3	67	53.8	72.8	46.6	54.4	34.5	46.6	47.3	54.4	67.6	69.8
12.03	100	99.7	22.9	23.5	22.9	58.2	98.7	52.2	100	77.7	95.2	25.6	53.7	91.7	49.8	25.7	27.1	100	47.6	94.3	29.4	26.1	20.4	41	56.4	46.2	100	79.8
12.04	63.4	63.3	43.3	30.8	40.9	50.6	64.8	49.8	71.2	53.8	95.2	33.3	37.1	63.7	45.4	41	51.4	65.6	48	72.3	34.9	50.5	36.3	43.9	48	40.5	71.6	67.5
12.05	93.5	96.5	79.2	80.3	74.9	87.9	95.6	80	93.4	100	100	89.2	87.7	89.7	100	72.6	76.1	73.4	67.9	100	90.7	88.4	78.9	80.5	81.2	97.9	98	100
12.06	100	87	31.4	32.9	41.4	61.6	98.1	60	100	91.5	100	43.6	55.9	80.7	76.4	39.6	47.1	88.2	57.9	95.9	47	45.5	26.7	42.1	73.9	61.7	100	84.9
12.07	100	81.9	31.9	28.5	15.2	65	100	49.8	96.8	74.4	95.9	31.9	45.9	50.5	44.5	20.8	34.7	42.9	25.6	67.1	33.4	42.6	16.3	39.3	73.7	40.7	100	56.8
12.08	5.23	24.5	2.6	3.6	2.3	23	17.2	2.9	17.7	100	100	16.2	9.9	11.8	90.8	1.3	4	0.5	0.4	40.7	39.8	20.7	10.8	5.8	4.1	100	26.7	100
12.09	45.2	57	39.1	28.6	50.5	32.6	50.7	46.2	62.5	49.8	66.1	35.5	29.7	55.4	48.2	33.7	38.5	66.5	46.2	59.7	40.4	46.5	28.6	33.7	41.5	39.8	61.5	61.4
12.10	100	96.3	88.6	79.3	100	88.4	99.3	97.4	97	92.7	97.3	96.8	83.4	96.6	93.6	87.6	88.3	100	100	99.7	86.3	92.9	77.8	84.9	96.8	95.4	99.1	94.7

subindicators of Pillar 11 'Business dynamism', second, in Subsect. 4.2, the intercriteria correlations in between the subindicators of Pillar 12 'Innovation capability', and third, in Subsect. 4.3, in between the subindicators of pillars 11 and 12. In this way, we will get a better understanding of the factors that form the innovation ecosystem of countries, from the European Union perspective.

4.1   ICA Results for the Subindicators Within Pillar '11 Business Dynamism'

In the frames of Pillar 11 'Business dynamism' the results from application of ICA (Table 4, Fig. 2) highest intercriteria positive consonances are detected in between three of the eight subindicators: 11.06 'Willingness to delegate authority', 11.07 'Growth of innovative companies' and 11.08 'Companies embracing disruptive ideas'. These three (out of a total of 28) pairs also form a well clustered group of the top 10% highest positive consonances in this selection. It is noteworthy that these three criteria form an intercriteria correlation triple, as proposed in [6, 14].

It is noteworthy that these three criteria also are among the best correlating with the aggregated Pillar 11 itself, where one other subindicator 11.03 'Insolvency recovery rate' is the one that exhibits highest positive consonance with Pillar 11, while in the same time exhibiting dissonance and weak positive consonance with the rest subindicators in the pillar.

One criterion, subindicator 11.04 'Insolvency regulatory framework' exhibits strong negative consonance with all the rest ones in the pillar, and with the pillar itself,

Table 3. Results of the interCriteria analysis from the input of Table 2 (a) membership, (b) non-membership.

(a)	Pillar 11	11.01	11.02	11.03	11.04	11.05	11.06	11.07	11.08	Pillar 12	12.01	12.02	12.03	12.04	12.05	12.06	12.07	12.08	12.09	12.10
Pillar 11	1.000	0.627	0.616	0.854	0.503	0.749	0.825	0.849	0.841	0.841	0.741	0.767	0.762	0.857	0.714	0.794	0.802	0.675	0.783	0.690
11.01	0.627	1.000	0.561	0.598	0.418	0.545	0.640	0.669	0.648	0.579	0.680	0.511	0.561	0.638	0.505	0.548	0.608	0.516	0.521	0.455
11.02	0.616	0.561	1.000	0.593	0.399	0.566	0.598	0.585	0.598	0.561	0.542	0.516	0.513	0.595	0.561	0.545	0.563	0.548	0.545	0.487
11.03	0.854	0.598	0.593	1.000	0.444	0.669	0.772	0.743	0.717	0.804	0.656	0.757	0.749	0.772	0.706	0.765	0.762	0.667	0.741	0.669
11.04	0.503	0.418	0.399	0.444	1.000	0.447	0.397	0.431	0.437	0.442	0.360	0.442	0.370	0.429	0.508	0.405	0.468	0.550	0.439	0.389
11.05	0.749	0.545	0.566	0.669	0.447	1.000	0.746	0.751	0.807	0.749	0.733	0.712	0.656	0.772	0.608	0.704	0.630	0.595	0.802	0.709
11.06	0.825	0.640	0.598	0.772	0.397	0.746	1.000	0.868	0.884	0.804	0.751	0.733	0.815	0.876	0.608	0.799	0.780	0.556	0.746	0.701
11.07	0.849	0.669	0.585	0.743	0.431	0.751	0.868	1.000	0.910	0.817	0.804	0.772	0.780	0.913	0.624	0.783	0.759	0.579	0.775	0.690
11.08	0.841	0.648	0.598	0.717	0.437	0.807	0.884	0.910	1.000	0.796	0.820	0.751	0.746	0.910	0.606	0.754	0.722	0.574	0.783	0.672
Pillar 12	0.841	0.579	0.561	0.804	0.442	0.749	0.804	0.817	0.796	1.000	0.704	0.862	0.839	0.852	0.772	0.915	0.833	0.720	0.825	0.685
12.01	0.741	0.680	0.542	0.656	0.360	0.733	0.751	0.804	0.820	0.704	1.000	0.709	0.659	0.796	0.561	0.659	0.624	0.553	0.741	0.648
12.02	0.767	0.511	0.516	0.757	0.442	0.712	0.733	0.772	0.751	0.862	0.709	1.000	0.788	0.820	0.754	0.812	0.754	0.680	0.796	0.669
12.03	0.762	0.561	0.513	0.749	0.370	0.656	0.815	0.780	0.746	0.839	0.659	0.788	1.000	0.812	0.667	0.899	0.860	0.603	0.757	0.693
12.04	0.857	0.638	0.595	0.772	0.429	0.772	0.876	0.913	0.910	0.852	0.796	0.820	0.812	1.000	0.653	0.815	0.783	0.608	0.812	0.696
12.05	0.714	0.505	0.561	0.706	0.508	0.608	0.608	0.624	0.606	0.772	0.561	0.754	0.667	0.653	1.000	0.717	0.725	0.873	0.659	0.532
12.06	0.794	0.548	0.545	0.765	0.405	0.704	0.799	0.783	0.754	0.915	0.659	0.812	0.899	0.815	0.717	1.000	0.857	0.653	0.783	0.701
12.07	0.802	0.608	0.563	0.762	0.468	0.630	0.780	0.759	0.722	0.833	0.624	0.754	0.860	0.783	0.725	0.857	1.000	0.661	0.701	0.648
12.08	0.675	0.516	0.548	0.667	0.550	0.595	0.556	0.579	0.574	0.720	0.553	0.680	0.603	0.608	0.873	0.653	0.661	1.000	0.598	0.450
12.09	0.783	0.521	0.545	0.741	0.439	0.802	0.746	0.775	0.783	0.825	0.741	0.796	0.757	0.812	0.659	0.783	0.701	0.598	1.000	0.751
12.10	0.690	0.455	0.487	0.669	0.389	0.709	0.701	0.690	0.672	0.685	0.648	0.669	0.693	0.696	0.532	0.701	0.648	0.450	0.751	1.000

(b)	Pillar 11	11.01	11.02	11.03	11.04	11.05	11.06	11.07	11.08	Pillar 12	12.01	12.02	12.03	12.04	12.05	12.06	12.07	12.08	12.09	12.10
Pillar 11	0.000	0.344	0.341	0.143	0.418	0.246	0.169	0.146	0.153	0.156	0.254	0.220	0.217	0.138	0.257	0.188	0.185	0.307	0.206	0.288
11.01	0.344	0.000	0.373	0.376	0.484	0.426	0.331	0.302	0.323	0.394	0.291	0.452	0.394	0.333	0.442	0.410	0.354	0.442	0.444	0.500
11.02	0.341	0.373	0.000	0.368	0.489	0.392	0.360	0.373	0.360	0.399	0.415	0.434	0.429	0.362	0.378	0.399	0.386	0.397	0.407	0.455
11.03	0.143	0.376	0.368	0.000	0.479	0.328	0.225	0.254	0.280	0.196	0.341	0.233	0.233	0.225	0.267	0.220	0.228	0.317	0.251	0.312
11.04	0.418	0.484	0.489	0.479	0.000	0.474	0.524	0.489	0.484	0.481	0.561	0.471	0.534	0.492	0.394	0.503	0.450	0.362	0.476	0.516
11.05	0.246	0.426	0.392	0.328	0.474	0.000	0.249	0.243	0.188	0.249	0.262	0.275	0.323	0.222	0.362	0.278	0.357	0.386	0.188	0.270
11.06	0.169	0.331	0.360	0.225	0.524	0.249	0.000	0.127	0.111	0.193	0.243	0.254	0.164	0.119	0.362	0.183	0.206	0.426	0.243	0.278
11.07	0.146	0.302	0.373	0.254	0.489	0.243	0.127	0.000	0.085	0.180	0.190	0.214	0.198	0.082	0.347	0.198	0.228	0.402	0.214	0.288
11.08	0.153	0.323	0.360	0.280	0.484	0.188	0.111	0.085	0.000	0.201	0.175	0.235	0.233	0.085	0.365	0.228	0.265	0.407	0.206	0.307
Pillar 12	0.156	0.394	0.399	0.196	0.481	0.249	0.193	0.180	0.201	0.000	0.294	0.127	0.143	0.146	0.201	0.069	0.156	0.265	0.167	0.296
12.01	0.254	0.291	0.415	0.341	0.561	0.262	0.243	0.190	0.175	0.294	0.000	0.278	0.320	0.198	0.410	0.323	0.362	0.429	0.249	0.331
12.02	0.220	0.452	0.434	0.233	0.471	0.275	0.254	0.214	0.235	0.127	0.278	0.000	0.183	0.167	0.209	0.161	0.225	0.294	0.185	0.302
12.03	0.217	0.394	0.429	0.233	0.534	0.323	0.164	0.198	0.233	0.143	0.320	0.183	0.000	0.167	0.288	0.082	0.116	0.362	0.217	0.275
12.04	0.138	0.333	0.362	0.225	0.492	0.222	0.119	0.082	0.085	0.146	0.198	0.167	0.167	0.000	0.317	0.167	0.204	0.373	0.177	0.283
12.05	0.257	0.442	0.378	0.267	0.394	0.362	0.362	0.347	0.365	0.201	0.410	0.209	0.288	0.317	0.000	0.241	0.238	0.101	0.307	0.423
12.06	0.188	0.410	0.399	0.220	0.503	0.278	0.183	0.198	0.228	0.069	0.323	0.161	0.082	0.167	0.241	0.000	0.122	0.315	0.193	0.265
12.07	0.185	0.354	0.386	0.228	0.450	0.357	0.206	0.228	0.265	0.156	0.362	0.225	0.116	0.204	0.238	0.122	0.000	0.312	0.280	0.323
12.08	0.307	0.442	0.397	0.317	0.362	0.386	0.426	0.402	0.407	0.265	0.429	0.294	0.362	0.373	0.101	0.315	0.312	0.000	0.378	0.516
12.09	0.206	0.444	0.407	0.251	0.476	0.188	0.243	0.214	0.206	0.167	0.249	0.185	0.217	0.177	0.307	0.193	0.280	0.378	0.000	0.222
12.10	0.288	0.500	0.455	0.312	0.516	0.270	0.278	0.288	0.307	0.296	0.331	0.302	0.275	0.283	0.423	0.265	0.323	0.516	0.222	0.000

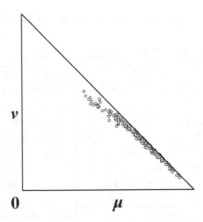

Fig. 1. Results of the InterCriteria analysis (Tables 3 (a,b)) plotted as points on the intuitionistic fuzzy interpretational triangle.

Table 4. ICA pairs of the subindicators (criteria) in Pillar 11, sorted ascendingly with respect to their distance ('d') from the intuitionistic fuzzy truth (i.e. point $\langle 0, 1 \rangle$).

C1	C2	μ	v	d
11.07	11.08	0.910	0.085	0.124
11.06	11.08	0.884	0.111	0.161
11.06	11.07	0.868	0.127	0.183
11.05	11.08	0.807	0.188	0.269
11.03	11.06	0.772	0.225	0.320
11.05	11.07	0.751	0.243	0.348
11.05	11.06	0.746	0.249	0.355
11.03	11.07	0.743	0.254	0.361
11.03	11.08	0.717	0.280	0.398
11.01	11.07	0.669	0.302	0.448
11.03	11.05	0.669	0.328	0.466
11.01	11.08	0.648	0.323	0.477
11.01	11.06	0.640	0.331	0.489
11.02	11.06	0.598	0.360	0.540

C1	C2	μ	v	d
11.02	11.08	0.598	0.360	0.540
11.02	11.03	0.593	0.368	0.549
11.01	11.03	0.598	0.376	0.550
11.02	11.07	0.585	0.373	0.558
11.01	11.02	0.561	0.373	0.576
11.02	11.05	0.566	0.392	0.584
11.01	11.05	0.545	0.426	0.623
11.04	11.05	0.447	0.474	0.728
11.03	11.04	0.444	0.479	0.733
11.04	11.08	0.437	0.484	0.743
11.04	11.07	0.431	0.489	0.750
11.01	11.04	0.418	0.484	0.757
11.02	11.04	0.399	0.489	0.775
11.04	11.06	0.397	0.524	0.799

and two other subindicators, exhibit dissonance to weak negative consonance, namely 11.01 'Cost of starting a business' and 11.02 'Time to start a business'.

The subindicator 11.05 'Attitudes toward entrepreneurial risk' is also worth commenting, as it exhibits negative consonance or dissonance with the first four subindicators in the pillar, and positive consonance with the last three, especially subindicator 11.08 'Companies embracing disruptive ideas'.

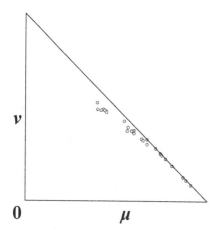 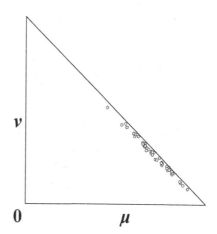

Fig. 2. Results of the ICA between the subindicators (criteria) in Pillar 11, plotted as points on the IF triangle

Fig. 3. Results of the ICA between the subindicators (criteria) in Pillar 12, plotted as points on the IF triangle

4.2   ICA Results for the Subindicators Within Pillar 12 'Innovation Capability'

In the frames of Pillar 12 'Innovation capability', as show on Table 5, Fig. 3, the highest intercriteria positive consonances are detected between the pairs 12.03 'International co-inventions' and 12.06 'Patent applications', 12.03 'International co-inventions' and 12.07 'R&D expenditures', 12.06 'Patent applications' and 12.07 'R&D expenditures', and 12.05 'Scientific publications' and 12.08 'Quality of research institutions'. Interestingly, these four (out of a total of 45) pairs also form a well clustered group of the top 10% highest positive consonances in this selection, and out of these four, 12.03, 12.06 and 12.07 also form an intercriteria correlation triple.

In Pillar 12, six out of ten subindicators exhibit high positive consonance (with $\mu \geq 0.8$) with the aggregate pillar, namely 12.02 'State of cluster development', 12.03 'International co-inventions', 12.04 'Multi-stakeholder collaboration', 12.06 'Patent applications', 12.07 'R&D expenditures', 12.09 'Buyer sophistication'. Three subindicators exhibit dissonance, namely 12.01 'Diversity of workforce', 12.08 'Quality of research institutions', and 12.10 'Trademark applications'.

Strongest negative consonance is exhibited between 12.01 'Diversity of workforce' and 12.10 'Trademark applications', on one hand, and 12.05 'Scientific publications' and 12.08 'Quality of research institutions', on the other (see the bottom of Table 5).

Interesting other observations are that the only criterion with which 12.08 'Quality of research institutions' exhibits strong positive consonance is criterion 12.05 'Scientific publications', and none of the rest.

Table 5. ICA pairs of the subindicators (criteria) in Pillar 12 'innovation capability', sorted ascendingly with respect to their distance ('d') from the IF truth.

C1	C2	μ	v	d
12.03	12.06	0.899	0.082	0.130
12.05	12.08	0.873	0.101	0.162
12.03	12.07	0.860	0.116	0.182
12.06	12.07	0.857	0.122	0.188
12.02	12.04	0.820	0.167	0.245
12.02	12.06	0.812	0.161	0.248
12.04	12.06	0.815	0.167	0.249
12.03	12.04	0.812	0.167	0.251
12.04	12.09	0.812	0.177	0.258
12.02	12.09	0.796	0.185	0.275
12.02	12.03	0.788	0.183	0.279
12.01	12.04	0.796	0.198	0.284
12.06	12.09	0.783	0.193	0.290
12.04	12.07	0.783	0.204	0.298
12.02	12.05	0.754	0.209	0.323
12.03	12.09	0.757	0.217	0.326
12.02	12.07	0.754	0.225	0.333
12.09	12.10	0.751	0.222	0.334
12.01	12.09	0.741	0.249	0.359
12.05	12.07	0.725	0.238	0.364
12.05	12.06	0.717	0.241	0.372
12.06	12.10	0.701	0.265	0.399
12.01	12.02	0.709	0.278	0.402
12.07	12.09	0.701	0.280	0.410

C1	C2	μ	v	d
12.03	12.10	0.693	0.275	0.412
12.04	12.10	0.696	0.283	0.416
12.02	12.08	0.680	0.294	0.434
12.03	12.05	0.667	0.288	0.441
12.02	12.10	0.669	0.302	0.448
12.05	12.09	0.659	0.307	0.459
12.07	12.08	0.661	0.312	0.461
12.01	12.03	0.659	0.320	0.468
12.06	12.08	0.653	0.315	0.468
12.01	12.06	0.659	0.323	0.470
12.04	12.05	0.653	0.317	0.470
12.07	12.10	0.648	0.323	0.477
12.01	12.10	0.648	0.331	0.483
12.01	12.07	0.624	0.362	0.522
12.03	12.08	0.603	0.362	0.537
12.04	12.08	0.608	0.373	0.541
12.08	12.09	0.598	0.378	0.552
12.01	12.05	0.561	0.410	0.601
12.01	12.08	0.553	0.429	0.619
12.05	12.10	0.532	0.423	0.631
12.08	12.10	0.450	0.516	0.754

4.3 ICA Results for the Subindicators Between Pillar '11 Business Dynamism' and Pillar 12 'Innovation Capability'

Given that Pillar '11 Business dynamism' and Pillar 12 'Innovation capability' are the top correlation of all the twelve pillars of competitiveness in the WEF's GCI, it is interesting to investigate which of the subindicators of both pillars exhibit highest intercriteria positive consonance (Table 6).

We first notice, just as in Sect. 4.1, that the three subindicators of pillar 11, 11.01 'Cost of starting a business', 11.02 'Time to start a business' and 11.04 'Insolvency regulatory framework' tend to exhibit negative consonance to dissonance with all the subindicators in Pillar 12. Similar is the behaviour of subindicators 12.05 'Scientific publications' and 12.08 'Quality of research institutions' with respect to all the subindicators in Pillar 11. Other negative consonances or dissonances are observed between the pairs 11.03 'Insolvency recovery rate' and 12.01 'Diversity of workforce', or 11.05 'Attitudes toward entrepreneurial risk' and 12.03 'International co-

Table 6. ICA pairs formed by the subindicators in Pillar 11 and those in Pillar 12, sorted ascendingly with respect to their distance ('d') from the IF truth.

C1	C2	μ	v	d
11.07	12.04	0.913	0.082	0.120
11.08	12.04	0.910	0.085	0.124
11.06	12.04	0.876	0.119	0.172
11.06	12.03	0.815	0.164	0.247
11.08	12.01	0.820	0.175	0.251
11.06	12.06	0.799	0.183	0.272
11.07	12.01	0.804	0.190	0.273
11.05	12.09	0.802	0.188	0.273
11.07	12.06	0.783	0.198	0.294
11.07	12.03	0.780	0.198	0.296
11.08	12.09	0.783	0.206	0.299
11.06	12.07	0.780	0.206	0.301
11.07	12.09	0.775	0.214	0.311
11.07	12.02	0.772	0.214	0.313
11.05	12.04	0.772	0.222	0.318
11.03	12.04	0.772	0.225	0.320
11.03	12.06	0.765	0.220	0.322
11.03	12.07	0.762	0.228	0.329
11.07	12.07	0.759	0.228	0.331
11.08	12.06	0.754	0.228	0.335
11.03	12.02	0.757	0.233	0.337
11.08	12.02	0.751	0.235	0.342
11.03	12.03	0.749	0.233	0.343
11.08	12.03	0.746	0.233	0.345
11.06	12.01	0.751	0.243	0.348
11.06	12.09	0.746	0.243	0.352
11.03	12.09	0.741	0.251	0.361
11.06	12.02	0.733	0.254	0.369
11.05	12.01	0.733	0.262	0.374
11.08	12.07	0.722	0.265	0.384
11.05	12.10	0.709	0.270	0.397
11.03	12.05	0.706	0.267	0.397
11.05	12.02	0.712	0.275	0.399
11.05	12.06	0.704	0.278	0.406
11.06	12.10	0.701	0.278	0.408
11.07	12.10	0.690	0.288	0.423
11.01	12.01	0.680	0.291	0.433
11.08	12.10	0.672	0.307	0.449
11.03	12.10	0.669	0.312	0.455
11.03	12.08	0.667	0.317	0.460

C1	C2	μ	v	d
11.05	12.03	0.656	0.323	0.472
11.03	12.01	0.656	0.341	0.485
11.01	12.04	0.638	0.333	0.492
11.07	12.05	0.624	0.347	0.511
11.05	12.07	0.630	0.357	0.515
11.01	12.07	0.608	0.354	0.528
11.05	12.05	0.608	0.362	0.534
11.06	12.05	0.608	0.362	0.534
11.08	12.05	0.606	0.365	0.537
11.02	12.04	0.595	0.362	0.543
11.05	12.08	0.595	0.386	0.559
11.04	12.08	0.550	0.362	0.578
11.02	12.05	0.561	0.378	0.580
11.07	12.08	0.579	0.402	0.582
11.02	12.07	0.563	0.386	0.583
11.08	12.08	0.574	0.407	0.589
11.01	12.03	0.561	0.394	0.590
11.02	12.08	0.548	0.397	0.602
11.02	12.06	0.545	0.399	0.605
11.01	12.06	0.548	0.410	0.611
11.02	12.09	0.545	0.407	0.611
11.06	12.08	0.556	0.426	0.616
11.02	12.01	0.542	0.415	0.618
11.04	12.05	0.508	0.394	0.630
11.02	12.03	0.513	0.429	0.649
11.02	12.02	0.516	0.434	0.650
11.01	12.09	0.521	0.444	0.653
11.01	12.08	0.516	0.442	0.655
11.01	12.05	0.505	0.442	0.663
11.01	12.02	0.511	0.452	0.666
11.02	12.10	0.487	0.455	0.686
11.04	12.07	0.468	0.450	0.696
11.04	12.02	0.442	0.471	0.730
11.04	12.09	0.439	0.476	0.736
11.01	12.10	0.455	0.500	0.740
11.04	12.04	0.429	0.492	0.754
11.04	12.06	0.405	0.503	0.779
11.04	12.10	0.389	0.516	0.800
11.04	12.03	0.370	0.534	0.826
11.04	12.01	0.360	0.561	0.851

inventions', or 11.05 'Attitudes toward entrepreneurial risk' and 12.07 'R&D expenditures'.

The strongest notable intercriteria positive consonances are between criterion 12.04 'Multi-stakeholder collaboration', on one hand, and the three subindicators 11.06 'Willingness to delegate authority', 11.07 'Growth of innovative companies' and 11.08 'Companies embracing disruptive ideas'. High (μ ≥ 0.8) are the consonances also in the pairs 11.07 'Growth of innovative companies' and 12.01 'Diversity of workforce'; 11.08 'Companies embracing disruptive ideas' and 12.01 'Diversity of workforce'; 11.06 'Willingness to delegate authority' and 12.03 'International co-inventions'; 11.05 'Attitudes toward entrepreneurial risk' and 12.09 'Buyer sophistication', as well as 11.06 'Willingness to delegate authority' and 12.06 'Patent applications' with $\mu = 0.799$.

5   Conclusion

In the present paper, we apply the intuitionistic-fuzzy sets based method of InterCriteria Analysis on the data about the 28 European Union Member States derived from the Global Competitiveness Index 2018 of the World Economic Forum according to the two traditionally most correlating pillars of competitiveness 11 'Business dynamism' and 12 'Innovation capability', and more specifically the eight and ten, respectively, subindicators on which these pillars are based. While the European competitiveness based on the WEF GCI reports has been discussed in a series of works over the years, and in some sense has been a playground for ICA innovation with many new ideas of theoretical nature stemming from the results of the application of the method on these data, this is the first time when we analyse the subindicators that build these two most strongly related pillars of competitiveness, and thus outline dependencies that aim to shed light on these aspects of national economic competitiveness. The detected pairwise relations between these factors of business dynamism and innovation capability are considered informative for the national decision and policy makers, especially in the light of the World Economic Forum's traditional appeal to them to identify the transformative forces in the national economies and strengthen them to drive future economic growth.

Acknowledgments. This research has been supported under Grant Ref. No. KP-06-N22/1/2018 "Theoretical research and applications of InterCriteria Analysis" funded by the Bulgarian National Science Fund.

References

1. Atanassov, K., Atanassova, V., Gluhchev, G.: Intercriteria analysis: ideas and problems. Notes Intuitionistic Fuzzy Sets **21**(1), 81–88 (2015)
2. Atanassov, K., Mavrov, K.D., Atanassova, V.: Intercriteria decision making: a new approach for multicriteria decision making, based on index matrices and intuitionistic fuzzy sets. Issues Intuitionistic Fuzzy Sets Generalized Nets **11**, 1–8 (2014)
3. Atanassov, K., Szmidt, E., Kacprzyk, J.: On intuitionistic fuzzy pairs. Notes Intuitionistic Fuzzy Sets **19**(3), 1–13 (2013)
4. Atanassova, V.: Interpretation in the intuitionistic fuzzy triangle of the results, obtained by the intercriteria analysis. In: 16th World Congress of the International Fuzzy Systems Association (IFSA), 9th Conference of the European Society for Fuzzy Logic and Technology (EUSFLAT), pp. 1369-1374, 30. June–03 July (2015). https://doi.org/10.2991/ifsa-eusflat-15.2015.193

5. Atanassova, V., Doukovska, L., Atanassov, K., Mavrov, D.: Intercriteria decision making approach to EU member states competitiveness analysis. In: Proceedings of the International Symposium on Business Modeling and Software Design – BMSD 2014, Luxembourg, pp. 289–294, 24–26 June 2014.https://doi.org/10.5220/0005427302890294

6. Atanassova, V., Doukovska, L., Michalikova, A., Radeva, I.: Intercriteria analysis: from pairs to triples. Notes on Intuitionistic Fuzzy Sets **22**(5), 98–110 (2016)

7. Atanassova, V., Doukovska, L., de Tre, G., Radeva, I.: Intercriteria analysis and comparison of innovation-driven and efficiency-to-innovation driven economies in the European union. Notes Intuitionistic Fuzzy Sets **23**(3), 54–68 (2017)

8. Atanassova, V., Vardeva, I., Sotirova, E., Doukovska, L.: Traversing and ranking of elements of an Intuitionistic fuzzy set in the intuitionistic fuzzy interpretation triangle. In: Atanassov, K., et al. (eds.) Novel Developments in Uncertainty Representation and Processing. AISC, vol. 401, pp. 161–174. Springer, Cham (2016). https://doi.org/10.1007/978-3-319-26211-6_14

9. Doukovska, L., Atanassova, V., Sotirova, E.: European union member states' performance in the 2018 global competitiveness index 4.0 through the prism of intercriteria analysis. In: Proceedings of the 4th International Conference on Numerical and Symbolic Computation Developments and Applications, Porto, Portugal, pp. 11–12, April 2019 (accepted)

10. Doukovska, L., Atanassova, V., Sotirova, E., Vardeva, I., Radeva, I.: Defining consonance thresholds in intercriteria analysis: an overview. In: Hadjiski, M., Atanassov, K.T. (eds.) Intuitionistic Fuzziness and Other Intelligent Theories and Their Applications. SCI, vol. 757, pp. 161–179. Springer, Cham (2019). https://doi.org/10.1007/978-3-319-78931-6_11

11. Mavrov, D., Radeva, I., Atanassov, K., Doukovska, L., Kalaykov, I.: Intercriteria software design: graphic interpretation within the intuitionistic fuzzy triangle. In: Proceedings of the Fifth International Symposium on Business Modeling and Software Design, 279–283 (2015)

12. Mavrov, D.: Software for intercriteria analysis: implementation of the main algorithm. Notes Intuitionistic Fuzzy Sets **21**(2), 77–86 (2015)

13. Mavrov, D.: Software for intercriteria analysis: working with the results. Ann. "Inform." Sect., Union Scientists Bulgaria **8**, 37–44 (2015–2016)

14. Roeva, O., Pencheva, T., Angelova, M., Vassilev, P.: Intercriteria analysis by Pairs and triples of genetic algorithms application for models identification. In: Fidanova, S. (ed.) Recent Advances in Computational Optimization. SCI, vol. 655, pp. 193–218. Springer, Cham (2016). https://doi.org/10.1007/978-3-319-40132-4_12

15. Schwab, K.: The Global Competitiveness Report, World Economic Forum (2018). ISBN-13: 978-92-95044-76-0. http://reports.weforum.org/global-competitiveness-report-2018/

16. InterCriteria Research Portal. http://intercriteria.net/publications/

Flexibility in Tools

InterCriteria Analysis of the Most Problematic Factors for Doing Business in the European Union, 2017–2018

Lyubka Doukovska[1]([⊠]) [iD] and Vassia Atanassova[2] [iD]

[1] Institute of Information and Communication Technologies,
Bulgarian Academy of Sciences,
2 Acad. Georgi Bonchev Street, Sofia, Bulgaria
doukovska@iit.bas.bg
[2] Institute of Biophysics and Biomedical Engineering,
Bulgarian Academy of Sciences,
105 Acad. Georgi Bonchev Street, Sofia, Bulgaria
vassia.atanassova@gmail.com

Abstract. In this paper, we use the method of the InterCriteria Analysis, based on the concepts of intuitionistic fuzzy sets and index matrices, to analyze a dataset extracted from the Global Competitiveness Index, concerning the most problematic factors for doing business in the European Union member states. The method is applied on the data of these 28 countries extracted from the Global Competitiveness Report 2017–2018.

Keywords: InterCriteria Analysis · Global Competitiveness Index ·
Problematic factors for doing business · Intuitionistic fuzzy sets ·
Decision making · Uncertainty

1 Introduction

Every year, the World Economic Forum (WEF) releases its Global Competitiveness Index report (GCI), which aims to be one of the most in-depth looks into the financial health and risks of nearly 140 countries around the world. It integrates twelve macroeconomic and the micro/business aspects of competitiveness into a single index, based on more than 100 subindicators that capture concepts that matter for productivity and long-term prosperity. GCI defines its purpose as a common framework populated with comparable data that allows national policy makers to monitor their annual progress along some long-term determinants of productivity, growth, income levels, and well-being.

A. Cuzzocrea et al. (Eds.): FQAS 2019, LNAI 11529, pp. 353–360, 2019.
https://doi.org/10.1007/978-3-030-27629-4_32

In the reports produced until 2018 [15], in addition to the countries' performance along these twelve 'pillars of competitiveness', charts were provided summarizing those factors seen by business executives as the most problematic for doing business in their economy. The information was drawn from the World Economic Forum's Executive Opinion Survey, where respondents were asked to select the five most problematic of a list of 16 factors, and rank them from 1 (most problematic) to 5. The results were then tabulated and weighted according to the ranking assigned by respondents [15]. As of the end of 2018, WEF restructured the methodology of the GCI, now labeled '4.0' [16], which does not include the charts of most problematic factors for doing business. Nevertheless, the availability and relevance of these data has motivated us to explore the relations between these sixteen factors, and for this purpose we used the instrumentation of the InterCriteria Analysis (ICA), which is based on the two underlying concepts of intuitionistic fuzzy sets and of index matrices, [1, 2]. It is noteworthy that ICA has been used in a series of research of data from the GCI [5, 7, 9] aimed at detecting relations between the twelve pillars of competitiveness of national economies, with some interesting and consistent results obtained over time. This is in line with the WEF's traditional appeal to policy makers to identify priorities based on the nation's economic performance, while also understanding the drivers of competitiveness and the underlying relations between them.

This paper is structured as follows. In Sect. 2, we describe shortly the intuitionistic fuzzy sets and the ICA method. In Sect. 3, we present the input data that will be analyzed with the proposed method. Section 4 contains the result of the application of ICA onto the presented input data, as well as discussion on the findings. The last section draws some conclusions and ideas of further research.

2   Presentation of the Method

InterCriteria Analysis (ICA) was originally introduced in 2014 as a method for detecting existing patterns and dependencies similar to correlation, between a set of criteria based on the evaluations of a set of objects against these criteria. A detailed presentation of the method is given in [2, 10]. The original motivation behind the method was derived from an problem from the field of industrial petro-chemistry, where some of the criteria were slower and/or more expensive to evaluate than others, and the decision maker's aim was to accelerate or lower the cost of the overall decision making process by eliminating the costly criteria on the basis of some detected correlations between them and the cheaper and faster ones. The method is based on intuitionistic fuzzy sets in order to render account of uncertainty, and returns as output a table of detected dependencies between any pair of criteria in the form of intuitionistic fuzzy pairs [3], i.e. tuples of numbers in the [0, 1]-interval, whose sum belongs to that interval as well and stay respectively for the intuitionistic fuzzy functions of membership and the non-membership. These tuples are then interpreted as presence of pairwise correlation between the respective pair of criteria (termed 'positive consonance'), or lack of correlation (termed 'negative consonance'), or uncertainty (termed 'dissonance'). Based on the decision maker's expertise and/or an algorithm (see [10]), the thresholds for the membership and the non-membership are set as two numbers in the [0, 1]-interval, and these are a problem-specific. Equipped with these thresholds and the method's ability to render account of the uncertainty, the decision maker can now decide if the pairwise positive consonances between the targeted criteria are high enough and whether the 'expensive' criteria can be eliminated from the further decision making process without compromising precision.

3 Presentation of the Input Data

The input data comes in the form of a matrix of 28 labeled rows staying for the analyzed European Union member states and 16 labeled columns with the most problematic factors for doing business (MPFDB) in these countries, namely, 'Access to financing' (ATF), 'Corruption' (COR), 'Crime and theft' (CAT), 'Foreign currency regulations' (FCR), 'Government instability/coups' (GIC), 'Inadequate supply of infrastructure' (ISI), 'Inadequately educated workforce' (IEW), 'Inefficient government bureaucracy' (IGB), 'Inflation' (INF), 'Insufficient capacity to innovate' (ICI), 'Policy instability' (PIN), 'Poor public health' (PPH), 'Poor work ethic in national labor force' (PWE), 'Restrictive labor regulations' (RLR), 'Tax rates' (TRA), 'Tax regulations' (TRE). We note that some of these factors are closely related to the defined twelve pillars of competitivness in the 2017–2018 GCI, for instance Pillar 1 'Institutions', Pillar 7 'Labor market efficiency' or Pillar 12 'Innovation'.

Table 1 shows the input dataset, which is conditionally formatted in a way to show the intensity of the problematic factor, as identified by the survey respondents. While the EU comprise member states in different stages of economic development (with one Stage 2 'Efficiency-driven' economy, Bulgaria, twenty Stage 3 'Innovation-driven' economies and seven transition Stage 2 to Stage 3 economies), the rather harmonized legislation of the 28 and their union political and economic union explains the relatively homogeneous performance with respect to the least and the most problematic factors, as seen on the average. The least problematic factors for the EU member states in 2017–2018 were 'Foreign currency regulations', 'Crime and theft', 'Poor public health' and 'Inflation' with 0.73% to 1.12% of average weight, and the most problematic factors were 'Tax regulations', 'Restrictive labor regulations', 'Inefficient government bureaucracy' and 'Tax rates', with 10.21% to 14.88% of average weight. This information will serve when analyzing the results of the application of ICA on the data, as the least problematic factors will be excluded from the discussion.

Table 1. ICA input with data for the 28 EU member states in 2017–2018 (objects) against the 16 most problematic factors for doing business (criteria), in %, as sorted by 'Average'

	Austria	Belgium	Bulgaria	Croatia	Cyprus	Czech Rep.	Denmark	Estonia	Finland	France	Germany	Greece	Hungary	Ireland	Italy	Latvia	Lithuania	Luxembourg	Malta	Netherlands	Poland	Portugal	Romania	Slovak Rep.	Slovenia	Spain	Sweden	UK	Average
FCR	0.4	0.1	0.3	0.3	1.7	0.3	0.3	0.0	1.2	1.1	4.0	0.5	0.7	2.5	0.0	0.0	0.0	0.2	2.0	0.8	0.8	0.3	0.0	0.5	0.7	0.1	1.0	0.6	0.7
CAT	0.0	0.0	2.5	2.4	0.3	0.8	1.8	0.5	0.0	0.0	3.8	0.1	2.0	0.7	1.3	0.8	0.3	0.0	0.0	2.7	0.7	0.0	1.1	0.6	0.0	0.0	1.4	1.2	0.8
PPH	0.2	0.3	0.8	0.3	2.3	0.0	0.8	1.5	0.3	0.0	3.1	0.7	4.3	2.9	0.1	1.8	0.8	0.0	0.1	0.2	1.5	0.1	1.0	0.3	0.6	0.9	1.0	1.0	1.0
INF	0.7	0.4	3.3	0.0	0.5	0.2	0.9	1.9	0.3	0.2	4.5	0.0	1.0	2.1	0.0	0.5	1.6	3.9	0.7	0.7	0.6	0.5	1.7	0.1	0.3	1.0	2.8	0.9	1.1
GIC	0.7	1.7	5.9	3.3	0.7	2.6	3.1	9.4	2.0	2.1	4.7	10.8	0.4	8.8	3.8	3.5	4.7	0.0	2.3	1.6	6.5	2.8	4.3	1.6	2.1	3.4	5.2	3.5	3.6
PWE	3.6	1.6	8.8	3.2	3.4	1.8	6.0	7.5	0.6	2.6	5.8	0.8	7.2	1.2	1.6	4.6	3.2	3.9	9.8	2.6	3.3	1.2	6.5	4.3	4.9	3.2	3.8	5.6	4.0
ISI	1.4	4.4	3.4	1.4	10.9	4.6	5.1	5.7	0.8	0.9	5.4	2.0	3.0	17.7	5.5	2.6	2.6	9.8	11.7	2.0	4.0	1.2	10.1	6.9	2.3	2.0	4.9	9.3	5.0
COR	0.1	0.4	17.8	11.5	7.7	9.6	0.5	2.2	0.0	1.8	3.2	5.5	14.9	0.0	4.6	8.0	4.6	0.9	7.9	0.6	1.5	3.2	11.7	19.1	5.4	5.0	1.6	0.0	5.3
ICI	5.1	6.4	2.9	5.2	11.1	6.7	4.6	7.9	8.9	5.9	6.4	1.4	5.7	7.5	5.3	2.8	3.7	8.7	12.4	8.8	3.3	4.8	2.8	3.9	3.8	11.3	3.5	8.4	6.0
PIN	3.5	5.2	6.7	13.4	2.8	9.8	3.2	4.3	6.1	7.7	4.8	13.8	7.7	4.3	8.2	7.2	5.2	0.0	3.0	3.2	11.5	13.1	6.1	5.2	8.4	7.4	3.0	11.3	6.7
ATF	2.1	5.0	8.5	5.0	19.5	2.8	9.3	5.4	7.7	6.5	3.9	10.0	7.9	9.7	9.6	7.1	5.3	6.1	11.7	8.6	6.9	10.2	11.9	0.8	7.7	9.6	4.9	8.6	7.6
IEW	5.8	4.1	8.2	3.7	5.1	7.3	9.5	17.9	1.7	3.1	8.1	0.5	15.2	3.6	3.4	7.5	9.7	23.5	11.2	11.3	7.0	4.5	11.9	8.5	4.4	6.9	9.3	10.3	8.0
TRE	11.3	16.0	5.3	12.4	2.8	17.6	13.3	3.6	11.7	17.6	10.7	14.1	9.8	3.6	10.5	13.0	11.7	8.3	3.7	10.2	17.6	6.5	3.1	10.1	10.8	5.4	13.4	11.9	10.2
RLR	23.2	16.1	4.3	5.0	10.2	8.3	10.3	5.6	27.3	19.1	10.5	1.2	3.2	7.0	11.0	4.4	13.2	18.9	5.0	18.0	12.5	13.8	1.8	8.8	13.9	13.5	14.8	6.3	11.0
IGB	21.3	14.6	12.0	21.8	19.4	16.9	10.9	8.5	9.8	11.8	9.0	18.1	6.3	11.9	17.6	18.2	15.6	11.1	14.6	15.5	8.4	19.1	12.9	15.7	16.5	15.2	6.9	10.5	13.9
TRA	20.4	23.7	9.3	11.0	1.7	10.9	20.5	18.1	21.5	19.6	12.1	20.3	10.4	16.7	17.3	17.9	17.8	4.8	4.0	13.1	13.8	18.7	13.0	13.6	18.2	15.1	22.6	10.6	14.9

4 Main Results and Discussion

The input data from Table 1 was analyzed with the software for ICA, developed by Mavrov [12, 13], freely available from the website http://intercriteria.net, [17]. The output represents two tables, Table 2 (a) and (b), for the membership and the non-membership parts of the IFPs, respectively, that stand collectively for the IF consonance / dissonance between any pair of criteria. While the input is objects (28 countries) against criteria (here, 16 MPFDBs), the output is two 16 × 16 matrices. Along the main diagonals of the two tables, all elements of the membership table are 1's and all elements of the non-membership table are 0's thus producing $\langle 0, 1 \rangle$'s as the IFPs, i.e. the intuitionistic fuzzy perfect 'truth', as every criterion correlates perfectly with itself. Also, the two tables are symmetrical according to the main diagonals, since the ICA method mandates that the intercriteria consonance between two criteria C_i and C_j is identical with the intercriteria consonance between C_j and C_i.

We can thus only concentrate on the 120 unique intercriteria pairs. Following the already established practice in the ICA research (see e.g. [5, 7, 9]), we graphically visualise the resultant intercriteria pairs as points on the intuitionistic fuzzy interpretational triangle [4, 8, 11], thus giving perception of what does the respective intuitionistic fuzzy set look like (Fig. 1). Many of the points belong to the hypotenuse (intuitionistic fuzzy values flattened to fuzzy), but also some are inside the triangle, i.e. their uncertainty, or hesitation margin is non-zero.

Table 2. Results of the intercriteria analysis from the input of Table 1: (a) the membership elements of the IF pairs, (b) the non-membership elements of the IF pairs

(a)	Crime and theft	Foreign currency regulations	Poor public health	Inflation	Poor work ethic in national labor force	Government instability/coups	Insufficient capacity to innovate	Policy instability	Tax regulations	Inadequate supply of infrastructure	Corruption	Access to financing	Inefficient government bureaucracy	Inadequately educated workforce	Tax rates	Restrictive labor regulations
CAT	1.000	0.434	0.571	0.526	0.553	0.540	0.365	0.450	0.444	0.503	0.526	0.423	0.376	0.558	0.323	0.288
FCR	0.434	1.000	0.492	0.463	0.442	0.399	0.577	0.397	0.471	0.481	0.397	0.471	0.368	0.405	0.426	0.532
PPH	0.571	0.492	1.000	0.624	0.595	0.627	0.386	0.455	0.402	0.587	0.484	0.521	0.333	0.545	0.431	0.320
INF	0.526	0.463	0.624	1.000	0.861	0.558	0.505	0.283	0.339	0.611	0.407	0.489	0.278	0.722	0.405	0.466
PWE	0.553	0.442	0.595	0.661	1.000	0.492	0.447	0.373	0.368	0.643	0.608	0.481	0.376	0.767	0.339	0.336
GIC	0.540	0.399	0.627	0.558	0.492	1.000	0.344	0.577	0.513	0.542	0.487	0.537	0.413	0.463	0.548	0.328
ICI	0.365	0.577	0.386	0.505	0.447	0.344	1.000	0.352	0.370	0.574	0.376	0.540	0.458	0.519	0.384	0.590
PIN	0.450	0.397	0.455	0.283	0.373	0.577	0.352	1.000	0.630	0.323	0.563	0.503	0.574	0.328	0.511	0.402
TRE	0.444	0.471	0.402	0.339	0.368	0.513	0.370	0.630	1.000	0.323	0.410	0.310	0.492	0.365	0.675	0.579
ISI	0.503	0.481	0.587	0.611	0.643	0.542	0.574	0.323	0.323	1.000	0.516	0.540	0.413	0.669	0.312	0.344
COR	0.526	0.397	0.484	0.407	0.608	0.487	0.376	0.563	0.410	0.516	1.000	0.511	0.601	0.548	0.328	0.262
ATF	0.423	0.471	0.521	0.489	0.481	0.537	0.540	0.503	0.310	0.540	0.511	1.000	0.542	0.476	0.426	0.386
IGB	0.376	0.368	0.333	0.278	0.376	0.413	0.458	0.574	0.492	0.413	0.601	0.542	1.000	0.357	0.505	0.476
IEW	0.558	0.405	0.545	0.722	0.767	0.463	0.519	0.328	0.365	0.669	0.548	0.476	0.357	1.000	0.331	0.399
TRA	0.323	0.426	0.431	0.405	0.339	0.548	0.384	0.511	0.675	0.312	0.328	0.426	0.505	0.331	1.000	0.669
RLR	0.288	0.532	0.320	0.466	0.336	0.328	0.590	0.402	0.579	0.344	0.262	0.386	0.476	0.399	0.669	1.000

(b)	Crime and theft	Foreign currency regulations	Poor public health	Inflation	Poor work ethic in national labor force	Government instability/coups	Insufficient capacity to innovate	Policy instability	Tax regulations	Inadequate supply of infrastructure	Corruption	Access to financing	Inefficient government bureaucracy	Inadequately educated workforce	Tax rates	Restrictive labor regulations
CAT	0.000	0.405	0.288	0.347	0.328	0.349	0.526	0.426	0.439	0.381	0.357	0.468	0.524	0.339	0.574	0.606
FCR	0.405	0.000	0.397	0.439	0.479	0.524	0.360	0.519	0.452	0.447	0.532	0.455	0.566	0.532	0.511	0.402
PPH	0.288	0.397	0.000	0.299	0.336	0.307	0.556	0.476	0.537	0.347	0.450	0.421	0.611	0.402	0.516	0.624
INF	0.347	0.439	0.299	0.000	0.288	0.394	0.455	0.661	0.619	0.341	0.545	0.471	0.685	0.243	0.561	0.497
PWE	0.328	0.479	0.336	0.288	0.000	0.479	0.532	0.590	0.603	0.328	0.362	0.492	0.606	0.217	0.646	0.646
GIC	0.349	0.524	0.307	0.394	0.479	0.000	0.638	0.389	0.460	0.431	0.487	0.439	0.571	0.524	0.439	0.656
ICI	0.526	0.360	0.556	0.455	0.532	0.638	0.000	0.622	0.611	0.407	0.606	0.444	0.534	0.476	0.611	0.402
PIN	0.426	0.519	0.476	0.661	0.590	0.389	0.622	0.000	0.341	0.643	0.402	0.466	0.402	0.651	0.468	0.574
TRE	0.439	0.452	0.537	0.619	0.603	0.460	0.611	0.341	0.000	0.651	0.563	0.667	0.492	0.622	0.312	0.405
ISI	0.381	0.447	0.347	0.341	0.328	0.431	0.407	0.643	0.651	0.000	0.458	0.437	0.571	0.317	0.675	0.640
COR	0.357	0.532	0.450	0.545	0.362	0.487	0.606	0.402	0.563	0.458	0.000	0.466	0.384	0.439	0.659	0.722
ATF	0.468	0.455	0.421	0.471	0.492	0.439	0.444	0.466	0.667	0.437	0.466	0.000	0.444	0.513	0.563	0.601
IGB	0.524	0.566	0.611	0.685	0.606	0.571	0.534	0.402	0.492	0.571	0.384	0.444	0.000	0.640	0.492	0.519
IEW	0.339	0.532	0.402	0.243	0.217	0.524	0.476	0.651	0.622	0.317	0.439	0.513	0.640	0.000	0.669	0.598
TRA	0.574	0.511	0.516	0.561	0.646	0.439	0.611	0.468	0.312	0.675	0.659	0.563	0.492	0.669	0.000	0.328
RLR	0.606	0.402	0.624	0.497	0.646	0.656	0.402	0.574	0.405	0.640	0.722	0.601	0.519	0.598	0.328	0.000

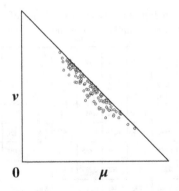

Fig. 1. Results of the InterCriteria Analysis (Table 2 (a, b)) plotted as points on the IF triangle.

In the Table 3 below, we will outline the top 10% of the ICA positive consonance pairs from Table 2.

Table 3. Top 10% of ICA positive consonance pairs, sorted according in ascending order to their distance to $\langle 1, 0 \rangle$

C_i	C_j	μ	v	d
Poor work ethic in national labor force	Inadequately educated workforce	0.767	0.217	0.318
Inflation	Inadequately educated workforce	0.722	0.243	0.369
Inflation	Poor work ethic in national labor force	0.661	0.288	0.445
Tax regulations	Tax rates	0.675	0.312	0.451
Inadequate supply of infrastructure	Inadequately educated workforce	0.669	0.317	0.458
Tax rates	Restrictive labor regulations	0.669	0.328	0.466
Poor public health	Inflation	0.624	0.299	0.480
Poor public health	Government instability/coups	0.627	0.307	0.483
Poor work ethic in national labor force	Inadequate supply of infrastructure	0.643	0.328	0.485
Policy instability	Tax regulations	0.630	0.341	0.504
Crime and theft	Poor public health	0.571	0.288	0.517
Inflation	Inadequate supply of infrastructure	0.611	0.341	0.517

It is noteworthy that the top three pairs are formed between 3 of the 16 factors, 'Poor work ethic in national labor force', 'Inadequately educated work-force' and 'Inflation' with consonances in the IFPs $\langle 0.767; 0.217 \rangle$, $\langle 0.722; 0.243 \rangle$, $\langle 0.661; 0.288 \rangle$, thus forming and intercriteria correlation triple, as described in [6, 14]. However, as we discussed in the previous section, four of the 16 factors, namely, 'Foreign currency regulations', 'Crime and theft', 'Poor public health' and 'Inflation', at least in the context of EU, have little to no weight. Hence, we remove them from the significant detected ICA consonances. On the other hand, four other factors, 'Tax regulations', 'Restrictive labor regulations', 'Inefficient government bureaucracy' and 'Tax rates' are ranked highest among the EU member states. Thus, the other IFPs in the top 10% are 'Tax regulations' and 'Tax rates' ranking with $\langle 0.675; 0.312 \rangle$, 'Tax rates' and 'Restrictive labor regulations' with $\langle 0.669; 0.328 \rangle$, and 'Tax regulations' and 'Policy instability' with $\langle 0.630; 0.341 \rangle$.

5 Conclusion

In the present paper, we apply the method of Inter-Criteria Analysis on the weighted data about the 16 most problematic factors for doing business, measured in the 28 European Union member states, as derived from the 2017–2018 Global Competitiveness Index of the World Economic Forum. The aim of the research is to identify, using this novel intuitionistic fuzzy sets-based method how these sixteen factors are related to each other, which can be indicative of what changes EU and its national economies are subject to if they are to foster their competitiveness and innovation, in the light of the World Economic Forum's traditional appeal to the national policy makers to identify the transformative forces in the national economies and strengthen them to drive future economic growth. While numerous research using the ICA method has been dedicated to the analysis of the twelve pillars of competitiveness in the WEF's methodology over the years, the present leg of research is the first that addresses these most problematic factors for doing business. Although in different annual editions of the Global Competitiveness Index these factors have been formulated with slight variations, and as of the 2018 Global Competitiveness Index v. 4.0, they have been completely dropped out of the report, we consider researching these factors useful and insightful, and encourage the national policy makers to consider the results presented of the detected relations in between them when building the future policies in this regard.

Acknowledgement. This research has been supported by the Bulgarian National Science Fund under Grant Ref. No. KP-06-N22/1/2018 "Theoretical research and applications of InterCriteria Analysis".

References

1. Atanassov, K., Atanassova, V., Gluhchev, G.: Intercriteria analysis: ideas and problems. Notes Intuitionistic Fuzzy Sets **21**(1), 81–88 (2015)
2. Atanassov, K., Mavrov, D., Atanassova, V.: Intercriteria decision making: a new approach for multicriteria decision making, based on index matrices and intuitionistic fuzzy sets. Issues Intuitionistic Fuzzy Sets Generalized Nets **11**, 1–8 (2014). ISBN: 978-83-61551-10-2
3. Atanassov, K., Szmidt, E., Kacprzyk, J.: On intuitionistic fuzzy pairs. Notes Intuitionistic Fuzzy Sets **19**(3), 1–13 (2013)
4. Atanassova, V.: Interpretation in the intuitionistic fuzzy triangle of the results, obtained by the intercriteria analysis. In: 16th World Congress of the International Fuzzy Systems Association (IFSA), 9th Conference of the European Society for Fuzzy Logic and Technology (EUSFLAT) 2015, Gijon, Spain, vol. 1369–1374, 30 June–03 July 2015. https://doi.org/10.2991/ifsa-eusflat-15.2015.193

5. Atanassova, V., Doukovska, L., Atanassov, K., Mavrov, D.: Intercriteria decision making approach to EU member states competitiveness analysis. In: Proceedings of the International Symposium on Business Modeling and Software Design – BMSD 2014, Luxembourg, pp. 289–294, 24–26 June 2014. https://doi.org/10.5220/0005427302890294

6. Atanassova, V., Doukovska, L., Michalikova, A., Radeva, I.: Intercriteria analysis: from pairs to triples. Notes Intuitionistic Fuzzy Sets 22(5), 98–110 (2016)

7. Atanassova, V., Doukovska, L., de Tre, G., Radeva, I.: Intercriteria analysis and comparison of innovation-driven and efficiency-to-innovation driven economies in the European Union. Notes Intuitionistic Fuzzy Sets 23(3), 54–68 (2017)

8. Atanassova, V., Vardeva, I., Sotirova, E., Doukovska, L.: Traversing and ranking of elements of an intuitionistic fuzzy set in the intuitionistic fuzzy interpretation triangle, chapter, novel developments in uncertainty representation and processing. Adv. Intell. Syst. Comput. 401, 161–174 (2016)

9. Doukovska, L., Atanassova, V., Sotirova, E.: European union member states' performance in the 2018 global competitiveness index 4.0 through the prism of intercriteria analysis. In: Proceedings of the 4th International Conference on Numerical and Symbolic Computation Developments and Applications, Porto, Portugal, pp. 11–12 April 2019. (accepted)

10. Doukovska, L., Atanassova, V., Sotirova, E., Vardeva, I., Radeva, I.: Defining consonance thresholds in intercriteria analysis: an overview. In: Hadjiski, M., Atanassov, K.T. (eds.) Intuitionistic Fuzziness and Other Intelligent Theories and Their Applications. SCI, vol. 757, pp. 161–179. Springer, Cham (2019). https://doi.org/10.1007/978-3-319-78931-6_11

11. Mavrov, D., Radeva, I., Atanassov, K., Doukovska, L., Kalaykov, I.: Intercriteria software design: graphic interpretation within the intuitionistic fuzzy triangle. In: Proceedings of the Fifth International Symposium on Business Modeling and Software Design, pp. 279–283 (2015)

12. Mavrov, D.: Software for intercriteria analysis: implementation of the main algorithm. Notes Intuitionistic Fuzzy Sets 21(2), 77–86 (2015)

13. Mavrov, D.: Software for intercriteria analysis: working with the results. Ann. "Inform." Sect. Union Scientists Bulgaria. 8, 37–44 (2015–2016)

14. Roeva,O., Pencheva, T., Angelova, M., Vassilev, P.: Intercriteria analysis by pairs and triples of genetic algorithms application for models identification. In: Recent Advances in Computational Optimization. Studies in Computational Intelligence, vol. 655, pp. 193–218 (2016). https://doi.org/10.1007/978-3-319-40132-4_12

15. Schwab, K.: The Global Competitiveness Report 2017–2018, World Economic Forum. ISBN-13: 978-1-944835-11-8. https://www.weforum.org/reports/the-global-competitivenes s-report-2017-2018

16. Schwab, K.: The Global Competitiveness Report 2018, World Economic Forum. ISBN-13: 978-92-95044-76-0. http://reports.weforum.org/global-competitiveness-report-2018/

17. InterCriteria Research Portal. http://intercriteria.net/publications/

An Effective System for User
Queries Assistance

Elio Masciari[1], Domenico Saccà[2], and Irina Trubitsyna[2(✉)]

[1] Federico II University of Naples, Naples, Italy
elio.masciari@unina.it
[2] DIMES-Università della Calabria, 87036 Rende (CS), Italy
{sacca,trubitsyna}@dimes.unical.it

Abstract. The Big Data paradigm has recently come on scene in a quite pervasive manner. Sifting through massive amounts of this kind of data, parsing them, transferring them from a source to a target database, and analyzing them to improve business decision-making processes is too complex for traditional approaches. In this respect, there have been recent proposals that enrich data while exchanging them, such as the Data Posting framework. This framework requires the ability of using domain relations and count constraints, which may be difficult to manage for non-expert users. In this paper, we propose *Smart Data Posting*, a framework using intuitive constructs that are automatically translated in the standard Data Posting framework. In particular, we allow the use of *smart mapping rules* extended with additional selection criteria and the direct use of tuple generating dependencies and equality generating dependences. We present a complexity analysis of the framework and describe the architecture of a system for advanced search, tailored for Big Data, that implements the Smart Data Posting framework.

1 Introduction

Big Data paradigm [1,10,25] recently come on scene in a quite pervasive manner, however this apparently sudden change of perspective had a long history before the term *Big Data* was coined. Indeed, both industry and research people have been entrenched in (big) data that have been stored in massive amounts, with an increasing speed and exhibiting a huge variety for over a decade before the Big Data paradigm was *officially* born. The major challenge has always been to unveil valuable insights for the industry to which that particular data belonged.

As a matter of fact, sifting through all of that data, parsing it, transferring it from a source to a target database, and analyzing all of it for purposes of improving business decision-making processes turn to be too complex for traditional approaches. In this respect, recent proposals have been made for enriching data while exchanging them like the Data Posting framework.

One of the most important features of Data Posting recently introduced in [8] is the improvement of data exchange between the sources and the target database. The idea is to adapt the well-known Data Exchange techniques to

A. Cuzzocrea et al. (Eds.): FQAS 2019, LNAI 11529, pp. 361–373, 2019.
https://doi.org/10.1007/978-3-030-27629-4_33

the new Big Data management and analysis challenges we find in real world scenarios. The *Data Posting setting* consists of a source and a domain database schemes, a target flat fact table, a set of source-to-target mapping rules and a set of target constraints. The *data posting problem* associated with this setting is: given finite source and domain database instances, find a finite instance for the target fact table that satisfies the internal integrity constraints and the mapping requirements. Data Posting approach use non-deterministic variables instead of the existentially quantified ones in the mapping rules (the so called, Source to Target Generating Dependencies). The values for the non-deterministic variables can be chosen non deterministically from the finite domain relation following the strategy indicated in the framework by using the target count constraints [23]. Obviously, the solution of the data posting problem could not be universal as it represents a specific choice. However, it is worth noticing that, in the context of Big Data we are often interested in the discovery of new knowledge and the overall analysis of the data, moreover some attributes of the target tables may be created for storing the discovered values. Thus, the choice of concrete values can be seen as a first phase of data analysis that solves uncertainties by enriching the information contents of the whole system. Consider the following application scenario that we will use as running example.

Example 1. The source database describes the objects by relation $R_S(I, P, V)$ with attributes I (object's identifier), N (property name) and V (value). The main problems in the data posting scenario are:

1. Extract the information about objects' compatibility in the source and target databases. This task can be considered as a kind of soft-clustering that aims at grouping similar objects.
2. Identify "relevant" properties and their values to be extracted in the target database. The strategy to be applied has to take into account two different needs: (i) decide if the property is relevant and (ii) select its value.

Suppose that we extract the information about objects' compatibility into a relation $C(I_T, I_S, L)$, where the first two attributes are object's identifiers and L is the level of compatibility. In order to enrich the target relation R_T with some "relevant" properties from S we can set the following strategy: *The combination property-value (n, v) taken from R_S is "relevant" to the target object with identifier I_T if the following conditions hold: (1) it occurs frequently, i.e. it belongs to at least 20 source objects with compatibility towards i_T at least 0.6; (2) for the same property only the most frequent value must be considered as "relevant".*

The description of this scenario with the standard data posting constructs can be done as follows. We can define an unary domain relation $\mathcal{D}$ containing only values 0, 1, and −1 and the target relations A and Rel described below.

- $A(I_T, I_S, N, V)$ stores the information of objects from R_S, whose compatibility level with the target object with identifier I_T is at least 0.6.
- $Rel(I_T, N, V, Flag)$ stores for each target object with identifier I_T the combinations property-value $\langle N, V \rangle$ and the flag Flag whose value has the following meaning:

−1 the combination $\langle N, V \rangle$ is not relevant, as it does not occur frequently in R_S;

0 the combination $\langle N, V \rangle$ is not relevant, although it occurs frequently in R_S, the value V is is not the most frequent one;

1 the combination $\langle N, V \rangle$ is relevant, as it occurs frequently and the value V is the most frequent value.

The source to target dependencies are

$$R_S(i_T, n, v) \wedge C(i_T, i_S, 1) \wedge 1 \geq 0.6 \rightarrow A(i_T, i_S, n, v)$$
$$R_S(i_T, n, v) \wedge C(i_T, i_S, 1) \wedge 1 \geq 0.6 \wedge \mathcal{D}(\texttt{flag}) \rightarrow \texttt{Rel}(i_T, n, v, \texttt{flag})$$

where all variables are universally quantified. Since $\mathcal{D}$ is domain relation, only one value between -1, 0 and 1 can be chosen as the flag value for each triple (i_T, n, v) in the relation Rel.

The following count constrains set the selection criteria:

$$\texttt{Rel}(i_T, n, v, 1) \rightarrow \#(\{\, I_S : A(i_T, I_S, n, v) \,\}) \geq 20$$
$$\texttt{Rel}(i_T, n, v, 0) \rightarrow \#(\{\, I_S : A(i_T, I_S, n, v) \,\}) \geq 20$$
$$\texttt{Rel}(i_1, n_2, v_2, -1) \rightarrow \#(\{\, I_S : A(i_T, I_S, n, v) \,\}) < 20$$
$$\texttt{Rel}(i_T, n, v, 1), \texttt{Rel}(i_1, n, v', 0) \rightarrow$$
$$\#(\{\, I_S : A(i_T, I_S, n, v) \,\}) \geq \#(\{\, I_S : A(i_T, I_S, n, v') \,\})$$

Intuitively, I_S is a count variable. The first three constraints establish frequently occurring combinations $\langle i_T, n, v \rangle$ in the relation A. The last constraint indicates that for the same property only the most frequent value must be considered as "relevant".   □

As shown in the example above, the data posting setting requires the ability to manage domain relations and count constraints. Recently, in [18,19], the use of *smart mapping rules* to support user suggestion in a big data environment has been proposed. The extraction of source data can be performed with *smart mapping rules* that allow us to express the selection criteria in a simple and intuitive way, thus avoiding the direct use of count constraints. In this paper we further investigate this idea and present a new version of data posting framework, called Smart Data Posting. In particular, we extend the selection conditions in the smart mapping rules and allow the direct use of Tuple Generating Dependencies (TGDs) and Equality Generating Dependencies (EGDs). The new framework simplifies the process of modelling by means of intuitive constructs that are automatically translated in the standard framework.

For instance, our running scenario can be modelled as follows: R_S and C are source relations; $\texttt{Rel}(I, N, V)$ is the target relation; the smart mapping rule is reported below:

$$R_S(i_S, n, v) \wedge C(i_T, i_S, 1) \wedge 1 \geq 0.6 \xrightarrow{\;i_S, 20, \langle v, \max \rangle\;} \texttt{Rel}(i_T, n, v)$$

Intuitively, the body of the rule takes the objects with compatibility level at least 0.6, the selection criterion has been synthesized on the arrow, indicating

(i) the count variable i$_S$, (ii) the minimum value of counting 20, and (iii) the variable v whose value should be the most frequent one (indication "*max*").

In the new framework we can also indicate that the property of any object must have a particular number of values. For instance, by changing the indication "*max*" in "*unique*" in the mapping rule we indicate that exactly one value is allowed. By changing the indication "*max*" in "*at least 2* ∧*at most 3*" in the mapping rule we indicate that the number of values may be 2 or 3.

Observe that the use of the smart mapping rules simplifies the implementation of the data posting setting in practice. The smart mapping rules, or similar formalism can be also profitable used in different logic-based settings (e.g., P2P Deductive Databases [6,7], prioritized reasoning in logic programming [5,16,24], efficient evaluation of logic programs [12,13], etc.).

Plan of the Paper. In the following, in Sect. 2 we describe the background of our approach. In Sect. 3 we present the Smart Data Posting framework. In Sect. 4 we describe the System for User Queries Assistance. Finally, in Sect. 5 we will draw our conclusion.

2   Background

Data Exchange. Data exchange [2,11] is the problem of migrating a data instance from a source schema to a target schema such that the materialized data on the target schema satisfies a number of given integrity constraints (mainly inclusion and functional dependencies). The integrity constraints are specified by TGDs (Tuple Generating Dependencies) and EGDs (Equality Generating Dependencies). *TGDs* are formulas of the form: $\forall \mathbf{x}[\phi(\mathbf{x}) \rightarrow \exists \mathbf{y} \ \psi(\mathbf{x}, \mathbf{y})]$, where $\phi(\mathbf{x})$ and $\psi(\mathbf{x}, \mathbf{y})$ are conjunctions of literals, and $\mathbf{x}, \mathbf{y}$ are lists of variables. Full TGDs are TGDs without existentially quantified variables. *EGDs* are formulas of the form: $\forall \mathbf{x}[\phi(\mathbf{x}) \rightarrow x_1 = x_2]$ where $\phi(\mathbf{x})$ is conjunctions of literals, while x_1 and x_2 are variables in $\mathbf{x}$. In the following we will often omit the universal quantifiers, when their presence is clear from the context.

The classical data exchange setting is: $(S, T, \Sigma_{ST}, \Sigma_T)$, where S is the source relational database schema, T is the target schema, Σ_T are dependencies on the target scheme T and Σ_{ST} are source-to-target dependencies. The dependencies in Σ_{ST} map data from the source to the target schema and are TGDs of the form $\forall \mathbf{x}(\phi_S(\mathbf{x}) \rightarrow \exists \mathbf{y} \ \psi_T(\mathbf{x}, \mathbf{y}))$, where $\phi_S(\mathbf{x})$ and $\psi_T(\mathbf{x}, \mathbf{y})$ are conjunctions of literals on S and T, respectively. Dependencies in Σ_T specify constraints on the target schema and can be either TGDs or EGDs.

The computation of an universal solution (the compact representation of all possible solutions) can be done by means of the fixpoint chase algorithm, when it terminates [9]. The execution of the chase involves inserting tuples possibly with null values to satisfy TGDs, and replacing null values with constants or other null values to satisfy EGDs. Specifically, the chase consists of applying a sequence of steps, where each step enforces a dependency that is not satisfied by the current instance. It might well be the case that multiple dependencies can be enforced and, in this case, the chase picks one non deterministically. Different choices lead to different sequences, some of which might be terminating, while others might not. Unfortunately, checking whether the chase terminates is an undecidable problem [9]. To cope with this issue, several "termination criteria" have been proposed, that is, (decidable) sufficient conditions ensuring chase termination [3,4,14,15,20,21].

Data Posting. The data posting framework [8] adapts the well-known data exchange techniques to the new Big Data management and analysis challenges we find in real world scenarios. The *data posting setting* $(\mathbf{S}, \mathcal{D}, \mathbf{T}, \Sigma_{st}, \Sigma_t)$ consists of a finite source database schema $\mathbf{S}$, a finite domain database scheme $\mathcal{D}$, a target schema $\mathbf{T}$, a set Σ_{st} of non-deterministic source-to-target TGDs and a set Σ_t of target count constraints. A *non-deterministic source-to-target TGD (NdTGD)* is a dependency over $\langle \mathbf{S}, \mathcal{D}, \mathbf{T} \rangle$ of the form $\forall \mathbf{x} [\phi_S(\mathbf{x} \cup \tilde{\mathbf{y}}) \rightarrow \phi_T(\mathbf{z})]$, where $\mathbf{x}$ and $\mathbf{z}$ are lists of universally quantified variables; $\tilde{\mathbf{y}}$ is a (possibly empty) list of variables, called *non deterministic*, these variables can occur in ϕ_S only in relations from $\mathcal{D}$; $\mathbf{x} \cap \tilde{\mathbf{y}} = \emptyset$ and $\mathbf{z} \subseteq \mathbf{x} \cup \tilde{\mathbf{y}}$; the formula ϕ_S and ψ_T are conjunctions of atoms with predicate symbols in $\mathbf{S} \cup \mathcal{D}$ and in $\mathbf{T}$, respectively. The structure of NdTGDs ensures that any target database on $\mathbf{T}$ is finite.

The NdTGD can be seen as the standard TGD, where existentially quantified variables are replaced with non-deterministic variables, whose values can be chosen from the finite domains defined by domain relations, i.e. relations from $\mathcal{D}$. The mapping process is performed as usual but presumes that for every assignment of $\mathbf{x}$ a subset of all admissible values for $\tilde{\mathbf{y}}$ can be chosen in an arbitrary way. As an example, consider the source relation $\mathtt{objs}$ and the domain relation $\mathcal{D}$ reporting all possible characterizations of objects, whose instances contains tuples $\mathtt{obj_s}(r)$, where r denotes a restaurant, and $\{\mathcal{D}(r, \mathtt{fish}), \mathcal{D}(r, \mathtt{meet}), \mathcal{D}(r, \mathtt{expensive}), \mathcal{D}(r, \mathtt{cheap})\}$, respectively. The NdTGD $\mathtt{objs}(n) \wedge \mathcal{D}(n, v) \rightarrow \mathtt{dscr_T}(n, v)$ can be used to assign characterization to the objects choosing them from the domain relation $\mathcal{D}$ non-deterministically. For instance, the mapping can produce the target instances $\{\mathtt{dscr_T}(r, \mathtt{fish}), (\mathtt{dscr_T}(r, \mathtt{cheap})\}$ or $\{\mathtt{dscr_T}(r, \mathtt{meat})\}$, but cannot produce $\{\mathtt{dscr_T}(r, \mathtt{green})\}$.

A *count constraint* is a dependency over $\mathbf{T}$ of the form $\forall \mathbf{x} [\phi_T(\mathbf{x}) \rightarrow \#(\{\mathbf{Y} : \exists \mathbf{z}\, \alpha(\mathbf{x}, \mathbf{Y}, \mathbf{z})\})$ <op> $\beta(\mathbf{x}))]$, where ϕ_T is a conjunction of atoms with predicate symbol in $\mathbf{T}$, <op> is any of the comparison operators $(=, >, \geq, <$ and $\leq)$, $H = \{\mathbf{Y} : \exists \mathbf{z}\, \alpha(\mathbf{x}, \mathbf{Y}, \mathbf{z})\}$ is a *set term*, $\#$ is an interpreted function symbol that computes the cardinality of the (possibly empty) set corresponding to H, $\#(H)$ is *count term*, and $\beta(\mathbf{x})$ is an integer or a variable in $\mathbf{x}$ or another count term with universally quantified variables in $\mathbf{x}$. The lists $\mathbf{x}$, $\mathbf{Y}$ and $\mathbf{z}$ do not share variables, $\alpha(\mathbf{x}, \mathbf{Y}, \mathbf{z})$ is a conjunction of atoms $T_i(\mathbf{x}, \mathbf{Y}, \mathbf{z})$ with $T_i \in \mathbf{T}$.

Let I_T be the instance of $\mathbf{T}$. The *active domain* AD_I is the set of all values occurring in I_T. Given a substitution $\mathbf{x}/\mathbf{v}$ assigning values in AD_I to universally quantified variables, $K_{\mathbf{v}} = \{\mathbf{Y} : \exists \mathbf{z}\, \alpha(\mathbf{v}, \mathbf{Y}, \mathbf{z})\}$ defines the set of values in AD_I assigned to the free variables in $\mathbf{Y}$ for which $\exists \mathbf{z}\, \alpha(\mathbf{v}, \mathbf{Y}, \mathbf{z})$ is satisfied by I_T and $\#(K_{\mathbf{v}})$ is the cardinality of this set. We say that I_T satisfies the count constraint if each substitution $\mathbf{x}/\mathbf{v}$ that makes true its body expression, makes also true its head expression. As an example, the count constraint $\mathtt{obj_T(n)} \rightarrow \#(\{V : \mathtt{dscr(n, V)}\}) = 2)$ states that every object must have exactly 2 characterizations.

The *data posting problem* is defined as follows: given finite source instance I_S and finite domain instance $I_{\mathcal{D}}$, find a finite target instance I_T, such that $\langle I_S, I_{\mathcal{D}}, I_T \rangle$ satisfies both Σ_{st} and Σ_t. This problem is $\mathcal{NP}$-complete under the data complexity. In the case than Σ_{st} does not contains non-deterministic variables, the data posting problem becomes polynomial.

3 Smart Data Posting

The Smart Data Posting setting is based on the idea that the standard source to target dependencies can be enriched with the selection criterion regarding the local exchange process. The obtained dependencies, that we call *smart mapping rules*, are expressive enough for different practical application and can be profitably used for simplifying and optimizing the standard Data Posting setting.

Definition 1. A *smart mapping rule* is of the form:

$$\forall \mathbf{z}[\ \phi(\mathbf{z}) \xrightarrow{\mathbf{y},k,\langle \mathbf{v},f \rangle} r(\mathbf{x}, \mathbf{v}) \ ]$$

where $\mathbf{x}, \mathbf{y}, \mathbf{z}, \mathbf{v}$ are vectors of variables, such that $\mathbf{x} \cup \mathbf{y} \cup \mathbf{v} \subseteq \mathbf{z}$ and $\mathbf{x}, \mathbf{y}$ and $\mathbf{v}$ do not share the variables; ϕ_S is the conjunction of literals and expressions involving comparison operators $(>, <, \geq, \leq, =, \neq)$ and variables in $\mathbf{z}$ or constants; r is a target relation; $\mathbf{y}$ is called a *support vector*; k is a natural number (greater than 1) which indicates the support value; $\mathbf{y}$ and k may be omitted together. The pair $\langle \mathbf{v}, f \rangle$ indicates how the choice for the values of $\mathbf{v}$ should be performed: f can be *"max"*, *"unique"*, *"exactly m"*, *"at most m"*, and *"at least l"* where m and l are natural numbers, $m > 1$, $l > 0$, or the conjunctions *"unique $\wedge$ max"*, *"exactly m $\wedge$ max"* , or the conjunction composed by *"at most m"*, *"at least l"* and *"max"*. The pair $\langle \mathbf{v}, f \rangle$ may be omitted.   □

Semantics. The smart mapping rule specifies that the tuple $\langle \mathbf{X}, \mathbf{V} \rangle$ is added to r only if it is supported by at least k (different) initializations $\{\mathbf{Y}_1, ... \mathbf{Y}_k\}$ of $\mathbf{y}$, i.e. for each $j \in [1..k]$ there exists an initialization $\mathbf{Z}_j$ of $\mathbf{z}$, that maps $\mathbf{x}, \mathbf{y}$ e $\mathbf{v}$ in $\mathbf{X}, \mathbf{Y}_j$ and $\mathbf{V}$ respectively, and that makes true $\phi(\mathbf{Z}_j)$. If both $\mathbf{y}$ and k are omitted, all initialization satisfying the body satisfy this first check.

In the case than no further indications of choice are specified (the third arrow label is omitted) all the tuples satisfying the first check are added to r. Otherwise, the set of tuples to be added is further reduced using f content for the selection of values in $\mathbf{v}$. For each assignment of values in $\mathbf{x}$ the indication

- *"max"* specifies that only tuples supported by a maximum number of initializations of $\mathbf{y}$ must be selected;
- *"unique"* specifies that the assignment of values in $\mathbf{v}$ must be unique;

– *"exactly m"* (resp., *"at most m"*, *"at least m"*) specifies that exactly (resp., at most, at least) m possible different assignments can be selected for **v**.

When several choices of tuples satisfy the indications *"unique"*, *"exactly m"*, *"at most m"*, and *"at least n"*, the selection among alternatives can be done arbitrarily.

The indications *"unique"* and *"exactly (resp., at most, at least) m"* cannot be applied together, but can be combined with *"max"*. The indications *"at most m"*, *"at least l"* and *"max"* can be combined.

Example 2. Consider again our running Example 1. Below we report some selection strategies and the corresponding smart mapping rules.

1. The relevant properties for the target object are the properties $\langle n, v \rangle$ "supported" by at least 7 source objects with compatibility level at least 0.9 towards it.

$$R_S(i_S, n, v) \wedge C(i_T, i_S, 1) \wedge 1 \geq 0.9 \xrightarrow{i_S, 7} Rel(i_T, n, v)$$

2. The relevant properties for the target object are those present in the source objects with compatibility level at least 0.5 towards it. Exactly three distinct values must be selected (arbitrarily) for the property of any object.

$$R_S(i_S, n, v) \wedge C(i_T, i_S, 1) \wedge 1 \geq 0.5 \xrightarrow{\langle v, \text{exactly } 3 \rangle} Rel(i_T, n, v)$$

□

We will call smart mapping rules *non-trivial* if the arrow has has at least one label, and *trivial* otherwise. Obviously, trivial mapping rules correspond to full TGDs.

Definition 2. *The Smart Data Posting setting $(S, T, \Sigma_{ST}, \Sigma_T)$ consists of a source and a target database schemes S and T, a set Σ_T of TGDs, EGDs and count constraints involving only target relations, and a set Σ_{ST} of smart mapping rules of the form $\forall \mathbf{z}[\ \phi_S(\mathbf{z}) \xrightarrow{y, k, \langle v, f \rangle} r(\mathbf{x}, \mathbf{v})\ ]$, where ϕ_S denotes the conjunction of source relations and r is target relation. Each target relation can be defined by exactly one non-trivial mapping rule or by any number of trivial mapping rules.*

The data posting problem associated with this setting is: given a finite source instance I_S for S, find a finite instance I_T of T such that $\langle I_S, I_T \rangle$ satisfies $\Sigma_{ST} \cup \Sigma_T$. □

The semantic of the Smart Data Posting setting can be done in terms of the standard Data Posting setting. In particular, we start traducing every non-trivial mapping rule ρ of the form $\forall \mathbf{z}[\ \phi_S(\mathbf{z}) \xrightarrow{y, k, \langle v, f \rangle} r(\mathbf{x}, \mathbf{v})\ ]$ into the constructs of the standard setting as follows.

We introduce the unary domain relation $\mathcal{D}_\rho$. If $\langle v, f \rangle$ is omitted, $\mathcal{D}_\rho$ contains values -1 and 1, otherwise $\mathcal{D}_\rho$ contains values -1, 0 and 1. We also introduce the target relations $A_\rho(\mathbf{X}, \mathbf{Y}, \mathbf{V})$ and $Rel_\rho(\mathbf{X}, \mathbf{V}, Flag)$, where $\mathbf{X}$, $\mathbf{Y}$ and $\mathbf{V}$ represent vectors of attributes corresponding to the vectors of variables $\mathbf{x}$, $\mathbf{y}$ e $\mathbf{v}$, respectively, while the decision weather to select the pair $\langle \mathbf{x}, \mathbf{v} \rangle$ in the target relation r is stored by the attribute $Flag$: -1 or 0 (not added) and 1 (added).

The set of source to target dependencies is enriched with the following rules:

$$\phi_S(\mathbf{z}) \rightarrow A_\rho(\mathbf{x}, \mathbf{y}, \mathbf{v})$$
$$\phi_S(\mathbf{z}) \wedge \mathcal{D}_\rho(\texttt{flag}) \rightarrow \texttt{Rel}_\rho(\mathbf{x}, \mathbf{v}, \texttt{flag})$$

The set of target count constraints is modified as follows. First, we traduce all TGDs and EGDs in terms of count constraints:

- the TGD of the form $\forall \mathbf{x}[\,\phi_S(\mathbf{x}) \rightarrow \exists \mathbf{y}\ \psi_T(\mathbf{x}, \mathbf{y})\,]$ corresponds to:

$$\forall \mathbf{x}[\,\phi_S(\mathbf{x}) \rightarrow \#(\{\mathbf{Y} : \psi_T(\mathbf{x}, \mathbf{Y})\}) \geq 1\,]$$

- the full TGD $\forall \mathbf{x}[\,\phi_S(\mathbf{x}) \rightarrow \psi_T(\mathbf{x})\,]$ can be formulated by the count constraint:

$$\forall \mathbf{x}[\,\phi_S(\mathbf{x}) \rightarrow \#(\{\mathbf{Y} : \psi_T(\mathbf{z}) \wedge \mathbf{x} = \mathbf{Y} \wedge \mathbf{z} = \mathbf{Y}\}) = 1\,]$$

where vectors $\mathbf{x}$, $\mathbf{Y}$, and $\mathbf{z}$ have the same cardinality and do not share variables;

- the EGD of the form $\forall \mathbf{x}[\,\phi(\mathbf{x}) \rightarrow x_1 = x_2\,]$, where $x_1, x_2 \in \mathbf{x}$ corresponds to:

$$\forall \mathbf{x}\,[\,\phi(\mathbf{x}) \rightarrow \#(\{Y : Y = x_1 \wedge Y = x_2\}) = 1\,]$$

where Y is a new variable not included in $\mathbf{x}$.

Next, we replace every occurrence of $r(\mathbf{z})$ with $\texttt{Rel}_\rho(\mathbf{z}, 1)$. Finally, we add the set of constraints that allow to establish the flag value:

1. We start by adding *support constraints*, that ensure that the value -1 is assigned to the variable *flag* iff the degree of support of the combination $\langle \mathbf{x}, \mathbf{v} \rangle$ does not reach k. First, we add constraint for values 1 and -1.

$$\texttt{Rel}_\rho(\mathbf{x}, \mathbf{v}, 1) \rightarrow \#(\{\mathbf{Y} : A_\rho(\mathbf{x}, \mathbf{Y}, \mathbf{v})\}) \geq k$$
$$\texttt{Rel}_\rho(\mathbf{x}, \mathbf{v}, -1) \rightarrow \#(\{\mathbf{Y} : A_\rho(\mathbf{x}, \mathbf{Y}, \mathbf{v})\}) < k$$

If $\langle \mathbf{v}, f \rangle$ is not omitted, we also add constraint for value 0:

$$\texttt{Rel}_\rho(\mathbf{x}, \mathbf{v}, 0) \rightarrow \#(\{\mathbf{Y} : A_\rho(\mathbf{x}, \mathbf{Y}, \mathbf{v})\}) \geq k$$

2. When $f =$ "*unique*" the *uniqueness choice constraint* is added:

$$\texttt{Rel}_\rho(\mathbf{x}, \_, \texttt{flag}) \wedge \texttt{flag} \geq 0 \rightarrow \#(\{\mathbf{V} : \texttt{Rel}_\rho(\mathbf{x}, \mathbf{V}, 1)\}) = 1$$

3. When $f =$ "*exactly m*" the *m-choice constraints* is added:

$$\texttt{Rel}_\rho(\mathbf{x}, \_, \texttt{flag}) \wedge \texttt{flag} \geq 0 \rightarrow \#(\{\mathbf{V} : \texttt{Rel}_\rho(\mathbf{x}, \mathbf{V}, 1)\}) = \mathtt{m}$$

4. When $f = $"*at most m*" the *at-most constraints* is added:

$$\text{Rel}_\rho(\mathbf{x}, \_, \text{flag}) \wedge \text{flag} \geq 0 \rightarrow \#(\{\mathbf{V} : \text{Rel}_\rho(\mathbf{x}, \mathbf{V}, 1)\}) \leq \mathbf{m}$$

5. When $f = $"*at least m*" the *at-least constraints* are added:

$$\text{Rel}_\rho(\mathbf{x}, \_, \text{flag}) \wedge \text{flag} \geq 0 \rightarrow \#(\{\mathbf{V} : \text{Rel}_\rho(\mathbf{x}, \mathbf{V}, 1)\}) \geq \mathbf{m}$$

6. When $f = $"*max*" we add (i) the *optimization constraint*

$$\text{Rel}_\rho(\mathbf{x}, \mathbf{v}, 1), \text{Rel}_\rho(\mathbf{x}, \mathbf{v}', 0) \rightarrow \#(\{\mathbf{Y} : \text{A}_\rho(\mathbf{x}, \mathbf{Y}, \mathbf{v})\}) \geq \#(\{\mathbf{Y} : \text{A}_\rho(\mathbf{x}, \mathbf{Y}, \mathbf{v}')\})$$

(ii) the *at-least constraint*, ensuring the selection of at least one initialization of $\mathbf{v}$ for each $\mathbf{X}$

$$\text{Rel}_\rho(\mathbf{x}, \_, \text{flag}) \wedge \text{flag} \geq 0 \rightarrow \#(\{\mathbf{V} : \text{Rel}_\rho(\mathbf{x}, \mathbf{V}, 1)\}) \geq 1$$

7. When $f = $"*unique* $\wedge$*max*" (resp. $f = $"*exactly m* $\wedge$*max*") we add the *uniqueness choice* (resp. *m-choice*) constraint and the *optimization constraint*.
8. When f is a combination of "*max*", "*at least m*" and "*at most m*" indications we add the corresponding combination of the *optimization*, *at-least* and *at-most* constraints.

Observe that the presented framework extends the one proposed in [19] with additional conditions and the direct use of TGDs and EGDs. The complexity results presented below follow from similar results provided in [19].

Theorem 1. *Given a Smart Data Posting setting* $(S, T, \Sigma_{ST}, \Sigma_T)$ *and a finite source instance* I_S *for* S, *the problem of deciding whether there exists a finite instance* I_T *of* T *such that* $\langle I_S, I_T \rangle$ *satisfies* $\Sigma_{ST} \cup \Sigma_T$ *is* $\mathcal{NP}$-*complete under the data complexity.* $\qquad\square$

The Smart Data Posting setting is called *semi-deterministic* if the *non determinism* in the data posting process *is locally-resolvable*, i.e. if the mapping rules having a label of the form $\langle v, f \rangle$ do not define target relations involved in Σ_T.

Theorem 2. *Given a semi-deterministic Smart Data Posting setting* $(S, T, \Sigma_{ST}, \Sigma_T)$ *and a finite source instance* I_S *for* S, *the problem of deciding whether there exists a finite instance* I_T *of* T *such that* $\langle I_S, I_T \rangle$ *satisfies* $\Sigma \cup \Sigma_T$ *is polynomial under the data complexity.*

Corollary 1. *Let* $(S, T, \Sigma_{ST}, \emptyset)$ *be a Smart Data Posting setting and* I_S *be a finite source instance for* S. *When a finite instance* I_T *of* T *such that* $\langle I_S, I_T \rangle$ *satisfies* Σ_{ST} *exists, it can be found in polynomial time (under the data complexity).*

4   Our System in a Nutshell

In this section we provide an high-level description of our System for User Queries Assistance that implements the smart data posting framework described in previous sections. In Fig. 1, we depict the overall process of information analysis, enrichment and delivery to the final user.

Data about user activities and interactions with heterogeneous systems, e.g. a social network, are collected by our *Big Data Storage System*, which performs the following preliminary operations: (i) it first computes some high level statistics about user search (e.g. most frequent search keywords) that will be refined during the information analysis and enrichment steps; (ii) it stores all the collected data in a staging area to overcome potential problems due to different speed, size and format of incoming data; (iii) it performs the proper extraction, transformation and loading operations for making data well suited for efficient storage (space saving) and analysis (fast execution time); (iv) finally, it stores the pre-processed data in a structure tailored for Big Data.

After data pre-elaboration takes place, we go through the *Smart Data Posting* layer, which includes three sub-modules. The first one is based on a suite of clustering algorithms that are devoted to the extraction of unsupervised information hidden in the collected data. The obtained clusters, are filtered by an evaluation module that identifies the dimensions exhibiting the potential to spread across the user network activities. After this filtering step, high level information will be used by the smart data posting module to enrich information sources. We stress that data posting differs from classical data exchange because, while moving data, the contents are enriched by supplying additional pieces of information. To this end, a source database is linked with additional tables, called *domain relations*, that store the dimensions to be added into the target database and aggregate data dependencies (in particular, count constraints) are used to select dimension values that better characterize the scenario being analyzed. We observe that the dimension-based structure of a target database can be

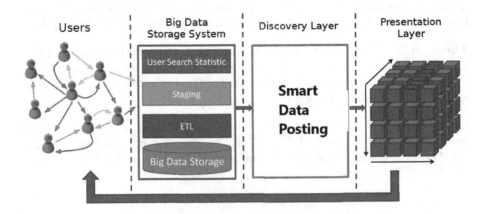

Fig. 1. Our system for user queries assistance

effectively supported by a column-based Big Data storage system – actually, in our implementation we used HBase [22].

Finally the *Presentation Layer* is used to personalize the enriched information for the current user query and to present portions of it (dimensions) into the search toolbar that are pertinent with entered keywords for enabling a kind of faceted browsing.

It is worth noticing that, in our architecture, Smart Data Posting considers the information extracted by the clustering algorithm and tries to derive new dimensions that could be added to the initial domain scheme while preserving the information richness. Moreover, commonly used search engines do not exploit such a refined information. Finally, we take into account the *count constraints* deriving from the data. Once new knowledge is obtained, we add the new dimension to the data store by exploiting the flexibility offered by the column family based data layer.

Currently, we are testing our approach in a real life scenario within the D-All project activities and the preliminary results are quite encouraging both in term of usability and effectiveness. Unfortunately, we cannot provide a detailed description of these results due to project constraints.

5   Conclusion and Future Work

In this paper we presented Smart Data Posting, a framework based on data enrichment, and the architecture of a system for advanced search, tailored for Big Data. The new framework extends the one proposed in [19] with additional conditions and the direct use of TGDs and EGDs. The proposal have been tested in a real scenario within the MISE Project Data Alliance (D-ALL). More in detail, we implemented a prototype that leverages the new framework in order to propose users a set of interesting analysis dimensions. Users can validate the proposed dimensions, in that case they are added to the system knowledge base. Our early experiments are quite encouraging and will be deeply refined as a future work after the project conclusion.

We stress that our user behavior oriented framework deals with a number of issues that are quite intriguing for to the big data paradigm. Indeed, we deal with all the big data "V"s [1,10,17,25]. First of all, data collected in the framework are typically high sized (**V**olume). In addition, the most challenging issues dealt with in our framework are the unpredictable arrival rate of fresh data (**V**elocity), heterogeneous information content and format (**V**ariety) and their concept drift (**V**ariability). Furthermore, our data need to be properly elaborated in order to be confident about their (**V**eracity). Finally, a great deal of attention must be devoted to the extraction of useful information in order to assess their **V**alue.

Acknowledgements. All authors have been supported by MISE Project Data Alliance (D-ALL).

References

1. Agrawal, D., et al.: Challenges and opportunities with big data. A community white paper developed by leading researchers across the United States (2012)
2. Arenas, M., Barceló, P., Fagin, R., Libkin, L.: Locally consistent transformations and query answering in data exchange. In: Beeri, C., Deutsch, A. (eds.) PODS, pp. 229–240. ACM (2004)
3. Calautti, M., Greco, S., Molinaro, C., Trubitsyna, I.: Rewriting-based check of chase termination. In: Proceedings of the 9th Alberto Mendelzon International Workshop on Foundations of Data Management, Lima, Peru (2015)
4. Calautti, M., Greco, S., Molinaro, C., Trubitsyna, I.: Exploiting equality generating dependencies in checking chase termination. PVLDB 9(5), 396–407 (2016)
5. Caroprese, L., Trubitsyna, I., Zumpano, E.: A framework for prioritized reasoning based on the choice evaluation. In: Proceedings of ACM Symposium on Applied Computing (SAC), Seoul, Korea, 11–15 March 2007, pp. 65–70 (2007)
6. Caroprese, L., Zumpano, E.: Aggregates and priorities in P2P data management systems. In: Proceedings of 15th International Database Engineering and Applications Symposium, IDEAS 2011, Lisbon, Portugal, pp. 1–7 (2011)
7. Caroprese, L., Zumpano, E.: Computing a deterministic semantics for P2P deductive databases. In: Proceedings of 21st International Database Engineering & Applications Symposium, IDEAS 2017, Bristol, United Kingdom, pp. 184–191 (2017)
8. Cassavia, N., Masciari, E., Pulice, C., Saccà, D.: Discovering user behavioral features to enhance information search on big data. TIIS 7(2), 7:1–7:33 (2017)
9. Deutsch, A., Nash, A., Remmel, J.B.: The chase revisited. In: Proceedings of the Twenty-Seventh ACM SIGMOD-SIGACT-SIGART Symposium on Principles of Database Systems, PODS 2008, Vancouver, BC, Canada, 9–11 June 2008, pp. 149–158 (2008)
10. The Economist: Drowning in numbers - digital data will flood the planet - and help us understand it better. The Economist, November 2011
11. Fagin, R., Kolaitis, P.G., Popa, L.: Data exchange: getting to the core. ACM Trans. Database Syst. 30(1), 174–210 (2005)
12. Greco, G., Greco, S., Trubitsyna, I., Zumpano, E.: Optimization of bound disjunctive queries with constraints. TPLP 5(6), 713–745 (2005)
13. Greco, S., Molinaro, C., Trubitsyna, I., Zumpano, E.: NP datalog: a logic language for expressing search and optimization problems. TPLP 10(2), 125–166 (2010)
14. Greco, S., Spezzano, F., Trubitsyna, I.: Stratification criteria and rewriting techniques for checking chase termination. PVLDB 4(11), 1158–1168 (2011)
15. Greco, S., Spezzano, F., Trubitsyna, I.: Checking chase termination: cyclicity analysis and rewriting techniques. IEEE Trans. Knowl. Data Eng. 27(3), 621–635 (2015)
16. Greco, S., Trubitsyna, I., Zumpano, E.: On the semantics of logic programs with preferences. J. Artif. Intell. Res. 30, 501–523 (2007)
17. Lohr, S.: The age of big data. nytimes.com, February 2012
18. Masciari, E., Saccà, D., Trubitsyna, I.: Simple user assistance by data posting. In: Proceedings of the 2nd IEEE International Conference on Artificial Intelligence and Knowledge Engineering, AIKE 2019, pp. 1–8 (2019, to appear)
19. Masciari, E., Saccà, D., Trubitsyna, I.: Simplified data posting in practice. In: Proceedings of 23rd International Database Engineering and Applications Symposium, IDEAS 2019, Athens, Greece (2019, to appear)

20. Meier, M., Schmidt, M., Lausen, G.: On chase termination beyond stratification. PVLDB **2**(1), 970–981 (2009)
21. Onet, A.: The chase procedure and its applications in data exchange. In: Data Exchange, Integration, and Streams, pp. 1–37 (2013)
22. Redmond, E., Wilson, J.R.: Seven Databases in Seven Weeks: A Guide to Modern Databases and the NoSQL Movement. Pragmatic Bookshelf, Raleigh (2012)
23. Saccà, D., Serra, E., Guzzo, A.: Count constraints and the Inverse OLAP problem: definition, complexity and a step toward aggregate data exchange. In: Lukasiewicz, T., Sali, A. (eds.) FoIKS 2012. LNCS, vol. 7153, pp. 352–369. Springer, Heidelberg (2012). https://doi.org/10.1007/978-3-642-28472-4_20
24. Sakama, C., Inoue, K.: Prioritized logic programming and its application to commonsense reasoning. Artif. Intell. **123**(1–2), 185–222 (2000)
25. Special Report: Big data. Nature, September 2008

On the Usefulness of Pre-Processing Step in Melanoma Detection Using Multiple Instance Learning

Eugenio Vocaturo[1]([⊠]) [iD], Ester Zumpano[1] [iD],
and Pierangelo Veltri[2] [iD]

[1] DIMES - Department of Computer Science, Modelling, Electronic
and System Engineering, University of Calabria, Rende, Italy
{e.vocaturo,e.zumpano}@dimes.unical.it
[2] DSMC- Bioinformatics Laboratory Surgical and Medical Science Department,
University Magna Graecia, Catanzaro, Italy
veltri@unicz.it

Abstract. Although skin cancers, and melanoma in particular, are characterized by a high mortality rate, on the other hand they can be effectively treated when the diagnosis is made at the initial stages. The research in this field is attempting to design systems aimed at automatically detecting melanomas on the basis of dermoscopic images. The interest is also motivated by the opportunity to implement solutions that favor self-diagnosis in the population. Determining effective detection methods to reduce the error rate in diagnosis is a crucial challenge.

Computer Vision Systems are characterized by several basic steps. Pre-processing is the first phase and plays the fundamental role to improve the image quality by eliminating noises and irrelevant parts from the background of the skin. In [1] we presented an application to image classification of a Multiple Instance Learning approach (MIL), with the aim to discriminate between positive and negative images. In [3] we subsequently applied this method to clinical data consisting of non-pre-processed melanoma dermoscopic images. In [2] we also investigated some pre-processing techniques useful for automatic analysis of melanoma images.

In this work we propose to use, after applying a pre-processing step, the MIL approach presented in [1] on the same melanoma data set adopted in [3]. The preliminary results appear promising for defining automatic systems that act as a "filter" mechanism to support physicians in detecting melanomas cancer.

Keywords: Multiple instance learning · Image pre-processing ·
Melanoma detection

1 Introduction

Melanoma is a particularly deadly form of skin cancer and is responsible for 75% of all skin cancer deaths. Melanoma is also one of the emerging diseases as evidenced by the International Agency for Research on Cancer (IARC). Every year there are more than

© Springer Nature Switzerland AG 2019
A. Cuzzocrea et al. (Eds.): FQAS 2019, LNAI 11529, pp. 374–382, 2019.
https://doi.org/10.1007/978-3-030-27629-4_34

160.000 new diagnoses of cutaneous melanoma and of these 62.000 occur in Europe [4]. However, if melanoma is diagnosed in its initial stages, it can be treated effectively [5]. A late diagnosis can be lethal for the patient, as melanoma can quickly grow deep and spread to other parts of the body. Medical imaging is transforming the diagnostic methods in various fields of medicine, including Dermatology. Imaging is used to support the diagnosis of skin diseases and to analyze the response to therapy. Thus, developing computerized diagnostic systems to facilitate early detection of melanoma becomes a necessity. The various proposals of computer vision systems are characterized by some basic common phases, including *image acquisition, pre-processing, segmentation, features extraction, features selection* and finally *classification*.

Since the output of each step is the input of the next one, all phases play a key role in enabling correct diagnosis. Pre-processing plays a fundamental role: the elimination of noise and not significant parts against the background of skin images [6]. Various pre-processing techniques are proposed for noise removal and image enhancement, which allow the removal of disturbing factors from dermoscopic images, such as hair. An efficient image pre-processing step will allow better image classification and accuracy. In the present work we apply our classification method proposed in [1], on a data set of pre-processed dermatoscope images obtained from the one used in [3]: the objective is to effectively appreciate the improvements in terms of precision and accuracy.

The paper is organized as follows. In Sect. 2, we highlight the rule of pre-processing step to perform automated diagnoses on melanoma, explaining the optimization operations made on the database used for the presented numerical experiments. In Sect. 3, we recall the outline of our model based on Multiple Instance Learning approach. In Sect. 4, we report the results obtained highlighting the classification improvement achieved thanks to pre-processing step. Finally, conclusions and directions to be followed in the future are reported.

2 Pre-processing for Melanoma Computer Detection

Distinguishing a melanoma from a melanocytic nevus is not easy, especially in the initial phase, even when expert dermatologists operate with the aid of dermoscopy.

Many medical protocols have been defined such as the seven-point checklist [7], the ABCDE rule [8] and the Menzies method [9] to support the diagnosis of melanoma skin cancer. These protocols inspire the implementation of Computer Vision Systems useful for increasing the accuracy and the timeliness of diagnosis. The computer is able to extract some information, in terms of color variation, asymmetry, texture features, which may not be easily perceived by human eyes. If these images are processed and analyzed through evolved mathematical algorithms, it is possible to obtain objective quantitative data, able to provide information on the underlying physio pathological phenomena; thus, it is possible to support diagnostic and surgical intervention [10]. The classical methodology would require removing a piece of tissue from the patient's body in order to perform histological analyzes. A more accurate diagnosis implies less recourse to invasive examinations, like biopsy, with consequent lower costs for both the patient and the community.

Imaging can be at the level of total body photography to detect changes in the size, shape or color of individual lesions, but also at the subcellular level with techniques such as confocal reflectance microscopy used to visualize atypical cells. The various imaging techniques are used upstream of computer vision systems with the aim to acquire images of specific lesions. The various image acquisition techniques used in Dermatology present specific characteristics as reported in [2].

Among the various possibilities, we have focused on Dermatoscopy, which guarantees also one of the cheapest ways to identify and classify skin cancer.

Dermatoscopy, dermoscopy or epiluminescience, is a non-invasive technique based on an optical instrument called dermatoscope that allows observing sub-cutaneous patterns not visible to the naked eye, favoring their recognition.

The optical dermatoscope is a small manual instrument based on a lens, able to provide magnifications mainly between 10 and 20 times, specially illuminated with incident light. It is now demonstrated how dermoscopy increases the diagnostic sensitivity for melanoma compared to simple vision with the naked eye of 20–30% allowing increasingly early diagnosis [11].

Dermoscopic images may be influenced by some artifacts, including the gradual transition between the lesion and the skin, the presence of hair, the transition effects of the gel and the water bubble, plus colored lesions and specular color reflections. The presence of these artifacts can generate incorrect assessments of the lesion and, therefore, of the classification of skin cancer. It is necessary to provide pre-processing step to properly manage image enhancement, image restoration and artifact removal. There are many techniques used for the acquisition of skin images, and depending on which one is used, different phases may be necessary in the preprocessing step. The applications of Gaussian, middle and median filters [12] and of the anti-stain filters [13] are the techniques of preprocessing more frequently used. In particular, the presence of short hair on small skin lesions is an impediment capable of infecting the segmentation phase and contributing to an inaccurate final diagnosis.

To remove thick hair in skin cancer images, researchers proposed methods based on mathematical morphology, on the detection of the curvilinear structure, on an in painting based method, on Top Hat transformations combined with bi-cubic interpolation. In [14] an interesting review on hair removal techniques. The dermatoscope photos we took into consideration for our numerical experiments were affected by the presence of hair. For the pre-processing step of our dataset we use Dull Razor [15], a dedicated software tool that removes hair from images by identifying the positions of dark hair, verifying that the dark pixel is a thin structure and finally smoothing the pixels replaced with an adaptive median filter. Figure 1(a) shows a lesion covered by thick hair and Fig. 1(b) shows the result after hair removal step.

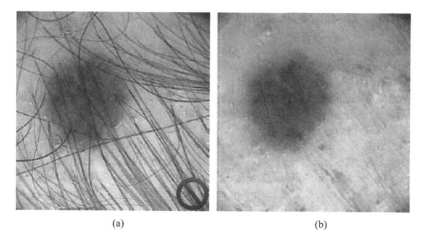

Fig. 1. An image of nevus: (a) with hair, (b) after pre-processing step.

The following figures show the dermatoscopic photos of melanomas (Fig. 2) and of common nevi (Fig. 3) we used. The red signal indicates the images that have been pre-processed to obtain a hairless version.

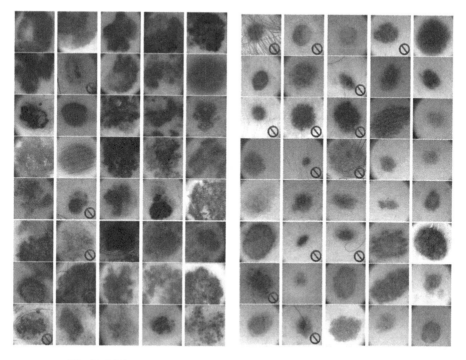

Fig. 2. Melanomas   **Fig. 3.** Common nevi

3   Multiple Instance Learning

Classification techniques aim to classify data into different classes, and this can be done by identifying appropriate separation surfaces. In [3] we presented a Multiple Instance Learning (MIL) approach, aimed at classifying melanoma images using a separating hyperplane. In melanoma detection, the result of a classification process leads either to dichotomous distinction between melanoma and benign lesion or to evaluate a probability of class membership. Typically, a MIL problem consists in classifying sets of items. In MIL terminology, such sets are called bags and the items inside them are called instances. The main peculiarity of such problems is that, in learning phase, only the labels of the bags are known, while the labels of the instances are unknown: thus, a bag is positive if it contains at least a positive instance and it is negative if it does not contain any positive instance.

In literature there are two different approaches for solving a MIL problem: one is the instance-level approach and the other one is the bag-level approach. In the first one, the classification is performed in the instance space, without looking at the global properties of the bags; vice versa, in a bag-space approach the classifier is constructed by separating directly the bags, each of them seen as a global entity.

MIL paradigm works very well with respect to a classical supervised approach also in the field of medical image diagnostics [16], where local analysis is relevant.

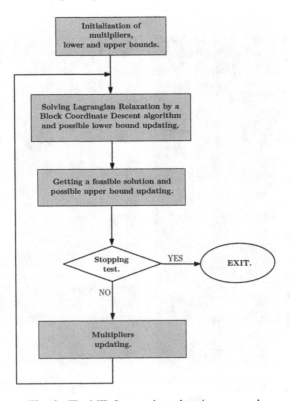

Fig. 4. The MIL Lagrangian relaxation approach

For further details and general considerations on the MIL paradigm we refer the reader to the surveys [17] and [18]. A simplified scheme of the MIL algorithm is reported in Fig. 4 and further details can be found in [19].

4 Numerical Experimentations

The MIL classification algorithm proposed in [19] and summarized in the previous section has been applied to classification of some medical dermoscopic images drawn from the dataset PH^2 [20]. Preliminary applications to image classification of the same algorithm have been done in [21].

The PH^2 database was set up by the Universidad do Porto and Tecnico Lisboa, in collaboration with the Dermatology Service of the Hospital Pedro Hispano (Portugal). The equipment used to acquire these dermoscopic images is the *Tubinger Mole Analyzer system*, by which it is possible to obtain high resolution images with a magnification factor of 20x. The images obtained are in 8-bit RGB color with a resolution of 768×560 pixels. Patients from whom the photos were taken correspond to phototype II or III, according to Fitzpatrick's skin type classification scale. This justifies the fact that the background color, not affected by injury, varies from white to creamy white.

These images have been classified as common nevus or melanoma by expert dermatologists considering the manual segmentation of the skin lesion, the clinical and histological diagnosis and dermoscopic criteria (asymmetry, colors, pigment network, particular structures) [20].

In our experiments, none of the features resulting from the manual analysis was used in the automatic classification process, but we have just considered the images of common nevi as negative and the images of melanomas as positive. The presence of hair in some images made a pre-processing step necessary. We used Dull Razor [15], a software tool dedicated to removing hair from images: in this way we obtained a hairless version of images.

The dataset considered consists of 40 images of melanoma (Fig. 2) and 40 images of common nevi (Fig. 3). To decrease the number of instances, we first reduced the image resolution to 128×128 pixels and subsequently we partitioned each image into square groups (blobs) of 32×32 pixel size. For each blob, we have computed the average of the RGB intensities of the blob and the differences between this value and the same quantity calculated for the adjacent blobs (up, down, left, right). As a consequence, we have obtained feature vectors of fifteen dimension and a database consisting of 80 bags (the images) and 320 instances (the blobs). The code corresponding to the MIL algorithm summarized in Sect. 3 (see also Fig. 4) was implemented in Matlab and was executed on a Windows 10 system characterized by a 2.21 GHz processor.

We performed two types of experiments: for each of them we report in Tables 1(a) and (b) the training correctness, the testing correctness and the CPU time. The last rows in both the tables are the average results obtained in [3], where no type of pre-processing technique has been adopted.

Table 1. Test on pre-processed Melanoma DB: (a) 10-fold cross-validation, (b) 5-fold cross-validation

(a)

Fold number	Training correctness	Testing correctness	CPU Time
1	94.44	100.00	0.47
2	94.44	100.00	0.38
3	97.22	87.50	0.46
4	94.44	87.50	0.35
5	91.67	87.50	0.18
6	95.83	62.50	0.23
7	93.06	100.00	0.33
8	93.06	75.00	0.26
9	94.44	62.50	0.23
10	90.28	87.50	0.39
Average	93.89	85.00	0.32
Average [3]	92.64	83.75	0.37

(b)

Fold number	Training correctness	Testing correctness	CPU Time
1	95.31	87.50	0.52
2	92.19	100.00	0.32
3	95.31	75.00	0.40
4	92.19	93.75	0.32
5	93.75	87.50	0.31
Average	93.75	88.75	0.38
Average [3]	93.13	88.75	0.29

In Table 1(a) we have used a be–level 10 cross-validation. The results appear promising, especially if we consider that they were obtained from a set of small-resolution photos. Moreover, we highlight that in three cases (folds n. 1, 2 and 7) the algorithm was able to correctly classify all the images in the test set. In Table 1(b) we report the results of a be–level 5 cross-validation: this second experiment is motivated by the idea to increase the test set which, in the first case, consisted of 8 images.

Also, in this second experiment, the results are promising: we note in fact that, in correspondence to the second fold, the entire test set consisting of 16 images (9 with melanoma and 7 without) is correctly classified.

The used approach is also effective in terms of CPU time, whose average, for both the experiments, is less than one second. Although we used only color features, the obtained results show a slight improvement in the classification performance with respect to the values obtained in [3].

Future research could be to investigate the classification performance, considering in addition geometry and textures features.

5   Conclusion

Automatic diagnostics has become an essential tool for doctors in deciding whether a skin lesion is a benign mole or a malignant melanoma. Research is attempting the automatic early diagnosis of melanoma by implementing Computer Vision Systems (CVS) that analyze digital images of skin lesions. Recent studies review the features of interest that can be used in CVS for melanoma detection [22]. Furthermore, the improvement of digital cameras, which are also equipped on smartphones and wearable devices, favors the possibility of patient's self-diagnosis [23]. Nowadays, great attention is devoted to effective solutions ensuring accuracy in the identification of groups of similar patients [45] and capturing valuable insights from medical sources [46]. Pre-processing assumes a fundamental role in the elimination of noise and irrelevant parts from the background of skin images.

In this paper we have presented an application of a Multiple Instance Learning approach to melanoma detection obtaining promising results, both in terms of classification accuracy and CPU times, using a pre-processing technique.

Future research could consist in the design of more sophisticated segmentation techniques, in order to further improve the classification results. We intend to evaluate the use of other features such as geometry and texture. In this way, our model could be able to benefit more broadly from the contribution of the pre-processing phase.

References

1. Astorino, A., Fuduli, A., Gaudioso, M., Vocaturo, E.: A Multiple instance learning algorithm for color images classification. In: Proceedings of IDEAS 2018, Villa San Giovanni, Italy, pp. 262–266 (2018). https://doi.org/10.1145/3216122.3216144
2. Vocaturo, E., Zumpano, E., Veltri, P.: Image pre-processing in computer vision systems for melanoma detection. In: IEEE International Conference on Bioinformatics and Biomedicine, BIBM 2018, Madrid, Spain, December 3–6 2018, pp. 2117–2124 (2018). http://doi.ieeecomputersociety.org/10.1109/BIBM.2018.8621507
3. Astorino, A., Fuduli, A., Veltri, P., Vocaturo, E.: Melanoma detection by means of Multiple Instance Learning. In: Interdisciplinary Sciences: Computational Life Sciences INSC-D-18-00327R1 (2019, submeeted)
4. Siegel, R.L., Miller, K.D., Jemal, A.: Cancer statistics. Cancer J. Clin. **68**(1), 7–30 (2018). https://doi.org/10.3322/caac.21442
5. Gutman, D., et al.: Skin lesion analysis toward melanoma detection: A challenge at the international symposium on biomedical imaging (ISBI) 2016. In: International Skin Imaging Collaboration (ISIC), CoRR, abs/1605.01397 (2016)
6. Mesquita, J., Viana, C.: Classification of Skin Tumours through the Analysis of Unconstrained Images. De Montfort University Leicester, UK (2008)
7. Argenziano, G., et al.: Seven-point checklist of dermoscopy revisited. Br. J. Dermatol. **164**(4), 785–790 (2011)
8. Rigel, D., Friedman, R., Kopf, A., Polsky, D.: Abcde an evolving concept in the early detection of melanoma. Arch. Dermat. **141**(8), 1032–1034 (2005)
9. Johr, R.H.: Dermoscopy: alternative melanocytic algorithms; the ABCD rule of dermatoscopy, menzies scoring method, and 7-point checklist. Clin. Dermatol. **20**(3), 240–247 (2002)
10. Iaquinta, P., et al.: eIMES 3D: an innovative medical images analysis tool to support diagnostic and surgical intervention. In: FNC - MobiSPC 2017, pp. 459–464 (2017)
11. Andreassi, L., et al.: Digital dermoscopy analysis for the differentiation of atypical nevi and early melanoma: a new quantitative semiology. Arch. Dermatol. **135**(12), 1459–1465 (1999). PMID 10606050
12. Cheng, H.D., Shan, J., Ju, W., Guo, Y., Zhang, L.: Automated breast cancer detection and classification using ultrasound images: a survey. Pattern Recogn. **43**(1), 299–317 (2010)
13. Michailovich, O., Tannenbaum, A.: Despeckling of medical ultrasound images. IEEE Trans. Ultrason. Ferroelectr. Freq. Control **53**, 64–78 (2006)
14. Abbas, Q., Celebi, M.E., García, I.F.: Hair removal methods: a comparative study for dermoscopy images. Biomed. Signal Process. Control **6**(4), 395–404 (2011)
15. Lee, T., Gallagher, R., Coldman, A., McLean, D.: Dull Razor: a software approach to hair removal from images. Comput. Biol. Med. **27**, 533–543 (1997)

16. Quellec, G., Cazuguel, G., Cochener, B., Lamard, M.: Multiple-instance learning for medical image and video analysis. IEEE Rev. Biomed. Eng. **10**, 213–234 (2017)
17. Amores, J.: Multiple instance classification: review, taxonomy and comparative study. Artif. Intell. **201**, 81–105 (2013)
18. Carbonneau, M., Cheplygina, V., Granger, E., Gagnon, G.: Multiple instance learning: a survey of problem characteristics and applications. Pattern Recogn. **77**, 329–353 (2018)
19. Astorino, A., Fuduli, A., Gaudioso, M.: A Lagrangian Relaxation Approach for Binary Multiple Instance Classification. In: IEEE Transactions on Neural Networks and Learning Systems (2019). https://doi.org/10.1109/tnnls.2018.2885852
20. Mendonça, T., et al.: PH^2-A dermoscopic image database for research and benchmarking. In: 35th IEEE International Conference on Engineering in Medicine and Biology Society, Osaka, Japan, July 2013, pp. 3–7, (2013)
21. Astorino, A., Fuduli, A., Veltri, P., Vocaturo, E.: On a recent algorithm for multiple instance learning. Preliminary applications in image classification. In: 2017 IEEE International Conference on Bioinformatics and Biomedicine (BIBM), pp. 1615–1619 (2017)
22. Vocaturo, E., Zumpano, E., Veltri, P.: Features for Melanoma Lesions Characterization in Computer Vision Systems. In: 9th International Conference on Information, Intelligence, Systems and Applications, IISA 2018, Zakynthos, Greece, 23–25 July 2018, pp. 1–8 (2018). https://doi.org/10.1109/IISA.2018.8633651
23. Vocaturo, E., Veltri, P.: On the use of networks in biomedicine. In: 14th International Conference on Mobile Systems and Pervasive Computing (MobiSPC 2017), 24–26 July 2017, Leuven, Belgium, pp. 498–503 (2017), ISSN 1877-0509. https://doi.org/10.1016/j.procs.2017.06.132
24. Masciari, E., Mazzeo, G.M., Zaniolo, C.: Analysing microarray expression data through effective clustering. Inf. Sci. **262**, 32–45 (2014)
25. Greco, S., Molinaro, C., Trubitsyna, I.: Computing approximate query answers over inconsistent knowledge bases. IJCAI **2018**, 1838–1846 (2018)

Systems and Miscellanea

Towards Flexible Energy Supply in European Smart Environments

Stefania Marrara[1] , Amir Topalović[1], and Marco Viviani[2(✉)]

[1] Consorzio C2T, Milan, Italy
{stefania.marrara,amir.topalovic}@consorzioc2t.it
[2] Department of Informatics, Systems and Communication,
University of Milano-Bicocca, Milan, Italy
marco.viviani@unimib.it
http://www.consorzioc2t.it/en/, http://www.ir.disco.unimib.it/

Abstract. Nowadays, electricity is the most widely used kind of energy, which is composed by a mix of traditional fossil sources and renewable energies. The use of renewable energies is increasingly incentivized at present, but, due to their characteristics connected for example to climatic conditions, they can be subject to temporary unavailability. Production plants, in order to function properly, and to guarantee a standard level of energy, must cope flexibly with this problem. In this article, we aim at presenting the main technologies and solutions that are connected to the considered problem, and we introduce the architecture of a flexible affiliation system that can optimize the use of electricity distribution networks efficiently, reducing energy waste.

Keywords: Flexible energy supply · Smart environments ·
Smart Grids · Smart cities

1 Introduction

Electricity is the most versatile and most widely used kind of energy, accessible by more than five billion people worldwide. For this reason, the electricity sector is driving the transformation of the world energy system, and electricity is the type of energy that shows the most sustained growth. Moreover, it is the sector that contributes more than any other to the reduction of the share of fossil sources within the world energy mix.

Renewable energies, an element of crucial importance in the world energy scenario, are rapidly gaining ground due to the growing sensitivity of the public opinion and governments towards *climate change* (IEA World Energy Outlook 2014) [1], a topic that is increasingly discussed also within the different social media, with different levels of depth and reliability [15]. Blocking climate change is one of the strategic objectives defined by the European Community for 2020, defined in the global Europe 2020 strategy for smart and sustainable growth.[1]

---

[1] https://tinyurl.com/yaq2phsr.

© Springer Nature Switzerland AG 2019
A. Cuzzocrea et al. (Eds.): FQAS 2019, LNAI 11529, pp. 385–395, 2019.
https://doi.org/10.1007/978-3-030-27629-4_35

In particular, the strategy aims to ensure that, by 2020, the EU's greenhouse gas emissions will be reduced by 20%, 20% of energy will come from renewable sources, and there will be a 20% increase in energy efficiency.

By defining the term "residual electricity demand" as the energy not supplied by renewable sources, but necessary to meet the energy demand, we notice that the greater the variability of the residual demand, the greater the flexibility required by the available production plants that are required to help to meet the demand but also to compensate for any unexpected unavailability typical of some renewable sources.

The availability of storage systems, the flexibility of some types of traditional plants and the amount of available renewable resources can mitigate this variability reducing the additional costs and technical difficulties of management; nevertheless, the issue is challenging. In this scenario, many traditional production plants will still be needed but will be increasingly used, especially in countries where the increase in renewable sources will be higher. This need arises from the variability and uncertainty of supply from renewable sources such as wind and photovoltaics, for which the production capacity to be relied on is much lower than the installed capacity.

If, therefore, the consumption of electricity and the level of decentralization of generation, mainly due to the use of renewable sources, is destined to increase considerably, technically the problem of management can be solved in two ways: increasing the capacity of the existing network (mainly the distribution network, then cables and transformers in medium and low voltage) or using the existing network capacity more efficiently, smarter, by developing a Smart Grid (Source: IEA World Energy Outlook 2014) [1].

Aim of this paper is to present the main technologies adopted to develop a Smart Grid, and to propose the architecture of a flexible affiliation system able to conciliate the different needs of heterogeneous devices w.r.t. the supply provided by a distribution network, reducing wastes of unused energy.

2   Background and Related Work

With the term "Smart Grid" we mean a new framework, in many ways revolutionary, to design and develop an active and intelligent electric network, modifying the classical architecture of an electricity grid to increase the respect for the environment, the energy efficiency, the reliability and the security of supply, but, above all, to put the consumer at the center of the electricity system.

The new Smart Grid approach is applicable not only to new plants, but also to the existing ones, a factor that underpins the overwhelming success of these applications, and is based on technologies that, although largely developed, must be used through application solutions that include also solutions still in an embryonic state, with strong growth perspectives and a considerable degree of technical and technological complexity [14].

Although Smart Grids also include the Generation and Electric Transmission in a transverse way, this paper is focused on Electrical Distribution, w.r.t. both

Customer Side applications (Advanced Metering and Home Area Network) and Grid Side (Distribution Network Automation), as these are the segments that are significantly growing in the market thanks to increasing investments and technologies mature for industrial and large-scale use [14].

Technically speaking, Smart Grids adopt the most advanced techniques in terms of network design and components to improve efficiency, safety and performance. Energy storage technologies can provide a significant contribution to integrating renewable sources into the grid. Moreover a more flexible management of electricity distribution and transmission is required to reduce generation fluctuations and increase efficiency. Control and monitoring systems can help to avoid malfunctions and out of service issues. By using all these intelligent technologies and their interconnection through an appropriate communication system, we obtain the Smart Grid in its most advanced concept.

In a broader sense, the Smart Grid is not a single network but a set of networks, aimed at connecting the structures of different energy producers on several levels, with automatic coordination, increasing connectivity, automation and coordination among suppliers, consumers and the network, in order to optimize the transmission and distribution of energy. Figure 1 shows the main elements involved a Smart Grid system, whose parts are interconnected in order to share and optimize sustainable energy sources.

SMART GRID

GENERATION → TRANSMISSION → DISTRIBUTION → POWER CONSUMERS

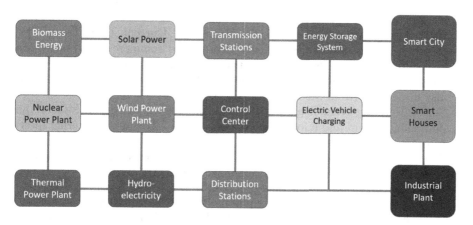

Fig. 1. Elements involved in a Smart Grid.

2.1 Basic Concepts

In this section, the main concepts (and related terminologies) of the Smart Grid framework for the development of electrical systems (both at high and very high voltage and medium and low levels) are presented, with reference to the European System currently settled and its evolutions. The evolution of the electrical system has been impressive due to the following factors:

- Attention to growth and sustainable development with a strong focus on environmental and social aspects and energy savings;
- Connection of medium and low voltage networks of renewable sources distributed throughout the territory, often volatile (photovoltaic and wind);
- Connection of high and very high voltage networks of concentrated renewable sources;
- The role of the market that is giving more and more space and power to the user/consumer (citizen) and to organized citizens (users/consumers), which favors the development of new technologies and applications related to Micro Grid (i.e., medium and low voltage electrical systems that contain generation (distributed renewable energy, but also traditional), loads, storage systems and an electrical network that connects these nodes), Smart Community and Smart City;
- A more and more delocalized and decentralized (in some federalist aspects) perspective management of electrical systems that is encouraging a greater participation of local communities.

It has also been based on the use of the following technologies and applications:

- Local Renewable Energy (Bulk Renewable Sources) [6], which must be transferred from peripheral areas of the system (Northern Europe for Wind Offshore, Southern Mediterranean for PV Solar Plant and Siberia for large hydroelectric basins) to the European load center through Super Grids;
- Power electronic systems (Facts, Flexible Active Current Transmission Systems) [9], which govern power flows according to commercial and operation considerations (e.g., resolution of network congestion problems);
- Advanced Direct Current(DC) technologies for high voltage applications, but also in perspective in Medium and Low Voltage;
- Smart Metering technologies, with particular regard to Digital Meters and data management and information systems (AMI - Advanced Metering Interface) [2];
- Smart Grid technologies applied to Medium Voltage, such as MV network teleconduction, secondary substation automation (MT/BT) [3].
- Renewable and Distributed Energy installed in Medium and Low Voltage;
- Storage technologies, such as pumped hydroelectric, or battery systems [7];
- Advanced and low cost systems of EMS (Energy Management System), and DMS (Distribution Management System) [13];
- Quality of service based on actual consumer needs;
- Network nodes that can be at the same time loads and generators: *prosumer* = producer + consumer).

This scenario has introduced new concepts and above all terminologies that are worth recalling and better defining. The European Electric System as a whole, consists of:

– Macro Grids: they perform a public function, regardless of the nature of their property. They consist of high and very high voltage systems, but also of medium and low voltage systems with AC/DC technologies and provide public services according to the standard parameters of quality and reliability (PQR);
– Micro Grids, that will be detailed in the following.

Macro Grids can be classified as follows:

– Super Grids (EHV Macro Grids): they are electrical power transmission systems, mainly based on direct current technology, designed to facilitate the production of large-scale renewable energy in remote areas for transmission to consumption centers. The Super Grids therefore represent a fourth level in addition to those of Transmission, Medium Voltage Distribution and Low Voltage Distribution;
– HV Macro Grids: they represent the current electrical transmission networks (380/220kV with AC technology);
– MV & LV Macro Grids: they represent the current medium voltage (20/10 kV with AC technology) and low voltage (380/220 V with AC technology) electricity distribution networks.

Micro Grids can be classified as follows:

– Mili Grid: often referred as MV Micro Grid [10]. These are electrical systems that group together generators and loads that can co-operate and often include also traditional distribution sections. They are networks designed to provide low PQR power (power quality and reliability) for those devices that require it. These networks are now subject to various rules and legal restrictions that may be different according to the various European contexts (in some European countries these networks are not currently allowed, if not on an experimental basis). In the future, these systems will be required to have operating procedures able to guarantee the public service no longer offered at the Macro Grid level. These networks are also defined as "microgrid utilities" or "community grids";
– Micro Grid: medium and mainly low voltage electrical systems that contain generation (distributed but also traditional renewable energy), loads, storage systems and an electrical grid that connects these nodes together. These networks are locally managed and can operate in an isolated way or connected to the Macro Grid. They are networks designed to provide even low PQR power for those devices that require it. Another important definition is that a Micro Grid is a Customer Micro Grid, i.e., a network consisting mainly of a limited number (e.g., 100–200) of prosumers (loads that can also become generators) and therefore of digital meters (intelligent meters). In this case, on the Macro Grid perspective, the Micro Grid is a simple load node (which can also become active). In this case, the electrical infrastructure inside the grid can be conceptually seen as a connection network between generators and small loads, instead of a low voltage public service distribution network.

This new approach may have very strong legal and regulatory implications in the near future. The Micro Grid is designed for autonomous operation (electrically isolated) from the Macro Grid, although many of these are normally interconnected to the Macro Grid by purchase/sale Energy and electrical services connected. In this perspective, thanks to the Micro Grid, the Macro Grid is free from the responsibility of service quality (continuity, interruptibility, etc.) and reliability; that responsibility will pass on the shoulders of the Micro Grid itself. It should also be noted that these responsibilities may concern the energy aspects as a whole, including the production and distribution of heat;

– Nano Grid (intelligent loads) [11]: these are networks that require critical and priority loads. An interesting case (often not considered in the planning of low voltage destruction system) of telecommunication systems that have completely different characteristics from the normal electricity distribution networks and that are in strong growth. These are low energy networks, often (but not always) in direct current, designed to provide high PQR energy for those devices that require it.

3 Energy Distribution Automation

The automation of electricity distribution systems or Distribution Automation (DA) is becoming increasingly important as the number of distributed power sources increases with the aim of improving the quality and reliability of the medium and low voltage networks. The focus is mainly on the primary and secondary distribution cabins of the electricity grid, owned and managed by the distributor, with increasing requirements in terms of automation, control and protection. The main objective of the automation level is monitoring the network status and the transmission of the measured quantities in order to increase the knowledge and the governability of the network through the remote control of the IED (Intelligent Electronic Device) located in the network itself. In this way it is possible to automatically detect and eliminate faults and possibly automatically or manually intervene to restore the supply in particular critical situations. The following activities are part of the automation of the distribution [8]:

– Real-time monitoring of devices located in the network and of all those sensors that can improve network control;
– Introduction and control of active components or that can automatically handle certain situations, for example transformers with automatic voltage regulator;
– Bidirectional communication between the IED and the control room;
– Integration of the devices in the information system of the electricity company in order to manage, for example, maintenance or emergency response in case of failure or for better customer management, etc.;
– Management of distributed resources, generators and loads.

The most demanding challenge for the electricity grids of the future is therefore represented by the integration of a high component of electricity produced from renewable sources while maintaining a high quality and reliability of supply. The level of distribution of electricity generation will tend to increase more and more, leading to an increase in the complexity of the distribution network in terms of bidirectional power flows, reliability, stability, network management, network capacity, etc. A first problem concerns, for example, the stability of the voltage put at risk by the power flows due to the distributed generation both in low and in medium voltage; the consequence is that the voltage could exceed the defined maximum and minimum limits. Moreover, the nominal values of the components of the network are not such as to withstand these flows and this results in the overload of fundamental components such as cables, overhead lines and transformers. Possible solutions to the problem are identifiable in the following activities [8]:

- Progressive transition from radial networks to mesh networks capable of distributing power flows; for this purpose, it may be necessary to increase the number of secondary distribution substations;
- Introduction or improvement of the Distribution Energy Management Systems (DEMS);
- Introduction of distributed systems of energy storage;
- Planned and balanced installation of loads such as charging systems for electric vehicles, in order to control and reduce power flows;
- Control of the power fed into the grid from renewable sources;
- Replacement of some passive components with as many assets, for example distribution transformers with automatic voltage regulators.

The introduction of information technology and modern communication systems can make a substantial contribution to solving the problem by decentralizing intelligence and implementing appropriate algorithms.

4 Architecture of a Flexible Affiliation System

In this section, we illustrate the design of the proposed architecture to build a prototype of a flexible *affiliation system*, i.e, a system that is able to collect and provide information, on request, on the type of electric engine connected to the power supply network, and guide the request of energy supply itself. The characteristics of the user's electric engines (e.g., power consumption class, electrical isolation degree, ...) is information useful to estimate how the user network will require energy in time. The information gathered from the prototype that will be developed, will be used to define energy saving policies based on real energy loads used.

In Fig. 2, the main components of the proposed architecture are illustrated. The first component is the *Meter*, which is simply in charge of measuring the energy consumption of the user net. In the following, the other components of the architecture are described in detail.

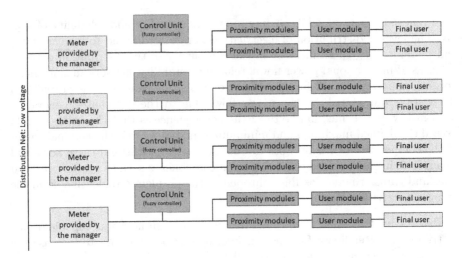

Fig. 2. Architecture of the system.

Control Unit. The *Control Unit* (CU) is a part of the plant connected to the low-voltage electricity network downstream of the energy outlet (see Fig. 2, after the *Meter Provided by the Manager* component). Its connection can be made at any point in the user network, but preferably in the main distribution panel of the system. The control panel will communicate with the user *Proximity Modules* (which will be detailed later and which are illustrated in Fig. 2) through a conveyed wave modem, or any other suitable technology. To this end, a study phase is foreseen for the selection of the most appropriate communication protocols among the most used in this context [5].

A Control Unit can be configured to manage a single network or to coordinate multiple user networks, communicating with other CUs with reduced functionality. The coordination among the different user networks is provided by a Mamdami fuzzy controller able to flexibly conciliate the requests of the users w.r.t. the supply guaranteed by the distribution network. Following the approach we used in [4] in the context of multi-modal authentication, the supply request value is computed by a fuzzy controller employing a Mamdani approach [12] with a *center of area* defuzzification. The set of rules describing the controller behaviour has been manually evaluated by a team of experts on a test period of 1 month.

This approach makes it possible to implement policies to manage electricity consumption at the highest level of aggregation (buildings, industrial sites, etc.). The Control Unit, in addition to the connection with the proximity modules, will be equipped to allow wired and/or wireless connections to external devices for the above purposes:

- communicate with a PC to insert or modify a custom configuration;
- communicate with auxiliary devices equipped with sensors useful for defining intervention policies.

Proximity Modules. The system requires the use of multiple *Proximity Modules* (PM), equipped with a standard socket for powering electrical devices. Their task will be to interrogate the *User Module* (detailed in the following) of the electrical device at the moment of the mechanical connection and to keep in memory the characteristics of the user device. The PMs will respond to the periodic queries made by the Control Unit providing data obtained from the User Module of the electrical device. Furthermore, they will implement the user power management policies decided by the Control Unit. The modules will be able to make consumption measurements on the connected user. The information will be made available to the control unit.

User Module. The element of the system that makes the user electric engine intelligent is the *User Module* (UM). It is able to provide to the Proximity Module to which it is connected, all the data useful to characterize the corresponding electrical device (e.g., its type, its energy consumption class, its peak power, etc.). In the testing phase, the User Module will be an external element to the associated electrical device, and will be of "general purpose" type [16], so as to be configurable to identify different and heterogeneous types of devices.

5   Conclusions and Further Research

The evolution of the European energy system requires a new role for networks (in particular of electricity grids) because an insufficient development of electricity grids risks compromising the achievement of the objectives of European energy policy, which aims at promoting more and more the use of renewable energies. In this paper, after a review of the main technologies composing a Smart Grid, we started to consider a small part of the problem, by proposing the design and the further development of a flexible affiliation system, able to collect and provide information, on request, on the type of electric engine connected to the power supply network. The information gathered from the prototype will be used to define energy saving policies based on real energy loads used.

In the future, our aim is, first of all, the refinement of the proposed architecture and the implementation and test of a first prototype. More in general, as regards the strategic lines in this area, it will be necessary to intervene on the following aspects:

- Security of supply:
  - Support diversification of energy sources (renewable, but also nuclear);
  - Making energy available where (overcoming spatial constraints) and when (coping with demand points) it serves to cope with the increased vulnerability of the electricity system.

- Environmental sustainability:
  - Take advantage of renewable and / or delocalized renewable sources (offshore wind);

- Increase energy efficiency in energy transformation by exploiting local energy resources (renewables, cogeneration);
- Allow the development of new energy services (e.g., electric cars).

- Competitiveness:
    - Facilitate energy exchanges. Take advantage of lower-cost production resources (reduce network congestion) and support competition (reduce market power);
    - Promote access to the electricity system and integration of European markets;
    - Support the technological development of new forms of generation;
    - Develop the end-user market (e.g., transfer of price signals to the user)
    - In the evolving energy scenario, the electricity grid must also be transformed to continue to perform its role in the best possible way;
    - Manage the relationship between generation and consumption, guaranteeing the safety and economy of the system.

References

1. AA.VV.: IEA World Energy Outlook 2014. https://www.iea.org/publications/freepublications/publication/WEO2014.pdf
2. AA.VV.: Smart meters. https://esmig.eu/page/smart-metering-technologies
3. AA.VV.: ZIV Smart Grid Solutions. https://www.zivautomation.com/ziv/ziv-smart-grid-solutions/
4. Azzini, A., Marrara, S.: Toward trust-based multi-modal user authentication on the web: a fuzzy approach. In: Proceedings of FUZZ-IEEE 2007, IEEE International Conference on Fuzzy Systems 2007, Imperial College, London, UK, 23–26 July, pp. 1–6 (2007). https://doi.org/10.1109/FUZZY.2007.4295594
5. Centenaro, M., Vangelista, L., Zanella, A., Zorzi, M.: Long-range communications in unlicensed bands: the rising stars in the IoT and smart city scenarios. IEEE Wireless Commun. 23(5), 60–67 (2016). https://doi.org/10.1109/MWC.2016.7721743
6. Denis, G.S., Parker, P.: Community energy planning in Canada: the role of renewable energy. Renew. Sustain. Energy Rev. 13(8), 2088–2095 (2009). https://doi.org/10.1016/j.rser.2008.09.030
7. Dunn, B., Kamath, H., Tarascon, J.M.: Electrical energy storage for the grid: a battery of choices. Science 334(6058), 928–935 (2011)
8. EPRI: Guide to implementing distribution automation systems using IEC 61850, Technical report, December 2002
9. Flourentzou, N., Agelidis, V.G., Demetriades, G.D.: VSC-based HVDC power transmission systems: an overview. IEEE Trans. Power Electron. 24(3), 592–602 (2009). https://doi.org/10.1109/TPEL.2008.2008441
10. Hassan, F., Ahmadi, A., Ault, G., Lee, M., Hopkins, R.: Islanded operation of renewables dominated MV microgrid with highly unbalanced loads. IET Conference Proceedings, p. 49.6 (2016)
11. Latha, S.H., Chandra Mohan, S.: Centralized power control strategy for 25 kw nano grid for rustic electrification. In: 2012 International Conference on Emerging Trends in Science, Engineering and Technology (INCOSET), pp. 456–461 December 2012. https://doi.org/10.1109/INCOSET.2012.6513949

12. Mamdani, E., Assilian, S.: An experiment in linguistic synthesis with a fuzzy logic controller. Int. J. Man-Mach. Stud. **7**(1), 1–13 (1975). https://doi.org/10.1016/S0020-7373(75)80002-2

13. Meliopoulos, A., Polymeneas, E., Tan, Z., Huang, R., Zhao, D.: Advanced distribution management system. IEEE Trans. Smart Grid **4**, 2109–2117 (2013). https://doi.org/10.1109/TSG.2013.2261564

14. Rinaldi, S., Ferrari, P., Flammini, A., Gringoli, F., Loda, M., Ali, N.: An application of IEEE 802.11ac to smart grid automation based on IEC 61850. In: IECON 2016-42nd Annual Conference of the IEEE Industrial Electronics Society, pp. 4645–4650 October 2016. https://doi.org/10.1109/IECON.2016.7793725

15. Viviani, M., Pasi, G.: Credibility in social media: opinions, news, and health information—a survey. Wiley Interdisc. Rev.: Data Mining Knowl. Disc. **7**(5), e1209 (2017)

16. Zanella, A., Bui, N., Castellani, A., Vangelista, L., Zorzi, M.: Internet of things for smart cities. IEEE Internet Things J. **1**(1), 22–32 (2014). https://doi.org/10.1109/JIOT.2014.2306328

Intelligent Voice Agent and Service (iVAS) for Interactive and Multimodal Question and Answers

James Lockett[1], Sanith Wijesinghe[1], Jasper Phillips[2], Ian Gross[2], Michael Schoenfeld[1], Walter T. Hiranpat[1], Phillip J. Marlow[1], Matt Coarr[2], and Qian Hu[2(✉)]

[1] The MITRE Corporation, 7515 Colshire Drive Virginia, Bedford, USA
[2] The MITRE Corporation, 202 Burlington Road, Bedford, MA 01730, USA
qian@mitre.org

Abstract. This paper describes MITRE's Intelligent Voice Agent and Service (iVAS) research and prototype system that provides personalized answers to government customer service questions through intelligent and multimodal interactions with citizens. We report our novel approach to interpret a user's voice or text query through Natural Language Understanding combined with a Machine Learning model trained on domain-specific data and interactive conversations to disambiguate and confirm user intent. We also describe the integration of iVAS with voice or text chatbot interface.

Keywords: Intelligent and multimodal · Interactive question and answer · NLU · Machine Learning

1 Introduction

Although voice assistants and text-based chatbots are commonly deployed for commercial product and service use cases, their ability and flexibility to respond to natural language queries specific to government customer service questions are minimal and emerging (Herman 2017; Hendry 2019). This is due to the large variation and expressiveness of human language across a diverse citizen demographic and the lack of domain knowledge specific to government services. In this study, we describe our approach to address this challenge using combined speech technology and natural language processing together with robust Natural Language Understanding (NLU), Machine Learning (ML) and Artificial Intelligence (AI). We describe use cases that demonstrate automated response to user query, call classification, and call routing. In Sect. 2, we describe the Intelligent Voice Agent and Service's (iVAS) NLU and ML model applied to use cases and discuss its classification performance. In Sect. 3, we further describe the iVAS application prototype's multimodal and intelligent question and response features.

© Springer Nature Switzerland AG 2019
A. Cuzzocrea et al. (Eds.): FQAS 2019, LNAI 11529, pp. 396–402, 2019.
https://doi.org/10.1007/978-3-030-27629-4_36

2 Robust Natural Language Understanding and Machine Learning to Interpret Users' Questions and Deliver Relevant Responses

Automatic Speech Recognition (ASR) technologies continue to advance and can now provide single-digit word error rate for conversational speech (Saon et al. 2017, Xiong et al. 2016, Park et al. 2019) to transcribe a caller's speech. ASR allows callers to express their questions through natural human language instead of using specific keywords or pressing numbers on a phone. However, even 100% transcription accuracy and complete sentence construction is insufficient for a purely rule-based language processing application. Due to the variations and expressiveness of human language understanding, interpreting a user's query or request remains a challenging task (Hu et al. 2019). For a system to generate the most relevant answer to a question, additional information is needed to refine the user's query, and this often requires a dynamic interaction between the user and the system.

In this study we describe our approach to enabling automated call and query classification and determining an appropriate response with domain-adapted word embeddings (Sarma et al. 2018). The approach combines speech technology with natural language processing and NLU, ML, and domain-specific AI. We use transfer learning from a pre-trained word-embedding model to provide features robust to lexical variation and word order in the user's speech or text query. Language model pre-training has been shown to be effective for improving many natural language processing tasks (Dai and Le 2015, Peters et al. 2018, Radford et al. 2018, Howard and Ruder 2018).

In the iVAS system, users are prompted by a synthesized voice agent or chatbot to express their needs in natural language. The user's speech is captured and transcribed as text input to a trained classifier that outputs a probability for each of the possible responses that are used by our system to intelligently deliver or execute the response to the query. Unlike rule-based systems or keyword matching, which need to be maintained by domain experts and are sensitive to both lexical and syntactic variations, our approach is data-driven and robust to variation in the user's natural speech or text query. Thus, it understands the semantic content even when it is represented by different words such as synonyms and acronyms, sentence structures such as questions or requests, and filler words. It allows users to express their needs or queries through natural language instead of relying on prescribed phrases or keywords.

2.1 Methodology

The use cases explored in this study look to automate the call routing function when a user calls into a service line. The objective is to reduce the wait times involved with talking to a customer service representative. We investigate how to automatically interpret a caller's intent through natural language and route the caller to the appropriate call center service department. For two separate use cases, we consider 7 and 10 different service department routing options. The automatic call interpretation and routing task is framed as an N-way classification given an arbitrary utterance of English text to determine the service department that has the highest probability of being associated with that utterance.

Ideally, there would be actual historic call routing data with either transcripts or recordings that detail what a caller said that led to be routed to a given service department. In the absence of historical call or text query data or transcripts, our classifier model is based on a pre-trained Glove model (Pennington et al. 2014) and trained using data scraped from various online sources, including: (1) review sites such as Yelp, and (2) community forums related to the domain of the call center. We extracted sentences from these sources and manually labeled them for each of the possible responses. Each sentence is preprocessed by standard NLP techniques, e.g., case normalization, stop word removal, and punctuation removal. A pre-trained word embedding model maps each word in a sentence to a 300-dimensional vector. The vectors are averaged to obtain a final averaged word embedding representing the entire sentence. We trained a logistic regression classifier on these sentence vectors with the route/specific phoneline as the target of prediction in the N-way classification.

2.2   Results

The study on 2 separate use cases yielded F1 scores that ranged from 84% to 97% and 56% to 94% respectively (using 5-fold cross validation) as shown in Tables 1 and 2. Natural language expression queries to the call center can be correctly classified for the user's intended destination of the call with an average of 91% correct classification rate for use case 1.

Table 1. Classification scores for use case 1 (7 service departments)

Department	Precision	Recall	F1-score
Human resource	0.98	0.97	0.97
Eyes	0.95	0.9	0.93
Dental	0.87	0.95	0.91
Laboratory	0.95	0.87	0.91
Pharmacy	0.9	0.92	0.91
Radiology	0.92	0.82	0.87
Mental health	0.87	0.81	0.84
Average			91%

Table 2. Classification scores for use case 2 (10 service departments).

Department	Precision	Recall	F1-score
Dental	0.86	0.95	0.90
Education benefits	0.87	0.94	0.90
Eyes	0.95	0.89	0.92
Human resource	0.80	0.81	0.80
Laboratory	0.95	0.88	0.91
Mental health	0.87	0.79	0.83
Burial service	1.00	0.89	0.94
Pharmacy	0.89	0.94	0.91
Radiology	0.95	0.80	0.87
Vocation & rehabilitation	0.65	0.49	0.56
Average	0.88	0.84	0.85

When the same ML model trained and tested for use case 1 is applied to use case 2, in which 3 new routing options are added, the classification rate drops to an average F-score of 85%. This may mean more training data is needed to extend the model. We suppose bidirectional and contextualized word embedding models (Howard and Ruder 2018; Peters et al. 2018; Radford et al. 2018) are needed for classification tasks with a larger set of class members.

2.3 Implication and Application

This data-driven, ML approach can be generalized to other classification and response domains to make the question and answer system more robust and flexible to a user's natural language queries. We expect our call classification and routing NLU model can be further refined when trained on actual historical call center data.

3 Intelligent, Interactive, and Multimodal iVAS Prototype

In this section, we describe the iVAS question and answer prototype that implements the underlying NLU and ML models, which enable intelligent natural language voice conversation or text-based dialogue to obtain relevant answers from the system. The iVAS system is designed to (1) interpret various permutations of natural language through semantic parsing, expansion, and context-sensitive NLU, (2) interact with users to obtain user-specific information to refine/confirm the question and generate more relevant answers based on application domain knowledge, and (3) perform multimodal interaction through speech and written text for question and answer as illustrated in Figs. 1 and 2 respectively.

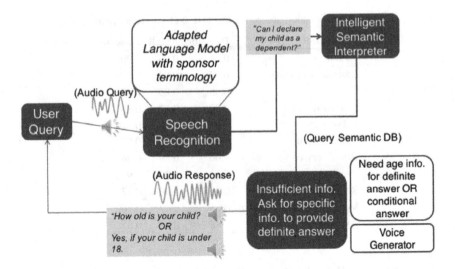

Fig. 1. Interactive natural language question and answer via speech

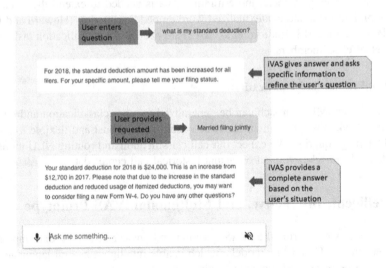

Fig. 2. Interactive natural language question and answer via chatbot

3.1   iVAS Prototype: Disambiguation via Interactive Conversation or Dialogue with the User

The iVAS voice and chatbot interface enables the conversation and dialogue between the user and the system. Even when the NLU and ML model finds a candidate response with a high system confidence, iVAS will still ask the user to confirm if the response is indeed what the user wants before executing the downstream process. This is illustrated in Fig. 3 in which iVAS finds the response with high probability.

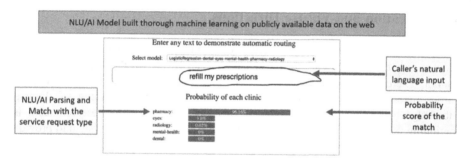

Fig. 3. iVAS interprets the user's query and identifies the service department with high probability.

Through natural language interaction via speech or text, the iVAS NLU and ML model automatically identifies the semantic underpinning of the user's intent or query and retrieves the response candidate from the system. If the system finds an answer or response to the question with a high system confidence, the answer or the response (such as routing to the matched service department) will be executed only after confirming with the user.

In cases when the iVAS NLU model finds two response candidates with close probability, the iVAS voice agent or chatbot asks the user to select the system-generated responses or make another query to ensure the system correctly interprets the user's intent or query.

3.2 iVAS Functional Blocks Supporting Additional Response Types

During the research and development of iVAS, it has become apparent that an intelligent system can provide other useful responses to a user's natural language query beyond just automatic call routing. The following is a list of the main response types the iVAS system can provide through interactive question and answer exchange: (1) automatically interpret/parse the intent of the incoming calls through NLU and a ML based domain-specific model, (2) interact with the caller/user when key information is needed to derive the most pertinent answer, (3) conduct automatic look-up and matching of the closest business facility/options based on the zip code or place name provided by the user, (4) verify/confirm the answer with the user before call routing, (5) automatically transfer the call to a live operator when urgent/crisis intent is identified/expressed, and (6) offer direct call transfer, provide a phone number or address, provide a relevant answer to the user's question or direct the user to a web portal to complete the business transaction.

3.3 iVAS Multimodal Architecture

iVAS is designed to be configuration driven and robust to voice and text question and answer interaction. Its architecture is agnostic of platform, device, and modalities (voice, text). Its NLU and decision-tree framework can be adapted to support various business and service needs for natural conversational query and answer systems.

4   Implication and Future Directions

The iVAS research and prototype demonstrates how, through natural conversation, relevant answers or responses to a user's query can be provided by speech or a text chatbot. There are larger classification tasks and more complex queries that require further investigation using efficient methodologies and deep learning of domain knowledge to provide the most relevant answers to a user. The research team is continuing the research of robust natural language query and answer system to provide efficient and useful answers to the users.

References

Herman, J.: U.S. federal AI virtual assistant pilot. In: Presentations Made at the U.S. General Services Administration Emerging Citizen Technology Program, Washington, D.C, 17 May 2017

Hendry, J.: DHS attempts most ambitious Microsoft digital assistant build yet, ITNews, 29 March 2019. https://www.itnews.com.au/news/dhs-attempts-most-ambitious-microsoft-digital-assistant-build-yet-523101

Saon, G., et al.: English conversational telephone speech recognition by humans and machines, [cs.CL], 6 March 2017. arXiv:1703.02136v1

Xiong, W., et al.: Achieving human parity in conversational speech recognition (2016). arXiv: 1610.05256

Park, D.S., et al.: Specaugment: a simple data augmentation method for automatic speech recognition, 18 April 2019. arXiv:1904.08779

Dai, A., Le, Q.: Semi-supervised sequence learning. In: Advances in Neural Information Processing (NIPS) (2015)

Hu, Q., Lockett, J., et al.: Automated call classification and routing with speech technology and artificial intelligence. In: SpeechTek Conference, Washington DC, USA (2019)

Sarma, P.K., Liang, Y., Sethares, W.A.: Domain adapted word embeddings for improved sentiment classification. In Proceedings of the Workshop on Deep Learning Approaches for Low-Resource NLP, pp. 51–59, Melbourne, Australia, 19 July 2018. c 2018 Association for Computational Linguistics

Pennington, J., Socher, R., Manning, C.D.: Glove: global vectors for word representation. In: Proceedings of the 2014 Conference on Empirical Methods in Natural Language Processing (EMNLP), Doha, Qatar, pp. 1532–1543, 25-29 October 2014. c 2014 Association for Computational Linguistics

Peters, M., et al.: Deep contextualized word representations. In: NAACL (2018)

Radford, A., Narasimhan, K., Salimans, T., Sutskever, I.: Improving language understanding with unsupervised learning, Technical report (2018). OpenAI

Howard, J., Ruder, S.: Universal language model fine-tuning for text classification. In: ACL. Association for Computational Linguistics (2018)

A Study on Topic Modeling for Feature Space Reduction in Text Classification

Daniel Pfeifer[1(✉)] and Jochen L. Leidner[2,3]

[1] Department of Medical Informatics, Heilbronn University of Applied Sciences,
Max-Planck-Str. 39, 74081 Heilbronn, Germany
`daniel.pfeifer@hs-heilbronn.de`
[2] Refinitiv Labs, 30 South Colonnade, London E14 5EP, UK
`leidner@acm.org`
[3] University of Sheffield, 211 Portobello, Sheffield S1 4DP, UK

Abstract. We examine two topic modeling approaches as feature space reduction techniques for text classification and compare their performance with two standard feature selection techniques, namely Information Gain (IG) and and Document Frequency (DF). Feature selection techniques are commonly applied in order to avoid the well-known "curse of dimensionality" in machine learning. Regarding text classification, traditional techniques achieve this by selecting words from the training vocabulary. In contrast, topic models compute topics as multinomial distributions over words and reduce each document to a distribution over such topics. Corresponding topic-to-document distributions may act as input data to train a document classifier. Our comparison includes two topic modeling approaches – Latent Dirichlet Allocation (LDA) and Topic Grouper. Our results are based on classification accuracy and suggest that topic modeling is far superior to IG and DF at a very low number of reduced features. However, if the number of reduced features is still large, IG becomes competitive and the cost of computing topic models is considerable. We conclude by giving basic recommendations on when to consider which type of method.

Keywords: Topic modeling · Text classification · Feature selection ·
Feature space reduction

1 Introduction

Feature space reduction is a common step for text classification in order to avoid the well-known "curse of dimensionality" ([3]). Standard approaches achieve this by reducing the *training vocabulary* V: E.g., [19] compare five respective techniques including Information Gain (IG), Document Frequency (DF) and Chi-Square, where all three performed well. [7] is a more extensive study comprising additional word selection techniques and over 200 datasets.

Over the last two decades, probabilistic topic modeling has become an active sub-field of information retrieval and machine learning. Hereby, each topic $t \in T$ is typically represented via a multinomial distribution $p(w|t)$ with $w \in V$ where

© Springer Nature Switzerland AG 2019
A. Cuzzocrea et al. (Eds.): FQAS 2019, LNAI 11529, pp. 403–412, 2019.
https://doi.org/10.1007/978-3-030-27629-4_37

the set of distributions $\Phi = \{p(w|t) \mid w \in V, t \in T\}$ forms the actual *topic model*. Related ideas and solutions were formed in the two seminal publications on *probabilistic Latent Semantic Indexing* (pLSI) ([9]) and *Latent Dirichlet Allocation* (LDA) ([5]). Related models are learned from a training collection D of documents d based on the frequency $f_d(w)$ of each word w per document d. To date, LDA is probably the most commonly used topic modeling approach, and it produces a fixed-size set of non-hierarchical topics (cf. [4] for a general introduction to topic modeling and LDA).

We can apply topic modeling as a feature space reduction method as follows: First, the topic model Φ must be learned from the training collection D. Using Φ, a document d can be characterized by multinomial distributions $p(t|d)$ expressing the prevalence of each topic t in d. Regarding training documents, $p(t|d)$ is an additional output of the topic model's learning procedure. Computing $p(t|d)$ for a test document is called a "fold-in" and will be detailed in Sect. 3. Instead of using word frequencies, a classifier may then be trained and tested via related distributions $p(t|d)_{t \in T}$. Since the number of topics $|T|$ is usually much smaller than the size of the training vocabulary $|V|$, this results in a feature space reduction for the classifier. Figure 1 contrasts the standard word selection and embedding approach with a corresponding approach based on topic modeling.

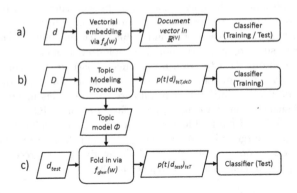

Fig. 1. (a) Standard word embedding for text classification with a potentially reduced vocabulary, (b) classification using topic modeling at training time and (c) classification using topic modeling at test time

To the best of our knowledge, our study is the first to explore *how the performance of topic model-based feature reduction for text classification relates to the number of features*. This covers the following aspects:

1. We describe in reasonable detail, how the steps (b) and (c) from Fig. 1 can be implemented, such that other machine learning practitioners can make best use of it.
2. Based on three datasets we run a direct comparison of feature reduction for text classification using word selection and topic modeling. We include IG, DF, two variants of LDA and Topic Grouper – a more recent topic modeling approach.
3. The results from (2) allow for conclusions and general recommendations on when to prefer which approach.

2   Related Work

We first give a brief overview of *Topic Grouper* (TG) from [15]. as it is incorporated in our study besides LDA: TG has no hyper parameters and partitions V via agglomerative clustering. In this case, a topic t consists of a set of words from V such that $\bigcup_{t \in T} t = V$ and $s \cap t = \emptyset$ for any $s, t \in T$. So each word $w \in V$ belongs to exactly one topic $t \in T$.

To begin with, TG produces a binary clustering tree over the vocabulary V forming a hierarchical topic model. In order to gain a number of non-hierarchical topics T, a dendrogram cut can be made in the produced clustering tree. Depending on the cut position, the range for $|T|$ lies between $|V|$ and 1. Figure 2 illustrates this for an artificial vocabulary $V = \{a, the, it, med, doc\}$. So in case of TG, the number of topics $|T|$ can be chosen *after* training the topic model by resorting to the tree produced *during* training.

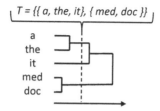

Fig. 2. Obtaining a flat topic model T with two topics via a dendrogram cut of a topic tree produced by Topic Grouper

Blei *et al.* [5] includes an experiment that reduces the feature space via LDA-based topic models in order to classify text using an SVM. However, the authors do not describe their method in detail and a direct comparison to standard word selection techniques is missing. We try to close this gap here.

The study in [16] has a similar focus as ours but it does not clarify how related topic models are generated. As we will show, classification performance depends very much on the details of topic model generation. More importantly, the author does *not* assess classification performance *under a varying number of features*. As will become clear, this aspect is crucial when comparing feature reduction techniques for the given purpose. In addition, it uses only a single dataset which is unsuitable general conclusions.

The authors of [1] study LDA, IG and others as a preprocessing step for text classification based on AdaBoost. Again they work with a fixed number of features for each setting while targeting AdaBoost only. [12] choose LDA as a feature reduction step for news text classification without comparing it to other methods.

The authors of [6] and [11] investigate on topic modeling as a feature reduction method for document clustering, whereas we target supervised document classification.

3   Method

3.1   Datasets

We work with three popular datasets according to Table 1. Regarding "Reuters 21578" we kept only documents with a unique class label, considered only the ten most frequent classes and adopted the so-called "ModApte split" (see [13]). Regarding "Twenty News Groups" we removed all tokens containing non-alphabetical characters or being shorter than three characters. In both cases we performed Porter stemming and stop word filtering. Regarding "OHSUMED" we used the preprocessed dataset extract "ohscal" from [7] with exactly one class label per document.

3.2   Topic Model Generation

To generate LDA models we use Gibbs sampling according to [8]. Moreover, we adopt a commonly used heuristic from [8] for LDA's hyper parameters implying $\beta = 0.1$ and $\alpha = 50/|T|$, and call it "LDA with Heuristics".

In addition, we perform a hyper parameter optimization for α and β using the so-called "Minka's Update" according to [14] and [2] and call it "LDA Optimized". For best possible results under "LDA Optimized" and in concordance with Wallach $et\ al.$ [17], we support an asymmetrical optimization for α such that $\alpha \in \mathbb{R}^{|T|}$. In this case, an estimation of α is based on an initially computed topic model Φ_1. The updated α can in turn be used to compute an updated model Φ_2 (while using Φ_1 as a starting point to compute Φ_2) an so forth. After several iterations of such alternating steps, the models Φ_i as well as α converge. [14] provides a theoretical basis for the estimation of Dirichlet parameters via sample distribution data. Regarding α, these are (samples of) estimated distributions $p(t|d)_i$ as computed along with an intermediate model Φ_i. In total, this results in an Expectation Maximization loop for α (but also for β) nesting the actual LDA procedure.

Regarding TG, we simply run the related algorithm according to [15] on the training documents and choose $|T|$ and with it T from the inferred topic tree according to Sect. 2. In order to obtain the distributions $p(w|t)$ as part of a model Φ, we estimate $p(w|t) := \sum_{d \in D} f_d(w) / (\sum_{w \in t} \sum_{d \in D} f_d(w))$ if $w \in t$ and $p(w|t) := 0$ otherwise.

3.3   Choice of Classifier

An important question affecting a our study is which type of classifier to use. Although not the best performing method, we chose Naive Bayes (NB) for the following reasons:

1. It lends itself well to all of the applied feature space reduction approaches as will be shown below.
2. It does *not* mandate additional hyper parameter settings such as SVM, which would complicate the comparison and potentially incur bias.

3. Approaches relying on a TF-IDF embedding (such as Roccio or SVM as in
   [10]) are problematic with regard to LDA because DF and IDF are undefined
   for topics.
4. Many classification methods incur a problem-specific preference to a certain
   number of features: They trade off happens when an increasing number features starts to degrade accuracy due to the curse of dimensionality. In contrast, NB is robust against a large number of features and is known to perform
   best without any feature space reduction (see [10]). So, by using by NB we
   avoid a related kind of bias, and we may expect accuracy to rise continuously
   with an increasing number of features.

To confirm our argument, we tried other classifiers such as SVM variants and
indeed experienced the issues according to (2) and (4) from above (not depicted).

3.4   Classification via Topic Models

Let $C = \{c_1, \ldots, c_m\}$ be the set of classes for the training documents D. We
assume that the class assignments $l(d) \in C, d \in D$ are unique and known with
regard to D. We define D_c as the subset of training documents belonging to class
c, so $D_c = \{d \in D | l(d) = c\}$.

As mentioned before we set $f_d(w)$ to be the frequency of $w \in V$ in document
d. Further, let $f_d(t)$ be the frequency of topic t in d, $|D|$ be the number of
documents in D and $|d| = \sum_{w \in V} f_d(w)$. When using topics, NB determines the
class of a test document d_{test} via

$$argmax_{c \in C} \log p(c|d_{test}) \approx argmax_{c \in C} \log(p(c) \cdot \prod_{t \in T} p(t|c)^{f_{d_{test}}(t)})$$

with $p(c) \approx |D_c|/|D|$.

For best possible results under LDA, we estimate $f_{d_{test}}(t) \approx |d_{test}| \cdot p(t|d_{test})$.
In order to compute $p(t|d_{test})$ accurately, we resort to the so-called fold-in
method: A word-to-topic assignment z_i is sampled for every word occurrence
w_i in d_{test} using Gibbs sampling according to [8]. This involves the use of the
underlying topic model Φ and leads to a respective topic assignment vector $\mathbf{z}$
of length $|d_{test}|$. The procedure is repeated S times leading to S vectors $\mathbf{z}^{(s)}$.
Together, these results form the basis of

$$p(t|d_{test}) \approx 1/S \cdot \sum_{s=1}^{S} 1/|d_{test}| \sum_{i=1}^{|d_{test}|} \delta_{\mathbf{z}_i^{(s)}, t}.$$

More details on this sampling method can be found in [18].

Moreover, we estimate $p(t|c) \approx (\sum_{d \in D_c} p(t|d) \cdot |d|)/\sum_{d \in D_c} |d|$. In this case,
an approximation of $p(t|d)$ is already known from running LDA on the training
documents.

Since TG partitions V, each word $w \in V$ belongs to exactly one topic t. So
we can determine $f_d(t) := \sum_{w \in t} f_d(w)$, which results in the following estimate
under TG: $p(t|c) \approx ((1 + \sum_{d \in D_c} f_d(t))/(|T| + \sum_{d \in D_c} |d|)).$[1]

---

[1] The "1+" and "$|T|+$" in the expression form a standard Lidstone smoothing account-
ing for potential zero probabilities. Other than that, its practical effect is negligible.

4   Results and Discussion

Figures 3, 4 and 5 present classification accuracy as a function of the number topics or selected words using micro averaging. Given a small number of topics, our findings confirm the impressive abilities of LDA for feature space reduction as reported in [5] when applying hyper parameter optimization. Beyond 700 topics, the heuristic setting degrades LDA's performance in two cases. In accordance with [19], the results confirm that IG performs better than DF. The performance of TG depends on the dataset and ranges below "LDA Optimized", is considerably above IG in Fig. 5 but remains below IG in Fig. 4. In Fig. 3 "LDA Optimized", IG and TG are close above 200 topics or words, respectively.

When applying topic modeling this way, an important point to consider is the computational overhead for topic model generation but also for feature space reduction of new documents at classification time: LDA's runtime is in $O(|T|(\sum_{d \in D} |d|)^2)$ (see [5]) without hyper parameter optimization. The additional EM loop for hyper parameter optimization further drives up the computational cost but as seen in Figs. 5 and 3 this kind of optimization is relevant. E.g., regarding our experiments, computing related topic models with more than a thousand topics took several hours. At test-time, LDA requires the relatively complex fold-in computation of $p(t|d_{test})$ which is on the order of $S \cdot |d_{test}| \cdot |T|$ for a test document.

The runtime of TG is on the order of $|V|^2|D|$ (see [15]), and therefore is it important to limit the size of the vocabulary of the training collection. Once a TG model is built, its use for feature space reduction incurs minimal overhead: i.e., a word from a test document d_{test} can be reduced in constant time via the unique word-to-topic assignment. Thus the total feature space reduction cost for a test document remains on the order of $|d_{test}|$. As noted before, TG assesses all values for $|T|$ between $|V|$ and one within an single training run. This allows to adjust the degree of feature space reduction in hindsight without the need for topic model recomputations.

Altogether, these observations lead us to the following recommendation on when to consider topic modeling as a feature reduction technique for text classification: The primary criterion for a related decision is *the desired number of features* for the classifier:

- If it is well over a few thousand, the computational overhead for LDA does not outweigh the potential improvement in classification accuracy. In this case TG might offer some improvement but our results show that this is also depends on the dataset. It is therefore advisable to try out IG first and then to consider TG for potential improvements in accuracy.
- If the desired number of features is well under a few hundred, then LDA with hyper parameter optimization becomes attractive. However, this case seems unlikely as many popular classifiers can well handle a few hundred features without suffering from the curse of dimensionality.

– If a classifier can deal with a few thousand features or more, standard word selection techniques are an overall good choice since in this case, at least IG approximates or matches approaches based on topic modeling. Also, it incurs lower complexity and less computational overhead.

The presented results can all be reproduced via a prototypical Java library named TopicGrouperJ published on GitHub.[2] Besides script code for the experiments, it features implementations of TG and offers an LDA Gibbs Sampler with options for hyper parameter optimization according to Sect. 3.2.

Table 1. Datasets used for the classification task ($|C|$ is the number of classes, MF is the minimum frequency to keep a stem)

Dataset	$|D|$	$|D_{test}|$	$|V|$	$|C|$	MF
Reuters 21578	7,142	2,513	9,567	10	3
OHSUMED	8,374	2,788	11,423	10	3
Twenty news groups	14,134	4711	25,826	20	5

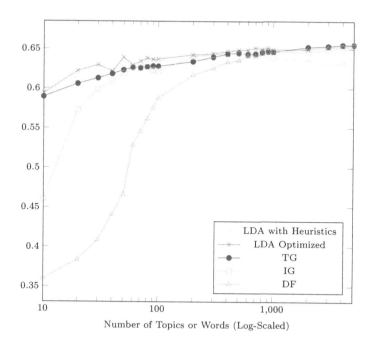

Number of Topics or Words (Log-Scaled)

Fig. 3. Accuracy for Reuters 21578

---

[2] See https://github.com/pfeiferd/TopicGrouperJ.

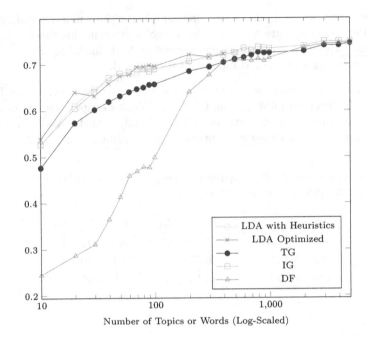

Fig. 4. Accuracy for OHSUMED

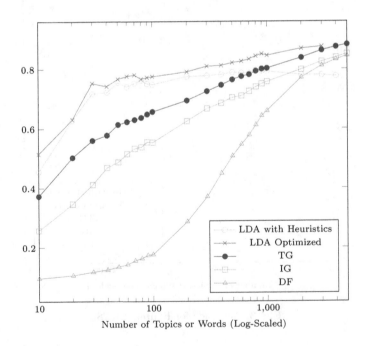

Fig. 5. Accuracy for twenty new groups

References

1. Al-Salemi, B., Ayob, M., Noah, S.A.M., Aziz, M.J.A.: Feature selection based on supervised topic modeling for boosting-based multi-label text categorization. In: 2017 6th International Conference on Electrical Engineering and Informatics (ICEEI), pp. 1–6 November 2017
2. Asuncion, A., Welling, M., Smyth, P., Teh, Y.W.: On smoothing and inference for topic models. In: Proceedings of the Twenty-Fifth Conference on Uncertainty in Artificial Intelligence, pp. 27–34. UAI 2009. AUAI Press, Arlington, VA, USA (2009)
3. Bellman, R.: Adaptive Control Processes: A Guided Tour. Princeton University Press, Princeton (1961)
4. Blei, D.M.: Probabilistic topic models. Commun. ACM **55**(4), 77–84 (2012)
5. Blei, D.M., Ng, A.Y., Jordan, M.I.: Latent Dirichlet allocation. J. Mach. Learn. Res. **3**, 993–1022 (2003)
6. Drummond, A., Vagena, Z., Jermaine, C.: Topic models for feature selection in document clustering. In: Proceedings of the SIAM International Conference on Data Mining, pp. 521–529 (2013)
7. Forman, G.: An extensive empirical study of feature selection metrics for text classification. J. Mach. Learn. Res. **3**, 1289–1305 (2003)
8. Griffiths, T.L., Steyvers, M.: Finding scientific topics. Proc. Nat. Acad. Sci. **101**(Suppl. 1), 5228–5235 (2004)
9. Hofmann, T.: Probabilistic latent semantic analysis. In: Proceedings of the Fifteenth Conference on Uncertainty in Artificial Intelligence, UAI 1999, pp. 289–296. Morgan Kaufmann, San Francisco (1999)
10. Joachims, T.: Text categorization with support vector machines: learning with many relevant features. In: Nédellec, C., Rouveirol, C. (eds.) ECML 1998. LNCS, vol. 1398, pp. 137–142. Springer, Heidelberg (1998). https://doi.org/10.1007/BFb0026683
11. Kumar, B.S., Ravi, V.: LDA based feature selection for document clustering. In: Proceedings of the 10th Annual ACM India Compute Conference, Compute 2017, pp. 125–130. ACM, New York (2017)
12. Li, Z., Shang, W., Yan, M.: News text classification model based on topic model. In: 2016 IEEE/ACIS 15th International Conference on Computer and Information Science (ICIS), pp. 1–5, June 2016
13. Manning, C.D., Raghavan, P., Schütze, H.: Introduction to Information Retrieval. Cambridge University Press, New York (2008)
14. Minka, T.P.: Estimating a Dirichlet distribution, Technical report, Carnegie Mellon University, Pittsburgh, PA, USA (2000). https://tminka.github.io/papers/dirichlet/minka-dirichlet.pdf
15. Azzopardi, L., Stein, B., Fuhr, N., Mayr, P., Hauff, C., Hiemstra, D. (eds.): ECIR 2019. LNCS, vol. 11437. Springer, Cham (2019). https://doi.org/10.1007/978-3-030-15712-8
16. Sriurai, W.: Improving text categorization by using a topic model. Adv. Comput. **2**(6), 21 (2011)
17. Wallach, H.M., Mimno, D.M., McCallum, A.: Rethinking LDA: why priors matter. In: Bengio, Y., Schuurmans, D., Lafferty, J.D., Williams, C.K.I., Culotta, A. (eds.) NIPS, pp. 1973–1981. Curran Associates, Inc. (2009)

18. Wallach, H.M., Murray, I., Salakhutdinov, R., Mimno, D.: Evaluation methods for topic models. In: Proceedings of the 26th Annual International Conference on Machine Learning, ICML 2009, pp. 1105–1112. ACM, New York (2009)
19. Yang, Y., Pedersen, J.O.: A comparative study on feature selection in text categorization. In: Proceedings of the Fourteenth International Conference on Machine Learning, ICML 1997, pp. 412–420. Morgan Kaufmann, San Francisco (1997)

Author Index

Printed in the United States
By Bookmasters